Community and Agency Counseling

Second Edition

Samuel T. Gladding
Wake Forest University

Deborah W. Newsome
Wake Forest University

PEARSON

Merrill
Prentice Hall

Upper Saddle River, New Jersey
Columbus, Ohio

Library of Congress Cataloging-in-Publication Data

Gladding, Samuel T.
    Community and agency counseling / Samuel T. Gladding, Deborah W. Newsome—2nd ed.
      p. cm.
    Includes bibliographical references and indexes.
    ISBN 0-13-093312-0
    1. Counseling. 2. Counseling—History. I. Newsome, Deborah W. II. Title.
BF637.C6G528   2004
361'.06—dc21

                            2003011223

Vice President and Executive Publisher: Jeffery W. Johnston
Publisher: Kevin M. Davis
Editorial Assistant: Autumn Crisp
Production Editor: Mary Harlan
Production Coordination: Karen Ettinger, The GTS Companies/York, PA Campus
Design Coordinator: Diane C. Lorenzo
Photo Coordinator: Sandy Schaefer
Text Design and Illustrations: The GTS Companies/York, PA Campus
Cover Design: Jason Moore
Cover Image: SuperStock
Production Manager: Laura Messerly
Director of Marketing: Ann Castel Davis
Marketing Manager: Amy June
Marketing Coordinator: Tyra Poole

This book was set in Garamond by The GTS Companies/York, PA Campus. It was printed and bound by R.R. Donnelley & Sons Company. The cover was printed by Phoenix Color Corp.

Photo Credits: Scott Cunningham/Merrill, pp. 45, 213, 274, 295; George Dodson/PH College, p. 2; Charles Gatewood/PH College, p. 135; Steve Gorton/Dorling Kindersley Media Library, p. 340, Michal Heron/ PH College, p. 240; Bruce Johnson/Merrill, p. 25; Don Klumpp/Getty Images Inc.–Image Bank, p. 157; Anthony Magnacca/Merrill, p. 69; PH College, p. 100; John Serafin/Silver Burdett Ginn, p. 368; Anne Vega/Merrill, p. 188.

Pearson Education Ltd.
Pearson Education Singapore, Pte. Ltd.
Pearson Education, Canada, Ltd.
Pearson Education–Japan

Pearson Education Australia Pty. Limited
Pearson Education North Asia Ltd.
Pearson Educación de Mexico, S.A. de C.V.
Pearson Education Malaysia, Pte. Ltd.

10 9 8 7 6 5 4 3 2 1
ISBN: 0-13-093312-0

In memory of Shirley Ratliff, Nicholas Vacc, and Mary Thomas Burke, who taught us through example and insight the art and science of community counseling.

About the Authors

Samuel T. Gladding is a professor and chair of the Department of Counseling at Wake Forest University in Winston-Salem, North Carolina. He has been a practicing counselor in both public and private community agencies. His leadership in the field of counseling includes service as president of the American Counseling Association (ACA), the Association for Counselor Education and Supervision (ACES), the Association for Specialists in Group Work (ASGW), and Chi Sigma Iota (international counseling honor society). He is also the former editor of the *Journal for Specialists in Group Work.*

In 1999, he was cited as being in the top 1 percent of contributors to the *Journal of Counseling and Development* for the 15-year period, 1978–1993. Some of Gladding's most recent books are: *The Counseling Dictionary* (2001), *Family Therapy: History, Theory, & Process* (3rd ed.) (2002), *Becoming a Counselor: The Light, the Bright, and the Serious* (2002), *Group Work: A Counseling Specialty* (4th ed.) (2003), and *Counseling: A Comprehensive Profession* (5th ed.) (2004).

Dr. Gladding is a National Certified Counselor (NCC), a Certified Clinical Mental Health Counselor (CCMHC), and a Licensed Professional Counselor (LPC) in North Carolina. He is married to the former Claire Tillson and the father of three children—Benjamin, Nathaniel, and Timothy. In his spare time, he enjoys swimming, playing tennis, writing poetry, and reading humor.

Deborah W. Newsome is an assistant professor in the Department of Counseling at Wake Forest University in Winston-Salem, North Carolina. She also works as an adjunct clinician at a not-for-profit counseling center, where she counsels children, adolescents, and their families. She has authored and co-authored several book chapters and journal articles and currently is secretary of the Association for Assessment in Counseling and Education (AACE). Her research interests focus on adolescents' career development, family interactions, and academic achievement.

Dr. Newsome received a Ph.D. in counseling and counselor education from the University of North Carolina at Greensboro. She is a National Certified Counselor (NCC), a Licensed Professional Counselor (LPC), and a Licensed School Counselor (LSC) in North Carolina. She and her husband, David Newsome, have two teenagers—David and Jennifer. In addition to writing, teaching, counseling, and supervising, Dr. Newsome enjoys running, reading, and playing the flute.

Preface

Community counseling represents a relatively recent specialty area in professional counseling, although its history is extensive. It began when a small group of counselors started working in community and agency settings, including mental health settings, not-for-profit organizations, hospitals, and other places outside traditional educational settings. Prior to the 1960s, little attention, few curricula courses in counseling programs, and few professional opportunities focused on counseling in nonschool environments. Yet, a core of counselors found themselves working in community settings. Thus, although the term *community counselor* was first introduced into the professional literature in the late 1970s, the concept and practice of community counseling date back further. A case can even be made that community counseling really began at the turn of the 20th century, when two founders of counseling in the United States, Frank Parson and Clifford Beers, focused their attention on social environmental concerns: specifically, career development and mental health.

Regardless of its roots, the practice and growth of community counseling were given a boost in the 1960s and 1970s. During this time, the Community Mental Health Centers Act of 1963 was enacted, resulting in the deinstitutionalization of people with mental illnesses and the establishment of broad-reaching, outpatient, community-based services. Also during this time, an epidemic of drug use necessitated the establishment of many substance-abuse treatment centers. Moreover, several not-for-profit and church-sponsored agencies began providing counseling services. As a consequence of these and other societal changes, counselors found new employment opportunities in settings other than schools and universities.

Gradually, a groundswell of counselors employed in agencies and other organizations advocated a name by which to identify themselves. Judith and Michael Lewis (1977) coined the descriptor "community counseling" to identify counseling activities outside educational institutions. Since that time, the definition and professional preparation of community counseling have evolved and expanded. Community counselors in the 21st century perform a broad range of therapeutic services among diverse client populations and in a variety of settings. They use multifaceted approaches that promote prevention, early intervention, wellness, and advocacy, taking into account the client, the environment, and the interactions between the two. Many community counselors are trained in counselor education programs that are recognized by the Council for Accreditation of Counseling and Related Educational Programs (CACREP) and are employed in venues that include community mental health centers, health care centers, not-for-profit organizations, private practice, career development centers, employee assistance programs, and other agencies.

In the second edition of *Community and Agency Counseling,* topics related to community counseling in the 21st century are addressed. Specifically, we examine the history and foundations of community counseling, roles and functions of community counselors, counseling with diverse populations, and settings in which community counselors practice.

NEW TO THIS EDITION

The second edition features much new content, including:

- An expanded description of the professional identity of community counselors
- Updated information regarding ethical and legal issues as they pertain to community counseling
- A focus on current and emerging influences on community counseling, including managed care, technology, wellness, and spirituality
- Detailed information describing intake services, treatment planning, and record keeping
- New chapters that address assessment and diagnosis, crisis intervention, prevention, advocacy, and program evaluation
- An expanded chapter on counseling diverse populations that addresses counseling with people who differ with respect to race, ethnicity, sexual orientation, and ability
- Additional information on counseling children and adolescents, focusing on developmental issues, contextual factors, and prevalent issues
- New or expanded chapters that examine community settings and the services offered in those settings
- Narratives from professional community counselors and other mental health workers describing their experiences in various settings with diverse clientele

ORGANIZATION OF THE TEXT

The content is designed to address pertinent topics in community counseling, with an emphasis on subjects highlighted by the Council for Accreditation of Counseling and Related Educational Programs (CACREP). Contents are organized under four headings:

- *Part I: Historical and Professional Foundations of Community Counseling.* The historical and professional foundations of community counseling are outlined, beginning with a recounting of the historical roots of the profession (Chapter 1). In Chapter 2, the concept of professional identity is explored, including the meaning of community counseling and credentialing associated with the profession. In Chapter 3, ethical and legal issues, particularly those that pertain to community counseling, are discussed. Chapter 4 addresses current and emerging influences on community counseling, including managed care, technology, and an emphasis on wellness and spirituality.

• *Part II: Roles and Functions of Community Counselors.* Community counselors are responsible for developing the knowledge and skills needed to conduct a broad array of counseling services. Part II opens with a general description of the counseling process and specific descriptions of activities that occur during the initial, working, and termination stages of counseling. In the next chapter, specific attention is given to two general functions that community counselors need to conduct skillfully: assessment and diagnosis. In Chapter 7, other essential counseling services are described, including crisis intervention, prevention, advocacy, and program evaluation. Two more important services are described in the last two chapters of the section: working with groups (Chapter 8) and counseling with couples and families (Chapter 9).

• *Part III: Working With Specific Populations.* In our diverse society, it is crucial for counselors to develop skills in working with people of different racial backgrounds, sexual orientations, levels of ability, and ages. Issues related to counseling with diverse populations are explored in Chapter 10, followed by a focus on counseling with adults across the life span (Chapter 11) and with children and adolescents (Chapter 12).

• *Part IV: Community Counseling Practice: Settings and Services.* Community counselors are employed in many different profit and not-for-profit settings that operate in both the public and the private sector. In Chapter 13, several settings in which community counselors might be employed are described, including community mental health centers (CMHCs), health care facilities, and child and family agencies. Other community settings, including career counseling centers, employee assistance programs, and private practices, are highlighted in Chapter 14.

The content of the second edition is based on current research and practices germane to community counseling. Information presented in the chapters is supplemented with narratives supplied by mental health professionals employed across counseling settings, who share their views of the rewards and challenges associated with the services they provide.

ACKNOWLEDGMENTS

It takes the efforts of a community to create and revise a textbook. We want to thank our professional colleagues in the various communities in which we have worked—Rockingham Community Mental Health Center (NC), the Trinity Center, Rockingham Community College (NC), Fairfield University (CT), the University of Alabama at

Birmingham, the University of North Carolina at Greensboro, and Wake Forest University (NC). We also want to acknowledge the dedicated mental health professionals who supplied narratives or personal interviews for the text, including Tom Buffkin, Tania Castillero, Kelli Coker, Ann Dixon Coppage, Robin Daniel, Pat DeChatelet, Jay Hale, Pamela Karr, Susanna Lund, Nick Mazza, Peg McEwen, Ellen Nicola, Peg Olson, Elizabeth Vaughan, Laura Veach, and Dorothy Walker. Throughout the course of the text revision, several Wake Forest graduate students provided invaluable assistance, including Jenny Cole, LaKicia Fuller, Beverly Huffstetler, Rolanda Mitchell, Priscilla Sloane, and Claudetta Wall. We also want to recognize the contributions of the staff at Merrill/Prentice Hall: Kevin Davis, Autumn Crisp, and Christina Tawney, whose patience and flexibility made the project manageable. We would like to thank the reviewers who provided invaluable comments and suggestions. They are Thomas J. DeStefano, Northern Arizona University; Don F. Keller, Clemson University; Simeon Schlossberg, Western Maryland College; and Christy Spears Sholola, University of Phoenix.

We are especially grateful for the contributions of our spouses (Claire Gladding and David Newsome) for their patience, encouragement, and suggestions during the textbook revision. We express gratitude to our children—Benjamin, Nathaniel, and Timothy Gladding; David and Jennifer Newsome—for the responsibility and understanding they demonstrated throughout the revision process. We appreciate our families for the humor, love, support, and sensitivity they provide on an ongoing basis.

During the course of revising this text, we were saddened by the loss of two loved and respected mentors in the counseling field—Dr. Nicholas Vacc and Sister Mary Thomas Burke. Nicholas and Sister Mary Thomas exemplified the traits that characterize counselors at their best, and they will be greatly missed. We are deeply grateful for their immeasurable contributions to the counseling profession in general and community counseling in particular.

REFERENCE

Lewis, J., & Lewis, M. (1977). *Community counseling: A human services approach.* New York: Wiley.

Discover the Companion Website Accompanying This Book

THE PRENTICE HALL COMPANION WEBSITE: A VIRTUAL LEARNING ENVIRONMENT

Technology is a constantly growing and changing aspect of our field that is creating a need for content and resources. To address this emerging need, Prentice Hall has developed an online learning environment for students and professors alike—Companion Websites—to support our textbooks.

In creating a Companion Website, our goal is to build on and enhance what the textbook already offers. For this reason, the content for each user-friendly Website is organized by topic and provides the professor and student with a variety of meaningful resources. Common features of a Companion Website include:

For the Professor—

Every Companion Website integrates **Syllabus Manager**™, an online syllabus creation and management utility.

- **Syllabus Manager**™ provides you, the instructor, with an easy, step-by-step process to create and revise syllabi, with direct links into Companion Website and other online content without having to learn HTML.
- Students may logon to your syllabus during any study session. All they need to know is the web address for the Companion Website and the password you've assigned to your syllabus.
- After you have created a syllabus using **Syllabus Manager**™, students may enter the syllabus for their course section from any point in the Companion Website.
- Clicking on a date, the student is shown the list of activities for the assignment. The activities for each assignment are linked directly to actual content, saving time for students.
- Adding assignments consists of clicking on the desired due date, then filling in the details of the assignment—name of the assignment, instructions, and whether it is a one-time or repeating assignment.

- In addition, links to other activities can be created easily. If the activity is online, a URL can be entered in the space provided, and it will be linked automatically in the final syllabus.
- Your completed syllabus is hosted on our servers, allowing convenient updates from any computer on the Internet. Changes you make to your syllabus are immediately available to your students at their next logon.

For the Student—

- **Counseling Topics**—17 core counseling topics represent the diversity and scope of today's counseling field.
- **Annotated Bibliogrphy**—includes seminal foundational works and key current works.
- **Web Destinations**—lists significant and up-to-date practitioner and client sites.
- **Professional Development**—provides helpful information regarding professional organizations and codes of ethics.
- **Electronic Bluebook**—send homework or essays directly to your instructor's emil with this paperless form.
- **Message Board**—serves as a bulletin board to post—or respond to—questions or comments to/from a national audience.
- **Chat**—real-time chat with anyone who is using the text anywhere in the country—ideal for discussion and study groups, class projects, etc.

To take advantage of these and other resources, please visit the *Community and Agency Counseling*, Second Edition, Companion Website at

www.prenhall.com/gladding

Research Navigator: Research Made Simple!

www.ResearchNavigator.com

Merrill Education is pleased to introduce Research Navigator—a one-stop research solution for students that simplifies and streamlines the entire research process. At www.researchnavigator.com, students will find extensive resources to enhance their understanding of the research process so they can effectively complete research assignments. In addition, Research Navigator has three exclusive databases of credible and reliable source content to help students focus their research efforts and begin the research process.

HOW WILL RESEARCH NAVIGATOR ENHANCE YOUR COURSE?

- Extensive content helps students understand the research process, including writing, internet research, and citing sources.
- Step-by-step tutorial guides students through the entire research process from selecting a topic to revising a rough draft.
- Research Writing in the Disciplines section details the differences in research across disciplines.
- Three exclusive databases—EBSCO's ContentSelect Academic Journal Database, *The New York Times* Search by Subject Archive and "Best of the Web" Link Library—allow students to easily find journal articles and sources.

WHAT'S THE COST?

A subscription to Research Navigator is $7.50 but is **free** when used in conjunction with this textbook. To obtain free passcodes for your students, simply contact your local Merrill/Prentice Hall sales representative, and your representative will send you the Evaluating Online Resource Guide, which contains the code to access Research Navigator as well as tips on how to use Research Navigator and how to evaluate research. To preview the value of this website to your students, please go to www.educatorlearningcenter.com and use the Login Name "Research" and the password "Demo."

Brief Contents

Contents

PART III

WORKING WITH SPECIFIC POPULATIONS   239

PART I

Historical and Professional Foundations of Community Counseling

CHAPTER 1

Historical Overview of the Counseling Profession

There is a quietness that comes
  in the awareness of presenting names
  and recalling places
    in the history of persons
      who come seeking help.
Confusion and direction are a part of the process
  where in trying to sort out tracks
  that parallel into life
    a person's past is traveled.
Counseling is a complex riddle
  where the mind's lines are joined
  with scrambling and precision
    to make sense out of nonsense,
  a tedious process
  like piecing fragments of puzzle together
  until a picture is formed.

Gladding, S. T. (1978). In the midst of the puzzles and counseling journey. *Personnel and Guidance Journal, 57,* 148. © ACA. Reprinted with permission. No further reproduction authorized without written permission of ACA.

The following story was popular when I (Gladding) first entered the counseling profession: A young man took a stroll by a river. As he was walking, he noticed an old woman flailing her arms in the midst of the river and yelling for assistance. Without hesitation, he jumped into the water, swam out, grabbed her, and pulled her to safety. Just as she was recovering, a boy floated past in dire straits. Again the young man dove into the water and rescued the boy in the same brave way he had done with the older woman. To the young man's chagrin and to the amazement of a small crowd that was gathering on the banks of the stream, a third person, a middle-aged executive, came floating by yelling for help. The young man was a hero once more with his rescue of the businessman.

Exhausted, he then started walking upstream. As he did, a bystander asked him, "Aren't you going to stay to rescue others who may fall in the river and need you?"

The young man replied, "No. I'm going farther up the river to find out why these people are falling in."

The story illustrates a key component of counseling in general and of community counseling in particular: Counseling focuses on prevention whenever possible and on altering people's environments to make them hospitable as opposed to hostile.

The term *community counseling* was initially coined by Amos and Williams (1972) and later by Lewis and Lewis (1977) to identify those counseling activities that took place outside other established domains, such as educational settings. In 1984, the Association of Counselor Educators and Supervisors (ACES) Committee on Community Counseling described community counseling as a process and orientation that:

- Favors using a multifaceted approach that is developmental and educative
- Emphasizes prevention
- Takes into account the effects of the community on the client
- Seeks to empower clients through advocacy (Hayes, 1984, March)

These basic premises, which highlight development, prevention, client–environment interaction, and empowerment, continue to characterize community counseling today, as well as the profession of counseling in general.

Remley and Herlihy (2001) summarized key points that provide the foundation for the professional identity of counselors. These guiding principles are:

1. The best perspective for helping people resolve their personal and emotional issues is the wellness model for mental health. From a wellness perspective, mental health is viewed as occurring on a continuum, and the goal of counseling is to help the person move toward a higher level of wellness, rather than to cure an illness.
2. Many of the personal and emotional issues people experience can best be understood from a developmental perspective. Understanding the dynamics of human growth and development and addressing clients' concerns accordingly are key components of successful counseling.
3. Prevention and early intervention are preferable to remediation, whenever possible. Prevention activities include psychoeducational groups, training seminars, career exploration groups, and a host of other activities. Early intervention,

which occurs when a client is at risk of experiencing personal or emotional problems, can help keep problems from escalating.

4. The goal of counseling is to empower clients to solve problems independently. Counseling is viewed as a transitory process through which clients increase their self-understanding and problem-solving ability. (pp. 19–23)

Community counselors provide services to a wide spectrum of people in a variety of settings. In some settings, the typical concerns expressed by clients may require short-term intervention. However, community counselors also are trained to work with clients dealing with more serious concerns, requiring interventions of longer duration. Counseling's emphasis on development, prevention, and treatment makes it attractive to those seeking healthy life-stage transitions and productive lives free from disorders (Romano, 1992).

Box 1–1

"Practicing counselors are concerned about pathology, but not from a myopic perspective. People develop difficulties (and in many cases pathology) at various times during their developmental life span. Effectively dealing with pathology does not preclude using a developmental framework. Furthermore, an understanding of the developmental course of numerous disorders is an important aspect of prevention, accurate diagnosis, and treatment."

—(Hinkle, 1999, p. 469)

Community counseling has not always been a specialty area in the profession of counseling. Rather, it has evolved over the years. Many people, unaware of its evolution, forget that professional counseling has always stressed growth and focused on people in many stages of life. Therefore, it is important to examine the history of community counseling in the broadest context possible. In the next section, the historical events and circumstances that have shaped the counseling profession are highlighted. Understanding the past can lead to a better appreciation of the present and future trends of community counseling.

A CHRONOLOGICAL OVERVIEW OF COMMUNITY COUNSELING

One way to chart the evolution of counseling is to trace important events and personal influences through the decades of the 20th century and into the 21st century. Keep in mind that the development of professional counseling, like the activity itself, was and is a process. Therefore, some names and events will not fit neatly into a rigid chronology.

Before 1900

Counseling is a relatively new profession (Aubrey, 1977, 1982), and its foundations are interdisciplinary. Some of the roles carried out by counselors were and are shared by other individuals in the helping professions (Herr & Fabian, 1993).

Before the 1900s, most counseling was informal and in the form of advice or information. Indeed, "no mention of counseling was made in the professional literature until 1931" (Aubrey, 1983). In the United States, counseling developed out of a humanitarian concern to improve people's lives in communities adversely affected by the Industrial Revolution of the mid- to late 1800s (Aubrey, 1983). The social welfare reform movement, the spread of public education, and various changes in population makeup of the time, such as the influx of a large number of immigrants, also influenced the growth of what would become the counseling profession and ultimately community counseling (Aubrey, 1977; Goodyear, 1984).

Most of the pioneers in counseling identified themselves as social reformers and educators. They focused on helping children and adults learn about themselves, others, and the world of work. Initially, these helpers were involved primarily in child/adult welfare, educational/vocational guidance, and even legal reform. Their work was built on specific information and lessons, such as moral instruction on being good and doing right (Nugent, 2000). They saw needs in American society and took steps to fulfill them. Teachers and administrators in agencies were the main practitioners. Activities that would commonly become community counseling were an early focus.

1900–1909

Community counseling began as an infant profession in the early 1900s, when the helping process was largely dominated by Freud's psychoanalytic theory and behaviorism. During this decade, three persons emerged as leaders: Frank Parsons, Clifford Beers, and Jesse B. Davis.

Frank Parsons, a Boston educator, focused on growth and prevention. Parsons has been characterized as a broad scholar, a persuasive writer, a tireless activist, and a great intellect (Davis, 1988; Zytowski, 1985). Often called the Father of Guidance, he is best known for having founded Boston's Vocational Bureau in 1908, which represented a major step in the development of vocational guidance.

Parsons worked with young people who were in the process of making career decisions. He theorized that choosing a vocation was a matter of relating three factors: a knowledge of work, a knowledge of self, and a matching of the two (Drummond & Ryan, 1995). Parsons devised a number of procedures to help his clients learn more about themselves and the world of work. His work provided the foundation on which modern career counseling is based (Kiselica & Robinson, 2001).

Parsons's book, *Choosing a Vocation* (1909), published 1 year after his death, was quite influential. For example, having been influenced by Parsons, Boston's school superintendent, Stratton Brooks, designated 117 elementary and secondary teachers as "vocational counselors" (Nugent, 2000). The "Boston example" soon spread to other major cities as others recognized the need for vocational planning. By 1910, thirty-five cities were attempting to emulate Boston (Lee, 1966). In any case, one emphasis in community counseling can be traced to the influence of Parsons.

Clifford Beers, a former Yale student, was hospitalized for mental illness several times during his life. He found conditions in mental institutions deplorable and exposed them in his book, *A Mind That Found Itself* (1908), which became quite popular. Beers advocated better mental health facilities and reform in the treatment of the mentally ill. His work had an especially powerful influence on the fields of psychiatry and psychology, in which many of the practitioners described their activities as counseling (Hansen, Stevic, & Warner, 1986). Although Beers died in a psychiatric facility at the age of 67, his Mental Hygiene Movement aroused the national conscience to act on behalf of those who were mentally ill (Kiselica & Robinson, 2001), and his legacy was a forerunner of the mental health emphasis in community counseling.

Jesse B. Davis was the first person to set up a systematized guidance program in the public schools (Aubrey, 1977). As superintendent of the Grand Rapids, Michigan, school system, he suggested in 1907 that classroom teachers of English composition teach their students lessons in guidance once a week, with the goal of building character and preventing problems. Davis, influenced by such progressive American educators as Horace Mann and John Dewey, believed that proper guidance would help cure the ills of American society (Aubrey, 1977). What Davis and other progressive educators advocated was not counseling in the modern sense but a forerunner of counseling: school guidance (a preventive educational means of teaching students how to effectively deal with life events).

1910s

The contributions of Parsons, Beers, and Davis during the initial decade of the century led to the emergence of several "firsts" during the next decade. The first university-level course in vocational guidance was offered at Harvard University in 1911. The first citywide school guidance program was established in Grand Rapids, Michigan, in 1912; and in 1913, the National Vocational Guidance Association (NVGA), the first national professional organization in the counseling field, was founded (Hershenson, Power, & Waldo, 1996).

The NVGA began publishing a bulletin in 1915 (Goodyear, 1984). In 1921, the *National Vocational Guidance Bulletin* started regular publication. It evolved in later years to become the *National Vocational Guidance Magazine* (1924–1933), *Occupations, The Vocational Guidance Magazine* (1933–1944), *Occupations, The Vocational Guidance Journal* (1944–1952), *Personnel and Guidance Journal* (1952–1984), and finally the *Journal of Counseling and Development* (1984). NVGA was important because it established an association offering guidance literature and united those with an interest in vocational counseling for the first time.

An interest in testing, especially group testing, emerged during this decade as a result of World War I. To screen its personnel, the U.S. Army commissioned the development of numerous psychological instruments, among them the *Army Alpha* and *Army Beta* intelligence tests. Several of the Army's screening devices were employed in civilian populations after the war, and psychometrics (psychological testing) became a popular movement.

Aubrey (1977) observes that because the vocational guidance movement developed without an explicit philosophy, it quickly embraced psychometrics to gain a legitimate foothold in psychology. Reliance on psychometrics had both positive and negative effects. On the positive side, it gave vocational guidance specialists a stronger and more "scientific" identity. On the negative side, it distracted many specialists from developments in other behavioral sciences, such as sociology, biology, and anthropology.

1920s

The 1920s were relatively quiet for the developing community counseling profession. This was a period of consolidation. Education courses for counselors, which had begun at Harvard in 1911, almost exclusively emphasized vocational guidance during the 1920s. The dominant influences on the emerging profession were the progressive theories of education and the federal government's use of guidance services with war veterans.

A notable event was the development of the first standards for the preparation and evaluation of occupational materials (Lee, 1966). Along with these standards came the publication of new psychological instruments such as Edward Strong's *Strong Vocational Interest Inventory* (SVII) in 1928. Although the publication of this instrument did not have an immediate impact on the field of counseling in general, it set the stage for future directions (Strong, 1943).

A final noteworthy event of the decade was Abraham and Hannah Stone's 1929 establishment of the first marriage and family counseling center in New York City. This event was followed by the establishment of other centers throughout the nation, marking the beginning of the specialty of marriage and family counseling.

1930s

The 1930s were not as quiet as the 1920s, in part because the Great Depression influenced researchers and practitioners, especially in university and vocational settings, to emphasize helping strategies and counseling methods that related to employment (Ohlsen, 1983). A highlight of the decade was the development of the first theory of counseling, which was formulated by E. G. Williamson and his colleagues (including John Darley and Donald Paterson) at the University of Minnesota. Williamson modified Parsons's theory and used it to work with students and the unemployed. His emphasis on a directive, counselor-centered approach came to be known by several names, including the *Minnesota point of view* and *trait-factor counseling*. Williamson's (1939) pragmatic approach promoted the counselor's teaching, mentoring, and influencing skills.

One premise of Williamson's theory was that persons had traits (e.g., aptitudes, interests, personalities, achievements) that could be integrated in a variety of ways to form factors (constellations of individual characteristics). Counseling was based on a scientific, problem-solving, empirical method that was individually tailored to each client to help him or her stop nonproductive thinking and become an effective decision maker (Lynch & Maki, 1981). Williamson's influence dominated counseling for the next 2 decades, and he continued to write about the theory into the 1970s (Williamson & Biggs, 1979).

Another major occurrence was the broadening of counseling beyond occupational concerns. The seeds of this development were sown in the 1920s, when Edward Thorndike and other psychologists began to challenge the vocational orientation of the guidance movement (Lee, 1966). The work of John Brewer completed this change in emphasis. His 1932 book, *Education as Guidance,* proposed that every teacher be a counselor and that guidance be incorporated into the school curriculum. Brewer believed that all education should focus on preparing students to live outside of the school environment. His emphasis helped counselors see vocational decisions as just one part of their responsibilities. Although this event initially had the most relevance for counselors who worked in schools, it later affected counselors working in community settings.

During the 1930s, the U.S. government became more involved in counseling, especially by establishing the U.S. Employment Service. This agency published the first edition of the *Dictionary of Occupational Titles* (DOT) in 1939. The DOT, which became a major source of career information for specialists working with the unemployed, described known occupations in the United States and coded them according to job titles.

1940s

Three major events of the 1940s radically shaped the practice of counseling: the theory of Carl Rogers, World War II, and the government's involvement in counseling after the war.

Carl Rogers rose to prominence in 1942 with the publication of his book *Counseling and Psychotherapy,* which challenged the counselor-centered approach of Williamson as well as major tenets of Freudian psychoanalysis. Rogers espoused a nondirective approach to counseling that focused on the client. His ideas were both widely accepted and harshly criticized. Rogers advocated giving clients the responsibility for their own growth. He thought that if clients had an opportunity to be accepted and heard, then they would begin to know themselves better and become more congruent (genuine). The counselor, acting in a nonjudgmental, accepting role, served as a mirror, reflecting the verbal and emotional manifestations of the client.

Aubrey (1977) has noted that before Rogers, the literature in counseling was very practical, dealing with topics such as testing, orientation, procedures, vocations, placement functions, and the goals and purposes of guidance. With Rogers, there was a new emphasis on the techniques and methods of counseling, research, selection and training of future counselors, and the goals and objectives of counseling. Guidance, for all intents and purposes, suddenly disappeared as a major consideration in the bulk of the literature and was replaced by a decade or more of concentration on counseling.

With the advent of World War II, the U.S. government needed counselors and psychologists to help select and train specialists for the military and for industry (Ohlsen, 1983). The war also brought about a new way of looking at vocations for men and women. During the war, many women worked outside the home.

Traditional occupational sex roles began to be questioned, and greater emphasis was placed on personal freedom.

Also during the war, mental health professionals worked successfully with a large number of military personnel who suffered emotional breakdowns. The National Institute of Mental Health was established, and in 1946, the National Mental Health Act was passed, which authorized funds for research and training to prevent and treat mental health disorders (Hershenson et al., 1996).

After the war, the U.S. Veterans Administration (VA) funded the training of counselors and psychologists by granting stipends and paid internships to students engaged in graduate study. Monies made available through the VA and the GI Bill (benefits for veterans) influenced teaching professionals in graduate education to define their curriculum offerings more precisely. Counseling, as a profession, began to move further away from its historical alliance with vocational development.

1950s

"If one decade in history had to be singled out for the most profound impact on counselors, it would be the 1950s" (Aubrey, 1977, p. 292). Indeed, the 1950s produced at least four major events that dramatically affected the history of counseling:

- The establishment of the American Personnel and Guidance Association (APGA)
- The establishment of Division 17 (Counseling Psychology) within the American Psychological Association (APA)
- The passage of the National Defense Education Act (NDEA)
- The introduction of new guidance and counseling theories

American Personnel and Guidance Association.   APGA grew out of the American Council of Guidance and Personnel Association (ACGPA), a loose confederation of organizations "concerned with educational and vocational guidance and other personnel activities" (Harold, 1985, p. 4). ACGPA operated from 1935 to 1951, but its major drawback was its inability to commit its members to any course of action. APGA was formed in 1952 with the purpose of formally organizing groups interested in guidance, counseling, and personnel matters. Its original four divisions were the American College Personnel Association (Division 1), the National Association of Guidance Supervisors and Counselor Trainers (Division 2), the NVGA (Division 3), and the Student Personnel Association for Teacher Education (Division 4). During its early history, APGA was more of an interest group than a professional organization, because it did not originate or enforce standards for membership (Super, 1955).

Division 17.   In 1952, the Division of Counseling Psychology (Division 17) of APA was formally established. Its formation required dropping the term *guidance* from what had formerly been the association's Counseling and Guidance Division. Part of the impetus for the division's creation came from the VA, but the main impetus came from APA members interested in working with a more "normal" population than the one seen by clinical psychologists (Whitely, 1984).

Once created, Division 17 became more fully defined. Super (1955), for instance, distinguished between counseling psychology and clinical psychology, holding that counseling psychology was more concerned with normal human growth and development and was influenced in its approach by both vocational counseling and humanistic psychotherapy. Despite Super's work, counseling psychology had a difficult time establishing a clear identity within the APA (Whitely, 1984). Yet the division's existence has had a major impact on the growth and development of counseling as a profession.

National Defense Education Act.   A third major event was the passage in 1958 of the National Defense Education Act (NDEA), which was enacted following the Soviet Union's launching of their first space satellite, *Sputnik I.* The Act's primary purpose was to identify scientifically and academically talented students and promote their development. Through Title V-B, funds were provided for upgrading school counseling programs. The NDEA also established counseling and guidance institutes and provided funds and stipends to train counselors. In 1964, NDEA was extended to include elementary counseling. By 1965, the number of school counselors exceeded 30,000 (Armour, 1969). Because of NDEA, school counselors were plentiful, and it became possible for counselor educators to consider offering programs in community and agency settings.

New theories.   Several new counseling theories emerged during the 1950s. Prior to that time, four main theories influenced the work of counselors: (a) psychoanalysis and insight theories (e.g., Sigmund Freud); (b) trait–factor or directive theories (e.g., E. G. Williamson); (c) humanistic and client-centered theories (e.g., Carl Rogers); and, to a lesser extent, (d) behavioral theories (e.g., B. F. Skinner). Debates among counselors usually centered on whether directive or nondirective counseling was more effective, and almost all counselors assumed that certain tenets of psychoanalysis (e.g., defense mechanisms) were true.

During the 1950s, debate gradually shifted away from this focus as new theories of helping began to emerge. Behavioral theories, such as Joseph Wolpe's systematic desensitization, began to gain influence. Cognitive theories made an appearance, as witnessed by the growth of Albert Ellis's rational-emotive therapy and Eric Berne's transactional analysis. Learning theory, self-concept theory, and advances in developmental psychology made an impact as well (Aubrey, 1977). By the end of the decade, the number and complexity of theories associated with counseling had grown considerably and were applicable in settings outside the educational environment.

1960s

The initial focus of the 1960s was on counseling as a developmental profession. Gilbert Wrenn set the tone for the decade in his widely influential book, *The Counselor in a Changing World* (1962). His emphasis, reinforced by other prominent professionals such as Leona Tyler and Donald Blocher, was on working with others to resolve developmental needs. Wrenn's book had influence throughout the 1960s, and he, along with Tyler, became one of the strongest counseling advocates in the United States.

The impact of the developmental model in counseling lessened, however, as the decade continued. The moderation came as a result of three events: the Vietnam War, the civil rights movement, and the women's movement. Each event stirred up passions and pointed out needs within society. Many counselors attempted to address social issues by concentrating their attention on special needs created by the events and by focusing on crisis counseling and other short-term intervention strategies.

Other powerful influences that emerged during the decade were the humanistic counseling theories of Dugald Arbuckle, Abraham Maslow, and Sidney Jourard. Also important was the phenomenal growth of the group movement (Gladding, 2003). The emphasis of counseling shifted from a one-on-one encounter to small-group interaction. Behavioral counseling grew in prominence with the appearance of John Krumboltz's *Revolution in Counseling* (1966), which promoted learning (beyond insight) as the root of change. Thus, the decade's initial focus on development became sidetracked, although an awareness of the need for counseling throughout society had grown.

Professionalism within APGA increased during the 1960s. In 1961, APGA published a "sound code of ethics for counselors" (Nugent, 1981, p. 28). In 1969, Division 17 of APA began publication of a professional journal, *The Counseling Psychologist,* with Gilbert Wrenn as its first editor. This journal, along with the *Personnel and Guidance Journal,* accepted articles representing a wide range of counseling interests.

Particularly important to the evolution of community counseling was the passage of the 1963 Community Mental Health Centers Act. The goal of this landmark act was to establish a nationwide system of community mental health centers (CMHCs) that would serve the needs of America's newly deinstitutionalized mentally ill population by focusing on outpatient, community-based services (Winegar, 1993). These centers opened up new counseling employment opportunities outside educational settings, and many counselor education programs changed their focus from preparing counselors for work in schools to preparing counselors for work in community agencies (Hershenson et al., 1996).

A final noteworthy milestone was the establishment of the ERIC Clearinghouse on Counseling and Personnel Services (CAPS) at the University of Michigan. Founded in 1966 by Garry Walz, ERIC/CAPS was funded by the Office of Educational Research and Improvement at the U.S. Department of Education and was another example of the impact of government on the development of counseling. Through the years ERIC/CAPS (now ERIC/CASS; http://www.ericcass.uncg.edu/) would become one of the largest and most utilized resources on counseling activities and trends in the United States and throughout the world. It also sponsored conferences on leading topics in counseling that brought national leaders together.

1970s

The 1970s saw the emergence of several trends. Among the more important were the rapid growth of counseling outside educational settings, the formation of helping-skills programs, the beginning of licensure for counselors, and the further development of APGA as a professional organization for counselors.

Diversification in counseling settings.   The rapid growth of counseling outside educational institutions started in the 1970s, when mental health centers and community agencies began to employ significant numbers of counselors. Before this time, the majority of counselors had been employed in educational settings, usually public schools. But the demand for school counselors decreased as the economy underwent several recessions and the number of school-age children began to decline. In addition, the number of counselor education programs increased from 327 in 1964 to about 475 by 1980 (Hollis & Wantz, 1980). This dramatic rise in the number of counselor education programs meant that more counselors were competing for available jobs (Steinhauser, 1985).

The diversification of counseling resulted in specialized training in counselor education programs and in the development of new concepts of counseling. For example, Lewis and Lewis (1977) used the term *community counselor* to describe a new type of counselor who could function in multidimensional roles regardless of employment setting. Many community counseling programs were established, and counselors became more common in such agencies as mental health clinics, hospices, employee assistance programs, psychiatric hospitals, and substance abuse centers. Equally as striking, and more dramatic in growth, was the formation of the American Mental Health Counselor Association (AMHCA) within APGA. Founded in 1976, AMHCA quickly became one of the largest divisions within APGA and united mental health counselors into a professional organization in which they could better define their roles and goals.

Helping-skills programs.   The 1970s saw the development of helping-skills programs that concentrated on relationship and communication skills. Initiated by Truax and Carkhuff (1967) and Ivey (1971), these programs taught basic counseling skills to professionals and nonprofessionals alike. The emphasis was humanistic and eclectic. It was assumed that there were certain fundamental skills that should be mastered to establish satisfactory personal interaction. A bonus for counselors who received this type of training was that they could teach the skills to others rather easily. Thus, counselors could now consult by teaching some of their skills to their colleagues.

State licensure.   By the mid-1970s, state boards of examiners for psychologists had become more restrictive. Some of their restrictions, such as barring graduates of counseling programs in education departments from taking the psychology licensure exam, caused considerable tension, not only between APA and APGA but also within the APA membership itself (Ohlsen, 1983). The result was APGA's move toward state and national licensure for counselors. In 1976, Virginia became the first state to adopt a counselor licensure law.

A strong APGA.   During the 1970s, APGA emerged as an even stronger professional organization. Several changes altered its image and function, one of which was the building of its own headquarters in Alexandria, Virginia. APGA also began to question its professional identification, because personnel and guidance seemed to be outmoded ways of defining the organization's emphases.

In 1973, the Association of Counselor Educators and Supervisors (ACES), a division of APGA, outlined the standards for a master's degree in counseling. In 1977, ACES approved guidelines for doctoral preparation in counseling (Stripling, 1978). During the decade, the membership of the organization increased to almost 40,000, and five new divisions (including AMHCA) were chartered.

1980s

The 1980s saw the continued growth of counseling as a profession, exemplified by proactive initiatives from counselors associated with APGA and Division 17. Among the most noteworthy events of the decade were those that standardized the training and certification of counselors, those that recognized counseling as a distinct profession, those that increased the diversification of counselor specialties, and those that emphasized human growth and development.

Standardization of training and certification.   The move toward standardized training and certification of counselors began early in the decade and grew stronger yearly. In 1981, the Council for Accreditation of Counseling and Related Educational Programs (CACREP) was formed as an affiliate organization of APGA. It refined the standards first proposed by ACES in the late 1970s and initially accredited four programs and grandparented programs already recognized as accredited by the California State Counselor Association and ACES (Steinhauser & Bradley, 1983). In 1987, CACREP achieved membership in the Council on Postsecondary Accreditation (COPA), thereby putting it on a par with such accreditation bodies as the APA (Herr, 1985). CACREP standardized counselor education programs for master's and doctoral programs in the areas of school, community/agency, mental health, marriage and family counseling/therapy, and personnel services for college students. The inclusion of community/agency counseling in CACREP accreditation further strengthened this specialty within the profession.

Complementing the work of CACREP, the National Board for Certified Counselors (NBCC), which was formed in 1983, began to certify counselors on a national level. The NBCC developed a standardized test, and defined eight major subject areas in which counselors should be knowledgeable: (a) human growth and development, (b) social and cultural foundations, (c) helping relationships, (d) groups, (e) lifestyle and career development, (f) appraisal, (g) research and evaluation, and (h) professional orientation. To become a National Certified Counselor (NCC), examinees were required to pass a standardized test and meet experiential and character reference qualifications. In 1984, NBCC set up standards for certifying career counselors, and as a result, many individuals became National Certified Career Counselors (NCCC) (Herr, 1985). By the end of the decade, there were approximately 17,000 NCC and NCCC professionals.

Finally, in collaboration with CACREP, the National Academy of Certified Clinical Mental Health Counselors (NACCMHC), an affiliate of AMHCA, continued to define training standards and certify counselors in mental health counseling, a process it had begun in the late 1970s (Seiler, Brooks, & Beck, 1987; Wilmarth, 1985). It also began training supervisors of mental health counselors in 1988. Both programs attracted thousands of new professionals into counseling and upgraded the credentials of those already in the field.

Counseling as a distinct profession.   A profession is characterized by its "role statements, codes of ethics, accreditation guidelines, competency standards, licensure, certification and other standards of excellence" (VanZandt, 1990, p. 243). The evolution of counseling in the 1980s as a distinct mental health profession came as a result of events, issues, and forces, both inside and outside APGA (Heppner, 1990). Inside APGA, there was a growing awareness among its leaders that the words *personnel* and *guidance* no longer described the work of its members. In 1983, after considerable debate, APGA changed its name to the American Association for Counseling and Development (AACD) to "reflect the changing demographics of its membership and the settings in which they worked" (Herr, 1985, p. 395). The name change symbolized the rapid transformation in identity that APGA members had been experiencing through the implementation of policies regarding training, certification, and standards. External events that influenced APGA to change its name and ultimately its focus included legislation, especially on the federal level, that recognized mental health providers and actions by other mental health services associations.

Moreover, professional commitment among members of AACD increased. Chi Sigma Iota, an international academic and professional honor society, was formed in 1985 to promote excellence in the profession. By the end of the decade, it had grown to over 100 chapters and 5,000 members (Sweeney, 1989). Furthermore, liability insurance policies, new counseling specialty publications, legal defense funds, legislative initiatives, and a variety of other membership services were made available to AACD members (Myers, 1990). By 1989, over 58,000 individuals had become members of AACD, an increase of over 18,000 members in 10 years.

Diversification of counseling.   During the 1980s, counselors became even more diversified. Large numbers of counselors continued to be employed in primary and secondary schools and in higher education in a variety of student personnel services. Mental health counselors and community/agency counselors were the two largest blocks of professionals outside formal educational environments. In addition, the number of counselors swelled in mental health settings for business employees, the aging, and married persons and families. Symbolic of that growth, the Association for Adult Development and Aging (AADA) and the International Association for Marriage and Family Counselors (IAMFC) were organized and chartered as divisions of the American Counseling Association (ACA) in 1987 and 1990, respectively.

Strong membership in AACD divisions dedicated to group work, counselor education, humanistic education, measurement and development, religious and value issues, employment and career development, rehabilitation, multicultural concerns, offender work, and military personnel further exemplified the diversity of counseling during the 1980s. Special issues of AACD journals focused on such topics as violence (*Journal of Counseling and Development,* March 1987), the gifted and talented (*Journal of Counseling and Development,* May 1986), the arts (*Journal of Mental Health Counseling,* January 1985), and prevention (*Elementary School Guidance and Counseling,* October 1989). These publications helped broaden the scope of counseling services and counselor awareness.

Increased emphasis on human growth and development.   Counseling's emphasis on human growth and development during the 1980s took several forms. For example, new emphasis was placed on developmental counseling across the life span (Gladstein & Apfel, 1987). New behavioral expressions associated with Erik Erikson's first five stages of life development were formulated (Hamachek, 1988). An increased emphasis on the development of adults and the elderly was most clearly represented by the formation of the Association for Adult Aging and Development (AAAD) and by the development of curriculum guides that infused gerontological counseling into counselor preparation programs.

A second way human growth and development was stressed was through increased attention to gender issues and sexual orientation (see, for example, O'Neil & Carroll, 1988; Pearson, 1988; Weinrach, 1987). Carol Gilligan's (1982) landmark study on the development of moral values in females, which helped introduce feminist theory into the counseling arena, forced human growth specialists to examine more thoroughly the differences between genders. There was more of an emphasis on moral development, as research in the area increased (Colangelo, 1985; Lapsley & Quintana, 1985).

Finally, the challenges of working with different ethnic and cultural groups were increasingly discussed (Ponterotto & Casas, 1987). The Association for Multicultural Counseling and Development (AMCD) assumed a leadership role in these discussions; but multicultural themes, such as the importance of diversity, became a central issue among all groups, especially in light of the renewed racism that developed in the 1980s (Carter, 1990).

Overall, the increased emphasis on human growth and development highlighted the need for counseling in a variety of settings. The events of the 1980s enhanced the professional status of community counselors in a number of areas, and the actual number of community counselors graduating from counselor education programs began to exceed the number of school counselors for the first time in history.

1990s

Changes in the evolution of the counseling profession continued into the 1990s—some of them symbolic and others structural. One change that was both symbolic and substantial was the 1992 decision by the American Association for Counseling and Development (AACD) to modify its name and become the American Counseling Association (ACA). The new name better reflected the membership and mission of the organization. Three new divisions within ACA were founded: the American College Counseling Association in 1991; the Association for Gay, Lesbian, and Bisexual

Issues in Counseling in 1996; and Counselors for Social Justice in 1999. By the end of the decade, ACA was composed of 18 different divisions:

1. *National Career Development Association (NCDA).* Founded in 1913; formerly the National Vocational Guidance Association.
2. *Counseling Association for Humanistic Education and Development (C-AHEAD).* Founded in 1931; formerly the Student Personnel Association for Teacher Education.
3. *Association for Counselor Education and Supervision (ACES).* Founded in 1938; formerly the National Association of Guidance Supervisors and Counselor Trainers.
4. *American School Counselor Association (ASCA).* Founded in 1953.
5. *American Rehabilitation Counseling Association (ARCA).* Founded in 1958; formerly the Division of Rehabilitation Counseling.
6. *Association for Assessment in Counseling and Education (AACE).* Founded in 1965; formerly the Association for Measurement and Evaluation in Guidance.
7. *National Employment Counseling Association (NECA).* Founded in 1966.
8. *Association for Multicultural Counseling and Development (AMCD).* Founded in 1972; formerly the Association for Non-White Concerns in Personnel and Guidance.
9. *International Association of Addictions and Offender Counselors (IAAOC).* Founded in 1972; formerly the Public Offender Counselor Association.
10. *Association for Specialists in Group Work (ASGW).* Founded in 1973.
11. *Association for Spiritual, Ethical, and Religious Values in Counseling (ASERVIC).* Founded in 1974; formerly the National Catholic Guidance Conference.
12. *American Mental Health Counselors Association (AMHCA).* Founded in 1978.
13. *Association for Counselors and Educators in Government (ACEG).* Founded in 1984; formerly the Military Educators and Counselors Association (MECA).
14. *Association for Adult Development and Aging (AADA).* Founded in 1986.
15. *International Association of Marriage and Family Counselors (IAMFC).* Founded in 1989.
16. *American College Counseling Association (ACCA).* Founded in 1991.
17. *Association for Gay, Lesbian, and Bisexual Issues in Counseling (AGLBC).* Founded in 1996.
18. *Counselors for Social Justice.* Founded as an organizational affiliate in 1999. Gained divisional status in September 2002.

A second noteworthy event of the decade was the continued strong emphasis on counseling issues related to multiculturalism and diversity. In 1992, Sue, Arredondo, and McDavis published a set of multicultural competencies and standards to guide professionals who were working with people of different races. This important publication set the stage for a larger debate about the nature of multiculturalism. Some leaders in the field adopted a more inclusive definition of multicultural counseling, taking into account differences in language, socioeconomic status, gender, sexual orientation, physical abilities, race, culture, and ethnicity (Lee, 1997). Much discussion occurred, and continues to occur, about what diversity and counseling within a pluralistic society entail (Weinrach & Thomas, 1998).

A third noteworthy event that had particular significance for community and mental health counselors also occurred in 1992. For the first time, counseling was included as a primary mental health profession in the health care human resource statistics compiled by the Center for Mental Health Services and by the National Institute of Mental Health (Manderscheid & Sonnenschein, 1992). This type of recognition put counseling on a par with other mental health specialties such as psychology, social work, and psychiatry. By the beginning of the 21st century, there were approximately 100,000 certified or licensed counselors in the United States (Wedding, 2000).

The provision of health care in general, including mental health care, significantly impacted the counseling profession during the 1990s. The explosive growth of managed care organizations during the decade has been described as a revolution in the private mental health care delivery system (Winegar, 1993). Conglomerates emerged, and many counselors became providers for health maintenance organizations (HMOs). Consequently, the number of independent counselors decreased, as did the number of sessions a counselor could offer under many managed health care plans. A new emphasis was placed on legislation connected with these organizations, motivating counselors to become increasingly informed and active as legislative proponents (Barstow, 1998).

Also within the decade, the importance of holistic approaches to counseling was emphasized. Counselors paid increased attention to the many contexts that affect mental health and well-being, including social and cultural influences, spirituality, and family and work environments.

Other developments within the decade included the following:

- The merger of NACCMHC with NBCC to credential over 22,000 counselors
- The growth of CACREP- and APA-accredited programs in counselor education and counseling psychology, both on the master's and on the doctoral levels (Hollis, 2000)
- An increased number of counseling-related publications by ACA, APA, commercial book companies, and ERIC/CASS (Counseling and Student Services Clearinghouse)
- The growth of Chi Sigma Iota to over 220 chapters and 22,000 members

CURRENT TRENDS IN THE NEW MILLENNIUM

In 2002, the counseling profession formally celebrated its 50th anniversary as a profession under the umbrella of the American Counseling Association. During 2001 and 2002, ACA paid special tribute to the counseling profession's history by chronicling the organization's first 50 years in a series of articles published in *Counseling Today*. These publications illustrated the fact that counseling is a dynamic profession that changes and adapts to meet emerging societal and individual needs.

Many topics that captured the profession's attention as the new century began and still continue to be salient are the changing roles of men and women, innovations in media and technology, the promotion of wellness, mental health parity legislation, and advocacy and social justice (Bass & Yep, 2002; Hackney & Wrenn, 1990; Lee & Walz, 1998). Concerns related to family dysfunction, poverty, violence, and aging are among a myriad of issues community counselors address. The manner in which mental health care is provided and funded, particularly as it relates to managed care organizations, remains a prominent area of concern.

Of particular importance to community counselors in the 21st century is the need to select counseling interventions based on outcome research. David Kaplan (2002) reminds us that counselors need to select interventions that empirically answer Gordon Paul's question: "What works best with this particular client, with this particular problem, with this particular counselor, in this particular setting?" Community counselors are challenged to refine, implement, and evaluate interventions that are empirically based.

Perhaps the most pressing concern of the 21st century is finding ways to deal with conflict, violence, and trauma. In the 1990s, heightened concern about conflict and safety emerged during a rash of school shootings and the Oklahoma City bombing, which resulted in the death of many innocent people (Daniels, 2002). However, a defining moment in conflict and violence occurred on September 11, 2001, when terrorists attacked the United States by crashing commercial airliners into the World Trade Center towers in New York City and into the Pentagon in Washington, DC. These acts signaled the beginning of an active, new emphasis in counseling on preparing and responding to trauma and tragedy (Bass & Yep, 2002; Walz & Kirkman, 2002). In the aftermath of the terrorist attacks, counselors have become increasingly aware of the need to develop crisis plans and strategies for working with different populations affected by violence and tragedy. As a response, ACA has created a Crisis Response Planning Task Force to prepare counselors to implement disaster mental health services on a large scale (Kaplan, 2002). Many community counselors have participated in disaster relief training coordinated by the American Red Cross, and others have made plans to do so. From both preventive and treatment perspectives, community counselors recognize the need to develop skills in dealing with violence, trauma, and tragedy.

Some of the topics that have particular relevance for community counselors practicing in the 21st century, including managed care challenges, technological influences, wellness, and spirituality, are discussed in more detail in Chapter 4. Other topics, including crisis counseling, advocacy, and outcome-based research, are addressed in conjunction with relevant chapters elsewhere in the text.

SUMMARY AND CONCLUSION

This chapter began with the story of a hero who went from being a rescuer to becoming a deliverer of preventive services. The story illustrates the assumptions of those who work as community counselors: that it is most important to focus on people's environments as opposed to their symptoms, that a multifaceted approach to treatment is better than one that is based on a single-service plan, and that prevention is more efficient than remediation. The chapter then briefly reviewed other premises of counseling in general and its evolution in the 20th century.

Counseling, especially community counseling, is distinguished from traditional psychotherapy and other human services professions by its concern with the developmental and situational difficulties of otherwise well-functioning persons. It is a short-term, theory-based approach to the resolution of problem areas, and it focuses on personal, social, vocational, and educational concerns within a number of environments.

The history of counseling shows that the profession has an interdisciplinary base that continues to this day. It began with the almost simultaneous concern and activity of Frank Parsons, Clifford Beers, and Jesse B. Davis to provide, reform, and/or improve services in the areas of vocational guidance, mental health treatment, and character development of children. Counseling is interlinked with but distinct from psychometrics, psychology, and sociology. Noteworthy events in the history of counseling include the involvement of the government in counseling during and after World War I, the Great Depression, World War II, and the launching of Sputnik. Ideas from innovators such as John Brewer, E. G. Williamson, Carl Rogers, Gilbert Wrenn, Leona Tyler, John Krumboltz, Alan Ivey, Carol Gilligan, and Derald Wing Sue have shaped the development of the profession and broadened its horizon. The emergence and growth of the American Counseling Association (which has its roots in the establishment of the National Vocational Guidance Association in 1913) has been a major factor in the growth of the profession, especially since the 1950s.

Community counseling programs emerged in universities in the 1970s, and community counseling was officially recognized as a specialty area in 1981, with the establishment of CACREP. The number of community counselors working in agency settings has dramatically increased since the beginning of the 1980s. In the first decade of the 21st century, community counselors can be found working with many different populations in a wide range of settings, including community mental health centers, medical settings, jails and prisons, businesses, and private practice. In the next chapter, attention shifts from the history of the counseling profession, including community counseling, to the importance of developing a professional identity as a community counselor.

SUMMARY TABLE

Highlights in the History of Community Counseling

1900s

Frank Parsons, the "Father of Guidance," establishes the Boston Vocational Bureau to help young people make career decisions; writes *Choosing A Vocation*.

Clifford Beers, a former mental patient, advocates for better treatment of the mentally ill; publishes influential book: *A Mind That Found Itself*.

Jesse B. Davis sets up first systematic guidance program in the public schools (Grand Rapids, Michigan).

1910s

National Vocational Guidance Association (NVGA) established; forerunner of American Counseling Association (ACA).

Psychometrics embraced by vocational guidance movement after World War I.

1920s

Publication of the *Strong Vocational Interest Inventory* (SVII).

Abraham and Hannah Stone establish the first marriage and family counseling center in New York City.

Counselors begin broadening focus beyond vocational interests.

1930s

E. G. Williamson and colleagues develop a counselor-centered trait-factor approach to work with the unemployed. It is the first theory of counseling, often called the Minnesota point of view.

John Brewer advocates education as guidance with vocational decision making as a part of the process.

Publication of the *Dictionary of Occupational Titles* (DOT), the first government effort to systematically code job titles.

1940s

Carl Rogers develops nondirective approach to counseling; publishes *Counseling and Psychotherapy*.

With advent of World War II, traditional occupational roles are questioned publicly; personal freedom is emphasized over authority.

U.S. Veterans Administration (VA) funds the training of counselors and psychologists.

1950s

American Personnel and Guidance Association (APGA) founded; forerunner of the American Counseling Association.

National Defense Education Act (NDEA) enacted. Title V-B provides training for counselors.

New theories (such as transactional analysis and rational-emotive therapy) are formulated. They challenge older theories (such as psychoanalysis, trait-factor, and client centered).

1960s

Emphasis in counseling on developmental issues. Gilbert Wrenn publishes *The Counselor in a Changing World*.

Leona Tyler writes extensively about counseling.

Behavioral counseling, led by John Krumboltz's *Revolution in Counseling,* emerges as a strong counseling theory.

Upheaval of civil rights and women's movements and Vietnam War. Counseling sidetracked from a developmental emphasis; counselors increasingly concerned with addressing social and crisis issues.

Community Mental Health Centers Act passed; establishes community mental health centers and future employment settings for community counselors.

Groups gain popularity as a way of resolving personal issues.

APGA publishes its first code of ethics.

ERIC/CAPS founded; begins building a database of research in counseling.

First publication of *The Counseling Psychologist* journal.

1970s

Diversification of counseling outside of educational settings. Term *community counseling* coined to describe this type of multifaceted counselor.

American Mental Health Counseling Association (AMHCA) formed.

Basic helping-skills programs begun by Robert Carkhuff, Allen Ivey, and colleagues.

State licensure of counselors begins; Virginia is first state to adopt a counselor licensure law.

APGA emerges as a strong professional association.

1980s

Council for Accreditation of Counseling and Related Educational Programs (CACREP) formed; begins accreditation of counseling programs, including community counseling.

National Board of Certified Counselors (NBCC) established.

Chi Sigma Iota (international academic and professional honor society) begun.

Growing membership continues in counseling associations. New headquarters building for AACD.

Human growth and development highlighted as an emphasis of counseling. *In a Different Voice* by Carol Gilligan focuses attention on the importance of studying women and women's issues in counseling.

1990s

AACD changes its name to the American Counseling Association (ACA).

Diversity and multicultural issues in counseling stressed by Paul Pedersen, Courtland Lee, Clemmont Vontress, Patricia Arredondo, Derald Wing Sue, and others.

Spiritual issues in counseling addressed more openly.

Increased focus on regulations and accountability for counselors.

National Academy for Clinical Mental Health Counselors merges with NBCC.

Counselors seek to be recognized as core providers as national health care reform is discussed and enacted.

Community counseling recognized more as a specialty within the counseling profession as agencies continue hiring a number of counselors.

2000 and Beyond

The counseling profession celebrates its 50th anniversary.
Current areas of focus include:

- Diversity, advocacy, and social justice
- Health maintenance organizations, managed care, and community counselors' roles as providers of mental health services
- Innovations in technology, especially the widespread use of the Internet
- An emphasis on holistic approaches, wellness, and spirituality
- The need for outcome-based research to determine "best practice" options
- Crisis management: finding ways to deal with conflict, violence, and trauma, both from a preventive and treatment standpoint

REFERENCES

Amos, W. E., & Williams, D. E. (1972). *Community counseling: A comprehensive model for developmental services*. St. Louis, MO: Warren H. Green.

Armour, D. J. (1969). *The American counselor*. New York: Russell Sage.

Aubrey, R. F. (1977). Historical development of guidance and counseling and implications for the future. *Personnel and Guidance Journal, 55*, 288–295.

Aubrey, R. F. (1982). A house divided: Guidance and counseling in twentieth century America. *Personnel and Guidance Journal, 60*, 198–204.

Aubrey, R. F. (1983). The odyssey of counseling and images of the future. *Personnel and Guidance Journal, 61*, 78–82.

Barstow, S. (1998, June). Managed care debate heats up in Congress. *Counseling Today, 1*, 26.

Bass, D. D., & Yep, R. (2002). *Terrorism, trauma, and tragedies: A counselor's guide to preparing and responding*. Alexandria, VA: American Counseling Association.

Beers, C. (1908). *A mind that found itself*. New York: Longman Green.

Brewer, J. M. (1932). *Education as guidance*. New York: Macmillan.

Carter, R. T. (1990). The relationship between racism and racial identity among white Americans: An exploratory investigation. *Journal of Counseling and Development, 69*, 46–50.

Colangelo, N. (1985). Overview. *Elementary School Guidance and Counseling, 19*, 244–245.

Daniels, J. A. (2002). Assessing threats of school violence: Implications for Counselors. *Journal of Counseling and Development, 80*, 215–218.

Davis, H. V. (1988). *Frank Parsons: Prophet, innovator, counselor*. Carbondale: University of Southern Illinois Press.

Drummond, R. J., & Ryan, C. W. (1995). *Career counseling: A developmental approach*. Upper Saddle River, NJ: Merrill/Prentice Hall.

Gilligan, C. (1982). *In a different voice*. Cambridge, MA: Harvard University Press.

Gladding, S. T. (1978). In the midst of the puzzles and counseling journey. *Personnel and Guidance Journal, 57,* 148.

Gladding, S. T. (2003). *Group work: A counseling specialty* (4th ed.). Upper Saddle River, NJ: Merrill/Prentice Hall.

Gladstein, G. A., & Apfel, F. S. (1987). A theoretically based adult career counseling center. *Career Development Quarterly, 36,* 178–185.

Goodyear, R. K. (1984). On our journal's evolution: Historical developments, transitions, and future directions. *Journal of Counseling and Development, 63,* 3–9.

Hackney, H., & Wrenn, C. G. (1990). The contemporary counselor in a changed world. In H. Hackney (Ed.), *Changing contexts for counselor preparation in the 1990s* (pp. 1–20). Alexandria, VA: Association for Counselor Education and Supervision.

Hamachek, D. E. (1988). Evaluating self-concept and ego development within Erikson's psychosocial framework: A formulation. *Journal of Counseling and Development, 66,* 354–360.

Hansen, J. C., Stevic, R. R., & Warner, R. W. (1986). *Counseling: Theory and process* (4th ed.). Boston: Allyn & Bacon.

Harold, M. (1985). Council's history examined after 50 years. *Guidepost, 27*(10), 4.

Hayes, R. L. (1984, March). Report on community Counseling. *ACES Newsletter,* 15.

Heppner, P. P. (1990). Life lines: Institutional perspectives [Feature editor's introduction]. *Journal of Counseling and Development, 68,* 246.

Herr, E. L. (1985). AACD: An association committed to unity through diversity. *Journal of Counseling and Development, 63,* 395–404.

Herr, E. L., & Fabian, E. S. (1993). The *Journal of Counseling and Development*: Its legacy and its aspirations. *Journal of Counseling and Development, 72,* 3–4.

Hershenson, D. B., Power, P. W., & Waldo, M. (1996). *Community counseling: Contemporary theory and practice.* Boston: Allyn & Bacon.

Hinkle, J. S. (1999). A voice from the trenches: A reaction to Ivey and Ivey (1998). *Journal of Counseling and Development, 77,* 474–483.

Hollis, J. W. (2000). *Counselor preparation 1999–2001: Programs, faculty, trends* (10th ed.). Philadelphia: Taylor & Francis.

Hollis, J. W., & Wantz, R. A. (1980). *Counselor preparation.* Muncie, IN: Accelerated Development.

Ivey, A. E. (1971). *Microcounseling: Innovations in interviewing training.* Springfield, IL: Thomas.

Kaplan, D. (2002, July). Celebrating 50 years of excellence. *Counseling Today, 1,* 45.

Kiselica, M. S., & Robinson, M. (2001). Bringing advocacy to life: The history, issues, and human dramas of social justice work in counseling. *Journal of Counseling and Development, 79,* 387–397.

Krumboltz, J. D. (Ed.). (1966). *Revolution in counseling.* Boston: Houghton Mifflin.

Lapsley, D. K., & Quintana, S. M. (1985). Recent approaches to the moral and social education of children. *Elementary School Guidance and Counseling, 19,* 246–259.

Lee, J. M. (1966). Issues and emphases in guidance: A historical perspective. In J. M. Lee & N. J. Pallone (Eds.), *Readings in guidance and counseling.* New York: Sheed & Ward.

Lee, C. C., & Walz, G. R. (Eds.). (1998). *Social action: A mandate for counselors.* Alexandria, VA: American Counseling Association.

Lee, C. C. (1997). The promise and pitfalls of multicultural counseling. In C. C. Lee (Ed.), *Multicultural issues in counseling* (2nd ed., pp. 3–13). Alexandria, VA: American Counseling Association.

Lewis, J., & Lewis, M. (1977). *Community counseling: A human services approach.* New York: Wiley.

Lynch, R. K., & Maki, D. (1981). Searching for structure: A trait-factor approach to vocational rehabilitation. *Vocational Guidance Quarterly, 30,* 61–68.

Manderscheid, R. W., & Sonnenschein, M. A. (1992). *Mental health in the United States, 1992* (DHHS Publication No. [SMA] 92-1942). Washington, DC: U.S. Government Printing Office.

Myers, J. E. (1989). *Infusing gerontological counseling into counselor preparation.* Alexandria, VA: American Association for Counseling and Development.

Myers, J. (1990). [Personal interview]. Greensboro, NC: Author.

National Board for Certified Counselors and National Academy of Certified Clinical Mental Health Counselors. (1988). *National directory of certified counselors.* Alexandria, VA: Author.

Nugent, F. A. (1981). *Professional counseling.* Monterey, CA: Brooks/Cole.

Nugent, F. A. (2000). *An introduction to the profession of counseling* (3rd ed.). Upper Saddle River, NJ: Merrill/Prentice Hall.

Ohlsen, M. M. (1983). *Introduction to counseling.* Itasca, IL: F. E. Peacock.

O'Neil, J. M., & Carroll, M. R. (1988). A gender role workshop focused on sexism, gender role conflict, and the gender role journey. *Journal of Counseling and Development, 67,* 193–197.

Parsons, F. (1909). *Choosing a vocation.* Boston: Houghton Mifflin.

Pearson, J. E. (1988). A support group for women with relationship dependency. *Journal of Counseling and Development, 66,* 394–396.

Ponterotto, J. G., & Casas, J. M. (1987). In search of multicultural competence within counselor education programs. *Journal of Counseling and Development, 65,* 430–434.

Remley, T. P., & Herlihy, B. (2001). *Ethical, legal, and professional issues in counseling.* Upper Saddle River, NJ: Merrill/Prentice Hall.

Rogers, C. R. (1942). *Counseling and psychotherapy.* Boston: Houghton Mifflin.

Romano, G. (1992, Spring). AACD's 40th Anniversary. *American Counselor, 1,* 18–26.

Seiler, G., Brooks, D. K., Jr., & Beck, E. S. (1987). Training standards of the American Mental Health Counselors Association: History, rationale, and implications. *Journal of Mental Health Counseling, 9,* 199–209.

Steinhauser, L. (1985). A new PhD's search for work: A case study. *Journal of Counseling and Development, 63,* 300–303.

Steinhauser, L., & Bradley, R. (1983). Accreditation of counselor education programs. *Counselor Education and Supervision, 25,* 98–108.

Stripling, R. O. (1978). ACES guidelines for doctoral preparation in counselor education. *Counselor Education and Supervision, 17,* 163–166.

Strong, E. K., Jr. (1943). *Vocational interests of men and women.* Stanford, CA: Stanford University Press.

Sue, D. W., Arredondo, P., & McDavis, R. J. (1992). Multicultural competencies and standards: A call to the profession. *Journal of Counseling and Development, 70,* 477–486.

Super, D. E. (1955). Transition: From vocational guidance to counseling psychology. *Journal of Counseling Psychology, 2,* 3–9.

Sweeney, T. (1989). Excellence vs elitism. *Newsletter of Chi Sigma Iota, 5,* 1, 11.

Truax, C. B., & Carkhuff, R. R. (1967). *Toward effective counseling and psychotherapy: Training and practice.* Chicago: Aldine.

United States Employment Service. (1939). *Dictionary of occupational titles.*

VanZandt, C. E. (1990). Professionalism: A matter of personal initiatives. *Journal of Counseling and Development, 68,* 243–245.

Walz, G. R., & Kirkman, C. J. (Eds.) (2002). *Helping people cope with tragedy and grief.* Greensboro, NC: ERIC/CASS and NBCC.

Wedding, D. (2000). Current issues in psychotherapy. In R. J. Corsini & D. Wedding (Eds.), *Current psychotherapies* (6th ed., pp. 445–460). Itasca, IL: F. E. Peacock.

Weinrach, S. G. (1987). Microcounseling and beyond: A dialogue with Allen Ivey. *Journal of Counseling and Development, 65,* 532–537.

Weinrach, S. G., & Thomas, K. R. (1998). Diversity-sensitive counseling today: A postmodern clash of values. *Journal of Counseling and Development, 76,* 115–122.

Whitely, J. M. (1984). Counseling psychology: A historical perspective. *Counseling Psychologist, 12,* 2–109.

Williamson, E. G. (1939). *How to counsel students: A manual of techniques for clinical counselors.* New York: McGraw-Hill.

Williamson, E. G., & Biggs, D. A. (1979). Trait-factor theory and individual differences. In H. M. Burks, Jr., & B. Stefflre (Eds.), *Theories of counseling* (3rd ed., pp. 91–131). New York: McGraw-Hill.

Wilmarth, R. R. (1985, Summer). Historical perspective, part two. *AMHCA News, 8,* 21.

Winegar, N. (1993). Managed mental health care: Implications for administrators and managers of community-based agencies. *Families in Society: The Journal of Contemporary Human Services, 74,* 171–178.

Wrenn, C. G. (1962). *The counselor in a changing world.* Washington, DC: American Personnel and Guidance Association.

Zytowski, D. (1985). Frank! Frank! Where are you now that we need you? *The Counseling Psychologist, 13,* 129–135.

CHAPTER 2

Professional Identity of Community Counselors

In the midst of a day
that has brought only grey skies, hard rain,
and two cups of lukewarm coffee,
You come to me with Disney World wishes
Waiting for me to change into:
a Houdini figure with Daniel Boone's style
Prince Charming's grace and Abe Lincoln's wisdom
Who with magic words, a wand,
frontier spirit, and perhaps a smile
Can cure all troubles in a flash.
But reality sits in a green-cushioned chair—
lightning has struck a nearby tree,
Yesterday ended another month,
I'm uncomfortable sometimes in silence,
And unlike fantasy figures
I can't always be
what you see in your mind.

Gladding, S. T. (1973). Reality sits in a green-cushioned chair. *Personnel and Guidance Journal*, *54*, 222. © ACA. Reprinted with permission. No further reproduction authorized without written permission of ACA.

I n Chapter 1, a definition of counseling and a description of the historical foundations of the counseling profession were presented. In this chapter, we focus on
the professional identity of community counselors. *Professional identity* refers
to the philosophy, training model, and scope of practice that characterize a particular
profession (MacCluskie & Ingersoll, 2001). A critical task for all counselors, including
community counselors, is to assume a professional identity and be able to explain
that identity to others (Remley & Herlihy, 2001).

At the beginning of this chapter, a general introduction to some of the therapeutic professionals with whom community counselors work is presented. Next, we
examine more closely the specific professional identity of community counselors.
The chapter closes with a description of professional credentialing that further
defines the roles and functions of professional counselors in general and community
counselors in particular.

THERAPEUTIC PROFESSIONALS IN COMMUNITY SETTINGS

Defining Therapeutic Professions

Counselors in community settings frequently work with several different therapeutic
professionals. To facilitate collaboration among mental health practitioners, it is
important to have an understanding both of one's own professional identity and the
professional identity of colleagues whose credentials differ but who perform similar
activities.

Therapeutic professionals can be defined as "mental health professionals
trained to help people with problems that manifest behaviorally or psychologically
and that may have roots in physical, psychological, or spiritual dimensions"
(MacCluskie & Ingersoll, 2001, p. 3). The problems people experience may range
from situational or developmental concerns to more severe psychological disorders.
Traditionally, attempts have been made to define specific mental health professions
based on the severity of client problems. However, professional definition based
strictly on client diagnosis may be somewhat misleading. Although the counseling
profession focuses on providing services that are developmental and preventive in
nature, community and agency counselors also are trained to work with clients experiencing more serious concerns, including problems described in the *Diagnostic
and Statistical Manual of Mental Disorders* (DSM-IV-TR, American Psychiatric Association [APA], 2000). Thus, it may be more helpful to categorize different therapeutic
professions by their training emphases and requirements, recognizing that similarities as well as differences exist among the various professions. In this section, we
provide a brief overview of the therapeutic professions of social work, psychiatry,
psychology, and counseling.

Social work.   Social workers who have trained at the graduate level earn the Master
of Social Work (MSW) degree by completing programs that range from 56 to 66
hours and include internships in social agencies. Some social workers elect to
pursue additional training at the doctoral level. Although it is possible to complete

social work programs at the undergraduate rather than at the graduate level, such programs do not lead to licensure, which allows the independent practice of mental health counseling. Social work educational programs are accredited by the Council on Social Work Education (CSWE) and are housed in schools of social work. The National Association of Social Workers (NASW) credentials professionals who demonstrate advanced clinical and educational proficiencies.

Social workers participate in a variety of activities, including helping individuals, groups, and communities enhance social functioning. They are trained to recognize the importance of clients' environments, status, and roles in society. Important goals include negotiating social systems and advocating for change (MacCluskie & Ingersoll, 2001). Some social workers administer government programs for the underprivileged and disenfranchised. Others engage in individual, group, and family counseling, emphasizing a systems and contextual approach rather than following a medical model.

Psychiatry.   In contrast, psychiatry represents a specialty area within the school of medicine. Psychiatrists earn a medical degree (MD) and then complete a residency in psychiatry. To earn the license to practice, they must pass both a national and a state examination.

There is some dispute within the field of psychiatry related to preferred models of training. Some psychiatrists primarily follow a strict biomedical model and spend most of their time with clients prescribing medications and evaluating their effects (MacCluskie & Ingersoll, 2001). Other psychiatrists adhere to a biopsychosocial model, which acknowledges the interaction of behavioral, psychological, and social factors on development and mental health. In general, psychiatrists specialize in treating people who have major psychological disorders, and, until recently, they were the only therapeutic professionals who had the authority to prescribe medication. In a few locations, some psychologists now have legal rights to prescribe psychopharmacological medications.

Psychology.   Psychology programs are accredited by the American Psychological Association (APA). Psychologists typically earn a PhD (doctor of philosophy), EdD (doctor of education), or PsyD (doctor of psychology), although some psychologists earn master's degrees but not doctorates. Areas of specialization within the field include clinical, social, cognitive, developmental, counseling, and school psychology. All states license psychologists, although requirements for licensure differ from state to state. Since the 1940s, psychologists have been viewed as experts in psychological assessment (Exner, 1995)—a view that has led to disagreement among therapeutic professionals about who should have access to various assessment instruments. In February 1996, responding to attempts by state psychology licensure boards to restrict assessment practices of other trained professionals, the National Fair Access Coalition on Testing (FACT) was formed. FACT represents some 525,000 counseling and mental health professionals who are interested in protecting their right to use psychological, educational, vocational, industrial, and other assessment instruments (National Fair Access Coalition on Testing, 2000).

Counseling psychology is a specialization area that derived from the APA Division of Counseling and Guidance in 1955 (Perry, 1955). Counseling psychology shares common roots and emphases with the field of counselor education, which is described in the following section.

Counselor education.   Professional counselors earn either a master's or a doctoral degree from a counselor education or closely related program. Programs are accredited by the Council for Accreditation of Counseling and Related Educational Programs (CACREP). On the master's level, CACREP accredits programs in community counseling, mental health counseling, school counseling, marriage and family counseling/therapy, and student affairs practice in higher education. CACREP-accredited master's programs range from a minimum of 48 to 60 semester hours depending on the area of specialization. Based on the 2003 CACREP guidelines, programs in community counseling, school counseling, and student affairs practice in higher education require a minimum of 48 semester hours, whereas mental health and marriage and family counseling programs require a minimum of 60 semester hours. Doctoral-level programs in counselor education require specialized course work, in-depth research, supervised field experiences, and instruction and practice in clinical supervision.

The number of accredited counselor preparation programs has increased steadily since 1981. Based on an April 2003 report, there are 389 accredited master's-level programs and 45 accredited doctoral programs in counseling and counselor education (see Table 2–1).

As noted in Chapter 1, there are several features of counseling that help distinguish it from other therapeutic professions. Although they may espouse different theoretical orientations, counselors from all specializations tend to work from a preventive, developmental, holistic framework, building on clients' strengths and assets. Counselors help clients with issues ranging from developmental concerns and problems in living to issues associated with pathology.

Box 2–1

"I treat everyone developmentally, but I want to recognize pathology when it is in the room with me."

—Robin Daniel, PhD, LPC, Director of Counseling and Student Disability Services, Greensboro College

Box 2–2
Who are professional counselors?

What makes professional counselors unique from their peers in other mental health disciplines is their "wellness" orientation. While trained to understand pathology and mental illness, professional counselors take a preventive approach to helping people and are trained to use counseling treatment interventions which include principles of development, wellness, and pathology that reflect a pluralistic society.

—American Counseling Association, 2003, http://www.counseling.org/resources/licensure.htm

Table 2–1

The Council for Accreditation of Counseling and Related Educational Programs Directory of Accredited Programs

Code	No. of Programs	Description
		Entry-level programs (Master's degree programs)
CC	129	Community Counseling (at least 48 semester hours)
ClC	2	College Counseling-2001 Standards (at least 48 semester hours)
CrC	6	Career Counseling (at least 48 semester hours)
GC	2	Gerontological Counseling (at least 48 semester hours)
MFC/T	26	Marital, Couple, and Family Counseling/Therapy (at least 60 semester hours)
MHC	29	Mental Health Counseling (at least 60 semester hours)
SC	150	School Counseling (at least 48 semester hours)
SA	1	Student Affairs-2001 Standards-(at least 48 semester hours)
SACC	33	Student Affairs Practice in Higher Education-College Counseling Emphasis-1994 Standards-(at least 48 semester hours)
SAPP	11	Student Affairs Practice in Higher Education-Professional Practice
	389	Emphasis-1994 standards-(at least 48 semester hours)
		Doctoral-level programs (PhD and/or EdD degree programs)
CE	45	Counselor Education and Supervision

Note. Reprinted with permission of the Council for Accreditation of Counseling and Related Educational Programs: 2003.

Some of the specific issues counselors are trained to help with include career and lifestyle issues, marriage and family concerns, stress management, crisis issues, and mediation (Smith, 1999). They help people grow mentally, emotionally, socially, spiritually, and educationally (American Counseling Association [ACA], 2003). Counselors typically follow a nonmedical approach that emphasizes the importance of biological, social, emotional, and psychological interactions.

Currently, 46 states and the District of Columbia legally regulate the counseling profession through licensure. Licensed, generalist practitioners are ethically bound to practice within their areas of competence and must participate in appropriate educational and supervision activities if they choose to add areas of specialization to their practice.

Other therapeutic professionals.   Community counselors who work in hospital settings are likely to interact with psychiatric nurses, who have been trained in schools of nursing, are registered nurses (RNs), and typically hold a master's degree.

Community counselors also may interact with counselors in various specialization areas, such as rehabilitation counseling, marriage and family therapy, or addictions counseling.

Collaboration among practitioners.   Although it is important to establish a specialized identity within the broad arena of therapeutic professions, it is equally important to recognize the ways in which professions interrelate. Ideally, understanding the differences and similarities among the various fields will enable professionals to collaborate and complement each other's work so that clients' needs are served effectively.

Box 2–3
Working Collaboratively With Other Therapeutic Professionals

I am a counselor educator who volunteers several hours each week at a nonprofit counseling center, where I counsel with children and families. Also working at the center are two clinical psychologists, a social worker, a substance abuse counselor, a grief counselor, and several community or mental health counselors. A psychiatrist acts as the center's medical director, and the agency director is a licensed professional counselor with a specialty in community counseling.

Each week, a two-hour block for group supervision is set aside. During this time, consultation is provided for clinicians who wish to present cases for feedback. Our combined knowledge, experiences, and training backgrounds contribute to a rich time of interaction and provide the presenting clinician with new skills and perspectives. We also discuss recent intakes and make decisions about which clinician, based on area of specialization, will be best suited to work with a particular client.

—Debbie Newsome, PhD, LPC, NCC

COMMUNITY COUNSELING AS A SPECIALTY

The specialty area within the field of counseling that is the focus of this text is community counseling. In this section, we provide an overview of the evolution of community counseling and discuss some of the characteristics of community counseling that distinguish it from other specialties.

Evolution of Community Counseling

Prior to the 1960s, the settings most commonly associated with counseling were schools and universities. With President John F. Kennedy's endorsement of the Community Mental Health Centers Act in 1963, the demand for counselors in community settings increased. The new law provided funding for the delivery of preventive mental health interventions in communities as well as in schools (Scileppi, Teed, & Torres, 2000). Responding to this need, counselor education programs began preparing students to work in community settings, with most community counseling programs beginning after 1970 (Hershenson & Berger, 2001). With the establishment of CACREP in 1981, master's programs in community and other agency settings, as well as programs in school counseling and college student personnel, were eligible to apply for accreditation.

Although no specialized division for community counseling was formed in what was then the American Association for Counseling and Development (AACD), a Committee on Community Counseling was developed in 1983 within the Association for Counselor Educators and Supervisors (ACES) (Hershenson & Berger, 2001). The committee proposed that community counseling be viewed as a process and an orientation rather than as a specialized work setting (Hayes, 1984). It was suggested that community counselors take into account the effects of the community environment on individuals and seek to empower individuals by serving as advocates, thereby affecting the community as a whole. Training of community counselors emphasized the delivery of preventive and rehabilitative services to a diverse clientele, and graduates of community counseling programs were employed in various positions and in many different settings (Hershenson & Berger, 2001).

Throughout the 1980s, no definitive criterion for community counseling programs was provided in the CACREP standards; instead, it was left up to each counseling program to define its own area of specialization (Hershenson & Berger, 2001). Consequently, there was a great deal of variation in course titles and content. Specific requirements for community counseling programs were delineated in the 1994 CACREP standards. These standards were further refined in the 2002 revision and are listed in Figure 2–1.

At the time of this writing, 129 master's-level counseling programs are accredited in community counseling (CACREP, 2003). The total number of programs represents an increase since 1999, when 104 community counseling programs were CACREP accredited, and closely approximates the number of accredited school counseling programs (150). In contrast, only 29 programs are accredited in mental health counseling, a specialty area that has many similarities to community counseling. However, community counseling, unlike school counseling and mental health counseling, never has established a specialized professional organization within ACA and has no identified representation on the CACREP board. It does not publish a professional journal, nor does it have a specialized certification procedure (Hershenson & Berger, 2001). Interestingly, in a recent survey of directors of community counseling programs, 42 of the 69 respondents did not believe that a professional division for community counseling within ACA was needed, although the majority of those surveyed did indicate that a newsletter, journal, and/or Web site focusing on community counseling should be developed (Hershenson & Berger).

Defining Community Counseling

During its evolution, community counseling has been defined in several different ways. Early in its formation, community counseling was viewed as counseling that took place in any setting other than schools or universities. Prior to the establishment

A. Foundations of Community Counseling

1. Historical, philosophical, societal, cultural, economic, and political dimensions of the current trends in the community human service/mental health movement
2. Roles, functions, preparation standards, credentialing, licensure and professional identity of community counselors
3. Policies, laws, legislation, recognition, reimbursement, right-to-practice, and other issues relevant to community counseling
4. Ethical and legal considerations specifically related to the practice of community counseling (e.g., the ACA Code of Ethics)
5. The role of racial, ethnic and cultural heritage, nationality, socioeconomic status, family structure, age, gender, sexual orientation, religious and spiritual beliefs, occupation, physical and mental status, and equity issues in community counseling

B. Contextual Dimensions of Community Counseling

1. The roles of community counselors in various practice settings and the relationships between counselors and other professionals in these settings
2. Organizational, fiscal, and legal dimensions of the institutions and settings in which community counselors practice
3. Strategies for community needs assessment to design, implement, and evaluate community counseling interventions, programs, and systems
4. General principles of community intervention, consultation, education, and outreach; and characteristics of human services programs and networks (public, private, and volunteer) in local communities

C. Knowledge and Skill Requirements for Community Counselors

1. Typical characteristics of individuals and communities served by a variety of institutions and agencies that offer community counseling services
2. Models, methods, and principles of program development and service delivery for a clientele based on assumptions of human and organizational development, including prevention, implementation of support groups, peer facilitation training, parent education, career/occupational information and counseling, and encouragement of self-help
3. Effective strategies for promoting client understanding of and access to community resources
4. Principles and models of biopsychosocial assessment, case conceptualization, theories of human development and concepts of normalcy and psychopathology leading to diagnoses and appropriate counseling plans
5. Knowledge of the principles of diagnosis and the use of current diagnostic tools, including the current edition of the *Diagnostic and Statistical Manual*
6. Effective strategies for client advocacy in public policy and other matters of equity and accessibility
7. Application of appropriate individual, couple, family, group, and systems modalities for initiating, maintaining, and terminating counseling, including the use of crisis intervention and brief, intermediate, and long-term approaches

D. Clinical Instruction

For the Community Counseling Program, the 600-clock hour internship (Standard III.H) occurs in a community setting under the clinical supervision of a site supervisor as defined by Section III, Standard C.1-2. The requirement includes a minimum of 240 direct service clock hours. The program must clearly define and measure the outcomes expected of interns, using appropriate professional resources that address Standards A, B, and C (Community Counseling Programs).

Figure 2–1
Standards for Community Counseling Programs (CACREP, 2003)
Note. Reprinted with permission of the Council for Accreditation of Counseling and Related Educational Programs Directory of Accredited Programs: 2003.

of the 1994 CACREP standards, concern was expressed about the lack of a clear definition of community counseling and the lack of consistency across programs (Cowger, Hinkle, DeRidder, & Erk, 1991). Since that time, a clearer definition of community counseling has emerged. Two of the more widely accepted definitions of community counseling are presented next.

Hershenson, Power, and Waldo (1996) defined *community counseling* as "the application of counseling principles and practices in agency, organizational, or individual practice settings that are located in and interact with their surrounding community" (p. 26). They suggested that community counseling is based on the following suppositions:

- The focus of assessment and intervention needs to include the community as well as the client.
- Interventions should take a proactive, health-promoting approach that is educative and empowering.
- Interventions are based on the principle of building on strengths, which include client and community resources.
- Community counselors working with specific populations or with particular issues may have to use skills developed by other counseling specialties (e.g., career, gerontological, or mental health counseling).
- Central functions of community counselors include counseling, coordinating, consulting, educating, programming, and advocacy.

Lewis, Lewis, Daniels, and D'Andrea (2003) also emphasized a multifaceted approach to community counseling that recognizes the importance of client–environment interaction. They defined *community counseling* as "a comprehensive helping framework of intervention strategies and services that promotes the personal development and well-being of all individuals and communities" (p. 6). They presented a model of community counseling comprised of four service components: (a) direct client services, (b) indirect client services, (c) direct community services, and (d) indirect community services. Examples of each service component are illustrated in Figure 2–2.

According to Lewis et al. (2003), effective community counselors reflect an awareness of society's effects on its members. They strive to understand the unique needs and experiences of people from diverse backgrounds and seek to prevent debilitating problems that occur in the community. Clients are viewed holistically, possessing strengths, resources, and limitations.

When clients learn to help themselves, they and their communities are strengthened. A common set of assumptions guide the work of community counselors, including the following:

- People's environments either nurture or limit them.
- The goal of counseling is to facilitate individual and community empowerment.
- A multifaceted approach to counseling is more effective than a single-service approach.
- Attention to the multicultural nature of clients' development is essential to the planning and delivery of counseling services.

	Client Services	**Community Services**
Direct	• Individual counseling • Crisis intervention • Substance abuse counseling • Family counseling	• Parent education programs • Stress management workshops • Conflict mediation workshops
Indirect	• Advocating for clients • Referring clients to appropriate human service agencies	• Lobbying for social change • Influencing public policy • Influencing systems that affect clients

Figure 2–2
Examples illustrating components of community counseling
Note. From *Community Counseling: Empowerment Strategies for a Diverse Society* (3rd ed.), by J. A. Lewis, M. D. Lewis, J. A. Daniels, and M. J. D'Andrea, 2003, Pacific Grove, CA: Brooks/Cole. Adapted with permission of Wadsworth, a division of Thomson Learning: www.thomsonrights.com. Fax 800 730-2215.

- Prevention is more efficient than remediation.
- The community counseling model can be used in a variety of human service, educational, and business settings (Lewis et al., 2003, p. 20).

The community counseling definitions provided by both Hershenson et al. (1996) and Lewis et al. (2003) address the fact that community counselors perform a broad range of therapeutic interventions among diverse client populations and in a variety of settings. Community counselors embrace multifaceted approaches that promote prevention, early intervention, and wellness, taking into account the client, the community, and the interactions between the two. *Community* can be conceptualized as the larger set of social systems in which the client lives and which directly affect functioning and development (Hershenson et al., 1996). A theoretical paradigm, or frame of reference, that is particularly suited to this conceptualization of community counseling is the bioecological model proposed by Uri Bronfenbrenner (1979, 1995). In the next section, a brief description of the environmental components of Bronfenbrenner's model is provided.

The Bioecological Model

The bioecological model of human development (Figure 2–3) focuses on the settings in which development occurs and on the interaction of individuals within and across those settings. According to the model, people grow and change through processes of progressively more complex reciprocal interactions between an active evolving individual and the persons, objects, and symbols in his or her immediate external environment (Bronfenbrenner, 1995). Specifically, the model integrates the

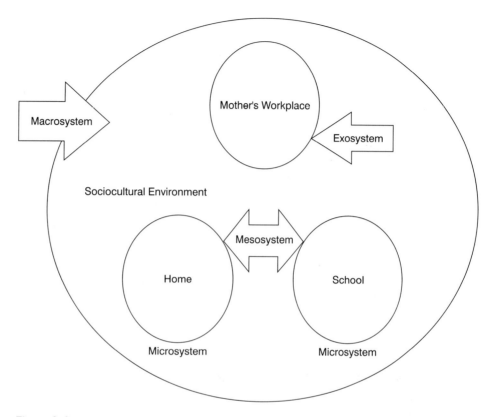

Figure 2–3
Multiple Systems of Interaction. Bronfenbrenner's Bioecological Model

various components that contribute to developmental outcomes, including the individual, the environment, and the processes of interaction that affect the individual in that environment.

People grow and develop within multiple environments that can be categorized into four nested systems: the microsystem, the mesosystem, the exosystem, and the macrosystem (Bronfenbrenner, 1979, 1995). The *microsystem* represents the most proximal environment within which an individual develops. Family, school, the peer group, and the workplace are all examples of specific microsystems. The next system, the *mesosystem,* is defined by interrelations among two or more microsystems at a particular point in an individual's development. An example of the dynamic interactions characterizing a mesosystem would be a situation in which a child's parents are going through a divorce and the child begins acting out at school. A more distal system, the *exosystem,* refers to a context that exerts indirect influence on an individual. For example, a parent's workplace may affect the parent in ways that then indirectly affect the child. At the fourth level of Bronfenbrenner's taxonomy is the *macrosystem,* which refers to an overarching belief system or culture. This broad, inclusive system exerts its effects indirectly through cultural tools and institutions. The macrosystem impacts the way society is structured and warrants special consideration when counseling with diverse populations.

Community counselors recognize that a client's development is affected both by the immediate systems in which he or she participates and by the broader sociocultural forces that have a more global impact. Consequently, all four systems and their interactions need to be considered when community counselors work with clients.

Community Counseling Settings

As stated earlier, from its inception, community counseling was viewed as an orientation rather than as a work setting (Hayes, 1984). Indeed, a common denominator shared by community counselors is that they work outside of educational settings, although there are some exceptions to this generalization. Community counseling practice settings include agencies, organizations, work sites, hospital environments, and individual practices. In a survey by Richardson and Bradley (1986), settings employing community counselors included community mental health centers, juvenile and adult probation agencies, family and children's service organizations, substance abuse programs, rehabilitation programs, hospitals, and educational agencies. Other settings that currently employ community counselors include geriatric centers, employee assistance programs, government programs, businesses and industries, religious institutions, health maintenance organizations, shelters for domestic violence victims, hospice programs, and programs for people living with HIV/AIDS. In Part IV of this text, we describe counseling practices in some of the more common settings in which community counselors are employed.

PROFESSIONAL IDENTIFICATION THROUGH CREDENTIALING

Legal Recognition of Counseling

Professional credentialing is an essential part of professional recognition and identification. One of the first steps toward professional credentialing is legal recognition. As recently as 1960, counseling did not have a strong enough identity as a profession to be recognized legally. In that year, a judge ruled in the case of *Bogust v. Iverson* that a counselor with a doctoral degree could not be held liable for the suicide of one of his clients because counselors were "mere teachers" who received training in a department of education.

It was not until 1971, in an *Iowa Law Review Note,* that counselors were legally recognized as professionals who provided personal as well as vocational and educational counseling. The profession was even more clearly defined in 1974 in *Weldon v. Virginia State Board of Psychologists Examiners.* The judgment rendered stated that counseling was a profession distinct from psychology. The U.S. House of Representatives further refined the definition of counseling and recognized the profession in

H. R. 3270 (94th Congress, 1976) by stating that *counseling* is "the process through which a trained counselor assists an individual or group to make satisfactory and responsible decisions concerning personal, educational and career development."

The initial state laws that regulated counseling, such as the one passed in Virginia in 1976, classified counseling as a generic profession with specialties, such as community or school counseling (Swanson, 1983). Further impetus for defining counseling as a profession came in 1981 with the establishment of CACREP, which provided professionwide standards and review procedures for training programs (Hershenson et al., 1996).

Professional Credentialing

With the recognition of counseling as a separate professional entity, a need developed for regulation through credentialing procedures. The process of credentialing counselors has evolved over the years. Obtaining professional credentials, especially certification and licensure, has become increasingly important in the counseling profession (Glosoff, 1992). Some credentials are conferred by the counseling profession, and others are provided by states to regulate who can legally practice in that state. Both types of credentialing are designed to protect the public and the profession.

National voluntary certification.   The National Board for Certified Counselors (NBCC), the leading national organization that certifies counselors, was established by the counseling profession in 1982 to certify counselors who have met requirements in training, experience, and performance on the National Counselor Examination (NBCC, 2003a). As of 2003, over 33,000 counselors are recognized as National Certified Counselors (NCCs). NCCs are certified for a period of 5 years, adhere to the NBCC *Code of Ethics,* and pay an annual maintenance fee. Specific requirements for initial certification are listed in Figure 2–4. At the end of each 5-year cycle, NCCs can apply for certification renewal by providing documentation of successful completion of a prescribed number of continuing education credits. For qualified counselors who hold the NCC credential, NBCC offers certification specialties in the following areas:

- Certified Clinical Mental Health Counselor (CCMHC) credential, which bases its standards on professional clinical mental health counselor competencies
- National Certified School Counselor (NCSC) credential, which identifies to the public those who have met national professional school counseling standards
- Master Addictions Counselor (MAC) credential, which identifies those counselors who have met national professional addictions counseling standards

Specific requirements for obtaining specialty credentials can be obtained by contacting NBCC at http://www.nbcc.org.

Professional certification is important because it ensures that counselors, rather than independent state legislators, set the national standards and minimum requirements for being a professional counselor (Remley & Herlihy, 2001).

What is the National Board for Certified Counselors?

The National Board for Certified Counselors, Inc., and Affiliates is an independent, not-for-profit credentialing body incorporated in 1982 to establish and monitor a national certification system. NBCC identifies and maintains a register of counselors who have voluntarily sought and obtained this certification. Counselors who have met predetermined NBCC standards in their training, experience, and performance on the National Counselor Examination for Licensure and Certification (NCE), the most portable test in counseling, are recognized as National Certified Counselors (NCC). Currently more than 33,000 professionals hold the NCC credential.

Created by the American Counseling Association (ACA), NBCC is an independent credentialing body with close ties to ACA. The main focus of NBCC is to promote quality counseling through certification.

Since October 1985, NBCC has been accredited by the National Commission for Certifying Agencies (NCCA), an independent national regulatory organization that monitors the credentialing processes of its member agencies. Accreditation by this commission represents the foremost organizational recognition in national certification.

NBCC offers the following specialty certifications*
- National Certified School Counselor (NCSC)
- Certified Clinical Mental Health Counselor (CCMHC)
- Master Addictions Counselor (MAC)

the NCC credential is a prerequisite for these specialty certifications.

What are the requirements?

General Requirements
- A master's degree with a major study in counseling from a regionally accredited college or university.
- A minimum of 48 semester/72 quarter hours of graduate level counseling coursework with at least one course in each of the following areas: Human Growth & Development, Social & Cultural Foundations, Helping Relationships, Group Work, Career & Lifestyle Development, Appraisal, Research & Program Evaluation, and Professional Orientation/Ethics in Counseling.
- Two academic terms of supervised field experience in a counseling setting. Applicants who have only one academic term of field experience may substitute one additional year of post-master's supervised experience beyond the otherwise required two years of post-master's supervised experience.
- Two years of post-master's counseling experience with 3,000 hours of work as a counselor and 100 hours of face-to-face counseling supervision, each over the two-year period.
- Two professional endorsements, one of which must be from a recent supervisor with an advanced degree (master's or higher) in counseling or a related mental health field (psychology or social work).
- A passing score on the National Counselor Examination for Licensure and Certification (NCE). If you have already passed the NCE for your state license or credential, you might be NCE exempt.

Figure 2–4
The National Board for Certified Counselors (NBCC, 2003a)
Note. Reprinted with permission of the National Board for Certified Counselors (NBCC)(2003).

Why Become Nationally Certified?

National certification is a continuing source of pride and career enhancement for the counseling professional.

Holding the NCC credential:

- Promotes professional accountability and visibility
- Ensures a national standard developed by counselors, not legislators
- Provides improved marketing through NBCC's referral service for the public
- Keeps NCCs in touch with current events in their profession through *The National Certified Counselor*, NBCC's newsletter
- Provides a source for research grants through the Research and Assessment Corporation for Counseling (RACC), an NBCC affiliate
- Furnishes NBCC backing to defend counselors' use of assessment instruments through the support of the National Fair Access Coalition on Testing (FACT).

Length of NBCC Certification

National Certified Counselors (NCCs) are certified for a period of five years and receive a professional certificate. NCCs must adhere to the NBCC Code of Ethics and must pay, on a yearly basis, an annual maintenance fee. At the conclusion of each five-year cycle, NCCs must be able to document the completion of 100 contact clock hours of continuing education or again take and pass the NCE.

Figure 2–4   *Continued*

National certification also provides referral sources and networking across state lines. However, possessing the national counseling certification credential does not regulate professional practice; it is not a license to practice. Therefore, counselors need to be aware of state licensure statutes before they begin to practice professionally.

State regulations: Licensure, certification, and registration.   Occupational licensure is one of the most important ways of defining an occupation as a profession (Hosie, 1991). Licensing defines scope of practice and determines who can and cannot offer certain services. Theoretically, the primary purpose of licensure is to protect the public (MacCluskie & Ingersoll, 2001). State laws that dictate requirements for licensure to practice counseling differ from state to state, especially with regard to training, experience, and examinations (Bradley, 1995). Once licensure requirements have been established, an individual cannot practice a profession legally without obtaining a license (Anderson & Swanson, 1994). There are some exceptions to this rule, depending on the setting in which one is practicing. For example, counselors who practice in educational institutions, nonprofit corporations, or in local, state, or federal agencies may be exempt from the licensure requirement (Remley & Herlihy, 2001). However, this exemption does not relate to reimbursement, and many third-party payors will not reimburse counselors who are not licensed.

States that have licensure statutes have established boards to oversee the issuing of credentials. Information about state credentials is presented in Table 2–2.

Table 2–2
State licensure legislation (NBCC, 2003b)

State	Year	Exam	Credentials
Alabama	1979	NCE	LPC
Alaska	1988	NCE	LPC
Arizona	1988	NCE or NCMHCE	CPC
Arkansas	1979	NCE	LPC, LAC
California	No licensure law at this time	NCE	In registry
Colorado	1988	NCE	LPC
Connecticut	1997	NCE/NCMHCE	LPC
Delaware	1987	NCE	LPCMH
District of Columbia	1992	NCE	LPC
Florida	1981 (Revised 1987)	NCMHCE	LMHC
Georgia	1984	NCE	LPC
Hawaii	No licensure law at this time		
Idaho	1982	NCE	LPC
Illinois	1992	NCE or NCMHCE	LPC or LCPC
Indiana	1997	NCMHCE	LMHC
Iowa	1991	NCE or NCMHCE	LMHC
Kansas	1987 (Legislature law passed 1996)	NCE/NCMHCE	LPC
Kentucky	1996	NCE	CPC
Louisiana	1987	NCE	LPC
Maine	1989	NCE	LPC or LCPC
Maryland	1985 and 1998	NCE or EMAC	LCPC
Massachusetts	1987	NCMHCE	LMHC
Michigan	1988	NCE	LPC
Minnesota	Licensure law passed in 2003	To be determined	To be announced
Mississippi	1985	NCE	LPC
Missouri	1985	NCE	LPC
Montana	1985	NCE or NCMHCE	LCPC
Nebraska	1986	NCE or NCMHCE	LPC or CPC or LMHP
Nevada	No legislature law at this time		Licensed alcohol and drug counselor, licensed MFT
New Hampshire	1992	NCMHCE	LMHC
New Jersey	1993	NCE	LPC
New Mexico	1993	NCE or NCMHCE	LPC or LPCC

Table 2–2   *(Continued)*

State	Year	Exam	Credentials
New York	2002 (Licensure law passed in 2002 and takes effect in 2005)	To be determined	To be announced
North Carolina	Registry law 1983 (licensure law 1993)	NCE	LPC
North Dakota	1989	NCE or NCMHCE	LPC or LPCC or LAPC
Ohio	1984	Ohio LPCE	LPC or LPCC
Oklahoma	1985	NCE	LPC
Oregon	1989	NCE	LPC
Pennsylvania	1998	NCE	LPC
Rhode Island	1987	NCMHCE	CCMH
South Carolina	1985	NCE or NCMHCE	LPC
South Dakota	1990	NCE or NCMHCE	LPC or LPC-MH
Tennessee	1984	NCE	LPC
Texas	1981	Texas PCE	LPC
Utah	1994	NCE or NCMHCE	LPC
Vermont	1988	NCE and NCMHCE	LCMHC
Virginia	1976	NCMHCE	LPC
Washington	1987	NCE or NCMHCE	CMHC
West Virginia	1986	NCE	LPC
Wisconsin	1992	NCE	CPC or PC
Wyoming	1987	NCE	LPC

Note. Adapted with permission of the National Board for Certified Counselors (NBCC).

Note. LPC = Licensed Professional Counselor; CPC = Certified Professional Counselor; LAC = Licensed Associate Counselor; LPCMH = Licensed Professional Counselor of Mental Health; LMHC = Licensed Mental Health Counselor; LCPC = Licensed Clinical Professional Counselor; LPCC = Licensed Professional Clinical Counselor; LAPC = Licensed Associate Professional Counselor; LCMHC = Licensed Clinical Mental Health Counselor; CMHC = Certified Mental Health Counselor; PC = Professional Counselor; MFT = Marriage and Family Therapist; LMHP = Licensed Mental Health Practitioner; CCMH = Clinical Counselor in Mental Health; NCE = National Counselor Examination for Licensure and Certification; NCMHCE = National Clinical Mental Health Counseling Examination; EMAC = Examination for Master Addictions Counselor.

Legal regulation can take the form of *licensure, certification,* or *registration.* The Council on Licensure, Enforcement and Regulation (1993) defines these three credentials in the following manner:

> *Licensure* is the most restrictive form of state regulation. Under licensure laws, it is illegal for a person to practice a profession without first meeting state-imposed standards. Under *certification,* the state grants title protection to persons meeting predetermined

standards. Those without title may perform the services of the occupation, but may not use the title. *Registration* is the least restrictive form of regulation, usually taking the form of requiring individuals to file their names, addresses, and qualifications with a governmental agency before practicing the occupation. (p. 1)

Because legal regulation of the counseling profession currently is not uniform among the 50 states, counselors who want to practice in a particular state need to "ascertain exactly what the state credential (whether it is a license, certificate, or registry) entitles the credentialed person to do" (Remley & Herlihy, 2001, p. 26).

Professional Affiliation

Another way community counselors establish and maintain a professional identity is through their affiliation with professional organizations. Being active in professional associations provides a number of benefits for community counselors. Through an association, members of a profession can address issues as a group rather than independently. Professional associations provide opportunities for continuing education, which is critical for maintaining credentials and updating skills. Professional associations also establish and enforce codes of ethics for their members, which provide consistent guidelines for conduct (Remley & Herlihy, 2001). The leading professional association for counseling is the American Counseling Association (ACA), which has over 55,000 members in 50 different countries (Schmitt, 2002).

In addition to joining ACA, community counselors may choose to join one or more of its 18 divisions, which are listed at the end of Chapter 1. Currently, community counseling is not represented by a specialized division in ACA. There are mixed feelings among professionals about the need for the establishment of a community counseling division within ACA (see Hershenson & Berger, 2001). Hershenson et al. (1996) contend that a specialty division is needed to advocate for community counseling and promote research and development within the field. Currently, with no such division in existence, many community counselors choose to join other ACA divisions, such as the American Mental Health Counselors Association (AMHCA), the Association for Specialists in Group Work (ASGW), the International Association of Addictions and Offender Counselors (IAAOC), or the National Career Development Association (NCDA). Also, community counselors can join state branches of ACA, which hold annual conventions, represent counselors in legislative matters, publish newsletters, and often provide workshops and training for members.

SUMMARY AND CONCLUSION

In this chapter, we examined the professional identification of community counselors, both in relation to other therapeutic professionals and within the counseling profession itself. We described some of the specific characteristics of community counseling, including the use of multifaceted approaches to promote prevention, early intervention, and wellness. Interactions between people and their environments are of particular interest to community counselors because of the way those interactions affect functioning and development. Consequently, counseling interventions include services to individuals, groups, families, and communities.

An important component of professional identification is credentialing, which includes professional certification and licensure. Community counselors are encouraged to earn the credentials needed to represent themselves professionally to the public. The credential conferred by the counseling profession is that of National Certified Counselor (NCC). Licensure and other forms of legal regulation are conferred by the state to define the scope of practice and to determine who is allowed to offer certain services. Community counselors need to be familiar with the specific regulatory requirements dictated by the state in which they live.

Another way to promote professional identification, interact with other counselors, and update knowledge and skills is through professional affiliation. Many community counselors choose to join the ACA. Depending on their interests and specializations, they also may choose to join one of ACA's 18 divisions. ACA and several of its divisions have established codes of ethics, which provide guidelines for conduct and are discussed in the next chapter.

REFERENCES

American Counseling Association (2003). Counselor licensure legislation: Protecting the public. Retrieved on May 4, 2003, from http://www.counseling.org/resources/licensure.htm

American Psychiatric Association. (2000). *Diagnostic and statistical manual of mental disorders* (4th ed., text rev.). Washington, DC: Author.

Anderson, D., & Swanson, C. D. (1994). *Legal issues in licensure.* Alexandria, VA: American Counseling Association.

Bradley, L. J. (1995). Certification and licensure issues. *Journal of Counseling and Development, 74,* 185–186.

Bronfenbrenner, U. (1979). *The ecology of human development.* Cambridge, MA: Harvard University Press.

Bronfenbrenner, U. (1995). The bioecological model from a life course perspective: Reflections of a participant observer. In P. Moen, G. H. Elder, & K. Luscher (Eds.), *Examining lives in context: Perspectives on the ecology of human development* (pp. 599–647). Washington, DC: American Psychological Association.

Council for Accreditation of Counseling and Related Educational Programs. (2003). *Directory of accredited programs.* Retrieved on May 2, 2003, from http://www.counseling.org/cacrep/directory.htm

Council on Licensure, Enforcement and Regulation (CLEAR). (1993). *The directory of professional and occupational regulation in the United States and Canada.* Lexington, KY: Author.

Cowger, E. L., Hinkle, J. S., DeRidder, L. M., & Erk, R. R. (1991). CACREP community counseling programs: Present status and implications for the future. *Journal of Mental Health Counseling, 13,* 172–186.

Exner, J. E. (1995). Why use personality tests? A brief historical view. In J. N. Butcher (Ed.), *Clinical personality assessment: Practical approaches* (pp. 10–18). New York: Oxford University Press.

Gladding, S. T. (1973). Reality sits in a green-cushioned chair. *Personnel and Guidance Journal, 54,* 222.

Glosoff, H. L. (1992). Accrediting and certifying professional counselors. *Guidepost, 34*(12), 6–8.

Hayes, R. L. (1984, March). Report on community counseling. *ACES Newsletter,* p. 15.

Hershenson, D. B., & Berger, G. P. (2001). The state of community counseling: A survey of directors of CACREP-accredited programs. *Journal of Counseling and Development, 79,* 188–193.

Hershenson, D. B., Power, P. W., & Waldo, M. (1996). *Community counseling: Contemporary theory and practice*. Boston: Allyn & Bacon.

Hosie, T. W. (1991). Historical antecedents and current status of counselor licensure. In F. Bradley (Ed.), *Credentialing in counseling* (pp. 23–52). Alexandria, VA: American Counseling Association.

Lewis, J. A., Lewis, M. D., Daniels, J. A., & D'Andrea, M. J. (2003). *Community counseling: Empowerment strategies for a diverse society* (3rd ed.). Pacific Grove, CA: Brooks/Cole.

MacCluskie, K. C., & Ingersoll, R. E. (2001). *Becoming a 21st century agency counselor: Personal and Professional Explorations*. Belmont, CA: Wadsworth.

National Fair Access Coalition on Testing. (2000). [Online]. Retrieved from http://www.fairaccess.org

National Board for Certified Counselors (2003a). *The National Certified Counselor (NCC) Credential: National certification for professional counselors*. Author: Greensboro, NC.

National Board for Certified Counselors. (2003b). State credentialing boards. Retrieved on May 4, 2003, from http://www.nbcc.org/exams/stateboards.htm

Perry, W. G. (1955). The findings of the commission in counseling and guidance. *Annals: New York Academy of Science, 63,* 396–407.

Remley, T. P. & Herlihy, B. (2001). *Ethical, legal, and professional issues in counseling*. Upper Saddle River, NJ: Merrill/Prentice Hall.

Richardson, B. K., & Bradley, L. J. (1986). *Community agency counseling: An emerging specialty in counselor preparation programs*. Alexandria, VA: American Association for Counseling and Development Foundation.

Schmitt, S. M. (2002). Kaplan takes over as ACA president. *Counseling Today, 1,* 45.

Scileppi, J. A., Teed, E. L., & Torres, R. D. (2000). *Community psychology: A common sense approach to mental health*. Upper Saddle River, NJ: Prentice Hall.

Swanson, C. D. (1983). The law and the counselor. In J. A. Brown & R. H. Pate, Jr. (Eds.), *Being a counselor* (pp. 26–46). Monterey, CA: Brooks/Cole.

CHAPTER 3

Ethical and Legal Aspects of Counseling

In the cool grey dawn of early September,
I place the final suitcase into my Mustang
And silently say "good-bye"
*   to the quiet beauty of North Carolina.*
Hesitantly, I head for the blue ocean-lined coast
*   of Connecticut.*
Bound for a new position and the unknown.
Traveling with me are a sheltie named "Eli"
*   and the still fresh memories of our last counseling session.*
You, who wrestled so long with fears
*   that I kiddingly started calling you "Jacob,"*
*   are as much a part of me as my luggage.*
Moving in life is bittersweet—
like giving up friends and fears.
The taste is like smooth, orange, fall persimmons,
*   deceptively delicious but tart.*

Gladding, S. T. (1984). Bittersweet. *Counseling and Values, 28*, 146. © ACA. Reprinted with permission. No further reproduction authorized without written permission of ACA.

Counseling is not a value-free or neutral activity (Grant, 1992; Schulte, 1990). Rather, counseling is a profession based on values, which are "orienting beliefs about what is good ... and how that good should be achieved" (Bergin, 1985, p. 99). Values are at the core of counseling relationships. All goals in counseling, whether for lifestyle modification or for symptom relief, are undergirded by value systems (Bergin, 1992). On the basis of the values they hold, counselors and clients take directions in the counseling process and make decisions. Community counselors need to be aware of their personal and professional values and beliefs if they are to act responsibly, ethically, and legally.

Counseling is also a moral enterprise that requires action based on careful, reflective thought about which response is most appropriate in any given situation (Tennyson & Strom, 1986). Counselors are guided in their thoughts and actions by moral values, professional and personal ethics, and legal procedures and precedents. It is impossible to apply a cookbook approach to counseling because both clients and counselors are unique in their life histories, psychological needs, and values (DePauw, 1986). In ideal situations, counselors are guided by an internal desire to be good as well as by external codes of ethics and laws directed toward how to do good (McGovern, 1994).

Counselors who are not clear about their personal values, ethics, and legal responsibilities, as well as about those of their clients, can cause harm despite their best intentions (Huber, 1994; Remley & Herlihy, 2001). Therefore, it is vital for counselors to be knowledgeable about both themselves and professional counseling guidelines before attempting to work with others. Ethical counselors demonstrate professional knowledge, concern, and good judgment in their work with clients. They are cautiously prudent in what they suggest and proactive in seeking consultation from other professionals when questionable circumstances arise. In this chapter, we explore ethical standards as well as legal constraints and mandates under which counselors operate. In some cases, but not in all, ethical and legal considerations overlap (Wilcoxon, 1993). Each is crucial to the work and well-being of community counselors and the clients they serve.

DEFINITIONS: ETHICS, MORALITY, AND LAW

The terms *ethics* and *morality* are often used synonymously, and in some ways their meanings are similar. Both deal with "what is good and bad or the study of human conduct and values" (Van Hoose & Kottler, 1985, p. 2). Yet, each term has a distinct definition.

Ethics can be defined as "a philosophical discipline that is concerned with human conduct and moral decision making" (Van Hoose & Kottler, 1985, p. 3). Ethics are normative in nature and focus on principles and standards that govern relationships between individuals, such as between counselors and clients. *Morality*, on the other hand, involves judgment or evaluation of action. It is associated with the employment of such words as *good, bad, right, wrong, ought,* and *should*

(Brandt, 1959; Grant, 1992). Even though some moral principles tend to be universally shared, moral conduct is defined within the context of a culture or society (Remley & Herlihy, 2001).

Kitchener (1984) described five moral principles that form the foundation for ethical guidelines and provide clarification for ethical decision making (Forester-Miller & Davis, 1996). These principles are as follows:

- *Autonomy,* which allows an individual the freedom of choice and action. Counselors are responsible for helping clients make their own decisions and act on their own values. Counselors also are responsible for helping clients consider the ramifications of their decisions and protect them from actions that may lead to harm of self or others.
- *Nonmaleficence,* which refers to not harming other people. Nonmaleficence, which is one of the oldest moral principles in the profession (Cottone & Tarvydas, 2003), is defined by the dictate followed by ancient Greek physicians to "above all, do no harm." Counselors are to refrain from actions that may intentionally or unintentionally harm others.
- *Beneficence,* which is a proactive concept implying doing things that contribute to the welfare of the client. When practicing beneficence, it is important for counselors to avoid taking a paternalistic approach toward clients that undermines their autonomy (Cottone & Tarvydas, 2003).
- *Justice,* which refers to treating all people fairly. The concept of justice implies that counselors should not discriminate on the bases of race, gender, sexual orientation, or any other factor. Counselors need to examine the degree to which justice is carried out through the policies of agencies, institutions, and laws that affect mental health practices (Cottone & Tarvydas, 2003).
- *Fidelity,* which means that counselors are loyal to their clients, honor their commitments, and fulfill their obligations.

These five principles provide a fundamental framework for guiding community counselors in making judgments about what actions they should take to promote their clients' welfare (Granello & Witmer, 1998).

The concept of professional ethics can be further clarified by differentiating between *mandatory ethics* and *aspirational ethics* (Corey, Corey, & Callanan, 1998). *Mandatory ethics* refers to a level of ethical functioning characterized by required compliance with basic, minimal standards. *Aspirational ethics,* in contrast, describes the highest level of conduct toward which counselors may aspire. Community counselors are guided by aspirational ethics when they make choices in accordance with the higher principles behind the literal meaning of ethical codes.

Law, which differs from ethics and morality, is the precise codification of governing standards that are established to ensure legal and moral justice (Hummell, Talbutt, & Alexander, 1985). Law is created by legislation, court decision, and tradition, as in English common law. Laws codify minimum standards of behavior that society will tolerate, whereas ethics represent ideal standards (Remley & Herlihy, 2001). The practice of community counselors is guided by ethical and legal standards, and it is important to be well informed about both.

Interactions Between Ethics and the Law

		Example
1. Ethical & Legal	Following a just law	Keeping a client's confidences that are also protected by law from disclosure
2. Ethical & Illegal	Disobeying an unjust law	Refusing to breach promised confidentiality even though ordered to do so by court
3. Ethical & Alegal	Doing good where no law applies	Offering free service to poor clients
4. Unethical & Legal	Following an unjust law	Following the Federal Trade Commission's edict that ethical codes cannot prohibit the use of testimonials in ads for counseling services
5. Unethical & Illegal	Breaking a just law	Disclosing confidential information protected by law from disclosure
6. Unethical & Alegal	Doing harm that no law prohibits	Promoting client dependency to enhance one's own feeling of power

Figure 3–1

Interactions between ethics and the law

Source: Adapted from *Ethical and Professional Issues in Counseling* (2nd ed.) (p. 46), by R. R. Cottone and V. M. Tarvydas, 2003, Upper Saddle River, NJ: Prentice Hall; and *Guide to Ethical Practice in Psychotherapy* by A. Thompson, 1990, New York: John Wiley & Sons. Copyright 1990 by John Wiley & Sons. This material is used by permission of John Wiley & Sons, Inc.

The law does not dictate what is ethical in a given situation; rather, it dictates what is legal. Sometimes what is legal at a given time—for example, matters of race, age, or sex—is considered unethical or immoral by some significant segments of society. A classic example of such a controversy is found in the segregation patterns that people of color endured in the United States between the end of the Civil War and the 1950s. This practice was legal; however, it was without ethical or moral rationale.

Ethical codes are not intended to supersede the law; instead, they typically clarify existing law and policy (Cottone & Tarvydas, 2003). At times, however, conflicts between the legal and the ethical codes of conduct occur (see Figure 3–1). Although laws tend to be more objective and specific than ethical or moral codes, interpretations of laws change over time and are often situationally dependent (Vacc & Loesch,

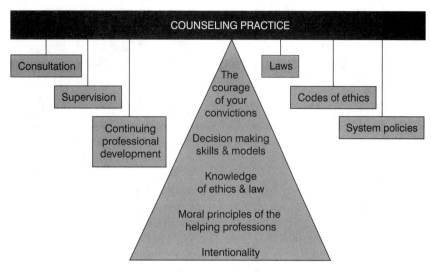

Figure 3–2
Professional practice—Built from within and balanced from outside the self
Source: From "Ethical, Legal, and Professional Issues in Counseling," by T. P. Remley, Jr., and B. Herlihy, ©
2001. Reprinted by permission of Pearson Education, Inc., Upper Saddle River, NJ.

2000). Therefore, it is necessary for community counselors to be aware of legal
issues that are applicable to their counseling situations and work to reconcile differences in legislative and ethical standards. Furthermore, when community counselors
act as consultants or advocates for clients, they need to be aware of the potential for
legal change and have sound principles upon which to advocate for modification of
existing systems.

Remley and Herlihy (2001) provide a model for professional practice that integrates moral and ethical principles, ethical and legal codes, and outside sources of
help. The model, depicted in Figure 3–2, illustrates the balance between the internal
beliefs and values that drive the counselor and the external forces that guide and
support counseling practice. Professional community counselors are committed to
developing a deep awareness of personal values and professional moral and ethical
principles, a thorough understanding of ethical and legal codes, and a willingness to
participate in consultation, supervision, and professional development activities.

ETHICS AND COUNSELING

Purpose of Ethical Codes

Many mental health professions have established codes of ethics that provide guidelines for practitioners, including the ACA (1995), the National Board of Certified
Counselors (NBCC, 1997), the American Psychological Association (APA, 1995), and

the National Association of Social Work (NASW, 1996). Typically, ethical codes consist of general statements that stipulate counseling duties to enhance client welfare (Granello & Witmer, 1998). Codes of ethics serve several purposes. They help promote ethical behavior by educating practitioners about sound ethical conduct, providing a mechanism for accountability and serving as catalysts for improving practice (Herlihy & Corey, 1996). They help clarify professionals' responsibilities to clients and society and protect clients and members of the profession from unethical or incompetent practice. Also, the establishment of codes and standards helps protect a profession from outside regulation by providing a method for self-regulation.

The ACA (1995) *Code of Ethics and Standards of Practice* represents the fifth version of the counseling profession's ethical code. The original version was initiated by Donald Super and was adopted by the American Personnel and Guidance Association (APGA) in 1961. It has been revised periodically since that date, and the 1995 *Code of Ethics and Standards of Practice* is currently under review. In addition to the *Code of Ethics and Standards of Practice,* ACA produces *A Practitioner's Guide to Ethical Decision Making* (Forester-Miller & Davis, 1996), video conferences on resolving ethical dilemmas (Salo, Forester-Miller, & Hamilton, 1997), and an *ACA Ethical Standards Casebook* (Herlihy & Corey, 1996).

Within the ACA, several divisions have developed separate codes of ethics, a practice that potentially can create confusion among practitioners (Herlihy & Remley, 1995). Community counseling is not represented as a separate ACA division, so there is no separate community counselors' code or set of standards. However, many community counselors are members of the American Mental Health Counselors Association (AMHCA)or other ACA divisions that do have their own ethical codes. Professional counselors who belong to multiple associations, hold national certifications, and are members of various divisions within the ACA are expected to comply with several different codes, which can be problematic and unwieldy. Remley and Herlihy (2001), as well as other counseling professionals, have recommended that a single, universally accepted code of ethics be established for the counseling profession. However, until this occurs, community counselors are responsible for understanding and adhering to the different ethical codes that govern the organizations to which they belong. In particular, community counselors will want to be familiar with the ethical codes established by ACA (1995) and NBCC (1997), as well as with any ethical standards created by the states in which they practice.

The ACA *Code of Ethics and Standards of Practice*

The ACA (1995) *Code of Ethics and Standards of Practice,* as implied by the title, consists of two different documents: an ethical code and a list of standards. The *Standards of Practice* are minimal behavioral statements based on the *Code of Ethics.* According to Herlihy and Corey (1996), the *Standards of Practice* "were developed in response to the needs of nonmembers of ACA to understand our minimal expectations for ethical behavior and to enforce these expectations in legal arenas" (p. 7). The *Standards of Practice* are specific, relatively brief, and describe what is mandatory and minimal in professional conduct (Granello & Witmer, 1998). The

Code of Ethics, in contrast, provides more detailed guidance regarding the standards of practice and represents the aspirational ethics that guide the counseling profession (Herlihy & Corey).

The *Code of Ethics and Standards of Practice* are arranged under eight major sectional headings:

- **Section A, The Counseling Relationship,** focuses on the nature of the relationship between counselors and clients. This section emphasizes client welfare as the counselor's primary responsibility. Twelve topics related to the counseling relationship are addressed, including the necessity to respect diversity, provide informed consent, and avoid dual relationships. The section also addresses the importance of recognizing personal needs and values and their effects on the counseling relationship. Sexual intimacies with clients are prohibited, and guidance is provided on issues such as fees, multiple clients, termination, and the use of computer technology.

- **Section B, Confidentiality,** outlines the client's right to privacy in a counselor–client relationship. Limitations to confidentiality are addressed, as are considerations in working with groups, families, children, and incompetent clients. Requirements regarding client records are described, and guidelines are prescribed to protect client confidentiality when conducting research, training others, or consulting.

- **Section C, Professional Responsibility,** provides guidelines related to professional knowledge and competence, advertising and solicitation, presentation of credentials, public responsibility, and respect for others who work in the mental health field.

- **Section D, Relationships With Other Professionals,** elaborates further on the counselor's interactions with other mental health workers. Attention is given to employment considerations, consultation, referral fees (which are unethical), and subcontractor arrangements. Counselors are expected to understand the roles of related professional groups and to collaborate with them effectively.

- **Section E, Evaluation, Assessment, and Interpretation,** presents guidelines on selecting, using, and interpreting assessment instruments. The section also addresses expectations related to informed consent, disclosure of test results, testing conditions and security, and proper diagnosis of mental disorders.

- **Section F, Teaching, Training, and Supervision,** provides guidelines for counselor educators and trainers, counselor education programs, and students and supervisees.

- **Section G, Research and Publication,** describes the responsibilities of researchers, including informed consent practices, the reporting of research results, the protection of research participants, and publication guidelines.

- **Section H, Resolving Ethical Issues,** focuses on counselors' responsibility to know the ethical standards. Procedures are described for dealing with suspected violations and cooperating with ethics committees.

NBCC Code of Ethics

Many community counselors choose to become nationally certified. A prerequisite for becoming a Nationally Certified Counselor (NCC) is formally agreeing to abide by the NBCC *Code of Ethics*. The NBCC *Code of Ethics* was developed in 1982 and revised in 1987, 1989, and 1997. It can be accessed through the NBCC Web site (http://www.nbcc.org). The NBCC ethical code consists of six sections, many of which parallel the sections of the ACA code. Unlike the ACA code, guidelines for consulting and private practice are each discussed in their own sections of the NBCC *Code of Ethics*. Counseling over the Internet is addressed, with further elaboration provided in NBCC's *Standards for the Ethical Practice of Internet Counseling*. We give more attention to the topic of ethics and Internet counseling in Chapter 4.

Limitations of Ethical Codes

Ethical codes are necessary but not sufficient for promoting ethical behavior (Pederson, 1997). Ethical standards are general and idealistic in nature, seldom answering specific questions (Remley & Herlihy, 2001). No ethical code can address every situation, and interpretation within the context of particular situations is crucial. Consequently, community counselors are responsible for exercising sound judgment and decision-making skills in their work with clients. They are guided by ethical guidelines but do not rely on them exclusively.

Several limitations exist in any ethical code. The following are among those most frequently listed (Corey, Corey, & Callanan, 1998; Mabe & Rollin, 1986; Talbutt, 1981):

- Some issues cannot be resolved by a code of ethics.
- Enforcing ethical codes is difficult.
- There may be conflicts within the standards delineated by the code.
- Some legal and ethical issues are not covered in codes.
- Sometimes conflicts arise between ethical and legal codes.
- Ethical codes do not address cross-cultural issues.
- Ethical codes do not address every possible situation.
- Ethical codes are historical documents. Thus, what may be acceptable practice at one time may be considered unethical later.
- There may be difficulty in bringing the interests of all parties involved in an ethical dispute together systematically.
- Ethical codes are not proactive documents that help counselors decide what to do in a given situation.

Thus, ethical codes are useful in many ways, but they have their limitations. Counselors need to be aware that they will not always find all the guidance they want when consulting these documents. Nevertheless, any time an ethical issue arises in counseling, the counselor should first consult ethical standards to see whether the situation is addressed.

Limitations of the ACA Code of Ethics and Standards of Practice.   In preparation for the upcoming review and revision of the current ACA *Code of Ethics and Standards of Practice,* the ACA Ethics Committee solicited comments from ACA members regarding limitations of the existing code in the following areas: (a) multicultural and diversity counseling; (b) professional responsibility and relationships; (c) teaching, training, and supervision; and (d) research and publication (Brown & Espina, 2000). Recommendations indicated a need for greater emphasis on or development of standards in the areas of spirituality, sexual orientation, culture, assisted suicide, school counseling, dual relationships for counselors in rural areas, and aggression and violence in professional relationships (Williams & Freeman, 2002).

Pedersen (1997) noted limitations in the ACA *Code of Ethics* with respect to cultural differences. He observed that the current ethical guidelines "represent a culturally biased perspective that minimalizes the importance of worldviews of ethnocultural minorities" (p. 27). As ethical guidelines are revised, efforts must be made to help counselors deal with the dilemmas that are inherent in contrasting cultures. Community counselors will want to be especially cognizant of cultural differences as they make ethical judgments.

Ethical Decision Making

It is not unusual for counselors to experience situations in which ethical guidelines are less than clear and an ethical decision must be made. In the absence of clear ethical guidelines, relying strictly on personal value judgments or doing what "seems right" is not adequate because not all value judgments are equally valid (Kitchener, 1984). Ethics is a critical component of counseling practice, and counselors need to be taught competent ways of making ethical decisions (Cottone & Claus, 2000). Numerous models have been developed to help counselors with the decision-making process (see Cottone & Claus for a review), although surprisingly little research has been conducted on the effectiveness of these models.

Kitchener's (1984) seminal work on ethical decision making in counseling and counseling psychology precipitated an increased interest in the topic among practitioners and educators. In her article, Kitchener emphasized the need for counseling professionals to develop a deeper understanding of the foundations of ethical decision making. Fundamental to the decision-making process are the five moral/ethical principles of autonomy, beneficence, nonmaleficence, justice, and fidelity. All these principles involve conscious decision making by counselors throughout the counseling process.

Among the many existing decision-making models, some are theoretically or philosophically based, others are practice based, and some draw from both theory and practice. Decision-making models bring order and clarity to the reasoning process, thereby helping counselors resolve ethical dilemmas more effectively. A model that is grounded in the five moral principles described earlier and that provides pragmatic, practice-oriented procedures was developed by Forester-Miller and Davis (1996) and is presented next. The model can be accessed through ACA's Web site at http://www.counseling.org.

Ethical decision-making model

1. *Identify the problem.* Gather information, being as specific and objective as possible, to help illuminate the situation. Ask questions such as, "Is this an ethical,

legal, professional or clinical problem, or some combination of each?" and "Is the issue related to my actions, the client's actions, or the agency and its policies?" Examine the problem from many different perspectives and avoid searching for an easy solution.

2. *Apply the ACA Code of Ethics.* After the problem is identified, refer to the *Code of Ethics and Standards of Practice* (1995) to determine which ethical standards apply. If one or more standards apply, follow the course of action indicated. If the problem is more complex, then there probably is a true ethical dilemma, and it will be necessary to take additional steps.

3. *Determine the nature and dimensions of the dilemma.* Several avenues should be followed to ensure that the problem has been fully examined, including:

- Consider the principles of autonomy, beneficence, nonmaleficence, justice, and fidelity. Which principles apply to the situation? Which principle takes priority in this case if two or more principles are in conflict?
- Review the relevant professional literature.
- Consult with experienced colleagues or supervisors. They may be able to identify aspects of the dilemma that are not readily apparent.
- Consult with state or national professional associations.

4. *Generate potential courses of action.* If possible, work with at least one colleague to brainstorm as many options as possible.

5. *Consider the potential consequences of all options and determine a course of action.* Evaluate each option and its potential consequences. What are the implications for the client, yourself, and others? Eliminate options with problematic consequences and determine which option best addresses the situation and the priorities you have identified.

6. *Evaluate the selected course of action.* Evaluate the selected course of action to determine whether it presents any new ethical considerations. Stadler (1986) suggests applying three simple tests:

- Would you treat others in this situation the same way?
- Would you want your behavior reported by the media?
- Would you recommend the same course of action to another counselor in the same situation?

If the answer to any of these questions is negative, reevaluate the problem and the course of action selected. If the answers are affirmative, thus passing the tests of justice, publicity, and universality, move on to implementation.

7. *Implement the course of action.* Taking the final step involves courage and strength of conviction. Document the action and include a rationale for selecting the particular course of action (Watts, 1999). After implementing the plan, follow up on the situation to determine whether your actions resulted in the anticipated consequences.

It is important to remember that different professionals may arrive at different solutions to the same ethical dilemma, particularly if it is complex. Forester-Miller and Davis (1996) remind us that following a systematic model to arrive at a decision provides a professional explanation for the course of action implemented. By evidencing good intentions, the knowledge and skill to make ethical decisions, and the moral courage to see those decisions through, community counselors are better able to engage consistently in ethical counseling behaviors (Morrissey, n.d.).

Other guidelines for acting ethically.   Swanson (1983) lists four guidelines deemed important in assessing whether counselors act in ethically responsible ways. The first is that counselors *act with personal and professional honesty*. Counselors must operate openly with themselves and those with whom they work. Hidden agendas and unacknowledged feelings hinder relationships and place counselors on shaky ethical ground. One way to overcome personal or professional honesty problems that may get in the way of acting ethically is to receive supervision (Kitchener, 1994).

A second guideline is that counselors *act in the best interest of clients*. This ideal is easier to discuss than to achieve. At times, a counselor may impose personal values on clients and ignore what the client really wants. At other times, a counselor may fail to recognize an emergency and too readily accept the idea that the best interest of the client is served by doing nothing.

A third guideline is that counselors *act without malice or personal gain*. Some clients are difficult to like or deal with, and counselors must be especially careful with these individuals. However, counselors must also be careful to avoid relationships with likeable clients on either a personal or a professional basis. Errors in judgment are most likely to occur when the counselor's self-interest becomes a part of the relationship with a client (St. Germaine, 1993).

A final guideline is whether counselors can justify an action "as the best judgment of what should be done based upon the current state of the profession" (Swanson, 1983, p. 59). To make such a decision, counselors must keep up with current trends by reading the professional literature, attending in-service workshops and conventions, and becoming actively involved in local, state, and national counseling activities.

The *ACA Ethical Standards Casebook* (Herlihy & Corey, 1996) can be especially helpful in many counseling situations. It presents case studies describing questionable ethical situations and provides guidelines and questions for reflection to assist counselors in making ethical responses. Each case study involves a standard of the ACA ethical code.

As helpful as the casebook may be, in some counseling situations the proper response still may not be obvious (Huber, 1994). For example, the question of confidentiality as it pertains to the individual rights of a person with AIDS and society's right to be protected from the spread of the disease is one with which some counselors struggle (Harding, Gray, & Neal, 1993). Likewise, there are multiple ethical dilemmas involved in counseling adult survivors of incest, including issues of confidentiality and the consequences of reporting abuse (Daniluk & Haverkamp, 1993). Therefore, when in doubt about what to do in a given situation, it is crucial for community counselors to consult with colleagues and/or seek supervision, in addition to referring to principles, guidelines, casebooks, and professional codes of ethics.

Unethical Behavior

Although most counselors strive to adhere to ethical standards, situations occasionally arise when such is not the case. In these circumstances, counselors must take some action. To do otherwise condones the unethical behavior and can be detrimental to both clients and the profession. A word of caution is in order, however. Remley and Herlihy (2001) remind us that "unless you are an ethics committee or licensure board member or are in a rare situation in which you should report a peer's suspected unethical conduct, you should be very reluctant to label another counselor's actions as unethical, illegal, or unprofessional" (p. 9). The caution against judging too quickly must be balanced against the obligation to address practices of peers that are viewed as unethical.

The ACA *Code of Ethics* (1995) states, "When counselors possess reasonable cause that raises doubt as to whether a counselor is acting in an ethical manner, they take appropriate action" (Standard H.2.a.). The phrases "reasonable cause" and "appropriate action" require careful attention (Remley & Herlihy, 2001). First, it is important to avoid making decisions based on secondhand information or rumors. Only direct knowledge of unethical behavior obligates a counselor to take action. Second, the procedures for determining what to do in situations when ethical conduct is in question vary according to the seriousness of the misconduct (Welfel, 2002). Minor breaches of conduct typically are more amenable to informal resolution than serious violations.

According to the ACA guidelines, a counselor should initially attempt to address issues of misconduct informally with the counselor whose behavior is in question. If an informal approach is unsuccessful or unfeasible, it may be necessary to report the offense to the supervisor or employer, state or national professional associations, or licensure or certification boards. Prior to making a report, it is best to consult with colleagues who are uninvolved in the situation.

The ACA Ethics Committee is responsible for managing formal reports of unethical practice on the part of ACA members (ACA, 1995). Guidelines for dealing with reports of misconduct are spelled out in ACA's (1997) *Policies and Procedures for Processing Complaints of Ethical Violations*. The number of formal complaints received by the Ethics Committee from 2001 to 2002 was 29; however, 20 of these were against non-ACA members and 1 was dismissed due to insufficient evidence (Williams & Freeman, 2002). During the same year, the Ethics Committee received 1,359 informal inquiries about ethical codes and standards. The majority of these inquiries dealt with issues of professional responsibility (e.g., professional competence, credentials, advertising, and soliciting clients) and confidentiality. Specific issues related to professional responsibility and confidentiality, as well as other issues that frequently confront community counselors, are addressed later in this chapter.

Counselors are not only responsible for acting in ways that are personally and professionally ethical but also for engaging in behavior that is lawful. At times, ethical and legal standards are in conflict. In the next section, we explore legal issues that affect the mental health profession, followed by descriptions of some of the more common ethical and/or legal issues that community counselors encounter.

THE LAW AND COUNSELING

The profession of counseling is governed by legal standards as well as by ethical ones. *Legal* refers to "law or the state of being lawful," and *law* refers to "a body of rules recognized by a state or community as binding on its members" (Shertzer & Stone, 1980, p. 386). The law plays a pervasive role in the personal and professional lives of counselors and affects almost all areas of counselor practice (Remley & Herlihy, 2001; Rowley & MacDonald, 2001).

The legal system of the United States is not static. Interpretations of law evolve over time and frequently are situationally contingent (Vacc & Loesch, 2000). Also, no general, comprehensive body of law regulates mental health professions (Van Hoose & Kottler, 1985). However, there are a number of court decisions and statutes that influence legal opinion in regard to community counseling, and counselors need to keep updated. The 1993 Napa County, California, case involving Gary Ramona is one such legal decision. In this widely publicized trial, Ramona sued his daughter's therapists, "charging that by implanting false memories of sexual abuse in her mind they had destroyed his life" (Butler, 1994, p. 10). Ramona was awarded $475,000 after the jury "found the therapists had negligently reinforced false memories" (Butler, p. 11). The legal concept on which the case was decided was *duty to care*—a legal obligation of health providers to not act negligently.

Another important legal case in recent years was the 1996 U.S. Supreme Court decision in *Jaffee v. Redmond,* which maintained that communications between licensed psychotherapists and their patients are privileged and do not have to be disclosed in cases held in federal court (Remley, Herlihy, & Herlihy, 1997). The importance of the case for counseling is that a legal precedent was set regarding privileged communication between a master's-level clinician (in this case, a social worker) and her client. The court decision affirmed the importance of protecting confidential communications between "psychotherapists" (the term used in this particular ruling) and their clients, thereby establishing a precedent that makes it more likely for judges to extend privilege in cases involving licensed counselors and clients (Glosoff, Herlihy, & Spence, 2000).

Stude and McKelvey (1979) observed that the law is "generally supportive or neutral" (p. 454) toward professional codes of ethics and toward counseling in general. The law supports licensure or certification of counselors as a means of ensuring that those who enter the profession attain at least minimal standards. It also supports the general "confidentiality of statements and records provided by clients during therapy" (p. 454). In addition, the law is neutral "in that it allows the profession to police itself and govern counselors' relations with their clients and fellow counselors" (p. 454). The only time the law overrides a professional code of ethics is when it is necessary "to protect the public health, safety, and welfare" (p. 454). This necessity is most likely to occur in situations concerning confidentiality, when disclosure of information is necessary to prevent harm. In such cases, counselors have a *duty to warn* potential victims about the possibility of a client's violent behavior (Costa & Altekruse, 1994).

Legal Mechanisms That Affect Community Counselors

Credentialing.   One way the community counseling profession is affected by our legal system is through credentialing. As explained in Chapter 2, legal regulation can take the form of licensure, certification, or registration, with licensure being the most powerful form of credentialing (Remley & Herlihy, 2001). Currently, 47 states license counselors. Licensure statutes specify minimum standards for becoming licensed to practice in a particular state. They also provide legal definitions of counselors' roles and legal recourse for alleged violations (Hershenson, Power, & Waldo, 1996). Community counselors will want to be aware of credentialing requirements and legal ramifications associated with credentialing that may affect their practice.

Criminal and civil law.   Another way community counselors are affected by the legal system is through two distinct types of law: criminal and civil. Criminal law applies to acts that are considered crimes against society and are prosecuted by the government, not by individuals (Anderson, 1996). Such acts are punishable by fines, imprisonment, or, in extreme cases, the death penalty. Fraud, civil disobedience, being an accessory to a crime, and contributing to the delinquency of a minor are examples of criminal offenses for which some mental health professionals have been found liable (Anderson, 1996; Vacc & Loesch, 2000).

Civil law applies to acts committed that affect the civil rights of individuals or other bodies (Anderson, 1996). Civil matters are settled in court when one individual brings suit against another, with sanctions applied to compensate the wronged individual. Civil liability is based on the concept of *tort,* which is a legal concept that refers to "a private injury against the person, property, or reputation of another individual that legal action is designed to set right" (Anderson, p. 45). The most common cause of legal liability for mental health professionals is *malpractice,* a term that refers to negligence in carrying out professional responsibilities or duties (Anderson; Cottone & Tarvydas, 2003).

Malpractice.   Professional malpractice is regulated by state law and therefore usually applies only when a person is credentialed according to state statute. However, counselors can still be held legally negligible or guilty of intentional infliction of distress even in cases when the term malpractice does not technically apply (Anderson, 1996).

Areas of potential malpractice for counselors include (Vacc & Loesch, 2000, pp. 249–250):

- Making a faulty diagnosis (e.g., attributing a physically based problem to a psychological condition)
- Failing to take action when someone other than the client is in danger
- Improperly certifying a client in a commitment hearing
- Engaging in behavior inappropriate to the accepted standards of the profession (e.g., unethical behavior)
- Failing to take adequate precautions for a suicidal client
- Providing services for which competence has not been established
- Breaching confidentiality

- Promising a "cure"
- Taking advantage of the counseling relationship for personal gain, monetary or otherwise
- Failing to use a technique that would have been more helpful
- Failing to provide informed consent

Until recently, there were relatively few counselor malpractice suits. However, with the increased number of licensed, certified, and practicing counselors, malpractice suits have become more common. Therefore, community counselors must make sure they protect themselves from such possibilities.

There are several proactive ways to avoid malpractice and protect oneself from liability. To avoid malpractice, community counselors will want to adhere to professional codes of ethics and provide counseling services viewed as acceptable by the profession (Anderson, 1996; Granello & Witmer, 1998). Regardless of how careful counselors are, however, malpractice lawsuits can still occur. Therefore, carrying professional liability insurance is essential. *Avoiding Counselor Malpractice* (Crawford, 1994) is an excellent book explaining the nature and scope of malpractice and ways to take reasonable precautions to avoid being implicated in lawsuits. Being cognizant of legal issues and obtaining legal advice when questions arise can help counselors protect themselves should their actions be challenged (Remley & Herlihy, 2001).

Other reasons for court appearances.   A relatively small number of counselors have to appear in court to face liability charges. More frequently, counselors find themselves in court for other reasons. For example, a counselor may be asked to serve as an expert witness. An *expert witness* is "an objective and unbiased person with specialized knowledge, skills, or information, who can assist a judge or jury in reaching an appropriate legal decision" (Remley, 1992, p. 33). A counselor who serves as an expert witness is compensated for his or her time financially.

A counselor may also be summoned to appear in court through a *court order* (i.e., a subpoena to appear in court at a certain time in regard to a specific case). Such a summons is issued with the intent of having the counselor testify on behalf of or against a present or former client. Because the legal system is adversarial, counselors are wise to seek the advice of attorneys before responding to court orders (Remley, 1991). In so doing, counselors may come to understand law, court proceedings, and options they have in response to legal requests. Role-playing possible scenarios before appearing in court may also help counselors function better in such situations.

To prepare for legal encounters, counselors should read some or all of the 12 volumes in the *American Counseling Association Legal Series*. These volumes, edited by Theodore P. Remley, Jr., are written by counseling experts who have either legal degrees or expert knowledge on important legal issues such as preparing for court appearances, documentation of counseling records, counseling minors, confidentiality and privileged communication, third-party payments, and managing a counseling agency.

COMMON ETHICAL AND LEGAL CONCERNS

Counselors in all settings, including community settings, deal with many issues that have ethical and legal ramifications. A number of authors (e.g., Anderson, 1996; Corey et al., 1998; Cottone & Tarvydas, 2003; Remley & Herlihy, 2001; Welfel, 2002) have authored texts that describe ethical and legal concerns that affect mental health practictioners. Also, these topics are frequently addressed in professional development and continuing education activities. The purpose of this section is not to provide a comprehensive overview of all the ethical and legal issues community counselors may encounter; instead, it is to provide information about some of the more common concerns that affect the practice of community counseling: shared communication, informed consent, dual relationships, and professional competence. Other issues, including record keeping, mandated counseling, payment issues, professional responsibilities, counseling minors, and issues related to managed care and technology, are addressed in other chapters.

Privacy, Confidentiality, and Privileged Communication

The relationship between counselors and clients is based on trust. For communication to occur freely, clients must have both their privacy and the information shared in session protected (Anderson, 1996). Ethical and legal issues related to communication and trust include privacy, confidentiality, and privileged communication.

Definitions.   *Privacy* is the client's right to determine what information about themselves will be shared with others (Remley & Herlihy, 2001). It is a broad term that includes not only the confidences shared during counseling sessions but also the fact that the client is participating in counseling. Several factors can jeopardize a client's privacy right, including waiting in a general reception area, using credit cards for billing, disposing of records, taping sessions, and other documentary or business activities associated with the counseling setting (Cottone & Tarvydas, 2003). Community counselors must use foresight and take the necessary steps to respect and protect the dignity and privacy of their clients.

Confidentiality is a professional's promise not to disclose information revealed during the privacy of the counselor–client relationship, except under the conditions agreed on (Cottone & Tarvydas, 2003; Glosoff, 2001). The assurance of confidentiality is considered one of the most fundamental obligations of counselors. Counselors should discuss confidentiality and its limits with clients before counseling begins. Except in certain situations, which are described later, counselors may share confidential information only with the direct written consent of clients or their legal guardians (Cottone & Tarvydas, 2003). If confidence is broken, either intentionally or unintentionally, the concern becomes a potentially legal as well as an ethical issue for counselors.

Privileged communication, a narrower concept, regulates privacy protection and confidentiality by protecting clients from having their confidential communications disclosed in court without their permission (Shah, 1969). For privilege to be recognized, the communication "must have been made in confidence, with the indicated desire that it remain so" (Anderson, 1996, p. 20). Typically, state law governs whether privilege exists in a counselor–client relationship (Glosoff et al., 2000). On the federal level, the U.S. Supreme Court set a precedent for protecting confidential communications by ruling that the confidences shared between a social worker and her client were privileged and not subject to disclosure (*Jaffee v. Redmond*).

Although the concept of privilege appears to be relatively straightforward, in reality it is complex and somewhat confusing (Glosoff et al., 2000). One major reason for the confusion is that laws regulating privilege, particularly in regard to exemptions, vary from state to state. Furthermore, new laws are enacted and existing statutes are modified on a regular basis. Consequently, counselors must be familiar with statutes and case law and participate in continuing education offerings to stay abreast of new developments (Glosoff et al., 2000)

Limits of confidentiality.   Confidentiality is not absolute: There are times when obligations to other individuals and society override the ethical responsibility of confidentiality. It is the counselor's responsibility to clarify for clients the exceptional circumstances when breaching confidentiality is either permissible or required (Corey et al., 1998).

A landmark court case that reflects the importance of limiting confidentiality is *Tarasoff v. Board of Regents of the University of California* (1976). In this case, a student, Prosenjit Poddar, who was a voluntary outpatient at the student health services on the Berkeley campus of the University of California, informed the psychologist who was counseling him that he intended to kill his former girlfriend, Tatiana Tarasoff, when she arrived back on campus. The psychologist notified the campus police, who detained and questioned the student about his proposed activities. The student denied any intention of killing Tarasoff, acted rationally, and was released. Poddar refused further treatment by the psychologist, and no further steps were taken to deter him from his intended action. Two months later, he killed Tarasoff. Her parents sued the Board of Regents of the University of California for failing to notify the intended victim of a threat against her. The California Supreme Court ruled in their favor, indicating that a therapist has a duty to protect the public that overrides any obligation to maintain client confidentiality.

Thus, there is a limit to how much confidentiality a counselor can or should maintain. The ruling in the Tarasoff case, sometimes called *duty to warn,* implies that counselors need to take reasonable action to help protect potential victims from dangerous clients. Subsequent court decisions have expanded on the Tarasoff doctrine of *duty to warn,* by extending the duty to warn unknown persons, bystanders who might be injured by a negligent act, and individuals whose property has been threatened (Remley & Herlihy, 2001).

If a counselor determines that a client is dangerous (either to himself/herself or to others), choices of action range from relatively unintrusive (e.g., asking the client to sign a no-harm contract) to highly intrusive (e.g., having the client involuntarily committed to a psychiatric facility), with many other options existing between these two extremes. In situations where counselors are faced with the duty to warn, they should consult with colleagues and supervisors to determine the course of action that is ethically and legally sound.

A number of additional limitations to confidentiality and privileged communication have been cited in the literature. A summary of the more common exceptions is presented in Figure 3–3. Because of the differences in state statutes and individual circumstances, community counselors will want to verify the limitations that are applicable to their counseling practice. Also, if confidentiality must be broken, it is good practice to talk with the client about the need to share information and to invite the client to participate in the process when feasible (Remley & Herlihy, 2001).

Potential Exceptions to Confidentiality and Privileged Communication	
To protect others from harm	• When there is suspected abuse or neglect of a child, an elderly person, a resident of an institution, or another vulnerable individual • When the client poses a clear and imminent danger to self or others • When the client has a fatal, communicable disease and the client's behavior is putting others at risk of contracting the disease
To help improve client services	• When working under supervision (Let the client know you are being supervised.) • When consulting with colleagues or peers (e.g., treatment teams) • When clerical assistants handle confidential information (e.g., managed care) • When other mental health professionals request information and the client has provided written consent to share
Other possible exceptions	• When clients raise the issue of their mental health in legal proceedings • When counselors need to defend themselves against a complaint made to a licensure or certifying board or in a court of law • When the client is involved in civil commitment proceedings • When ordered by a court (The counselor should request privilege on behalf of the client, although the right to privilege may be legally overridden, depending on the circumstances.)

Figure 3–3
Potential exceptions to confidentiality and privileged communication
(Corey et al., 1998; Glosoff, 2001)

Informed Consent

Clients have a number of legal as well as ethical rights in counseling, but they frequently do not know about them. One of the counselor's first tasks is to learn what rights clients have and to inform the clients of those rights. The process of informed consent refers to clients' right to know what they are getting into when they engage in counseling. It allows them to make informed decisions about their treatment and the release of confidential information (Glosoff, 2001). Informed consent provides clients with information about how the counseling process works and makes them active partners in the counseling relationship (Remley & Herlihy, 2001).

Although informed consent may be either implied (behavioral) or expressed (written or verbal with witnesses), expressed consent in written form provides a more professional way to protect clients' rights (Glosoff, 2001; Vacc & Loesch, 2000). Two criteria are central to the concept of informed consent: *disclosure* and *free consent* (Glosoff). *Disclosure* refers to providing clients with the information they need to make informed decisions about entering into counseling, remaining in counseling, and sharing personal information. *Free consent* means that clients choose to engage in an activity without undue pressure or coercion. For informed consent to be legally recognized, clients must demonstrate *capacity* (the ability to make rational decisions) and know that they are free to withdraw consent at any time, except in court-ordered situations. When working with minors and others unable to legally provide informed consent, special considerations, such as those discussed in Chapter 12, are necessary.

Professional disclosure statements prepared by counselors are contracts that formalize the informed consent process. Disclosure statements are described in more detail in Chapter 5. The ACA *Code of Ethics* (1995) specifies the elements that ethically are part of informed consent procedures and therefore need to be included in disclosure statements (Remley & Herlihy, 2001):

- The purposes, goals, techniques, procedures, limitations, risks, and benefits of the proposed services
- The implications of diagnosis and the intended use of tests and reports
- Information about fees and billing
- Confidentiality and its limitations
- Clients' rights to obtain information about their case notes and to participate in ongoing counseling plans
- Clients' rights to refuse any recommended services and be advised of the consequences of refusal

In addition to preparing a comprehensive, understandable professional disclosure statement for clients to sign, counselors need to talk with clients face to face to clarify any information that may be confusing. Also, ongoing discussion throughout the counseling process helps ensure that client and counselor are working together effectively. Informed consent begins when counseling is initiated, but the process should continue throughout the time the client is in counseling (Glosoff, 2001; Remley & Herlihy, 2001).

Dual Relationships

The issue of dual relationships as an ethical consideration is relatively new, emerging from debates in the 1970s on the ethical nature of counselor–client sexual intimacies. Indeed, sexual dual relationships are among the most serious boundary violations and should always be avoided. Sexual activity between a therapist and a client is considered a felony in at least 12 states, and several other states have passed laws making it probable that practitioners found guilty of sexual misconduct will lose their licenses (Glosoff, 2001). Unfortunately, sexual misconduct continues to be the leading cause of malpractice among mental health practitioners (Morrissey, n.d.).

When professional groups concluded that sexual relationships between counselors and clients were unethical, questions were raised about the formation of other types of relationships between counselors and clients, such as business deals or friendships. Although opinions on the subject vary, the general rule followed by community counselors is to avoid dual or multiple relationships with clients. The reason is "that no matter how harmless a dual relationship seems, a conflict of interest almost always exists, and any professional counselor's judgment is likely to be affected" (St. Germaine, 1993, p. 27). What follows is potentially harmful, because counselors lose their objectivity and clients may be placed in situations in which they cannot be assertive and take care of themselves. For example, if a business transaction takes place between a counselor and a client at the same time that counseling is occurring, either party may be negatively affected if the product involved does not meet expectations. The resulting emotions will most likely impact the therapeutic relationship. Therefore, as a matter of ethics, counselors need to keep boundaries clear and avoid dual or multiple relationships whenever possible. This means refraining from entering into counseling relationships with friends, family members, students, fellow workers, and others with whom one has a preexisting relationship. To maintain healthy boundaries in existing counseling relationships, community counselors are advised to avoid socializing, exchanging gifts, or conducting business with clients.

Although the principles underlying the ethics of dual relationships seem clear, implementing them is sometimes difficult. Indeed, it may be impossible to avoid all forms of multiple relationships, particularly in small isolated communities (Glosoff, 2001). Remley and Herlihy (2001) note that many "small worlds" exist, even in urban environments, and that people's political affiliation, ethnic identity, sexual orientation, and substance-dependence recovery status all can potentially lead to dual-relationship dilemmas. To avoid exploitation or other difficulties that may result from unavoidable multiple relationships, Glosoff (1997) suggests that counselors recognize the complexity of therapeutic relationships, exercise sound clinical judgment, attend to self-care, and engage in ongoing self-evaluation and peer consultation.

Professional Competence

Another area that has particular legal and ethical significance for community counselors is that of professional competence. Section C.2.a. of the ACA *Code of Ethics and Standards of Practice* (1995) addresses professional competence in this manner:

Counselors practice only within the boundaries of their competence, based on their education, training, supervised experience, state and national professional credentials, and appropriate professional experiences. Counselors will demonstrate a commitment to gain knowledge, personal awareness, sensitivity, and skills pertinent to working with a diverse client population.

The concept of counselor competence is multidimensional. On one hand, it can be defined according to minimum requirements and minimum performance levels required by outside sources (e.g., licensure boards, counseling graduate programs). It also can be viewed as an ideal state of maximum knowledge and skills toward which counselors strive. Remley and Herlihy (2001) remind us that competence is not an either/or concept; rather, it is multileveled and spans a continuum.

Counselors are required to practice within their boundaries of competence; however, those boundaries are not always easy to delineate. Boundaries of competence involve the levels of training, experience, and credentialing required to perform certain procedures or interventions (Tarvydas & Cottone, 2003). From a legal standpoint, competence refers to the capability of providing the accepted *standards of care* required for working in a particular situation. *Standards of care* has been defined as "the professional conduct as practiced by reasonable and prudent practitioners who have special knowledge and ability for the diagnosis and treatment of clinical conditions" (Granello & Witmer, 1998, pp. 371–372). For example, standards of care procedures are demonstrated when a community counselor with trained, supervised experience in cognitive–behavioral therapy and anxiety disorders selects a cognitive–behavioral intervention to use with a client dealing with panic disorder.

Professional competence can be developed and maintained through education, formal training, and supervised practice in particular areas. It is important to recognize the impossibility of universal competence: No single professional counselor will be competent in all areas (Welfel, 2002). When counselors attempt to expand their competencies, whether in a new practice area or with a new population of individuals, they need to evaluate the time, training, and supervision that will be required to develop the skills needed to work effectively with their clients.

Competent practice also involves an ability to work with a diverse population of clients. Both the ACA and the NBCC codes of ethics state that counselors have the responsibility to respect the diversity of their clients and act in ways that are nondiscriminatory. If a counselor does not have the training and supervised practice needed for working with culturally diverse clients, he or she may be practicing unethically by providing services to them (Remley & Herlihy, 2001). Community counselors have an ethical obligation to develop the knowledge and skills needed to work in a culturally diverse society. The *Multicultural Competencies and Standards* (Sue, Arredondo, & McDavis, 1992) provide guidelines for practicing culturally sensitive counseling with diverse populations. Community counselors need to be aware of their own cultural values and biases and learn ways to work effectively with those from different cultural backgrounds.

Often, counselors will find themselves in situations in which the needs of a particular client are greater than their professional competence. When this occurs, the best course of action is to refer that client to someone with the necessary training. At other times, counselors may need to refer clients on the basis of personal factors affecting competence, such as stress, illness, or some form of impairment (Remley & Herlihey, 2001). The key to practicing responsibly is being aware of one's capabilities and level of functioning and making sound judgments based on that awareness.

Concerns related to confidentiality, informed consent, dual relationships, and professional competence are only a few of the many ethical and legal issues that community counselors are likely to encounter. To practice in ways that are ethically and legally sound, community counselors will want to participate actively in self-examination, consultation, and continuing education.

SUMMARY AND CONCLUSION

The community counseling profession is influenced by ethical and legal constructs that affect the counselor–client relationship and the practice of counseling. Counselors, like other mental health professionals, have established codes of ethics to guide them in the practice of helping others. The ACA *Code of Ethics and Standards of Practice* and the NBCC *Code of Ethics* are the main documents community counselors should consult when they face ethical dilemmas. Acting ethically is not always easy, comfortable, or clear.

In making ethical decisions, counselors rely on personal values as well as on ethical standards and legal precedents. Following a decision-making model and documenting reasons for selecting certain actions can promote ethical practice. To help with ethical dilemmas, community counselors can consult with professional colleagues and refer to casebooks and other professional literature. It is imperative that counselors become well informed in the area of ethics for the sake of their own well-being and for that of their clients.

In addition, it is crucial that counselors be informed about state and national legislation and legal decisions. These will affect the ways in which counselors work. Counselors are liable for civil and criminal malpractice suits if they violate client rights or societal rules. One way to protect themselves legally is for counselors to review and follow the ethical standards of the professional organizations with which they are affiliated and to operate according to recognized standard practices. Community counselors also need to have professional liability insurance in the event that their practices are questioned.

Ethical standards and legal codes reflect current conditions and are ever-evolving documents. They do not cover all situations, but they do offer help to counselors beyond that found in their own personal beliefs and values. Community counselors will want to be especially aware of ethical and legal obligations that relate to confidentiality, informed consent, dual relationships, and professional competence. They also will want to be knowledgeable about evolving ethical and legal standards that relate to managed care and the use of technology, topics that are addressed in the next chapter.

REFERENCES

American Counseling Association. (1995). *Ethical standards of the American Counseling Association.* Alexandria, VA: Author.

American Counseling Association. (1997). *Policies and procedures for processing complaints of ethical violations.* Alexandria, VA: Author.

American Psychological Association. (1995). *Ethical principles of psychologists and code of conduct.* Washington D.C.: Author.

Anderson, B. S. (1996). *The counselor and the law* (4th ed.). Alexandria, VA: American Counseling Association.

Bergin, A. E. (1985). Proposed values for guiding and evaluating counseling and psychotherapy. *Counseling and Values, 29,* 99–115.

Bergin, A. E. (1992). Three contributions of a spiritual perspective to counseling, psychotherapy, and behavior change. In M. T. Burke & J. G. Miranti (Eds.), *Ethical and spiritual values in counseling* (pp. 5–15). Alexandria, VA: American Counseling Association.

Brandt, R. (1959). *Ethical theory.* Upper Saddle River, NJ: Prentice Hall.

Brown, S. P., & Espina, M. R. (2000). Report of the ACA ethics committee: 1998–1999. *Journal of Counseling and Development, 78,* 237–241.

Butler, K. (1994, July/August). Duty of care. *Family Therapy Networker, 18,* 10–11.

Corey, G., Corey, M. S., & Callanan, P. (1998). *Issues and ethics in the helping professions* (5th ed.). Pacific Grove, CA: Brooks/Cole.

Costa, L., & Altekruse, M. (1994). Duty-to-warn guidelines for mental health counselors. *Journal of Counseling and Development, 72,* 346–350.

Cottone, R. R., & Claus, R. E. (2000). Ethical decision-making models: A review of the literature. *Journal of Counseling and Development, 78,* 275–283.

Cottone, R. R., & Tarvydas, V. M. (2003). *Ethical and professional issues in counseling* (2nd ed.). Upper Saddle River, NJ: Merrill/Prentice Hall.

Crawford, R. L. (1994). *Avoiding counselor malpractice.* Alexandria, VA: American Counseling Association.

Daniluk, J. C., & Haverkamp, B. E. (1993). Ethical issues in counseling adult survivors of incest. *Journal of Counseling and Development, 72,* 16–22.

DePauw, M. E. (1986). Avoiding ethical violations: A timeline perspective for individual counseling. *Journal of Counseling and Development, 64,* 303–305.

Forester-Miller, H., & Davis, T. D. (1996). *A practitioner's guide to ethical decision making.* Alexandria, VA: American Counseling Association.

Gladding, S. T. (1984). Bittersweet. *Counseling and Values, 28,* 146.

Glosoff, H. L. (1997). Multiple relationships in private practice. In B. Herlihy & G. Corey (Eds.), *Boundary issues in counseling* (pp. 114–120). Alexandria, VA: American Counseling Association.

Glosoff, H. L. (2001, November). *Ethical practice in a complex era: Clients' rights, counselors' responsibilities.* Workshop presentation at Wake Forest University, Winston-Salem, NC.

Glosoff, H. L., Herlihy, B., & Spence, E. B. (2000). Privileged communication in the counselor–client relationship. *Journal of Counseling and Development, 78,* 454–462.

Granello, P. F., & Witmer, J. M. (1998). Standards of care: Potential implications for the counseling profession. *Journal of Counseling and Development, 76,* 371–380.

Grant, B. (1992). The moral nature of psychotherapy. In M. T. Burke & J. G. Miranti (Eds.), *Ethical and spiritual values in counseling* (pp. 27–35). Alexandria, VA: American Counseling Association.

Harding, A. K., Gray, L. A., & Neal, M. (1993). Confidentiality limits with clients who have HIV: A review of ethical and legal guidelines and professional policies. *Journal of Counseling and Development, 71,* 297–304.

Hershenson, D. B., Power, P. W., & Waldo, M. (1996) *Community counseling: Contemporary theory and practice.* Needham Heights, MA: Allyn & Bacon.

Herlihy, B., & Corey, G. (1996). *ACA ethical standards casebook* (5th ed.). Alexandria, VA: ACA.

Herlihy, B., & Remley, T. P., Jr. (1995). Unified ethical standards: A challenge for professionalism. *Journal of Counseling and Development, 74,* 130–133.

Huber, C. H. (1994). *Ethical, legal and professional issues in the practice of marriage and family therapy* (2nd ed.). New York: Macmillan.

Hummell, D. L., Talbutt, L. C., & Alexander, M. D. (1985). *Law and ethics in counseling.* New York: Van Nostrand Reinhold.

Jaffee v. Redmond, WL 314841 (U.S. June 13, 1996).

Kitchener, K. S. (1984). Intuition, critical evaluation, and ethical principles: The foundation for ethical decisions in counseling psychology. *The Counseling Psychologist, 12,* 43–55.

Kitchener, K. S. (1994, May). Doing good well—The wisdom behind ethical supervision. *Counseling and Human Development,* 1–8.

Mabe, A. R., & Rollin, S. A. (1986). The role of a code of ethical standards in counseling. *Journal of Counseling and Development, 64,* 294–297.

McGovern, T. F. (1994, May/June). Being good and doing good: An ethical reflection around alcoholism and drug abuse counseling. *The Counselor,* 14–18.

Morrissey, M. (Ed.) (n.d.). Ethics in professional counseling discussed at national videoconference. Retrieved July 24, 2002, from http://www.counseling.org/ctonline/archives/epc.htm

National Association of Social Workers (1996). *Code of ethics.* Washington D.C.: Autohr.

National Board for Certified Counselors (NBCC). (1997). *NBCC code of ethics.* Retrieved May 4, 2003 from http://www.nbcc.org

Pedersen, P. B. (1997). The cultural context of the American Counseling Association code of ethics. *Journal of Counseling and Development, 76,* 23–28.

Remley, T. P., Jr. (1991). *Preparing for court appearances.* Alexandria, VA: American Counseling Association.

Remley, T. P., Jr. (1992, Spring). You and the law. *American Counselor, 1,* 33.

Remley, T. P., Jr., & Herlihy, B. (2001). *Ethical, legal, and professional issues in counseling.* Upper Saddle River, NJ: Merrill/Prentice Hall.

Remley, T. P., Jr., Herlihy, B., & Herlihy, S. B. (1997). The U.S. Supreme Court decision in *Jaffee v. Redmond:* Implications for counselors. *Journal of Counseling and Development, 75,* 213–218.

Rowley, W. J. & MacDonald, D. (2001). Counseling and the Law: A cross-cultural perspective. *Journal of counseling and development, 79,* 422–429.

Salo, M., Forester-Miller, H., & Hamilton, W. M. (1997). Report of the ACA ethics committee: 1995–1996. *Journal of Counseling and Development, 75,* 174–175.

Schulte, J. M. (1990). The morality of influencing in counseling. *Counseling and Values, 34,* 103–118.

Shah, S. A. (1969). Privileged communications, confidentiality, and privacy: Privileged communications. *Professional Psychology, 1,* 59–69.

Shertzer, B., & Stone, S. (1980). *Fundamentals of Counseling* (3rd ed.). Boston: Houghton Mifflin.

St. Germaine, J. (1993). Dual relationships: What's wrong with them? *American Counselor, 2,* 25–30.

Stude, E. W., & McKelvey, J. (1979). Ethics and the law: Friend or foe? *Personnel and Guidance Journal, 57,* 453–456.

Sue, D. W., Arredondo, P., & McDavis, R. J. (1992). Multicultural competencies/standards: A pressing need. *Journal of Counseling and Development, 70,* 477–486.

Swanson, C. D. (1983). Ethics and the counselor. In J. A. Brown & R. H. Pate, Jr. (Eds.), *Being a counselor* (pp. 47–65). Monterey, CA: Brooks/Cole.

Talbutt, L. C. (1981). Ethical standards: Assets and limitations. *Personnel and Guidance Journal, 60,* 110–112.

Tarasoff v. Board of Regents of the University of California. (1976). 551 p2d 334, 131, Cal Rptr 14 (Cal. Sup. Ct. 1976).

Tennyson, W. W., & Strom, S. M. (1986). Beyond professional standards: Developing responsibleness. *Journal of Counseling and Development, 64,* 298–302.

Vacc, N. A., & Loesch, L. (2000). *Professional orientation to counseling* (3rd ed.). Philadelphia: Brunner-Routledge.

Van Hoose, W. H., & Kottler, J. (1985). *Ethical and legal issues in counseling and psychotherapy* (2nd ed.). San Francisco: Jossey-Bass.

Watts, R. E. (1999). Confidentiality and duty to report: A case study. *Family Journal, 7,* 65–67.

Welfel, E. R (2002). *Ethics in counseling and psychotherapy: Standards, research, and emerging issues* (2nd ed.). Pacific Grove, CA: Brooks/Cole.

Wilcoxon, S. A. (1993, March/April). Ethical issues in marital and family counseling: A framework for examining unique ethical concerns. *Family Counseling and Therapy, 1,* 1–15.

Williams, C. B., & Freeman, C. T. (2002). Report of the ACA Ethics Committee: 2000–2001. *Journal of Counseling and Development, 30,* 251–254.

CHAPTER 4

Current and Emerging Influences on Community Counseling

I feel at times that I'm wasting my mind
as we wade through your thoughts and emotions.
With my skills I could be in a world-renowned clinic
with a plush, private office, soft padded chairs,
and a sharp secretary at my command.
Instead of here in a pink cinderblock room
where it leaks when it rains
and the noise seeps under the door like water.
But in leaving, you pause for a moment
as your voice spills out in a whisper:
"Thanks for being here when I hurt."
With those words my fantasies end, as reality,
like a wellspring begins filling me
with life-giving knowledge, as it cascades through my mind,
That in meeting you, when you're flooded with pain,
I discover myself.

Gladding, S. T. (1975). Here and now. *Personnel and Guidance Journal, 53,* 746. © ACA. Reprinted with permission. No further reproduction authorized without written permission of ACA.

I n the last section of Chapter 1, we described some of the current issues and trends that are influencing the counseling profession in general and the community counseling profession in particular. Among those influences are multiculturalism and diversity, professional recognition and reimbursement, evidence-based treatment protocols, and advocacy and social justice issues. Although these topics are all significant, they are not addressed in Chapter 4 because attention is given to them in other sections of the book. In this chapter, we focus on three topics which are not addressed in as much depth in other chapters, but have had a widespread influence on the practice of community counseling: managed care, technology, and wellness and spirituality.

Managed care has had a pervasive impact on the delivery of mental health services. It has profoundly impacted the manner in which counseling is provided, with the majority of practitioners who work in managed care environments reporting an increased use of brief-term and solution-focused interventions (Mitchell, 1998). Working in managed care organizations has led to the rise of ethical concerns in regard to client care, confidentiality, competence, and integrity. In this chapter, we examine the development of managed care organizations, their influence on community counseling, ethical issues associated with managed care practices, and recommendations for community counselors who work in managed care environments.

Innovations in technology also have created opportunities and challenges for community counselors. In particular, the widespread use of the Internet has led to new options for individual and group counseling, as well as to increased access to mental health resources for the general public. Advances in technology do not come without a cost, however, and with new technological advances also come ethical concerns about a host of issues, including confidentiality, accountability, and viability of online resources. Thus, a second topic explored in this chapter is that of computer applications in counseling.

Finally, during the past decade there has been a renewed interest in promoting wellness and integrating spirituality into the counseling process. In many settings, community counselors are responding to the need to view clients holistically and to work with them from a multidimensional perspective. Whereas the counseling profession has always stressed development and prevention, the current emphasis on wellness extends previous assumptions. A related but unique focus on spirituality also has influenced community counseling in the 21st century. Spirituality is manifested in many different ways among people; consequently, it is important for counselors to avoid making assumptions and to let clients take the lead in integrating spirituality into the counseling process.

Each of these three topics—managed care, technological innovations, and wellness and spirituality—has had a distinct effect on the current practice of community counseling. It is likely that they will continue to affect counselors and the services they provide in the years that lie ahead. As counselors provide services in a dynamic, changing society, they will want to be aware of factors that influence clients and the counseling profession and make informed decisions about how to respond professionally to those influences.

MANAGED CARE

One event that has had a tremendous impact on community counselors, especially during the past 15 years, is the explosive growth of managed health care organizations. *Managed care* is a general term used to describe the systems of businesses and organizations that arrange for the financing and delivery of health services, including medical and mental health practices (Phelps, Eisman, & Kohout, 1998). *Managed behavioral health care,* which represents a growing segment of the managed care industry, specializes in mental health and substance abuse treatment.

The influx of managed care has caused significant changes in the manner in which mental health treatment is provided and financed. Indeed, according to some mental health professionals, managed care has emerged as the "single most important influence on the practice of counseling and psychotherapy" (Davis & Meier, 2001, p. vii). To function effectively as a community counselor in the 21st century, an understanding of key concepts and implications associated with managed care is essential. In this section, we describe the development and key functions of managed care systems and discuss some of the implications for community counselors, particularly in regard to ethical considerations.

The Development of Managed Care Systems

In many ways, health care today is equated with managed care. Prior to the 1980s, however, managed care organizations were uncommon. Mental health care was generally funded by major medical insurance, which utilized a fee-for-service system (Huber, 1998). Within such a system, insurance companies paid for services rendered by practitioners after consumers met specified deductible amounts. These third-party health care systems were founded on the premise that a large group of persons would pay a premium to offset the cost of care for those who were ill (Cooper & Gottlieb, 2000).

When third-party insurance systems such as Blue Cross were first established, mental health benefits were not included in their plans. Indeed, it was not until the 1950s that such insurance plans began to include mental health benefits, with services being provided more frequently on an outpatient, rather than on an inpatient, basis (Austad & Berman, 1991).

With more employers offering insurance coverage, and with the establishment of federally funded programs such as Medicare and Medicaid in 1965, the cost and the utilization of medical and mental health services increased dramatically. Escalating costs and growing demands for coverage and service led to increasingly greater portions of the federal budget and corporate profits being earmarked for health insurance costs (Mitchell, 1998).

In response to the rising cost of health coverage associated with existing plans, insurance companies, employers, and the federal government began to grapple with ways to curb expenses. Managed care provided an alternative to the traditional fee-for-service system. The Health Maintenance Organization Act of 1973 designated federal funding for the development of managed care programs and required

Term	Definition
Managed Care Organization (MCO)	The oversight of health care delivery by a third party whose purpose is to limit costs and monitor and influence services. The term refers to any HMO or managed behavioral care entity.
Health Maintenance Organization (HMO)	An organization that provides comprehensive health care to its members in return for a fixed monthly membership fee. Health services are coordinated by a primary care physician, who serves as the gatekeeper and makes all decisions regarding referral for specialty examinations and services.
Individual or Independent Practice Association (IPA)	An organization that typically is created by physicians and marketed to employers. An IPA may contract services with several different HMOs. Practitioners in the IPA serve clients from the HMOs as well as their individual clients.
Preferred Provider Organization (PPO)	Groups of hospitals, physicians, or other practitioners who contract with employers, insurance companies, or third-party groups to provide comprehensive medical care for a fee that is typically discounted. This plan allows patients to visit specialists outside the plan's network, but at a higher cost.
Health Care Finance Agency (HCFA)	The federal agency that oversees health financing policies for Medicare and the Office of Prepaid Health Care
Joint Commission on Accreditation of Health care Organizations (JCAHO)	A nonprofit organization whose goal is to improve the quality of health care services.
National Committee for Quality Assurance (NCQA)	A private, nonprofit group composed primarily of representatives from managed care companies and employers whose purpose is to evaluate the quality of managed care plans and accredit MCOs based on standardized reviews.

Figure 4–1
Types of Managed Care Organizations and Managed Care Regulators
Note. Definitions compiled from various sources, including Davis; Meier, 2001; Lawless, Ginter, & Kelly, 1999; & Winegar & Hayter, 1998.

employers to offer managed care options to employees (Cooper & Gottlieb, 2000). Health maintenance organizations (HMOs) are one of several forms of managed care systems designed to reduce total health care costs by shifting care to less expensive forms of treatment (Luck, 1999; Madonna, 2000). According to the U.S. Surgeon General's Report on Mental Health (1999), 72 percent of Americans are enrolled in some type of managed mental health care. In the 21st century, managed health care has emerged as a major factor influencing health care in general and mental health services in particular (Cooper & Gottlieb, 2000).

What Is Managed Care?

Corcoran and Vandiver (1996) noted that *managed care* refers to the administration of health care services by a party other than the client or practitioner. Managed care systems assume the financial risks as well as oversee the services provided by practitioners to clients. Generally speaking, the two primary goals of managed care systems are to (a) contain costs and (b) ensure quality of care. Costs are controlled by limiting the amount and type of services, monitoring services, and changing the nature of services offered (Foos, Ottens, & Hill, 1991). Managed care systems typically use treatment guidelines, peer review, and financial incentives and penalties to influence providers, payors, and financial intermediaries to manage the cost, financing, utilization, and quality of health care services (Luck, 1999).

Most of today's mental health professionals have at least some degree of involvement with managed care systems (Glosoff, 1998). Consequently, community counselors need to be familiar with terms and procedures associated with managed care environments. According to Alperin and Phillips, as cited by Glosoff (1998), the three most common models of managed care are HMOs, preferred provider organizations (PPOs), and government-funded health programs (i.e., Medicaid, Medicare, and Civilian Health and Medical Programs of the Uniformed Services). Descriptions of various managed care systems and terms associated with those systems are presented in Figures 4–1 and 4–2.

Today, there are hundreds of managed care companies operating in both the public and the private sectors (American Federation of State, County and Municipal Employees [AFSCME], 1998). These companies contract with approved mental health providers and facilities to provide mental health services for consumers at reduced fees. Providers and facilities that contract with MCOs agree to comply with company procedures, including preadmission screening and utilization reviews. Some companies are more restrictive than others, so prospective providers are encouraged to explore the potential effects the policies may have on their work with clients (Glosoff, 1998).

Implications for Counselors

How has managed care affected the work of professional counselors? According to Anderson (2000), working within managed care systems has changed the way mental health professionals perform clinical duties. Short-term, highly focused interventions that follow treatment guidelines and protocols are the norm (Mitchell, 1998). The

Term	Definition
Capitation	A form of payment in which the provider is paid on a per-member basis.
Carve-outs	The separation or carving out of specific types of health care from the overall benefit package. For example, the mental health and substance abuse portion of health care benefits may be "carved out" of the overall package, with separate contracts being made with managed behavioral care organizations.
Case/Care Management	A coordinated set of professional activities focused on treatment planning and assurance of treatment delivery that addresses the clients' needs while maintaining quality, cost-effective outcomes.
Case Rate	A preestablished fee paid for the entire course of treatment for one case.
Clinical Review Criteria	The written protocols or decision trees used by a utilization review organization to determine medical necessity and level of care decisions.
Closed Panel Health Plan	The managed care organization (MCO) requires participants to utilize practitioners, facilities, and pharmacies with which it has a contractual relationship.
Covered Services	Professional services of health care providers that have been authorized by the health care plan or HMO.
Gatekeeper	An individual (usually a clinician) who controls the access to health care services for members of a specific group. Often, the gatekeeper is the *primary care physician (PCP)*. In some health care delivery systems, the gatekeeper is a case manager.

Figure 4–2
Terms associated with managed care systems
Note. Definitions compiled from various sources, including Davis; Meier, 2001; Lawless, Ginter, & Kelly, 1999; & Winegar & Hayter, 1998.

Gag Clause	A stipulation made by an MCO that prevents counselors from discussing alternative treatments outside the boundaries of approved services (gag clauses are less common now than in the past after having been successfully challenged in court).
Intensive Outpatient Program (IOP)	In behavioral health care, IOP refers to an outpatient treatment program that provides 2 to 4 hours of care two or more times per week (both individual and group counseling).
Level of Care	Refers to treatment alternatives on a continuum of care (e.g., inpatient, partial hospitalization, outpatient, long-term residential treatment).
Medically Necessary	When a particular treatment or evaluation is required, appropriate, and in agreement with acceptable standards of medical practice and cannot be provided in a less intensive setting.
Network	Contracts made by an HMO with two or more independent group practices to provide services to HMO members.
Open Panel (HMO)	The HMO allows members to receive services outside of the provider network without referral authorization. Members usually pay an additional deductible and/or co-pay for these services.
Primary Care Physician (PCP)	Physician who oversees the provision of health care for defined subsets of HMO members. Some managed care plans require PCP screening and referral for mental health or substance abuse treatment as well as for other types of health care.
Practice Guidelines	Recommended interventions and procedures for treatments of specific conditions so as to achieve optimum results as efficiently as possible.
Provider Contract	A written agreement between a licensed health care provider (e.g., physician, counselor, facility) and a health plan.
Utilization Review	Process by which the MCO reviews the diagnosis, treatment plan, and response to treatment before authorizing the use or extension of the client's benefit plan.

Figure 4–2   *Continued*

emphasis is on demonstrating the efficacy of services while containing costs. Counselors working in managed care environments are expected to write specific treatment plans, participate in utilization reviews, and comply with the limits placed on the amount of therapy authorized by managed care organizations. Cooper and Gottlieb (2000), citing several sources, highlight the defining characteristics of counseling and psychotherapy in a managed care system:

- Brief therapy is mandated and characterized by immediate assessment of the client's presenting problem, clearly delineated treatment goals, and an active counselor.
- The counselor forms a pragmatic therapeutic relationship with the client for the purpose of providing the most efficient and effective treatment.
- Required communication with the client's PCP is usually required, as well as increased interaction with other health care professionals.
- The counseling process is monitored by the MCO and typically includes documentation of treatment necessity and regular submission of treatment plans. The process of monitoring the therapeutic process is called *utilization review* (UR) and may occur before, during, and after treatment.

Advantages and Disadvantages of Managed Care

Proponents of managed care assert that managed care services contain costs while simultaneously maintaining quality service (Paulson, 1996; Winegar, 1993). Supporters claim that time-limited treatment is a research-supported practice that is as effective as traditional treatment for most clients (see Austad & Berman, 1991; Hoyt, 1995). Other potential advantages associated with managed care include greater access to mental health services, increased numbers of referrals for some practitioners, and the implementation of quality control and standards of practice (Lawless, Ginter, & Kelly, 1999). Accredited managed behavioral care organizations typically require providers to document the quality of their work in several areas, including client satisfaction, clinical outcomes, and adherence to best-practice guidelines, thus increasing practitioner accountability.

Even though working in managed care settings may benefit practitioners and clients in some ways, recent studies indicate that most mental health professionals believe that managed care has negatively affected their work with clients and presents significant ethical challenges (Cooper & Gottlieb, 2000; Danzinger & Welfel, 2001; Phelps et al., 1998). Practitioners have expressed several concerns related to counseling in managed care environments. One concern is that standardized treatment guidelines fail to take into account the unique nature of clients' needs and compromise counselors' autonomy in determining specific interventions (Mitchell, 1998). The systems that set up treatment protocols usurp much of the clinical judgment and professionalism of the practitioner (Smith, 1999). Other concerns include arbitrary time limits, caps on the number of sessions approved, increased paperwork, difficulties in being placed on provider lists, and insufficient qualified personnel acting as gatekeepers (Glosoff, Garcia, Herlihy, & Remley, 1999). Managed mental health care systems are based on a medical model, which requires the labeling of pathology before services are authorized (Glosoff, 1998), rather than on a growth-based developmental model, which characterizes the counseling profession. Services that do not constitute a medical necessity will not be reimbursed, and many policies exclude coverage for certain types of counseling and mental health conditions, including marriage counseling, career counseling, educational services, experimental interventions, and personality disorders (Luck, 1999). Particularly distressing to many clinicians are the ethical dilemmas encountered when attempting to balance managed care dictums with professional codes of ethics. Indeed, Phelps et al. (1998) reported that negative appraisals of managed care organizations often stem from the difficult ethical issues with which practitioners are faced.

Ethical Considerations

A growing body of literature addresses ethical dilemmas that face community coun-selors working in managed care environments (e.g., Cooper & Gottlieb, 2000; Daniels, 2001; Danzinger & Welfel, 2001; Davis & Meier, 2001; Glosoff et al., 1999; Smith, 1999). Ethical concerns related to client welfare, confidentiality, informed consent, counselor competence, and integrity are among the issues frequently encountered in managed care environments, requiring counselors to engage in thoughtful decision-making practices.

Client welfare.   A professional counselor's first and foremost responsibility is to respect the dignity and promote the welfare of clients (American Counseling Associ-ation [ACA], 1995). At times, counselors working in managed care environments are faced with the difficulty of supporting the client's right to quality care as a priority over the counselor's relationship with the reimburser. According to the ACA (1995) *Code of Ethics and Standards of Practice,* treatment plans should be clinically viable, offer a reasonable likelihood of effectiveness, be consistent with the client's abilities and situations, and be respectful of the client's freedom of choice (Standard A.1.c.). However, because treatment plans must conform to MCO protocols and be approved by MCO representatives, counselors may not be free to plan and imple-ment treatments independently. When professional judgments differ from MCO mandates, practitioners must decide whether to implement the approved but less suitable treatment plans or risk denial of reimbursement (Danzinger & Welfel, 2001).

Time-limited treatment imposed by MCOs also can affect client welfare in that it may compromise quality, providing the client with partial treatment, which may result in early termination. Miller (1996) refers to this practice as *rationing* and cau-tions that it is imperative for counselors to inform clients in advance about the possi-bility of rationed services. In some cases, clinicians may determine that clients will benefit from brief therapy. Even so, the number of sessions recommended by the clinician for a satisfactory outcome may be greater than the number allocated by the MCO (Davis & Meier, 2001). When this is the case, counselors need to make appro-priate arrangements for those who cannot be served effectively following MCO guidelines. Such arrangements may include negotiating longer treatment with

MCOs, having clients pay out of pocket, referring clients to alternative treatment sources, and working *pro bono* (Glosoff et al., 1999). Standard A.10.d. of the ACA (1995) *Code of Ethics and Standards of Practice* addresses the issue of early termination by stating that counselors are not to abandon their clients and are responsible for making arrangements for continuation of care.

There are legal as well as ethical ramifications of time-limited treatment and early termination. In court cases dealing with the issue of responsible treatment of clients, most decisions have found the practitioners primarily responsible for their clients' care, regardless of MCO guidelines (Glosoff et al., 1999). For example, in *Wickline v. State of California* (1987), the provider was held liable for the HMO's decision to limit hospitalization, even though the provider had recommended additional treatment. In this case, which dealt with the delivery of medical services rather than of needed mental health services, the court maintained that the provider did not protest the HMO's denial of services aggressively enough (Davis & Meier, 2001). In another case, *Muse v. Charter Hospital of Winston-Salem, Inc.* (117 N.C. App. 468 [1995]), the court ruled that it was the duty of the mental health facility to provide care to patients based on patients' medical conditions, not on the needs of insurance companies.

Box 4–1
Muse v. Charter Hospital of Winston-Salem, Inc.

> In *Muse,* plaintiffs brought an action for the wrongful death of their son, Joe, who was an inpatient in a psychiatric hospital for treatment of depression with suicidal thoughts. When Joe's insurance was about to expire, the hospital sought a promissory note of payment from the parents. The parents agreed to pay for 2 extra days, after which Joe was released as an outpatient. Shortly thereafter, Joe took an overdose of drugs and killed himself. In this case, the court held that the hospital "had a duty not to institute a policy or practice which required that patients be discharged when their insurance expired and which interfered with the medical judgment of [the doctor]" (117 N.C. App. 468 [1995], LEXIS at *2).
>
> —(Madonna, 2000, p. 26)

Confidentiality.   Assurance of confidentiality is at the heart of the counseling relationship. Without this assurance, many clients would not feel safe discussing private, intimate aspects of their lives (Remley & Herlihy, 2001). Section B of ACA's (1995) *Code of Ethics and Standards of Practice* extensively addresses the issue of confidentiality. Traditionally, counselors have been able to assure clients of confidentiality, with certain exceptions (i.e., threat of harm to self or others). With the advent of managed care, however, the issue of confidentiality has become much more complex (Barnett, 1998). Danzinger and Welfel (2001) reported that one of the most frequently listed ethical challenges associated with managed care was that of confidentiality. Eighty percent of the counselors and counselor educators surveyed in their study stated that interactions with MCOs either often or occasionally compromised client confidentiality.

MCOs often request extensive, personal information about clients and detailed reports of their treatment (Cooper & Gottlieb, 2000). Once information is shared with MCOs, counselors have little control over what happens to that information (Danzinger & Welfel, 2001). Cooper and Gottlieb offer several recommendations to practitioners to help them address ethically the issue of confidentiality:

- Provide a comprehensive informed consent form to help clients understand the ramifications of MCO reimbursement policies.
- Only release the minimal amount of information needed so that the client's privacy is protected.
- Make sure clients understand the nature of any release forms signed.
- Avoid sending case notes to MCOs; instead, send treatment summaries.
- Exercise precaution when transmitting information via e-mail, fax machines, and cellular phones. Whenever possible, mail requested paperwork to the MCO.

Informed consent.   Standard A.3.a. of the ACA (1995) *Code of Ethics* states that counselors are to inform clients of the purposes, goals, procedures, limitations, risks, and benefits of counseling, both at the onset of the counseling relationship and throughout the process as necessary. The *Code of Ethics* also states that counselors should take steps to make sure clients understand the implications of diagnosis, the use of tests and reports, the procedures for fee-setting and billing, and the limits of confidentiality. Counselors working within a managed care context may need to expand their informed consent procedures to ensure that clients are aware of their benefit plans, MCO-related limits to confidentiality, and potential limits to treatment (Daniels, 2001). Cooper and Gottlieb (2000) recommend that practitioners view informed consent as an ongoing process rather than as a single event. When clients begin counseling, they may not be fully able to understand what they are told, especially if they are experiencing stress, anxiety, or depression. Revisiting issues related to informed consent ensures that the client truly comprehends the information that was presented initially.

Competence.   Most MCOs endorse brief-therapy models of treatment. Although many counselor education programs now include brief-therapy models as part of their curricula, there are some counselors who have not been adequately trained or prepared to practice brief therapy. Standard C.2.b. of the *Code of Ethics and Standards of Practice* states that counselors are to practice only within the boundaries of their competence. If counselors are not adequately trained to provide treatments authorized by an MCO, then they must either receive proper training or refrain from joining particular managed care panels (Cooper & Gottlieb, 2000; Daniels, 2001).

Integrity.   *Integrity* refers to honesty and fairness and includes being accurate and unbiased when reporting to other parties, including to MCOs (Cooper & Gottlieb, 2000). Honesty in diagnosing and reporting is addressed in Standard E.5.a. and Standard C.5.c. of ACA's ethical code. However, when client diagnoses do not fall within reimbursement guidelines, counselors may be tempted to diagnose inappropriately to gain reimbursement (Danzinger & Welfel, 2001). For example, a practitioner might assign a more serious diagnosis than is warranted to obtain more authorized sessions, a process known as *upcoding* (Cooper & Gottlieb, 2000). In other situations, the counselor may be tempted to *downcode,* or apply a less serious diagnosis, so that the client is able to receive treatment. For example, if a client presents with borderline personality disorder—an Axis II condition that typically is not reimbursable—a counselor who downcodes would record only an Axis I condition, such as depression (Cooper & Gottlieb, 2000). In a national survey of clinical counselors, over 70 percent of the respondents stated that they were aware of at least occasional occurrences of downcoding, and over 60 percent indicated awareness of upcoding (Mead, Hohenshil, & Singh, 1997). Both practices, sometimes called "diagnosing for dollars" (Wylie, 1995, p. 22), are unethical and probably constitute insurance fraud.

Recommendations for Counselors

When working in a managed care environment, counselors need to be aware of and plan for ethical conflicts (Glosoff et al., 1999). If an ethical dilemma does arise, it is important to have a decision-making plan in place. An example of an ethical decision-making model was presented in Chapter 3. In solving ethical dilemmas related to managed care, Cooper and Gottlieb (2000) suggest using Haas and Malouf's model of ethical decision making, which includes the following steps:

1. Gather information about the problem.
2. Consult with colleagues and look at relevant literature to consider pertinent legal and ethical principles.
3. Create a list of appropriate responses.
4. Conduct a cost–benefit analysis of each potential response.
5. Choose the option that best resolves the dilemma.
6. Act on that option and evaluate its effectiveness.

In addition to knowing how to solve ethical dilemmas effectively, counselors can do several things to facilitate their work with clients affiliated with MCOs. Counselors are encouraged to gain a complete understanding of the terms and functions of MCOs, including preauthorization, cost containment, clinical criteria requirements, and use review procedures (Glosoff et al., 1999). Counselors also need to be aware of client benefits, referral procedures, criteria for medical necessity, procedures for completing claim forms, and emergency procedures (Anderson, 2000). Other ways to prepare for work in a managed care environment include developing knowledge and skills related to DSM-IV categories, treatment-plan writing (Figure 4–3), brief and solution-focused counseling, and procedures for getting on provider panels (Lawless, Ginter, & Kelly, 1999). Combining clinical expertise with knowledge of MCO procedures and skill in working collaboratively with MCO personnel can help community counselors provide quality mental health services in the age of managed care.

Just as managed care has precipitated changes in the delivery of mental health services, technological advances have brought about new options in regard to counseling service delivery. In the next section, we direct our attention to computer applications in counseling.

- A clear statement of the client's problem
- A statement of goals with specific, measurable criteria to measure goal attainment
  - Goals can be listed as short term, intermediate, and long term, depending on the issues that are addressed.
- A clear statement of objectives or activities that will be implemented to help the client meet the established goals
  - Ask yourself, "How will I know if the client accomplished the objective?"
- A time frame within which goals and objectives will be accomplished

Example:
The client currently exhibits flat affect, depressed mood, and reports disturbed sleep (no more than 4 hours a night for the past month) and decreased appetite (has been eating one meal a day for the past 2 weeks). The goals are (1) to make a list of three pleasurable activities from which client will choose one and perform 3 days out of the week, (2) to eat two well-balanced meals a day for one week, and (3) to identify triggers to depression by writing in a journal three times a week. I plan to see the client in weekly individual sessions. I will be using cognitive behavioral techniques to help identify triggers to depression as well as client-centered therapy to enhance the therapeutic relationship. I am requesting 12 sessions. At the end of these sessions, the client's progress will be reevaluated.

(Anderson, 2000, p. 345)

Figure 4–3
What to include in a treatment plan written for an MCO
Reprinted with permission of AMHCA.

TECHNOLOGY AND COUNSELING

Of the many developments that have profoundly influenced the mental health profession, those related to technology have been especially salient. The widespread availability of computer networking and the Internet in the 1990s dramatically increased the use of computers in counseling (Oravec, 2000). Community counselors are challenged to make decisions about ways they will choose to use, or not use, computers in their work. As noted by Walz (2000), "All counselors must come to grips with this exponentially expanding medium and decide for themselves what to do and what not to do" (p. xii).

Throughout the past several decades, efforts to integrate technology into mental health care have increased significantly (Oravec, 2000). The impact of technology in general and computers in particular on the counseling profession accelerated with the advent of the microcomputer in the 1970s. During the 1970s and 1980s, computer applications were developed for a variety of counseling-related activities, including assessment and test interpretation, career guidance, and client data management (Granello, 2000). By 1994, more than 70 computer-assisted guidance systems and software programs were in use. Currently, a wide range of technologies influence counseling, including the telephone, microcomputers, video, CD-ROM, e-mail, and the World Wide Web. The accelerated use of technologies presents counselors with new opportunities as well as potential challenges. Consequently, "healthy management of technological tools may be one of the most critical competencies a counseling professional can model and teach" (Casey, 2000, p. 18).

The Internet and Community Counseling

Whereas technological applications in the mental health field are widespread and numerous, the evolution of the Internet in the 1990s has had, perhaps, the most pervasive effect on the counseling profession. Over 50 percent of American homes now have Internet access, and many more people gain access through their places of employment (Harris-Bowlsbey, 2000). Indeed, the increased accessibility of the Internet has "revolutionized communication technology and opened new horizons for the dissemination of mental health information and services" (Rosik, 2001, p. 106).

Box 4–2

> *The boom in Internet access and use, first in academic circles and then with the general public, has created an entire new chapter in the computer-counseling relationship.*
>
> —(Granello, 2000, p. 11)

Although its origins date back to post-World War II days, the Internet has only recently become readily accessible to the general public (Guterman & Kirk, 1999). In particular, the development of the World Wide Web (WWW, or "the Web") has transformed the Internet into an information highway (Sampson & Bloom, 2001), providing the general public with global interconnection and instantly accessible information. Counseling-related Internet applications include electronic mail (e-mail) counseling, list servers, computer conferencing, chat rooms, and bulletin board systems. Assessments, information, and instruction also are delivered in a wide array of formats on the Internet (Sampson & Bloom).

As individuals spend more time interacting with each other online, mental health services that make use of the Internet are becoming increasingly more widespread (Oravec, 2000). In this section, attention will be given to two emerging forms of online mental health services: *counseling* and *guidance*. Sampson and Bloom (2001) defined *computer applications in counseling* as those situations in which a relationship has been established between a counselor and a client over time for the purpose of helping the client (or clients). They defined *computer applications in guidance* as the use of text, graphic, audio, and video resources for self-help purposes (e.g., Internet career guidance services).

Online Counseling

"WebCounseling," "cybercounseling," and "technology-assisted distance counseling" are commonly used terms to describe the process of counseling with individuals, families, or groups over distance using the Internet (NBCC, 2001; Oravec, 2000). Online counseling can occur through e-mail interaction, teleconferencing, and video-conferencing. Of the three processes, videoconferencing most closely approximates traditional face-to-face counseling. Videoconferencing and teleconferencing are both forms of *synchronous counseling* (i.e., the interaction takes place during the moment of Internet connection). Online counseling using e-mail is *asynchronous counseling,* meaning there is a time lapse in communication between the counselor and the client. In this section, we focus on asynchronous counseling using e-mail, because currently, fewer people have access to videoconferencing, although options are likely to increase with continued technological advances (Sampson & Bloom, 2001).

Online e-mail counseling.   Many people are quite adept at using e-mail as a primary means of communication. For some, using e-mail for therapeutic purposes is a logical next step. In situations where face-to-face contact is geographically or physically not feasible, or when it creates excessive anxiety for the client, online counseling using e-mail may provide access to mental health services that otherwise would not be a possibility (Tait, 1999).

Online individual counseling can take several different forms. In some cases, a question-and-answer format is used: An individual states a problem, and the mental health professional responds within a fixed time period with information, recommendations, or a counseling referral (Sampson, Kolodinsky, & Greeno, 1997). In other situations, the online counseling acquires a more formal structure, in which client and counselor make arrangements to communicate therapeutically, using e-mail as the mode of communication for each session. *Therapy Online* is an example of an e-mail counseling and therapy practice initiated by Murphy and Mitchell (1998). Depending on the client's needs, counseling can range from a few brief exchanges to more long-term interactions. The client–counselor relationship is initiated when the client completes a worksheet available at the *Therapy Online* Web site (http://www.therapyonline.ca). If online counseling seems to be an appropriate option, the counselor(s) and client design a plan to structure future correspondence (Oravec, 2000). Typically, Murphy and Mitchell use narrative and solution-focused approaches to serve the needs of their clients.

In an online interview discussing their e-mail counseling practice (Collie, Mitchell, & Murphy, 2000), Mitchell and Murphy noted several benefits associated with electronic counseling, including "convenience, privacy, schedule flexibility, the possibility of communicating thoughts and feelings right away rather than waiting until the weekly appointment, and the potential for leveling the power imbalances" (p. 234). Murphy and Mitchell described the importance of developing specific online counseling skills to compensate for the lack of visual cues. These skills, which include the use of metaphorical language, the use of special fonts, and descriptive immediacy, enable the counselor to contextualize and enhance the meaning of the printed word, thus enabling the counselor to convey warmth and caring to the client. Murphy and Mitchell also emphasized the importance of informing clients at the outset of the possibility of technical glitches interfering with communication pathways. They suggested providing clients with a window of time in which they should expect a response, and if no response is forthcoming, to contact the counselor.

Online support groups and *online group counseling* represent other ways to offer computer-assisted mental health services (Oravec, 2000). Online support groups provide opportunities for global communication among individuals dealing with issues such as grief, depression, and chronic illness. Many participants perceive these computer-based support groups as helpful and validating, although research about their efficacy is limited (Gary & Remolino, 2000). Online group counseling also has received some support in the literature (Riemer-Reiss, 2000). With online group counseling, the counselor coordinates exchanges among members, sets ground rules, and takes steps to ensure that all participants have the opportunity to benefit from the proceedings. Until more research is conducted on these and other online services, counselors need to be alert to potential dangers and complications associated with their uses.

How prevalent is the practice of online counseling? In a search of Internet counseling home pages, Sampson et al. (1997) located approximately 275 practitioners offering direct counseling services via the Internet. In contrast, Heinlen, Welfel, Richmond, and Rak (2003) conducted a search for Web sites offering options of online counseling services and located 136 sites. So although the prevalence of online counseling at this point in time may not be high, counseling is being conducted on the Internet, and future enhancements in technology may lead to an increase in cybercounseling services.

Sampson et al. (1997) noted that the credentials of counselors offering online services varied, including M.D., Ph.D, L.P.C., and M.A. Some "counselors" identified no credentials at all. Certainly, this raises concerns in regard to unlicensed people promoting themselves as counselors (Hughes, 2000). Some Web sites included disclaimers stating all information provided was advice (or education), not "therapy"; however, even with the disclaimer, the implications are problematic. To confirm the credentials of online therapists, clients are advised to access online verification centers, such as *Credential Check* (http://www.mentalhelp.net/check); (Sampson & Bloom, 2001).

In response to some of the professional, ethical, and legal issues potentially associated with online counseling, NBCC organized a task force in 1995 to develop a set of technology-assisted counseling guidelines. These guidelines evolved into the *Standards for the Ethical Practice of WebCounseling,* which were adopted formally in 1997 and updated in November 2001 (NBCC, 2001). Now called the *Standards for the Practice of Internet Counseling,* the guidelines address practices that are unique to Internet counseling and are based on the principles of ethical practice that embody the NBCC *Code of Ethics* (NBCC, 2001). Specific areas that are addressed include the counseling relationship, confidentiality, data security, licensure, and certification. The *Standards for the Ethical Practice of Internet Counseling* are listed in Figure 4–4 and also can be accessed through the NBCC Web site (http://www.nbcc.org).

In October 1999, the ACA Governing Council approved a separate set of ethical guidelines for online counseling. These guidelines address many of the same issues

Internet Counseling Relationship

1. In situations where it is difficult to verify the identity of the Internet client, steps are taken to address impostor concerns, such as by using code words or numbers.
2. Internet counselors determine if a client is a minor and therefore in need of parental/guardian consent. When parent/guardian consent is required to provide Internet counseling to minors, the identity of the consenting person is verified.
3. As part of the counseling orientation process, the Internet counselor explains to clients the procedures for contacting the Internet counselor when he or she is offline and, in the case of asynchronous counseling, how often e-mail messages will be checked by the Internet counselor.
4. As part of the counseling orientation process, the Internet counselor explains to clients the possibility of technology failure and discusses the alternative modes of communication, if that failure occurs.
5. As part of the counseling orientation process, the Internet counselor explains to clients how to cope with potential misunderstandings when visual cues do not exist.
6. As a part of the counseling orientation process, the Internet counselor collaborates with the Internet client to identify an appropriately trained professional who can provide local assistance, including crisis intervention, if needed. The Internet counselor and Internet client should also collaborate to determine the local crisis hotline telephone number and the local emergency telephone number.
7. The Internet counselor has an obligation, when appropriate, to make clients aware of free public access points to the Internet within the community for accessing Internet counseling or Web-based assessment, information, and instructional resources.
8. Within the limits of readily available technology, Internet counselors have an obligation to make their Web site a barrier-free environment to clients with disabilities.
9. Internet counselors are aware that some clients may communicate in different languages, live in different time zones, and have unique cultural perspectives. Internet counselors are also aware that local conditions and events may impact the client.

Confidentiality in Internet Counseling

10. The Internet counselor informs Internet clients of encryption methods being used to help ensure the security of client/counselor/supervisor communication. Encryption methods should be used whenever possible. If encryption is not made available to clients, clients must be informed of the potential hazards of unsecured communication on the Internet. Hazards may include unauthorized monitoring of transmissions and/or records of Internet counseling sessions.

Figure 4–4

Standards for the ethical practice of Internet counseling

Note. Reprinted with permission of the National Board for Certified Counselors (NBCC, 2001, http://www.nbcc.org/ethics).

11. The Internet counselor informs Internet clients if, how, and how long session data are being preserved. Session data may include Internet counselor/Internet client e-mail, test results, audio/video session recordings, session notes, and counselor/supervisor communications. The likelihood of electronic sessions being preserved is greater because of the ease and decreased costs involved in recording. Thus, its potential use in supervision, research, and legal proceedings increases.

12. Internet counselors follow appropriate procedures regarding the release of information for sharing Internet client information with other electronic sources. Because of the relative ease with which e-mail messages can be forwarded to formal and casual referral sources, Internet counselors must work to ensure the confidentiality of the Internet counseling relationship.

13. Internet counselors review pertinent legal and ethical codes for guidance on the practice of Internet counseling and supervision. Local, state, and national statutes, as well as codes of professional membership organizations, professional certifying bodies, and state or provincial licensing boards need to be reviewed. Also, as varying state rules and opinions exist on questions pertaining to whether Internet counseling takes place in the Internet counselor's location or in the Internet client's location, it is important to review codes in the counselor's home jurisdiction as well as in that of the client. Internet counselors also consider carefully local customs regarding age of consent and child abuse reporting, and liability insurance policies need to be reviewed to determine if the practice of Internet counseling is a covered activity.

14. The Internet counselor's Web site provides links to Web sites of all appropriate certification bodies and licensure boards to facilitate consumer protection.

Figure 4–4   *Continued*

that the NBCC *Standards* address and can be accessed through ACA's homepage (http://www.counseling.org). Even with the passage of ethical standards by ACA and NBCC, major challenges exist regarding the use of online counseling services. Issues related to certification, requisite training, safeguarding of clients' rights, dealing with emergency situations, third-party payments, and insufficient research on the efficacy of online counseling have yet to be resolved. Sussman (1998) reminds us that one of our duties as counseling professionals is to take an active role in guiding the development and implementation of this new method of service delivery, both now and in the future.

Computer-Assisted Guidance: Online Mental Health Resources

The Internet provides people in today's society with quick access to multimedia-based psychoeducational resources (Riemer-Reiss, 2000; Sampson & Bloom, 2001).

These resources can be used without counselor assistance for self-help purposes, or they may be prescribed to supplement traditional counseling. Online psychoeducational resources address a wide range of topics, including mental illness, parenting, conflict resolution, stress management, child development, and career-related issues. Often, the Internet sites allow people to select media formats that best suit their individual learning styles (Sampson & Bloom). They typically include links to other Web sites, making it possible to access multiple sources of information very rapidly. A downside of the proliferation of information is that Internet-based "assessments, information, and instruction may be attractively presented but inherently invalid and potentially harmful" (Sampson & Bloom, 2001, pp. 623–624).

A specialty area that has many useful computer-based applications, both for personalized computer-based software and for online use, is that of career development. The first computer-based career planning systems were developed in the 1960s (Casey, 2001). Since that time, numerous comprehensive computer-assisted career guidance systems, such as the SIGI-PLUS and DISCOVER, have been created to help people learn about their career interests, skills, and values. More recently, a plethora of career-related materials have been made available online. Either on their own or with the help of a counselor, people can use the Web to:

- Get information about employment opportunities, job resources, and occupational outlooks
- Get information about company profiles
- Get information about graduate schools and financial aid
- Create and submit electronic resumes
- Complete assessments of interests, personality, skills, and values
- Visit virtual career centers

As with other psychoeducational material available online, some sources are more reputable than others. Harris-Bowlsbey, Dikel, and Sampson (as cited by Casey, 2001) have created a comprehensive guide to Internet career resources. Potential problems associated with online career resources include varied qualities of services, the possibility of invalid or unreliable assessment tools, lack of follow-up and support, misinformation, and, in some cases, compromised confidentiality.

The National Career Development Association (NCDA, 1997) developed the NCDA *Guidelines for the Use of the Internet for Provision of Career Information and Planning Services*. These guidelines, which can be accessed through the NCDA Web site, provide detailed information for counselors who plan to use Web-based career services in their practices.

Issues and Implications for Counselors

Technology in general and the Internet in particular have led to a broad spectrum of counseling-related computer applications (Casey, 2001). Computer applications, when used prudently, can enhance counseling services in multiple ways and lead to professional growth. However, there are benefits and costs associated with technology. Some of the major concerns that have accompanied increased Internet access include Internet addiction, cybersex addiction, Internet pornography, and online predators (e.g., Hall & Parsons, 2001; Pennington, 2002). Thus, in addition to developing skills for using technology effectively in counseling, counselors need to be aware of the signs and symptoms associated with Internet-related disorders and develop the skills needed for intervention.

Another issue related to mental health services and technology is that of equality of access. The U.S. Department of Commerce (1999) reported that households with incomes of $75,000 or higher are 20 times more likely to have Internet access than those at the lowest income levels and 9 times more likely to have a computer at home (cited in Lee, 2000). Because of this gap, Lee warns that "basing the opportunity for quality mental health and educational services on access to the new network technologies is potentially to consign many to marginalization and disenfranchisement" (p. 85). Lee goes on to state, "It is an ethical and moral imperative that the digital divide be bridged" (p. 92). Counselors can take necessary steps to ensure that computer-related counseling services are available to all clients, regardless of their socioeconomic status.

To work effectively in our rapidly advancing technological society, counselors need to stay abreast of emerging developments. Engaging in research, participating in ongoing technological training, being familiar with the resources available online, and being involved in continued refinement of guidelines for Internet use in counseling are just a few of the ways counselors can responsibly manage the opportunities and challenges that accompany the inevitable expansion of computer use that will continue to influence the provision of mental health services.

As advancements are made in technology, accompanied by increased access to data and communication options, many Americans have found themselves on "accessibility overload" (Swenson, 1998, p. 45). With progress comes a pushing of personal and professional limits, which can result in fatigue, frustration, and disorganization. Finding ways to balance progress with a respect for limits is essential to maintaining physical and psychological health. It is not surprising, then, that promoting wellness and integrating spirituality have emerged as strong influences on the counseling profession during the 21st century. It is to those influences that we direct our attention next.

WELLNESS AND SPIRITUALITY

During the past decade, there has been a renewed interest in promoting wellness and integrating spirituality. The interest in these areas springs from an increased emphasis in the profession on working with clients from a multidimensional perspective. Those who come to counseling are seen as individuals who have a variety of mental, physical, emotional, social, and spiritual needs. These needs must be met if clients are to grow in positive directions.

The focus on wellness comes from the developmental arena of counseling which has always been one of the principle foundations of the profession (Gladding, 2004). Although wellness was not initially stressed in counseling, it was assumed that counselors dealt with primarily healthy people who were experiencing difficulties because of a variety of factors. The focus on wellness in counseling today, however, extends further than the original assumption on health. Rather, it is assumed that in order to optimize clients' growth there must be an active concentration on helping them develop health and wellness in multiple ways.

Spirituality has grown as a part of counseling in a different way. Initially, counselors followed the lead of other helping professionals in not dealing with spiritual concerns of clients. The subject area was seen as one peripheral to counseling and one that counselors were not equipped to handle. Yet over the years, counselors from many walks of life have grown to see spirituality as a dimension that most clients have an interest in and that sometimes needs addressing in counseling sessions (Sperry, 2001). There are various forms of spirituality, and counselors must have both an open mind and a broad knowledge base to work with clients on this aspect of their lives.

Different aspects of wellness and spirituality will be examined in this section because community counselors regularly deal with them.

Wellness

In recent years, the idea of promoting wellness within the counseling profession has grown (Myers, Sweeney, & Witmer, 2001; Witmer & Sweeney, 1999). Wellness involves many aspects of life including the physical, intellectual, social, psychological, emotional, and environmental. Myers, Sweeney, and Witmer (2000) define wellness as

> a way of life oriented toward optimal health and well-being in which body, mind, and spirit are integrated by the individual to live life more fully within the human and natural community. Ideally, it is the optimum state of health and well-being that each individual is capable of achieving. (p. 252)

A model for promoting wellness has been developed by Myers et al. (2000). It revolves around five life tasks—spirituality, self-direction, work and leisure, friendship, and love. Some of these tasks, such as self-direction, are further subdivided into a number of subtasks, such as sense of worth, sense of control, problem solving and creativity, sense of humor, and self-care. The premise of the wellness model, which is discussed further in Chapter 7, is that healthy functioning occurs on a developmental continuum, and healthy behaviors at one point in life affect subsequent development and functioning as well.

An overall emphasis in counseling, however, is not just on wellness but on *positive wellness* (i.e., health-related activities that are both preventive and remedial and have a therapeutic value to individuals who practice them consistently). Such activities include eating natural foods, taking vitamins, going to health spas, meditating, participating in regular exercise, and exploring a variety of humanistic and transpersonal approaches to helping (O'Donnell, 1988). "For the person to be a whole, healthy, functioning organism, one must evaluate the physical, psychological, intellectual, social, emotional, and environmental processes" (Carlson & Ardell, 1988, p. 383).

Research supports the basis for the wellness movement, at least on the physiological level. In an extensive review of the literature on the effectiveness of physical fitness on measures of personality, Doan and Scherman (1987) found strong support for the idea that regular exercise can have a beneficial effect on people's physical and psychological health. Chung and Baird's (1999) review of the literature on psychological effects of exercise found that exercise can positively affect mood state, anxiety level, and self-esteem. Both reviews support counselors who prescribe health habits to accompany regular counseling practices. Other strategies for working from a wellness perspective are more cognitively based and include having counselors dwell on positive, life-enhancing things they can do.

In counseling per se, two approaches based on a wellness model are *solution-focused theory* (SFT) (deShazer, 1988) and *stress inoculation training* (SIT) (Meichenbaum, 1993). In SFT, problems are not seen as "evidence of an underlying pathology" (Mostert, Johnson, & Mostert, 1997, p. 21). Rather, the emphasis in this approach is on finding solutions to difficulties regardless of causes. In SIT, a proactive, psychoeducational intervention (Israelashvili, 1998), individuals are helped to understand their problematic situations, acquire skills for coping with them, and apply this knowledge to current and future events through the use of imagery or simulated rehearsal.

Overall, a cornerstone of the wellness approach is an emphasis on prevention and education in addition to treatment, if needed (Kleist & White, 1997). Wellness emphasizes the positive nature and health of human beings (Myers, 1992). Thus, counselors help "their clients identify their strengths and build on their strengths" (Rak & Patterson, 1996, p. 368). Individuals are seen as having the resources to solve their own problems in a practical, immediate way.

Spirituality

Spirituality has some common linkage with wellness in that it is often incorporated as a part of wellness, and like wellness, there is currently "no generally agreed on definition of spirituality" (Ganje-Fling & McCarthy, 1996, p. 253). However, as a rule, "spirituality includes concepts such as transcendence, self-actualization, purpose and meaning, wholeness, balance, sacredness, altruism, and a sense of a Higher Power" (Stanard, Sandhu, & Painter, 2000, p. 209). Thus, as a concept, *spirituality* usually refers to a unique, personally meaningful experience of a transcendent dimension that is associated with wholeness and wellness (Hinterkopf, 1998; Westgate, 1996).

In a comprehensive overview of spirituality, religion, and counseling, Ingersoll (1994) points out dimensions that are most characteristic of spirituality including:

- A concept of the divine or a force greater than oneself
- A sense of meaning
- A relationship with the divine
- Openness to mystery
- A sense of playfulness
- Engagement in spiritually enhancing activities
- Systematic use of spiritual forces as an integrator of life

Thus, one's spiritual journey is often developmental in nature. It involves an active search toward overcoming current centricity to becoming more connected with the meaning of life, including an awareness of ultimate being (Chandler, Holden, & Kolander, 1992; Kelly, 1995).

Within counseling there is a tradition of including spirituality as an important dimension of human life. For example, such luminaries as Victor Frankl, Abraham Maslow, and Rollo May emphasized the importance of spirituality in living. In addition, Adler believed that besides the three main tasks of life—society, work, and sexuality—there are two other challenges of life: spirituality and coping with self (Dreikurs & Mosak, 1966). Furthermore, Jung believed spirituality is a vital part of life, with those over the age of 40 uniquely qualified to explore its many dimensions.

Likewise, a key component of some counseling-related organizations has been an emphasis on spirituality. For instance, in Alcoholics Anonymous (AA) there is the use of a 12-step program that has at its basis a spiritual foundation. Group discussions in AA meetings center on helping members realize they need and have the support of others and a dependence on a higher power. The spiritual dimension in AA results in an emphasis on members admitting their powerlessness over alcohol (or other substances).

In addition to these theoretical and practical aspects of spirituality within counseling, there is an increased emphasis on spirituality and its importance in the well-being of those seeking help and wishing to maintain their own health (Burke & Miranti, 1995; Hudson, 1998). For many people who seek counseling, spirituality and religion are key factors in their lives (Burke et al., 1999). In addition, many counselors are drawn to spiritual and religious values and practices. Consequently, "spiritual competencies for counselors have been proposed and distributed nationally and are beginning to be assimilated into counselor training programs" (Myers & Truluck, 1998, p. 120).

The Association for Spiritual, Ethical, and Religious Values in Counseling (ASERVIC), a division within the ACA, is devoted to exploring the place of spirituality in counseling. ASERVIC can be helpful to counselors in exploring themselves as spiritual persons (Goud, 1990; Kottler, 1986) and in helping them use clients' spiritual values to aid progress in counseling (Aust, 1990; Goldberg, 1994).

Ingersoll (1994) states that counselors interested in working well with clients committed to a particular spiritual view can best do so by affirming the importance of spirituality in the client's life, using language and imagery in problem solving and treatment that is congruent with the client's worldview, and consulting with other "healers," such as ministers, in the client's life. This process calls for cultural sensitivity as well as for ethical practices of the highest standard. For example, spirituality and the role of the minister in African American culture are factors influencing members of this group as a "source of mental and emotional sustenance" (Priest, 1991, p. 214). Native Americans, too, may find spiritual elements different from non-Native-American traditions important in helping them. Therefore, counselors who work with this population may want to consult a medicine man or medicine woman before trying to work with persons or groups seeking recovery (Vick, Smith, & Herrera, 1998).

Sometimes spirituality is manifested in a particular philosophy or religious belief, such as Taoism or Christianity. When spirituality is in the form of religious beliefs, counselors need to be respectful and work with clients to maximize the positive nature of their beliefs and values in connection with the difficulties they are experiencing. Counselors who work best with religious issues in counseling are either pluralistic, that is, "recognizing the existence of a religious or spiritual absolute reality" but allowing for multiple interpretations and paths toward it; or constructivist, that is, recognizing a client worldview that includes God or spiritual realities (Zinnbauer & Pargament, 2000, p. 167).

Regardless of the form spirituality takes, spiritual aspects of clients' lives can be enhanced through creating rituals or other ways for clients to focus on their lives that help them appreciate life rather than depreciate themselves. For example, one ritual that distraught clients might be invited to engage in is writing down five things for which they are grateful (Hudson, 1998). Such an assignment can help them move away from bitterness and transcend the adversity of the moment.

In addition to helping clients, forms of spirituality, such as meditation and prayer, may be important aspects of counselors' lives as well. Kelly (1995) found in a nationally representative sample of ACA-affiliated counselors that the majority of respondents valued spirituality in their lives (even more than institutionalized religion). In many cases, a "counselor's personal spirituality/religiousness may prove a value base for being attuned to clients' spiritual and religious issues" (Kelly, 1995, p. 43). Therefore, counselors should first assess their own spirituality as well as that of their clients. Then their job is to assist clients in dealing with psychosocial tasks, such as maintaining a meaningful quality of life, coping with loss of function, and confronting existential or spiritual issues. Regardless, asking about a client's spirituality or spiritual resources has become a fundamental intake question in many counseling practices, as counselors address the total person of the client.

SUMMARY AND CONCLUSION

As the field of counseling continues to evolve, it is essential to respond to the diverse and dynamic needs of clients, organizations, and society in general. In this chapter, we have examined three distinct forces that influence the counseling profession and the delivery of counseling services.

Managed care is a term used to describe the systems of organizations that arrange for the delivery of health services. The expansion of managed care into the 21st century has changed the way mental health care services are provided and financed. Practitioners who work in managed care environments are likely to employ brief, highly focused interventions that follow treatment guidelines. There are advantages and disadvantages associated with the proliferation of managed care organizations. Among the advantages that have been cited are increased access to mental health services, higher rates of referrals, controlled costs, and the implementation of quality control and standards of practice. However, many mental health practitioners indicate that managed care has negatively impacted their work with clients and created significant ethical challenges. Community counselors who work in managed care environments need to be aware of potential ethical concerns and engage in thoughtful, informed decision-making practices as they confront those concerns.

Technological innovations have precipitated rapid changes in American society: changes that will continue to influence education and lifestyles in ways that cannot yet be envisioned. The increased availability and use of computers and the Internet have brought additional opportunities and challenges to the counseling profession. In particular, online computer applications, including counseling and guidance, have created new possibilities for mental health services offered by community counselors. As with managed care, advances in technology have been accompanied by ethical challenges that warrant careful consideration. Community counselors will want to stay informed about technological developments and make well-informed decisions about integrating technology into their counseling practices.

Both wellness and spirituality have taken on increased importance in counseling over the years. Wellness is connected with activity on the part of clients as they proactively take steps to improve their physical and psychological health. The promotion of wellness incorporates many dimensions, including physical, intellectual, social, psychological, emotional, and environmental factors. Spirituality also is an active process that may benefit clients and counselors as they explore the dimensions of their own development in this area. Most clients are not offended by inquiries into their spiritual life and may actually want to work on aspects of their spiritual development in counseling. As with wellness, clients may choose not to focus therapeutically on spirituality, but counselors can give them the choice by asking relevant questions about this important dimension of life.

REFERENCES

American Counseling Association. (1995). *Code of ethics and standards of practice.* Alexandria, VA: Author.

American Federation of State, County and Municipal Employees. (1998). Managed care comes to mental health. Retrieved May 15, 2001, from http://www.afscme.org/pol-leg/mcmh05.htm

Anderson, C. E. (2000). Dealing constructively with managed care: Suggestions from an insider. *Journal of Mental Health Counseling, 22,* 343–353.

Aust, C. F. (1990). Using client's religious values to aid progress in therapy. *Counseling and Values, 34,* 125–129.

Austad, C. S., & Berman, W. H. (1991). Managed care and the evolution of psychotherapy. In C. S. Austad & W. H. Berman (Eds.), *Psychotherapy in managed health care: The optimal use of time and resources* (pp. 3–18). Washington, DC: American Psychological Association.

Barnett, J. E. (1998). Confidentiality in the age of managed care. *The Clinical Psychologist, 51,* 30–33.

Burke, M. T., & Miranti, J. G. (1995). *Counseling: The spiritual dimension.* Alexandria, VA: American Counseling Association.

Burke, M. T., Hackeny, H., Hudson, P., Miranti, J., Watts, G. A., & Epp, L. (1999). Spirituality, religion, and CACREP curriculum standards. *Journal of Counseling and Development, 77,* 251–257.

Carlson, J., & Ardell, D. E. (1988). Physical fitness as a pathway to wellness and effective counseling. In R. Hayes & R. Aubrey (Eds.), *New directions for counseling and human development* (pp. 383–396). Denver: Love.

Casey, J. A. (2000). Managing technology wisely: A new counselor competency. In J. W. Bloom & G. R. Walz (Eds.), *Cybercounseling and cyberlearning: Strategies and resources for the new millennium* (pp. 17–28). Alexandria, VA: American Counseling Association.

Casey, J. A. (2001). Counseling and technology. In D. Capuzzi & D. R. Gross (Eds.), *Introduction to the counseling profession* (3rd ed.); (pp. 106–120). Needham Heights, MA: Allyn & Bacon.

Chandler, C. K., Holden, J. M., & Kolander, C. A. (1992). Counseling for spiritual wellness: Theory and practice. *Journal of Counseling and Development, 71,* 168–175.

Chung, Y. B., & Baird, M. K. (1999). Physical exercise as a counseling intervention. *Journal of Mental Health Counseling, 21,* 124–135.

Collie, K. R., Mitchell, D., & Murphy, L. (2000). Skills for online counseling: Maximum impact at minimum bandwidth. In J. W. Bloom & G. R. Walz (Eds.), *Cybercounseling and cyberlearning: Strategies and resources for the new millennium* (pp. 219–236). Alexandria, VA: American Counseling Association.

Cooper, C. C., & Gottlieb, M. C. (2000). Ethical issues with managed care: Challenges facing counseling psychology. *The Counseling Psychologist, 28,* 179–236.

Corcoran, K., & Vandiver, V. (1996). *Maneuvering the maze of managed care: Skills for mental health practitioners.* New York: The Free Press.

Daniels, J. A. (2001). Managed care, ethics, and counseling. *Journal of Counseling and Development, 79,* 119–122.

Danzinger, P. R., & Welfel, E. R. (2001). *Journal of Mental Health Counseling, 23,* 137–150.

Davis, S. R., & Meier, S. T. (2001). *The elements of managed care.* Belmont, CA: Wadsworth.

deShazer, S. (1988). *Clues: Investigating solutions in brief therapy.* New York: Norton.

Doan, R. E., & Scherman, A. (1987). The therapeutic effect of physical fitness on measures of personality: A literature review. *Journal of Counseling and Development, 66,* 28–36.

Dreikurs, R. R., & Mosak, H. H. (1966). The task of life. I: Adler's three tests. *Individual Psychologist, 4,* 18–22.

Foos, J. A., Ottens, A. J., & Hill, L. K. (1991). Managed mental health: A primer for counselors. *Journal of Counseling and Development, 69,* 332–336.

Ganje-Fling, M. A., & McCarthy, P. (1996). Impact of childhood sexual abuse on client spiritual development: Counseling implications. *Journal of Counseling and Development, 74,* 253–258.

Gary, J. M., & Remolino, L. (2000). Coping with loss and grief through online support groups. In J. W. Bloom & G. R. Walz (Eds.), *Cybercounseling and cyberlearning: Strategies and resources for the new millennium* (pp. 95–114). Alexandria, VA: American Counseling Association.

Giles, T. R. (1993). Managed mental health care. Boston: Allyn & Bacon.

Gladding, S. T. (2004). *Counseling: A comprehensive profession* (5th ed.). Upper Saddle River, NJ: Prentice Hall.

Glosoff, H. L. (1998). Managed care: A critical ethical issue for counselors. *Counseling and Human Development, 31,* 1–16.

Glosoff, H. L., Garcia, J., Herlihy, B., & Remley, T. P. (1999). Managed care: Ethical considerations for counselors. *Counseling and Values, 44,* 8–16.

Goldberg, J. R. (1994, June). Spirituality, religion and secular values: What role in psychotherapy? *Family Therapy News, 25*(9), 16–17.

Goud, N. (1990). Spiritual and ethical beliefs of humanists in the counseling profession. *Journal of Counseling and Development, 68,* 571–574.

Granello, P. G. (2000). Historical context: The relationship of computer technologies and counseling. In J. W. Bloom & G. R. Walz (Eds.), *Cybercounseling and cyberlearning: Strategies and resources for the new millennium* (pp. 3–16). Alexandria, VA: American Counseling Association.

Guterman, J. T., & Kirk, M. A. (1999). Mental health counselors and the Internet. *Journal of Mental Health Counseling, 21,* 309–325.

Hall, A. S., & Parsons, J. (2001). Internet addiction: College student case study using best practices in cognitive behavior therapy. *Journal of Mental Health Counseling, 23,* 312–327.

Harris-Bowlsbey, J. (2000). The Internet: Blessing or bane for the counseling profession? In J. W. Bloom & G. R. Walz (Eds.), *Cybercounseling and cyberlearning: Strategies and resources for the new millennium* (pp. 39–50). Alexandria, VA: American Counseling Association.

Heinlen, K. T., Welfel, E. R., Richmond, E. N., & Rak, C. F. (2003). The scope of WebCounseling: A survey of services and compliance with *NBCC Standards for the Ethical Practice of WebCounseling*. *Journal of Counseling and Development, 81,* 61–69.

Hinterkopf, E. (1998). *Integrating spirituality in counseling: A manual for using the experiential focusing method.* Alexandria, VA: American Counseling Association.

Hoyt, M. F. (1995). *Brief therapy and managed care: Readings for contemporary practice.* San Francisco: Jossey-Bass.

Huber, C. H. (1998). Time-limited counseling, invisible rationing, and informed consent. *Family Journal, 6,* 325–327.

Hudson, P. (1998, April/May). Spirituality: A growing resource. *Family Therapy News, 29*(2), 10–11.

Hughes, R. S. (2000). Cybercounseling and regulations: Quagmire or quest? In J. W. Bloom & G. R. Walz (Eds.), *Cybercounseling and cyberlearning: Strategies and resources for the new millennium* (pp. 321–338). Alexandria, VA: American Counseling Association.

Ingersoll, R. E. (1994). Spirituality, religion, and counseling: Dimensions and relationships. *Counseling and Values, 38,* 98–111.

Israelashvili, M. (1998). Preventive school counseling: A stress inoculation perspective. *Professional School Counseling, 1,* 21–25.

Kelly, E. W., Jr. (1995). *Spirituality and religion in counseling and psychotherapy.* Alexandria, VA: American Counseling Association.

Kleist, D. M., & White, L. J. (1997). The values of counseling: A disparity between a philosophy of prevention in counseling and counselor practice and training. *Counseling and Values, 41,* 128–140.

Kottler, J. A. (1986). *On being a therapist.* San Francisco: Jossey-Bass.

Lawless, L. L., Ginter, E. J., & Kelly, K. R. (1999). Managed care: What mental health counselors should know. *Journal of Mental Health Counseling, 21,* 50–65.

Lee, C. C. (2000). Cybercounseling and empowerment: Bridging the digital divide. In J. W. Bloom & G. R. Walz (Eds.), *Cybercounseling and cyberlearning: Strategies and resources for the new millennium* (pp. 85–94). Alexandria, VA: American Counseling Association.

Luck, R. S. (1999). Rehabilitation counseling credentialing as a professional specialty. In G. L. Gandy, E. D. Martin, & R. E. Hardy (Eds.), *Counseling in the rehabilitation process: Community services for mental and physical disabilities* (2nd ed.), (pp. 271–288). Springfield, IL: Thomas.

Madonna, T. I. (2000). Providing mental health services under managed care arrangements: The challenges. *Hospital Topics, 78,* 23–27.

Mead, M. A., Hohenshil, T. H., & Singh, K. (1997). How the DSM system is used by clinical counselors: A national study. *Journal of Mental Health Counseling, 19,* 383–401.

Meichenbaum, D. (1993). Changing conceptions of cognitive behavior modification: Retrospect and prospect. *Journal of Consulting and Clinical Psychology, 61,* 202–204.

Miller, I. J. (1996). Managed care is harmful to outpatient mental health services: A call for accountability. *Professional Psychology: Research and Practice, 27,* 349–363.

Mitchell, C. G. (1998). Perceptions of empathy and client satisfaction with managed behavioral health care. *Social Work, 43,* 404–411.

Mostert, D. L., Johnson, E., & Mostert, M. P. (1997). The utility of solution-focused, brief counseling in schools: Potential from an initial study. *Professional School Counseling, 1,* 21–24.

Murphy, L., & Mitchell, D. (1998). When writing helps to heal: E-mail as therapy. *British Journal of Guidance and Counselling, 26,* 21–32.

Muse v. Charter Hospital of Winston-Salem, Inc., 117 N.C. App.468 (1995).

Myers, J. E. (1992). Wellness, prevention, development: The cornerstone of the profession. *Journal of Counseling and Development, 71,* 136–138.

Myers, J. E., Sweeney, T. J., & Witmer, J. M. (2000). The wheel of wellness: Counseling for wellness: A holistic model for treatment planning. *Journal of Counseling and Development, 78,* 251–266.

Myers, J. E., Sweeney, T. J., & Witmer, J. M. (2001). Optimization of behavior. In D. C. Locke, J. E. Myers, & E. L. Herr (Eds.), *The handbook of counseling* (pp. 641–652). Thousand Oaks, CA: Sage.

Myers, J. E., & Truluck, M. (1998). Human beliefs, religious values, and the counseling process: A comparison of counselors and other mental health professionals. *Counseling and Values, 42,* 106–123.

National Board of Certified Counselors. (2001). Standards for the ethical practice of Internet counseling.

Retrieved November 20, 2001, from http://www.nbcc.org/ethics

National Career Development Association (1997). NCDA guidelines for the use of the Internet for the provision of career information and planning services. Alexandria, VA: Author.

Newman, R., & Bricklin, P. (1991). Parameters of managed mental health care: Legal, ethical, and professional guidelines. *Professional Psychology: Research and Practice, 22,* 26–35.

O'Donnell, J. M. (1988). The holistic health movement: Implications for counseling theory and practice. In R. Hayes & R. Aubrey (Eds.), *New directions for counseling and human development* (pp. 365–382). Denver: Love.

Oravec, J. A. (2000). Online counselling and the Internet: Perspectives for mental health care supervision and education. *Journal of Mental Health, 9,* 121–135.

Paulson, R. I. (1996). Swimming with the sharks or walking in the Garden of Eden: Two visions of managed care and mental health practice. In P. R. Raffoul & C. A. McNeece (Eds.), *Future issues of social work practice* (pp. 85–96). Needham Heights, MA: Allyn & Bacon.

Peck, M. S. (1978). *The road less traveled.* New York: Simon & Schuster.

Pennnington, D. A. (2002, December). Breaking free. *Counseling Today 6,* 45.

Phelps, R., Eisman, E. J., & Kohout, J. (1998). Psychological practice and managed care: Results of the CAPP practitioner study. *Professional Psychology: Research and Practice, 29,* 31–36.

Priest, R. (1991). Racism and prejudice as negative impacts on African American clients in therapy. *Journal of Counseling and Development, 70,* 213–215.

Rak, C. F., & Patterson, L. E. (1996). Promoting resilience in at-risk children. *Journal of Counseling and Development, 74,* 368–373.

Remley, T. P., Jr., & Herlihy, B. (2001). *Ethical, legal, and professional issues in counseling.* Upper Saddle River, NJ: Merrill/Prentice Hall.

Riemer-Reiss, M. L. (2000). Utilizing distance technology for mental health counseling. *Journal of Mental Health Counseling, 22,* 189–203.

Rosik, C. H. (2001). Professional use of the Internet: Legal and ethical issues in a member care environment. *Journal of Psychology and Theology, 29,* 106–120.

Sampson, J. P., Jr., & Bloom, J. W. (2001). The potential for success and failure of computer applications in counseling and guidance. In D. C. Locke, J. E. Myers, & E. L. Herr (Eds.), *The handbook of counseling* (pp. 613–627). Thousand Oaks, CA: Sage.

Sampson, J. P., Jr., Kolodinsky, R. W., & Greeno, B. P. (1997). Counseling on the information highway: Future possibilities and potential problems. *Journal of Counseling and Development, 75,* 203–212.

Smith, H. B. (1999). Managed care: A survey of counselor educators and counselor practitioners. *Journal of Mental Health Counseling, 21,* 270–283.

Sperry, L. (2001). Spirituality in clinical practice: *Incorporating the spiritual dimension in psychotherapy and counseling.* New York: Brunner-Routledge.

Stanard, R. P., Sandhu, D. S., & Painter, L. C. (2000). Assessment of spirituality in counseling. *Journal of Counseling and Development, 78,* 204–210.

Sussman, R. J. (1998). Counseling online. Retrieved January 14, 2003, from *CTOnline,* http://www.counseling.org

Swenson, R. A. (1998). *The overload syndrome: Learning to live within your limits.* Colorado Springs, CO: NavPress.

Tait, A. (1999). Face-to-face and at a distance: The mediation of guidance and counselling through the new technologies. *British Journal of Guidance and Counselling, 27,* 113–122.

U.S. Surgeon General's Report on Mental Health. (1999). Washington, DC: Office of the Surgeon General.

Vick, R. D., Smith, L. M., & Herrera, C. I. R. (1998). The healing circle: An alternative path to alcoholism recovery. *Counseling and Values, 42,* 133–141.

Walz, G. R. (2000). Preface. In J. W. Bloom & G. R. Walz (Eds.), *Cybercounseling and cyberlearning: Strategies and resources for the new millennium* (pp. xi–xvii). Alexandria, VA: American Counseling Association.

Warfield, R. D., & Goldstein, M. B. (1996). Spirituality: The key to recovery from alcoholism. *Counseling and Values, 40,* 196–205.

Welfel, E., Heinlen, K., & Rak, C. (2000, March). *Buyer beware! Data on Web counselors' (non)compliance with ethical standards.* Paper presented at the annual conference of the American Counseling Association, Washington, DC.

Westgate, C. E. (1996). Spiritual wellness and depression. *Journal of Counseling and Development, 75,* 26–35.

Wickline v. State of California, 239 Cal. Rptr. 805, 741 P.2d 613 (1987).

Winegar, N. (1993). Managed mental health care: Implications for administrators and managers of community-based agencies. *Families in society: The Journal of Contemporary Human Services, 74,* 171–178.

Winegar, N., & Hayter, L. M. (1998). *Guidebook to managed care and practice management terminology.* New York: Haworth Press.

Witmer, J. M., & Sweeney, T. J. (1999). Toward wellness: The goal of helping. In T. J. Sweeney (Ed.), *Adlerian counseling: A practitioner's approach.* Philadelphia: Taylor & Francis.

Wylie, M. S. (1995, May/June). The power of the DSM-IV: Diagnosing for dollars. *Networker,* 22–32.

Zinnbauer, B. J., & Pargament, K. I. (2000). Working with the sacred: Four approaches to religious and spiritual issues in counseling. *Journal of Counseling and Development, 78,* 162–171.

PART II

Roles and Functions of Community Counselors

CHAPTER 5

The Counseling Process

Your words splash heavily upon my mind
*   like early cold October rain*
*   falling on my roof at dusk.*
The patterns change like an Autumn storm
*   from violent, rumbling, crashing sounds*
*   to clear, steady streams of expression.*
Through it all I look at you
*   soaked in past fears and turmoil;*
Then patiently I watch with you in the darkness
*   for the breaking of black clouds*
*   that linger in your turbulent mind*
And the dawning of your smile
*   that comes in the light of new beginnings.*

Community counselors promote mental health on multiple levels by providing prevention services, treatment, and advocacy for a wide range of clients in diverse settings. In upcoming chapters, information is presented about ways to work effectively with individuals, groups, families, and specific populations. Prior to presenting that information, however, it is important to consider information that is applicable across populations for community and agency counselors. Much of this information is general, and you will need to adapt it to meet the needs of clients in the particular environments in which you work.

The chapter begins with a description of physical factors that affect the counseling environment and thus the counseling process. Next, we focus on the initial, working, and termination stages of counseling. Counselor and client behaviors associated with each stage are highlighted.

One component of working effectively with clients is maintaining careful records of counseling activities. Throughout the chapter, specific documentation procedures associated with the different stages of counseling are addressed, including professional disclosure statements, intake interviews, treatment plans, and case notes.

THE PHYSICAL SETTING OF COUNSELING

The physical settings in which community counselors work vary in size, comfort, and appearance. How much control counselors have over their working environments varies as well, depending on the agency or organization. Counseling can occur almost anywhere, but some physical settings help promote the process better than others. Environmental factors influence individuals physically, psychologically, and emotionally. Thus, it is important to consider physical elements that enhance or detract from the counseling process.

Pressly and Heesacker (2001) reviewed counseling-relevant literature on various physical conditions that affect counseling, including accessories, color, room design, and other factors. Although there are no universal qualities that compose the "ideal" counseling setting, certain features appear to be more conducive to the counseling process than others. Therefore, it is helpful to be aware of different environmental elements that can affect the counseling process.

Aesthetic Qualities and Room Design

People are influenced by room appearance in different ways. Although a few people may be oblivious to their surroundings, it is likely that both counselors and clients will be affected by room décor at some level. Artwork, photographs, and objects that counselors consider meaningful or attractive help make the counseling environment more appealing to counselors and clients. In regard to wall hangings, research has shown that people prefer texturally complex images of natural settings to posters of people, urban life, or abstract works (Pressly & Heesacker, 2001). Plants, which represent growth, can enhance the office's appeal. Preference for office colors varies, depending on the age and sex of clients. Children and young adults tend to associate light colors with positive emotions and dark colors with negative emotions. Neutral colors may be soothing as well as practical and may be preferred when space is shared with other counselors.

Lighting research indicates that brightly lit rooms may enhance general conversation, whereas softer light is more conducive to intimate conversation. Lighting that highlights furniture, artwork, and plants can be especially effective. In addition to lighting, room temperature influences the mental concentration of counselors and clients. In places where community counselors can control the thermostat, keeping the temperature within a comfortable range, while being sensitive to client differences, is preferable (Pressly & Heesacker, 2001).

The room design itself also affects the counseling process. Whenever possible, the counseling room should be private and free from distracting sounds or smells. Research on furniture placement indicates that most clients prefer an intermediate distance between themselves and the counselor. What is considered optimal, however, is influenced by a number of factors, including cultural background, gender, and the nature of the relationship. Pressly and Heesacker (2001) cite studies that suggest clients may feel a greater degree of autonomy and comfort in offices where they have some control over the furniture arrangement. For example, couches and movable chairs allow clients to place themselves in positions that are comfortable. Also, it is important for counseling offices to be physically accessible to individuals with disabilities.

The arrangement of the furniture depends on what the counselor is trying to accomplish. Some counselors prefer to sit behind a desk during sessions, but most do not. A desk can be a physical and symbolic barrier to the development of a close relationship. Benjamin (1987) recommends that counselors include two chairs and a nearby table in the setting. The chairs should be set at a 90-degree angle from each other so that clients can look either at their counselors or straight ahead. The table can be used for many purposes, such as a place for a box of tissues. Benjamin's ideas are strictly his own; each counselor must find a physical arrangement that is comfortable for him or her.

Regardless of the arrangement within the room, counselors should not be interrupted during counseling sessions. Phone calls should be held, and, in some cases, a *do-not-disturb* sign should be hung on the door to keep others from entering. Auditory and visual privacy are mandated by professional codes of ethics and facilitate maximum self-disclosure.

THE COUNSELING PROCESS

Initial Sessions: Building a Counseling Relationship

Counseling by its very nature is a process that occurs over time. Although counseling is not a linear process, it can be helpful conceptually to divide the process into three stages: initial, working, and termination. Various tasks and responsibilities are associated with each stage, including securing informed consent, conducting intake interviews, and record keeping. Also, different client factors, including motivation for change and responsiveness to treatment, need to be considered. Throughout the counseling process, practitioners continually work to establish and maintain a positive counseling alliance with their clients.

During the first few sessions of the counseling process, counselors focus on building a therapeutic relationship and helping clients explore issues that directly affect them. There are two struggles that go on at this time (Napier & Whitaker, 1978). One is the *battle for structure,* which involves issues of administrative control (e.g., scheduling, fees, and participation in sessions). The other is the *battle for initiative,* which relates to client motivation for change and responsibility. It is essential for counselors to win the first battle and for clients to win the second battle. If there are failures at these points, the counseling effort may be prematurely terminated, and both counselors and clients may feel worse for the experience.

Structure

Clients and counselors sometimes have different perceptions about the purpose and nature of counseling. By providing structure to the process, counselors can help clarify expectations and prevent misunderstandings. Structure in counseling, which also is called *role induction,* refers to counselor–client understanding about the conditions, procedures, and nature of counseling. It helps protect rights, define roles, provide direction, and verify obligations of both parties.

Structure is provided throughout all the stages of counseling, but it is especially important at the beginning. Clients often seek counseling when they are in a state of crisis or flux, which can leave them feeling out of control. To help clients regain stability and find new directions in their lives, counselors provide constructive guidelines. Counselors' decisions about how to establish structure are based on their theoretical orientation to counseling, their areas of expertise, and the personalities of their clients. Finding a balance between too much and too little structure can be challenging. It helps for counselors to be flexible and to negotiate the nature of the structure with their clients on an ongoing basis.

Establishing practical guidelines is essential to the structure-building process. Guidelines include *time limits* (such as a 50-minute session), *action limits* (for the prevention of destructive behavior), *role limits* (what will be expected of each participant), and *procedural limits* (in which the client is given the responsibility to work on specific goals or needs); (Brammer, 1993; Goodyear & Bradley, 1980; Kelly & Stone, 1982). Guidelines also provide information on fee schedules and on other important concerns of clients. In general, structure promotes counseling development by providing a framework in which the process can take place.

At the outset, counselors will want to provide clients with an opportunity to give informed consent to participate in counseling. Informed consent has ethical and legal implications that are discussed in depth in Chapter 3. Glosoff (2001), citing several sources, suggests using an informed consent content checklist to guide the counseling process, which includes the following topics:

- **Counselor's Background and Professional Affiliations**. Include education, areas of specialization, licensure and certification, professional affiliations, and contact information for appropriate regulatory or certification boards and professional organizations.

- **Therapeutic Process Issues**. Describe the nature of the counseling process and counseling relationships, boundaries of the professional relationship, your theoretical orientation and how that affects the counseling process, and clients' rights to participate in ongoing counseling plans.

- **Risks, Benefits, and Alternatives**. Make sure that clients understand that results cannot be guaranteed. Discuss the limitations, potential risks, and benefits of counseling. Explain the client's right to refuse recommended services and to be advised of potential consequences of that refusal.

- **Fees**. Describe fees associated with services, cancellation and "no-show" policies, arrangements with any managed care organizations, and issues related to insurance reimbursement.

- **Confidentiality and Privileged Communication**. Describe confidentiality and its limits, information that may need to be shared with insurance companies, plans for dealing with any exceptions to confidentiality that may arise, and clients' rights to obtain information about their records. Also include information about any supervisory or peer consultation arrangements.

- **Structure of the Counseling Relationship**. Describe the frequency and length of sessions, approximate duration of counseling, any known limitations to the length of treatment, and procedures for termination.

- **Diagnostic Labels**. How will diagnostic labels be used? How do insurance companies use diagnostic labels to determine reimbursement? What are the potential ramifications of diagnostic labels (e.g., preexisting conditions)? What are your limitations to control what insurance companies do with the information you provide them?

- **Emergency Situations and Interruptions in Counseling**. What are the normal hours of operation? What constitutes an "emergency," and what should clients do if you cannot be reached? Explain what happens when you are on vacation and the possibility of unexpected interruptions in counseling services, as well as ways to handle those interruptions.

- **Involuntary Clients**. What information will be shared, with whom, and for what purposes? How will participation in counseling affect legal issues (e.g., parole)? Involuntary clients have the right to refuse treatment but need to be informed of the legal consequences if that action is taken.

To help ensure the provision of informed consent, community counselors will want to prepare a professional disclosure statement, which provides information to clients about the counselor and about the counseling process. Such statements, like the one in Figure 5–1, often define a counselor's qualifications and theoretical orientation as well as the purposes, expectations, responsibilities, methods, and ethics of counseling. Professional disclosure statements differ, depending on the counseling setting and the clientele (e.g., adult or child, agency or private practice, involuntary or voluntary clients). As counselors develop new competencies, they will want to modify their disclosure statements to reflect the new areas of expertise.

Professional Disclosure Statement

A COUNSELOR–CLIENT CONTRACT

By Joseph Wittmer, Ph.D., NCC, and Theodore P. Remley, J.D., Ph.D., NCC
The following statement was written by Joe Wittmer, Ph.D., NCC, and Theodore P. Remley, J.D., Ph.D., NCC. Wittmer is Distinguished Service Professor and Department Chair, Department of Counselor Education, at the University of Florida, Gainesville. Remley holds both a law degree and a Ph.D. in Counselor Education. He is chairperson of the Counselor Education Department at the University of New Orleans.

Our profession is becoming more attuned to client rights as well as to counselor accountability. The client–counselor contract given here addresses both of these important issues. Please feel free to change and use the contract as you deem appropriate. However, be aware of the laws in your state, the uniqueness of your own setting, and your own competencies in your use of the contract. NBCC considers this document particularly helpful to those formulating state-mandated disclosure statements used in most licensure states.

INFORMATION AND CONSENT

Qualification/Experience:
I am pleased you have selected me as your counselor. This document is designed to inform you about my background and to ensure that you understand our professional relationship.

I am licensed by (your state) as a Professional Counselor. In addition, I am certified by the National Board for Certified Counselors, a private national counselor certifying agency. My counseling practice is limited to (types of clients, i.e., adolescents, personal, career, marriage, etc.).

Nature of Counseling:
I hold a (your postgraduate degree or degrees relevant to counseling) from (name of institution[s]) and have been a professional counselor since (year of your master's degree in counseling or related field.)

I accept only clients who I believe have the capacity to resolve their own problems with my assistance. I believe that as people become more accepting of themselves, they are more capable of finding happiness and contentment in their lives. However, self-awareness and self-acceptance are goals that sometimes take a long time to achieve. Some clients need only a few counseling sessions to achieve these goals, while others may require months or even years of counseling. Should you decide to end our counseling relationship at any point, I will be supportive of that decision. If counseling is successful, you should feel that you are able to face life's challenges in the future without my support or intervention.

Although our sessions may be very intimate emotionally and psychologically, it is important for you to realize that we have a professional relationship rather than a personal one. Our contact will be limited to the paid sessions you have with me.

Figure 5–1

Professional disclosure statement

Note. From "A Counselor–Client Contract," by J. Wittmer and T. P. Remley, 1994 (Summer), *NBCC News Notes, 2,* 12–13. Reprinted with permission of NBCC.

Please do not invite me to social gatherings, offer gifts, or ask me to relate to you in any way other than in the professional context of our counseling sessions. You will be best served if our relationship remains strictly professional and if our sessions concentrate exclusively on your concerns. You will learn a great deal about me as we work together during your counseling experience. However, it is important for you to remember that you are experiencing me only in my professional role.

Referrals:
If at any time for any reason you are dissatisfied with my services, please let me know. If I am not able to resolve your concerns, you may report your complaints to the Board for Professional Counselors in (your state) at (phone number) or the National Board for Certified Counselors in Greensboro, NC, at 336-547-0607.

Fees, Cancellation and Insurance Reimbursement:
In return for a fee of $_____ per individual session, $_____ per couple/family session, and/or $_____ per group session, I agree to provide services for you. The fee for each session will be due and must be paid at the conclusion of each session. Cash or personal checks are acceptable for payment. In the event that you will not be able to keep an appointment, you must notify me 24 hours in advance. If I do not receive such advance notice, you will be responsible for paying for the session that you missed.

Some health insurance companies will reimburse clients for my counseling services and some will not. In addition, most will require that I diagnose your mental health condition and indicate that you have an "illness" before they will agree to reimburse you. Some conditions for which people seek counseling do not qualify for reimbursement. If a qualifying diagnosis is appropriate in your case, I will inform you of the diagnosis I plan to render before I submit it to the health insurance company. Any diagnosis made will become part of your permanent insurance records.

If you wish to seek reimbursement for my services from your health insurance company, I will be happy to complete any forms related to your reimbursement provided by you or the insurance company. Because you will be paying me each session for my services, any later reimbursement from the insurance company should be sent directly to you. Please do not assign any payments to me.

Those insurance companies that do reimburse for counselors usually require that a standard amount be paid (a "deductible") by you before reimbursement is allowed, and then usually only a percentage of my fee is reimbursable. You should contact a company representative to determine whether your insurance company will reimburse you and what schedule of reimbursement is used.

Records and Confidentiality:
All of our communication becomes part of the clinical record, which is accessible to you on request. I will keep confidential anything you say to me, with the following exceptions: a) you direct me to tell someone else, b) I determine that you are a danger to yourself or others, or c) I am ordered by a court to disclose information.

By your signature below (please sign both copies, keep one for your files and return the other copy to me), you are indicating that you have read and understood this statement, and/or that any questions you have had about this statement have been answered to your satisfaction.

(Counselor's Name and Signature)   (Client's Name and Signature)
Date: Date:

Figure 5–1   *Continued*

Initiative

Initiative can be thought of as the motivation to change. Ritchie (1986) notes that most counselors and counseling theories assume that clients will be cooperative. Indeed, many clients come to counseling on a voluntary or self-referred basis. They experience tension and concern about themselves or others, but they are willing to work hard in counseling sessions. Other clients, however, are more reserved about participating in counseling. Vriend and Dyer (1973) estimate that the majority of clients who visit counselors are reluctant to some degree. When counselors meet clients who seem to lack initiative, they often do not know what to do with them, much less how to go about doing it. Therefore, some counselors are impatient, irritated, insensitive, and ultimately give up trying to work with such persons (Doyle, 1998). They may end up blaming themselves or their clients if counseling is not successful. Such recriminations need not occur if counselors understand the dynamics involved in working with reluctant or resistant clients.

Reluctant and resistant clients.   A *reluctant client* is one who has been referred by a third party and is frequently "unmotivated to seek help" (Ritchie, 1986, p. 516). Many children, adolescents, and court-referred clients are good examples. They do not wish to be in counseling, let alone talk about themselves. Many reluctant clients terminate counseling prematurely and report dissatisfaction with the process.

A *resistant client* is a person in counseling who is unwilling or opposed to change. Such an individual may actively seek counseling but does not wish to go through the pain that change demands. Instead, the client clings to the certainty of present behavior, even when such action is counterproductive and dysfunctional. Some resistant clients refuse to make decisions, are superficial in dealing with problems, and take any action to resolve a problem (i.e., do anything a counselor says). According to Sack (1988), "the most common form of resistance is the simple statement 'I don't know'" (p. 180). Such a response makes the counselor's next move difficult.

Resistance can take many forms and may be active or passive. Otani (1989, p. 459) has proposed four broad categories of resistance: "[1] amount of verbalization; [2] content of message; [3] style of communication; and [4] attitude toward counselors and counseling sessions." The 22 forms of resistance included in these categories are represented in Figure 5–2.

Resistance can also be considered within the context of clients' motivation for change. The *transtheoretical model of change,* developed by Prochaska and associates (e.g., Prochaska, DiClemente, & Norcross, 1992; Prochaska & Norcross, 2003), provides a way to conceptualize different levels of readiness for change: *precontemplation, contemplation, preparation, action,* and *maintenance.* A description of each level is provided in Figure 5–3. Assessing a client's readiness for change according to these levels informs decisions regarding treatment and interventions.

Whereas some clients enter counseling already in the preparation stage, others may still be in the precontemplation or contemplation stage, where they are denying either the existence or the seriousness of a problem. Reluctant clients, including people who have been court-ordered to participate in counseling, typically are in one of

Category A: Response quantity resistance
Definition: The client limits the amount of information to be communicated to the counselor.
Forms
Silence
Minimum talk
Verbosity

Category B: Response content resistance
Definition: The client restricts the type of information to be communicated to the counselor.
Forms
Intellectual talk
Symptom preoccupation
Small talk
Emotional display
Future/past preoccupation
Rhetorical question

Category C: Response style resistance
Definition: The client manipulates the manner of communicating information to the counselor.
Forms
Discounting
Thought censoring/editing
Second-guessing
Seductiveness
Last-minute disclosure
Limit setting
Externalization
Counselor focusing/stroking
Forgetting
False promising

Category D: Logistic management resistance
Definition: The client violates basic rules of counseling.
Forms
Poor appointment keeping
Payment delay/refusal
Personal favor-asking

Figure 5–2
Twenty-two forms of resistance
Source: From "Client Resistance in Counseling: Its Theoretical Rationale and Taxonomic Classification," by A. Otani, 1989, *Journal of Counseling and Development, 67,* 459. © 1989 by ACA. Reprinted with permission. No further reproduction authorized without written permission of the American Counseling Association.

Stage of Change	Characteristics	Possible Interventions
Precontemplation	Client is unaware that a problem exists.	Awareness exercises Support Motivational interviewing Feedback Education
Contemplation	Client is aware that a problem exists but denies that the problem is serious or requires treatment.	Exploration of values, personal goals, and desired changes Motivational interviewing Exploration of strategies for making changes Promoting ownership and responsibility
Preparation	Client has taken small steps toward change, indicating potential commitment.	Explore reasons for and against changing Strengths and weaknesses inventory Gestalt techniques
Action	Client has demonstrated commitment to change through overt behaviors.	Behavioral strategies (e.g., rehearsal, reinforcement, tasks, ordeals, and homework)
Maintenance	Client has made positive changes in the desired area and is attempting to change his or her lifestyle to maintain the changes.	Continuing support Reinforcement management Follow-up contracts Support groups Relapse prevention

Figure 5–3
The stages of change
Note. Based on Petrocelli, 2002; Prochaska, DiClemente, & Norcross, 1992; Young, 2001.

these two stages of readiness. For such clients, processes that increase arousal and provide support are more likely to be effective than are approaches that focus on tasks or behavioral schedules (Petrocelli, 2002). To be effective, community counselors need to be aware of a client's level of readiness and motivation for change, as well as specific tasks and interventions that are most suitable for that level.

Winning the battle for initiative.   There are several ways counselors can help clients win the battle for initiative and achieve success in counseling. One way is to anticipate the anger, frustration, defensiveness, or ambivalence that some clients display (Ritchie, 1986). Indeed, such responses are to be expected with involuntary clients, as well as other clients who are fearful of the helping process. Counselors who anticipate client resistance are better prepared to deal effectively with it when it is encountered (Young, 2001).

A second way to deal with a lack of initiative is to show acceptance, patience, understanding, and a general nonjudgmental stance. Demonstrating these supportive attitudes helps build and strengthen the therapeutic relationship, which is perhaps the most powerful predictor of successful client outcome (Seligman, 2001, p. 19). An empathic, nonjudgmental approach helps promote trust and open communication. When open communication exists, clients are more likely to be honest with themselves and the counselor and better able to recognize and express reasons for resistance or noncompliance (Young, 2001).

A third way to win the battle for initiative is through the use of persuasion (Kerr, Claiborn, & Dixon, 1982). All counselors have some influence on clients and vice versa (Dorn, 1984; Strong, 1982). How a counselor responds to the client, directly or indirectly, can make a significant difference in whether the client takes the initiative in working to produce change. *Persuasiveness,* also referred to as *social influence,* is "the process of encouraging clients to take reasonable and growth-producing risks, to make thoughtful decisions and healthy choices, to disclose and process feelings and experiences that may reawaken pain, and to move forward toward their goals" (Seligman, 2001, p. 19). When clients view the counselor as reliable, credible, and competent, they are more likely to respond positively to counselor persuasiveness.

A fourth way counselors can assist clients in gaining the initiative is through confrontation. *Confrontation* involves pointing out discrepancies in clients' beliefs, actions, words, or nonverbal behaviors (Young, 2001). Clients then take responsibility for responding to the confrontation. There are three primary ways of responding: denial, accepting some aspect of the confrontation as true, and fully accepting the confrontation and agreeing to try to resolve the inconsistency (Young, 2001). Doing something differently or gaining a new perspective on a problem can be a beneficial result of confrontation, especially if what has previously been tried has not worked.

Although winning the battle for initiative is associated with the initial sessions, client resistance can be evidenced at any point during the counseling process. Counselors can help clients move forward by recognizing resistance when it is evidenced and helping clients assume ownership for the change process.

Initial Counseling Interviews

The counseling process begins with the initial session, which serves as the foundation for subsequent interventions (Mitchell, 2001). Initial sessions set the tone for the counseling process and strongly influence the likelihood of future sessions.

In the first session, both counselors and clients work to determine whether they want to continue the relationship. Counselors should quickly assess whether they are capable of working with particular clients and their issues through being honest, open, and appropriately confrontational (Okun, 1997). Clients must ask themselves if they feel comfortable with and trust the counselor before they can enter into the relationship wholeheartedly. Although the client–counselor relationship evolves over time, clients are likely to form perceptions about the quality of the relationship early, and those perceptions tend to be stable (Seligman, 2001).

Frequently in community settings, the initial session is used primarily to gather information about the client for the purpose of *assessment* and *diagnosis,* topics that are discussed more extensively in Chapter 6. Counselors who are employed by medical, mental health, correctional, rehabilitation, and social agencies are likely to conduct formal intake interviews to gather information and form diagnostic impressions. Usually, these agencies have intake questionnaires designated for initial session use (see Figure 5–4). Examples of topics addressed during intake interviews include the following:

- **Identifying information about the client** (age, race, birth date, marital status, occupation, contact information)
- **The presenting concern(s) and level of client distress** (intensity or severity of concern)
- **History of the presenting concern** (onset of concern, duration and frequency, surrounding events)
- **Family background** (marital status, number of children, other relatives in the home, influences of family on presenting concern)
- **Personal history** (educational, medical, vocational, other)
- **Previous counseling experiences** (duration, outcome, what was helpful or not helpful)
- **Risk assessment** (suicidal or homicidal ideation)
- **Clinical impression and/or diagnosis** (case conceptualization, current level of functioning)
- **Client's goals for counseling** (What does the client want to happen in counseling? To what degree does he or she believe the problem is changeable?)

Although intake interviews tend to be structured and focused, counselors will want to be attentive to relationship-building skills throughout the session. In some settings, the intake forms are lengthy and may prohibit building rapport, unless the counselor takes definite steps to counteract that possibility. For example, the counselor may begin the interview by stating something like:

> During the first session, it is important for me to ask several questions in order to get a clearer picture of what brings you here and to be able to make decisions about what might be most helpful for you. So please bear with me through the process, even though it may seem rather formal and structured. At times, I will ask you to explain things in more detail. If there are questions you would rather not answer, please let me know and we'll move on to another question.

In other settings, the intake interview is less structured. In an unstructured interview, the counselor has a general concept of topics to cover, but the questions are geared toward the individual needs of the client (Whiston, 2000). With less formal initial interviews, it often is not necessary to follow a particular sequence in gathering the needed information; instead, the counselor follows the client's lead. An advantage

I. Identifying data
   A. Client's name, address, telephone number through which client can be reached. This information is important in the event the counselor needs to contact the client between sessions. The client's address also gives some hint about the conditions under which the client lives (e.g., large apartment complex, student dormitory, private home, etc.).
   B. Age, sex, marital status, occupation (or school class and year). Again, this is information that can be important. It lets you know when the client is still legally a minor and provides a basis for understanding information that will come out in later sessions.

II. Presenting problems, both primary and secondary
   It is best when these are presented in exactly the way the client reported them. If the problem has behavioral components, these should be recorded as well. Questions that help reveal this type of information include
   A. How much does the problem interfere with the client's everyday functioning?
   B. How does the problem manifest itself? What are the thoughts, feelings, etc., that are associated with it? What observable behavior is associated with it?
   C. How often does the problem arise? How long has the problem existed?
   D. Can the client identify a pattern of events that surround the problem? When does it occur? With whom? What happens before and after its occurrence?
   E. What caused the client to decide to enter counseling at this time?

III. Client's current life setting
   How does the client spend a typical day or week? What social and religious activities, recreational activities, etc., are present? What is the nature of the client's vocational and/or educational situation?

IV. Family history
   A. Father's and mother's ages, occupations, descriptions of their personalities, relationships of each to the other and each to the client and other siblings.
   B. Names, ages, and order of brothers and sisters; relationship between client and siblings.
   C. Is there any history of mental disturbance in the family?
   D. Descriptions of family stability, including number of jobs held, number of family moves, etc. (This information provides insights in later sessions when issues related to client stability and/or relationships emerge.)

V. Personal history
   A. Medical history: any unusual or relevant illness or injury from prenatal period to present.
   B. Educational history: academic progress through grade school, high school, and post–high school. This includes extracurricular interests and relationships with peers.
   C. Military service record.

Figure 5–4
Sample intake interview
Source: From *Counseling Strategies and Interventions* (pp. 66–68), by H. Hackney and L. S. Cormier, 1999, Boston, MA: Allyn & Bacon. © 1999 by Pearson Education. Reprinted by permission of the publisher.

D. Vocational history: Where has the client worked, at what types of jobs, for what duration, and what were the relationships with fellow workers?

E. Sexual and marital history: Where did the client receive sexual information? What was the client's dating history? Any engagements and/or marriages? Other serious emotional involvements prior to the present? Reasons that previous relationships terminated? What was the courtship like with present spouse? What were the reasons (spouse's characteristics, personal thoughts) that led to marriage? What has been the relationship with spouse since marriage? Are there any children?

F. What experience has the client had with counseling, and what were the client's reactions?

G. What are the client's personal goals in life?

VI. Description of the client during the interview

Here you might want to indicate the client's physical appearance, including dress, posture, gestures, facial expressions, voice quality, tensions; how the client seemed to relate to you in the session; client's readiness of response, motivation, warmth, distance, passivity, etc. Did there appear to be any perceptual or sensory functions that intruded upon the interaction? (Document your observations.) What was the general level of information, vocabulary, judgment, abstraction abilities displayed by the client? What was the stream of thought, regularity, and rate of talking? Were the client's remarks logical? Connected to one another?

VII. Summary and recommendations

In this section you will want to acknowledge any connections that appear to exist between the client's statement of a problem and other information collected in this session. What type of counselor do you think would best fit this client? If you are to be this client's counselor, which of your characteristics might be particularly helpful? Which might be particularly unhelpful? How realistic are the client's goals for counseling? How long do you think counseling might continue?

Figure 5–4   *Continued*

to a less structured interview is that it can be intentionally adapted to meet the client's unique needs. However, unstructured interviews have more room for error and may result in spending too much time on relatively minor issues (Whiston, 2000).

Regardless of the type of intake interview conducted, counselors will use a combination of closed and open questions to gather information about the client. *Closed questions* can be effective in eliciting a large amount of information in a short time, but they do not encourage elaboration, which might be needed. An example of a closed question is, "How long have you been separated from your husband?" In contrast to the closed question is the *open question,* which typically begins with words such as *what, how,* or *could* and allows the client more latitude to respond. "I wonder how you feel about that," "Help me understand what you mean," and "Could you tell me more?" are examples of open questions. Both types of questions can be used effectively by community counselors during intake interviews to gain information and spur the client's thinking (Young, 2001).

Another form of communication used by counselors during initial sessions is a *request for clarification,* which helps the counselor make sure that he or she understands what the client is saying. These requests require the client to repeat or elaborate on material just covered. For example, a counselor might say, "Please help me understand this relationship" or "I don't see the connection here."

Building a Relationship During Initial Sessions

During the initial interview, it is important to take the steps needed to make clients feel comfortable, respected, supported, and heard. For this to happen, counselors need to set aside their own agendas and focus exclusively on the client. *Rapport* is established and maintained by counselors who are genuinely interested in and accepting of the individuals with whom they work. The counselor can help build rapport by intentionally using specific helping skills, such as reflecting feelings, summarizing, clarifying, and encouraging. It is critical for counselors to develop a repertoire of helping skills and an ability to use them appropriately throughout the counseling process. Ivey (1994) states that the two most important skills for rapport building are basic attending behavior and client-observation skills. A counselor needs to focus on what the client is thinking and feeling and how the client is behaving. Establishing and maintaining rapport is vital for the disclosure of information and the ultimate success of counseling.

One way that counselors help establish rapport is by inviting clients to describe their reasons for seeking help. Such noncoercive invitations to talk are called *door openers* (Bolton, 1979); these contrast with judgmental or evaluative responses known as *door closers*. Appropriate door openers include inquiries and observations such as "What brings you to see me?", "What would you like to talk about?", and "You look like you are in a lot of pain. Tell me about it." These types of unstructured, open-ended invitations allow clients to take the initiative (Cormier & Hackney, 1999; Young, 2001). In such situations, clients are most likely to talk about priority topics.

The amount of talking that clients engage in and the insight and benefits derived from the initial interview can be enhanced by the counselor through appropriately conveyed empathy, encouragement, support, caring, attentiveness, acceptance, and genuineness. Of all of these qualities, *empathy* is the most important.

Empathic counselors are able to share a client's experiences through deep and subjective understanding (Vacc & Loesch, 2000). Of particular importance is being able to perceive the cultural frame of reference from which the client operates. Carl Rogers (1987) described two factors that make empathy possible: (a) realizing that "an infinite number of feelings" do not exist and (b) having a personal security where "you can let yourself go into the world of this other person and still know that you can return to your own world. Everything you are feeling is 'as if'" (pp. 45–46).

Empathy is expressed through active listening, which is the intentional use of attending abilities that enable the counselor to respond to the client's verbal and nonverbal messages and emotional experiences (Vacc & Loesch, 2000). Counselors can make responses at several levels that reflect different aspects of empathy. A scale formulated by Carkhuff (1969), *Empathic Understanding in Interpersonal Process,* provides a classic measure of these levels. Each of the five levels either adds to or subtracts from the meaning and feeling tone of a client's statement:

1. The verbal and behavioral expressions of the counselor either do not attend to or detract significantly from the verbal and behavioral expressions of the client.
2. Although the counselor responds to the expressed feelings of the client, he or she does so in a way that subtracts noticeable affect from the communications of the client.
3. The expressions of the counselor in response to the expressions of the client are essentially interchangeable.
4. The responses of the counselor add noticeably to the expressions of the client in a way that expresses feelings a level deeper than the client was able to express.
5. The counselor's responses add significantly to the feeling and meaning of the expressions of the client in a way that accurately expresses feeling levels deeper than what the client is able to express.

Responses at the first two levels are not considered empathic; in fact, they inhibit the creation of an empathic environment. For example, if a client expresses distress over the loss of a job, a counselor operating on either of the first two levels might reply, "Well, you might be better off in a different line of work." Such a response misses the pain that the client is feeling.

At Level 3, a counselor's response is rated as "interchangeable" with that of a client. The cartoon in Figure 5–5 depicts the essence of such an interchange.

Figure 5–5
Source: From N. Goud, 1983, *Personnel and Guidance Journal, 61,* 635. © 1983 by ACA. Reprinted with permission. No further reproduction authorized without written permission of the American Counseling Association.

At Levels 4 and 5, a counselor either "adds noticeably" or "adds significantly" to what a client has said. It is this ability to go beyond what clients say that distinguishes counseling from conversation or other less therapeutic forms of behavior (Carkhuff, 1972). The client's reaction determines whether or not a counselor's response accurately reflected the client's implicit message.

Throughout the initial phase of counseling, counselors are involved in developing a therapeutic relationship and assessing the client's problems and possible causes of those problems. During the initial sessions, counselors work with clients to determine what will help them heal, change, and cope more effectively with life. The work carried out during the initial sessions leads to the collaborative establishment of therapeutic goals, which are recorded in the form of a treatment plan.

Throughout the counseling process, an important part of a community counselor's work is documenting what goes on during intake interviews and subsequent sessions. Because careful, intentional record keeping is an essential skill, information about keeping client records is presented next.

Client Records

There are a number of helpful sources community counselors can refer to for assistance in record keeping and documentation. Also, most community agencies have guidelines for maintaining client records, and counselors need to familiarize themselves with those guidelines. One book that is particularly pertinent is *Documentation in Counseling Records* (Mitchell, 2001). Much of the material that follows comes from that source.

What are client records? *Client records* refers to all client information that is needed for treatment (Piazza & Baruth, 1990). Although most client records are in printed or electronic form, client records also include any video- or audiotapes of client–counselor interactions. The number and types of forms vary depending on the needs of the client, agency, and practitioner. Piazza and Baruth note that most client records fall within one of the following six categories: (a) identifying or intake information, (b) assessment information, (c) the treatment plan, (d) case notes, (e) the termination summary, and (f) other data (e.g., signed consent for treatment, copies of correspondence, consent for release of information forms, copies of correspondence). Identifying information, assessment information, and treatment plans are usually documented during initial counseling sessions; case notes provide a written record of treatment and intervention; and termination documentation is compiled at the end of the counseling process. Client records provide documentation of what transpires between a counselor and a client. They protect the interests of both parties and promote continuity of care.

Reasons for careful record keeping.   For many counselors, completing paperwork can be tedious and less fulfilling than actually working with clients. However, professional documentation is a key component of the counseling process. Mitchell (2001, pp. 1–2) points out several reasons careful record keeping is essential:

- The American Counseling Association (ACA) *Code of Ethics and Standards of Practice* (1995) requires counselors to "maintain records necessary for rendering professional services to their clients and as required by laws, regulations, or agency or institution procedures" (Section B.4.).
- Adequate documentation helps protect counselors from malpractice allegations.
- Inadequate or incomplete documentation may be harmful to the client as well as to the counselor.
- In the event that the primary counselor is unable to provide services, client records can ensure appropriate continuity of care.
- Funding sources require documentation that verifies the need for services as well as the nature of the services rendered.
- Utilization review, peer review, and quality assurance review, which often are based on client records, are essential to the work that occurs in many agencies.

Confidentiality and access to client records.   Counselors are responsible for ensuring the safety and confidentiality of any client records they create, maintain, or destroy. This means that counselors make sure client documents are secured in locked files or protected computer programs. Efforts should be made to ensure that all client charts remain in the agency. When records are maintained electronically, the computer used to create and store records needs to have a security component to protect confidential information (Mitchell, 2001). Password protection and the ability to know who is logged on or off are examples of ways computer systems in agencies can help protect client confidentiality.

Although ownership of the content of client records technically belongs to the mental health professional, clients have the right to access copies of their records and control their dissemination (Welfel, 2002). Therefore, counselors have an ethical and a legal obligation to provide competent clients access to their records if requested, unless the content would be detrimental to client welfare. Also, clients have the right to demand that copies of clinical records be transferred to other professionals. It is important for community counselors to keep clients' access rights in mind as client records are created.

If counselors need to transfer or disclose client records to legitimate third parties, written consent should be obtained from the client. In such cases, it is preferable to mail documents rather than to fax them, unless the situation is critical (Mitchell, 2001). If records must be faxed, the cover letter needs to indicate that the information is confidential, intended for use only by the designated person, and that receipt must be acknowledged.

Client records can be subpoenaed in litigation situations, sometimes despite client objection and/or claims of privilege. Subpoenas are court orders that cannot be ignored. When subpoenas are issued, counselors should consult with a lawyer before turning over records or appearing in court (Remley & Herlihy, 2001). If records must be turned over, copies of the originals should be sent and should not include documentation from other professionals. In some cases, the attorney who issued the subpoena will allow counselors to write and submit treatment summaries rather than submit copies of the actual case notes themselves.

Suggestions for record keeping. Mitchell (2001) provides several recommendations for documenting intake sessions, treatment plans, and case notes. Among those suggestions are:

- Make notes grammatically clear and correct.
- Use precise language, avoiding jargon, clichés, and qualifiers.
- Enter only the information that is pertinent to the client's situation.
- Write legibly and in an organized manner.
- Eliminate unfounded opinions or assumptions.
- Logically relate the recorded intervention to the treatment plan.
- Avoid including personal feelings in client records.
- Describe the client's behavior or quote what was said during the session.
- Do not use Wite-Out. If you need to alter a document, use pen to draw a line through the entry. Above the line, write *error* and *corrected entry,* then add the correct information.
- Write notes within 24 to 48 hours of the session.
- Document outcomes of sessions.
- Sign each record, including your full name and credentials. In some cases, it is necessary to obtain a co-signature (e.g., supervisor or medical director).

In addition to these suggestions, Remley and Herlihy (2001) suggest writing notes with the assumption that they will become public information at some later date. However, the counselor should not be so cautious that insufficient information is recorded.

Careful record-keeping procedures will serve counselors well in any of the community settings in which they work. Although the process is somewhat time consuming, it benefits the counselor and the client in many ways. In particular, keeping accurate professional records facilitates the provision of quality services to clients and provides self-protection for the counselor (Remley & Herlihy, 2001). Treatment plans and case notes, which represent the most common form of documentation kept by community counselors, are discussed in the next section, which focuses on the working phase of counseling.

THE WORKING PHASE OF COUNSELING

In the initial phase of counseling, counselors concentrate on gathering information and getting their clients involved in the helping process. The initial sessions of counseling conclude with a treatment plan that serves as the basis for the next phase of counseling—the action or working phase. During this phase, specific objectives are refined and interventions for achieving those objectives are implemented. It is important to remember that the division between the *initial phase* and the *working phase* is arbitrary. For example, assessment, although associated with the initial phase of counseling, continues through all phases of counseling. Treatment plans, which usually come at the conclusion of the initial phase of counseling, also signify the beginning of the working phase of counseling and are described next.

Treatment Plans

Treatment plans help set the course for further counseling interventions. They are required by managed care organizations and many insurance companies for service approval and reimbursement. A *treatment plan* explains why the client is receiving services and what is going to take place in counseling. It lists measurable and desired outcomes of treatment and is sometimes called a *plan of care, service plan, individual habitation plan, residential plan,* or *case management plan*, depending on the type of services provided and the agency providing those services (Mitchell, 2001).

Mitchell (2001, pp. 20–21) recommends including the following components in a treatment plan:

- **Problem statement.** The presenting problem or concern is clearly described.
- **Goal statement and expected date of achievement.** List specific, measurable goals that relate to the presenting problem(s). Include expected dates that goals will be accomplished.
- **Treatment modality.** Describe the interventions that will be used to help meet the stated goals. To be a billable service, the intervention must be provided by a professional who is considered qualified by the funding source.
- **Clinical impression or diagnosis.** Clinical impressions need to accurately reflect the client's mental health as described in the assessment. Diagnostic terms, when used, should be listed according to DSM (Diagnostic and Statistical Manual of Mental Disorders) or ICD (International Classification of Diseases) codes. A client's condition must not be overstated or understated.
- **Names and credentials.** List the names and credentials of people who participated in the development of the treatment plan. Also list the name of the assigned clinician. The person who writes the plan needs to sign and date it.

Treatment plans should represent a collaborative effort between client and counselor. The ACA *Code of Ethics and Standards of Practice* (1995) stipulates that plans should offer a "reasonable promise of success," taking into account "the abilities and circumstances of the client" (Section A.1.). Throughout the course of counseling, the treatment plan should be reevaluated and adapted as needed (Piazza & Baruth, 1990).

Interventions, Skills, and Techniques

Counseling interventions are outlined in the treatment plan and are determined by several factors, including the nature of the presenting problem, client characteristics (e.g., cultural background, age, personality); counselor characteristics, theoretical orientation and training; and the organization in which the counselor works. For example, a counselor with a strong existential orientation is likely to interact and intervene differently with clients than a counselor with a cognitive–behavioral orientation (Granello & Witmer, 1998).

Throughout the mental health profession, there is a push to determine what interventions tend to yield the best outcomes for specific conditions. Outcome research indicates that, in general, counseling is effective across settings and theoretical orientations (see Sexton, Whiston, Bleuer, & Walz, 1997, for a review). What, then, leads to successful outcomes? A summary of counseling research reveals that client outcome is determined by client variables, a set of *common factors*, and specific interventions applied to particular problems (Granello & Witmer, 1998). It is important for counselors to provide the most effective treatments possible by selecting interventions and techniques that have been demonstrated as effective.

Following in the tradition of the medical profession, which adopts procedures or protocols based on research for treatment of specific problems, the American Psychiatric Association, American Psychological Association, psychiatric nursing profession, and American Counseling Association have independently made strong efforts to summarize outcome research to guide mental health practices. One responsibility of community counselors is to find ways to integrate research and practice so that the interventions they select coincide with professional standards of care (Granello & Witmer, 1998). When interventions are informed by research, successful outcomes during the working phase of counseling are more likely. At the same time, however, it is important to remember that not all clients experience the same problem in the same way, and focusing too much on immediate problem resolution rather than taking a more broad-based approach to healthy emotional functioning may be counterindicated (Vacc and Loesch, 2000).

Lambert and Bergin (1994) suggested that the common curative factors of effective counseling can be organized into three categories (Table 5–1): (a) *support factors* (e.g., the therapeutic alliance, trust, empathy, catharsis), (b) *learning factors* (e.g., cognitive learning, affective experiencing, feedback), and (c) *action factors* (e.g., reality testing, rehearsal, mastery efforts). During the working phase, counselors may find it beneficial to use various combinations of these factors to help clients make positive changes. Earlier in the chapter, we examined support factors that facilitate the development of a therapeutic client–counselor relationship. In this section, particular attention will be given to three of the learning and action factors: cognitive learning (ways of thinking), affective experiencing (ways of feeling), and rehearsal (ways of behaving).

Cognitive learning.   Often, clients come to counseling with distorted or dysfunctional cognitions, making them more susceptible to problems related to life events (Seligman, 2001). Cognitive distortions affect the way people think, feel, and act on multiple levels. Counselors can help clients change distorted or unrealistic cognitions

Table 5–1

Common Factors Across Therapies Associated With Positive Outcomes

Support Factors	Learning Factors	Action Factors
Catharsis	Advice	Behavioral regulation
Identification with therapist	Affective experiencing	Cognitive mastery
Mitigation of isolation	Assimilation of problematic experiences	Encouragement of facing fears
Positive relationship	Changing expectations for personal	Taking risks
Reassurance	effectiveness	Mastery efforts:
Release of tension	Cognitive learning	• Modeling
Structure	Corrective emotional experience	• Practice
Therapeutic alliance	Exploration of internal frame of reference	• Reality testing
Therapist/client active	Feedback	Success experience
participation	Insight	Working through
Therapist expertness	Rationale	
Therapist warmth, respect,		
empathy, acceptance,		
genuineness		
Trust		

Note. From "The Effectiveness of Psychotherapy," by M. J. Lambert and A. E. Bergin, 1994, In A. E. Bergin and S. L. Garfield (Eds.), *Handbook of Psychotherapy and Behavior Change* (4th ed., pp. 143–189). New York: Wiley. Copyright © 1994 by John Wiley & Sons. Reprinted with permission. This material is used by permission of John Wiley & Sons, Inc.

by offering them the opportunity to explore thoughts and beliefs within a safe, accepting, and nonjudgmental environment.

Cognitive distortions are negative, inaccurate biases that can result in unhealthy misperceptions of events. For example, a worker may assume that his or her boss considers him or her less capable than others, when in reality, the boss is pleased with his or her performance. Cognitive theorists have identified several types of distortions, including exaggerating the negative, minimizing the positive, overgeneralizing, catastrophizing, and personalizing. Cognitive distortions also are evidenced when people engage in all-or-nothing thinking or *selective abstraction* (taking a detail out of context and using it to negate an entire experience). Such perceptions can result in negative automatic thoughts, which then negatively affect emotions and mood states. Counselors can teach clients to evaluate and challenge the validity of their cognitions (Beamish, Granello, & Belcastro, 2002). Teaching clients ways to correct faulty information processing can help them view situations from a more realistic perspective and react accordingly.

The goal of cognitive learning and restructuring is to help clients formulate new cognitions that are more realistic and adaptive (Beck, 1995). One way counselors can help clients modify cognitions is through the process of *reframing,* which offers the client another probable and positive viewpoint of what a situation is or why an event might have happened. Such a changed point of view provides the client with an opportunity to respond differently to the situation (Young, 2001). For example, if an adolescent client (e.g., a young boy) insists that his mother is always worrying and nagging him, the counselor might be able to help the client reframe the situation by suggesting that it sounds like his mother is concerned about his well-being and appears to care about him very much.

Affective experiencing.   Just as it is important to help clients examine their cognitions, or to think about their thinking patterns, it also is important to help clients recognize and explore the emotions they experience. Although there are numerous emotions common to the human experience, people experience emotions uniquely. Seligman (2001, pp. 199–201) describes eight dimensions that characterize emotions:

- **Emotional, physical, or a combination**. Emotions are physically embedded. For example, worry (an emotion) can lead to nausea and/or headaches (physical symptoms).
- **Overt, covert, or a combination of both**. Overt feelings are evident to other people, whereas covert feelings are kept inside and not revealed.
- **Positive, negative, or mixed**. Joy, happiness, and amusement are positive emotions. Anger, worry, and fear are negative emotions. Emotions that typically fall into one category may be experienced differently by certain people.
- **In or out of awareness**. Some people are more aware of their emotional states than are others. People who are unaware of their emotions often experience problems in relationships. Feelings that are considered "unacceptable" may be particularly challenging in treatment.
- **Level of intensity**. The intensity with which emotions are felt varies, depending on the person and the circumstances. Intense expression of negative emotions can lead to misunderstandings and relationship difficulties.
- **Appropriateness for context and stimulus**. Emotional expression that may be appropriate in one context may not be appropriate in another context.
- **Congruence**. When emotions are expressed congruently, verbal and nonverbal behaviors match.
- **Helpful or harmful**. Depending on the way and the context in which they are expressed, emotions may enhance lives and relationships or contribute to struggles intrapersonally and interpersonally.

There are a number of skills and techniques counselors can use to increase clients' emotional awareness. The skill of accurately reflecting feelings is used by many counselors to help clients focus on emotions they may be avoiding (Young, 2001). Helping clients identify the feeling associated with a particular incident, reflecting the feeling back to them, and then encouraging them to determine where in their body that feeling is experienced can help clients develop emotional awareness. By asking them to think of a time in their lives they had the same bodily sensations and emotional feelings that were just experienced, counselors can assist clients in exploring patterns of emotional responses. Also, many Gestalt techniques, when used properly, provide powerful ways for clients to connect with their emotions (Corey, 2001). However, in some cases, interventions that focus on emotions are not recommended, particularly when clients are in high levels of pretreatment distress (Sexton et al., 1997).

Simply releasing emotions, also called *catharsis,* can have some value in counseling, but it should not be the final goal. Corey (2001, p. 70) emphasizes, "Following an emotional release, it is essential to work with the associated insights and the cognitions underlying the emotional patterns. It is important to link emotional exploration to cognitive and behavioral work." The goal of increasing affective experiencing, then, is to help clients connect their emotions with cognitions and behaviors in a way that leads to new insights and changed behavior.

Rehearsal.   Whereas cognitive learning focuses on thoughts and affective experiencing focuses on emotions, *rehearsal* focuses on client behavior. Counselors can help clients maximize the possibility of accomplishing their goals by giving them opportunities to rehearse or practice new behaviors. The old adage that practice makes perfect is as true for clients who wish to reach a goal as it is for athletes or artists. Clients can rehearse in two ways: overtly and covertly (Cormier & Cormier, 1998). *Overt rehearsal* requires clients to verbalize or act out what they are going to do. For example, if a woman is going to ask a man out for a date, she will want to rehearse what she is going to say and how she is going to act before she actually encounters the man. *Covert rehearsal* involves mentally preparing for a specific course of action through imagination and reflection. For example, business people who have to give a speech can first imagine the conditions under which they will perform and then reflect on how to organize the subject matter for presentation. Imagining the situation beforehand can alleviate unnecessary anxiety and help improve performance.

Sometimes a client needs counselor coaching during the rehearsal period. Coaching may involve providing temporary written or visual aids to help clients remember what to do next in a given situation. At times, it may simply involve giving clients corrective feedback. Feedback provides clients with accurate information about the behavior they are practicing. For feedback to be received, it is helpful to talk about the feedback process ahead of time and share observations in a nonthreatening, objective manner. To maximize its effectiveness, feedback should be given both orally and in writing.

Another way to help clients practice and generalize the skills learned in counseling sessions is by assigning homework. Homework provides clients with opportunities to work on particular skills outside of the counseling session. Homework has numerous advantages, including:

- Keeping clients focused on relevant behavior between sessions
- Helping them see clearly what kind of progress they are making
- Motivating clients to change behaviors
- Helping them evaluate and modify their activities
- Helping clients assume more responsibility for their own behaviors

- Celebrating a breakthrough achieved in counseling (Hay & Kinnier, 1998; Hutchins & Vaught, 1997)

Almost all counselors use homework at some time to get clients to help themselves. For homework to be most effective, it needs to be relevant to the situation and specifically tied to some measurable behavior change (Okun, 1997; Young, 2001).

Cognitive learning, affective experiencing, and rehearsal are just a few of the many interventions counselors use during the working phase of counseling. Throughout the process, effective counselors will continue to employ basic helping skills (e.g., clarifying, summarizing, probing, immediacy, confrontation, reflecting content and feeling) and specific theory-grounded techniques (e.g., the empty-chair technique) to help clients make progress toward their goals. As counseling progresses, it is important to work with the client to reevaluate goals and progress, making changes when necessary.

An important task that accompanies all phases of counseling, including the working phase, is documenting counselor–client interactions. After each counseling session, counselors will need to write case notes to document what occurred. Information about writing case notes is presented next.

Case Notes

Each time a counselor meets with a client, he or she is responsible for documenting the activity. This documentation is sometimes referred to as a *case note, clinical entry, progress note, group note,* or *service log* (Mitchell, 2001). Prior to the advent of managed care services, the primary purpose of case notes was to enable counselors to record information about the content of the counseling session and to guide professional practice. This purpose still is paramount. However, 21st-century community counselors operating in managed care environments must write case notes with the understanding that the content may be used to determine reimbursement for services. With this in mind, Mitchell recommends that notes be precise and contain the following elements (pp. 21–22):

- **Confirmation of a Service.** What did the counselor do during the session? What did the client do? Use verbs to describe the services rendered (e.g., *focused, identified, discussed, recommended*).
- **Verification of the Information Implied Within the Billing Code.** The content of the case note should confirm the date of service, length of session, and type of service provided.
- **An Original, Legible Signature.** Some notes need co-signatures. To determine whether a co-signature is necessary, counselors need to read and comply with the state licensure and funding source regulations.

There are many acceptable formats that can be followed when writing case notes. Examples of three useful formats are presented in Figure 5–6. In many instances, the agency for which a counselor works will have a predetermined outline that is to be followed when writing case notes, and it is incumbent on the counselor

STIPS Format (from Prieto & Scheel, 2002)	
Signs and symptoms	Record the client's current level of functioning and clinical signs and symptoms, especially as they relate to the presenting issues. Record any changes from previous level of functioning. Note observable client behaviors (e.g., appearance, affect, speech).
Topics of discussion	Describe the major issues discussed in the session. Include any developments that have occurred since the previous session.
Interventions	Record specific interventions used during the session. Interventions should relate to the identified problem and treatment goals. Track client's completion of "homework" assignments and record any new assignments. Summarize progress clients have made toward established goals.
Progress and plans	Record plans for the next session, including specific topics of discussion, planned interventions, and anticipated outcomes. Note any changes to the overall treatment plan.
Special issues	Record any newly developed or ongoing critical issues that need to be tracked (e.g., suicidal ideation, homicidal threats, concerns about referrals, suspected abuse). Document ways these issues are being handled (e.g., consultation, supervision, reporting to outside agencies).

Goals and Action Plan Format (from Piazza & Baruth, 1990)	
Goals for the session	State goals for the session that relate to the client's treatment plan and are connected to previous sessions. (Goals should be flexible to accommodate more pressing concerns when necessary.)
Goal attainment	Describe the techniques and interventions used in the session and evaluate their effectiveness. If the interventions were ineffective, what could have been done differently?
Clinical impressions	Record clinical impressions based on client behavior and statements. Avoid recording subjective impressions that are not supported by data.
Action plan	State plans for the next session. These plans will be used to provide the goal statement for that session.

Figure 5–6
Three sample formats for case notes

SOAP Format (from Cameron & turtle-song, 2002)	
Subjective	Record information about the problem from the client's perspective (and from that of significant others). Include the client's feelings, thoughts, and goals. Describe the intensity of the problem and its effect on relationships.
Objective	Record factual observations made by the counselor. Observations include any physical, interpersonal, or psychological findings noted by the counselor (e.g., appearance, affect, client strengths, mental status, responses to the counseling process).
Assessment	Summarize clinical thinking about the client's issues. This section synthesizes and analyzes data from the subjective and objective observations. When appropriate, include the DSM-IV-TR diagnosis. (Section may also include clinical impressions used to make a diagnosis.)
Plan	Record plans for future interventions and a prognosis. Include the date of the next session, proposed interventions, and anticipated gains from treatment.

Figure 5–6   *Continued*

to adhere to that format. Remley and Herlihy (2001) remind us that the primary purposes of keeping case notes are to provide quality services to clients and to document decisions made and actions taken as a counselor.

Documenting Work With High-Risk Clients

Special considerations need to be taken when counselors work with clients classified as *high risk*. Examples of high-risk cases include clients who are potentially violent, suicidal, homicidal, or engaged in criminal behavior. Clients who have experienced or committed abuse also are considered high risk. Some of the legal and ethical considerations counselors are faced with when working with such clients are explored in Chapter 3. Suicide assessment and crisis intervention are described in Chapters 6 and 7. In this section, the focus is on documentation issues that need to be taken into account for the counselor's self-protection.

If a counselor determines that a client is potentially dangerous, three things must be done: (a) explain how the conclusion was reached, (b) take action, and (c) document the action (Mitchell, 2001). There are a number of actions a counselor might take, depending on the situation. In some cases, it is necessary to notify the potential target and/or appropriate law enforcement agencies. Other action options include consulting with a psychiatrist and taking steps toward an involuntary hospitalization. Before taking action, it is advisable to consult with coworkers, a supervisor, and a lawyer and then document those consultations. Take any threat of suicide or homicide seriously and write down the client's exact words (as closely as possible) when documenting the threats. At times, suicide or homicide contracts can be developed with the client and are clinically useful. Mitchell encourages practitioners to involve clients in the documentation process when feasible because it can "enhance the service relationship, promote empowerment, and make paperwork easier" (p. 59).

If a counselor suspects abuse, neglect, or criminal behavior, it is advisable to discuss the case with a lawyer and contact the proper authority if a report is required (Mitchell, 2001). When documenting concerns about abuse, be sure to record the client's words and behaviors rather than express unsubstantiated opinions. By sticking to the facts and avoiding impressionistic or defamatory statements, objectivity is maintained and the counselor is in a better position to carry out the next step. A general rule of thumb is to be precise and specific in all documentation, especially in cases of high risk.

TERMINATION

Why Termination Is Important

Termination is the last phase of counseling and refers to the decision made by the client, counselor, or both parties to stop counseling. It is probably the least researched and most neglected phase of counseling. Many counselors assume that termination with a client will occur naturally, with satisfying outcomes for both parties. Goodyear (1981) states that "it is almost as though we operate from a myth that termination is a process from which the counselor remains aloof and to which the client alone is responsive" (p. 347).

But the termination of a counseling relationship has an impact on all involved, and it is often complex and difficult. Termination may well produce mixed feelings on the part of both the counselor and the client (Cowger, 1994; Kottler, Sexton, & Whiston, 1994). For example, a client may be both appreciative and regretful when the time comes to end a particular counseling relationship. Unless it is handled properly, termination has the power to harm as well as heal (Doyle, 1998).

Historically, addressing the process of termination directly has been avoided for several reasons. Ward (1984) suggested two of the most prominent reasons. First, termination is associated with loss—a traditionally taboo subject in all parts of society. Even though loss may be associated with re-creation, transcendence, greater self-understanding, and new discoveries (Hayes, 1993), counseling is generally viewed as emphasizing growth and development unrelated to endings. Second, termination is not directly related to the microskills that facilitate counseling relationships (Ivey, 1994). Therefore, termination is not a process usually highlighted in counselor education.

However, termination serves several important functions. First, termination signals that something is finished. Throughout life, individuals enter into and leave a succession of experiences, including jobs, relationships, and life stages. Growth and adjustment depend on an ability to make the most of these experiences and learn from them. To begin something new, a former experience must be completed and resolved (Perls, 1969). Termination is the opportunity to end a learning experience properly, whether on a personal or professional level (Hulse-Killacky, 1993). Counselors who manage the termination process appropriately can help clients learn healthy ways to end relationships for the purpose of moving on to the next stage of life.

Second, termination gives clients the opportunity to maintain changes already achieved and generalize problem-solving skills to new areas. Successful counseling results in significant changes in the ways clients think, feel, or act. These changes are rehearsed in counseling, but they must be practiced in the real world. Termination provides an opportunity for such practice. The client can always go back to the counselor for any needed follow-up, but termination is the natural point for the practice of independence to begin. It is a potentially empowering experience for clients that enables them to address the present in an entirely new or modified way. At termination, the opportunity to put "insights into actions" (Gladding, 1990, p. 130) is created. Thus, what seems like an exit becomes an entrance.

Finally, termination serves as a reminder that the client has matured (Vickio, 1990). Besides offering clients new skills or different ways of thinking about themselves, effective counseling that ends with an appropriate termination marks a time in clients' lives when they are less absorbed by and preoccupied with personal problems and better able to deal with outside people and events. This ability to handle external situations may result in more interdependent relationships that are mutually supportive and that consequently lead to a life that is more balanced and satisfying.

Timing of Termination

When to terminate a relationship is a question that has no definite answer. If the relationship is ended too soon, clients may lose the ground they gained in counseling and regress to earlier behaviors. If termination is never addressed, clients can become dependent on the counselor and fail to resolve difficulties and grow as persons. There are, however, several pragmatic considerations related to the timing of termination (Hackney & Cormier, 1996; Young, 2001):

* *Have clients achieved behavioral, cognitive, or affective contract goals?* When both clients and counselors have a reason to believe that particular goals have been reached, the timing of termination is easier to determine. The key to this consideration is setting up a mutually agreed upon contract before counseling begins.

* *Can clients concretely show where they have made progress in what they wanted to accomplish?* In this situation, specific progress may be the basis for making a decision about termination.

* *Is the counseling relationship helpful?* If either client or counselor senses that what is occurring in counseling sessions is not helpful, termination is appropriate.

* *Has the context of the initial counseling arrangement changed?* In cases where there is, for example, a move or a prolonged illness, termination (as well as a referral) should be considered.

Overall, there is no one right time to terminate a counseling relationship. The "when" of termination must be determined in accordance with the uniqueness of the situation and with overall ethical and professional guidelines.

Early termination.   Issues related to termination for counselors working in managed care environments are explored in Chapter 4. In many cases, counselors may be expected to provide time-limited services to clients. In these situations, counselors need to explain the time limits at the outset of counseling. If the client reaches the end of an HMO-imposed time limit before he or she is ready to terminate, the counselor will want to negotiate for additional sessions with the service provider, refer the client to alternative sources for help, ask the client to pay out-of-pocket, or provide *pro bono* services (Glosoff, 1998). The ACA *Code of Ethics and Standards of Practice* (1995) makes it clear that counselors cannot abandon their clients (Section A.11.a.). However, the *Code of Ethics* also stipulates that it is permissible for counselors to discontinue services in the following circumstances:

- It is clear that the client is no longer benefiting from counseling.
- The client does not pay the designated fees.
- Agency limits do not allow services to continue.
- An appropriate referral is made, but the client declines the referral.

Facilitating the Termination Process

Counseling relationships vary in length and purpose. It is vital to the health and well-being of everyone involved that the subject of termination be brought up early so that the time in counseling is used as effectively as possible. Individuals need time to prepare for the end of meaningful relationships. There may be some sadness even if the relationship ends in a positive way. Thus, termination should not necessarily be presented as the zenith of the counseling experience. It is better to play down the importance of termination rather than to play it up (Cormier & Hackney, 1999).

Ideally, counselor and client should agree on when it is time to end the counseling relationship (Young, 2001). Often, verbal messages may indicate a readiness to terminate. For example, a client may say, "I really think I've made a lot of progress over the past few months"; or a counselor may state, "You appear to be well on your way to no longer needing my services." Statements of this nature suggest client recognition of growth or resolution. At other times, client behaviors signal that it is time to end the counseling relationship. Examples include a decrease in the intensity of work between counselor and client; the use of more humor or intellectualizing; and less denial, withdrawal, anger, mourning, or dependence.

How much time should counselors and clients devote to the termination process? Cormier and Hackney (1999) believe that when a relationship has lasted more than 3 months, the final 3 to 4 weeks should be spent discussing the impact of termination. For instance, counselors may inquire how their clients will cope without the support of the relationship. Counselors may also ask clients to talk about the meaning of the counseling relationship and how they will use what they have learned in the future. Shulman (1979) suggested that, as a general rule of thumb, one sixth of the time spent in a counseling relationship be devoted to focusing on termination. Although the exact amount of time termination should take is a matter of judgment, there needs to be a time of preparation before ending a counseling relationship (Young, 2001).

To help with the termination process, counselors can use a procedure called *fading*, in which counseling appointments are spaced over increasing lengths of time. Counselors can also help with termination by encouraging clients to articulate ways they will utilize their newly developed coping skills in upcoming life experiences.

Termination Documentation

When the counseling process is over, a closing statement, or termination summary, needs to be written and added to the client's record. Mitchell (2001) lists two reasons for carefully documenting termination: (a) the client may return for additional services, and (b) a client or the legal representative may initiate a law practice suit. Well-written termination summaries, particularly in cases of premature termination, can protect counselors against the accusation of abandonment.

Termination documentation provides a clinical summary of the course of treatment and its outcomes. Piazza and Baruth (1990) and Mitchell (2001) recommend including the following information in the termination summary:

- A synopsis of the initial assessment, treatment plan, interventions, and outcomes
- An evaluation of the client's current level of functioning
- Reasons for termination
- Final diagnostic impressions
- Follow-up plan. (When clients are moving from inpatient to outpatient care, an aftercare plan is needed that states identifying information about the new counselor and a plan for services.)

As with case notes, the format of the termination summary may be determined by the organization in which a counselor practices. Community counselors will want to be familiar with all record-keeping procedures associated with their work sites.

Follow-Up

Follow-up entails checking to see how the client is doing, with respect to the presenting issue, sometime after counseling has ended (Okun, 1997). In essence, it is a type of positive monitoring process that encourages client growth (Doyle, 1998; Egan, 1998). Although some counselors neglect following up on clients, the process is important because it reinforces the gains clients have made in counseling and helps both counselor and client reevaluate the counseling experience. Follow-up also emphasizes the genuine care and concern counselors have for their clients. Short-term follow-up is usually conducted 3 to 6 months after a counseling relationship terminates. Long-term follow-up is conducted at least 6 months after termination.

Follow-up may take many forms, but there are four main ways it is usually conducted (Cormier & Cormier, 1998). The first is to invite the client in for a session to discuss any progress the client has continued to make in achieving desired goals. A second way is through a telephone call to the client. A call allows the client to report directly to the counselor, though there is only verbal interaction. A third way is for the counselor to send the client a letter asking about the client's current status. A fourth and more impersonal way is for the counselor to mail the client a questionnaire dealing with current levels of functioning. Many public agencies use this type of follow-up as a way of showing accountability. Such procedures do not preclude the use of more personal follow-up procedures by individual counselors. Although time consuming, a personal follow-up is probably the most effective way of evaluating past counseling experiences. It helps assure clients that they are cared about as individuals and are more than just statistics.

Referral and Recycling

Counselors are not able to help everyone who seeks assistance. When counselors realize that a situation is unproductive, it is important for them to either terminate the relationship or make a referral. A *referral* involves arranging other assistance for clients (Okun, 1997). There are many reasons for referral, including the following (Goldstein, 1971):

- The client has a problem the counselor does not know how to handle.
- The counselor is inexperienced in a particular area (e.g., substance abuse) and does not have the necessary skill to help the client.
- The counselor knows of a nearby expert who would be more helpful.
- The counselor and client have incompatible personalities.
- The relationship between counselor and client is stuck in the initial phase of counseling.

Referrals involve a *how* and a *when*. The *how* involves knowing how to make a referral in a manner that maximizes the possibility that clients will follow through with the referral process. Clients may resist a referral if they feel rejected by the counselor. Patterson and Welfel (2000) suggest spending at least one session with clients in preparation for referrals. Some clients will need several sessions.

The *when* of making referrals involves timing. The longer clients work with a counselor, the more reluctant they may be to see someone else. Thus, timing is crucial. If a counselor reaches an impasse with a certain client, the counselor should refer that client as soon as possible. On the other hand, if the counselor has worked with a client for a while, the counselor should demonstrate sensitivity by giving the client enough time to get used to the idea of working with someone else.

Recycling is an alternative when the counselor thinks the counseling process has not yet worked but can be made to do so. *Recycling* involves the reexamination of all phases of the therapeutic process (Baruth & Huber, 1985). It may be that goals were not properly defined or an inappropriate strategy was chosen. Whatever the case, by reexamining the counseling process, counselor and client can decide how or whether to revise and reinvest in the counseling process. Counseling, like other experiences, is not always successful on the first attempt. Recycling gives both counselor and client a second chance to achieve positive change.

SUMMARY AND CONCLUSION

Before counseling even begins, consideration needs to be given to the physical setting in which counselors work. Research indicates that several factors, including room décor, lighting, temperature, and furniture arrangement, influence the counseling process.

Effective community counselors know how to work with clients throughout the counseling process, including the initial phase, the working phase, and termination. In the initial counseling sessions, counselors work to establish rapport and set up a structure for success. During this stage, issues related to informed consent are addressed, including the nature of counseling, the counselor's background, fees, and expectations. Counselors also make efforts to get clients to take the initiative in the change process. Clients enter counseling for different reasons, and many are reluctant or resistant. Counselors accept clients where they are, establish rapport, and provide motivation. During the initial sessions, counselors gather information about clients either formally (e.g., structured intake interviews) or less formally for the purpose of assessment. At the end of the initial phase, the counselor and client work collaboratively to set goals and design a treatment plan for change.

During the working phase of counseling, clients move toward achieving goals. The emphasis therefore shifts from understanding to activity. In selecting interventions, effective counselors integrate research with practice so that they can implement counseling procedures that are most likely to produce positive outcomes. Various common curative factors have been linked with effective counseling, including cognitive learning, affective experiencing, and rehearsal.

In the termination phase, counselors and clients gradually end their relationship and clients leave counseling. An important part of termination is follow-up. In follow-up, client progress is monitored through phone calls, personal interviews, or the mail.

Throughout the counseling process, practitioners need to document their interactions with clients. In this chapter, several recommendations associated with careful record keeping were made, particularly as they apply to writing treatment plans, case notes, and termination summaries. As community counselors provide quality services to their clients, they simultaneously manage the necessary documentation with a high degree of professionalism.

REFERENCES

American Counseling Association. (1995). *Code of Ethics and Standards of Practice.* Alexandria, VA: Author.

Baruth, L. G., & Huber, C. H. (1985). *Counseling and psychotherapy.* Columbus, OH: Merrill.

Beck, J. S. (1995). *Cognitive therapy: Basics and beyond.* New York: Guilford.

Beamish, P. M., Granello, D. H., & Belcastro, A. L. (2002). Treatment of panic disorder: Practical guidelines. *Journal of Mental Health Counseling, 24,* 224–246.

Benjamin, A. (1987). *The helping interview* (4th ed.). Boston: Houghton Mifflin.

Bolton, R. (1979). *People skills: How to assert yourself, listen to others, and resolve conflicts.* Upper Saddle River, NJ: Prentice Hall.

Brammer, L. M. (1993). *The helping relationship* (5th ed.). Boston: Allyn & Bacon.

Cameron, S., & turtle-song, i. (2002). Learning to write case notes using the SOAP format. *Journal of Counseling and Development, 80,* 286–292.

Carkhuff, R. R. (1969). *Helping and human relations.* New York: Holt, Rinehart & Winston.

Carkhuff, R. R. (1972). *The art of helping.* Amherst, MA: Human Resource Development Press.

Corey, G. (2001). *The art of integrative counseling.* Belmont, CA: Brooks/Cole.

Cormier, W. H., & Cormier, L. S. (1998). *Interviewing strategies for helpers: Fundamental skills and cognitive behavioral interventions* (4th ed.). Pacific Grove, CA: Brooks/Cole.

Cormier, L. S., & Hackney, H. (1999). *Counseling strategies and interventions* (5th ed.). Needham Heights, MA: Allyn & Bacon.

Cowger, E. (1994, November). *Dealing with grief and loss.* Presentation at the Southern Association for Counselor Education and Supervision conference, Charlotte, NC.

Dorn, F. J. (1984). The social influence model: A social psychological approach to counseling. *Personnel and Guidance Journal, 62,* 342–345.

Doyle, R. E. (1998). *Essential skills & strategies in the helping process* (2nd ed.). Pacific Grove, CA: Brooks/Cole.

Egan, G. (1998). *The skilled helper* (6th ed.). Pacific Grove, CA: Brooks/Cole.

Gladding, S. T. (1975). Autumn storm. *Personnel and Guidance Journal 54,* 149.

Gladding, S. T. (1990). Coming full cycle: Reentry after the group. *Journal for Specialists in Group Work, 15,* 130–131.

Glosoff, H. (1998). Managed care: A critical ethical issue for counselors. *Counseling and Human Development, 31,* 1–16.

Glosoff, H. L. (2001, November). *Ethical practice in a complex era: Clients' rights, counselors' responsibilities.* Workshop presentation at Wake Forest University, Winston-Salem, NC.

Goldstein, A. (1971). *Psychotherapeutic attraction.* New York: Pergamon.

Goodyear, R. K. (1981). Termination as a loss experience for the counselor. *Personnel and Guidance Journal, 59,* 349–350.

Goodyear, R. K., & Bradley, F. O. (1980). The helping process as contractual. *Personnel and Guidance Journal, 58,* 512–515.

Granello, P. F., & Witmer, J. M. (1998). Standards of care: Potential implications for the counseling profession. *Journal of Counseling and Development, 76,* 371–380.

Hackney, H., & Cormier, L. S. (1996). *The professional counselor* (4th ed.). Boston: Allyn & Bacon.

Hay, C. E., & Kinnier, R. T. (1998). Homework in counseling. *Journal of Mental Health Counseling, 20,* 122–132.

Hayes, R. L. (1993). Life, death, and reconstructive self. *Journal of Humanistic Education and Development, 32,* 85–88.

Hulse-Killacky, D. (1993). Personal and professional endings. *Journal of Humanistic Education and Development, 32,* 92–94.

Hutchins, D. E., & Vaught, C. G. (1997). *Helping relationships and strategies* (3rd ed.). Pacific Grove, CA: Brooks/Cole.

Ivey, A. E. (1994). *Intentional interviewing and counseling* (3rd ed.). Pacific Grove, CA: Brooks/Cole.

Kelly, K. R., & Stone, G. L. (1982). Effects of time limits on the interview behavior of type A and B persons within a brief counseling analog. *Journal of Counseling Psychology, 29,* 454–459.

Kerr, B. A., Claiborn, C. D., & Dixon, D. N. (1982). Training counselors in persuasion. *Counselor Education and Supervision, 22,* 138–147.

Kottler, J. A., Sexton, T. L., & Whiston, S. C. (1994). *The heart of healing.* San Francisco: Jossey-Bass.

Lambert, M. J., & Bergin, A. E. (1994). The effectiveness of psychotherapy. In A. E. Bergin & S. L. Garfield (Eds.), *Handbook of psychotherapy and behavior change* (pp. 143–189). New York: Wiley.

Mitchell, R. M. (2001). *The ACA Legal Series: Documentation in counseling records* (2nd ed.). Alexandria, VA: American Counseling Association.

Napier, A., & Whitaker, C. (1978). *The family crucible.* New York: Harper & Row.

Okun, B. F. (1997). *Effective helping* (5th ed.). Pacific Grove, CA: Brooks/Cole.

Otani, A. (1989). Client resistance in counseling: Its theoretical rationale and taxonomic classification. *Journal of Counseling and Development, 67,* 458–461.

Patterson, L. E., & Welfel, E. R. (2000). *Counseling process* (5th ed.). Pacific Grove, CA: Brooks/Cole.

Perls, F. S. (1969). *Gestalt therapy verbation.* Lafayette, CA: Real People Press.

Petrocelli, J. V. (2002). Processes and stages of change: Counseling with the transtheoretical model of change. *Journal of Counseling and Development, 80,* 22–30.

Piazza, N. J., & Baruth, N. D. (1990). Client record guidelines. *Journal of Counseling and Development, 68,* 313–316.

Pressly, P. K. & Heesacker, M. (2001). The physical environment and counseling: A review of theory and research. *Journal of Counseling and Development, 79,* 148–160.

Prieto, L. R., & Scheel, K. R. (2002). Using case documentation to strengthen trainees' case conceptualization skills. *Journal of Counseling and Development, 80,* 11–21.

Prochaska, J. O., DiClemente, C. C., & Norcross, J. C. (1992). In search of how people change: Applications to addictive behaviors. *American Psychologist, 47,* 1102–1114.

Prochaska, J. O., & Norcross, J. C. (2003). *Systems of psychotherapy: A transtheoretical analysis* (5th ed.). Pacific Grove, CA: Brooks/Cole.

Remley, T. P., Jr., & Herlihy, B. (2001). *Ethical, legal, and professional issues in counseling.* Upper Saddle River, NJ: Merrill/Prentice Hall.

Ritchie, M. H. (1986). Counseling the involuntary client. *Journal of Counseling and Development, 64,* 516–518.

Rogers, C. R. (1987). The underlying theory: Drawn from experience with individuals and groups. *Counseling and Values, 32,* 38–46.

Sack, R. T. (1988). Counseling responses when clients say "I don't know." *Journal of Mental Health Counseling, 10,* 179–187.

Seligman, L. (2001). *Systems, strategies, and skills of counseling and psychotherapy.* Upper Saddle River, NJ: Merrill/Prentice Hall.

Sexton, T. L., Whiston, S. C., Bleuer, J. C., & Walz, G. R. (1997). Integrating outcome research into counseling practice and training. Alexandria, VA: American Counseling Association.

Shulman, L. (1979). *The skills of helping individuals and groups.* Itasca, IL: F. E. Peacock.

Strong, S. R. (1982). Emerging integrations of clinical and social psychology: A clinician's perspective. In G. Weary & H. Mirels (Eds.), *Integrations of clinical and social psychology* (pp. 181–213). New York: Oxford University Press.

Vacc, N. A., & Loesch, L. (2000). *Professional orientation to counseling* (3rd ed.). Philadelphia: Brunner-Routledge.

Vickio, C. J. (1990). The goodbye brochure: Helping students to cope with transition and loss. *Journal of Counseling and Development, 68,* 575–577.

Vriend, J., & Dyer, W. W. (1973). Counseling the reluctant client. *Journal of Counseling Psychology, 20,* 240–246.

Ward, D. E. (1984). Termination of individual counseling: Concepts and strategies. *Journal of Counseling and Development, 63,* 21–25.

Welfel, E. R. (2002). *Ethics in counseling and psychotherapy: Standards, research, and emerging issues* (2nd ed.). Pacific Grove, CA: Brooks/Cole.

Whiston, S. C. (2000). *Principles and applications of assessment in counseling.* Belmont, CA: Wadsworth.

Young, M. E. (2001). *Learning the art of helping: Building blocks and techniques* (2nd ed.). Upper Saddle River, NJ: Merrill/Prentice Hall.

CHAPTER 6

Client Assessment and Diagnosis

She works in a world I have never known
Full of rainbow pills and lilac candles
Woven together with simple time-stitches
A pattern of color in a gray fabric factory
Where she spends her days
spinning threads
that go to Chicago by night.
Once with a little girl smile and a giggle
She flew to Atlanta in her mind,
Opening the door to instant adventures
far from her present fatigue,
That was a journal we shared
arranging her thoughts in a patchwork pattern
until the designs and desires came together.

Gladding, S. T. (1974). Patchwork. *Personnel and Guidance Journal, 53,* 39. © ACA. Reprinted with permission. No further reproduction authorized without written permission of ACA.

Community counselors are responsible for carrying out many different functions, some which may depend on the settings in which they work. Two general functions that most community counselors need to conduct skillfully are assessment and diagnosis. Assessment is an ongoing process in which counselors gather information about clients from several different sources and use that information to make decisions about treatment planning. Diagnosis is closely related to assessment and, although somewhat controversial, is used by counselors in many private and public settings to describe clients' conditions, guide treatment planning, and apply for third-party reimbursement. In this chapter, information about assessment and diagnosis is provided, and issues related to the two processes are examined.

ASSESSMENT IN COUNSELING

Assessment is a multifaceted activity that is integral to the counseling process. Although some people associate assessment with the early stages of counseling, it actually is an ongoing activity that takes place throughout the counseling process, from referral to follow-up (Hohenshil, 1996). Formal and informal methods of assessment help counselors gather information to determine the nature of clients' issues, the prevalence of their problems, their strengths and skills, and whether counseling is likely to be beneficial (Whiston, 2000). Conducting systematic assessment helps counselors and clients develop a better understanding of the presenting problems and issues, plan for future sessions, and evaluate progress made in counseling.

Assessment begins with the first counselor–client contact, as the counselor listens to the client's story and observes behaviors (Young, 2001). During this initial stage, important data about the client are collected, counselors begin to hypothesize about the nature of the client's concerns, and decisions are made about whether counseling will be beneficial. To gather information about clients, community counselors typically conduct intake interviews, which were described in Chapter 5. In this section, additional information is provided about assessment in counseling, including methods and purposes of assessment, principles of sound assessment, and issues related to assessment and diagnosis.

Assessment Defined

The term *assessment* has been defined in numerous ways. The *Standards for Educational and Psychological Testing* (American Educational Research Association [AERA], American Psychological Association [APA], & National Council on Measurement in Education [NCME], 1999, p. 172), a key authoritative source in the assessment field, defines *assessment* as "any systematic method of obtaining information from tests and other sources, used to draw inferences about characteristics of people, objects, or programs." Whiston (2000, p. 5) defines *assessment* as "a broad term that implies the evaluation of individuals through a process that may involve test results and other sources of information." *Psychological testing,* a term often associated with assessment, is just one of several methods counselors use to collect client information. Other methods include interviews, checklists, rating scales, and qualitative or experiential approaches. Counselors integrate and interpret the results of these evaluation methods to increase their understanding of clients and their situations (Hood & Johnson, 2002).

As part of their training, community counselors take at least one course in appraisal procedures, in which they learn methods and principles of assessment. It would be beyond the scope and purpose of this chapter to describe those methods and principles in depth. However, a brief overview is presented here to highlight important factors related to assessment in counseling.

Methods of Assessment

Assessment procedures may be formal or informal, standardized or nonstandardized, and objective or subjective. They can be used to measure attributes and behaviors in many domains, including personality, cognition, affect, ability, interests, values, and relationships. Community counselors can choose from a wide spectrum of methods for assessing clients, including the following:

- **Standardized Tests.** Psychological tests that are standardized must meet certain standards for test construction, administration, and interpretation. Such tests use representative norm groups for scoring and interpretation and typically have been evaluated for reliability and validity (Hood & Johnson, 2002). Examples of areas measured by standardized tests include aptitude, achievement, personality, interests, values, and skills.
- **Rating Scales and Checklists.** Rating scales and checklists provide subjective estimates of behaviors or attitudes based on observations made by the client or other observers. With checklists, clients or observers simply mark words or phrases that apply to them or their situation. Such tools can provide valuable information to counselors in a relatively brief time. With rating scales, the rater indicates the degree or severity of the characteristic being measured (Whiston, 2000). For example, a client may be asked to rate his or her energy level on a graded scale, from lethargic (1) to energetic (5). Informal rating scales may be used to determine the client's perception of the intensity of the presenting problem. Standardized rating scales that are completed by the client and significant others can be especially helpful for measuring a wide spectrum of behaviors. The Child Behavior Checklist (Achenbach, 1991) and Symptom Checklist-90-Revised (SCL-90–R, Derogatis, 1994) are examples of standardized rating scales that are commonly used in community counseling settings.
- **Other Inventories.** Community counselors may use a number of other inventories besides rating scales and checklists to assess client concerns. For example, the Minnesota Multiphasic Personality Inventory-2 (MMPI–2)is widely used by counselors in community settings (Bubenzer, Zimpfer, & Mahrle, 1990). The MMPI–2 consists of 567 affirmative statements that clients respond to in one of three ways: true, false, or cannot say. In addition to identifying individuals who may

be experiencing psychiatric problems, the MMPI–2 is able to discern important characteristics such as anger, alienation, depression, and social insecurity. Counselors need extensive training and experience to use the instrument accurately and appropriately (Austin, 1994).

• **Structured and Semistructured Interviews.** Interviews, which are described in Chapter 5, are commonly conducted by counselors to assess clients. Interviews can vary in format, ranging from relatively open and unstructured to highly structured. During the past several years, many structured clinical interviews have been published for research and practice purposes (see Vacc & Juhnke, 1997, for examples). Structured clinical interviews can be especially useful in the current era of managed care, which stresses precision, time-limited counseling, and demonstrated effectiveness (Vacc & Juhnke).

A structured clinical interview consists of "a list of relevant behaviors, symptoms, and events to be addressed during an interview, guidelines for conducting the interview, and procedures for recording and analyzing the data" (Vacc & Juhnke, 1997, p. 471). The questions are usually asked in an ordered sequence and typically are either diagnostic (specifically related to the *Diagnostic and Statistical Manual*) or descriptive (providing data on emotional, behavioral, and social issues, but not for the purpose of diagnosis).

Whereas structured clinical interviews specify the order and wording of questions, semistructured interviews are less restrictive. Semistructured interviews address the same issues as structured interviews do, but they provide more flexibility in sequence, wording, and interpretation.

• **Mental Status Examination.** The mental status examination (MSE) has been used by psychiatrists, psychologists, and social workers for over 50 years (Hinkle, 1992). In recent years, the MSE has also been used by community counselors who work in settings in which mental disorders are diagnosed and treated (Polanski & Hinkle, 2000). A skillfully administered MSE provides information about a client's level of functioning and self-presentation. It may be conducted formally or informally during the initial interview and provides a format for organizing objective and subjective data gathered during the interview (Polanski & Hinkle, 2000).

The MSE assesses behaviors and attitudes that can be organized under the following six categories: (a) appearance, attitude, and activity; (b) mood and affect; (c) speech and language; (d) thought process, thought content, and perception; (e) cognition; and (f) insight and judgment (Trzepacz & Baker, 1993). A brief description of each category is presented in Figure 6–1. When conducted proficiently, the MSE provides biological, social, and psychological information about the client that facilitates diagnosis and treatment planning (Polanski & Hinkle, 2000).

• **Qualitative Methods.** Qualitative assessment procedures include card sorts, structured exercises, creative activities, genograms, time lines, and other open-ended approaches. These methods are usually less formal than quantitative techniques, allowing for greater counselor and client flexibility and adaptability, which may make them especially suitable for a diverse clientele (Goldman, 1990). Qualitative methods elicit active client participation and provide ways for the counselor to understand the client's current problems within the context of his or her

APPEARANCE, ATTITUDE, AND ACTIVITY

- *Appearance: Appearance* refers to the client's physical presentation, dress, grooming, cleanliness, and presence or absence of any disabilities. It can also include body position, posture, and use of eye contact.
- *Attitude: Attitude* refers to the client's approach to the interview and interactions with the counselor. Observations about attitude include tone of voice, facial expressions, attentiveness, and degree of evasiveness in responses. Attitude may change during the course of the interview. Examples of terms used to describe attitude include *cooperative, uncooperative, suspicious, hostile,* and *open.*
- *Activity:* This category refers to the client's level and quality of motor activity. Any observation of tics, tremors, mannerisms, compulsions, and perseveration is documented. Physical manifestations of emotions (e.g., laughing, crying, fist clenching, and grunting) are documented, as well.
- *Mood and affect: Mood* refers to the client's predominant internal feeling state, as reported by the client. *Affect* refers to the client's outward expression of an emotional state, as observed by the counselor, and varies in range and intensity.
- *Speech and language: Language* refers to the client's ability to comprehend word meanings and express them through writing and speaking. Speech and language defects include *defects of association* (the way words are grouped to make phrases) and *defects of rate and rhythm of speech* (e.g., pressured or delayed speech patterns).
- *Thought process, thought content, and perception:* During the MSE, thought content and process are inferred from what the client says and what the counselor observes. Disturbances of thought process, content, and perception can include delusions and hallucinations. Appraising a client's thoughts of violence to self or others is a crucial part of thought content assessment.
- *Cognition: Cognition* refers to the client's ability to use logic, intellect, reasoning, memory, and other higher order cognitive functioning. During the MSE, cognition is assessed in a structured manner. Areas to be evaluated include attention, concentration, orientation, memory, and abstract thinking. Counselors can assess attention and concentration by asking the client to count backward by 7s or 3s from 100. Assessment of long- and short-term memory and orientation to person, place, time, and circumstance also help evaluate cognitive functioning.
- *Insight and judgment:* These are the most advanced areas of mental functioning. *Insight* refers to the degree to which a client is aware of how personal traits and behaviors contribute to his or her current situation. *Judgment* refers to the ability to make decisions about an appropriate course of action.

Figure 6–1

The Mental Status Examination

(From *Polanski & Hinkle, 2000; Trzepacz & Baker, 1993*).

unique developmental history. The active nature of qualitative assessment promotes counselor–client interaction and client self-awareness. The activities themselves are potentially change generating, thus making it possible for the assessment process to serve as an intervention.

Purposes of Assessment

The primary goal of assessment is to collect data about clients' behaviors, characteristics, and contexts that will then facilitate clinical decision making and evaluation. With this general purpose in mind, it is helpful to look at some of the specific ways assessment facilitates counseling throughout the different stages of the process: in early stages for treatment planning, during the treatment phase as an actual intervention, and throughout the process and after termination for evaluation (Whiston, 2000).

Assessment to inform the clinician and guide treatment planning.   At the outset of counseling, clients may talk about a wide spectrum of concerns. One of the goals of assessment during this early stage of counseling is to work with the client to clarify and prioritize the issues. A systematic assessment helps ensure that counselors are helping clients with the most important issues. In addition to helping clients prioritize their concerns, Young (2001, pp. 149–150) suggests seven other reasons counselors need to spend sufficient time assessing clients during initial sessions:

- Assessment provides crucial information that facilitates realistic goal planning. It informs treatment planning and often is used to provide a diagnosis.
- Assessment helps clients explore the problem and discover events that may be triggering it.
- Assessment helps counselors focus on the uniqueness of individuals by providing information about culture, family, and other contextual factors.
- Assessment uncovers the potential for self-harm or violence (i.e., suicidal or homicidal ideation; Figure 6–2).
- Assessment reveals important historical data.
- Assessment highlights strengths as well as concerns.
- Assessment can help clients become more aware of the severity of a problem (e.g., substance abuse).

In summary, a thorough assessment helps the counselor gain a more complete understanding of the client. Information provided through assessment helps the counselor make sound decisions about treatment goals and intervention strategies. In some settings, early assessment also is used to render a formal diagnosis.

Assessment as an intervention.   Beyond providing the counselor with information for diagnosis and treatment, assessment methods have the potential to be therapeutic in and of themselves. Formal and informal appraisal procedures can encourage client self-exploration and catalyze decision making. For example, discussing the results of

A Suicide Risk Awareness Index

Check your knowledge by responding to the following true/false statements:

1. More women than men commit suicide.
2. In 1999, suicide was the 11th leading cause of death in the United States.
3. The group with the highest suicide rate is African American females over the age of 65.
4. Marital status is not associated with suicide potential.
5. All depressed clients should be evaluated to determine suicidal ideation.
6. Adolescent suicide has increased by 85 percent in the last 20 years.
7. One of the most important signs to look for in suicide assessment is a sense of hopelessness or helplessness.
8. The strongest risk factors for suicide in adults are depression, alcohol abuse, cocaine use, and separation or divorce.
9. Firearms are the most commonly used method of suicide for men and women.
10. Discussing suicide potential with a client increases the likelihood that it will be carried out.

Answers to Suicide Awareness Index:

1. False; Although women are more likely than men to attempt suicide, more men die by suicide at a ratio of 4:1.
2. True
3. False; The highest rate of suicide, when categorized by gender and race, is among white men over the age of 85.
4. False; Rates for people who are single, widowed, or divorced are higher than rates for married individuals.
5. True; It is important to evaluate all clients for suicidal ideation, and depression is a risk factor for suicide.
6. False; Adolescent suicide has increased by 300 percent in the past 20 years and is the third leading cause of death among young people between 15 and 24 years of age.
7. True; Most suicidal clients exhibit a degree of hopelessness and/or helplessness.
8. True
9. True; Death by firearms accounted for 57 percent of all suicides in 1999.
10. False; All clients should be evaluated for suicidal ideation.
   (Statistics were obtained from the National Institute of Mental Health, 2000, 2002.)

Figure 6–2
Suicide risk assessment and intervention

Most counselors will, at some point, encounter the challenge of working with a suicidal client (Rogers, 2001). One of the key areas counselors need to evaluate during the initial session, as well as at other points in the counseling process, is the risk of suicide (Hood & Johnson, 2002; Whiston, 2000). The risk of suicide can be assessed informally by asking the client about his or her thoughts. Hood and Johnson (2002, pp. 292–293) suggest a series of graded questions, such as:

- How have you been feeling lately?
- How bad does it get?
- Has it ever been so bad that you wished you were dead?
- Have you ever had thoughts of suicide?
- Tell me about those thoughts.

If the client indicates that he or she has thought about suicide, the counselor will want to conduct a more in-depth assessment. The suicide risk assessment becomes part of the treatment in that talking about suicidal thoughts validates the client's experiences and communicates hope that the problem can be addressed (Hood & Johnson, 2002).

There are several formal and informal ways to assess suicide risk. Hood and Johnson (2002) and Whiston (2000) cite Stelmachers' recommendation that clinicians focus on seven areas:

- *Verbal Communication*. What has the client verbalized or hinted at? It is important to listen closely; the client may couch the ideation as a joke. Themes of escape, reducing tension, or self-punishment can all be indications of suicidal ideation.
- *Plan*. If the client gives any indication of suicidal thoughts, the counselor should determine if there is an actual suicide plan by asking questions such as "Have you thought about how you might do it?" or "How would you do it?" Generally, more specific, thought-out plans indicate a greater risk of an attempt, although with impulsive clients, this may not be the case.
- *Method*. If the client has a plan, determine what has already been put in place to carry out the plan. What methods are being considered and how available are they? Is the plan feasible? Determine the exact location of any lethal means (e.g., firearms and drugs).
- *Preparation*. To what degree has the client already put plans in place? For example, has he or she written a note or secured the lethal means? Has a place been determined? Sometimes people who are considering suicide give away possessions or get financial matters in order. The amount of preparation usually relates directly to the level of client risk.
- *Stressors*. Assess past, present, and future stressors. Stressors associated with suicide include loss of a loved one, physical illness, and economic difficulties. Anniversaries or special dates related to the stressors may exacerbate the client's sense of loss or depression, increasing the risk of suicide. Also, multiple stressors can compound a client's sense of hopelessness.
- *Mental State*. Mental disorders such as depression, substance abuse, and schizophrenia heighten the risk of suicide. Evaluating the client's mental and emotional state is crucial. Does the client express despondence, helplessness, anger, guilt, or torment? If so, he or she will need to be monitored closely. On the other hand, a sudden improvement of mood can indicate that the client has decided to "end the pain," and may be a sign for further evaluation.
- *Hopelessness*. What are the client's thoughts about the future? A sense of hopelessness is strongly associated with attempted suicide (Stelmachers, 1995) and serves as a red flag for suicide risk.

Figure 6–2   *Continued*

Suicide Intervention: What To Do If a Client Appears Suicidal

In terms of immediate treatment, counselors need to do whatever is necessary to keep the client safe (MacCluskie & Ingersoll, 2001). Past history, current assessment of the client's condition, and prognosis will determine the type of intervention that needs to occur. MacCluskie and Ingersoll describe treatment options as either *inpatient treatment* or *outpatient treatment*.

Inpatient treatment. If it is determined that the client is of danger to self, the prospect of voluntary hospitalization should be discussed. Ideally, the client then is taken to the hospital, where he or she is signed in. In this case, the client should be accompanied by a family member, a trusted friend, or by the clinician to ensure safety. Under no circumstances should the suicidal client be left alone, even briefly.

In situations when the counselor has determined that the client is of immediate danger to self but the client will not agree to voluntary hospitalization, involuntary hospitalization may be necessary. Family members and friends can be helpful in this process, although at times it is necessary for the counselor to commit the client, even though taking such a step can be detrimental to the counseling relationship (MacCluskie & Ingersoll, 2001).

Outpatient treatment. When the danger to self is not immediately imminent, outpatient treatment may be the best option. In this situation, "the goal is to obtain follow-up counseling soon—preferably in the next 48 hours, to provide support and re-assess the client" (MacCluskie & Ingersoll, 2001, p. 174). If the counselor's agency cannot provide continued, ongoing services, the counselor is responsible for scheduling the client with another professional at another agency, and follow-up should occur within the next few days. The client needs to be given emergency contact information and asked to sign a no-harm contract. In many cases, family members need to be consulted, preferably with the client's permission. With both inpatient and outpatient treatment, the counselor should consult with other professionals and document activities and decisions.

When working with suicidal clients, counselors can engage in specific behaviors to help clients overcome suicidal ideation and behaviors. Helpful interventions include building a strong therapeutic relationship with the client, validating other relationships in the client's life, helping the client resolve intense emotions, confronting self-destructive behaviors, encouraging personal autonomy, and helping clients acknowledge and overcome feelings of helplessness and despair (Paulson & Worth, 2002). Collaborating with medical personnel to arrange for medical evaluation may also be indicated (Laux, 2002).

Figure 6–2   *Continued*

a career interest inventory can help clients crystallize their understanding of personal interests, particularly as those interests relate to the world of work. Completing checklists of personal qualities can promote recognition and appreciation of strengths. Instruments like the *Wellness Evaluation of Lifestyle—Form J* (Myers, Sweeney, Witmer, & Hattie, 1998), which assesses different lifestyle factors associated with wellness, provide clients with an opportunity to examine areas of their lives that may be out of balance, thus serving as a motivator for change. Qualitative methods such as card sorts or time lines encourage clients to engage in self-reflection, which can then facilitate movement in new directions. It is the interactive dialog between counselor and client, either during an activity like a card sort or during the interpretation of the results of a psychological test, that transforms the assessment process from an information-gathering activity to a therapeutic intervention.

Assessment for evaluation and accountability.   The need to evaluate the effectiveness of counseling has become increasingly more important as managed care organizations and other agencies demand accountability. For evaluation to occur, goals and objectives need to be specified clearly during the early stages of counseling. Follow-up assessment can take several forms, including goal attainment scaling, self-monitoring techniques, posttests, client satisfaction surveys, and outcome questionnaires (Hood & Johnson, 2002).

Using assessment for evaluation is not a straightforward activity. Counseling is a complex process, and its effectiveness depends on many variables. Also, demonstrating the effectiveness of counseling varies, depending on who completes the outcome measure (e.g., the client, the counselor, or an outside observer) (Whiston, 2000). For evaluation to be meaningful, counselors will want to consider measuring change from multiple perspectives, using several different methods.

In addition to outcome evaluation at the conclusion of counseling, assessment can be conducted at various points throughout the process to determine what has been helpful and what needs to be changed. By obtaining objective and subjective feedback from clients, counselors can modify interventions so that clients are more likely to meet their goals.

Principles of Sound Assessment

The process of psychological assessment is both a science and an art (Hood & Johnson, 2002). Counselors need to have a comprehensive knowledge about psychological assessment instruments and their psychometric properties. They also need to integrate that knowledge with strong communication and counseling skills as they select, administer, and interpret assessment instruments. To help counselors conduct assessment skillfully, Hood and Johnson (2002, pp. 8–11) have suggested several basic principles:

- Determine the purpose of assessment. Focusing on that purpose will help counselors identify which assessment procedures to conduct.
- Involve the client in selecting areas to be assessed and in the interpretation of assessment results.
- Never rely on a single assessment tool; instead, use multiple methods of assessment. For example, a counselor may use information gained from an intake interview, the *Beck Depression Inventory,* an informal checklist, and outside observers to form an impression about whether a client is depressed.
- Consider the possibility of multiple issues, many of which may be interconnected (e.g., substance abuse, depression, and physical problems).

- Assess the client's environment. Problems occur in a social context and are rarely related to just one factor.
- Evaluate client strengths, as well as areas of concern. Identifying strengths and resources can help shift the focus from the problem to potential solutions (White, 2002).
- Consider alternative hypotheses, rather than simply looking for evidence to support a favorite hypothesis. What else might be going on with the client?
- Treat assessment results as tentative. As more information becomes available, initial assumptions may change.
- Be aware of cultural and personal biases that may influence decisions. Incorporate cultural data, such as measures of acculturation levels, into the assessment process.
- Consult with other professionals on a regular basis.
- Provide feedback about assessment results to clients. The feedback process can improve self-understanding and lead to change.

Issues Related to Assessment

Counselors are responsible for conducting ethically sound assessment procedures. Several documents have been developed to help guide professionals who use assessment instruments with the public. The *Standards for Educational and Psychological Testing* (AERA, APA, NCME, 1999) was developed by experts in several fields, including research, measurement, psychology, and counseling. It addresses a wide range of issues related to assessment practices, including test–user competencies, assessing testing applications, and diversity considerations. A document prepared by the Association for Assessment in Counseling, *Applying the Standards for Educational and Psychological Testing—What a Counselor Needs to Know* (2003), clarifies applications of the *Standards* (1999) for counselors. Both sources can help community counselors use assessment instruments responsibly and ethically.

Counselor competence.   Before using psychological assessment instruments, counselors need to consider their levels of training and experience. Different instruments require different degrees of competence, and counselors need to be able to demonstrate skill in using a particular instrument before administering it. To monitor competence, many test publishers require professionals to provide a record of their educational background before allowing them to purchase assessment instruments. Tests are graded by levels in regard to education and experience (i.e., Levels A, B, and C) and are sold only to those professionals who meet the requirements for a particular level (Hood & Johnson, 2002).

Diversity considerations.   A number of concerns have been raised about the misuse of assessment instruments with ethnic and racial minorities, people with disabilities, women, and other special populations (Whiston, 2000). Indeed, one of the most controversial issues in assessment relates to whether appraisal instruments are fair to people from different racial or ethnic groups (Suzuki & Kugler, 2001). When selecting instruments, counselors need to consider the client's cultural background, gender, language, developmental level, and level of physical ability. Counselors can expect to work with diverse populations and need to be skilled in cross-cultural assessment (Whiston, 2000). Specific considerations related to assessing diverse clientele include the following:

- Select instruments that are appropriate for the population being tested by examining the purpose of the test, norming groups, and sensitivity of content. Be aware of cultural limitations of certain appraisal instruments.
- Determine the client's language proficiency and, when possible, use tests that are written in that language.
- When administering tests to individuals with disabilities, do everything possible to ensure that the instrument accurately measures the skills or aptitudes it is designed to measure, rather than any characteristics associated with the disability. Be aware of options available for clients with disabilities who require testing accommodations.
- Consider the potential effects of counselor–client cultural differences on the test-taking process and its results. Be culturally sensitive in establishing rapport, conducting the assessment, and interpreting the results.

A booklet published by the Association for Assessment in Counseling (AAC), *Multicultural Assessment Standards* (Prediger, 1994), addresses assessment practices and applications for counselors who work with multicultural populations. The publication lists 34 standards from different sources that provide information on selecting, administering, scoring, and interpreting appraisal instruments for diverse clientele. Counselors can refer to this document, which is currently under revision, for guidance in conducting assessment with multicultural populations.

Use of results.   Client welfare is the counselor's primary consideration. In assessment, issues related to privacy, confidentiality, and communication of results come into play. Typically, community counselors have fewer ethical problems in these areas than other professionals because of the purpose and nature of assessment in counseling: to help clients in decision making or to provide additional information for goal planning and self-understanding (Hood & Johnson, 2002). In situations where test results are used for such high-stake purposes as selection, promotion, or placement, ethical dilemmas are more likely.

An issue related to the use of assessment results that does affect community counselors on a regular basis is that of diagnosis. Community counselors employed privately or by public mental health agencies routinely diagnose and treat clients with problems ranging from developmental concerns to more serious mental health conditions (Hohenshil, 1996). Indeed, almost all settings in which community and mental health counselors work require a diagnosis for reimbursement of services (White, 2002). A *DSM-IV-TR* (APA, 2000) multiaxial assessment and diagnosis provides essential information that helps counselors and clients with goal setting and treatment planning. However, diagnostic procedures have the potential for abuse, in that "an inappropriate label could follow a person throughout life, affecting family, social, educational, and occupational status" (Hohenshil, 1996, p. 65). Consequently, as we turn our attention to the diagnosis, it is important to remember that diagnosis is an ongoing process that is conducted not to label clients or for purposes of reimbursement but instead to aid in treatment planning and intervention.

DIAGNOSIS

Community counselors in the 21st century need to be skilled at assessing and diagnosing clients. Although some professionals believe that diagnosis contradicts a developmental approach to counseling (Ivey & Ivey, 1999), others maintain that "without an accurate diagnosis, counselors will probably have difficulty determining the proper treatment for a disorder and assessing whether a person is likely to benefit from counseling" (Seligman, 2001, p. 271). Hohenshil (1996) reminds us that many employers, licensing agencies, and insurance companies expect counselors to know how to formally diagnose mental disorders. He goes on to state that diagnosis, either formal or informal, has always been a part of counseling. For example, making a decision about whether a client's problem is a developmental issue or a form of pathology is, in fact, a form of diagnosis. In addition to making informal diagnoses, in recent years, community counselors have been expected to accrue skills in diagnosing using a formal diagnostic system, such as the *DSM-IV-TR* (Whiston, 2000).

Diagnosis is "the process of comparing the symptoms exhibited by the client with the diagnostic criteria of some type of classification system" (Hohenshil, 1996, p. 66). A diagnosis is a description of a person's condition and not a judgment of a person's worth (Rueth, Demmitt, & Burger, 1998). The purposes of diagnosis are to (a) define clinical entities so that clinicians have a common ground for understanding what a diagnostic category means and (b) help counselors determine appropriate treatment (Maxmen & Ward, 1995). Seligman (2001, pp. 271–272) outlines several reasons for becoming skilled in diagnosis:

- A diagnostic system provides a consistent framework and set of criteria for naming and describing mental disorders.
- Accurate diagnosis enables counselors to understand client symptoms and anticipate the typical course of a disorder.
- Diagnosis enables counselors to make use of the growing body of research on treatment effectiveness and promotes accountability.
- Diagnosis provides a common language for mental health professionals, which facilitates parity, communication, and collaboration.
- When counselors make diagnoses and treatment plans according to an accepted system, they are less vulnerable to malpractice suits.
- Sharing diagnoses with clients, when appropriate, can help them better understand their condition. Knowing that other people deal with the same condition and that there is information available can be reassuring.
- Diagnosis can help counselors determine whether they have the skills and training needed to help a particular client or whether it would be better to refer that client to another mental health professional.

Although there certainly is justification for developing diagnostic skills, there also are risks and concerns associated with the diagnostic process. Some of those risks include (Ivey & Ivey, 1999; Seligman, 2001):

- Diagnostic labels can be stigmatizing if misused and may lead to misperceptions of that person if the diagnosis becomes known.
- Diagnosis is part of the medical illness–cure tradition and is not consistent with a holistic, developmental approach to counseling that emphasizes multicultural concerns, contextual influences, and strength-based approaches.
- Diagnosis is historically contingent and socially constructed, not absolute reality.
- Diagnosis can lead to pathologizing the client so that he or she is viewed "as" the disorder (e.g., schizophrenic, borderline), rather than as a person with particular concerns.
- Diagnosis may have a negative impact on people's ability to obtain insurance and, in some situations, affect their employment opportunities.
- The most common diagnostic systems (i.e., the *DSM-IV-TR* and the *ICD-10*) are steeped in the Western concept of mental illness and may not be relevant to people from other cultures.

Although there are risks associated with the process of diagnosis, many of those risks can be avoided by conducting skillful and comprehensive assessments, presenting diagnostic information in such a way that it is understood by clients and families, and honoring client confidentiality (Seligman, 2001). To make proper diagnoses, counselors must receive extensive training and supervision. They should know diagnostic categories, particularly those described in the *DSM-IV-TR*. Therefore, it is to the *DSM-IV-TR* that we direct our attention next.

Using the *DSM-IV-TR* in Counseling

In the United States, the most widely used system for psychiatric diagnosis is the *Diagnostic and Statistical Manual of Mental Disorders* (DSM). Currently in its fourth edition, the *DSM-IV-TR* includes over 200 diagnoses, which are divided into 17 general categories and clearly defined by objective criteria (Maxmen & Ward, 1995). Whereas the *DSM-IV* was published in 1994, the text revision (*TR*) was published in 2000 to bridge the span between the *DSM-IV* and the *DSM-V*, which is scheduled for publication in 2006 or 2007. The text revision includes some changes to text sections of the *DSM* (e.g., Associated Features and Disorders, Prevalence) but no substantive changes in criteria sets for mental disorders (APA, 2000).

What is a mental disorder?   According to the *DSM-IV-TR* (2000), the term *mental disorder* can be defined as:

> a clinically significant behavior or psychological syndrome or pattern that occurs in an individual and that is associated with present distress (e.g., a painful symptom) or disability (i.e., impairment in one or more important areas of functioning) or with a significantly increased risk of suffering death, pain, disability, or an important loss of freedom. (p. xxxi)

DSM diagnoses are made based on the clinician's evaluation of certain criteria. Counselors are not trained to work with all of the disorders represented in the DSM; however, they are expected to be knowledgeable about the disorders and aware of their own areas of competence (Whiston, 2000).

Multiaxial diagnosis. The *DSM-IV-TR* uses a multiaxial diagnostic system that involves assessment on five different axes. The multiaxial system allows counselors to organize information based on clients' symptoms, their physical conditions, their levels of coping, and current stressors (Seligman, 2001). An overview of the five axes is presented in Table 6–1.

All clinical conditions or disorders are listed on Axis I or Axis II. Axis I disorders include all mental disorders and conditions except for personality disorders and mental retardation, which are listed on Axis II. Clients may have one or more diagnoses listed on these two axes. The principal diagnosis is the first disorder listed on Axis I, unless otherwise specified. When a diagnosis is listed, clinicians include the name and code number specified by the DSM. The severity of the disorder is specified as well, using the terms *Mild, Moderate, Severe, In Partial Remission, or In Full Remission* (Seligman, 2001).

Clinicians use Axis III to describe general medical conditions that may be related to the client's mental and emotional conditions. For example, recurring stomachaches or headaches might be related to an anxiety disorder. If the clinician does not have the client's medical records, he or she should specify that the medical conditions were self-reported.

On Axis IV, clinicians list psychosocial and environmental stressors that the client has experienced during the past year. Examples of stressors that may impact clients include family problems, finances, living situations, lack of social support, and negative life events (Maxmen & Ward, 1995).

Axis V is used to provide a global assessment of functioning (GAF) rating, which is based on a scale ranging from 1 to 100. Higher GAF ratings indicate higher levels of functioning. Scores below 50 usually indicate that the client is experiencing severe

Table 6–1
Multiaxial Assessment

Axis	What Is Rated	Example
Axis I	Clinical disorders, developmental disorders, and other conditions that may be a focus of clinical attention	305.00; alcohol abuse; moderate
Axis II	Personality disorders and mental retardation	317.00; mild mental retardation
Axis III	General medical conditions	Chronic pain
Axis IV	Psychosocial and environmental problems	Divorced, unemployed, no social support
Axis V	Global assessment of functioning (GAF)	30 (present) 45 (highest level in past year)

symptoms (Seligman, 2001). The rating typically depicts the client's current level of functioning, although sometimes clinicians also include the client's highest level of functioning within the past year. Although some research indicates that the GAF is an inadequate measure of adaptive functioning (Bacon, Collins, & Plake, 2002), in mental health settings the GAF is used more frequently than any other diagnostic tool to measure adaptive functioning and impairment.

Each of the five axes that comprise a DSM assessment and diagnosis contribute unique information about a client's overall situation. By examining all the information provided through multiaxial assessment, counselors can make decisions about diagnosis, treatment planning, and prognosis. When making a diagnosis, the counselor will want to begin with an initial broad observation and screening of the client. Next, he or she directs attention toward how the client's symptoms are evidenced. What types of symptom syndromes is the client experiencing (e.g., frequency, duration, and onset of symptoms)? The counselor then forms a tentative hypothesis about the type of disorder the client is experiencing, followed by a careful, diagnosis-specific inquiry to determine if the symptoms meet the specified criteria for a DSM diagnosis (Fong, 1995). A diagnosis should be given only if the specific criteria outlined in the DSM are met.

Overview of Mental Disorders and Conditions

It would be beyond the scope of this chapter to describe each of the 200-plus mental disorders and conditions contained in the *DSM-IV-TR*. The DSM is divided broadly into 17 sections, each of which is reviewed briefly in this section. People entering the field of community counseling will want to master DSM terminology and differential diagnosis by attending workshops, reading supplementary material (e.g., *Study Guide to DSM-IV*, Fauman, 1994), and consulting with experienced professionals.

• **Disorders Usually First Diagnosed in Infancy, Childhood, or Adolescence**. This large, comprehensive category includes disorders that usually originate early in life, with some disorders persisting into adulthood. Examples of early onset disorders include mental retardation (which is included in this section but listed as an Axis II disorder), learning disorders (e.g., dyslexia), communication disorders (difficulties in speech and language), and pervasive developmental disorders (e.g., autism and Rett's disorder). Also included in this category are attention-deficit and disruptive behavior disorders (e.g., oppositional-defiant disorder and conduct disorder), feeding and eating disorders of infancy or early childhood (e.g., pica), tic disorders, elimination disorders, and other disorders that are not included in the previous categories (e.g., separation anxiety).

• **Delirium, Dementia, and Amnestic and Other Cognitive Disorders**. Each of these disorders is organic in nature and involves some form of impairment to the brain. The impairment may be temporary or permanent and is characterized by deficits in cognition or memory. Examples of cognitive disorders include delirium (characterized by a clouding of consciousness and reduced environmental awareness), dementia (characterized by a deterioration of intellectual functions), and amnestic disorders (characterized by memory impairment). In most cases, counselors do not diagnose or treat cognitive disorders, but they need to be familiar with the symptoms in order to refer clients who demonstrate such deficits (Seligman, 2001).

• **Mental Disorders Due to a General Medical Condition.** At times, a medical condition that is described on Axis III manifests itself not only as a physical problem but also as a mental or emotional condition. For example, if catatonia results from encephalitis, the differential diagnosis would be *catatonic disorder due to a general medical condition.* Technically, psychological problems that result from medical conditions are not considered *mental disorders,* but they are included for identification purposes.

• **Substance-Related Disorders.** This category includes psychological and behavioral conditions related to substance use, including substance dependence and substance abuse. Abuse may involve alcohol, illegal drugs, prescription or over-the-counter medication, and toxins. Substance abuse and substance dependence often adversely affect performance and relationships. Successful intervention usually requires a multifaceted treatment plan (Seligman, 1999).

• **Schizophrenia and Other Psychotic Disorders.** The key feature of these disorders is a loss of contact with reality (Seligman, 2001). Usually, counselors are not trained to work with psychotic clients, although it is crucial for counselors to recognize the symptoms so that a referral can be made. According to Maxmen and Ward (1995), "Schizophrenia devastates as no other, for no other disorder causes as pervasive and profound an impact—socially, economically, and personally" (p. 173). Approximately 2.2 million American adults have schizophrenia in a given year (National Institute of Mental Health, 2001). Some of the symptoms exhibited by people with psychotic disorders include hallucinations, delusions, disorganized speech, catatonia, grossly disorganized behavior, and flat affect.

• **Mood Disorders.** Mood disorders are characterized by manic or depressive episodes. Examples include major depressive disorder (severe depression lasting at least 2 weeks), dysthymic disorder (moderate but long-lasting depression), bipolar disorders (characterized by manic and depressive episodes), and cyclothymic disorder. In a given year, approximately 18.8 million American adults, or 9.5 percent of the population, have a depressive disorder, with women twice as likely to be affected (NIMH, 2001). Cognitive–behavioral counseling, frequently in conjunction with medication, is often used to treat mood disorders.

• **Anxiety Disorders.** Anxiety disorders are the second most commonly occurring category of mental disorders, following substance abuse (cf. Fong & Silien, 1999). Anxiety is a multidimensional construct, characterized by feelings of apprehension, dysphoria, and/or symptoms of tension. Because anxiety is also a symptom of other mental disorders, counselors need to know how to diagnose anxiety disorders accurately. Examples of anxiety disorders include social phobia, agoraphobia, obsessive–compulsive disorder, specific phobias (fear of a specific object or situation, such as spiders), posttraumatic stress disorder (PTSD), and acute stress disorder. Anxiety disorders often co-occur with other disorders, such as depression.

• **Somatoform Disorders.** People with somatoform disorders present with physical symptoms that initially appear to be medical in nature but cannot fully be explained as medical conditions. The physical symptoms are not feigned in that physical symptoms of some sort do exist. Examples of somatoform disorders include somatization disorder, conversion disorder (e.g., blindness without a physical cause), hypochondriasis, and body dysmorphic disorder (characterized by an imagined or minimal flaw in one's appearance).

• **Factitious Disorders**. Clients with factitious disorders feign illness or disability because they enjoy assuming the role of "patient." They may fabricate complaints or inflict injury on themselves. A particularly troublesome disorder in this category is *Munchausen's syndrome by proxy,* characterized by caregivers using a child to gain access to medical treatment, often by injuring or even killing the person in their care. People with factitious disorders usually are resistant to treatment and may leave counseling prematurely.

• **Dissociative Disorders**. Dissociative disorders involve an alteration of consciousness that is neither organic nor psychotic (Seligman, 2001). Dissociative identity disorder (DID), which used to be called multiple personality disorder, is the most familiar of these conditions. Other examples are dissociative fugue, dissociative amnesia, and depersonalization disorder.

• **Sexual and Gender Identity Disorders**. This category includes three subcategories: sexual dysfunction, paraphilias, and gender identity disorders. Sexual dysfunction refers to difficulties related to sexual desire, sexual arousal, orgasm, and sexual pain. Paraphilia refers to an abnormal or unnatural attraction, such as *pedophilia* (sexual activity with children). Gender identity disorder is characterized by intense discomfort with one's biological gender and is not to be confused with sexual orientation issues.

• **Eating Disorders**. This new section in the DSM-IV-TR is composed of the three main types of eating disorders: anorexia nervosa, bulimia nervosa, and binge-eating disorder. Females are much more likely to develop these disorders than are males. Clients with anorexia nervosa do not maintain a minimally normal body weight, although they tend to view themselves as "too fat." Clients with bulimia nervosa engage in binge eating followed by purging (vomiting, using laxatives) to rid themselves from what they have eaten. Binge-eating disorder is similar to bulimia nervosa, except that clients do not engage in purging. Adolescent females, in particular, have a high rate of eating disorders, which, "if untreated, can be severely damaging or even fatal" (Seligman, 2001, p. 283).

• **Sleep Disorders**. This category is also new to the DSM-IV-TR. Sleep disorders are categorized as *primary* (the cause is undetermined and unrelated to another condition), *related to another mental disorder, due to a medical condition,* and *substance induced.* The inclusion of sleep disorders in the DSM reflects a growing awareness of the effects sleep deprivation can have on an individual's functioning (Seligman, 1999). Diagnosing sleep disorders is somewhat difficult and often takes place in sleep-disorder clinics.

• **Impulse–Control Disorders Not Elsewhere Classified**. The defining characteristic of impulse–control disorders is the client's difficulty in resisting impulses, drives, or temptations. For many of these disorders, the client feels a buildup of tension that is released when the act is committed but later may be followed by feelings of remorse or guilt. Examples include kleptomania (stealing objects that are not needed), pyromania (setting fires), pathological gambling, and intermittent explosive disorder (characterized by engagement in aggressive or destructive behaviors). Stress management and behavioral approaches are often part of the treatment plan for impulse–control disorders (Seligman, 2001).

• **Adjustment Disorders**. Adjustment disorders are characterized by mild to moderate impairment associated with a stressor experienced within 3 months of the onset of symptoms. The disorder may develop as the result of a single stressor or multiple stressors (e.g., divorce, job loss, and moving). If the disorder lasts less than 6 months, it is described as acute. If it lasts longer, it is considered chronic. Adjustment disorders are among the mildest of the disorders listed in the DSM and generally are responsive to crisis intervention or solution-focused counseling (Seligman, 2001).

• **Personality Disorders**. Clients with personality disorders demonstrate enduring patterns of functioning that are maladaptive, inflexible, and significantly impair social and occupational functioning or cause subjective distress (Maxmen & Ward, 1995). The maladaptive behavior is manifested in at least two of the following areas: cognition, interpersonal functioning, affectivity, or impulse control.

Personality disorders are coded on Axis II and are "among the most treatment-resistant of the disorders" (Seligman, 2001, p. 285). Ten personality disorders are described in the *DSM-IV-TR* and grouped into three clusters: Cluster A (paranoid, schizoid, and schizotypal personality disorders), Cluster B (antisocial, borderline, histrionic, and narcissistic personality disorders), and Cluster C (avoidant, dependent, and obsessive–compulsive personality disorders). People with Cluster A personality disorders often appear odd or eccentric. Clients with Cluster B disorders tend to appear dramatic, emotional, or erratic. In contrast, individuals diagnosed with Cluster C disorders appear anxious or fearful.

Diagnosis of a personality disorder involves evaluating the client's long-term patterns of functioning, with the particular characteristics of the disorder being evidenced by early adulthood (APA, 2000). It is important to take into account the client's ethnic, cultural, and social background to avoid misdiagnosis.

• **Other Conditions That May Be a Focus of Clinical Attention**. The conditions or problems coded in this category are not considered to be disorders, but they may still be a focus in counseling. Some of the conditions are listed as V-codes, and all are recorded on Axis I except for borderline intellectual functioning. Conditions listed in this category include relational problems (e.g., parent–child, sibling, or partner), problems related to abuse or neglect (physical and/or sexual abuse), and "additional conditions" such as bereavement, academic problems, or occupational problems. Often, people presenting with these conditions are emotionally healthy but are going through a difficult time, making counseling an especially suitable option.

Diagnosis and Treatment

Diagnosis is just one part of a comprehensive assessment that leads to treatment planning. It is a crucial part, however, in that it affects the delivery of counseling services, third-party reimbursement, and professional credibility.

Seligman (1996, 2001) has developed a model to help counselors integrate assessment, diagnosis, and treatment planning based on the DSM-IV-TR diagnostic system. The title of the model is a mnemonic device called DO A CLIENT MAP. Each letter of the mnemonic addresses one of the areas to be considered during diagnosis and treatment planning, thus providing a comprehensive organized guide for working with a client (Seligman, 2001, p. 287):

1. Diagnosis according to the *DSM-IV-TR* multiaxial system
2. Objectives of treatment (written as treatment goals)
3. Assessment procedures (formal and informal procedures)
4. Clinician (considerations related to clinical background, gender, ethnicity, and other issues)
5. Location of treatment (inpatient or outpatient, site)
6. Interventions (theoretical approach and specific interventions)
7. Emphasis of treatment (e.g., supportive, probing)
8. Numbers (individual, group, or family counseling)
9. Timing (duration and scheduling of sessions)
10. Medication (determine whether a referral for medication is needed)
11. Adjunct Services (additional activities to supplement the counseling process, such as tutoring)
12. Prognosis (based on the diagnosis, the GAF score, and levels of support)

Counselors will want to use the DSM-IV-TR responsibly, recognizing the importance of cultural influences and social context on client behaviors (Whiston, 2000). They will need to examine assessment information and diagnostic criteria critically, so that the diagnostic process is used for its intended purpose: to inform and guide treatment.

SUMMARY AND CONCLUSIONS

In this chapter, assessment and diagnosis—two essential elements of counseling in most community settings—were described. Assessment is a process that occurs throughout counseling and serves several purposes. It helps counselors and clients gain a better understanding of presenting problems, serves to guide treatment planning, acts as an intervention, and helps counselors evaluate progress and outcomes. Counselors can choose from a variety of assessment tools, including standardized tests, rating scales, interviews, the mental status examination, and qualitative approaches. There are a number of sound appraisal principles that counselors will want to follow, including the use of multiple methods to assess clients.

To help counselors conduct ethically sound assessments, several documents have been developed, including the *Standards for Educational and Psychological Testing* (AERA, APA, NCME, 1999). Some of the issues that affect the assessment process include counselor competence, assessing diverse populations, and use of assessment results.

Closely related to the process of assessment is diagnosis. Although the topic is somewhat controversial, diagnosis has become increasingly important for counselors over the course of the past 20 years (Seligman, 1999). Consequently, community counselors will want to be familiar with the most commonly used system of diagnosis of mental and emotional conditions: the *Diagnostic and Statistical Manual of Mental Disorders* (APA, 2000). The DSM-IV-TR provides a way for clinicians to assess clients on five broad dimensions, or axes. All mental disorders are recorded on Axis I or Axis II and are classified into 17 categories. Although community counselors do not treat all types of diagnoses, they will want to be familiar with signs and symptoms associated with each so that they can either plan appropriate interventions or make appropriate referrals.

Assessing and diagnosing are only two of several important functions carried out by community counselors. In the next chapter, we consider other counseling roles, including crisis intervention, primary prevention, advocacy, and program evaluation.

REFERENCES

Achenbach, T. M. (1991). *Manual for the Child Behavior Checklist/4-18 and 1991 profile.* Burlington: University of Vermont, Department of Psychiatry.

American Educational Research Association, American Psychological Association, and National Council on Measurement in Education. (1999). *Standards for educational and psychological testing* (2nd ed.). Washington, DC: American Educational Research Association.

American Psychiatric Association. (2000). *Diagnostic and statistical manual of mental disorders* (4th ed., text rev.). Washington, DC: Author.

Association for Assessment in Counseling. (2003, January). *Applying the Standards for Educational and Psychological Testing—What a Counselor Needs to Know.* Baltimore: Author.

Austin, J. T. (1994). Minnesota Multiphasic Personality Inventory (MMPI–2). *Measurement and Evaluation in Counseling and Development, 27,* 178–185.

Bacon, S. F., Collins, M. J., & Plake, E. V. (2002). Does the global assessment of functioning assess functioning? *Journal of Mental Health Counseling, 24,* 202–212.

Bubenzer, D. L., Zimpfer, D. G., & Mahrle, C. L. (1990). Standardized individual appraisal in agency and private practice: A survey. *Journal of Mental Health Counseling, 12,* 51–66.

Derogatis, L. R. (1994). *The SCL-90-R: Administration, scoring and procedures manual* (3rd ed.). Minneapolis, MN: NCS.

Fauman, M. A. (1994). *Study guide to DSM-IV.* Washington, DC: American Psychiatric Association.

Fong, M. L. (1995). Assessment and DSM-IV diagnosis of personality disorders: A primer for counselors. *Journal of Counseling and Development, 73,* 635–639.

Fong, M. L., & Silien, K. A. (1999). Assessment and diagnosis of DSM-IV anxiety disorders. *Journal of Counseling and Development, 77,* 209–217.

Goldman, L. (1990). Qualitative assessment. *The Counseling Psychologist, 18,* 205–213.

Hinkle, J. S. (1992). The mental status examination via computer: An evaluation of the mental status checklist computer report. *Measurement and Evaluation in Counseling and Development, 24,* 188–189.

Hohenshil, T. H. (1996). Role of assessment and diagnosis in counseling. *Journal of Counseling and Development, 75,* 64–67.

Hood, A. B., & Johnson, R. W. (2002). *Assessment in counseling: A guide to the use of psychological assessment procedures* (3rd ed.). Alexandria, VA: ACA.

Ivey, A. E., & Ivey, M. B. (1999). Toward a developmental diagnostic and statistical manual: The vitality of a contextual framework. *Journal of Counseling and Development, 77,* 484–490.

Laux, J. M. (2002). A primer on suicidology: Implications for counselors. *Journal of Counseling and Development, 80,* 380–383.

MacCluskie, K. C., & Ingersoll, R. E. (2001). *Becoming a 21st century agency counselor: Personal and professional explorations.* Belmont, CA: Wadsworth.

Maxmen, J. S., & Ward, N. G. (1995). *Essential psychopathology and its treatment* (2nd ed.). New York: Norton.

Myers, J. E., Sweeney, T. J., Witmer, J. M., & Hattie, J. H. (1998). *The Wellness Evaluation of Lifestyle—Form J.* Greensboro, NC: Author.

National Institute of Mental Health. (2000). Frequently asked questions about suicide. Retrieved June 25, 2002, from http://www.nimh.nih.gov/research/suicidefaq.cfm

National Institute of Mental Health. (2001). Depression research at the National Institute of Mental Health. Retrieved May 30, 2002, from http://www.nimh.nih.gov/publicat/depresfact.cfm

National Institute of Mental Health. (2002). NIMH suicide facts. Retrieved June 25, 2002, from http://www.nimh.nih.gov/research/suifact.htm

Paulson, B. L., & Worth, M. (2002). Counseling for suicide: Client perspectives. *Journal of Counseling and Development, 80,* 86–93.

Polanski, P. J., & Hinkle, J. S. (2000). The mental status examination: Its use by professional counselors. *Journal of Counseling and Development, 78,* 357–364.

Prediger, D. J. (1994). Multicultural assessment standards: Compilation for counselors. *Measurement and Evaluation in Counseling and Development, 27,* 68–73.

Rogers, J. R. (2001). Suicide risk assessment. In E. R. Welfel & R. E. Ingersoll (Eds.), *The mental health desk reference: A sourcebook for counselors and therapists* (pp. 259–264). New York: Wiley.

Rueth, T., Demmitt, A., & Burger, S. (1998, March). *Counselors and the DSM-IV: Intentional and unintentional consequences of diagnosis.* Paper presented at the American Counseling Association World Conference, Indianapolis, IN.

Seligman, L. (1996). *Diagnosis and treatment planning in counseling* (2nd ed.). New York: Plenum.

Seligman, L. (1999). Twenty years of diagnosis and the DSM. *Journal of Mental Health Counseling, 21,* 229–239.

Seligman, L. (2001). Diagnosis in counseling. In D. Capuzzi & D. R. Gross (Eds.), *Introduction to the counseling profession* (3rd ed., pp. 270–289). Needham Heights, MA: Allyn & Bacon.

Stelmachers, Z. T. (1995). Assessing suicidal clients. In J. N. Butcher (Ed.), *Clinical personality assessment: Practical approaches* (pp. 367–379). New York: Oxford University Press.

Suzuki, L. A., & Kugler, J. F. (2001). Multicultural assessment. In E. R. Welfel & R. E. Ingersoll (Eds.), *The mental health desk reference: A sourcebook for counselors and therapists* (pp. 279–286). New York: Wiley.

Trzepacz, P. T., & Baker, R. W. (1993). *The psychiatric mental status examination.* New York: Oxford University Press.

Vacc, N. A., & Juhnke, G. A. (1997). The use of structured clinical interviews for assessment in counseling. *Journal of Counseling and Development, 75,* 470–480.

Whiston, S. C. (2000). *Principles and applications of assessment in counseling.* Belmont, CA: Wadsworth.

White, V. E. (2002). Developing counseling objectives and empowering clients: A strength-based intervention. *Journal of Mental Health Counseling, 24,* 270–279.

Young, M. E. (2001). *Learning the art of helping: Building blocks and techniques* (2nd ed.). Upper Saddle River, NJ: Merrill/Prentice Hall.

CHAPTER 7

Essential Counseling Services: Crisis Intervention, Prevention, Advocacy, and Evaluation

She stands
  leaning on his outstretched arm
    sobbing awkwardly
Almost suspended between
  the air and his shoulder
    like a leaf being blown
      in the wind from a branch of a tree
        at the end of summer.
He tries to give her comfort
  offering soft words
    and patting her head.
"It's okay," he whispers
  realizing that as the words leave his mouth
    he is lying
And that their life together has collapsed
  like the South Tower of the World Trade Center
    that killed their only son.

Sam Gladding, *September 27th,* 2002.

I n Chapters 5 and 6, we focused primarily on individual counseling services: the counseling relationship, the counseling process, client assessment, and client diagnosis. Certainly, individual counseling is one of many important mental health services offered in community settings. Other essential services include crisis intervention, prevention programs, advocacy, and program evaluation. We begin this chapter by describing crisis intervention, which sometimes occurs with individual clients and other times is conducted with groups of people. We then focus on prevention, advocacy, and program evaluation—three key components of service delivery in community mental health organizations. Two other key services—group and family counseling—are discussed in the following two chapters.

Problems in living are an intrinsic part of life. Although the nature and intensity of problems faced by people vary, most individuals encounter crisis of some type during the course of their life journeys. Being able to work effectively with people facing crisis situations is a crucial counseling role. Therefore, in the first part of the chapter, we focus on the important service of crisis intervention.

Whereas crises may be inevitable and community counselors need to know how to intervene appropriately, a proactive mental health service that can help people manage crises more effectively and perhaps avoid certain crises altogether is prevention. Indeed, one of the defining characteristics of the counseling profession is an emphasis on preventing mental health problems by building on strengths and developing resources. Primary prevention strategies provide the most efficient way to promote mental health among large numbers of people; consequently, community counselors need to be skilled at designing and implementing prevention programs. In the second part of the chapter, we describe three prevention models and provide suggestions for implementing stress management programs.

Related to prevention is the service of advocacy, which steps outside the traditional role of counseling by focusing on injustices and environmental conditions that need to change for client welfare to be maximized (Kiselica & Robinson, 2001). The American Counseling Association (ACA) and other mental health organizations have made advocacy a priority in recent years. Advocates can engage in a spectrum of activities to address systemic needs, ranging from empowering clients to actively lobbying for social justice. Advocacy, both for clients and for the profession of counseling, has been described as a "professional imperative" (Myers, Sweeney, & White, 2002). Thus, in the third section of this chapter, we describe advocacy and outline skills and attributes needed to advocate successfully.

Although program evaluation is described at the end of the chapter, it does not occur only at the end of counseling service delivery. Instead, effective evaluation is an ongoing process that is integral to all aspects of community counseling programs, from start to finish. Ongoing, systemic, well-planned evaluation is a vital component of comprehensive community counseling programs. Evaluation enables counselors to make decisions about which services are effective and which need to be changed. It provides ways to ensure that services are being implemented as planned and that specific goals and outcomes are being met. Evaluation provides a way for counselors and community agencies to be accountable to clients, other professionals, accrediting agencies, and the community at large. We close the chapter with an overview of program evaluation, focusing on process and outcome evaluation as they relate to community counseling.

CRISIS INTERVENTION

During the past 2 decades, the need for crisis intervention services has increased significantly. One reason more services are needed is the recent upsurge of large-scale violent acts occurring in the United States, as evidenced by the terrorist attacks on New York City and Washington, DC, in 2001; the 1999 shootings at Columbine High School; and the 1995 bombing of the Federal Building in Oklahoma City, to name just a few of the more publicized catastrophic events. Violent acts occur "with such frequency and indiscriminateness that no one can consider him- or herself safe" (Myer, 2001, p. 3). Other disasters, including earthquakes, floods, fires, hurricanes, and tornadoes, result in tragic losses of lives and homes. Automobile and plane accidents, injury, illness, and disease can have devastating effects on victims and their families.

Experiences of violence, disaster, and any form of trauma can leave people without the sufficient resources needed for coping. In such cases, crisis intervention services are needed. Crises may affect a large group of people, as with the September 11 terrorist attacks, or be more personal in nature, as evidenced when individuals threaten suicide. When people experience a crisis situation, either within their communities or intrapersonally, finding ways to resolve the crisis effectively is essential to mental health and well-being.

Definition of Crisis

Box 7–1

> When written in Chinese, the word crisis is composed of two characters. One represents danger and the other represents opportunity.
>
> —John F. Kennedy

Before discussing crisis intervention services, it is important to clarify what is meant by the term *crisis*. Many definitions have been proposed, including:

- Crisis is a perception or experiencing of an event or situation as an intolerable difficulty that exceeds the person's current resources and coping mechanisms. Unless the person obtains relief, the crisis has the potential to cause severe affective, behavioral, and cognitive malfunctioning. (James & Gilliland, 2001, p. 3)
- Crises are personal difficulties or situations that immobilize people and prevent them from consciously controlling their lives. (Belkin, 1984, p. 424)

- Crisis is a state of disorganization in which people face frustration of important life goals or profound disruption of their life cycles and methods of coping with stressors. The term *crisis* usually refers to a person's feelings of fear, shock, and distress *about* the disruption, not to the disruption itself. (Brammer, 1985, p. 94)
- A crisis is a critical phase in a person's life when his or her normal ways of dealing with the world are suddenly interrupted. (Lewis, Lewis, Daniels, & D'Andrea, 2003, p. 117)

The concept of crisis is not simple or straightforward. Although a single event may precipitate a crisis, a combination of personal traits, environmental factors, and interpersonal support systems affect the manner in which the event is perceived and managed. An event that is perceived as relatively minor by one individual, such as failing a final examination, may be perceived as a crisis by someone else. Also, the timing, intensity, and number of other stressors the person is experiencing can impact the complexity of the crisis situation.

James and Gilliland (2001, pp. 5–6) emphasized the importance of distinguishing between different types of crises. Building on the research of other crisis specialists, they described four crisis domains:

1. *Developmental Crises.* Developmental crises occur during the normal flow of human growth and maturation. As people move through different developmental stages in their lives, they may experience crisis during certain changes or shifts. For example, a developmental crisis may occur when the last child leaves home or when a person retires. When the event corresponds to culturally accepted patterns and timetables, it is less likely to be experienced as a crisis than when it does not (e.g., teenage pregnancy or forced early retirement) (Myer, 2001).

2. *Situational Crises.* A situational crisis occurs when an unexpected, extraordinary event occurs that the person had no way of anticipating or controlling. Examples include automobile accident, rape, job loss, sudden illness, and death of a loved one. A situational crisis is "random, sudden, shocking, intense, and often catastrophic" (James & Gilliland, 2001, p. 5).

3. *Existential Crises.* An existential crisis is equated with intense, pervasive inner conflict and anxiety associated with the existential issues of purpose, meaning, responsibility, freedom, and commitment. At times, existential crises are precipitated by *nonevents,* such as realizing that one is never going to have children or make a significant difference in a particular field of work.

4. *Environmental Crises.* Environmental crises refer to natural or human-caused disasters that overtake a person or group of people who "find themselves, through no fault or action of their own, inundated in the aftermath of an event that may adversely affect virtually every member of the environment in which they live" (James & Gilliland, p. 6). In many ways, environmental crises are situational crises that have widespread ramifications. The terrorist attacks of September 11, 2001, exemplify a human-caused environmental crisis with wide-reaching effects.

Although crises represent highly stressful and disruptive situations, they do not imply mental illness (Lewis et al., 2003). The period of crisis is time limited, usually lasting no longer than 6 to 8 weeks, after which the major symptoms of distress diminish (Janoski, 1984). However, crises can have long-term physical and psychological outcomes, depending on how the crisis is resolved (James & Gilliland, 2001). In many instances, crisis intervention services are needed to help people resolve crises in ways that will prevent negative outcomes in the future.

Unresolved trauma can, in some instances, lead to the development of posttraumatic stress disorder (PTSD). With PTSD, the trauma lasts in an individual's mind long after the event itself has passed. People with PTSD may exhibit a number of symptoms, including reexperiencing the traumatic event through flashbacks, avoidance of trauma-related activities, emotional numbing, and a range of coexisting disorders (e.g., substance abuse, obsessive–compulsive disorder, and panic disorders) (American Psychiatric Association [APA], 2000). Counselors who work with PTSD clients need specialized training in empirically validated treatments to help reduce the impact of the trauma and improve functioning.

In contrast, when people experiencing crisis do manage to resolve their cognitive, affective, and behavioral reactions effectively, they can change and grow in a positive manner (James & Gilliland, 2001). As noted by Aguilera and Messick (1982):

> The Chinese characters that represent the word "crisis" mean both danger and opportunity. Crisis is a danger because it threatens to overwhelm the individual and may result in suicide or a psychotic break. It is also an opportunity because during times of crises, individuals are more receptive to therapeutic influence. Therefore, prompt and skillful intervention may not only prevent the development of a serious long-term disability but may allow new coping patterns to emerge that can help the individual function at a higher level of equilibrium than before the crisis. (p. 1)

Definition of Crisis Intervention

Crisis intervention differs from traditional counseling in that it is a "time-limited treatment directed at reactions to a specific event in order to help the client return to a precrisis level of functioning" (Myer, 2001, p. 5). It is an action-oriented approach used to help clients cope with a particular life situation that has thrown them off course. According to the National Organization for Victim Assistance (NOVA), goals of crisis response include helping the client defuse emotions, rearrange cognitive process, organize and interpret what has happened, integrate the traumatic event into his or her life story, and interpret the traumatic event in a way that is meaningful (Bauer, 2001).

Crisis intervention, also called *crisis management,* typically does not last longer than 6 weeks and may even be much briefer (Myer, 2001). It is not to be confused with more long-term postcrisis counseling, which can include the treatment of posttraumatic stress disorder (PTSD). Postcrisis counseling is another important mental health service, but it is not the focus of this section.

Because crisis intervention differs from traditional counseling, community counselors need to be trained to intervene effectively in crisis situations. The overview of crisis intervention provided in this section is not designed to be exhaustive, nor will it sufficiently prepare counselors to become crisis workers. However, it is important to be knowledgeable about specific strategies and skills associated with crisis management. To that end, we review the six-step model of crisis intervention presented by James and Gilliland (2001). The model, which is depicted in Figure 7–1, has been used successfully by professionals and trained lay workers to help people cope with many different types of crises.

As can be seen in Figure 7–1, three primary counselor functions are carried out at various stages of crisis intervention: (a) assessment, which occurs throughout crisis intervention; (b) listening, which is especially important during Steps 1, 2, and 3; and (c) acting, which varies in degrees of directiveness and occurs primarily during Steps 4, 5, and 6. Because assessment occurs throughout the intervention process and is the key to effective intervention, we address that topic first.

Crisis Assessment

The first step in crisis intervention is to assess the nature of the crisis. The purpose of crisis assessment is to provide information about (a) the severity of the crisis; (b) the client's current emotional, behavioral, and cognitive status; (c) the coping mechanisms, support systems, and additional resources available to the client; and (d) whether the client is of danger to self and others (James & Gilliland, 2001).

One method of crisis assessment that provides an efficient model for obtaining information about the severity of the crisis and the client's range of responses is the Triage Assessment Model (Myer, Williams, Ottens, & Schmidt, 1992). The model provides a framework for assessing a client's reactions in three domains: affective, behavioral, and cognitive (ABC). Each domain is composed of three categories of reactions that represent the range of responses clients typically experience in crisis situations. To use the model effectively with diverse populations, counselors need to be sensitive to cultural differences, recognizing that reactions may have different meanings in certain cultures (Myer, 2001).

- Responses in the *affective domain* include anger/hostility, anxiety/fear, and sadness/melancholy. Clients are assessed to determine which of these emotions is being experienced by the client and which appears to be dominant. People in crisis may be experiencing intense emotions and may scream or sob uncontrollably (Myer, 2001). At the other extreme, clients may appear emotionally numb, withdrawn, or shut down. Impaired emotional expression is an indication of the disequilibrium that usually accompanies crisis experiences. Counselors can help reestablish equilibrium by demonstrating empathy and using reflective listening skills to validate feelings.
- Responses in the *cognitive domain* include client perceptions of transgression (i.e., violation), threat, and loss. According to Myer (2001), perception of transgression is focused on the present (what is happening now, during the crisis). Perception of threat is future oriented, and perceptions of loss are focused on the past (recognizing that something is irrevocably gone). Perceptions may occur in any of several life dimensions: (a) physical, (b) psychological, (c) social relationships, and (d) moral/spiritual.
- Reactions in the *behavioral domain* are approach, avoidance, and immobility. Clients usually adopt one of the three behaviors in reacting to the crisis. When clients try to implement strategies to address the crisis event, they are using *approach* behaviors. *Avoidance* behaviors are those by which the client tries to ignore, deny, or

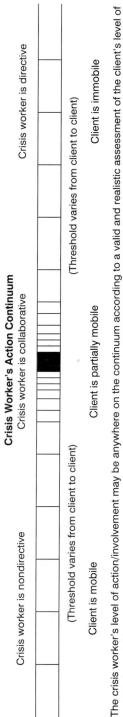

ASSESSING:

Overarching, continuous, and dynamically ongoing throughout the crisis; evaluating the client's present and past situational crises in terms of the client's ability to cope, personal threat, mobility or immobility, and making a judgment regarding type of action needed by the crisis worker. (See crisis worker's action continuum, below.)

Listening

LISTENING: Attending, observing, understanding, and responding with empathy, genuineness, respect, acceptance, nonjudgment, and caring.

1. *Define the problem.* Explore and define the problem from the client's point of view. Use active listening, including open-ended questions. Attend to both verbal and nonverbal messages of the client.

2. *Ensure client safety.* Assess lethality, criticality, immobility, or seriousness of threat to the client's physical and psychological safety. Assess both the client's internal events and the situation surrounding the client, and, if necessary, ensure that the client is made aware of alternatives to impulsive, self-destructive actions.

3. *Provide support.* Communicate to the client that the crisis worker is a valid support person. Demonstrate (by words, voice, and body language) a caring, positive, nonpossessive, nonjudgmental, acceptant, personal involvement with the client.

Acting

ACTING: Becoming involved in the intervention at a nondirective, collaborative, or directive level, according to the assessed needs of the client and the availability of environmental supports.

4. *Examine alternatives.* Assist client in exploring the choices he or she has available to him or her now. Facilitate a search for immediate situational supports, coping mechanisms, and positive thinking.

5. *Make plans.* Assist client in developing a realistic short-term plan that identifies additional resources and provides coping mechanisms —definite action steps that the client can own and comprehend.

6. *Obtain commitment.* Help client commit himself or herself to definite, positive action steps that the client can own and realistically accomplish or accept.

Crisis Worker's Action Continuum

| Crisis worker is nondirective | Crisis worker is collaborative | Crisis worker is directive |

(Threshold varies from client to client)   (Threshold varies from client to client)

Client is mobile   Client is partially mobile   Client is immobile

The crisis worker's level of action/involvement may be anywhere on the continuum according to a valid and realistic assessment of the client's level of mobility/immobility.

Figure 7–1

The six-step model of crisis intervention

Source: From *Crisis Intervention Strategies* (4th ed.), by R. K. James and B. E. Gilliland, © 2001. Reprinted with permission of Wadsworth, a division of Thomson Learning: www.thomsonrights.com. Fax 800 730-2215.

escape the crisis event. *Immobility* refers to a set of behaviors characterized by nonproductive, disorganized, or self-defeating attempts to cope with the crisis. Behavioral reactions may be constructive or maladaptive. To determine the helpfulness or harmfulness of the response, counselors can evaluate the potential outcome of the reaction by asking themselves, "Will the behavior aid or hinder the resolution of the crisis?" (Myer, 2001).

• During the assessment process, counselors need to be alert to any possibility of suicidal or homicidal ideation. Usually, the potential for violent reactions increases when the client's responses are intense or extreme. If a counselor has reason to believe that a client is a danger to self or others, he or she needs to assess the situation to determine *intent* (whether immediate or future), *availability of means, lethality of means,* and *whether there is a definite plan.* (See Chapter 6 for a more complete description of suicide assessment and intervention.)

When assessing each of the three domains, the counselor must determine not only the client's predominant response in each category but also the severity of the reactions on each scale. Myer (2001) suggests that crisis intervention should focus initially on the client's most severe reaction, realizing that the intensity of responses varies throughout the crisis experience, so continued assessment, flexibility, and adaptation are needed.

As stated earlier, assessment takes place throughout the crisis intervention process. Two other counselor functions that occur during crisis intervention are *listening* and *acting*. To explain how these functions are enacted, we next describe James and Gilliland's (2001) *six-step model of crisis intervention.*

Six-Step Model of Crisis Intervention

Step 1: Defining the Problem. The first step in James and Gilliland's (2001) model is to "define and understand the problem from the client's point of view" (p. 33). Core counseling skills, which include empathy, genuineness, and unconditional positive regard, are essential to this step of intervention. Giving the client a chance to tell his or her story not only helps with assessment but also helps the client "turn down the volume" of powerful feelings and reengage cognitive processes (Bauer, 2001). An important purpose of crisis intervention is to help clients take steps toward stabilizing emotionally and reengaging cognitively.

Box 7–2

Human beings are not wired to think after a crisis; we are wired to act and react. Unfortunately, many important decisions must be made and problems solved in postcrisis moments. Poor choices can complicate and increase the painful impact of surviving a tragedy. The sooner survivors have access to relatively clear thinking, the sooner they can begin making thoughtful decisions. Crisis responders facilitate this reconnection to thinking by helping survivors turn their experience from jumbled fragments into a coherent story.

—(Bauer, 2001, p. 242)

Step 2: Ensuring Client Safety.   Ensuring client safety means "minimizing the physical and psychological danger to self and others" (James & Gilliland, 2001, p. 33). Throughout crisis intervention, keeping clients safe must be of primary concern. Both the external environment and the client's internal processing of events need to be taken into account. Specific ways to assess the lethality of suicidal clients and provide for their safety are described in Chapter 6.

Step 3: Providing Support.   Through words, actions, and body language, the counselor needs to convey to the client genuine caring and support. It is not sufficient for the counselor to simply think he or she is being supportive. Rather, a key goal is to find ways to ensure that *the client perceives the counselor* as supportive, nonjudgmental, and involved.

Step 4: Examining Alternatives.   The next three steps of crisis intervention involve the use of strategies to help clients make appropriate choices and restore equilibrium. In Step 4 of the model, the counselor helps the client explore a range of options and alternatives. Part of the exploration includes encouraging the client to identify available support sources and coping mechanisms. Identifying resources and coping mechanisms and exercising constructive thinking patterns can help lessen clients' stress and anxiety (James & Gilliland, 2001).

Step 5: Making Plans.   This step is the logical follow-up to Step 4. Clients are encouraged to select from the different alternatives that were explored and then make specific plans for implementing the selected option. In this step, it is important for the counselor to work collaboratively with the client, thereby supporting his or her independence, power, and self-respect. Clients need an opportunity to restore their personal sense of control, which often is severely shaken in crisis situations.

Step 6: Obtaining Commitment.   In this step, the counselor encourages commitment to definite positive action steps that will help the client move toward precrisis equilibrium (James & Gilliland, 2001). It is important for action steps to be uncomplicated and clearly articulated, thereby increasing the probability of their being enacted. It also is essential to make plans for follow-up with the client. Depending on the situation, follow-up may include ongoing counseling or a referral to an appropriate source for continued assistance.

The six-step model provided by James and Gilliland (2001) presents an organized framework to guide counselors in crisis intervention. It provides a way to help manage the emerging feelings, concerns, and situations that clients experiencing trauma might present. Throughout the crisis intervention process, counselors assess the person and the situation to ensure that the client is safe, evaluate resources, and make decisions about how to intervene most effectively. Counselors use effective listening, communication, and problem-solving skills to help clients in crisis regain equilibrium, make sense of their situation, and resolve the crisis in a healthy manner.

Reflections on Counseling After Crisis

Crisis intervention is demanding, intensive work that requires specific skills, attributes, and attitudes on the part of the counselor. Prolonged exposure to clients who have experienced tragedy can lead to *compassion fatigue,* or *secondary traumatization* (James & Gilliland, 2001). Finding ways to prevent compassion fatigue or burnout are critical if counselors are going to provide crisis services effectively.

Box 7–3

After the September 11 terrorist attacks, I (Gladding) was asked to go to New York to work as a "mental health technician" for the American Red Cross. For a week, I worked at the Family Assistance Center on Pier 94. There I saw survivors of the tragedy and worked with them to help process the wide range of feelings—from denial to grief—that they felt. My job was to assist individuals in making applications for death certificates of their loved ones. I was an escort who walked with families from the front of the building to the back and talked with them about what they were feeling, what they had felt, or what they were doing in regard to the emotions that would be coming. I also accompanied families to Ground Zero so they could see for themselves the horror and finality of the event. The view of the site helped many individuals begin the process of grieving in depth as they realized in a stark and striking way that those they had loved and cherished in so many ways were indeed dead and would not be coming back to be with them.

From these experiences and other related incidents, I learned a great deal more than I ever anticipated about the nature of counseling, clients, and even myself. The lessons I learned have some universal application for persons who enter almost any crisis situation. They are especially applicable to crises that may seem on the surface overwhelming. In the midst of working with people who are in a crisis, counselors need to make sure they:

- Are mentally healthy to begin with
- Interact in positive and professional ways with colleagues
- Stay flexible and prepare for the unexpected
- Find out about resources and support personnel in the community to whom they can make referrals
- Realize the power of small acts of kindness, such as a sympathetic word
- Be mindful of the influence of nonverbal actions that lend support to those in need, from giving them tissues to offering them symbols of comfort
- Take care of themselves through physical exercise, keeping a journal, taking in needed nourishment, and debriefing regularly

Counseling after a crisis is a time filled with heavy emotion. It is a time of opportunity as well as one of turmoil. It demands much of counselors. Knowing what to expect can make the experience both positive and productive. The lessons I took away from my experiences in New York can be applied to many types of crisis situations—both large-scale community trauma and individualized, personal crisis events.

Because of the unique nature of crisis intervention, counselors who intend to work as crisis responders are encouraged to participate in disaster training, such as that offered by the American Red Cross and the National Organization for Victim

Assistance (NOVA). Through specialized training, accompanied by personal and professional competence, counselors can make a positive difference in the lives of people experiencing crisis.

Whereas crises are, to some extent, a part of life, the manner in which people cope with crises and other stressors depends largely on their ability to access resources and personal strengths. Proactive, preventive actions can lead to the avoidance of some crises altogether and build resilience in people so that unavoidable crises are managed more effectively. In the next section, we focus on the essential community counseling service of prevention.

PREVENTION

Definition of Prevention

A primary philosophical emphasis throughout the history of the counseling profession has been on preventing psychological distress by building on strengths and facilitating healthy development. The term *prevention,* however, is somewhat ambiguous, and professionals in mental health fields have struggled with its definition (Romano & Hage, 2000). The literal definition of prevention is to stop something from happening (e.g., cancer, depression, or teenage pregnancy). Gerald Caplan added to this definition as early as 1964 by differentiating among three types of prevention: *primary, secondary,* and *tertiary. Primary prevention* occurs "before the fact" and refers to prevention efforts that attempt to reduce the number of new occurrences of a disorder. The goal of primary prevention is to keep healthy people healthy by increasing environmental resources or bolstering personal competencies (Scileppi, Teed, & Torres, 2000). *Secondary prevention* is targeted toward people at risk of developing a mental health problem or who are exhibiting early symptoms of a disorder. The goal is to work with these individuals to forestall or alleviate problems before they become more severe. *Tertiary prevention* refers to efforts aimed at reducing the debilitating effects of an existing disorder. Tertiary prevention can also be conceptualized as treatment, remediation, or reactive intervention.

Box 7–4

Thus, a preventive perspective is not concerned with pathology but with health. It is not focused on reparation of existing problems but on helping people and human systems to avoid problems in living and more intractable dysfunctions. It is directed at larger numbers of people, not at individuals taken one at a time. And, it embraces an ecological, multicultural, systemic approach to help giving.

—(Conyne, 2000, p. 840)

Although the lines differentiating among the three types of prevention are not always distinct, in this section we focus on primary prevention and its implementation. Primary prevention can include doing something in the present to prevent something undesirable from happening in the future, or doing something in the present that will permit or increase desirable outcomes in the future (Albee & Ryan-Finn, 1993). The following descriptions provide clarification about the nature of primary prevention (Conyne, 2000, p. 840):

- Primary prevention is intended to decrease the incidences of new cases of any designated disorder.
- Primary prevention occurs through intentionally and collaboratively planned programs that are comprehensive, multilevel, multimethod, and interdisciplinary.
- Primary prevention programs are designed and implemented from a contextual, ecological perspective, taking into account multicultural and societal variables.
- Primary prevention is conducted to reduce risk factors (e.g., stressors, exploitation) while building protective factors (e.g., self-esteem, career aspirations).
- Primary prevention results in an empowered concordance between people and systems. Efforts are made to help make the person–environmental fit more satisfying, effective, and productive.

Primary prevention promotes healthy lifestyles by introducing preventive maneuvers that reduce the chances that a health problem will occur (Kaplan, 2000). It involves reducing negative influences, such as toxic lifestyles and environments, and strengthening resistance to stress through the development of coping skills, interpersonal skills, intrapersonal strengths, and support systems. Prevention may involve direct services, aimed at helping people build competencies, and indirect services, targeted toward changing specific environmental factors (Lewis et al., 2003).

Rationale for Prevention

Box 7–5

Comprehensive models of prevention must legitimize indirect services that enhance the lives of our client populations.

—(Vera, 2000, p. 835)

Prevention provides the most efficient way of helping promote mental health among the largest number of people. Whereas unquestionably there will continue to be a need for reactive interventions—individuals will continue to experience emotional distress and direct counseling may be needed to help alleviate that distress—greater emphasis on proactive, primary prevention provides opportunities to reach more people before distress is experienced. Albee (2000) argues for increased attention to major preventive efforts for these reasons:

The data are clear: At least a third of the population of the United States suffers debilitating emotional distress, yet the overwhelming majority of publications, public information, volunteer citizen's groups, news releases, presidential commissions, White House conferences, and so forth focus on individual treatment. To me, this whole situation is a flagrant example of denial. We have pitifully few resources with which to offer one-to-one treatment, yet we deny the importance of primary prevention. And too often when we discuss prevention, it is in terms of small-scale educational or inspirational programs, not major efforts. (p. 846)

Primary prevention is time efficient and cost efficient. It also is consistent with the bioecological approach to community counseling outlined in Chapter 2. When primary prevention efforts are targeted toward the proximal and distal environments in which people live and work, the likelihood of promoting mental health among individuals, communities, and the society at large is enhanced.

Although the need for prevention is theoretically at the core of professional counseling, there has been a general resistance to implementing large-scale prevention efforts (Lewis et al., 2003). To illustrate, surveys of mental health journals (e.g., the *Journal of Mental Health Counseling*) reveal that considerably more attention is devoted to treatment of conditions than to preventive counseling (Kiselica & Look, 1993; Kleist, 1999). Several factors contribute to this resistance. First, only small portions of budgets for mental health services are allocated for prevention programs (Scileppi et al., 2000). Monetary resources are limited, and from a political perspective, it is difficult to divert scarce resources from people who are already suffering from mental disorders. Similarly, most third-party reimbursement is based on a medical diagnosis and typically does not cover preventive interventions (Myers, 1992). Also, it has been noted that many training programs for counselors and other mental health workers do not offer specific courses on preventive interventions (Kleist, 1999). Consequently, even though strong arguments have been made for primary prevention, agencies may lack the funds and mental health workers may lack the knowledge and skills needed to implement comprehensive preventive programs (Romano & Hage, 2000).

Many scholars and practitioners have called for a renewed emphasis on prevention among counseling professionals (e.g., Albee, 2000; Conyne, 2000; Kleist, 1999; Romano & Hage, 2000). Prevention outcome research provides strong evidence that prevention is "a highly effective strategy for enhancing the quality of mental health in the community" (Scileppi et al., 2000, p. 80). Prevention efforts targeted toward wellness, health promotion, and resiliency can help people circumvent avoidable problems of living and navigate the unavoidable problems more effectively. For prevention programs to be successful, they need to be well designed, skillfully implemented, targeted toward a specific population and/or setting, and culturally sensitive. It also is important, after implementation, to evaluate their effectiveness (Conyne, 1991).

Prevention Models

Various models of effective primary prevention have been described in prevention literature. One such model is Bloom's (1996) *configural equation* of prevention, which focuses on three broad dimensions. Prevention efforts can be directed toward:

a. Increasing individual strengths and decreasing individual limitations (e.g., enhancing self-efficacy or teaching stress-reduction techniques)
b. Increasing social supports and decreasing social stresses (e.g., promoting self-help groups or drug information hotlines)

$$\text{Psychological health} = \frac{\text{Coping Skills} + \text{Self-Esteem} + \text{Social Support} + \text{Personal Power}}{\text{Organic Factors} + \text{Stress} + \text{Powerlessness}}$$

Figure 7–2
An equation for psychological health

   c. Enhancing environmental resources (e.g., community programs) and minimizing environmental pressures (e.g., targeting poverty, providing services
following natural disasters)

Albee's *incidence formula* (Albee & Gullotta, 1997) provides another way to
conceptualize the prevention of psychological difficulties. The incidence formula
model emphasizes the need to bolster people's coping skills, self-esteem, and support systems. Prevention strategies also can be directed at reducing negative effects
of certain biological conditions (e.g., predispositions to physical and mental conditions) and environmental stress. Lewis et al. (2003) adapted Albee's original formula,
adding the variables of *personal power* and *powerlessness*. The adapted formula is
depicted in Figure 7–2.

   Preventive programs designed to increase personal attributes, skills, and support
and decrease external and internal stressors may be directed toward individuals
and/or the environments in which they live and work. Strategies to increase personal
power and decrease powerlessness may involve systemic interventions directed at
unjust social conditions, which we describe later in the section on advocacy.

Wheel of Wellness model.   In Chapter 4 we described the renewed focus the counseling profession has placed on wellness, based on the assumption that optimal
growth involves an active concentration on developing the body, mind, and spirit so
that optimum health and well-being are achieved (Myers, Sweeney, & Witmer, 2000).
A holistic model of wellness and prevention was presented originally by Sweeney
and Witmer (1991) and Witmer and Sweeney (1992). Guided by research and clinical
practice, Myers et al. (2000) modified the original model to include additional characteristics associated with healthy people. The modified wellness model is depicted
in Figure 7–3.

   As can be seen in the diagram, the wheel consists of five major life tasks:
spirituality, self-direction, work and leisure, friendship, and *love.* Twelve subtasks
associated with the five major tasks are listed in the spokes of the wheel: *sense of
worth, sense of control, realistic beliefs, emotional awareness and coping, problem
solving and creativity, sense of humor, nutrition, exercise, self-care, stress management, gender identity,* and *cultural identity*. Life tasks are influenced by life forces,
including family, community, education, religion, and government. Life forces and
life tasks are influenced by external global factors, both natural (e.g., catastrophic
events) and human (e.g., war) (Myers et al., 2000).

Figure 7–3

The Wheel of Wellness

Note. From *The Wheel of Wellness*
(p. 10), by J. M. Witmer, T. J. Sweeney,
and J. E. Myers, 1998, Greensboro, NC:
Authors. Copyright 1998 by Witmer et
al. Reprinted with permission.

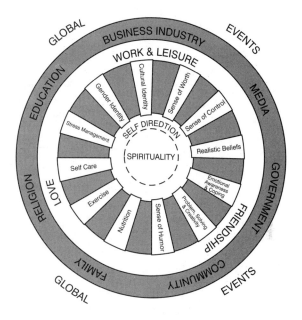

The Wheel of Wellness model can be used to guide the planning of prevention programs as well as counseling interventions. Myers et al. (2000) suggest a four-stage implementation of the model, which includes:

1. *Introduction of the Wheel of Wellness Model.* Wellness is defined, the model is introduced, and the connection between healthy living and overall well-being is described.

2. *Informal and/or Formal Assessment of Wellness.* Informal assessment of wellness involves asking people to rate their overall wellness on each dimension, on a scale of 1 to 10, with 10 representing a very high level of wellness. If a more formal method of assessment is preferred, counselors can administer the Wellness Evaluation of Lifestyle (WEL) (Myers & Sweeney, 1999; Hattie, Myers, & Sweeney, in press).

3. *Intentional Interventions to Enhance Wellness.* This step can be conducted individually when designing counseling interventions. When designing prevention programs, counselors can use the information gained from the initial assessment to determine which areas of focus might benefit the most people and then design programs accordingly. For example, if stress management appears to be an area that needs attention, counselors can implement a stress management program, such as the one that is described in the next section.

4. *Evaluation and Follow-Up.* Plans for evaluation and follow-up need to accompany whatever prevention strategy is implemented. Counselors can help participants identify markers of change to indicate short- and long-term goal accomplishment and to evaluate the overall success of the program.

During the time this text was written, Myers and Sweeney (2003) were in the process of publishing new, evidence-based research about their wellness model. The new model, called the Indivisible Self (IS-WEL), addresses individual and contextual factors that are grounded in Adlerian theory. Interested readers are encouraged to examine current literature describing the IS-WEL model.

General prevention models, including those constructed by Bloom (1996), Albee and Gullotta (1997), and Myers et al. (2000), serve as road maps for guiding the development of prevention programs. Although each model is distinct, the three share common characteristics, including a holistic emphasis that takes into account individual and environmental factors. Guided by these or other models, counselors will want to design prevention strategies based on the specific needs of the populations with which they are working.

Examples of exemplary prevention programs are numerous. One source that describes effective primary prevention programs is *14 Ounces of Prevention: A Casebook for Practitioners* (Price, Cowen, Lorion, & Ramos-McKay, 1988). Efficacious prevention programs have been implemented with preschoolers, children, adolescents, and adults. Many of the programs directed toward children and youth focus on life skills, such as interpersonal communication, problem solving and decision making, physical fitness and health maintenance, and identity development (e.g., Darden, Gazda, & Ginter, 1996; Ginter, 1999). Prevention programs for adults also address life skills, with some programs geared toward specific concerns, such as eating disorders, violence, parenting, and stress management. Because everyone suffers from physical and emotional stress of some nature, stress management is an especially important area to consider when designing prevention programs. Stress management programs can be adapted for all ages and provide a variety of physical and mental health benefits. For these reasons, a brief overview of stress, coping, and stress management is provided next.

Stress Management

The relationship among stress, coping, and well-being has received much attention during the past several decades (Romano, 2001). *Stress* is a construct that has been defined in multiple ways. It can be viewed as a relationship between the events that happen to us and our physical, cognitive, emotional, and behavioral responses to them (McNamara, 2000). Stress can refer to an internal state, an external event, or the interaction between a person and the environment. A more formal definition, offered by Lazarus and Folkman (1984), describes stress as "a particular relationship between the person and the environment that is appraised by the person as taxing or exceeding his or her resources and endangering his or her well-being" (p. 19). Perceptions of what is stressful vary widely among individuals, with some people viewing certain events as quite stressful and others being nonplussed by them.

Anything perceived as a source of threat, harm, loss, or challenge has the potential to be stressful. Stressors may be chronic (e.g., living in poverty), acute (e.g., death of a spouse), or ongoing daily aggravations (e.g., arguing between siblings). Exposure to stress triggers several physical, emotional, and cognitive changes. Immediate, short-term reactions to stress can potentially motivate people toward action; however, long-term exposure can lead to physical and psychosocial difficulties (Sharrer & Ryan-Wenger, 2002). Coping with stress is the process by which a person handles stressful situations and the thoughts and emotions they generate.

Prevention programs to help people manage stress effectively typically focus on (a) identifying sources of stress, (b) recognizing the physical and emotional consequences of stress, and (c) learning and implementing adaptive coping responses. McNamara (2000) suggests that counselors include the following eight components in stress management programs:

1. *Education about the causes and consequences of stress.* This includes helping people recognize sources of stress in their own lives and their cognitive, physical, and emotional responses to stress.
2. *Training in methods to reduce psychological and physical arousal.* Counselors can use deep breathing and relaxation exercises to help people reduce their reactions to stress.
3. *General problem-solving and decision-making skills.* Helping people construct a model for problem solving and decision making can help establish a healthy sense of control.
4. *General cognitive skills.* Cognitive restructuring, including reducing negative or catastrophic thinking, can also provide a sense of control that helps reduce stress.
5. *Physical ways of coping with stress.* Nutrition, physical activity, and sleep quality all impact people's psychological well-being. Developing and practicing good habits in each of these areas can help reduce stress.
6. *Time management.* Time management tools are essential for handling stress effectively. Setting achievable goals, balancing work and leisure, and organizing tasks are examples of time management tools. Additional examples are listed in Figure 7–4.

• Clarify your goals.	What is the most important and why?
• Avoid procrastination.	Establish a routine and reward yourself for completing tasks.
• Keep a calendar or day-timer.	Write down meetings, scheduled events, assignments, etc.
• Break down large tasks into manageable units.	Make plans for completing each unit.
• Keep a daily and weekly "to do" list.	Prioritize activities and tasks and check them off when they are completed.
• Recognize the need for balance and flexibility.	Include breaks and recreational times that coincide with your body clock.
• Keep things in perspective.	Worry saps time and energy and is nonproductive. If you find yourself getting anxious, take time to relax and practice deep breathing.

Figure 7–4
Time management tools

7. *Skills for increasing self-control and self-esteem.* Anger management skills can be taught to facilitate self-control. Counselors also can help people identify and develop personal strengths, thus building resilience.

8. *Social skills.* Social skills training includes effective communication, conflict resolution, and assertiveness training.

Stress management programs are often implemented in schools, work settings, universities, and community agencies. It is important for community counselors to be able to plan, implement, and evaluate stress management programs for the populations with which they work.

Many chronic stressors, including poverty, discrimination, and prejudice, are systemic in nature and need to be addressed accordingly. Albee (2000) states, "The longer I work in the field of prevention, the more convinced I become that economic, social-class variables are most important in perpetuating stress, social injustice, and exploitation" (p. 850). Lewis et al. (2003) collectively refer to individuals who experience a similar kind of stress for an extended time as *vulnerable populations.* Examples of vulnerable populations include people who are poor, homeless, and unemployed; families undergoing divorce; pregnant teenagers; people with chronic diseases such as AIDS; and people victimized by discrimination. To address the needs of vulnerable populations, counselors are urged to engage in advocacy, outreach, and social action, which are described next.

ADVOCACY

Box 7–6

Advocacy is an important aspect of every counselor's role. Regardless of the particular setting in which he or she works, each counselor is confronted again and again with issues that cannot be resolved simply through change within the individual. All too often, negative aspects of the environment impinge on a client's well-being, intensifying personal problems or creating obstacles to growth. When such situations arise, effective counselors speak up!

—(Lewis & Bradley, 2000, p. 3)

The 1999 Presidential Theme for the American Counseling Association was *Advocacy: A Voice for Our Clients and Communities.* During recent years, much attention has been directed toward the advocacy role of counselors. Advocacy counseling expands the traditional role of individual counseling, which focuses on intrapersonal concerns, to a broader focus that addresses injustices and environmental conditions that need to improve for the benefit of an individual or group (Kiselica & Robinson, 2001). In this section, we define advocacy as it relates to community counseling and discuss roles counselors can take to advocate for their clients.

What Is Advocacy?

Several definitions of advocacy have been proposed. For example, Toporek (2000) defines *advocacy* as actions taken by counseling professionals to help remove environmental barriers that hamper clients' well-being. Ezell (2001) describes advocacy as "purposive efforts to change specific existing or proposed policies or practices on behalf of or with a specific client or group of clients" (p. 23). Lewis et al. (2003) note that advocacy serves two purposes: (a) to increase clients' sense of personal power and (b) to foster environmental changes that reflect greater responsiveness to clients' personal needs.

Outreach, empowerment, social action, and *social justice* are all terms associated with advocacy. *Outreach* refers to initiating behaviors toward people in need for the purpose of making a helpful difference. It involves reaching out to vulnerable populations in their communities and helping them find new ways to cope with stressors (Lewis et al., 2003). *Empowerment* is a process through which clients gain the resources and skills needed to have more control over their environments and their lives (McWhirter, 1997). *Social action* refers to actions taken to reduce problems such as poverty, inequalities, and prejudice (Lee, 1998). *Social justice* involves taking action to eradicate oppressive systems of power and privileges (Counselors for Social Justice, 2002). Oppression occurs when power is used to limit or obstruct vulnerable groups' access to basic societal rights, a topic that is discussed in more depth in Chapter 10. Advocacy counseling can include outreach, empowerment, social action, and promoting social justice. Advocacy serves to enhance a client's sense of personal power and/or foster change in the broader sociopolitical environment.

As noted earlier, empowering individuals and diminishing societal forces that cause powerlessness among certain groups are ways to promote psychological health (refer back to Figure 7–2). Advocacy counseling can be conceptualized on a continuum, with empowerment of the individual client on one end of the continuum and social action to reduce oppression, discrimination, and other forms of injustice on the other end of the continuum (Toporek, 2000). Consequently, the counselor's role as an advocate can range from designing interventions that empower individual clients to taking action to influence public policy and institutional change.

Empowerment.   Facilitating empowerment in counseling is a way to focus on the individual client within the context of his or her sociopolitical environment. It may involve helping a woman who is being abused become aware of the inappropriate use of power and privilege that her partner is claiming. Or it may involve helping a client recognize an environmental barrier (e.g., discrimination in the workplace) and then make a plan to overcome it (Toporek, 2000). According to McWhirter (1994, 1997), empowerment is a lifelong process that involves critical self-reflection and action, an awareness of the power dynamics in the environment that affect diverse populations, and the development of skills to gain personal power and empower others.

To help counselors understand the concept of empowerment, McWhirter (1994, 1997) designed a "5 C's" model of empowerment for counseling, which includes the following components:

- *Collaboration,* which involves working collaboratively with clients to define the problem and plan for change. It also includes taking steps to decrease the inherent power differential between counselor and client.

- *Context,* which refers to acknowledging the role of factors such as poverty, racism, sexism, and other barriers in maintaining or exacerbating clients' problems.
- *Critical consciousness,* which is fostered by critical self-reflection and power analysis. The goal is to raise client awareness of the social, economic, and other power dynamics that affect their well-being.
- *Competence,* which focuses on clients' strengths, resources, and skills that can be used to help resolve the problem.
- *Community,* which may be defined broadly to include family, friends, ethnicity, faith, organizational affiliations, or other bonds. Connection with the community is essential to the empowerment process because it provides resources and support as well as opportunities for the client to "give back" by empowering others.

Key outcomes of empowerment are an enhanced sense of personal control and the ability to advocate for oneself. To facilitate self-advocacy in clients, counselors first need to be aware that counseling has the potential to encourage dependence in that it presupposes neediness (McWhirter, 1997; Steinbock, 1988). Rather than act as "rescuers," effective advocates help clients develop and utilize strengths and resources, both personally and in their communities.

Box 7–7

My First Professional Role in a Community Counseling Setting: Counselor, Advocate, and Team Member

After graduating from Wake Forest University with a master's degree in counselor education with an emphasis on community counseling, I joined a county mental health agency as a mental health practitioner, serving clients who have severe and persistent mental illness (SPMI). I am part of a team modeled after PACT (Program for Assertive Community Treatment), a nationally known model developed by Deborah J. Allness, M.S.S.W. M.D. and William H. Knoedler, M.D. The program is designed specifically for mental health professionals serving the SPMI population within the communities in which they live. Our treatment team is multi-disciplined, meeting each day to plan and coordinate care for clients, before going out into the community.

I realized early that I could apply the principles, theories, and counseling traditions learned during my educational training, practicum, and internship, as well as from my previous life experiences. My most challenging lesson to date is *patience*—not as much with clients, but rather with systems—the systems and agencies that must be choreographed and coerced in order to provide services. Building rapport and relationships among colleagues and others in the larger support system is especially important. It has taken little time to discover that I am not only a client's counselor, but also an advocate. Thus, I have also learned to advocate for myself as a professional counselor as well as ONE member of a dynamic mental health team.

Advocating for clients requires addressing stigmas every day, personal as well as those of the health, welfare, social services systems, and correctional facilities. In this environment, it is paramount to remember that ALL clients have rights, privileges, and expectations. Respecting differences and using power judiciously means sometimes adjusting MY counseling expectations to a new reality. In the classroom, diagnosis, treatment, and outcomes are stressed and garner importance. Working with the SPMI population teaches an additional lesson: Maintaining psychiatric stability is often an outcome to be celebrated.

Additional considerations that accompany the formidable tasks of effective assessment, diagnosing, and treatment planning are client issues of substance abuse, physical illness, intellectual functioning deficits, criminal history, and poor family support. A team approach incorporating biopsychosocial assessment that leads to the development of treatment plans that can be actualized is extremely important. The services we provide our clients are often their most consistent resources and activities available, thus demanding that each intervention encourage support and greater self-sufficiency rather than building dependence.

In summary, counseling in a community agency setting and working with SPMI clients has many unique and difficult challenges. In addition, the possibilities for personal and professional growth are tremendous. My decision to become a counselor is validated by the struggles and triumphs that I share each day with the clients, members of my team, and the larger pool of mental health professionals with whom I work.

—Tom Buffkin, M.A.Ed., LPC, NCC

Social action.   Counselors committed to social action are involved in confronting barriers faced by clients or client groups in their sociopolitical context (Toporek, 2000). Social action may be directed toward agencies, communities, the legal system, and legislation (Ezell, 2001). Social action can address immediate environmental concerns (e.g., advocating for changes to make a specific facility more accessible to people with disabilities) or more global concerns (e.g., becoming actively involved in legislative or policy issues that adversely affect groups of people). Advocating for mental health parity to ensure that mental health care benefits are covered in the same way as other health care benefits is one form of social action. Other examples of social action include advocating for public policy changes on behalf of the homeless and making community presentations to advocate for fair and respectful treatment of lesbian, gay, and bisexual individuals.

The most recently formed division in ACA, Counselors for Social Justice, provides an organized forum through which counselors can advocate for oppressed populations. Counselors for Social Justice (CSJ) was established in 1999 as an organizational affiliate and officially became an ACA division in September 2002. The mission statement of CSJ defines the organization as "a community of counselors and other professionals who recognize that many of the issues and concerns we address in our work result from social injustice and oppression" (CSJ, 2002). CSJ promotes individual and collective social responsibility, provides a support network for counselors engaged in social justice activities, and collaborates with other organizations in ACA and the larger community to implement social action strategies.

Advocacy Skills and Attributes

A number of skills and attributes are needed to engage in advocacy successfully. At the core of successful advocating is a compassionate spirit that is sensitive to human suffering and committed to helping alleviate that suffering (Kiselica & Robinson, 2001). Compassion and commitment provide the necessary motivation to take action related to an identified need (Myers, Sweeney, & White, 2002). Once a need is identified, counselors need skills to identify specific areas to target, keeping the bigger picture in mind. Social change usually does not occur quickly, and when changes are made, it takes time to implement and evaluate those changes (Ezell, 2001). To this end, advocates demonstrate planfulness, persistence, and patience.

To advocate successfully, counselors use many of the same verbal and nonverbal communication skills that are essential to effective counseling. Advocates need to be able to listen and respond empathically to vulnerable clients so that they feel understood and heard. Beyond that, counselors need to develop strong skills in persuasion, conflict resolution, compromise, and negotiation (Ezell, 2001). Also, to advocate successfully, counselors need skills in communicating effectively with the power sources from which change will originate. For example, when communicating with legislators, it is important to be organized, concise, and concrete. The use of jargon, exaggeration, or rambling hurts a counselor's presentation.

Other skills associated with advocacy include integrity, flexibility, resourcefulness, and the ability to prioritize. In addition, advocates need skills in assessing situations accurately; knowledge of laws, policies, and legal processes; capabilities in using the media and technology; an understanding of community organization and development; and a commitment to ethical standards (Kurpius & Rozecki, 1992).

In summarizing skills and practices related to advocacy, Ezell (2001) states that effective advocates do the following:

- Provide vigorous representation for their clients
- Use multiple methods to understand their clients' needs, issues, and problems
- Target specific policies or practices for change
- Map the decision systems responsible for targeted policies and practices
- Recast larger problems into solvable pieces
- Propose concrete solutions to problems
- Utilize several strategies and skills simultaneously and sequentially
- Actively counter negative stereotypes and misbeliefs
- Use the least conflictual tactics necessary to accomplish their objectives
- Exhibit cultural awareness and respect as they relate to colleagues, clients, and decision makers
- Place a high priority on impacting budgets
- Closely monitor the implementation of changed policies and practices (p. 193)

Challenges of Advocacy

Advocacy can be challenging work, particularly if efforts are not made to avoid certain pitfalls. Because of the personal investment involved, advocacy can be emotionally draining and lead to burnout if professionals do not set limits and boundaries

(Ezell, 2001). Also, it is important for advocates to evaluate themselves and their motives, being careful to avoid overzealousness and blind idealism (Kiselica & Robinson, 2001). Out of the desire to help vulnerable populations, it is possible to move ahead too quickly, not respecting existing barriers and perhaps even creating additional ones. Similarly, in attempting to right a wrong, advocates may tend to exaggerate claims about specific problems, an action which is unethical.

In addition to moving too quickly, it also is possible to assume responsibility for too much. McWhirter (1997) notes that "the number of issues that lend themselves to social activism is virtually endless" (p. 10). Focusing on specific issues, such as violence against women, affordable housing, or community assistance for seniors, enables counselors to channel energies more effectively than attempting to address an assortment of societal ills. Albee (2000) reminds us that not everyone needs to become a revolutionary; there is room in the field for all levels of intervention.

Advocacy for the Profession

Although our primary purpose in this section is to describe advocacy for client well-being, a related form of advocacy is for the counseling profession itself, which, according to Myers et al. (2002), is a professional imperative. Professional advocacy includes contributing to the development of a strong professional identity, lobbying for professional recognition, and demonstrating professional pride and accountability. It may include working through the political process by influencing legislation that affects the profession of counseling, such as obtaining Medicare reimbursement for licensed professional counselors. Engaging in professional advocacy benefits clients, because it helps ensure that counselors are recognized as competent and credible mental health service providers.

A key purpose of the services described thus far—crisis intervention, prevention, and advocacy—is to enhance client and community well-being. To make decisions about which services are working effectively and which need to be improved, a systematic form of evaluation needs to occur on an ongoing basis. In the final section of this chapter, we address the essential service of program evaluation.

PROGRAM EVALUATION

Another key component of community counseling services is program evaluation. Evaluation enables counselors and administrators to know whether the planned services have taken place as expected and whether specific goals and outcomes were achieved (Lewis, Lewis, Packard, & Soufleé, 2001). Evaluation results are used to make decisions about current and future services, including prevention programs; individual, group, and family counseling services; crisis programs; and outreach efforts. Systematic evaluation provides a way for counselors to reflect carefully on their counseling practices and make improvements as needed (Hadley & Mitchell, 1995; May, 1996).

Counselors who lack or fail to employ evaluation procedures place themselves and the counseling profession in jeopardy with the general public, third-party payers, and specific clients who rightfully demand accountability. A failure to evaluate counseling methods and related outcomes also puts counselors in danger of being unethical because they cannot prove that the counseling services implemented have a reasonable promise of success as the ethical codes of professional counseling associations require (Sexton & Whiston, 1996).

Purposes of Evaluation

Evaluation usually involves gathering meaningful information on various aspects of a counseling program and using those data to inform program planning and service delivery (Lewis et al., 2003; Loesch, 2001). Evaluation has a quality of immediate utility. In clinical settings, it gives counselors direct feedback on the services they provide and insight into what new services they need to offer. It also enables clients to have systematic, positive input into a counseling program. In describing counseling program evaluation (CPE), Loesch emphasized:

> The purpose of CPE is to maximize the efficiency and effectiveness of service delivery through careful and systematic examination of program components, methodologies, and outcomes. It is not the purpose of CPE simply to provide a rationale for what currently exists or is being done. Rather, CPE is used primarily to change counseling service delivery for the better. (p. 513)

Lewis et al. (2001) suggest that program evaluation serves five specific purposes. First, it aids in administrative decision making. Information gathered about the outcomes of services helps administrators make informed decisions about which programs to continue and expand and which programs to eliminate or reduce. Second, evaluation can help service providers make improvements in current programs by comparing them with what was originally planned. Third, evaluation provides a way to demonstrate accountability to funding and accrediting agencies, clients, and other stakeholders. Demonstrated accountability through evaluation can help agencies gain increased support from the larger community, which is a fourth purpose of evaluation. Finally, outcome evaluation can add to the growing body of research relevant to *best practices,* also called empirically validated (or supported) treatments (Sexton, 2001). For these purposes to be accomplished, evaluation results need to be disseminated to policymakers, consumers, and service providers (Lewis et al., 2001).

Steps in Evaluation

For program evaluation to be effective, it needs to comprehensive, systematic, and sequential. Plans for evaluation need to be made at the front end of program design, not afterwards (Lewis et al., 2001). To plan and implement an effective evaluation program, it is helpful to follow a sequential process, such as the following five-step procedure outlined by Burck and Peterson (1975).

According to Burck and Peterson, the first step in formulating an evaluation program involves a needs assessment. If counselors are to be accountable, they must first identify problems or concerns within their programs. *Needs assessment* refers to a set of methods or approaches used to determine if there is a need for a certain program or intervention (Duffy & Wong, 2000). Assessments can be conducted through surveys, interviews, focus groups, and other observational or descriptive methods.

Information gathered through the needs assessment is used to identify program goals and performance objectives. Here, both *terminal program outcomes* (those that are most immediately recognizable) and *ultimate program outcomes* (those that are most enduring) are described in terms of measurable performance objectives. In formulating goals and objectives, it is important to identify current program strengths, limitations, and resources and prioritize within that framework.

The third step in evaluation is designing and implementing a program. Program activities are selected to address the specific goals and objectives that have been delineated. To be successful, a program needs "a well-developed plan that integrates content, methods, resources, services, marketing, and evaluation" (Lusky & Hayes, 2001, p. 32).

Program design and implementation leads to the fourth step, which is revising and improving the program. No matter how well a program is planned, responses and outcomes are not always predictable. Consequently, ongoing evaluation of the process is required, accompanied by program revisions when necessary.

The fifth and final step is assessing the program's effectiveness in relation to the stated goals and objectives. Burck and Peterson (1975) refer to this step as "noting and reporting program outcome" (p. 567). This task is performed primarily by disseminating the findings of the program evaluation to the general public. Such consumer information is vital for potential clients if they are to make informed decisions, and counselors within a clinical program need this kind of feedback to improve their skills and services. Specific ways to gather outcome information are described in a subsequent section.

Comprehensive evaluation involves many people, including service providers, administrators, clients, and often the larger community. Each of these stakeholders plays a part in determining how the evaluation is conducted. Their degree of involvement in the process varies, depending on their interests and needs, but "all help determine the nature of effective evaluation practices" (Loesch, 2001, p. 515).

Process and Outcome Evaluation

Several different models of evaluation have been described in counseling literature. Most comprehensive models provide ways to evaluate *processes* and *outcomes*. In process evaluation, the focus is on the manner in which services are being delivered. In outcome evaluation, the focus is on whether the programs produced the desired results. Both are essential components of comprehensive program evaluation.

Process evaluation, also called *formative evaluation,* provides information about how well a program is being implemented (Lewis et al., 2003). During process evaluation, evaluators determine whether the programs are operating in accordance with stated plans, objectives, and expectations. Process evaluation involves ongoing monitoring of what services are being provided, by whom, for whom, to how many, when, and at what cost (Lewis et al., 2001).

Results obtained through process evaluation inform service providers about potential changes that need to be made to enhance program delivery. For example, if a support group for battered women is not being well attended, perhaps the group is meeting at an inopportune time, or perhaps the content used during group meetings is not addressing the most pertinent needs of the participants. By conducting process evaluation, counselors can determine what is or is not working and adapt accordingly.

Outcome evaluation provides information about whether, and to what degree, the goals and objectives of the program have been achieved. Also called *summative evaluation,* outcome evaluation provides one way for counselors to demonstrate accountability for their services. *Outcomes* are the benefits that clients received as a result of participating in a particular program (Scileppi et al., 2000). Although both process and outcome evaluations rely on clearly specified objectives, process evaluation objectives usually relate to projected activities, whereas outcome evaluation objectives are stated in terms of expected results.

Outcomes can be measured in various ways, several of which are described in Figure 7–5. Some of the more common measures include goal attainment scaling, consumer satisfaction surveys, and standardized outcome assessment devices (Dougherty, 2000). Ideally, evaluators will use multiple methods of assessment that are selected to measure client changes in skills, knowledge, behaviors, or adjustment (Lewis et al., 2001). Formal, in-depth outcome evaluation that is part of a well-designed research plan can help counselors and program administrators distinguish between changes that are a result of treatment and those that are simply a result of chance occurrences. However, implementing a formal, research-oriented outcome evaluation can be very time consuming, and efforts often focus on only one program component at a time (Lewis et al., 2001). Less formal outcome evaluation methods can be implemented more efficiently but are less likely to yield definitive results about treatment effects.

In some agencies, data gathered through process and outcome evaluations are used to conduct an *efficiency evaluation.* An efficiency evaluation connects the costs of implementing a particular program with the benefits achieved by the participants. In analyzing costs, resources required for program implementation are assessed, including time, effort, and financial expenditures. A key goal of an efficiency evaluation is to determine whether the same results can be achieved by reducing time, effort, or financial cost (Lewis et al., 2001).

Quality Assurance

In many settings, *quality assurance* (QA) is an ongoing process by which the agency and outside groups monitor the quality of services offered (MacCluskie & Ingersoll, 2001). Because of the demands of accrediting organizations such as the Joint Committee of Accreditation of Healthcare Organizations (JCAHO) and the National Committee for Quality Assurance (NCQA), documented outcome evaluation that provides evidence of quality of care is crucial. Quality of care is a multidimensional

Measurement	Purpose	Examples
Client satisfaction surveys	To evaluate the degree to which clients feel they have received services that are useful	Client Satisfaction Questionnaire-8 (CSQ-8); (Attkisson & Greenfield, 1994)
		Service Satisfaction Scale-30 (SSS-30); (Attkisson & Greenfield, 1994)
Goal attainment scaling	To help determine the efficacy of services according to preestablished criteria	Clients evaluate their progress toward achieving specific goals using a 5-point Likert scale.
Assessments of client functioning	To measure functional status along general or specific dimensions	Global Assessment of Functioning (GAF); (*DSM-IV-TR;* APA, 2000)
		Life Functioning Scales (Howard, Orlinsky, & Bankoff, 1994)
Assessments of client symptomatology	To rate the frequency or intensity of presenting complaints	Brief Symptom Inventory (Derogatis & Lazarus, 1994)
		Brief Psychiatric Rating Scale (Faustman, 1994)
Alternative assessment approaches	To gather information about clients using methods other than traditional paper-and-pencil approaches	Performance assessment (evaluating how a person acts or behaves in given situations)

Figure 7–5
Measuring outcomes: Examples of evaluation methods
From Loesch, 2001; and Steenberger and Smith, 1996.

construct that encompasses access and availability of care, client satisfaction with services, and adherence to recognized standards of care and service delivery (Steenbarger & Smith, 1996). It is in the best interest of community agencies to document evidence that quality services are being delivered and to seek external accreditation. External accreditation lets the public know that agencies have met certain minimum criteria for service delivery, thereby placing agencies in a better position to negotiate contracts with third-party providers (MacCluskie & Ingersoll, 2001).

Issues and Challenges of Evaluation

In principle, the concept of evaluation is relatively straightforward. In reality, however, evaluation is a complex process that can pose several challenges. One of the greatest challenges, according to Steenbarger and Smith (1996), involves the logistics of data collection. Administration and scoring of paper-and-pencil measures can be tedious and time consuming, leading to delays in calculating and disseminating results. Another challenge relates to the gathering and interpretation of evaluation data. Finding valid and reliable methods of measuring program effectiveness is a difficult task, and method selection varies from setting to setting. Consequently, what one agency considers "effective service" may or may not be truly effective. In addition to methodological concerns, professionals may resist evaluation because of concerns about how the results are going to be used. People do not like to be judged, especially if the results of the evaluation may be used against them (Duffy & Wong, 2000). When evaluators take steps to use evaluations constructively rather than punitively and clarify the intended purposes of the evaluation from the outset, people are more likely to respond favorably.

Although the challenges described in the preceding paragraph can create barriers to program evaluation, they can be overcome if handled sensitively. When evaluation is viewed as an integral component of service delivery that benefits both staff and clients, resistance to the process is minimized and opportunities for growth and improvement are enhanced.

SUMMARY AND CONCLUSION

In this chapter, we have provided an overview of four essential counseling services: crisis intervention, prevention, advocacy, and evaluation. It is important for community counselors to develop skills in each of these areas. The demand for crisis intervention has risen during recent years. Many forms of trauma, including violence, natural disasters, and developmental crises, can leave people without sufficient resources to cope effectively. In such cases, counselors need to be prepared to offer services to help people navigate the uncertainty and confusion that ensue. James and Gilliland's (2001) six-step model of crisis intervention provides a guide to help counselors work effectively in crisis situations.

Preventing psychological distress by helping people develop resources and strengths while reducing negative influences represents a fundamental value of the counseling profession. Primary prevention programs, which take into account individual and environmental influences, provide the most efficient way of promoting mental health among the largest number of people. The three prevention models described in the chapter emphasize the importance of enhancing individual strengths and environmental resources and decreasing individual limitations and social stresses. The Wheel of Wellness model (Myers et al., 2000) provides a guideline for optimizing health and well-being by enhancing specific life tasks, including spirituality, self-direction, work and leisure, friendship, and love.

A third service that is vital to community counseling is advocacy. Advocacy services go beyond the traditional role of individual counseling by focusing on ways to address social injustices and environmental conditions that impinge upon the well-being of individuals or groups. There are many ways counselors can serve as advocates for their clients, ranging from facilitating personal empowerment to political involvement aimed at improving societal conditions. Advocating for the counseling profession also benefits clients by ensuring that the profession is recognized as a viable, credible provider of mental health services.

A fourth example of essential community counseling services is program evaluation. Evaluation provides information that is used to make decisions about current and future counseling services. Systematic evaluation, which occurs throughout the course of service delivery, provides a way to demonstrate accountability and maximize the quality of the services that are provided. Two common types of evaluation are process evaluation, which supplies information about how well a program is being implemented, and outcome evaluation, which indicates the degree to which service goals and objectives are being met.

Each of the services described in this chapter—crisis intervention, prevention, advocacy, and program evaluation—has been researched and written about extensively by professionals in the field. The information presented here provides only a brief overview of the four topics. As part of your professional preparation, we encourage you to examine some of the many excellent resources related to these service components to enhance your knowledge and skills.

REFERENCES

Aguilera, D. C., & Messick, J. M. (1982). Crisis intervention: Theory and methodology (4th ed.). St. Louis: C. V. Mosby.

Albee, G. W. (2000). Commentary on prevention in counseling psychology. *Counseling Psychologist, 28,* 845–853.

Albee, G. W., & Gullotta, T. P. (1997). *Primary prevention works.* Thousand Oaks, CA: Sage.

Albee, G. W., & Ryan-Finn, K. D. (1993). An overview of primary prevention. *Journal of Counseling and Development, 72,* 115–123.

American Psychiatric Association. (2000). *Diagnostic and statistical manual of mental disorders* (4th ed., text rev.). Washington, DC: Author.

Attkisson, C. C., & Greenfield, T. K. (1994). Client Satisfaction Questionnaire-8 and Service Satisfaction Scale-30. In M. Maruish (Ed.), *The use of psychological testing for treatment planning and outcome assessment* (pp. 402–422). Hillsdale, NJ: Erlbaum.

Bauer, A. (2001). Responding to a community crisis: Frontline counseling. In E. R. Welfel & R. Elliott Ingersoll (Eds.). *The mental health desk reference* (pp. 239–245). New York: Wiley.

Belkin, G. S. (1984). *Introduction to counseling* (2nd ed.). Dubuque, IA: William C. Brown.

Bloom, M. (1996). *Primary prevention practices.* Thousand Oaks, CA: Sage.

Brammer, L. M. (1985). *The helping relationship: Process and skills* (3rd ed.). Upper Saddle River, NJ: Prentice Hall.

Burck, H. D., & Peterson, G. W. (1975). Needed: More evaluation, not research. *Personnel and Guidance Journal, 53,* 563–569.

Caplan, G. (1964). *Principles of preventive psychiatry.* New York: Basic Books.

Conyne, R. K. (1991). Gains in primary prevention: Implications for the counseling profession. *Journal of Counseling and Development, 69,* 277–279.

Conyne, R. K. (2000). Prevention in counseling psychology: At long last, has the time now come? *Counseling Psychologist, 28,* 838–844.

Corey, G. & Corey, M. S. (1990). *I never knew I had a choice* (4th ed.). Pacific Grove, CA: Brooks/Cole.

Counselors for Social Justice. (2002). CSJ mission statement. Retrieved on January 9, 2003, from http://www.counselorsforsocialjustice.org

Darden, C. A., Gazda, G. M., & Ginter, E. J. (1996). Lifeskills and mental health counseling. *Journal of Mental Health Counseling, 18,* 134–141.

Derogatis, L. R., & Lazarus, L. (1994). SCL-90-R, Brief Symptom Inventory, and Matching Clinical Rating Scales. In M. Maruish (Ed.), *The use of psychological testing for treatment planning and outcome assessment* (pp. 217–248). Hillsdale, NJ: Erlbaum.

Dougherty, A. M. (2000). *Psychological consultation and collaboration in school and community settings* (3rd ed.). Belmont, CA: Wadsworth.

Duffy, K. G., & Wong, F. Y. (2000). *Community psychology* (2nd ed.). Needham Heights, MA: Allyn & Bacon.

Ezell, M. (2001). *Advocacy in the human services.* Belmont, CA: Wadsworth.

Faustman, W. O. (1994). Brief psychiatric rating scale. In M. Maruish (Ed.), *The use of psychological testing for treatment planning and outcome assessment* (pp. 371–401). Hillsdale, NJ: Erlbaum.

Ginter, E. J. (1999). David K. Brooks' contribution to the developmentally based life-skills approach. *Journal of Mental Health Counseling, 21,* 191–202.

Hadley, R. G., & Mitchell, L. K. (1995). *Counseling research and program evaluation.* Pacific Grove, CA: Brooks/Cole.

Hattie, J. A., Myers, J. E., & Sweeney, T. J. (in press). A multidisciplinary model of wellness: The development of the Wellness Evaluation of Lifestyle. *Journal of Counseling and Development.*

Howard, K. I., Orlinsky, D. E., & Bankoff, E. A. (1994). The research project on long-term psychotherapy: A qualitative analysis. *Journal of Counseling Psychology, 43,* 207–217.

James, R. K., & Gilliland, B. E. (2001). *Crisis intervention strategies* (4th ed.). Pacific Grove, CA: Brooks/Cole.

Janoski, E. H. (1984). *Crisis counseling: A contemporary approach.* Monterey, CA: Wadsworth Health Sciences Division.

Kaplan, R. (2000). Two pathways to prevention. *American Psychologist, 55,* 382–396.

Kiselica, M. S., & Look, C. T. (1993). Mental health counseling and prevention: Disparity between philosophy and practice? *Journal of Mental Health Counseling, 15,* 3–14.

Kiselica, M. S., & Robinson, M. (2001). Bringing advocacy counseling to life: The history, issues, and human dramas of social justice work in counseling. *Journal of Counseling and Development, 79,* 387–397.

Kleist, D. M. (1999). The state of prevention in mental health counseling and counselor education. In J. S. Hinkle (Ed.), *Promoting optimum mental health through counseling: An overview* (pp. 35–40). Greensboro, NC: ERIC/CASS.

Kurpius, D. J., & Rozecki, T. G. (1992). Outreach, advocacy, and consultation: A framework for prevention and intervention. *Elementary School Guidance and Counseling, 26,* 176–189.

Lazarus, R. S., & Folkman, S. (1984). *Stress, appraisal and coping.* New York: Springer.

Lee, C. C. (1998). Counselors as agents for social change. In C. C. Lee & G. R. Walz (Eds.), *Social action: A mandate for counselors* (pp. 3–16). Alexandria, VA: American Counseling Association.

Lewis, J., & Bradley, L. (2000). Introduction. In J. Lewis & L. J. Bradley (Eds.), *Advocacy in counseling: Counselors, clients, and community* (pp. 3–4). Greensboro, NC: Caps Publications.

Lewis, J. A., Lewis, M. D., Daniels, J. A., & D'Andrea, M. J. (2003). *Community counseling: Empowerment strategies for a diverse society* (3rd ed.). Pacific Grove, CA: Brooks/Cole.

Lewis, J. A., Lewis, M. D., Packard, T., & Soufleé, F., Jr. (2001). *Management of human service programs* (3rd ed.). Belmont, CA: Wadsworth.

Loesch, L. C. (2001). Counseling program evaluation: Inside and outside the box. In D. C. Locke, J. E. Myers, & E. L. Herr (Eds.), *The handbook of counseling* (pp. 513–525). Thousand Oaks, CA: Sage.

Lusky, M. B., & Hayes, R. L. (2001). Collaborative consultation and program evaluation. *Journal of Counseling and Development, 79,* 26–38.

MacCluskie, K. C., & Ingersoll, R. E. (2001). *Becoming a 21st century agency counselor: Personal and professional explorations.* Belmont, CA: Wadsworth.

May, K. M. (1996). Naturalistic inquiry and counseling: Contemplating commonalities. *Counseling and Values, 40,* 219–229.

McNamara, S. (2000). *Stress in young people: What's new and what can we do?* New York: Continuum.

McWhirter, E. H. (1994). *Counseling for empowerment.* Alexandria, VA: American Counseling Association.

McWhirter, E. H. (1997). Empowerment, social activism, and counseling. *Counseling and Human Development, 29,* 1–14.

Myer, R. A. (2001). *Assessment for crisis intervention: A triage assessment model.* Belmont, CA: Wadsworth.

Myer, R. A., Williams, R. C., Ottens, A. J., & Schmidt, A. E. (1992). Crisis assessment: A three-dimensional model for triage. *Journal of Mental Health Counseling, 14,* 137–148.

Myers, J. E. (1992). Wellness, prevention, development: The cornerstone of the profession. *Journal of Counseling and Development, 71,* 136–139.

Myers, J. E., & Sweeney, T. J. (in press). A multidisciplinary model of wellness: The development of the Wellness Evaluation of Lifestyle. *Journal of Counseling and Development.*

Myers, J. E., & Sweeney, T. J. (1999). The Five Factor WEL (WEL-J). Greensboro, NC: Authors.

Myers, J. E., Sweeney, T. J., & White, V. E. (2002). Advocacy for counseling and counselors: A professional imperative. *Journal of Counseling and Development, 80,* 394–402.

Myers, J. E., Sweeney, T. J., & Witmer, J. M. (2000). The wheel of wellness counseling for wellness: A holistic model for treatment planning. *Journal of Counseling and Development, 78,* 251–266.

Price, R., Cowen, E., Lorion, R., & Ramos-McKay, J. (Eds.). (1988). *14 ounces of prevention: A casebook for practitioners.* Washington, DC: American Psychological Association.

Romano, J. L. (2001). Stress, coping, and well-being: Applications of theory to practice. In E. R. Welfel & R. Elliott Ingersoll (Eds.), *The mental health desk reference* (pp. 44–50). New York: Wiley.

Romano, J. L., & Hage, S. M. (2000). Prevention and counseling psychology: Revitalizing commitments for the 21st century. *Counseling Psychologist, 28,* 733–763.

Scileppi, J. A., Teed, E. L., & Torres, R. D. (2000). *Community psychology: A common sense approach to mental health.* Upper Saddle River, NJ: Prentice Hall.

Sexton, T. L. (2001). Evidence-based counseling intervention programs. In D. C. Locke, J. E. Myers, & E. L. Herr (Eds.), *The handbook of counseling* (pp. 499–512). Thousand Oaks, CA: Sage.

Sexton, T. L., & Whiston, S. C. (1996). Integrating counseling research and practice. *Journal of Counseling and Development, 74,* 588–589.

Sharrer, V. W., & Ryan-Wenger, N. A. (2002). School-age children's self-reported stress symptoms. *Pediatric Nursing, 28,* 21–27.

Steenbarger, B. N., & Smith, H. B. (1996). Assessing the quality of counseling services: Developing accountable helping systems. *Journal of Counseling and Development, 75,* 145–150.

Steinbock, A. J. (1988). Helping and homogeneity: Therapeutic interactions as the challenge to power. *Quarterly Journal of Ideology, 12,* 31–46.

Sweeney, T. J., & Witmer, J. M. (1991). Beyond social interest: Striving toward optimal health and wellness. *Individual Psychology, 47,* 527–540.

Toporek, R. L. (2000). Developing a common language and framework for understanding advocacy in counseling. In J. Lewis & L. J. Bradley (Eds.), *Advocacy in counseling: Counselors, clients, and community* (pp. 5–14). Greensboro, NC: Caps Publications.

Vera, E. M. (2000). A recommitment to prevention work in counseling psychology. *Counseling Psychologist, 28,* 829–837.

Witmer, J. M., & Sweeney, T. J. (1992). A holistic model for wellness and prevention over the life span. *Journal of Counseling and Development, 71,* 140–148.

CHAPTER 8

Working with Groups

*Who am I in this pilgrim group
whose members differ so in perception?
Am I timid like a Miles Standish,
letting others speak for me
because the experience of failure is softened
if a risk is never personally taken?
Or am I more like a John Alden
speaking boldly for others in the courting of beauty
but not seeking such for myself?
Perhaps I am more than either man
or maybe I'm both at different times!
In the silence and before others, I ponder the question anew.*

Gladding, S. T. (1979). A restless presence: Group process as a pilgrimage. *School Counselor, 27,* 126. © 1979 by ACA. Reprinted with permission. No further reproduction authorized without written permission of ACA.

W orking in groups is a counseling specialty that is relatively new, but one that is often effective in helping individuals resolve personal and interpersonal concerns. Organized groups make use of people's natural tendency to gather and share thoughts and feelings as well as work and play cooperatively.

This chapter examines the following aspects of groups:

- Their place in counseling
- Types of groups most often used
- Realities and misperceptions about groups
- Uses of as well as advantages and limitations of groups
- The theoretical basis for conducting groups
- Stages and issues in groups
- Qualities of effective group leaders

Counselors, especially in community settings, who restrict their competencies to individual counseling and do not learn how to run groups at different levels limit their options for helping.

THE PLACE OF GROUPS IN COUNSELING

A *group* is generally considered to be "a collection of two or more individuals who meet in face-to-face interaction, interdependently, with the awareness that each belongs to the group and for the purpose of achieving individual and/or mutually agreed upon goals" (Gladding, 2001, p. 55). The exception to this definition is found in some groups who meet on the Internet where there is no face-to-face interaction (Page et al., 2000).

Groups have a unique place in counseling. Everyone typically spends some time in group activities each day, for example, with colleagues, schoolmates, neighbors, or business associates. Gregariousness is a part of human nature, and many personal and professional skills are learned through group interactions. It is only natural, then, for community counselors to make use of this primary way of human interaction. Groups are an economical and effective means of helping individuals who share similar problems and concerns (Sleek, 1995).

Groups are not a new phenomenon in therapeutic work. They have a long and distinguished place in the service of counseling. Joseph Hersey Pratt is generally credited with starting the first psychologically oriented group. He did so in 1905 with tuberculosis outpatients at Massachusetts General in Boston. He found their regular group experience to be informative, supportive, and therapeutic. The following professionals were also pioneers in the group movement in the 20th century:

- Jacob L. Moreno, who introduced the term *group psychotherapy* into the counseling literature in the 1930s
- Kurt Lewin, whose field theory concepts in the 1930s and 1940s became the basis for the Tavistock small study groups in Britain and the T-group movement in the United States

- Fritz Perls, whose Gestalt approach to groups attracted new energy and interest in the field
- W. Edwards Deming, who conceptualized and implemented the idea of quality work groups to improve the processes and products people produced and to build morale among workers in businesses
- William Schutz and Jack Gibb, who emphasized a humanistic aspect to groups that focused on personal growth as a legitimate goal
- Carl Rogers, who devised the basic encounter group in the 1960s that became the model for growth-oriented group approaches.

Thus, organized groups are over 100 years old. Those who have engineered and created ways of conducting them have established various types of groups as a main component within counseling.

TYPES OF GROUPS

Groups come in many forms: "There seems to be a group experience tailored to suit the interests and needs of virtually anyone who seeks psychotherapy, personal growth, or simply support and companionship from others" (Lynn & Frauman, 1985, p. 423). There are a number of group models appropriate for a wide variety of situations. Although lively debate persists about how groups should be categorized, especially in regard to goals and process (Waldo & Bauman, 1998), the following types of groups have training standards developed by the Association for Specialists in Group Work (ASGW) (2000): psychoeducational, counseling, psychotherapy, and task/work (see Figure 8–1).

Psychoeducational Groups

Psychoeducational groups were originally developed for use in educational settings, specifically in public schools. They are also known simply as "educational" or "guidance" groups. The primary function of these types of groups is the prevention of personal or societal disorders through the conveying of information and/or the

Figure 8–1
The Group Work Rainbow
Note. From Robert K. Conyne, University of Cincinnati. Used with permission.

examining of values. Psychoeducational groups stress growth through knowledge. Content includes, but is not limited to, personal, social, vocational, and educational information. For instance, group participants may be taught how to deal with a potential threat (e.g., AIDS), a developmental life event (e.g., growing older), or an immediate life crisis (e.g., the death of a loved one). Preventive and growth activities can take many forms but usually they are presented as nonthreatening exercises or group discussions (Carroll, Bates, & Johnson, 1997).

Psychoeducational group activities are offered throughout the life span in a variety of settings. Sometimes these groups take the form of life-skill development, especially for those who have a deficit of appropriate interpersonal behaviors (Gazda et al., 1999). This "how-to" approach may include the use of films, plays, demonstrations, role-plays, and guest speakers. The size of the group varies with the setting (e.g., a self-contained classroom), but the typical group size ranges from 10 to 40 individuals. The group leader has expertise in the topic being discussed and is in charge of group management and disseminating information. One of the most important parts of the process that goes on in such groups revolves around group discussions of how members will personalize the information presented in the group context. These groups are designed to meet the needs of generally well-functioning people.

Counseling Groups

Counseling groups focus on prevention, growth, and remediation. They seek to help group participants to resolve the usual, yet often difficult, problems of living through interpersonal support and problem solving. An additional goal is to help participants develop their existing interpersonal problem-solving competencies so they may be better able to handle future problems. Nonsevere career, educational, personal, social, and developmental concerns are frequently addressed (ASGW, 1990, 2000).

Because the focus of group counseling is on each person's behavior and growth or change within the group, the interaction among persons, especially in problem solving, is highlighted. Group dynamics and interpersonal relationships are emphasized. Whereas psychoeducational groups are recommended for everyone on a continuous basis, group counseling is more selective. It focuses on individuals experiencing "usual, but often difficult, problems of living" (ASGW, 1990, p. 14) that information alone will not solve.

The size of these groups varies with the ages of the individuals involved, ranging from 3 or 4 in a children's group to 8 to 12 in an adult group. The number of group meetings also fluctuates but generally ranges from 6 to 16 sessions. The leader is in charge of facilitating the group interaction but becomes less directly involved as the group develops. Usually, the topics covered in group counseling are developmental or situational in nature, such as educational, social, career, and personal. Counseling groups tend not to be of long-standing duration. Compared with psychoeducational groups, this type of group offers a more direct approach to dealing with troublesome behaviors. The major advantages of group counseling are the interaction, feedback, and contribution of group members with each other over a period of time.

Psychotherapy Groups

Psychotherapy groups are set up to help individual group members resolve their in-depth psychological problems. They are described in the professional literature as remedial types of groups (Luchins, 1964). "Because the depth and extent of the psychological disturbance is significant, the goal is to aid each individual to reconstruct major personality dimensions" (ASGW, 1992, p. 13).

At times, there is overlap in group counseling and group psychotherapy, but the emphasis on major reconstruction of personality dimensions usually distinguishes the two. The setting of group psychotherapy is often in inpatient facilities, such as hospitals or mental health facilities, because of greater control of the people involved. As an entity, psychotherapy groups may be either open ended (admitting new members at any time) or closed (not admitting new members after the first session). Certain types of individuals are poor candidates for outpatient, intensive group psychotherapy. Among these individuals are depressives, incessant talkers, paranoids, schizoid and sociopathic personalities, suicidal personalities, and extreme narcissists (Yalom, 1995). It may be easier to identify group psychotherapy candidates who should be excluded than to pick those who should be included. Regardless, group psychotherapy is an American form of treatment and has provided much of the rationale for group counseling.

One of the primary aims of the group psychotherapy process is to reconstruct, through in-depth analysis, the personalities of those involved in the group (Brammer, Abrego, & Shostrom, 1993; Gazda, Ginter, & Horne, 2001). The size of the group varies from two or three to a dozen, and members meet for a period of months, or even years. The group leader has expertise in one of the mental health disciplines (psychiatry, psychology, counseling, social work, or psychiatric nursing) as well as in training and expertise in dealing with people who have severe emotional problems. The responsibilities of the leader are to confront as well as to facilitate.

Task/Work Groups

Task/work groups assist their members in applying group dynamics principles and processes to improve practices and the accomplishment of identified work goals. "The task/work group specialist is able to assist groups such as task forces, committees, planning groups, community organizations, discussion groups, study circles, learning groups, and other similar groups to correct or develop their functions" (ASGW, 1992, p. 13). The prototype of a task/work group is a quality circle where members of a work unit discuss the processes under which they operate and try to make continuous improvements.

There are as many types of task/work groups as there are kinds of tasks and work. Regardless of type or form, all task/work groups emphasize accomplishment and efficiency in completing identified work goals. They are united in their emphasis on achieving a successful performance or a finished product through collaborative efforts. Unlike other groups examined, there is no emphasis in task/work groups on changing individuals. Whether the group is successful or not depends on group dynamics, which are the interactions fostered through the relationships of members and leaders in connection with the complexity of the task involved. Because task/work groups run the gamut from informal subcommittee meetings to major Hollywood productions, the number of members within a task/work group may be large, but such a group usually works best when kept below 12. The length of a task/work group varies, but most are similar to other groups in that they have a beginning, a working period, and an ending. A difference in task/work groups compared with others is that often little attention is paid by members or leaders to the termination stage, and some of these groups end abruptly.

Mixed Groups

Most groups belong in one of the four categories of specialty groups just discussed. However, some do not fit well into any category. The most notable of these, so-called mixed groups, encompasses multiple ways of working with members and may change emphasis frequently. For example, some groups that are instructive are also simultaneously or consequentially therapeutic. The prototype for such a mixed type of group is a self-help group.

Self-help groups take two forms: those that are organized by an established professional-helping organization or individual (support groups) and those that originate spontaneously and stress their autonomy and internal group resources ("self-help" groups in the truest sense) (Riordan & Beggs, 1987). Although there are distinctions between support groups and self-help organizations, these groups share numerous common denominators including that they are composed of individuals who have a common focus and purpose. They are psychoeducational, therapeutic, and usually task driven. In addition, members of these groups frequently employ counseling techniques, such as reflection, active listening, and confrontation.

Many support and self-help groups seem to be successful in helping their members to take more control over their lives and to function well. Some that lack professional leadership make up for this deficiency in terms of experienced lay leaders. The narrow focus of these groups is both an asset in achieving a specific goal and a deficit in helping participants expand their horizons in many areas.

REALITIES AND MISPERCEPTIONS ABOUT GROUPS

Because group work is so important and prevalent in counseling and therapeutic circles, national organizations have been established for professionals engaged primarily in leading groups. Prominent group organizations include the American Group Psychotherapy Association (AGPA), the American Society of Group Psychotherapy and Psychodrama (ASGPP), and the Group Psychology and Group Psychotherapy division of the American Psychological Association (APA) (Division 49). However, probably the most comprehensive of these organizations, and the one to which most professional counselors belong, is the Association for Specialists in Group Work

(ASGW), a division of the American Counseling Association (ACA). This organization, which has a diverse membership, was chartered by the ACA in 1974 (Carroll & Levo, 1985). It has been a leader in the establishment of educational and best practices guidelines for group leaders (ASGW, 1998, 2000) and publishes a quarterly periodical, the *Journal for Specialists in Group Work*.

Despite these group organizations and the long history of different types of groups in society, certain misperceptions about groups are prevalent in the general public (Gladding, 1994, 2003). Most misperceptions involve counseling and psychotherapy groups (as opposed to psychoeducational and task/work groups). The following are some prevalent myths about groups:

- They are artificial and unreal experiences.
- They are second-rate structures for dealing with problems.
- They force people to lose their identity by tearing down psychological defenses.
- They require that people become emotional and spill their guts.
- They are touchy-feely, confrontational, hostile, and brainwashing experiences (Childers & Couch, 1989).

The reality is that none of these myths are true, at least in well-run groups. Indeed, quite the contrary of these ideas is actually the case. Therefore, it is important that individuals who are unsure about groups ask questions before they consider becoming members of them. In such a way, doubts and misperceptions can be addressed, anxiety may be lessened, and people may benefit significantly within a group environment.

USES OF, ADVANTAGES OF, AND LIMITATIONS OF GROUPS

Although there are specialty groups and best practices associated with such groups, whether an environment or a person is right for a group is always a question that should be asked before setting up a group. Furthermore, the advantages and limitations of groups should always be considered in establishing a group.

Uses of Groups

Most counselors must make major decisions about when, where, and with whom to use groups. There are some situations in which group use is not appropriate. For instance, a counselor employed by a company would be unwise to use groups to counsel employees with personal problems who are unequal in rank and seniority in the corporate network. Likewise, an agency counselor would be foolish to use a group setting as a way of working with children who are all behaviorally disruptive. But a group may be ideal for helping people who are not too disruptive or unequal in status and who have common concerns. In such cases the procedure is for counselors to schedule a regular time in a quiet, uninterrupted setting for such people to meet and interact together.

Groups differ in purpose, composition, and length, but basically they all involve work. Gazda et al. (2001) describe work as "the dynamic interaction between collections of individuals for prevention or remediation of difficulties or for the enhancement of personal growth/enrichment" (p. 297). Hence, the term *group work* is often used in connection with what goes on in groups. Group work is

> a broad professional practice involving the application of knowledge and skill in group facilitation to assist an interdependent collection of people to reach their mutual goals, which may be intrapersonal, interpersonal, or work related. The goals of the group may include the accomplishment of tasks related to work, education, personal development, personal and interpersonal problem solving, or remediation of mental and emotional disorders. (ASGW, 2000, p. 3)

Advantages of Groups

Groups have a number of general advantages. For example, group members can come to realize that they are not alone, unique, or abnormal in their problems and concerns. Through their interaction with one another, they learn more about themselves in social situations. In groups, clients can try out new behaviors and ways of interacting, because the group atmosphere provides a safe environment to experiment with change and receive feedback. Members also observe how others attack and resolve problems, thereby picking up skills vicariously. Finally, the group may serve as a catalyst to help persons realize a want or a need for individual counseling or the accomplishment of a personal goal.

If set up properly, groups have specific advantages that can be beneficial in helping individuals with a variety of problems and concerns. For instance, research has shown that breast cancer patients live longer and have a better quality of life when they undergo group therapy as a part of their recovery (Sleek, 1995). Groups can also be powerful and effective experiences for clients dealing with social phobias, developmental disabilities, and insomnia. There are literally hundreds of studies that describe group approaches and statistically support the effectiveness of various forms of groups. Documentation of group experiences is occurring at such a fast rate that it is difficult to stay abreast of the latest developments.

Some researchers in the field, such as Zimpfer (1990), regularly write comprehensive reviews on select group activities that help practitioners become better informed. The following are some relevant findings that are advantages of groups:

- Group counseling can be used to help motivate low-performing students and improve the grades and self-concepts of at-risk students. (Campbell & Myrick, 1990; Page & Chandler, 1994)
- Groups can promote career development in general (Pyle, 2000) and can be used effectively in vocational planning with some underserved populations, such as battered and abused women. (Peterson & Priour, 2000)

- Learning groups geared toward cooperative sharing can help participants achieve their goals more easily. (Avasthi, 1990)
- Support groups can be of benefit in helping older women cope with divorce and its aftermaths. (Blatter & Jacobsen, 1993)
- Group intervention with adolescent offenders can help them increase their maturational processes, especially their ability to work in a sustained way and to achieve a sense of relationship with others. (Viney, Henry, & Campbell, 2001)
- Group counseling and psychoeducational programs can help persons who have sustained a heart attack deal better with stressors in their lives. (Livneh & Sherwood-Hawes, 1993)

Limitations of Groups

Yet despite their many uses and advantages, groups are not a panacea for all people and problems. There are definite limitations and disadvantages of groups (Gladding, 2003). For example, many client concerns and personalities are not well suited for groups. The problems of individuals may not be dealt with in enough depth in groups. In addition, group pressure may force a client to take action, such as self-disclosure, before being ready. Groups may also lapse into a groupthink mentality, in which stereotypical, defensive, and stale thought processes become the norm while creativity and problem solving are squelched.

Another drawback to groups is that individuals may try to use them for escape or for selfish purposes and thereby disrupt the group process. Furthermore, it may be difficult for leaders to find a suitable time to conduct groups so that all who wish to can participate.

A sixth concern is whether groups will reflect the social milieu in which individual members normally operate. Otherwise, what is learned from the group experience may not be relevant. Finally, if groups do not work through their developmental stages successfully, they may become regressive and engage in nonproductive and even destructive behaviors such as scapegoating, group narcissism, and projection (McClure, 1994).

THEORETICAL APPROACHES IN CONDUCTING GROUPS

Theoretical approaches to counseling in groups vary as much as individual counseling approaches. In many cases, the theories are the same. For instance, within group work there are approaches that are based on psychoanalytic, Gestalt, person centered, rational-emotive, transactional analysis, and behavioral theories. Yet, the implementation of any theoretical approach differs when employed with a group because of group dynamics (the interaction of members within the group).

In an evaluation of seven major theoretical approaches to groups, Ward (1982) analyzes the degree to which each approach pays attention to the (a) individual, (b) interpersonal, and (c) group levels of the process (Table 8–1). For instance,

Table 8–1
Rating of theory strength at three group levels

Theory	Levels			Limiting Factors
	Individual	**Interpersonal**	**Group**	
Freud	Strong	Weak	Weak	Task, members, leader
Perls	Strong	Weak	Weak	Task, members, leader
Behavioral	Strong	Weak	Weak	Task, leader
Ellis	Strong	Medium	Weak	Task, leader
Berne	Strong	Strong	Weak	Task
Rogers	Strong	Medium	Medium	Style

Note. From "A Model for the More Effective Use of Theory in Group Work," by D. E. Ward, 1982, *Journal for Specialists in Group Work, 7,* 227. © 1982 by ACA. Reprinted with permission. No further reproduction authorized without written permission of the American Counseling Association.

the psychoanalytic, Gestalt, and behavioral approaches to groups are strong in focusing on the individual but weak on the other two components of the group process. However, the Rogerian approach is strong on the individual level and medium on the interpersonal and group levels. Ward points out the limiting aspects of each approach and the importance of considering other factors, such as the group task and membership maturity, in conducting comprehensive group assignments.

In a similar way, Frey (1972) outlines how eight approaches to group work can be conceptualized on continuums from insight to action and from rational to affective (Figure 8–2), and Hansen, Warner, and Smith (1980) conceptualize group approaches on continuums from process to outcome and from leader centered to member centered (Figure 8–3). Group leaders and potential group members must know how theories differ in order to make wise choices.

Overall, multiple theoretical models provide richness and diversity for conducting groups. Three additional factors are useful for group leaders to consider in arriving at a decision on what approach to take:

1. Does one need a theoretical base for conducting the group?
2. What uses will the theory best serve?
3. What criteria will be employed in the selection process?

A theory is a lot like a map. In a group, a theory provides direction and guidance in examining basic assumptions about human beings. Theory is also useful in determining goals for the group, in clarifying one's role and functions as a leader, and in explaining the group interactions. Finally, a theory can help in evaluating the outcomes of the group. Trying to lead a group without an explicit theoretical rationale is similar to attempting to fly an airplane without a map and knowledge of instruments. Either procedure is foolish, dangerous, and likely to lead to injury.

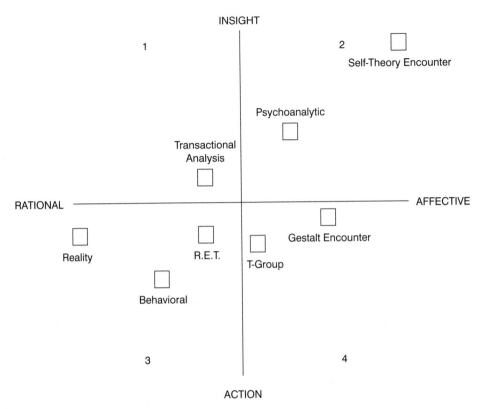

Figure 8–2

Group approaches conceptualized

Note. From "Conceptualizing Counseling Theories," by D. H. Frey, 1972, *Counselor Education and Supervision, 11*, 245. © 1972 by ACA. Reprinted with permission. No further reproduction authorized without written permission of the American Counseling Association.

A good theory also serves practical functions (Gladding, 2003; Vander Kolk, 1985). For example, it gives meaning to and a framework for experiences and facts that occur within a setting. Good theory helps make logical sense out of what is happening and leads to productive research. With so many theories from which to choose, the potential group leader is wise to be careful in selecting an approach.

Ford and Urban (1963) contend there are four main factors that should be considered when selecting a theory: personal experience, consensus of experts, prestige, or a verified body of knowledge. There are liabilities and advantages to all of these criteria. Therefore, it is crucial for counselors to listen to others and to read the professional literature critically to evaluate the theories that are most verifiable and that fit in with their personality styles.

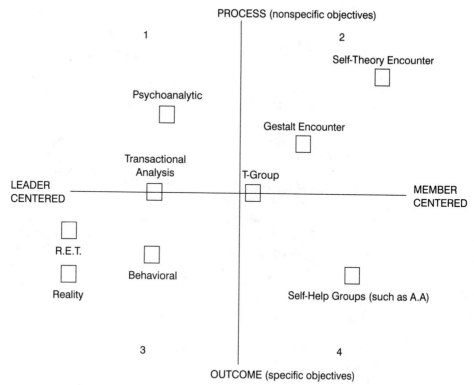

Figure 8–3
Group approaches conceptualized
Note. From James C. Hansen, Richard W. Warner, and Elsie J. Smith, *Group Counseling: Theory and Process,* 2nd Ed., Copyright © 1980 by Houghton Mifflin Company. Reprinted with permission.

STAGES IN GROUPS

Groups, like other living systems, go through stages. If an individual or group leader is not aware of these stages, the changes that occur within the group may appear confusing rather than meaningful, and the benefits may be few. Leaders can maximize learning by either setting up conditions that facilitate the development of the group or "through using developmentally based interventions, at both individual and group levels" (Saidla, 1990, p. 15). In either case, everyone in the group benefits.

There is debate within the professional literature about what and when groups go through stages. Developmental stages have been identified in various types of groups, such as learning groups and training groups, yet much of the debate about stages centers around group counseling. The most agreed-on number of group counseling stages is four or five, but there are models for as few as three and as many as six stages. Tuckman's stage model is considered mainstream.

Tuckman (1965) was one of the first theorists to design a stage process for group counseling. He believed there were four stages of group development: forming, storming, norming, and performing. This concept was later expanded to include a fifth stage of group development: adjourning (Tuckman & Jensen, 1977), or mourning/morning (Waldo, 1985). In each stage certain tasks are performed. For example, in the *forming stage,* the foundation is usually laid down for what is to come and who will be considered in or out of group deliberations. In this stage (the group's infancy), members express anxiety and dependency and talk about nonproblematic issues. One way to ease the transition into the group at this stage is to structure it so that members are relaxed and sure of what is expected of them. For example, prior to the first meeting members may be told they will be expected to spend 3 minutes telling others who they are (McCoy, 1994).

In the *storming stage,* there is usually considerable turmoil and conflict, as in adolescence. Group members seek to establish themselves in the hierarchy of the group and to deal successfully with issues concerning anxiety, power, and future expectations. Sometimes the group leader is attacked at this stage.

The *norming stage* is similar to young adulthood, where "having survived the storm the group often generates enthusiasm and cohesion. Goals and ways of working together are decided on" (Saidla, 1990, p. 16). This stage is sometimes combined with the storming stage and leads to the *performing stage,* which parallels adulthood in a developmental sense. At this stage, the group members become involved with each other and with their individual and collective goals. This is the time when the group, if it works well, is productive. Finally, in the *adjourning,* or *mourning/morning stage,* the group comes to an end, and members say good-bye to one another and to the group experience. In this death stage, members feel either fulfilled or bitter. There is often a celebration experience at this point or at least a closure ceremony.

One of the easiest ways to conceptualize groups, regardless of the type being led, is through the four-stage group model: forming, norming, working, and terminating. Table 8–2 gives a brief breakdown of the emphasis of each stage, its dynamics/characteristics, the role of the leader, the role of the members, possible problems, interventions, and ideal outcomes.

Overall, the developmental stages of a group are not readily or even clearly differentiated. "A group does not necessarily move step by step through life stages, but may move backward and forward as a part of its general development" (Hansen et al., 1980, p. 476). It is necessary that a group have at least a beginning, a middle, and a closing (Jacobs, Masson, & Harvill, 2002). After that, the question of what stage a group is in and where it is heading is one that is primarily answerable through either retrospection or insightful perception.

ISSUES IN GROUPS

There are a number of issues involved in conducting successful groups. Some deal with procedures for running groups; others deal with training and ethics.

Table 8–2

Four stages of groups

	FORMING	NORMING	WORKING	TERMINATING
Emphasis	Help members feel they are part of the group. Develop trust and inclusiveness.	Leader and members work through overt and covert tension, frustration, and conflict as they find their place in the group and develop a sense of cohesiveness (i.e., "we-ness").	Productivity, purposefulness, constructiveness, achievement, and action are highlighted.	Completeness, closure, and accomplishment of tasks/goals are highlighted along with celebration and ultimately the dismissal of the group.
Dynamics/ Characteristics	Members initiate conversations/ actions that are safe; interactions are superficial.	Energy, anxiety, and anticipation increase temporarily. Focus on functioning of group as an entity heightens. Cooperation and security increase toward end of this stage.	Members are more trusting of self and others. Increased risk taking, hopefulness, problem solving, and inclusiveness of others in achieving goals/objectives. Leader less involved in directing or structuring group. Members become increasingly responsible for running group.	About 15 percent of the group's time is spent concentrating and reflecting on events signifying the end of the group, such as completion of a task. Members deal with the issue of loss, as well as celebration, individually or collectively.
Role of Leader	Leader sets up a structured environment where members feel safe; clarifies purpose of group; establishes rules; makes introductions. Leader models appropriate behaviors; initiates ice-breaker activities; engages in limited self-disclosure; outlines vision of the group.	Leader manages conflict between members; emphasizes rules and regulations regularly; helps group become a more unified entity.	Leader concentrates on helping members and group as a whole achieve goals by encouraging interpersonal interactions. Prevention of problems through use of helping skills and renewed focus on reaching goal(s). Modeling of appropriate behavior(s) by leader.	The leader helps members assess what they have learned from the group and encourages them to be specific. Leader provides a structure for dealing with loss and celebration of group as well as its ending; arranges for follow-up and evaluation.

Table 8–2   *continued*

	FORMING	**NORMING**	**WORKING**	**TERMINATING**
Role of Members	Members need to dedicate themselves to "owning" the group and becoming involved. They need to voice what they expect to get out of the group as well as what they plan to give to it.	Members seek and receive feedback from others, which changes from more negative to neutral/positive as group works through power issues and becomes more unified. "I state-ments" become more necessary and prevalent.	Members concentrate on individual and group accomplishments; give and receive input in the form of feedback about their ideas and behaviors.	Group members focus on the work they have accomplished and what they still need to achieve. Members celebrate their accomplishments, resolve unfinished business with others, and incorporate their group experiences in both unique and uni-versal ways.
Problem Areas	Inactive, unfocused, or uninvolved group members will inhibit the group from progressing. Too much openness is also detrimental. Anxiety that is denied or unaddressed will surface again.	Group may deteriorate and become chaotic and conflictual with less involved members. Corrective feedback may be misunderstood and underused. A sense of cohesiveness may fail to develop, and group may regress and become more artificial.	Unresolved conflicts or issues may resurface. Inappropriate behaviors may be displayed and inhibit the growth of the group. Rules may be broken.	Members may deny the group is ending and be unprepared for its final session(s). Members may also be reluctant to end the group and may ask for an extension. Leaders may not prepare members for the ending and may in fact foster dependency.
Intervention Techniques	Set up the group room where it is conducive to interpersonal interaction, such as arranging chairs in a circle. Help group members feel relaxed, welcomed, and valued. Invest energy in giving group members a say or air time so they are energized and invested in the group.	Leader may introduce structured experiences, rely more on spontaneity, and use increased self-discloure. Leader may employ helping skills, such as active listening and linking, to build trust and sense of togetherness and purposefulness. Leader and members may take limited risks. Acknowledgment of differences as strengths.	More time may be allotted for discussion and interaction of goals and processes. Group may try acknowledgment of what is occurring and using the ideas of the group in reaching a resolution. A reminder to the group of agreed on goal(s) and the finiteness of the group's time may be helpful.	Both the group leader and members may actively remind each other of the conclusion of the process. Groups may be helped through good-bye events, such as celebrations, written or verbal feedback assignments on what they have learned from the group experience, and the joint planning of last sessions and the date of a follow-up.

	FORMING	NORMING	WORKING	TERMINATING
Ideal Outcome	Leader and members are clear on purpose of group, dedicated to that purpose, and feel a sense of trust in the group and their ability to contribute to it. Anxiety within the group lessens as members get to know each other and the purposes of the group better. Enthusiasm and commitment are heightened.	Differences and similarities within group members are recognized and used. Group becomes cooperative and leader/members invest in it with shared goals/ objectives. Conflicts between members are resolved. Group becomes poised to begin the working stage.	Group stays focused and productive; works as a team. Risk taking, creativity, and pride in group and its accomplishments occur. Group makes a transition toward termination.	Group members will have pride in having accomplished planned projects/goals and be able to point to tangible results. Everyone in the group will have dealt successfully with the loss in ending the group. Everyone will leave the group stronger and better connected with other group participants. Everyone will make a successful transition back from the life of the group to everyday life.

Selection and Preparation of Group Members

Screening and preparation are essential for conducting a successful group. Some individuals who wish to be members of groups are not appropriate for them. If such persons are allowed to join a group, they may end up being difficult group members (e.g., by monopolizing or manipulating) and cause the group leader considerable trouble (Kottler, 1994) or they may join with others, at an equally low level of functioning, and contribute to the regression of the group. When this happens, members become psychologically damaged, and the group is unable to accomplish its goals (McClure, 1990).

Screening and preparation are usually accomplished through pregroup interviews and training between the group leader and prospective members. During a pregroup interview, group members shall be selected whose needs and goals are compatible with the established goals of the group; who will not impede the group process; and whose well-being will not be jeopardized by the group experience. Research indicates that pregroup training, where members learn more about a group and what is expected of them, provides important information for participants and gives them a chance to lower their anxiety (Sklare, Petrosko, & Howell, 1993).

In the process of setting up a group, certain individuals may need to be screened out or may elect to screen themselves out. Screening is a two-way process. Potential group members may not be appropriate for a certain group at a particular time with a designated leader. Prospective group members should be advised of their options if they are not selected for a group, such as joining another group or waiting for a group to form that is better able to address their situation. In selecting group members, a group leader should select individuals in the group who can identify with other group members at least on some issues. In essence, the screening interview "lays the foundation upon which the group process will rest" (McCoy, 1994, p. 18).

Group members and leaders need to be informed as much as possible about group process before the group begins. Group process has to do with at least three basic questions: Who am I? Who am I with you? Who are we together? (Hulse-Killacky, Killacky, & Donigian, 2001). In other words, group process is the interaction of group members based on intrapersonal and interpersonal dynamics. Group process can be thought of as the chemistry between members; that is, it attracts or repels. It is the process of the group, not the content, focus, or purpose that will eventually determine whether a group succeeds. In other words, group process must be balanced with group content (Donigian, 1994). "When either the content or the process of . . . groups becomes disproportionate, the group may experience difficulty accomplishing work" (Nelligan, 1994, p. 8). Veterans of group experiences usually need minimal information about how a group will be conducted; novice participants may require extensive preparation. The point is that members who are informed about the procedures and focus of a group before they begin will do better in the group once it starts. This is true for any of the major types of groups, that is, psychoeducational, counseling, therapy, or task/work.

Before joining a group, potential members should check with the group organizer about what possibilities and outcomes are expected in a group experience. Corey (2001) lists a number of issues that potential participants have a right to expect clarification on before they enroll in a group. Among the most important of these, potential group members need the following information:

- A clear statement of the group's purpose
- A description of the group format, ground rules, and basic procedures
- A statement about the educational and training qualifications of the group leader(s)
- A pregroup interview to determine whether the potential group leader and members are suited for one's needs at the time
- A disclosure about the risks involved in being in a group and the rights and responsibilities of group members
- A discussion about the limitations of confidentiality and the roles group leaders and participants are expected to play within the group setting

Regardless of the perceived need for information, research supports the idea that "providing a set of expectations for participants prior to their initiation into a group improves the possibility of members having a successful group . . . experience"

So, what's your problem tonight?

Sounds to me like you're angry!

Na! sounds jealous.

I think you are bottling up rage!

I appreciate your concern for me, but I'd really like to begin tonight's group with a round of how *you're* feeling.

K. L. K. © '95

Figure 8–4
The Group
Source. © 1995 by Kurt Kraus. Used with permission.

(Sklare, Keener, & Mas, 1990, p. 145). Specific ways group leaders can facilitate "here and now group counseling are by discouraging 'you' and 'we' language, questioning, speaking in the third person, seeking approval, rescuing, and analyzing." Group leaders must model the behaviors they wish others to emulate. They must be able to make the covert overt and do away with hidden agendas, as the cartoon by Kraus (1995) humorously shows in Figure 8–4.

Finally, group leaders must know how to handle resistance and challenges to their leadership. Sklare et al. (1990, pp. 146–147) give methods of productively dealing with these behaviors.

Group Size and Duration

The size of a group is determined by its purpose and preference. Large groups are less likely to spotlight the needs of individual members. Therefore, outside of group guidance there is an optimal number of people that should be involved. A generally agreed-on number of group members is 6 to 8, though Gazda (1989) notes that if groups run as long as 6 months, up to 10 people may productively be included. Group size and duration affect each other. Corey (2001) states that

for ongoing groups with adults, about eight members with one leader seems to be a good size. Groups with children may be as small as three or four. In general, the group should have enough people to afford ample interaction so it doesn't drag and yet be small enough to give everyone a chance to participate frequently without . . . losing the sense of "group" (p. 93).

Open Versus Closed Groups

Open-ended groups admit new members after they have started; closed-ended groups do not. Lynn and Frauman (1985) point out that open-ended groups are able to replace lost members rather quickly and maintain an optimal size. Many long-term outpatient groups are open ended (Gladding, 2003; Sleek, 1995). Closed-ended groups, though not as flexible in size, promote more cohesiveness among group members and may be very productive in helping members achieve stated goals.

Confidentiality

Groups function best when members feel a sense of confidentiality; that is, what has been said within the group setting will not be revealed outside. To promote this sense of confidentiality and build trust, a group leader must be active. The subject of confidentiality should be raised in the prescreening interview. The importance of confidentiality needs to be stressed during the first meeting of the group and on a regular basis thereafter (Corey, Corey, & Callanan, 2003). The American Counseling Association and a number of other professional groups have published guidelines on confidentiality that emphasize the role group leaders have in protecting their members by clearly defining what confidentiality is and the importance and difficulty of enforcing it. Whenever there is any question about the betrayal of confidentiality within a group, it should be dealt with immediately. Otherwise, the problem grows and the cohesiveness of the group breaks down. Olsen (1971) points out that counselors must realize they can only guarantee their own adherence to the principles of confidentiality. Still, they must ensure the rights of all group members.

Physical Structure

Where a group is conducted is either an asset or a liability. Yalom (1995), among other prominent specialists in group work, emphasizes the need for a physical structure (i.e., a room or setting) that ensures the safety and growth of group members. Groups within community agencies need to be conducted in places that promote the well-being of the group. Attractive furnishings and the way the group is assembled (preferably in a circle) can facilitate the functioning of the group.

Co-Leaders

It is not necessary for groups to have co-leaders (two leaders); however, such an arrangement can be beneficial to the group and to the leaders, especially if the group has over 10 members. With co-leaders, one leader can work with the group while the other monitors the group process. A co-leader arrangement may also be beneficial when an inexperienced leader and an experienced leader are working together. In such a setup, the inexperienced leader can learn from the experienced one. Many group specialists advocate that an inexperienced leader co-lead a group first before attempting the process alone (Ritter, 1982).

Dinkmeyer and Muro (1979) suggest that successful, experienced co-leaders (a) possess a similar philosophical and operational style, (b) have similar experience and competence, (c) establish a model relationship for effective human interaction, (d) be aware of splitting member loyalty ties to one leader or the other and help the group deal with this, and (e) agree on counseling goals and the processes to achieve them so that power struggles are avoided.

Pietrofesa, Hoffman, and Splete (1984) recommend that co-leaders sit opposite each other in a group so that leader responsibility and observation are maximized. They point out that it is not necessary for group co-leaders to be of the opposite sex; skills, not gender, matter most.

Self-Disclosure

Self-disclosure is defined as "here and now feelings, attitudes, and beliefs" (Shertzer & Stone, 1981, p. 206). The process of self-disclosure is dependent on the trust that group members have for one another (Bunch, Lund, & Wiggins, 1983). If there is high trust, there will be greater self-disclosure. An interesting aspect of this phenomenon is that self-disclosure builds on itself and also builds cohesion among group members (Forsyth, 1999). During the first stages of the group, self-disclosure may have to be encouraged. Morran (1982) suggests that in the beginning sessions of a group, leaders make self-disclosures often in order to serve as a model for others and to promote the process. As Stockton, Barr, and Klein (1981) document, group members who make few verbal self-disclosures are more likely than others to drop out of a group or have a less positive experience in the group.

Feedback

Feedback is a multidimensional process that consists of group members' responding to the verbal messages and nonverbal behaviors of one another. It is one of the most important and abused parts of any group experience. When feedback is given honestly and with care, group members can gauge the impact of their actions on others and attempt new behaviors. Corey (2001) distinguishes between group feedback given at the end of a session and that given at the termination of a group. During the latter process, Corey encourages group members to be clear, concise, and concrete with one another. Group members should give themselves feedback about how they have changed during the group experience. After processing feedback information, group members should record some of the things said during final feedback sessions so they will not forget and can make use of the experience in evaluating progress toward their goals.

To promote helpful feedback, the following criteria should be taken into consideration (Donigian & Hulse-Killacky, 1999; Gladding, 2003; Yalom, 1995):

- Feedback should be beneficial to the receiver and not serve the needs of the giver.
- Feedback is more effective when it is based on describable behavior.
- In the early stages of group development, positive feedback is more beneficial and more readily accepted than negative feedback.
- Feedback is most effective when it immediately follows a stimulus behavior and is validated by others.
- Feedback is of greater benefit when the receiver is open and trusts the giver.

Follow-Up

Follow-up is used to keep "in touch" with members after the group has terminated to determine how well individuals are progressing on personal or group goals. Often group leaders fail to conduct proper follow-up. This failure is especially prevalent in short-term counseling groups or in groups led by an outside leader (Gazda, 1989). Leaders should provide for follow-up of group members after termination of a group as needed or requested. Follow-up helps group members and leaders assess what they gained in the group experience and allows the group leader to make a referral of a group member for help, if appropriate. Follow-up sessions maximize the effects of a group experience and encourage members to keep pursuing original goals (Jacobs et al., 2002).

Corey (2001) suggests that a follow-up session for a short-term group be conducted about 3 months after termination of the group experience. He points out that the process of mutual feedback and support from other group members at this time can be very valuable. If group members are aware during the termination stage of their group that they will meet again for a follow-up, they are more likely than not to continue pursuing their goals. In addition to a whole group follow-up, individual follow-up between leaders and group members is important, even if these sessions are conducted by phone.

QUALITIES OF EFFECTIVE GROUP LEADERS

There are distinguishing qualities of effective and ineffective group leaders (Johnson & Johnson, 2000). For instance, group leaders who are authoritarian, aggressive, confrontational, or removed emotionally from the group are ineffective and produce group casualties (i.e., members who drop out or are worse after the group experience) (Yalom & Lieberman, 1971). The following are four leadership qualities that have a positive effect on the outcome of groups, if not used excessively:

1. *Caring:* the more the better
2. *Meaning attribution:* includes clarifying, explaining, and providing a cognitive framework for change

3. *Emotional stimulation:* includes being active, challenging content, risk taking, and self-disclosure

4. *Executive function:* includes developing norms, structuring, and suggesting procedures (Yalom, 1995)

It is vital that group leaders find a position between the two extremes of emotional stimulation and executive function for the well-being of the group. Group leaders should not allow members to experience so much emotion that they are unable to process the material being discovered in the group; nor should they structure the situation so rigidly that no emotion is expressed.

Ohlsen (1977) states that effective leaders are those who understand the forces operating within a group, recognize whether these forces are therapeutic, and if they are not, take steps to better manage the group with the assistance of its members. His assessment of leadership complements that of Yalom (1995) and Osborne (1982), who believe that good group leaders behave with intentionality because they are able to anticipate where the group process is moving and recognize group needs. An example of this phenomenon is the ability of group leaders to treat the group homogeneously when there is a need to manage group tensions and protect group members and to treat them heterogeneously when the group has become too comfortable and is not working.

In addition, Corey (2001) maintains that effective group leaders are committed "to the never-ending struggle" to become more effective as human beings. He lists a number of personal qualities that are "vitally related to effective group leadership" (p. 29). Among these qualities are presence, personal power, courage, willingness to confront oneself, sincerity, authenticity, enthusiasm, sense of identity, and inventiveness/creativity.

Gill and Barry (1982) agree that group leadership skills are crucial to effectiveness. They trace the evolution of the emphasis on skills in groups through four classification systems (Dyer and Vriend, 1977; Ivey, 1973; Lieberman, Yalom, & Miles, 1973; Ohlsen, 1977). Gill and Barry's conceptualization of needed group skills is based on Egan's (2002) model of counseling, which involves three stages: group formation, group awareness, and group action.

A final quality of effective group leaders is that they are well educated in group theory and practice. In 1984, the Council for Accreditation of Counseling and Related Educational Programs (CACREP) adopted ASGW guidelines for the education of group leaders. These detailed guidelines, which were revised in both 1990 and 2000, are vital for potential group leaders to consult and follow.

SUMMARY AND CONCLUSION

Groups are an exciting, diversified, necessary, and effective way to help people and can take an educational, preventive, or remedial form. Standards have been formulated by the ASGW for psychoeducational groups, counseling groups, psychotherapy groups, and task/work groups. The theories used in groups are often the same as those employed in working with individuals. There are differences in application, however, especially in regard to an emphasis on dynamics, process, and content.

Group leaders must be competent in dealing with individual as well as with group issues if they are to be maximally effective. Learning how to do this is a developmental process. Good group leaders know what types of groups they are leading and share this information with potential members. Group leaders follow ethical, legal, and procedural guidelines of professional organizations. They are concerned with the general well-being of their groups and the people in them. They anticipate problems before they occur and take proactive steps to correct them. They systematically follow up with group members after the group has terminated. They keep up with the professional literature about groups and are constantly striving to improve their personal and professional levels of functioning.

Overall, groups are a stage-based, effective, and expanding way of working with people to achieve individual and collective goals. Professional counselors, especially those in community settings, must acquire group skills if they are to be well rounded and versatile.

REFERENCES

Association for Specialists in Group Work (ASGW). (1990). *Standards for training group workers.* Alexandria, VA: Author.

Association for Specialists in Group Work (ASGW). (1992). Professional standards for the training of group workers. *Journal for Specialists in Group Work, 17,* 12–19.

Association for Specialists in Group Work (ASGW). (1998). *Best practice guidelines.* Alexandria, VA: Author.

Association for Specialists in Group Work (ASGW). (2000). *Professional standards for the training of group workers.* Alexandria, VA: Author.

Avasthi, S. (1990). Native American students targeted for math and sciences. *Guidepost, 33*(6), 1, 6, 8.

Blatter, C. W., & Jacobsen, J. J. (1993). Older women coping with divorce: Peer support groups. *Women and Therapy, 14,* 141–154.

Brammer, L. M., Abrego, P. J., & Shostrom, E. L. (1993). *Therapeutic counseling and psychology.* Upper Saddle River, NJ: Prentice Hall.

Bunch, B. J., Lund, N. L., & Wiggins, F. K. (1983). Self-disclosure and perceived closeness in the development of group process. *Journal for Specialists in Group Work, 8,* 59–66.

Campbell, C. A., & Myrick, R. D. (1990). Motivational group counseling for low performing students. *Journal for Specialists in Group Work, 15,* 43–50.

Carroll, M., Bates, M. M., & Johnson, C. D. (1997). *Group leadership: A manual for group counseling leaders* (rev. ed.). Denver: Love.

Carroll, M. R., & Levo, L. (1985). The association for specialists in group work. *Journal for Counseling and Development, 63,* 453–454.

Childers, J. H., Jr., & Couch, R. D. (1989). Myths about group counseling: Identifying and challenging misconceptions. *Journal for Specialists in Group Work, 14,* 105–111.

Corey, G. (2001). *Theory and practice of group counseling* (5th ed.). Pacific Grove, CA: Brooks/ Cole.

Corey, G., Corey, M. S., & Callanan, P. (2003). *Issues and ethics in the helping profession* (6th ed.). Pacific Grove, CA: Brooks/Cole.

Dinkmeyer, D. C., & Muro, J. J. (1979). *Group counseling: Theory and practice* (2nd ed.). Itasca, IL: F. E. Peacock.

Donigian, J. (1994, Fall). Group reflections. *Together, 23,* 6.

Donigian, J., & Hulse-Killacky, D. (1999). *Critical incidents in group therapy* (2nd ed.). Pacific Grove, CA: Brooks/Cole.

Dyer, W. W., & Vriend, J. (1977). *Counseling techniques that work.* New York: Funk & Wagnalls.

Egan, G. (2002). *The skilled helper* (7th ed.). Pacific Grove, CA: Brooks/Cole.

Ford, D., & Urban, H. (1963). *Systems of psychotherapy: A comparative study*. New York: Wiley.

Forsyth, D. R. (1999). *Group dynamics* (3rd ed.). Belmont, CA: Wadsworth.

Frey, D. H. (1972). Conceptualizing counseling theories. *Counselor Education and Supervision, 11,* 243–250.

Gazda, G. M. (1989). *Group counseling: A developmental approach* (4th ed.). Boston: Allyn & Bacon.

Gazda, G. M., Asbury, F. A., Balzer, F. J., Childers, W. C., Phelps, R. E., & Walters, R. P. (1999). *Human relations development* (6th ed.). Boston: Allyn & Bacon.

Gazda, G. M., Ginter, E. J., & Horne, A. M. (2001). *Theory and practice of group psychotherapy*. Boston: Allyn & Bacon.

Gill, J. G., & Barry, R. A. (1982). Group focused counseling: Classifying the essential skills. *Personnel and Guidance Journal, 60,* 302–305.

Gladding, S. T. (1979). A restless presence: Group process as a pilgrimage. *The School Counselor, 27,* 126–127.

Gladding, S. T. (1994). *Effective group counseling*. Greensboro, NC: ERIC/CASS.

Gladding, S. T. (2001). *The counseling dictionary: Concise definitions of frequently used terms*. Upper Saddle River, NJ: Prentice Hall.

Gladding, S. T. (2003). *Group work: A counseling specialty* (4th ed.). Upper Saddle River, NJ: Prentice Hall.

Hansen, J. C., Warner, R. W., & Smith, E. J. (1980). *Group counseling* (2nd ed.). Chicago: Rand McNally.

Hulse-Killacky, D., Killacky, J., & Donigian, J. (2001). *Making task groups work in your world*. Upper Saddle River, NJ: Prentice Hall.

Ivey, A. E. (1973). Demystifying the group process: Adapting microcounseling procedures to counseling in groups. *Educational Technology, 13,* 27–31.

Jacobs, E. E., Masson, R. L., & Harvill, R. L. (2002). *Group counseling* (4th ed.). Pacific Grove, CA: Brooks/Cole.

Johnson, D. W., & Johnson, F. P. (2000). *Joining together: Group theory and group skills* (7th ed.). Boston: Allyn & Bacon.

Kottler, J. A. (1994). Working with difficult group members. *Journal for Specialists in Group Work, 19,* 3–10.

Lieberman, M. A., Yalom, I. D., & Miles, M. B. (1973). *Encounter groups: First facts*. New York: Basic Books.

Livneh, H., & Sherwood-Hawes, A. (1993). Group counseling approaches with persons who have sustained myocardial infarction. *Journal of Counseling and Development, 72,* 57–61.

Luchins, A. S. (1964). *Group therapy*. New York: Random House.

Lynn, S. J., & Frauman, D. (1985). Group psychotherapy. In S. J. Lynn & J. P. Garske (Eds.), *Contemporary psychotherapies: Models and methods* (pp. 419–458). Columbus, OH: Merrill.

McClure, B. A. (1990). The group mind: Generative and regressive groups. *Journal for Specialists in Group Work, 15,* 159–170.

McClure, B. A. (1994). The shadow side of regressive groups. *Counseling and Values, 38,* 77–89.

McCoy, G. A. (1994, April). A plan for the first group session. *The ASCA Counselor, 31,* 18.

Morran, D. K. (1982). Leader and member self-disclosing behavior in counseling groups. *Journal for Specialists in Group Work, 7,* 218–223.

Nelligan, A. (1994, Fall). Balancing process and content: A collaborative experience. *Together, 23,* 8–9.

Ohlsen, M. M. (1977). *Group counseling* (2nd ed.). New York: Holt, Rinehart & Winston.

Olsen, L. D. (1971). Ethical standards for group leaders. *Personnel and Guidance Journal, 50,* 288.

Osborne, W. L. (1982). Group counseling: Direction and intention. *Journal for Specialists in Group Work, 7,* 275–280.

Page, R. C., & Chandler, J. (1994). Effects of group counseling on ninth-grade at-risk students. *Journal of Mental Health Counseling,* 340–351.

Page, B. J., Delmonico, D. L., Walsh, J., L'Amoreaux, N. A., Danninhirsh, C., & Thompson, R. S. (2000). Setting up on-line support groups using The Palace software. *Journal for Specialists in Group Work, 25,* 133–145.

Peterson, N., & Priour, G. (2000). Battered women: A group vocational counseling model. In N. Peterson & R. C. Gonzalez (Eds.), *Career counseling models for diverse populations* (pp. 205–218). Pacific Grove, CA: Brooks/Cole.

Pietrofesa, J. J., Hoffman, A., & Splete, H. H. (1984). *Counseling: An introduction* (2nd ed.). Boston: Houghton Mifflin.

Riordan, R. J., & Beggs, M. S. (1987). Counselors and self-help groups. *Journal of Counseling and Development, 65,* 427–429.

Ritter, K. Y. (1982). Training group counselors: A total curriculum perspective. *Journal for Specialists in Group Work, 7,* 266–274.

Saidla, D. D. (1990). Cognitive development and group stages. *Journal for Specialists in Group Work, 15,* 15–20.

Shertzer, B., & Stone, S. C. (1981). *Fundamentals of guidance* (4th ed.). Boston: Houghton Mifflin.

Sklare, G., Keener, R., & Mas, C. (1990). Preparing members for "here-and-now" group counseling. *Journal for Specialists in Group Work, 15,* 141–148.

Sklare, G., Petrosko, J., & Howell, S. (1993). The effect of pregroup training on members' level of anxiety. *Journal for Specialists in Group Work, 18,* 109–114.

Sleek, S. (1995, July). Group therapy: Tapping the power of teamwork. *APA Monitor, 26* (1), 38–39.

Stockton, R., Barr, J. E., & Klein, R. (1981). Identifying the group dropout: A review of the literature. *Journal for Specialists in Group Work, 6,* 75–82.

Terres, C. K., & Larrabee, M. J. (1985). Ethical issues and group work with children. *Elementary School Guidance and Counseling, 19,* 190–197.

Tuckman, B. (1965). Developmental sequence in small groups. *Psychological Bulletin, 63,* 384–399.

Tuckman, B. W., & Jensen, M. A. (1977). Stages of small group development revisited. *Group and Organizational Studies, 2,* 419–427.

Vander Kolk, C. J. (1985). *Introduction to group counseling and psychotherapy.* Columbus, OH: Merrill.

Viney, L. L., Henry, R. M., & Campbell, J. (2001). The impact of group work on offender adolescents. *Journal of Counseling and Development, 79,* 373–381.

Waldo, M. (1985). Curative factor framework for conceptualizing group counseling. *Journal for Counseling and Development, 64,* 52–58.

Waldo, M., & Bauman, S. (1998). Regrouping the categorization of group work: A goal and process (GAP) matrix for groups. *Journal for Specialists in Group Work, 23,* 164–176.

Ward, D. E. (1982). A model for the more effective use of theory in group work. *Journal for Specialists in Group Work, 7,* 224–230.

Yalom, I. D. (1985). *The theory and practice of group psychotherapy* (3rd ed.). New York: Basic Books.

Yalom, I. D. (1995). *The theory and practice of group psychotherapy* (4th ed.). New York: Basic Books.

Yalom, I. D., & Lieberman, M. (1971). A study of encounter group casualties. *Archives of General Psychiatry, 25,* 16–30.

Zimpfer, D. G. (1990). Publications in group work, 1989. *Journal for Specialists in Group Work, 15,* 179–189.

CHAPTER 9

Marriage and Family Counseling

At thirty-five, with wife and child
  a Ph.D.
    and hopes as bright as a full moon
      on a warm August night,
He took a role as a healing man
  blending it with imagination,
    necessary change and common sense
To make more than an image on an eye lens
  of a small figure running quickly up steps;
Quietly he traveled
  like one who holds a candle to darkness
  and questions its power
So that with heavy years, long walks,
  shared love, and additional births
He became as a seasoned actor,
  who, forgetting his lines in the silence,
    stepped upstage and without prompting
      lived them.

Gladding, S. T. (1974). Without applause. *Personnel and Guidance Journal, 52,* 586. © 1974 by ACA. Reprinted with permission. No further reproduction authorized without written permission of ACA.

The profession of marriage and family counseling is relatively new. Its formal beginnings are traced to the 1940s and early 1950s, but its real growth occurred in the 1970s and 1980s (Brown & Christensen, 1999; Nichols, 1993). It differs from individual counseling and group counseling in both its emphasis and its clientele (Gladding, 2003; Hines, 1988; Trotzer, 1988). For instance, marriage and family counseling usually concentrates on making changes in systems, whereas individual counseling and group counseling primarily focus on intrapersonal and interpersonal changes.

This chapter explores various aspects of marriage and family counseling as they relate to community counselors. It begins with an examination of what a family is, the family life cycle, various family life forms, and the issues prevalent in each. It then looks at family stressors, outcome research, and the organizations and associations of those most involved in the profession. In addition, this chapter explains, briefly, some of the major theories employed in both marriage counseling and family counseling including those that are systemic as well as nonsystemic. The chapter then concludes with an overview of marriage and family enrichment.

Counselors who know how to work with couples and families are at a distinct advantage in offering services to a wide variety of clientele. It is essential for those who are employed in community settings to master the skills of helping those in various family life situations.

WHAT IS A FAMILY?

Families come in many forms (e.g., nuclear, single-parent, remarried, multigenerational, gay/lesbian) and may be defined in a number of ways (Goldenberg & Goldenberg, 2002). In this chapter, a *family* is considered to be those persons who are biologically and/or psychologically related through historical, emotional, or economic bonds and who perceive themselves to be a part of a household (Gladding, 2002). Such a definition allows for maximum flexibility in defining the boundaries of family life and fosters an understanding of the different forms of family life available without describing each in great detail. Furthermore, this definition engenders an appreciation of persons within family units and the roles they play.

Overall, families are characterized in multiple ways, and those that are healthy function efficiently according to form and need. Within most families there is a dual emphasis on fostering the development of individuals while simultaneously offering family members stability, protection, and preservation of the family unit structure (Burr, Hill, Nye, & Reiss, 1979; Strong, DeVault, & Sayad, 2001).

FAMILY LIFE AND THE FAMILY LIFE CYCLE

Family life and the optimal growth and development that take place within it are at the heart of marriage and family counseling. The *family life cycle* is the name given to the stages a family goes through as it evolves over the years. These stages sometimes parallel and complement those in the individual life cycle (e.g., Erikson, 1959; Levinson,

1978), but often they are unique due to the number of people involved and to the diversity of tasks to be accomplished. In Table 9–1, a 9-stage family life-cycle model is illustrated, which is derived from several sources (see Becvar & Becvar, 2000). The cycle, which is primarily applicable to middle-class Americans, begins with the unattached adult and continues through the family in later life. In each stage of the family life cycle there are practical, emotional, and relational challenges as well as potential crises that need to be addressed in a timely and adequate way.

Some families and family members are more "on time" in achieving stage-critical tasks that go with the family cycle of life shown here. In such cases, a better sense of well-being is achieved (Carter & McGoldrick, 1999). Other families, such as those in poverty, the wealthy, or new immigrants, have different ways of navigating through the life cycle. Regardless of timing, all families have to deal with family cohesion (i.e., emotional bonding) and family adaptability (i.e., ability to be flexible and change). Each of these two dimensions has four levels, as represented by Olson (1986) in what is known as the Circumplex Model of Marital and Family Systems (see Figure 9–1). "The two dimensions are curvilinear in that families that apparently are very high or very low on both dimensions seem dysfunctional, whereas families that are balanced seem to function more adequately" (Maynard & Olson, 1987, p. 502).

Families that are most successful, functional, happy, and strong are not only balanced but are highly social (Watts, Trusty, & Lim, 2000). According to researchers (Stinnett & DeFrain, 1985), healthy families (a) are committed to one another, (b) appreciate each other, (c) spend time together, (d) have good communication patterns, (e) have a high degree of religious orientation, and (f) are able to deal with crisis in a positive manner.

Wilcoxon (1985) notes the importance of marriage and family counselors' being aware of the different stages within the family while being concurrently attuned to developmental tasks of its individual members. When counselors are sensitive to individual family members and to the family as a whole, they are able to realize that some individual manifestations, such as depression (Lopez, 1986), career indecisiveness (Kinnier, Brigman, & Noble, 1990), and/or substance abuse (Stanton, 1999), are related to family structure and functioning. Consequently, they are able to be more inclusive in their treatment plans.

When evaluating family patterns and the mental health of everyone involved, it is crucial that an assessment be based on the form and developmental stage of the family constellation. To facilitate this process, Carter and McGoldrick (1999) propose sets of developmental tasks for traditional and nontraditional families. Bowen (1978) suggests terms, such as *enmeshment* and *triangulation*, to describe family dysfunctionality. (*Enmeshment* refers to family environments where members are overly dependent on each other or are undifferentiated. *Triangulation* refers to family fusion situations where one person is pulled in two different directions by the other members of the triangle.) Counselors who effectively work with couples and families have guidelines for determining how, where, when, or whether to intervene in the family process. They do not fail to act, such as neglecting to engage everyone in the therapeutic process, nor do they overreact, such as placing too much emphasis on verbal expression (Gladding, 2002).

Table 9–1
Stages of the Family Life Cycle

Stage	Emotional Issues	Stage-Critical Tasks
1. Unattached adult	Accepting parent–offspring separation	a. Differentiation from family of origin b. Development of peer relations c. Initiation of career
2. Newly married adults	Commitment to the marriage	a. Formation of marital system b. Making room for spouse with family and friends c. Adjusting career demands
3. Childbearing adults	Accepting new members into the system	a. Adjusting marriage to make room for child b. Taking on parenting roles c. Making room for grandparents
4. Preschool-age child	Accepting the new personality	a. Adjusting family to the needs of specific child(ren) b. Coping with energy drain and lack of privacy c. Taking time out to be a couple
5. School-age child	Allowing child to establish relationships outside the family	a. Extending family/society interactions b. Encouraging the child's educational progress c. Dealing with increased activities and time demands
6. Teenage child	Increasing flexibility of family boundaries to allow independence	a. Shifting the balance in the parent–child relationship b. Refocusing on midlife career and marital issues c. Dealing with increasing concerns for older generation
7. Launching center	Accepting exits from and entries into the family	a. Releasing adult children into work, college, marriage b. Maintaining supportive home base c. Accepting occasional returns of adult children
8. Middle-aged adults	Letting go of children and facing each other again	a. Rebuilding the marriage b. Welcoming children's spouses, grandchildren into family c. Dealing with aging of one's own parents
9. Retired adults	Accepting retirement and old age	a. Maintaining individual and couple functioning b. Supporting middle generation c. Coping with death of parents, spouse d. Closing or adapting family home

Note. From *Family Therapy: A Systematic Integration* (4th ed.), by Dorothy Stroh Becvar and Raphael J. Becvar, 2000, Needham Heights, MA: Allyn & Bacon. © 2000 by Allyn & Bacon. Reprinted with permission.

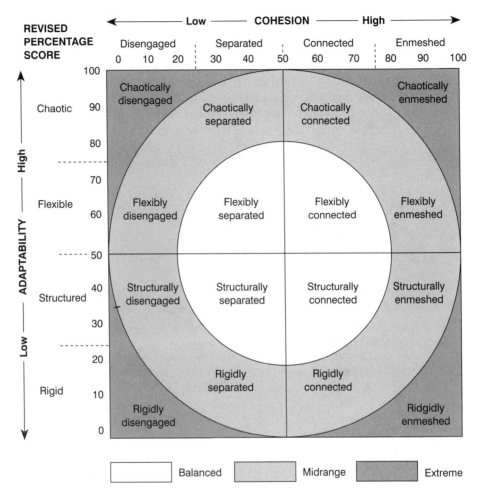

Figure 9–1
The circumplex model
Note. From *Family Social Science,* by David H. Olson, Ph.D., Professor, University of Minnesota,
St. Paul, MN. © 1979 (rev. 1986). Reprinted with permission.

DIFFERENT TYPES OF FAMILIES AND THEIR ISSUES

Prior to the 1980s, family therapy, with some notable exceptions, concentrated on working with traditional, middle-class nuclear families. Since that time, however, it has become evident that the future of the profession of family therapy is dependent on the ability and flexibility of professionals to work with a wide variety of families. Some of the most prevalent of these family forms are minority ethnic family groups, dual-career, single-parent, childless, remarried, gay/lesbian, aging, and multigenerational.

Minority Ethnic Families

Past research has indicated that distinct and relatively small-sized ethnic family groups are often misunderstood by majority cultures. This misunderstanding is associated with cultural prejudices, flaws in collecting data about minorities, stereotyping, and unrecognized economic differences (Hampson, Beavers, & Hulgus, 1990; Thomas, 1990). Bias is unfortunate because it perpetuates myths that may cause harm. Ethnic families need to be seen in regard to their strengths and liabilities both collectively and individually.

One trend now is to study ethnic families from the perspective of their competencies, social class, and observed family styles (Hampson et al., 1990). This type of approach makes it more likely that significant differences and similarities of families from various ethnic backgrounds will be reported accurately and fairly and that any treatment offered will be appropriate.

Dual-Career Families

Dual-career families are those in which both marital partners are engaged in work that is developmental in sequence and to which they have a high commitment (Hertz & Marshall, 2001). Over 50 percent of married couples in the United States are pursuing careers, and the likelihood is that their numbers will continue to increase. The reasons for this trend are complex, but they are related to the large number of women in the work force, economic pressures, and the tendency for professionals to marry other professionals.

"Balancing the dual-career and family life can lead to conflict and create a considerable source of stress" (Thomas, 1990, p. 174). Such a situation is likely if one or both members of the couple are inflexible in redefining traditional gender roles related to their careers and family obligations. In the past, men have reported that their career interests interfered with their fathering roles, and women have stated that parenting interfered with their career roles (Gilbert, 1985; Nicola, 1980). Current research indicates that working women are more likely to experience conflict between their work and family roles than are working men (Werbel, 1998). Learning new skills, staying flexible, and continually assessing and revising work and family life are necessary if dual-career couples are to thrive. Because there are multiple variables in family life that affect the quality of these couples, their coping strategies over time must be dealt with, as well as their career and personal patterns.

Single-Parent Families

Single-parent families continue to be a challenge for marriage and family counselors. These families are often some of the poorest and neediest (Waggonseller, Ruegamer, & Harrington, 1998). Although mothers predominantly head single-parent families (85 percent), each year there is an increasing number of fathers who gain custody of their children (Bumpass & Sweet, 1989; Davis & Borns, 1999).

The primary challenge for family counseling professionals is determining how to help these families find the support and services they need. The theoretical work of Nagy, which emphasizes community connectedness, is probably one of the most functional yet least utilized theories to date available for working with single-parent families (Boszormenyi-Nagy, 1987).

Childless Families

For many couples the option of whether they will have a child (or children) is one they consciously make. For others, the decision is a result of chance (such as marrying late) or biology (infertility). For couples born between 1946 and 1955 (the initial wave of the baby boomers), "nearly one in five is childless. For college educated women in their 40s, the rate is one in four" (Shulins, 1992, p. 14). This significant rate of childlessness is expected to continue for women born in the 1960s. It is not an all-time high, but it is equal to the childless rate of "women born around World War I who matured during the Depression" (Usdansky, 1993, 8A).

Childless couples, especially women, face pressures related to electing to be childless. Women who are childless are sometimes stigmatized and made to feel out of place in social gatherings. Extended family relationships are sometimes strained, especially when siblings of the childless couple have children. Childless couples may also have difficulty in mourning the children they never had or in coming to terms with the choices they made not to have children (McGoldrick & Walsh, 1999).

In any of these situations, family counselors may need to involve other family members related to the couple. They may also need to emphasize the opportunities available to childless couples and advantages of being childless, such as having less stress, more discretionary income, and greater opportunities to serve in the community.

Remarried Families

Remarried families (along with first-married and single-parent families) are one of three predominant types of American families. One reason for the growth of this type of family is associated with the fact that approximately three out of every four people who divorce eventually remarry (Goldenberg & Goldenberg, 2002).

Overall, remarried families are quite complex in regard to relationships. Individuals within them often have to establish new roles and new rules. Family counselors need to be prepared to deal with the multifaceted nature of these families and help individual members bridge physical and psychological gaps in relating to each other.

Gay/Lesbian Families

Since the 1970s same-sex couples have become increasingly prevalent in the United States. Census data suggest that partners of gays and lesbians are better educated than those of heterosexuals. Therefore, gay couples have higher incomes than heterosexual couples, whereas lesbian couples approach the average income of heterosexual couples.

The high education and income levels contribute to the varied lifestyles of gay/lesbian couples. The families they create range in composition from those that only include a significant other to those that are composed of a number of people. Some of these families have children from previous marriages, and others, especially lesbian couples, conceive children through biological means. Almost all gay/lesbian couples face some form of discrimination and prejudice in the communities in which they live, which tend to be large cities (Johnson & Colucci, 1999).

A challenge for counselors working with these families is understanding them. These families have traditionally had fluid boundaries and flexible composition. A second challenge of helping these families is assisting them in relating positively to the heterosexual families from which most came, to the communities in which they live, and to themselves and their partners.

Aging Families

The American family is aging in proportion to the population of the United States. It is estimated that by the year 2020, the typical family will consist of at least four generations. Furthermore, by the year 2040, nearly a quarter of the population of the United States will be 65 years and older. Yet, the study of aging families is a new frontier that "still lacks identifiable landmarks and road maps" (Goldberg, 1992, p. 1).

What we do know is that with increased age, families become concerned with different personal, family, and societal issues. For instance, on an individual level there is more emphasis on physical health (Goldin & Mohr, 2000). This focus spills over into family and institutional relationships as well. In addition to health, aging families are involved with the launching or relaunching of their young adult children. This crisis is especially acute during hard financial times, such as recessions, when the number of young unmarried adults return to live with their parents.

Another factor associated with aging families is increased stress and rewards as elderly relatives move into their children's homes (Montalvo & Thompson, 1988). In these situations, couples and families have to change their household and community routines and sometimes become involved in the caretaking of their parents. This type of situation can increase tension, anger, joy, guilt, gratitude, and grief among all involved. It is an uneven experience that fluctuates in its rewards and restrictions. It is a process that marriage and family counselors must become familiar with if they are to help aging families and their members cope.

Multigenerational Families

The number of multigenerational families has grown over the years. These are households that include a child, a parent, and a grandparent, according to the U.S. Bureau of the Census definition. Common before World War II, the number of multigenerational families decreased from that time until the 1980s. Now there are two factors influencing the increase in the number of these families. The first is economic, that is, when the economy is in recession fewer people maintain separate households. The second factor is medical. The aging population of the United States is living longer because of advances in medicine. Many individuals, especially those past their mid-70s, cannot maintain a house by themselves and, therefore, move in with their children.

The advantages of multigenerational families are many. Different generations get to interact and enjoy each other more directly. There are often more people to help with household and childcare duties, which can lessen stress. However, the disadvantages of this type of arrangement can be considerable. For instance, there may be increased stress on the parent subunit to take care of children and grandparents. There can also be new financial and psychological difficulties as the parent subunit has to take care of more people with the same amount of money and is simultaneously squeezed to provide adequate living space.

FAMILY LIFE STRESSORS

Stress is an inevitable part of life in all families. As with individuals, families attempt to keep stressful events from becoming distressful (Selye, 1976). They do this through a variety of means, some of which are healthier than others. The ways that families cope with stressors is sometimes related to whether they are prepared to deal with these situations.

Carter and McGoldrick (1999) have categorized family stressors into two types: vertical and horizontal (see Figure 9–2). Among the *vertical stressors* are those

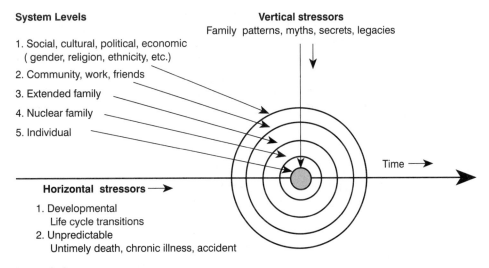

Figure 9–2
Horizontal and vertical stressors
Note. From *The Changing Family Life Cycle: A Framework for Family Therapy* (2nd ed.), by Betty Carter and Monica McGoldrick, 1989, Boston: Allyn & Bacon. © 1989 by Allyn & Bacon. Reprinted by permission.

dealing with family patterns, myths, secrets, and legacies. These are stressors that are historical and that families inherit from previous generations. *Horizontal stressors* are those related to the present. Some horizontal stressors are developmental, such as life cycle transitions; others are unpredictable, such as an accident. The Carter and McGoldrick model is systemic and in line with how most family therapists view families.

Although families have universally expected stressors that accompany life transitions, families are unique too. For example, the rates at which families plan for their children to grow up, leave home, and start families of their own differ. Families with a British American background usually expect a much faster shift in these events than Italian American families. Anticipating when events may happen helps family members prepare themselves mentally and physically for changes and even failure. In many cases, family life stages and individual life stages complement each other (Bowen, 1978).

Expected Life Stressors

There are a number of stressors that families can expect regardless of their level of functioning. Some are developmental stressors (i.e., age and life stage related), and others are situational stressors (i.e., interpersonal, such as dealing with feelings) (Figley, 1989). Some stressors are related to present events such as work, school, and social functions (Kaslow, 1991); others are more historical in nature (i.e., family life heritage).

When surveyed, family members frequently cite prevalent stressors in their families as those associated with (a) economics and finances, (b) children's behaviors, (c) insufficient couple time, (d) communicating with children, (e) insufficient personal time, and (f) insufficient family play time (Curran, 1985). Some of these everyday stressors deal with deficiencies, such as not having enough time. In these types of stress situations, families can resolve problems through planning ahead, lowering their expectations, or both. They are then better able to cope. The flip side of this solution-based stress relief is that families and their members may experience stress from not accomplishing enough of what they planned and from overscheduling family calendars.

Unexpected Life Stressors

Some family life situations take family members by surprise or are beyond the control of the family. If life events come too soon, are delayed, or fail to materialize, the health, happiness, and well-being of all involved may be affected (Schlossberg, 1984). Intensified emotionality and/or behavioral disorganization in families and their members are likely to occur as a result.

Timing is crucial to the functioning of families and their members, especially in dealing with the unexpected. If timing is off, families struggle. For example, if a first wedding is either relatively early in one's life (e.g., before age 20) or relatively late (after age 40), the difficulty of accepting or dealing with the circumstances surrounding the event, such as interacting with the new spouse, is increased for both the persons marrying and their families (Carter & McGoldrick, 1999).

Family development and environmental fit (Eccles et al., 1993) is a crucial variable in unexpected stress as well. Some environments are conducive to helping families develop and resolve unexpected crises; others are not. For example, a family that lives in an impoverished environment and experiences the loss of its major wage earner may not recover to its previous level of functioning, despite that family's best effort. Such would probably not be the case with a family experiencing the same circumstance but living in a more affluent and supportive environment.

RESEARCH AND ASSOCIATIONS

Interest in marriage and family counseling has grown rapidly since the 1970s, and the number of individuals receiving training in this specialty has increased accordingly. One reason for these increases is the growing need for services. Gurman and Kniskern (1981) report that approximately 50 percent of all problems brought to counselors are related to marriage and family issues. These issues include unemployment, poor school performance, spouse abuse, depression, rebellion, and self-concept.

Further, research studies summarized by Pinsof and Wynne (1995, 2000) report a number of interesting findings. First, family counseling interventions are at least as effective as individual interventions for most client complaints and lead to significantly greater durability of change. Second, some forms of family counseling (such as using structural/strategic family therapy with substance abusers) are more effective in treating problems than individual counseling approaches. Third, the presence of both parents, especially noncompliant fathers, in family counseling situations greatly improves the chances for success. Similarly, the effectiveness of marriage counseling when both partners meet conjointly with the counselor is nearly twice that of counselors working with just one spouse. Finally, when marriage and family counseling services are not offered to couples conjointly or to families systemically, the results of the intervention may be negative and problems may worsen. Overall, the basic argument for employing marriage and family counseling is its proven efficiency. This form of treatment is logical, fast, satisfactory, and economical.

Four major professional associations attract specialists in this area. The largest and oldest (established in 1942) is the American Association for Marriage and Family Therapy (AAMFT). The second association, the International Association of Marriage and Family Counselors (IAMFC), a division within the American Counseling Association, was chartered in 1986. The third association, Division 43 (Family Psychology), a division within the American Psychological Association (APA), was formed in 1984 to provide a professional affiliation for family practitioners who wanted to maintain their identity as psychologists (Kaslow, 1990). Finally, there is the American Family Therapy Association (AFTA), which was formed in 1977 and is identified as an academy of advanced professionals interested in the exchange of ideas (Gladding, 2002).

MARRIAGE COUNSELING

Couples seek marriage counseling for a wide variety of reasons, including issues of finance, children, fidelity, communication, and compatibility. Almost any situation can serve as the impetus to seek help.

Regardless of who initiates the request, it is crucial in almost all cases that the counselor sees both members of the couple from the beginning. Trying to treat one spouse alone for even one or two sessions increases both the other spouse's resistance to counseling and his or her anxiety. Also, if one member of a couple tries to change without the knowledge or support of the other, conflict is bound to ensue. Thus, Whitaker (1977) notes that if a counselor is not able to structure sessions so that both partners can attend, the counselor will probably not help the couple and possibly will do harm.

To combat possible negative results from occurring when one member of a couple is reluctant or refusing to attend counseling, Wilcoxon and Fenell (1983) developed a therapist-initiated letter explaining the process of marriage therapy to an absent partner. It outlines the perils of treating just one partner and is sent by counselors to the nonattending partner to help him or her see the possibilities that can accrue when working with both members of the couple (see Figure 9–3).

Depending on whether both partners decide to enter marriage counseling, a variety of approaches may be taken. Among the most popular approaches are psychoanalytic, social learning, Bowen family systems, structural–strategic, and rational emotive behavior therapy. A number of other treatment methods will not be covered here because of their lack of proven effectiveness.

Psychoanalytic Theory

Psychoanalytical marriage counseling is based on the *theory of object relations,* a theory that addresses how relationships are developed across the generations (Scarf, 1995; Slipp, 1988). *Objects* are significant others in one's environment, such as a mother, with whom children form an interactive emotional bond. The basis of preferences for certain objects as opposed to others is developed in early childhood in parent–child interactions. Individuals bring these unconscious forces into a marriage relationship.

In order to help the marriage, the counselor focuses with each partner on obtaining emotional insight into early parent–child relationships. The treatment may be both individual and conjoint. The counselor uses the process of *transference* where each partner restructures internally based perceptions of, expectations of, and reactions to self and others and projects them onto the counselor. Other techniques employed in this approach include taking individual histories of each partner and taking a history of the marriage relationship. Interpretation, dream work, and an analysis of resistance are often incorporated into the treatment. *Catharsis,* the expression of pent-up emotion, is a must. The goal of this approach is for individuals and couples to gain new insights into their lives, leading to changed behaviors.

(Date)

Mr. John Jones
111 Smith Street
Anytown, USA 00000

Dear Mr. Jones,

As you may know, your wife, Jill, has requested therapy services for difficulties related to your marriage. However, she has stated that you do not wish to participate in marital therapy sessions.

As a professional marriage therapist, I have an obligation to inform each of you of the possible outcome of marital therapy services to only one spouse. The available research indicates that one-spouse marital therapy has resulted in reported increases in marital stress and dissatisfaction for both spouses in the marriage. On the other hand, many couples have reported that marital therapy which includes both spouses has been helpful in reducing marital stress and enhancing marital satisfaction.

These findings reflect general tendencies in marital research and are not absolute in nature. However, it is important for you and Jill to be informed of potential consequences which might occur through marital therapy in which only your spouse attends. Knowing this information, you may choose a course of action which best suits your intentions.

After careful consideration of this information, I ask that you and Jill discuss your options regarding future therapy services. In this way, all parties will have a clear understanding of another's intentions regarding your relationship.

As a homework assignment for Jill, I have asked that each of you read this letter and sign in the spaces provided below to verify your understanding of the potential consequences to your relationship by continuing one-spouse marital therapy. If you are interested in joining Jill for marital therapy, in addition to your signature below, please contact my office to indicate your intentions. If not, simply sign below and have Jill return the letter at our next therapy session. I appreciate your cooperation in this matter.

Sincerely,

Therapist X
_____

We verify by our signatures below that we have discussed and understand the potential implications of continued marital therapy with only one spouse in attendance.

_____   _____
Attending Spouse   Date

_____   _____
Non-Attending Spouse   Date

Figure 9–3

Letter to engage a nonattending spouse

Note. From "Engaging the Non-Attending Spouse in Marital Therapy Through the Use of Therapist-Initiated Written Communication," by A. Wilcoxon and D. Fenell, 1983, *Journal of Marital and Family Therapy, 9*(32), 199–203. © 1983 by the American Association for Marriage and Family Therapy. Reprinted with permission.

Social-Learning Theory

Social-learning theory is a form of behaviorism that stresses learning through modeling and imitation (Bandura, 1977; Horne & Sayger, 2000). The premises underlying the theory are that behaviors are learned through observing others and that marriage partners either have a deficit or an excess of needed behaviors. A deficit may be the result of one or both partners never having witnessed a particular skill, such as how to fight fairly. An excess may come as a result of one or both partners' thinking that just a little more of a certain behavior will solve their problems. For example, one partner tells the other everything he or she likes and does not like in the marriage in the hope that honest communication will be beneficial. Although such honesty may be admired, research shows that marriages grow more through positive reciprocity than through negative feedback (Gottman & Silver, 2000). Selective communication and interaction with one's spouse seem to work best.

The focus in social-learning marriage counseling is on skill building in the present. Events that have disrupted the marriage in the past may be recognized but receive little focus. Within the treatment process, counselors may use a wide variety of behavioral strategies to help couples change, such as self-reports, observations, communication-enhancement training exercises, contracting, and homework assignments (Stuart, 1980, 1998). Much of social learning theory is based on linear thinking.

Bowen Family Systems Theory

The focus of Bowen family systems marital theory is on *differentiation,* or distinction, of one's thoughts from one's emotions and of one's self from others (Kerr & Bowen, 1988). Couples marry at varying levels of emotional maturity, with those who are less mature having a more difficult time in their marriage relationships. When there is a great deal of friction within a marriage, the partners who compose it are characterized by a high degree of *fusion* (undifferentiated emotional togetherness) or *cutoff* (physical or psychological avoidance). They have not separated themselves from their families of origin in a healthy way nor have they formed stable self-concepts. When they experience stress within the marriage, they tend to *triangulate,* or focus on a third party (Aylmer, 1986). The third party can be the marriage itself, a child, an outside agency, or even a somatic complaint. Regardless, it leads to unproductive couple interactions.

Techniques used in this approach focus on ways to differentiate one's self from one's extended family-of-origin system. In the process, there is an attempt to create an individuated person with a healthy self-concept who can couple and not experience undue anxiety every time the relationship becomes stressful. Ways of achieving this goal include assessment of self and family through the use of a *genogram* (a visual representation of a person's family tree depicted in geometric figures, lines, and words) and a focus on *cognitive processes* such as asking content-based questions of one's family (Bowen, 1976). The sequencing and pacing of this process differ from spouse to spouse, and the therapeutic interaction takes place either with one spouse and the counselor or ideally with both spouses and the counselor together.

Structural–Strategic Theory

Structural–strategic theory is based on the belief that when dysfunctional symptoms occur in a marriage they are an attempt to help couples adapt. This approach combines the best techniques of the structural and strategic schools of marriage and family therapy and sees problems as occurring within a developmental framework of the family life cycle. Marital difficulties are generated by the system the couple is in, and these symptoms consequently help maintain the marital system in which they operate (Todd, 1986). Therefore, the job of a structural–strategic marriage counselor is to get couples to try new behaviors because their old behaviors are not working. Usually, a specific behavior is targeted for change. If this behavior can be modified, it will tend to have a spillover effect, helping couples make other behavior changes as well.

To bring about change, counselors are active, direct, and goal oriented as well as problem focused, pragmatic, and brief (Todd, 1986). *Relabeling,* or giving a new perspective to a behavior, is frequently used as are *paradoxing,* or insisting on just the opposite of what one wants, and *prescribing the symptom,* or having the couple display voluntarily what they had previously manifested involuntarily, such as fighting (Gladding, 2002). The counselor often asks clients to pretend to make changes or to carry out homework assignments (Madanes, 1984; Minuchin, 1974). The objective is to bring about new functional behaviors that will help couples achieve a specific goal.

Rational Emotive Behavior Theory (REBT)

The premise behind REBT is that couples, like individuals, often become disturbed because of what they think rather than because of specific actions that occur in the relationship (Ellis, 2000). *Irrational thinking* that is "highly exaggerated, inappropriately rigid, illogical, and especially absolutist" is what leads to neurosis and relationship disturbance (Ellis, Sichel, Yeager, DiMattia, & DiGiuseppe, 1989, p. 17). To combat disturbances, couples need to challenge and change their belief systems about activating events. Otherwise they continue to "awfulize" and "catastrophize" about themselves and their marriage. The essence of this theory is essentially what Ellis (1988) calls "double systems therapy," where emphasis is placed on personal and family systems change.

As with individual counseling, the REBT counselor concentrates on thinking, but within a couple context. The focus is on helping individuals first and marriages second (Ellis, 2000). After assessing what is occurring with the couple, the REBT counselor works with the individuals separately and together in the ABC method of REBT. There is a special emphasis, however, on some particular marital problems, such as jealousy and issues of sexuality.

FAMILY COUNSELING

Families enter counseling for a number of reasons. Usually, there is an identified patient, or an individual who is seen as the cause of trouble within the family structure, that family members use as their ticket of entry. Most family counseling practitioners do not view one member of a family as the problem but instead work with the whole family system. Occasionally, family therapy is conducted from an individual perspective.

Family counseling has expanded rapidly since the mid-1970s and encompasses many aspects of couples counseling. Seven of its main theoretical orientations will be covered here. Although some family counselors are linearly based and work on cause and effect relationships, most are not. Rather, the majority of family counselors operate from a general systems framework and conceptualize the family as an open system that evolves over the family life cycle in a sociocultural context. Functional families follow rules and are flexible in meeting the demands placed on them by family members and outside agencies. Family systems counselors stress the idea of *circular causality;* that is, family members affect each other for better or worse, and the family as a whole, through their multiple interactions. These counselors also emphasize the following concepts:

- **Nonsummativity.** The family is greater than the sum of its parts. It is necessary to examine the patterns within a family rather than the actions of any specific member alone.
- **Equifinality.** The same origin may lead to different outcomes, and the same outcome may result from different origins. Thus, the family that experiences a natural disaster may become stronger or weaker as a result. Likewise, healthy families may have quite dissimilar backgrounds. Therefore, the focus of treatment is on interactional family patterns rather than on particular conditions or events.
- **Communication.** All behavior is seen as communicative. It is important to attend to the two functions of interpersonal messages: content (i.e., factual information) and relationship (i.e., how the message is to be understood). The *what* of a message is conveyed by how it is delivered.
- **Family Rules.** A family's functioning is based on both explicit and implicit rules. Family rules provide expectations about roles and actions that govern family life. Most families operate on a small set of predictable rules, a pattern known as the *redundancy principle.* To help families change dysfunctional ways of working, family counselors have to help them define and/or expand the rules under which they operate.
- **Morphogenesis.** The ability of the family to modify its functioning to meet the changing demands of internal and external factors is known as *morphogenesis.* Morphogenesis usually requires a *second-order change* (i.e., the ability to make an entirely new response) instead of a *first-order change* (i.e., continuing to do more of the same things that have been done previously; Watzlawick, Weakland, & Fisch, 1974). Instead of just talking, family members may need to try new behaviors.
- **Homeostasis.** As with biological organisms, families have a tendency to remain in a steady, stable state of equilibrium unless otherwise forced to change. When a family member unbalances the family through his or her actions, other members quickly try to rectify the situation through *negative feedback loops* (morphostasis). The model of functioning is similar to a furnace that comes on when a house falls below a set temperature and cuts off once the temperature is reached. Sometimes homeostasis can be

advantageous in helping a family achieve life cycle goals, but often it prevents the family from moving on to another stage in its development.

Counselors who operate from a family systems approach work according to the concepts just covered. For instance, if family rules are covert and cause confusion, the counselor helps the family make these regulations overt and clear. All members of the family are engaged in the process so that communication channels are opened. Often, a genogram is constructed in order to help family members and the counselor detect intergenerational patterns of family functioning that have an impact on the present (McGoldrick, Gerson, & Shellenberger, 1999).

Overall, the popularity of family counseling may be attributed to the realization that persons become healthier when their families function better. The economy of using family counseling and its encompassing nature are intrinsically appealing and make it attractive for counselors who wish to work on complex, multifaceted levels within their communities.

Psychodynamic Family Counseling

As traditionally practiced, psychoanalysis concentrates on individuals instead of social systems such as the family. Ackerman (1966) broke with tradition by working with intact families. He believed that family difficulties resulted from *interlocking pathologies,* or unconscious and dysfunctional ways of acting, present in the couple and family system. An initial goal of psychodynamic family counseling is to change the personalities of family members so they can work with one another in a healthy and productive way. Nichols and Schwartz (2001) point out that psychodynamic counselors who follow Ackerman most often employ an eclectic mix of psychoanalytic and systems concepts.

A unique contribution that psychodynamic practitioners have made to the field of family counseling is the use of *object relations* as a primary emphasis in treatment. Object relations, as mentioned previously, are internalized residues of early parent–child interactions. In dysfunctional families, object relations continue to exert a negative influence in present interpersonal relationships. Dysfunctional families are those with a greater degree of unconscious, unresolved conflict or loss (Paul & Paul, 1975). Three main ways of working with these families are (a) developing a stronger parent coalition, (b) defining and maintaining generation boundaries, and (c) modeling sex-linked roles (Walsh, 1982).

Overall, psychodynamic family counselors concentrate on (a) helping family members obtain insight and resolve family-of-origin conflicts/losses, (b) eliminating distorted projections, (c) reconstructing relationships, and (d) promoting individual and family growth. Prominent practitioners associated with this approach are Nathan Ackerman, James Framo, Theodore Lidz, and Norman Paul.

Experiential Family Counseling

Experientialist family counselors are concerned as much with individuals as with family systems and consider intrapsychic problems when explaining psychopathology.

Unlike most other family counselors, experientialists describe patterns of family dysfunction using the individual or a dyad as the unit of analysis. They believe that dysfunctional families are made up of people who are unaware of their emotions, or if they are aware of their emotions, they suppress them, making real intimacy very difficult. This tendency not to feel or express feelings creates a climate of *emotional deadness.* Therefore, the goal of counseling is to emphasize sensitivity and feeling expression, thus opening family members to new experiences.

Two prominent practitioners in the experiential school are Virginia Satir and Carl Whitaker. Satir (1967, 1972) stresses the importance of clear communications in her approach. Whitaker (1976, 1977) is more of an existential maverick whose interactions with families have sometimes been unconventional but always are very creative. Satir believes that when family members are under stress they may handle their communications in one of four nonproductive roles:

1. *Placater:* agrees and tries to please
2. *Blamer:* dominates and finds fault
3. *Responsible Analyzer:* remains emotionally detached and intellectual
4. *Distractor:* interrupts and constantly chatters about irrelevant topics

Satir helps families by teaching members to own personal feelings and express them clearly, a process she calls *leveling.* Individuals are instructed to listen to one another to promote intimacy. Satir further stresses the importance of obtaining and providing feedback and negotiating differences when they arise. Her primary focus is on communication skills. She uses experiential exercises and props to help families and their members become more aware.

Whitaker, who takes a less structured approach to working with families, represents the extreme side of the experiential school. He advocates nonrational, creative experiences in family counseling and lets the form of his methods develop as he works. He is unconventional and sometimes uses *absurdity* (i.e., a statement that is half-truthful and even silly if followed out to its conclusion) in working with families. To be effective, Whitaker uses a co-therapist. He has been known to go to sleep, have a dream, and share it with a family. Messages that come from such events are hard for family members to dismiss or resist. Families begin to change their patterns of behaving and become more honest, open, and spontaneous with each other as a result. Overall, Whitaker (1989) emphasizes uncovering and utilizing the unconscious life of the family.

Behavioral Family Counseling

Behavioral family counselors use theory techniques originally devised for treating individuals. With the exception of functional family therapists (e.g., Alexander & Parsons, 1982), they are nonsystemic in conceptualizing and in clinically working with families. Instead, most behavioral family counselors stress the importance of learning. They emphasize the importance of family rules and skill training and believe that behaviors are determined by consequences rather than by antecedents (Gladding, 2002).

The goals of behavioral family counseling are specific and limited. Behaviorists try to modify troublesome behavior patterns to alleviate undesirable interactions. Much of their work focuses on changing dyadic interaction through teaching, modeling, and reinforcing new behaviors. Behaviorists believe that change is best achieved through accelerating positive behavior rather than decelerating negative behavior. Most of their work is concentrated in three main areas of (a) behavioral parent training (Patterson, 1971), (b) behavioral marriage counseling (Stuart, 1980), and (c) treatment of sexual dysfunctions (LoPiccolo, 1978; Masters & Johnson, 1970).

Structural Family Counseling

Structural family counseling, founded by Salvador Minuchin (1974), is based on general systems theory. Its practitioners advocate structural changes in the organization of the family unit, with particular attention on changing interactional patterns in subsystems of the family, such as the marital dyad, and establishing clear boundaries between family members (Minuchin, Montalvo, Guerney, Rosman, & Schumer, 1967).

In working with families, structural family counselors join with the family in a position of leadership. They try to formulate a structure in their minds of the family to determine how it is stuck in dysfunctional patterns. These counselors then employ a number of techniques aimed at getting the family to change the way it operates (Minuchin & Fishman, 1981). One primary technique is to work with the family's interaction patterns. When family members repeat nonproductive sequences of behavior or demonstrate either a detached or enmeshed position in the family structure, the counselor will rearrange the physical environment so they have to act in a different way. The technique may be as simple as having people face each other when they talk. Structural family counselors also use *reframing,* or helping the family see its problem from a different and more positive perspective. For example, if a child is misbehaving, the behavior may be labeled "naughty" instead of "crazy." As a consequence, the child and actions will be viewed as less pathological. By helping families change their structure, reframe their problems, establish a hierarchy with the parents in charge, and create clear boundaries and appropriate ways of interacting, structuralists help families use their own inner resources to function in a productive and healthy way.

Strategic Family Counseling

Jay Haley (1973), Cloe Madanes (1991), and the Milan Group (Selvini-Palazzoli, Boscolo, Cecchin, & Prata, 1978) are prominent leaders within the strategic school of family counseling. Strategic counselors take a systemic view of problem behaviors and focus on the process rather than on the content of dysfunctional interactions. They strive to resolve presenting problems and pay little attention to instilling insight. One powerful technique often used by strategic counselors is to *prescribe the symptom.*

This approach places targeted behaviors, such as family fights, under the control of the counselor by making a behavior voluntary if family members comply and eliminating a behavior if the family group resists the counselor's instructions. Strategic family counselors accept the presenting problems of families and view symptoms as serving the positive purpose of communication.

The Milan Group uses the technique of *ordeals:* for example, doing something a person does not want to do (such as buying a gift for somebody who is disliked), during the treatment process. The idea is that if families have to make sacrifices to get better, then the long-term improvements of treatment are enhanced. A major aspect of strategic family counseling is the assignment of original homework tasks, often given in the form of prescriptions that are to be completed between sessions. Many strategic counselors work in teams and limit the number of treatment sessions as a motivational factor. Overall, this treatment is short term and pragmatic.

Brief Solution-Focused Family Counseling

Brief solution-focused family counseling is both an extension of strategic family counseling and a distinct entity. It traces its roots to the work of Milton Erickson (1954), particularly his *utilization principle:* using whatever clients presented in counseling "as a basis and means for client solutions and change" (Lawson, 1994, p. 244). Erickson believed that people have within themselves the resources and abilities to solve their own problems. "Additionally, Erickson . . . believed that a small change in one's behavior is often all that is necessary to lead to more profound changes in a problem context" (Lawson, 1994, p. 244). This viewpoint was adopted from Erickson by Jay Haley and has been formulated into brief solution-focused family counseling by Steve deShazer and Bill O'Hanlon.

The essence of brief solution-focused family counseling is that clients create problems because of their perceptions, such as "I am always depressed." Brief solution-focused family counselors try to help clients get a different perspective on their situations through having them notice exceptions to the times they are distressed. Client families are then directed toward solutions to situations that already exist as found in these exceptions. Thus, the focus of sessions and homework is on positives and possibilities either now or in the future (Walter & Peller, 1992). One way to help individuals change perspective from concentrating on the negative to emphasizing the positive is by asking the *miracle question* (deShazer, 1991). In this intervention clients are asked to imagine that their problem is suddenly solved. What will then happen in regard to their behaviors, and how will they know the problem is solved?

Narrative Family Therapy

Narrative family therapy emphasizes the reauthoring by individuals and families of their life stories. The most prominent professionals associated with narrative family therapy are Michael White and David Epston from Australia and New Zealand,

I have found, both personally and professionally, that life is a series of losses and opportunities often reshaping the very structure of families. To learn about each family's *story* and community is a privilege, responsibility, and challenge. To effect positive change on individual, family, group, and community levels is intrinsically rewarding. My role as a practitioner is to restore or instill choice, help clients pass through transitions; and when appropriate, engage in advocacy. In working with problems relating to partner abuse, child abuse, suicide, physical health, and poverty, I have found that all problems have a family and social context; however, the appropriate treatment is not always couple/family therapy. Practicing in a time when services are limited by managed care requires the engagement of clients in understanding/creating their *story* (individual, couple, and family) while also problem-solving, and establishing links to community resources in a brief time-frame. As a social worker and educator with an interdisciplinary background, I have found that *joining* and *letting go* ultimately shapes the pain and the promise of working with couples and families.

Figure 9–4

Reflections: Working With Couples and Families

Nicholas Mazza, Ph.D., is a Professor of Social Work at Florida State University. He holds Florida licenses in clinical social work, marriage and family therapy, and psychology. He is the editor of the *Journal of Poetry Therapy* and serves on the editorial board of the *Journal of Family Social Work*. Dr. Mazza's integrative theoretical framework has a strengths perspective involving systems, narrative, and cognitive–behavioral components.

respectively. The approach distinguishes between logicoscientific reasoning, which is characterized by empiricism and logic, and narrative reasoning, which is characterized by stories, substories, meaningfulness, and liveliness. According to the narrative viewpoint, "people live their lives by stories" (Kurtz & Tandy, 1995, p. 177). Thus, the emphasis within narrative family therapy is helping people change their life stories (Figure 9–4).

The process of change in life stories is undertaken by externalization of the problem, which means that all family members can objectively address unproductive behaviors (White, 1995). In addition, the influence of the problem on a person or persons is noted as well as the influence of a person or persons on a problem. Narrative family therapists also predict setbacks in treatment so families and individuals can plan ahead as to how they will act when those times come. As with solution-focused family counseling, there is a major focus on exceptions to the problem and on how families act when there is not a problem. The goal is to challenge a family's view of the world and to offer them hope that their lives can be different because some changes have taken place and they are moving toward putting other changes in place.

When the family or individuals have been successful in overcoming the externalized problem, narrative family therapists offer them certificates of achievement and celebrations to signify their victory or achievement (White & Epston, 1990).

MARRIAGE AND FAMILY ENRICHMENT

Although the majority of this chapter focuses on different treatment modalities for working with couples and families, it ends on a positive note with a primary prevention emphasis—enrichment. The idea of marriage enrichment is based on the concept that couples and consequently their families stay healthy or get healthier by actively participating in certain activities with other couples (Mace & Mace, 1977). In such settings, couples learn about themselves; they also learn from other couples. There are over two dozen enrichment organizations in the United States on a national level, and the material in this field has mushroomed (Mace, 1987).

Couple retreats, engagement in interactive cooperative activities, and involvement in family councils are among the most recommended ways of achieving health in marriages and families. The research on enrichment shows that it can be helpful to couples and families who are not in distress. However, enrichment experiences, especially those involving marriage encounter weekends, can be quite disruptive and damaging to distressed couples and can lead to further deterioration of their relationships (Doherty, Lester, & Leigh, 1986). Care must be exercised in selecting couples and families to participate in these programs.

A part of marriage and family enrichment involves self and couple help. This type of help is often in the form of structured exercises that theoretically and practically bring couples closer together through sharing information and experiences (Calvo, 1975; Guerney, 1977). For instance, couples may learn to give and receive nonverbal and verbal messages and to reflect on positive times in their life together. They may also be able to give and receive feedback on important relationship topics such as sexuality, finance, parenting, and household chores (Johnson, Fortman, & Brems, 1993).

SUMMARY AND CONCLUSION

Family life in the United States is very diverse with a number of family forms. Regardless of form, all families go through life cycles that influence their development. Expected and unexpected events can lead to stress and even distress. One way to help couples and families is through marriage and family counseling.

The professions of marriage and family counseling have grown rapidly in recent years for a number of reasons, including theory development, needs within the population, and proven research effectiveness. There are five main approaches to marriage counseling: psychoanalytic, social-learning, Bowen family systems, structural–strategic, and rational emotive behavior therapy. Family counseling has a wider range of approaches (e.g., behavioral, brief solution-focused, and narrative), but the dominant ones are family systems oriented.

In working as either a marriage counselor or a family counselor, the helping professional must be aware of the theoretical basis of the approach being implemented and must keep in mind where marriage and/or family members are in their individual and family life cycles. Counseling couples and families is important and gratifying for counselors. Likewise primary prevention in the form of enrichment experiences can and should be a part of counselors' work in community settings. Through enrichment experiences and exercises, couples learn more about each other and how to relate to one another and their families.

REFERENCES

Ackerman, N. W. (1966). *Treating the troubled family.* New York: Basic Books.

Alexander, J., & Parsons, B. V. (1982). *Functional family therapy.* Pacific Grove, CA: Brooks/Cole.

Aylmer, R. C. (1986). Bowen family systems marital therapy. In N. S. Jacobson & A. S. Gurman (Eds.), *Clinical handbook of marital therapy* (pp. 107–148). New York: Guilford Press.

Bandura, A. (1977). *Social learning theory.* Upper Saddle River, NJ: Prentice Hall.

Becvar, D. S., & Becvar, R. J. (2000). Family therapy: A systematic integration (4th ed.). Needham Heights, MA: Allyn & Bacon.

Boszormenyi-Nagy, I. (1987). *Foundations of contextual therapy.* New York: Brunner/Mazel.

Bowen, M. (1976). Theory in the practice of psychotherapy. In P. J. Guerin, Jr. (Ed.), *Family therapy: Theory and practice* (pp. 42–90). New York: Gardner Press.

Bowen, M. (1978). *Family therapy in clinical practice.* New York: Jason Aronson.

Brown, J. H., & Christensen, D. N. (1999). *Family therapy: Theory & practice* (2nd ed.). Pacific Grove, CA: Brooks/Cole.

Bumpass, L. L., & Sweet, J. A. (1989). Children's experience in single-parent families: Implications of cohabitation and marital transitions. *Family Planning Perspectives, 21,* 256–260.

Burr, W. R., Hill, R., Nye, F. I., & Reiss, I. L. (1979). *Contemporary theories about the family.* New York: The Free Press.

Calvo, G. (1975). *Marriage encounter: Official national manual.* St. Paul, MN: Marriage Encounter.

Carter, B., & McGoldrick, M. (1999). *Expanded family life cycle: Individual, family, and social perspectives.* Boston: Allyn & Bacon.

Curran, D. (1985). *Stress and the healthy family.* San Francisco: Harper & Row.

Davis, R. F., & Borns, N. E. (1999). *Solo dad survival guide: Raising your kids on your own.* New York: NTC/Contemporary Publishing.

deShazer, S. (1991). *Putting differences to work.* New York: Norton.

Doherty, W. J., Lester, M. E., & Leigh, G. (1986). Marriage encounter weekends: Couples who win and couples who lose. *Journal of Marital and Family Therapy, 12,* 49–61.

Eccles, J. S., Midgley, C., Wigfield, A., Buchanan, C. M., Reuman, D., Flanagan, C., & MacIver, D. (1993). Development during adolescence: The impact of stage–environment fit on young adolescents' experiences in schools and families. *American Psychologist, 48,* 90–101.

Ellis, A. (1988). *How to stubbornly refuse to make yourself miserable about anything—yes, anything!* Secaucus, NJ: Lyle Stuart.

Ellis, A. (2000). Rational–emotive behavior in marriage and family therapy. In A. M. Horne (Ed.), *Family counseling and therapy* (3rd ed., pp. 489–514). Itasca, IL: F. E. Peacock.

Ellis, A., Sichel, J. L., Yeager, R. J., DiMattia, D. J., & DiGiuseppe, R. (1989). *Rational–emotive couples therapy.* New York: Pergamon Press.

Erikson, E. H. (1959). *Identity and the life cycle: Psychological issues.* New York: International Universities Press.

Erickson, M. (1954). Special techniques of brief hypnotherapy. *Journal of Clinical and Experimental Hypnosis, 2,* 109–129.

Figley, C. R. (1989). *Helping traumatized families.* San Francisco: Jossey-Bass.

Gilbert, L. A. (1985). *Men in dual-career families: Current realities and future prospects.* Hillsdale, NJ: Lawrence Erlbaum Associates.

Gladding, S. T. (1974). Without applause. *Personnel and Guidance Journal, 52,* 586.

Gladding, S. T. (2003). *Group work: A counseling specialty* (4th ed.). Upper Saddle River, NJ: Prentice Hall.

Gladding, S. T. (2002). *Family therapy: History, theory, and practice*. Upper Saddle River, NJ: Prentice Hall.

Goldberg, J. R. (1992, August). The new frontier: Marriage and family therapy with aging families. *Family Therapy News, 23,* 1, 14, 21.

Goldenberg, H., & Goldenberg, I. (2002). *Counseling today's families* (4th ed.). Pacific Grove, CA: Brooks/Cole.

Goldin, E., & Mohr, R. (2000). Issues and techniques for counseling long-term, later-life couples. *The Family Journal, 8,* 229–235.

Gottman, J., & Silver, N. (2000). *The seven principles of making marriage work*. New York: Three Rivers Press.

Guerney, B. (1977). *Relationship enhancement*. San Francisco, CA: Jossey-Bass.

Gurman, A., & Kniskern, D. (1981). Family therapy outcome research: Knowns and unknowns. In A. Gurman & D. Kniskern (Eds.), *Handbook of family therapy* (pp. 742–775). New York: Brunner/Mazel.

Haley, J. (1973). *Uncommon therapy*. New York: Norton.

Hampson, R. B., Beavers, W. R., & Hulgus, Y. (1990). Cross-ethnic family differences: Interactional assessment of white, black, and Mexican-American families. *Journal of Marital and Family Therapy, 16,* 307–319.

Hertz, R. & Marshall, N. L. (2001). *Working families: The transformation of the American home*. Berkeley: University of California Press.

Hines, M. (1988). Similarities and differences in group and family therapy. *Journal for Specialists in Group Work, 13,* 173–179.

Horne, A., & Sayger, T. V. (2000). Behavioral approaches to couple and family therapy. In A. M. Horne (Ed.), *Family counseling and therapy* (3rd ed., pp. 454–488). Itasca, IL: F. E. Peacock.

Johnson, T. W., & Colucci, P. (1999). Lesbian, gay men, and the family life cycle. In B. Carter & M. McGoldrick (Eds.), *The expanded family life cycle* (3rd ed., pp. 346–361). Boston: Allyn & Bacon.

Johnson, M. E., Fortman, J. B., & Brems, C. (1993). *Between two people: Exercises toward intimacy*. Alexandria, VA: American Counseling Association.

Kaslow, F. (1990). *Voices in family psychology*. Newbury Park, CA: Sage.

Kaslow, F. W. (1991). The art and science of family psychology. *American Psychologist, 46,* 621–626.

Kerr, M. E., & Bowen, M. (1988). *Family evaluation: An approach based on Bowen theory*. New York: Norton.

Kinnier, R. T., Brigman, S. L., & Noble, F. C. (1990). Career indecision and family enmeshment. *Journal of Counseling and Development, 68,* 309–312.

Kurtz, P. D., & Tandy, C. C. (1995). Narrative family interventions. In A. C. Kilpatrick & T. P. Holland (Eds.), *Working with families* (pp. 177–197). Boston: Allyn & Bacon.

Lawson, D. (1994). Identifying pretreatment change. *Journal of Counseling and Development, 72,* 244–248.

Levinson, D. (1978). *The seasons of a man's life*. New York: Knopf.

Lopez, F. G. (1986). Family structure and depression: Implications for the counseling of depressed college students. *Journal of Counseling and Development, 64,* 508–511.

LoPiccolo, J. (1978). Direct treatment of sexual dysfunction. In J. LoPiccolo & L. LoPiccolo (Eds.), *Handbook of sex therapy*. New York: Plenum.

Mace, D. (1987). Three ways of helping married couples. *Journal of Marital and Family Therapy, 13,* 179–186.

Mace, D., & Mace, V. (1977). *How to have a happy marriage: A step-by-step guide to an enriched relationship*. Nashville, TN: Abington.

Madanes, C. (1984). *Behind the one-way mirror: Advances in the practice of strategic therapy*. San Francisco: Jossey-Bass.

Madanes, C. (1991). Strategic family therapy. In A. S. Gurman & D. P. Kniskern (Eds.), *Handbook of family therapy* (Vol. II, pp. 396–416). New York: Brunner/Mazel.

Masters, W. H., & Johnson, V. E. (1970). *Human sexual inadequacy*. Boston: Little, Brown.

Maynard, P. E., & Olson, D. H. (1987). Circumplex model of family systems: A treatment tool in family counseling. *Journal of Counseling and Development, 65,* 502–504.

McGoldrick, M., Gerson, R., & Shellenberger, S. (1999). *Genograms: Assessment and intervention*. New York: Norton.

McGoldrick, M., & Walsh, F. (1999). Death and the family life cycle. In B. Carter & M. McGoldrick (Eds.),

The expanded family life cycle (3rd ed., pp. 185–201). Boston: Allyn & Bacon.

Minuchin, S. (1974). *Families and family therapy*. Cambridge, MA: Harvard University Press.

Minuchin, S., & Fishman, H. C. (1981). *Family therapy techniques*. Cambridge, MA: Harvard University Press.

Minuchin, S., Montalvo, B., Guerney, B., Rosman, B., & Schumer, F. (1967). *Families of the slums*. New York: Basic Books.

Montalvo, B., & Thompson, R. F. (1988, July/August). Conflicts in the caregiving family. *Family Therapy Networker, 12*, 30–35.

Nicola, J. S. (1980). *Career and family roles of dual-career couples: Women in academia and their husbands*. Ann Arbor, MI: University Microfilms International.

Nichols, W. C. (1993). *The AAMFT: 50 years of marital and family therapy*. Washington, DC: AAMFT.

Nichols, M., & Schwartz, R. C. (2001). *Family therapy: Concepts and methods* (5th ed). Boston: Allyn & Bacon.

Olson, D. H. (1986). Circumplex model VII: Validation studies and FACES III. *Family Process, 25*, 337–351.

Patterson, G. R. (1971). *Families: Applications of social learning to family life*. Champaign, IL: Research Press.

Paul, N. L., & Paul, B. B. (1975). *A marital puzzle: Transgenerational analysis in marriage*. New York: Norton.

Pinsof, W., & Wynne, L. (Eds.). (1995). Special issue: The effectiveness of marital and family therapy. *Journal of Marital and Family Therapy, 21*, 339–613.

Pinsof, W. M., & Wynne, L. C. (2000). Toward progress research: Closing the gap between family therapy practice and research. *Journal of Marital and Family Therapy, 26*, 1–8.

Satir, V. M. (1967). *Conjoint family therapy*. Palo Alto, CA: Science and Behavior Books.

Satir, V. M. (1972). *Peoplemaking*. Palo Alto: Science and Behavior Books.

Scarf, M. (1995). *Intimate worlds: Life inside the family*. New York: Random House.

Schlossberg, N. K. (1984). *Counseling adults in transition: Linking practice with theory*. New York: Springer.

Selvini-Palazzoli, M., Boscolo, L., Cecchin, G., & Prata, G. (1978). *Paradox and counterparadox*. New York: Monson.

Selye, H. (1976). *The stress of life* (2nd ed.). New York: Guilford Press.

Shulins, N. (1992, June 27). Baby-boomers are waking up to childlessness. *Winston-Salem Journal, 14*, 17.

Slipp, S. (1988). *The technique and practice of object relations family therapy*. New York: Aronson.

Stanton, M. D. (1999, May). Alcohol use disorders. *AAMFT Clinical Update, 1*(3), 1–8.

Stinnett, N., & DeFrain, J. (1985). *Secrets of strong families*. Boston: Little, Brown.

Strong, B., DeVault, C., & Sayad, B. W. (2001). *The marriage and family experience: Intimate relationships in a changing society* (8th ed.). Belmont, CA: Wadsworth.

Stuart, R. B. (1980). *Helping couples change: A social learning approach to marital therapy*. New York: Guilford Press.

Stuart, R. B. (1998). Updating behavior therapy with couples. *The Family Journal: Counseling and Therapy for Couples and Families, 6*, 6–12.

Thomas, V. G. (1990). Determinants of global life happiness and marital happiness in dual-career black couples. *Family Relations, 39*, 174–178.

Todd, T. C. (1986). Structural-strategic marital therapy. In N. S. Jacobson & A. S. Gurman (Eds.), *Clinical handbook of marital therapy* (pp. 71–105). New York: Guilford Press.

Trotzer, J. P. (1988). Family theory as a group resource. *Journal for Specialists in Group Work, 13*, 180–185.

Usdansky, M. L. (1993, July 14). Many women in 30s won't have kids. *USA Today*, 8A.

Waggonseller, B. R., Ruegamer, L. C., & Harrington, M. C. (1998). *Coping in a single-parent home*. New York: Rosen.

Walsh, F. (1982). Conceptualizations of normal family functioning. In F. Walsh (Ed.), *Normal family processes* (pp. 3–42). New York: Guilford Press.

Walter, J., & Peller, J. (1992). *Becoming solution-focused in brief therapy*. New York: Brunner/Mazel.

Watts, R. E., Trusty, J., & Lim, M.-G. (2000). Characteristics of healthy families as a model of social interest. *Canadian Journal of Adlerian Psychology, 26*, 1–12.

Watzlawick, P., Weakland, J., & Fisch, R. (1974). *Change: Principles of problem formation and problem resolution*. New York: Norton.

Werbel, J. (1998). Intent and choice regarding maternal employment following childbirth. *Journal of Vocational Behavior, 53,* 372–385.

Whitaker, C. (1976). The hindrance of theory in clinical work. In P. J. Guerin (Ed.), *Family therapy: Theory and practice* (pp. 154–164). New York: Gardner Press.

Whitaker, C. (1977). Process techniques of family therapy. *Interaction, 1,* 4–19.

Whitaker, C. (1989). *Midnight musings of a family therapist.* New York: Norton.

White, M. (1995). *Re-authoring lives.* Adelaide, South Australia: Dulwich Centre Publications.

White, M., & Epston, D. (1990). *Narrative means to therapeutic ends.* New York: Norton.

Wilcoxon, S. A. (1985). Healthy family functioning: The other side of family pathology. *Journal of Counseling and Development, 63,* 495–499.

Wilcoxon, S. A., & Fenell, D. (1983). Engaging the non-attending spouse in marital therapy through the use of therapist-initiated written communication. *Journal of Marital and Family Therapy, 9,* 199–203.

PART III

WORKING WITH SPECIFIC POPULATIONS

CHAPTER 10

Community Counseling in a Diverse Society

I walk among groups of uniformed people
in a bustling, well-planned, unfamiliar land
that looks in many ways like my own.
As I hear the sound of language
alien to my ear
I futilely search for meaningful words
but end up with disappointments.
I am a foreigner
different from the rest
in looks, in style, and in expectations,
I stand out as a visitor in Osaka
who still veers right instead of left
to avoid the crowds in subways.
Amidst it all, I am filled with new awareness
as I step from cultural shelters
into a driving rain
to become drenched in falling water
and flooded with a rush of feelings.
The challenge of understanding
both myself and others
comes with each encounter.

From "Visitor in Osaka," by S. T. Gladding. Copyright 2002 by S. T. Gladding. Reprinted by
permission.

The effectiveness of counseling depends on many factors, but among the most important is for the counselor and client to be able to understand and relate to each other. Such a relationship is usually easier to achieve if the client and counselor are similar in such diverse factors as age, culture, disability, educational level, ethnicity, race, gender, language, religion, sexual orientation, and socioeconomic background (Weinrach & Thomas, 1996). Because similarities in all these categories at any one time is rare, it is imperative that counselors be acutely sensitive to their clients' backgrounds and special needs and equally attuned to their own values, biases, and abilities (Brinson, 1996; Holiday, Leach, & Davidson, 1994). Understanding and dealing positively with differences is a matter of developing both self-awareness (from the inside out) and an awareness of others (from the outside in) (Okun, Fried, & Okun, 1999). Differences between counselors and clients should never be allowed to influence the counseling process negatively.

In this chapter, issues related to counseling distinct populations in a culturally diverse world are addressed. As Coleman (1998) pointed out, "Culturally neutral counseling does not exist" (p. 153). As the United States population becomes increasingly more diverse, it is imperative for community counselors to develop the awareness, knowledge, and skills needed to interact successfully with people from different cultural backgrounds. Methods that work well with one client may be irrelevant or even inappropriate for other clients. Therefore, counselors must be constant lifelong learners, finding new and effective ways to work successfully with a diverse clientele. Topics covered in this chapter include working with culturally and ethnically distinct clients, sexual minority clients, and clients with disabilities.

COUNSELING ACROSS CULTURE AND ETHNICITY

Many distinct cultural and ethnic groups live in the United States. Currently, European Americans make up the largest group (approximately 70 percent), with four other distinct groups—African Americans, Native Americans, Asian Americans, and Hispanic Americans/Latina(o)s—composing the majority of the rest of the population (approximately 30 percent) (U.S. Census Bureau, 2000). These figures represent continued growth in minority population numbers, and it has been projected that numbers within these groups will constitute a majority at some point within the 21st century (Sue & Sue, 1999). Consequently, developing skills in multicultural counseling is imperative.

Several factors influence the counseling of cultural and ethnic groups, such as understanding a client's identity, education, age, religion, socioeconomic status, and experiences with racism (Brinson, 1996). An understanding of these factors is especially important when the counselor and client's cultural backgrounds differ. A guide that can help counselors systematically consider various cultural influences is the ADRESSING model (Hayes, 1996), shown in Figure 10–1. Letters of the model stand for "Age and generational influences, Disability, Religion, Ethnicity (which may include race), Social status, Sexual orientation, Indigenous heritage, National origin,

Figure 10–1
The ADRESSING model:
Nine cultural factors,
related minority groups,
and forms of oppression
Source: From "Addressing the
Complexities of Culture and
Gender in Counseling," by P. A.
Hayes, 1996, *Journal of Coun-*
seling and Development, 74,
p. 334. © ACA. Reprinted with
permission. No further repro-
duction authorized without
written permission of the
American Counseling
Association.

Cultural Factor	Minority Group	Biases with Power
Age/generational	Older adults	Ageism
Disability	People with disabilities	___ [a]
Religion	Religious minorities	___ [b]
Ethnicity/race	Ethnic minorities	Racism
Social status	People of lower status	Classism
Sexual orientation	Sexual minorities	Heterosexism
Indigenous heritage	Native peoples	Racism
National origin	Refugees, immigrants, and international students	Racism and colonialism
Gender	Women	Sexism

[a]Prejudice and discrimination against people with disabilities.
[b]Religious intolerance includes anti-Semitism (i.e., against both Jewish and Muslim people) and oppression of other religious minorities (e.g., Buddhists, Hindus, Mormons).

and Gender" (p. 332). This model is transcultural specific, placing an emphasis both on culture-specific expertise and also on a wide range of cross-cultural issues.

About a quarter of those who initially use mental health facilities are from minor-ity cultural and ethnic groups (Cheung, 1991). Yet researchers have consistently found that clients from minority groups who enter counseling tend to be less satis-fied with the services they receive than do clients from majority groups. Some 50 percent of minority-culture group members who begin counseling terminate after one session, as compared with about 30 percent of majority-culture clients (Sue & Sue, 1999). Several hypotheses have been proposed to explain why minority-culture clients underutilize counseling services. One explanation is that minority clients do not find traditional settings or psychotherapy helpful. They may distrust the counsel-ing process, considering it intrusive, dehumanizing, or stigmatizing (West-Olatunji, 2001). To meet the needs of racial and ethnic minority populations more effectively, community counselors need to develop cultural competencies characterized by respect for and understanding of ethnic and racial groups, including their histories, traditions, beliefs, and value systems.

Defining Culture and Multicultural Counseling

Culture may be defined in several ways. The term can be conceptualized as a combi-nation of "*ethnographic variables* such as ethnicity, nationality, religion, and lan-guage, as well as *demographic variables* of age, gender, place of residence, etc., *status variables* such as social, economic, and educational background and a wide range of formal or informal memberships and affiliations" (Pedersen, 1990, p. 550; emphasis added). Either consciously or unconsciously, culture affects and defines our thoughts, perceptions, values, and goals (Cohen, 1998).

A broad, inclusive definition of *culture* is "any group of people who identify or associate with one another on the basis of some common purpose, need, or similarity of background" (Axelson, 1993, p. 2). Common cultural elements include heritage, experiences, beliefs, and values. These aspects of culture are "webs of significance" that give coherence and meaning to life (Geertz, 1973). They help create the lenses through which people view and experience the world.

An individual's cultural identity is often complex and not readily apparent. People's identities are embedded in multiple levels of experiences and contexts (Robinson & Howard-Hamilton, 2000; Sue, Ivey, & Pedersen, 1996). The salience of various cultural elements differs from person to person. For example, one person may base his or her cultural identity on shared physical characteristics, whereas another person may identify more with shared history and beliefs. Furthermore, many people have multiple group-referenced identities, such as being a physically challenged African American female. To facilitate empathic understanding, community counselors can intentionally help clients articulate their cultural identity and the associated values and beliefs they consider important (West-Olatunji, 2001).

Just as the word *culture* is multifaceted, the terms *multicultural and multicultural counseling* have been conceptualized in numerous ways. There is no universal definition of *multicultural,* although accrediting groups such as the Council for Accreditation of Counseling and Related Programs (CACREP) have chosen to define the term broadly. Defined broadly, *multiculturalism* takes into account differences in areas such as language, race, ethnicity, gender, socioeconomic status, sexual orientation, and physical ability (C. Lee, 1997). Therefore, *multicultural counseling* may be viewed generally as counseling "in which the counselor and client differ" (Locke, 1990, p. 18). West-Olatunji (2001) emphasizes that multicultural counseling refers to "multiple perspectives or multiple cultural viewpoints within the counseling relationship in which none are dominant or considered more 'normal' than others" (p. 418).

Recognizing that all people are unique cultural beings and that no two people experience culture in exactly the same way (Ho, 1995), how, then, do counselors approach multicultural counseling? Historically, counselors have taken either an *etic* or an *emic* approach to the issue. The *etic* perspective emphasizes the universal qualities of counseling that are culturally generalizable. In contrast, the *emic* perspective focuses on the indigenous characteristics of each cultural group that influence the counseling process (W. Lee, 1999). Neither approach is singularly sufficient. The etic approach has been criticized for emphasizing universality to the extent of ignoring important cultural differences. The emic approach has been criticized for overemphasizing specific, culturally appropriate techniques to facilitate client change. Conceivably, the most constructive approach to multicultural counseling is one that merges etic and emic perspectives by focusing on both universal themes and specific cultural considerations.

As counseling professionals and researchers continue to build on the foundation of multicultural knowledge, one point remains clear: Community counselors need to develop cultural sensitivity and competency to work effectively with clients who differ from them. Counselors who disregard cultural differences and operate under the assumption that all counseling theories and techniques are equally applicable to all clients are, according to Wrenn (1962), *culturally encapsulated.* Insensitivity to the actual experiences of clients from different cultural backgrounds can lead to discrimination as well as to ethical misconduct.

Challenges and Issues in Multicultural Counseling

Developing multicultural counseling competencies can present both challenges and opportunities for community counselors. Skillful multicultural counseling involves being sensitive and flexible, tolerating ambiguity, and understanding and accepting different *worldviews* (Locke, 2001). *Worldview* refers to the way people perceive their relationship to the world, including nature, other people, objects, and religion (Sue, 1981). Worldviews, which are grounded in culture-based attitudes and experiences, influence people's thoughts, feelings, behaviors, and perceptions.

One challenge related to multicultural counseling is being able to recognize difficulties that arise from living in poverty and discrimination. Such difficulties may be associated with, but do not necessarily define, an individual's cultural identity. A failure to distinguish between cultural identity and systemic oppression can lead to *overculturalizing*—that is, "mistaking people's reactions to poverty and discrimination for their cultural pattern" (Smith & Vasquez, 1985, p. 533). Historically, members of ethnic minority groups in the United States have an average income that is lower than the average income of majority group members. A disproportionate number of minority group families have limited financial resources (Surgeon General, 2002). When people live in an environment characterized by poverty and powerlessness, they may exhibit behaviors and attitudes that appear dysfunctional but are, in fact, healthy coping mechanisms for living in that environment (West-Olatunji, 2001). Community counselors need to be aware of the multiple environmental and societal factors that affect their clients, some that are culturally based and others that are not.

Box 10–1

We cannot assume that racism will disappear just by our being good people, or by leaving people of color to deal with it. We cannot assume that sexism will disappear just by our being good people, or by leaving women to deal with it. We cannot assume that homophobia will disappear just by our being good people, or by leaving lesbians and gay men to deal with it. We cannot assume that discrimination against the "differently-abled" will disappear just by our being good people, or by leaving people who are differently-abled to deal with it. We can no longer tolerate the barriers that have kept us separate for so long. To take pleasure and strength in the particular heritage to which we were born is fine; to buttress our own identities by humiliating or demonizing or rendering invisible those of other heritages is a sure recipe for our own disaster. Alone, we will be mystified, silenced, invalidated; we will burn out in the struggle. But together, we can help each other pull down the walls that separate us and demolish the invisible barriers that keep us from the connection that is our human birthright.

—(Locke, 2001, p. 245–246)

A pressing issue that affects counseling in a diverse society is racism. *Racism* is prejudice displayed in blatant or subtle ways due to recognized or perceived differences in the physical and psychological backgrounds of people. It demeans all who participate in it and is a form of projection usually displayed out of fear or ignorance. *Cultural racism* occurs when one cultural group considers another group inferior, and the first group has the power to impose its standards on the other group. *Institutionalized racism* refers to the established use of policies, laws, customs, and norms to perpetuate discrimination and prejudice. It may be difficult for someone who is part of a majority group to recognize his or her own racism, although doing so is vital to the development of cultural self-awareness (W. Lee, 1999).

Another challenge in multicultural counseling is the dominance of theoretical approaches based on Euro-American cultural values (Sue et al., 1996). Some of the predominant Euro-American cultural values include individualism, autonomy, an action-oriented approach to problem solving, the work ethic, the scientific method, and an emphasis on rigid time schedules (Axelson, 1993; Sue et al., 1996). A liability of these values in counseling is that theories built around them may not always be applicable to clients from other cultural traditions (C. Lee, 1997; Nwachuka & Ivey, 1991; Sue, 1992). Indeed, such culture-bound values may contradict the value systems of other cultural groups, and intentionally or unintentionally imposing them on racial/ethnic minorities may be detrimental. Community counselors are challenged to move beyond Eurocentric biases that characterize traditional counseling theories and develop new conceptual frameworks that provide a "more complete, accurate, and culturally respectful understanding of human development" (D'Andrea & Daniels, 2001, p. 537).

A fourth factor that affects multicultural counseling is the client's level of *acculturation,* which refers to the process of acquiring the salient elements of the dominant culture (National Institute of Mental Health [NIMH], 1999). During the acculturation process, individuals are simultaneously influenced by elements of more than one culture. Coping with the conflict created by this experience can be difficult. Research indicates that challenges in trying to balance contrasting values of two or more different cultures include "psychological stress, guilt, apathy, depression, delinquency, resentment, disorientation, and poor self-esteem" (Yeh & Hwang, 2000, p. 425). Whereas historically the concept of acculturation has been applied to immigrant groups, it also has meaning for minority groups living in a mainstream majority culture (NIMH, 1999). Community counselors need to determine where clients are on a continuum of acculturation in order to provide them with appropriate services (Weinrach & Thomas, 1998).

Poverty, racism, value differences, and acculturation all can potentially influence the counseling process. Each of these issues in multicultural counseling must be recognized, understood, and empathically managed if counselors are to be effective with clients from different cultural backgrounds.

Developing Multicultural Counseling Competencies

In 1996, the Association for Multicultural Counseling and Development (AMCD) published a document, *Operationalization of the Multicultural Counseling Competencies* (Arredondo et al., 1996) designed to help counselors work effectively in an ethnically diverse society. At the time of this writing, the professional divisions in the American Counseling Association (ACA) were in the process of making decisions about whether to endorse the Competencies. Much debate about the need to provide formal endorsement of the Competencies has occurred, with critics maintaining that the Competencies place too much emphasis on race, as opposed to other cultural considerations (Weinrach & Thomas, 2002). Regardless of the stance one takes regarding endorsement, community counselors will want to be familiar with the multicultural competencies outlined in the publication. Specifically, the 31 competencies are organized into three categories: (a) *awareness* of one's own personal worldview and the effect of cultural conditioning on personal development, (b) *knowledge* of the worldviews of culturally different clients, and (c) *skills* needed to work with culturally different clients (Arredondo et al., 1996). Courtland Lee (2001) described ethnically responsive counselors as professionals who have intentionally found ways to grow and develop in each of these three categories.

Self-awareness.   For counselors to work successfully with clients from ethnically diverse backgrounds, it is important "to fully experience themselves as racial/ethnic beings" and "be anchored in perceptions of their own ethnic realities" (C. Lee, 2001, p. 584). They need to be aware of their own cultural values and biases before they can work effectively with people from different cultures. To develop self-awareness, counselors and counselors-in-training need to examine their own ethnic heritage and their personal ethnic identity development. This process is facilitated when counselors ask themselves questions such as, "How do I see myself as a member of my ethnic group?", "How do I see other people in my ethnic group?", and "How do I perceive people from different ethnic backgrounds?" (C. Lee, p. 584). Self-exploration leads to self-awareness, which enables counselors to be cognizant of ways their worldviews might influence the counseling process.

Knowledge.   In addition to developing self-awareness, counselors and counselors-in-training need to acquire a knowledge base that guides their work in a diverse society. To that end, C. Lee (2001) offers the following suggestions:

- Acquire an understanding of how economic, social, and political systems impact the psychosocial development of ethnic-minority groups.
- Acquire general knowledge about the histories, experiences, customs, and values of people from ethnically diverse groups. Understand how these contexts influence personal and social development.
- Read the literature and use the media to learn about the lifestyles, customs, values, and traditions of different ethnic groups. For example, view diversity-focused films about specific cultures, such as the ones listed in Figure 10–2, to understand and experience these cultures vicariously.
- Experience ethnic diversity firsthand by interacting with people in their cultural environments (e.g., attend festivals and ceremonies). In counselor-training programs, invite people from other cultures to speak, either individually or as part of a panel.

African American
Autobiography of Miss Jane Pittman
Boyz'n the Hood
The Color Purple
Colors
Do the Right Thing
Driving Miss Daisy
Eye on the Prize
Guess Who's Coming to Dinner
I Know Why the Caged Bird Sings
Jungle Fever
Long Walk Home
Malcolm X
Matewan
Mississippi Masala
Mo' Better Blues
Raisin in the Sun
Roots I & II
Sounder
To Kill a Mockingbird
White Man's Burden

Asian American
Come See the Paradise
Dim Sum
Double Happiness
Farewell to Manzanar
Joy Luck Club
The Wash
Wedding Banquet

Latino/Latina
American Me
Ballad of Gregorio Cortez
Born in East L.A.
El Norte
Like Water for Chocolate
Mi Familia
Milagro Bean Field War
Romero
Stand and Deliver

People with Disabilities
Born on the Fourth of July
Children of a Lesser God
Coming Home
Frankie Starlight
If You Can See What I Can Hear
Miracle Worker
My Left Foot
One Flew over the Cuckoo's Nest
The Other Side of the Mountain
A Patch of Blue
Waterdance
What's Eating Gilbert Grape

Gay, Lesbian, and Bisexual
And the Band Played On
Long Time Companion
Personal Best
Philadelphia
Priest
Strawberries and Chocolate
Torch Song Trilogy

Native American
Dances With Wolves
The Last of the Mohicans
The Mission
Never Cry Wolf
Pow Wow Highway
Thunderheart

Asian Indian
Mississippi Masala

Elderly
Cocoon
Driving Miss Daisy
Foxfire
Fried Green Tomatoes
Nobody's Fool
On Golden Pond

Figure 10–2

Sample list of films focusing on diverse populations

Source: From "The Diversity Video Forum: An Adjunct to Diversity Sensitive Training in the Classroom," by E. J. Pinterits and D. R. Atkinson, 1998, *Counselor Education and Supervision, 37,* pp. 213–214. © 1998 by ACA. Reprinted with permission. No further reproduction authorized without written permission of the American Counseling Association.

Although it is unrealistic to expect counselors to be knowledgeable about all cultures, they can intentionally learn about different ethnic groups, particularly those that they are most likely to encounter in counseling. By developing knowledge about different cultural groups, counselors are better prepared to work with clients in an ethnically responsive manner.

Skills.   Ethnically responsive counselors are able to help people resolve problems or make decisions in ways that are consistent with the realities of their cultural experiences (C. Lee, 2001). Lee suggests that skills should be grounded in three premises:

1. Ethnic diversity is real and should not be ignored.
2. Ethnic differences are not deficiencies. Counselors need to meet clients where they are, recognizing differences and responding accordingly.
3. Counselors need to avoid stereotypes and consider the multiple contexts that affect client development.

With these premises in mind, Lee goes on to describe five influences and attitudes that need to be taken into account when counseling with people from different ethnic groups (pp. 586–587).

- **Kinship Influences**. Kinship influences refer to the roles played by immediate and extended family, friends, and the community itself. Ethnically responsive counselors understand and appreciate those roles and, when appropriate, find ways to involve the kinship system in the counseling process. For example, in *network therapy* (Attneave, 1982), counseling takes place during a network meeting that includes the client, his or her immediate and extended family, and any significant people in the community who might be able to help with problem resolution (W. Lee, 1999).
- **Language Preference**. Ethnically responsive counselors appreciate and are sensitive to a client's language preference. Differences in language can refer to dialect, style, fluency, and nonverbal communication. The language used in counseling may or may not be the language used in the client's home. When possible, counselors should communicate with clients in their preferred language. When this is not feasible, a referral to a bilingual counselor may be appropriate.
- **Gender-Role Socialization**. Gender is a multifaceted construct that encompasses more than just biological sex. Gender roles are socially constructed and affect expectations, behaviors, and attitudes. An awareness of gender-role socialization can facilitate the counselor's ability to respond sensitively.
- **Religious/Spiritual Influences**. As with kinship influences, the roles played by religion and spirituality differ both within and between ethnic groups. Counseling may be enhanced if the influences of these forces are recognized and, when appropriate, included as a dynamic in the counseling process.
- **Help-Seeking Attitudes and Behaviors**. In some cultures, seeking outside help from a professional is neither understood nor valued. It may be necessary to offer services in nontraditional ways, perhaps outside of the counseling setting.

Box 10–2

As a new bilingual practitioner working with Latino/a clients and their families, I learned that I was expected not only to be a counselor but also to serve as advocate for clients who were not able at times to speak for themselves; that is, to speak English. I was faced with the dual challenges of establishing myself as a beginning counselor and creating a safe environment for my clients. Being a bilingual counselor allows me the opportunity to use my language skills to counsel Spanish-speaking clients in a more direct and empathic way than would occur through using a translator. A blessing indeed, but it also has proved to be a bit of a struggle getting my peers to view me as a trained therapist. They initially viewed me as a *translator*, asking "What are they [the family members] saying?" rather than as a *counselor,* asking "What do you think is going on with this family?"

As an advocate for my clients, I often must help them understand that my role is to help them with mental health issues, not to pass judgment regarding their immigration status in the United States. Through my continued work with Latino/a clients, I have experienced the joy of facilitating the removal of cultural and emotional *paredes* (walls) within individuals and families.

—(Tania Castillero, M.A. Ed., NCC, *Casa Guadalupe,* Catholic Social Services)

Becoming Ethnically Responsive Counselors: Integrating Awareness, Knowledge, and Skills

Developing multicultural counseling competencies is a complex process that integrates personal growth with learning and skill development (W. Lee, 1999). One training technique that helps counselors improve their multicultural counseling skills while increasing sensitivity and understanding is Pedersen's (1977, 1978, 2002) triad role-play model. In the role-play, participants take the roles of counselor, client, and problem. They simulate a counseling session in which they strive to:

• Articulate the problem from the client's cultural perspective
• Anticipate resistance from a culturally different client
• Diminish defensiveness by studying one's personal defensive responses
• Learn and practice recovery skills when culturally related problems occur.

Pedersen (2002) recommends that counselors-in-training videotape their role-plays to facilitate greater learning. By discussing the videotaped role-plays, students can enhance their understanding of how cultural differences can impact the counseling process.

Use of theories.   Another way counselors can develop skills in working with people from different cultures is by intentionally examining and implementing existing theories that have cross-cultural applications (e.g., Corsini & Wedding, 2000; Sue et al., 1996; Vontress, 1996). For example, existential counseling is a holistic approach that has applications across cultures and socioeconomic groups (Epp, 1998). Existential theory deals with the meaning of life, freedom, human relationships, and the ultimate realities of life and death. These basic human conditions transcend culture and, for many clients, are primary counseling concerns.

An exciting development in multicultural counseling is the renewed emphasis on theories specifically designed for different cultures (C. Lee, 1997). For example, traditional Asian psychotherapies, which have existed for more than 3,000 years, have recently become more popular in the West (Walsh, 2000). Many of these Eastern traditions stress existential and transpersonal health and development rather than pathology, employing such techniques as meditation and yoga. They can have beneficial effects on wellness and psychological growth, whether used alone or in concert with other approaches.

Conveying cultural empathy.   An essential component of working effectively with culturally diverse clients is the counselor's ability to communicate cultural empathy (Chung & Bemak, 2002). For cultural empathy to be conveyed, Chung and Bemak (pp. 156–157) make the following recommendations:

- Demonstrate a genuine interest in learning more about the client's culture. Become knowledgeable about the historical and sociopolitical background of clients and demonstrate sensitivity about specific cultural issues.
- Convey genuine appreciation for cultural differences between the client and counselor.
- Incorporate culturally appropriate interventions and outcome expectations into the counseling process. Implement indigenous healing practices from the client's culture when possible.
- Understand and accept the context of family and community for clients of different backgrounds.
- Recognize the psychosocial adjustment that must be made by clients who have moved from one environment to another.
- Be sensitive to oppression, discrimination, and racism that are encountered by many people, often on a regular basis.
- Be prepared to advocate for and empower clients who feel underprivileged and devalued.

Counselors who are able to convey cultural empathy are more likely to develop therapeutic relationships with clients from different cultural backgrounds, thus increasing the likelihood of positive counseling outcomes.

Summary

As community counselors develop ethnically responsive counseling skills, it is crucial to remember that *each individual, like each counseling session, is unique.* There are *probably more within-group differences than between-group differences among different ethnic groups* (Swartz-Kulstad & Martin, 1999). To counsel effectively, counselors must take steps to understand their clients and their specific concerns, taking into account their unique experiences as well as the broader contexts in which they live and interact.

As stated earlier, people frequently have multiple identities, some of which are more visible than others. In addition to focusing on ways to become an ethnically responsive counselor, it is also important to consider other issues related to counseling in a diverse society. In Chapter 11, counseling issues related to gender differences and working with older adults are addressed. In this next section, however, we turn our attention to counseling issues related to a client's sexual orientation.

COUNSELING AND SEXUAL ORIENTATION

Sexual orientation represents one of many dimensions that comprise an individual's identity. Unlike ethnicity, sexual orientation is, in many ways, an "invisible identity" (Bringaze & White, 2001). Consequently, counselors may not be aware of a client's sexual orientation unless the client chooses to reveal it. It is believed that between 5 and 15 percent of the population in the United States is lesbian, gay, or bisexual (Miller & House, 2001; Moursund & Kenny, 2002). Because of the stigmatization that continues to be associated with homosexuality in our society, many lesbians, gays, and bisexuals experience discrimination and lack of acceptance. Research indicates that nonheterosexual clients are more likely to seek counseling than are heterosexual clients; however, they also report being less satisfied with their experiences in counseling (Lidderdale & Whitman, 2000).

Professional mental health organizations, including the American Counseling Association (ACA), the American Psychological Association (APA), and the National Association of Social Workers (NASW), forbid discrimination based on sexual orientation. For example, the ACA *Code of Ethics and Standards of Practice* (1995) mandates that professional counselors actively attempt to understand the diverse cultural backgrounds of the clients with whom they work and avoid discrimination based on sexual orientation. To work effectively with lesbian, gay, or bisexual clients (hereafter referred to as *LGB*), community counselors need to develop a clear understanding of their own sexual identity, knowledge about issues related to LGB identity development and lifestyles, and skills for working competently with this population. In this section, information is presented about sexual orientation and sexual identity, special concerns related to working with LGB clients, and implications for counseling.

Definitions and Terminology

Although research strongly indicates that sexual orientation is biological in origin, there continue to be people who refer to sexual orientation as *sexual preference,* a term that is vague and unhelpful (Chen-Hayes, 2000). The suggested terminology is *sexual orientation,* which refers to past, present, and ideal feelings about who is attractive and desirable in sexual and/or romantic ways (Chen-Hayes, 2000). Sexual orientation—which can be heterosexual, homosexual, or bisexual—is a multidimensional construct that many researchers believe exists on a continuum (e.g., the Kinsey Studies). It is important to avoid making generalizations about sexual orientation because generalities may not necessarily represent the experience of a specific client (W. Lee, 1999). For the sake of clarity, in this chapter the term *gay* refers to men who are sexually oriented to other men, *lesbian* refers to women who are sexually oriented to other women, and *bisexual* refers to individuals who are sexually oriented to both men and women.

Community counselors will want to select terminology prudently in their work with all clients, regardless of sexual orientation. In particular, referring to someone as *homosexual* is discouraged because of the psychopathological connotations ascribed to that term in early editions of the *Diagnostic and Statistical Manual of Mental Disorders* (American Psychiatric Association [APA], 1968), when homosexuality was classified as a mental illness. Because the use of language can affect self-esteem, stigmatize, and be offensive, it is important for counselors to be cognizant of their use of language and check with clients to determine their preferences in regard to terminology (Miller & House, 2001).

Researchers distinguish among the terms *sexual attraction, sexual behavior,* and *sexual identity.* A person may be erotically attracted to someone of the same sex but engage exclusively in heterosexual behavior. Sexual identity, on the other hand, includes both the affectional and sexual dimensions of self that are evidenced by thoughts, feelings, and behaviors (Palma & Stanley, 2002). The development of sexual identity is a dynamic process that is influenced by personal and cultural experiences. Issues related to sexual identity development are often of particular concern to LGB clients, particularly when they have experienced prejudice and oppression.

Homophobia and Heterosexism

Prejudicial beliefs and attitudes, principally homophobia and heterosexism, have pervasive adverse effects on sexual minority clients, as well as on society as a whole. *Homophobia* refers to an antigay bias, or fear of individuals who are perceived as lesbian, gay, or bisexual. Homophobic attitudes are evidenced by stereotyping and downgrading LGB individuals. In extreme cases, these negative, derogatory responses become violent, resulting in harassment and hate crimes (Miller & House, 2001). As many as 92 percent of gay men and lesbians have experienced antigay verbal abuse, and some 24% report being victims of physical violence (W. Lee, 1999). An important role of community counselors is to combat homophobia when it is evidenced in any form.

Perhaps a more insidious form of discrimination and prejudice is *heterosexism,* which refers to the viewpoint that "heterosexuality is or should be the only acceptable sexual orientation" (Miller & House, 2001, p. 394). Heterosexism is the societal norm in the United States, as evidenced by prevailing attitudes that reinforce heterosexuality as the only acceptable life option. Heterosexism is evidenced when, for example, workplaces do not provide health care or bereavement benefits for same-sex partners or states fail to recognize same-sex life commitments as legal. Even more subtle forms of heterosexism may be evidenced in counseling agencies, when intake forms include blanks for *spouse* or counselors assume that their clients are heterosexual.

Although general trends indicate that people are more accepting of minority sexual identities than they have been in past years, many LGB individuals continue to combat homophobia and heterosexism on a regular basis. Counselors need to be aware of their own beliefs and responses, avoid discrimination, and learn skills for counseling effectively with LGB clients. When counselors hold beliefs that compromise their ability to do this, they need to inform their clients of the conflict and then make an appropriate referral (Palma & Stanley, 2002).

Box 10–3

When society categorizes an individual using only one dimension of humanness, a significant part of that person is omitted. This omission leads to stereotyping and labeling, which have a significant and detrimental impact on the individual. Examples of such stereotyping and labeling include "He is a dumb jock; what is he doing with a philosophy major?" "She's a woman; she shouldn't do that kind of work." "He's gay; he should not be working with children." "She is married; she couldn't possibly be bisexual." All of these statements focus on only one aspect of the individual. By focusing on an isolated aspect, the person in each of these examples is minimized and reduced to that one aspect—an unfair and inaccurate characterization of the whole person. The more holistic approach to human behavior focuses on the integration of all aspects of the individual, including the emotional, social, intellectual, spiritual, and physical dimensions of each person.

—(Miller & House, 2001, p. 392)

Sexual Identity Development and Coming Out

Models of identity development.   Several theoretical explanations of minority sexual identity development have been proposed, each with unique counseling implications (Palma & Stanley, 2002). Identity models explain the cognitive, emotional, and behavioral changes that occur as an individual moves toward identifying him- or herself as gay, lesbian, or bisexual. One of the first models was published by Cass (1979, 1984), whose six-stage model provided a framework for understanding sexual minority identity development while also influencing mental health professionals to move away from a pathological view of homosexuality (Degges-White, Rice, & Myers, 2000). Whereas Cass's model was based on a study of gay men, other models have been developed that point out different developmental paths experienced by women and bisexual individuals. In particular, lesbians often experience feelings of connectedness and attraction to women before associating those feelings with a specific sexual orientation (Bringaze & White, 2001). Bisexual identity development, which has not been researched as extensively as gay and lesbian identity development, involves dimensions that are unique to the bisexual experience and need to be taken into consideration during counseling (Horowitz & Newcomb, 1999). Being sensitive to issues that affect sexual minority identity development, as well as to issues that affect overall identity development, is crucial to counseling effectively.

It is helpful to view sexual identity development as a process that is unique for each individual and is influenced by personal and cultural factors (Palma & Stanley, 2002). Movement from one stage of development to another may be fluid and nonlinear, with no one formula or path that is "best." Bringaze and White (2001) emphasize that the process of achieving a positive lesbian, gay, or bisexual identity can take many years, with some people getting stuck during the process and never developing a positive, integrated identity. Counselors will want to take into account each client's unique sociocultural background, experiences, and perspectives and meet that client where he or she is in regard to sexual identity formation.

Sexual and ethnic minority identity.   Lesbian, gay, and bisexual individuals from ethnic minority groups may face a unique set of issues that differ from those facing other LGB clients. In some ways, LGB people of color face a double indemnity as they attempt to function in several communities simultaneously (W. Lee, 1999). They may be more likely to face social discrimination on many levels, which can lead to psychological distress. For example, Latino communities largely reject sexual minority identities (Sager, 2001). In Latino communities, *familism,* or the primary importance of family, is often valued above individual needs. Coming out in a Latino family may accentuate feelings of guilt and alienate clients from their family, church, and community. Consequently, LGB Latino clients may "face the difficult choice of remaining closeted in the heterosexist Latin American community or dealing with racism in the LGB and European American communities" (Sager, p. 25). The fear of rejection, cultural disinheritance, and loss of ties to one's ethnic community can make it especially difficult for clients from Latino and other ethnic groups to develop healthy, integrated sexual identities.

Coming out.   A key component of minority sexual identity development is the *coming out process. Coming out,* or letting other people know that one is lesbian, gay, or bisexual, is not a one-time event, but instead is an ongoing process, affected largely by an individual's life circumstances (Miller & House, 2001). The process may begin at any age and can be especially difficult for adolescents, who may be more vulnerable and subject to ridicule. At any age, making the decision to reveal one's sexual orientation to others can have serious consequences, both positive and negative (Winter, 2002). Community counselors can help clients sort through the various issues associated with that decision and examine the risks and benefits associated with coming out (Figure 10–3).

It is generally accepted that coming out is positively associated with mental health and relationship satisfaction (W. Lee, 1999). Coming out contributes to identity acceptance, integration, and authenticity. However, coming out also carries with it the risk of abandonment, ridicule, and disapproval. The process may be psychologically painful, as the old sense of self is grieved before the new sense of self emerges (W. Lee, 1999). Community counselors can help clients cope with coming out issues through the use of role play, cognitive rehearsal, and bibliotherapy. Providing information about support groups, hot lines, and other community resources also can be beneficial to LBG clients struggling with coming out issues.

Other Counseling Issues and Implications

Because of the stigma associated with homosexuality, LGB clients often enter counseling to help them come to terms with their orientation (Bringazc & White, 2001). However, the issues clients bring to counseling may or may not be related to sexual identity, and counselors need to avoid making premature assumptions about presenting concerns. With this caution in mind, there are some specific issues that

1. What kind of reactions do you expect when you tell family members, friends, co-workers, etc.?
2. How can you determine what the reactions might be?
3. What would be the worst possible reaction?
4. What can you do to prepare yourself against that reaction?
5. What happens when or if you tell your parents?
6. Should you tell your parents together or individually?
7. Should you tell both of your parents?
8. What happens if you do not tell certain people?
9. Is it necessary to tell everyone?
10. What are the best ways to tell people?
11. Can you think of alternative ways to tell people?
12. Are you aware that responses may change over time?

Figure 10–3
The consequences of coming out: Questions to consider
Source: From *Introduction to the Counseling Profession* (3rd ed., p. 402), by D. Capuzzi and D. R. Gross. Published by Allyn & Bacon, Boston, MA. Copyright © 2002 by Pearson Education. Reprinted by permission of the publisher.

are unique to sexual minority clients. Often, LGB clients struggle to understand themselves and their relationships within a predominantly heterosexual society. Internalized homophobia and self-image, interpersonal relationships, career-related concerns, and conflicted religious values are just a few of the issues that LGB clients may choose to work on in counseling.

Internalized homophobia and self-image.   Internalized homophobia occurs when a lesbian, gay, or bisexual individual internalizes negative societal attitudes about homosexuality (Miller & House, 2001; Sophie, 1987). Such internalization can result in cognitive dissonance, low self-esteem, depression, and other forms of psychological distress. Typically, a person's internalized messages are tied to childhood experiences, family roles, and societal expectations. LGB individuals receive messages from many sources, including friends, family members, church, school, and the media. Counselors can help clients explore and articulate the internalized messages they have received about homosexuality. By encouraging the exploration of thoughts and feelings, counselors can then help clients challenge inaccuracies and reconstruct meanings about sexuality that are more positive and acceptable (Bringaze & White, 2001).

For clients to explore thoughts and feelings about their sexual orientation, they need to sense unconditional positive regard on the part of the counselor. They may test the counselor to determine his or her stance toward homosexuality or bisexuality (Palma & Stanley, 2002). Community counselors can be proactive in establishing an environment in which clients feel safe exploring issues related to sexual identity. Suggestions for counselors include (Black & Underwood, 1998; Miller & House, 2001; Palma & Stanley; Winter, 2002):

- Demonstrate respect for the client's current experiences and presenting issues. These issues may or may not be related to sexual orientation.

- Be sincere, open, genuine, and ethical, respecting confidentiality and honoring differences.
- Explore personal issues related to sexuality and heterosexism. Covert, unexplored issues or attitudes are likely to impact the counseling experience negatively.
- Be aware of societal prejudices and oppression and advocate for an LGB-affirmative environment. Offices with books, brochures, and symbols that are relevant to LGB individuals suggest that the counselor is affirmative and nonjudgmental.
- Be sensitive to nonverbal or covert client messages that may signal permission for the counselor to address issues related to sexual identity.
- Be knowledgeable about sexual identity development issues. Provide support, normalize feelings, and anticipate confusion and ambiguity.
- Help clients explore feelings. Many LGB clients, especially adolescents, feel isolated, guilty, afraid, ashamed, and angry. Listen empathically, providing them with a safe space in which feelings can be validated.
- Use role-play to help clients handle a variety of situations, including coming out to family members and friends, if clients choose to do so.
- Be aware of the potential for depression and self-esteem issues and address them accordingly.
- Provide accurate information about sexually transmitted diseases, including AIDS.
- Be informed about community resources and support groups and share that information with LGB clients.

Family relationships.   Relationships with family members, particularly in regard to disclosure, can present unique sources of concern for LGB clients. When family members are supportive and accepting of sexual minority clients, relationships are enhanced, and clients report a higher degree of life satisfaction and adjustment (Bringaze & White, 2001). Unfortunately, however, many families do not support non-heterosexual orientations, and counselors need to help clients evaluate whether or not disclosure is advisable. Disadvantages associated with not coming out to family members include having to monitor and censor one's interactions and guilt associated with being unauthentic. On the other hand, when family values and cultural messages are such that an "out" sexual minority client will be alienated from his or her family, it may be in the client's best interest to avoid disclosure. Community counselors can help clients explore the realistic consequences of coming out to family, and if the client decides to disclose, the counselor can facilitate the process through rehearsal, empty-chair activities, and/or letter writing (Bringaze & White, 2001). Counselors also may be in a position to help families work through questions and confusion that arise in relation to their family member's sexual orientation (Winter, 2002).

Other relationships.   Relationships with heterosexual friends and colleagues also may be sources of concern for LGB clients. Palma and Stanley (2002) point out that there often is a time lag between disclosure of one's sexual identity and the acceptance and/or affirmation that friends and colleagues are capable of providing. Counselors can help clients develop appropriate expectations of others by reminding them of the time it took for them to acknowledge their own sexual identity.

Associating with other people who are gay, lesbian, or bisexual can be especially helpful for LGB clients. Social and professional groups that provide support have been established in most urban areas and can serve as powerful resources for LGB clients. Groups exist that address multiple issues, including sexism, legal concerns, aging, health, and religion. Counselors in rural communities will want to be aware of resources available nationally and in nearby cities (Miller & House, 2001).

LGB couples may seek counseling to work through relationship issues. Although some issues are common to same-sex and heterosexual couples (e.g., finances and communication problems) and are responsive to traditional therapeutic interventions, others are unique to gay and lesbian couples. For example, in many states, same-sex couples are denied most of the legal, religious, economic, and social benefits typically received by heterosexual couples. Likewise, same-sex couples do not have the social, legal, and moral sanctions that sustain opposite-sex couples (Miller & House, 2001). Same-sex couples have fewer visible role models and may experience unique difficulties in regard to role definition. Gay men may have difficulty with competition and may be prone to seek isolation when problems arise. Lesbians may have difficulty with autonomy, differentiation, and maintaining a sense of self (W. Lee, 1999). Attempting to define roles in the same ways they are defined in heterosexual relationships can be counterproductive or detrimental. Community counselors who plan to work with same-sex couples will need to participate in education, training, and supervision in order to meet the needs of their clients.

Career concerns.   Career choice, workplace benefits and stresses, and career advancement may present unique challenges to LGB clients (W. Lee, 1999). Sexual minority clients may not be able to integrate their personal lives into the workplace as easily as their heterosexual counterparts. They also may be more likely to face work discrimination, which refers to unfair and negative treatment based on personal attributes that are unrelated to job performance (Chung, 2002). Although many companies have adopted corporate nondiscrimination policies, discrimination in the workplace is still a reality faced by many sexual minority individuals. Counselors can help LGB clients examine their perceptions of discrimination and evaluate potential coping strategies, which may include open confrontation or changing jobs. In other situations, clients may choose to remain closeted in the workplace, in which case counselors can help the client cope with the additional stress that accompanies nondisclosure (W. Lee, 1999).

Other issues.   Other concerns that may be of particular significance to LGB clients include issues related to religious beliefs, AIDS, and advocacy. Often, LGB individuals struggle with conflicting values between their sexual orientation and their religious beliefs. Certain religious doctrines view homosexuality as sinful, and it may be difficult for LGB clients to find a place of worship where they are accepted. It is important for counselors to be aware of their own religious values, conflicts related to religion and sexual identity, and methods of helping clients address these difficult issues (Miller & House, 2001).

A myriad of counseling-related issues are associated with AIDS. AIDS, which was first identified in 1981, currently has no known cure. Initially, the group hardest hit by AIDS was gay men, resulting in a "secondary epidemic of prejudice, fear, and igno-rance" (Miller & House, 2001, p. 410). Counselors can address issues related to AIDS by challenging uninformed opinions, providing psychoeducation for the larger com-munity, and assisting with the multiple needs that afflict clients, friends, and family members living with HIV/AIDS. It also is important for counselors to be aware of the profound effect AIDS-related bereavement has had on gay men. Often, feelings asso-ciated with multiple losses, including denial, anger, depression, and guilt, need to be worked through in counseling sessions.

Community counselors are in a position to serve as advocates for LGB clients. Joining the Association of Gay, Lesbian, and Bisexual Issues in Counseling (AGLBIC), a division of ACA, is one way counselors can advocate for sexual minority clients. Counselors also can take proactive steps to counteract bias on all fronts, whether it exists in relation to a person's sexual orientation, gender, ethnicity, or any other characteristic subject to discrimination.

(Reader's Note: In this section, we did not elaborate on concerns specific to transgendered clients. Although transgendered persons have experiences similar to LGB populations, they also have "social and psychological dimensions unique to their identity" [Palma & Stanley, 2002, p. 74]. Although some of the counseling implications outlined in this section are applicable to transgendered clients, we encourage counselors to refer to other sources [e.g., Carroll, Gilroy, & Ryan, 2002] to become informed about issues specific to the transgender community.)

COUNSELING PEOPLE WITH DISABILITIES OVERVIEW

Box 10-4

> People with disabilities, like all people, want to participate fully in the society in which they live. The desire to achieve and to be successful is not diminished by a disability; indeed, the opportunity to work and contribute to the support of self and family is considered a basic right in a free, democratic society, and as Ameri-can citizens, people with disabilities have a right to equality of opportunity of edu-cation, employment, transportation, housing, health care, and leisure. A person's disability should not interfere with full participation in any of these activities.
>
> —(Martin, 1999, p. 25)

People with disabilities constitute our nation's largest minority group (W. Lee, 1999). Approximately 54 million Americans report some level of disability, and 26 mil-lion Americans describe their disability as severe (Holmes, 1999). Disabilities are mani-fested in a variety of ways and may be physical, emotional, cognitive, and/or behavioral in nature. Examples of specific disabilities include orthopedic, visual, speech, and hear-ing impairments; cerebral palsy; chronic diseases; developmental disabilities; neurologi-cal disorders; psychiatric illness; and substance addiction. In this section, a general overview about working with people with disabilities is provided.

In addition to variation in types of disabilities, there is much divergence in regard to age of onset, cause, severity, and manifestation of the disability. Consequently, the population of individuals with disabilities comprises one of the most diverse groups discussed thus far. Furthermore, people with disabilities represent the only minority group of which a person may unexpectedly become a member at any time (Foster, 1996).

Definitions and Terminology

The Americans With Disabilities Act of 1990 (ADA) defines *disability* as a physical or mental impairment that substantially limits a major life activity. Recently, the Supreme Court narrowed the ADA definition of disability by ruling that in order for a person to be considered substantially limited, the impairment must prevent or severely restrict the individual from doing activities that are of central importance to most people's daily lives, and that the impairment must be permanent or long term (Thomas, 2002). Disability status is dynamic, due to the transitory nature of health and to the connection between a person's level of functioning and the barriers in his or her environment (Fujiura, 2001).

When working with people who are disabled, counselors must put the client first, not the disability (Martin, 1999). One way to accomplish this is by avoiding labels and stereotyping. Related to this concept is the need to choose language respectfully, making sure that terms are not pejorative or dehumanizing. For example, it is better to refer to someone as a "person with a disability" rather than as a "disabled person" (Martin, 1999). Similarly, terms like "physically or mentally challenged" should be avoided. Because there are literally hundreds of physical and mental conditions that qualify as disabilities, no single source of information on terminology provides suggestions that are appropriate for all people (National Victim Assistance Academy [NVAA], 1999). Therefore, as in other counseling situations, counselors will want to check with clients to determine their preferences regarding terminology and language use.

The degree to which a disability impedes an individual's functioning is situational. The presence of a disability and its subsequent effects vary, depending on the individual and the circumstances. For example, two people may have the same type of spinal cord injury but react and adapt to the injury differently. Or someone may have epilepsy that is well controlled by medication, so that the disease does not pose a major impediment to the activities of daily living. Counselors can determine the degree to which a disability poses a barrier by carefully assessing and evaluating the client and the environment(s) in which he or she lives and works. Through careful assessment, stereotyping and overgeneralization can be avoided.

Factors Associated With Increased Rates of Disability

According to the U.S. Census Bureau's Survey of Income and Program Participation (SIPP), nearly 20 percent of Americans have specific functional losses or limitations classified as disabilities (cited in Fujiura, 2001). A number of demographic, socioeconomic, and medical trends have been linked with rising rates of disabilities. These

- **Aging.** Approximately three out of every four Americans over the age of 80 has a disability of some type, and over half of this age group has a disability classified as "severe." With longevity continuing to increase, there also comes an increase in disabilities associated with the aging process.
- **Poverty.** Poverty has been linked to disability as both a consequence and a cause. According to 1997 SIPP data, nearly 28 percent of adults with a severe disability live in poverty, in contrast to 8 percent of the general population. Americans with disabilities are at a substantial disadvantage in regard to employment, access to private health insurance, and levels of educational achievement.
- **Medical Advances.** Due to medical advances, survival rates for spinal cord and severe brain injury, as well as other medical conditions, have improved dramatically. Also, survival rates for low-birth-rate infants have increased 70-fold during the past 25 years, affecting the prevalence of developmental disabilities.
- **Emerging conditions.** Over the past years, certain medical conditions have either emerged as new syndromes (e.g., chronic fatigue syndrome) or increased in incidence (e.g., asthma, autism, attention-deficit/hyperactivity disorder). It is unclear whether the higher numbers represent an increase in prevalence or an increase in the recognition and reporting of such conditions.

Figure 10–4
Factors associated with increased disability
From Fujiura, 2001.

factors, which include aging, poverty, medical advances, and emerging medical conditions, are summarized in Figure 10–4.

Attitudes and Myths About Disabilities

Misconceptions and biases toward individuals with disabilities often reflect lack of knowledge and negative stereotyping. Such societal attitudes are often subtle and may include reactions of disgust, pity, or discomfort expressed verbally or nonverbally (NVAA, 1999). Some of the negative attitudes and myths that may be held by members of society who are not currently disabled include (W. Lee, 1999; Martin, 1999; NVAA, 1999; Tyiska, 1998):

- **The Charity or Helplessness Myth.** People with disabilities are suffering and should be extended charity instead of rights and responsibilities. Such an attitude also implies that people with disabilities are not capable of making decisions for themselves and need others to manage their lives.
- **The Spread Phenomenon Myth.** If one disability is present, there must be other disabilities as well.
- **The Dehumanization or Damaged Merchandise Myth.** A person with a disability is less than a full member of society or is inferior in some way.
- **The Feeling No Pain Myth.** People with disabilities are immune from pain and suffering or have no feelings.

- **The Disabled Menace Myth**. Because they are perceived as "different," people with disabilities are considered unpredictable and dangerous (e.g., people who fear having group homes for adults with mental retardation in their neighborhoods).

Box 10–5

> Stereotypes of people with disabilities portray them as abnormal; helpless; heroic and inspirational; childlike; in need of pity or charity; and as the smiling poster child, appreciative of even second-class status.
>
> —(W. Lee, 1999, p. 177)

Negative attitudes and perceptions tend to undermine self-advocacy efforts and increase the vulnerability of people with disabilities. To counteract this effect, counselors and others who work with people with disabilities need to take lead roles in helping change negative societal attitudes, beginning with an examination of any personal attitudes that might interfere with effective interactions and interventions (Figure 10–5).

- Treat the person with dignity and respect.
- Ask the person how to communicate most effectively with him or her.
- Address and speak directly to the person, even if he or she is accompanied by a third party.
- When introduced to a person with a disability, you may shake hands. People with limited hand use or who wear an artificial limb can usually shake hands.
- If you offer assistance, wait until the offer is accepted, then listen to or ask for instructions.
- With regard to most accommodations, take your cue from the individual.
- Do not tell the person that you admire his or her courage or determination for living with the disability.
- When speaking to a person who uses a wheelchair or crutches, place yourself at eye level in front of the person to facilitate the conversation.
- When communicating with a person who is hard of hearing and who prefers to lip-read, face the person. Make sure you have the person's attention before you begin speaking. Speak slowly and distinctly, in a normal tone of voice without shouting.
- When using a sign language interpreter, have him or her sit next to you so that the hearing-impaired person can easily shift his or her gaze back and forth.
- When meeting with someone who is visually impaired, indicate your presence verbally, identify yourself by name, and speak in a normal tone of voice. If other people are present, ask them to identify themselves.
- If someone has a developmental disability, give that person time to respond. Talk slowly and calmly, using easy-to-understand language.
- Obtain expert consultation on how to communicate effectively with individual victims with developmental disabilities and people with serious mental illness.

Figure 10–5

Suggestions for interacting with people who have disabilities
From NVAA, 1999; and Tyiska, 1998.

Federal Regulation Related to Disability

Through the years, federal legislation has taken a key role in protecting the civil rights of people with disabilities. During the past 2 decades, several federal initiatives to provide education and related services to individuals with disabilities have been enacted as laws. The Americans with Disabilities Act of 1990 (ADA) provided a clear, comprehensive mandate for the elimination of discrimination against individuals with disabilities (Middleton, Rollins, & Harley, 1999). Specifically, the ADA was enacted to protect people with disabilities from discrimination in employment, public accommodations, transportation, and telecommunication. Other important legislative measures that have been implemented during the past 2 decades are outlined in Figure 10–6.

To provide effective preventive and remedial services, counselors must actively seek to understand the laws, regulations, and programs that affect people with disabilities (Middleton et al., 1999). By being aware of the legislation and policy issues that shape the alternatives available to individuals with disabilities, counselors will be better prepared to meet the specific needs of the clients they serve.

- *Americans with Disabilities Act* (ADA, PL 101–336, 1990): A wide-ranging legislation intended to make American society more accessible to people with disabilities and to protect them from discrimination.
- *Individuals with Disabilities Education Act* (IDEA, PL 101–476, 1990) and the 1997 reauthorization of IDEA (PL 105–17, 1997): A set of laws mandating that all individuals between the ages of 0 and 21 receive a free and appropriate public education with access to a wide range of services. IDEA helps ensure that the rights of children with disabilities and their parents or guardians are protected.
- *Workforce Investment Act* (WIA, PL 105–220, 1998): Legislation intended to guide the implementation of One-Stop Career Centers. One-Stop Career Centers provide a single location where an applicant can gain information needed to choose an occupation, find access to training, be placed in a job, and have access to all public services needed to continue in employment. Under the WIA, all services available through a One-Stop Career Center must be accessible to everyone who uses them.
- *Ticket to Work and Work Incentives Improvement Act* (WIAA, H.R. 1180, 1999): Legislation designed to enhance the rights of consumers with disabilities to make a choice of service providers between private nonprofit, state rehabilitation agency, and private proprietary providers.

Figure 10–6
Legislation protecting the rights of individuals with disabilities (1990–2002)

COUNSELING CONSIDERATIONS

Overview of Goals and Interventions

The provision of counseling services to clients with disabilities can be categorized into three phases: *prevention* or *primary intervention, intervention,* and *postvention* or *rehabilitation* (Livneh & Wosley-George, 2001). In *prevention,* the emphasis is on preventing disease or disability before it occurs. Programmatic efforts are levied at increasing public awareness of specific activities or situations that are likely to lead to physical and/or emotional problems (e.g., stress, unhealthy behaviors, etc.). *Intervention* refers to direct, time-limited strategies that often are implemented with crisis-like situations, such as spinal cord injury, myocardial infarction, or severe psychological distress. *Postvention,* also called *rehabilitation counseling,* focuses on helping people with permanent or chronic physical, psychiatric, and mental disabilities cope successfully and adjust to life with that disability. Community counselors may be involved in each of these three phases of service. In this section, primary attention is given to the rehabilitation phase of counseling.

The major goal of rehabilitation counseling is to help individuals with the disabilities maximize their potential in terms of acceptance, independence, productivity, and inclusion (Martin, 1999). Interventions can be targeted toward the individual client or toward the environment in which the client lives and works. Client-aimed interventions include personal adjustment counseling, vocational counseling, behavioral modification, and skill development in performance of the *activities of daily living* (ADL). In contrast, environment-aimed interventions are targeted toward barriers in the external environment that may need modification to meet the client's goals. Examples may include helping the client find ways to use assistive aids (e.g., hearing aids, prostheses, and wheelchairs), facilitating the removal of architectural barriers, and placing the client in a group home (Livneh & Wosley-George, 2001). Both types of interventions often are carried out by counselors involved in rehabilitation work.

Training, Roles, and Functions of Rehabilitation Counselors

Most counselors whose primary work is with clients with disabilities have participated in rehabilitation education counselor education (RCE) programs. The Council of Rehabilitation Education (CORE) accredits institutions that offer rehabilitation counseling. Rehabilitation counselors receive certification through the Commission on Rehabilitation Counselor Certification (CRCC), which offers the following certifications: Certified Rehabilitation Counselor (CRC), Certified Disability Management Specialist (CDMS), Certified Case Manager (CCM), and Certified Alcohol Counselor (CAC). Currently, nearly 14,000 rehabilitation counselors have been certified by CRCC.

Many rehabilitation counselors belong to the American Rehabilitation Counseling Association (ARCA), a division of ACA whose mission is to enhance the development of people with disabilities and promote excellence in the rehabilitation

What is ARCA?

ARCA is an organization consisting of counseling practitioners, educators, and students who are devoted to improving the lives of people with disabilities. ARCA's mission is to always seek to improve the profession of rehabilitation counseling to better serve persons with disabilities. ARCA promotes research and collaborates with other rehabilitation counselors, educators, administrators, and national professional organizations and groups that are dedicated to serving the same population.

What are ARCA's goals?

- To provide positive leadership that promotes excellence in the areas of rehabilitation counseling practice, research, consultation, and professional development
- To eliminate obstacles that hinder people with disabilities from accessing desirable education opportunities, employment, and community activities
- To advocate for people with disabilities through educating the public and participating in legislative activities
- To increase public awareness of rehabilitation counseling and to extend the influence of the organization
- To help its members develop leadership skills through participating in the organization's activities

The Scope of Practice for Rehabilitation Counseling: What are the assumptions?

- The knowledge and skills necessary for effective rehabilitation counseling to persons with disabilities are outlined in the Scope of Practice Statement.
- Rehabilitation counseling is differentiated from other counseling fields as counseling serves as the core for a greater system of rehabilitation disciplines and related processes (e.g., vocational evaluation, job development and job placement, work adjustment, case management).
- There is a difference between the professional scope of rehabilitation counseling practice and the more specializing individual scope of practice.

The Scope of Practice for Rehabilitation Counseling: What are the underlying values?

- Promotion of independence, integration, and inclusion of people with disabilities in employment and the community
- Belief in valuing all people
- Commitment to equal justice, rights and privileges for all people, and a commitment to support persons with disabilities through advocacy to achieve this equality and empower themselves
- Emphasis on the holistic nature of human function (i.e., considering the individual's support systems and environment)

Figure 10–7

Source: The American Rehabilitation Counseling Association (ARCA, 2002), http://www.nchrtm.okstate.edu/ARCA/index.html. Reprinted with permission.

The Scope of Practice Statement

Rehabilitation counseling is a systematic process which assists persons with physical, mental, developmental, cognitive, and emotional disabilities to achieve their personal, career, and independent living goals in the most integrated settings possible through the application of the counseling process. The counseling process involves communication, goal setting, and beneficial growth or change through self-advocacy, psychological, vocational, social, and behavioral interventions. The specific techniques and modalities utilized within this rehabilitation counseling process may include, but are not limited to:

- assessment and appraisal;
- diagnosis and treatment planning;
- career (vocational) counseling;
- individual and group counseling treatment interventions focused on facilitation adjustments to the medical and psychosocial impact of disability;
- case management, referral, and service coordination;
- program evaluation and research;
- interventions to remove environmental, employment, and attitudinal barriers;
- consultation service among multiple parties and regulatory systems;
- job analysis, job development, and placement services, including assistance with employment and job accommodations; and
- the provision of consultation about access to rehabilitation technology.

Figure 10–7   *continued*

counseling profession (see Figure 10–7). Other professional organizations for counselors who specialize in working with clients with disabilities include the National Rehabilitation Counseling Association (NRCA) and the National Association of Rehabilitation Professionals in the Private Sector (NARPPS).

Rehabilitation counselors carry out several roles and functions in serving clients with disabilities. Initially, the role of the counselor is to assess the client's current level of functioning and the surrounding environmental influences that either hinder or assist functionality. Based on the results of that assessment, counselors help clients formulate goals. Depending on the nature of the goals, counselors may need to carry out several different roles. Versatility is important, as the counselor will not only provide services directly but also coordinate services with other professionals and monitor clients' progress in gaining independence and self-control.

Hershenson (1998) describes five different functions of rehabilitation counselors: counseling, consulting, coordinating services, case management, and critiquing effectiveness. In making decisions about what services to provide, Hershenson suggests that counselors take into account the client's personality (e.g., motivation, outlook on life, and reaction to the disability), interpersonal skills and socialized behavior, learning capacities, personal and work goals, and the extent of available supports and barriers. To achieve desired goals, the rehabilitation counselor may need to *counsel* with the client about specific coping issues, *consult* with the client's family and employer about expectations, *coordinate* a skills training program, engage in *case management* to monitor the delivery of services, and conduct an ongoing *critique (evaluation)* of the effectiveness of the interventions. Throughout the process, the counselor needs to be aware of the various systems and subsystems that influence the client's well-being. How do those systems and subsystems promote or impede rehabilitation? What physical and attitudinal resources or barriers do they present? It may be necessary to work with the client's friends, family, and employers to redesign the environment to maximize access and opportunities (Wright & Martin, 1999).

Counseling Issues and Implications

Livneh and Wosley-George (2001) state that counseling people with disabilities is quantitatively rather than qualitatively different from other types of counseling, particularly in regard to the prevalence of specific themes that emerge during the process, such as independence versus dependence, personal loss, coping with crises, and maintaining employment. Some of the common problems that arise in the personal and interpersonal domains are illustrated in Figure 10–8. Other counseling issues that may confront people with disabilities include coping and adjusting to an acquired disability, family concerns, career-related concerns, and abuse.

Coping with an acquired disability.   When someone sustains an unexpected disability, whether through bodily injury or the onset of a disease, that individual is suddenly faced with an array of physical and emotional challenges. Individuals who become disabled may feel lost, terrified, and confused about what the future holds.

Personal Domain	**Interpersonal Domain**
• Lack of motivation • Reluctance to participate in rehabilitation tasks • Increased depression and/or anxiety • Damaged body image • Insult to self-concept • Loss of sense of control • Loss of reward and pleasure sources • Loss of physical and economic independence • Difficulty accepting and adjusting to the disability • Inability to access the environment	• Increased dependence (financial, medical, psychosocial, other) • Impaired social and/or vocational roles • Changing family dynamics and relationships • Disruption of social life • Negative attitudes toward disability • Societal rejection and/or social isolation • Disuse or lack of appropriate social skills • Decreased sexual activity

Figure 10–8
Common issues in the personal and interpersonal domains
Cited in Livneh and Wosley-George, 2001.

In such cases, a primary counseling goal is to help the client make order out of chaos, recognizing that acceptance and adjustment take time. Frequently, the client is faced with grief and loss issues, much like those experienced after a death. Livneh and Evans (1984) outlined 12 phases of adjustment associated with an acquired disability: shock, anxiety, bargaining, denial, mourning, depression, withdrawal, internalized anger, externalized aggression, acknowledgment, acceptance, and adjustment/adaptation. Different interventions are appropriate for different phases. It is important for counselors to be aware of the adjustment process and work with it rather than against it. At times, client behaviors may seem bizarre or confusing, but that may be necessary for progress (Rothrock, 1999).

During the initial stages after a disability is sustained, crisis intervention and supportive counseling are often called for. Offering support and reassurance, listening and attending, and allowing the client to ventilate feelings can be especially helpful. Also, it is important to recognize that the client may be using defense mechanisms and that those mechanisms serve a purpose. Without them, "reality could overwhelm the individual, and the situation could be perceived as being impossible to address" (Rothrock, 1999, p. 210). In time, the client can deal more effectively with the reality of the disability.

As counseling continues, the counselor will want to help the client develop resources for accepting, coping, and adjusting to life with a disability. One way to encourage clients to draw from their own coping abilities is to find out what helped them cope with difficult events in the past. Modifications of previously successful coping behaviors can facilitate adjustment to the new lifestyle (Rothrock, 1999). For example, if a client has a supportive family, inviting the family to participate in counseling sessions could help with decision making and make life more manageable.

Cognitive therapy may help a client with a disability reinterpret life experiences in a manner that enhances resilience and a sense of coherence (Lustig, Rosenthal, Strauser, & Haynes, 2000). A strong sense of coherence increases the chances that a person will mobilize available resources and seek out new resources when handling stressful situations. A client's sense of coherence is determined by his or her perceptions of: (a) comprehensibility (the degree to which the world is perceived as predictable, ordered, and explicable), (b) manageability (the degree to which a person believes that he or she has the resources needed to handle a demand), and (c) meaningfulness (the belief that demands are worthy of investment and commitment). People with a strong sense of coherence are able to cope more effectively with stressors and thereby are more likely to adjust better to life with a disability (Lustig et al., 2000). Perceptions associated with a sense of coherence may be adaptive or dysfunctional. The goal of cognitive therapy is to help clients modify assumptions and perceptions that are maladaptive so that adjustment and quality of life are enhanced.

Adjusting to an acquired disability takes time and perseverance. Counselors can facilitate the process by fostering independence rather than dependence, finding ways to turn failures into learning experiences, respecting their clients as fellow human beings, and helping them take ownership of their rehabilitation.

Family issues.   Disabilities in family members can affect family functioning in numerous ways. Family responses to disability vary, depending in part on which phase of adaptation the family is in. Three common phases include the *crisis phase,* the *chronic phase,* and the *terminal phase* (W. Lee, 1999; Roland, 1994).

Families in the *crisis phase* are either waiting for a diagnosis or have just received information about a family member's disability. In this phase, family members often deal with feelings of shock, denial, anger, and depression. As when working with individuals, counselors can provide the family with supportive counseling characterized by empathic listening and attending. A primary goal during the crisis phase is to help the family consider what will remain the same and what will need to change as a consequence of the disability and then determine how to manage that change as it occurs (Roland, 1994).

Families in the *chronic phase* are coping with the day-to-day issues related to the disability (Roland, 1994). The degree to which adjustment and coping are needed is affected by numerous factors, including the nature and severity of the disability and the temperament and stamina of family members. Useful counseling interventions during this phase include helping family members find ways to manage stress, building on strengths, developing realistic expectations, and anticipating problems before they arise so that they can be managed more effectively.

Certain disabilities, such as cancer and amyotrophic lateral sclerosis (ALS), have a prognosis different from that of other disabilities, and in some cases, the condition is terminal. Family members typically need support as they deal with the many different emotions associated with anticipated loss. Counselors also can help families prepare for their loved one's death by making connections with hospice and other community resources. During the terminal phase, the primary caretakers frequently are under a tremendous amount of stress, and family interactions may be strained. Counselors can normalize the tension and encourage family members to find ways to take care of themselves as well as their loved one during this difficult time.

Career issues.   Although two out of three people with disabilities want to work, only 50 percent of those individuals are employed (W. Lee, 1999). Indeed, individuals with disabilities are likely to have the highest rate of unemployment or underemployment in the United States (National Organization on Disability, 2000). Consequently, counselors working with clients with disabilities need to be skilled in career counseling and cognizant of the types of skills that can be acquired through rehabilitation training.

The specific nature of a client's disability affects the type of career counseling that needs to take place. For example, if a person has emotional or communicative disabilities, he or she may not interview well. In such cases, nontraditional job-seeking strategies, such as networking, are recommended (cf. W. Lee, 1999). Also, skills training that includes role-play and fantasy enactment may help the client become more adept at interpersonal interactions. In other situations, a client may have a disability that would not keep him or her from performing a particular job if adaptations are provided. Then the counselor's role may include increasing client awareness of vocational options, particularly as they relate to the Americans With Disabilities Act.

Approximately 4 to 5 million adults in the United States have severe psychiatric disabilities (Garske, 1999). These individuals may experience deficits in social skills, personal management, symptom and medication management, cognition, and coping with stress. Many of them have not been successful in seeking employment; in fact, around 85 percent of the working-age people with severe psychiatric disabilities are unemployed (McReynolds & Garske, 1999). The demands of working with this population are complex and can present a strong challenge to mental health workers. To help people with severe mental illness become and remain contributing members of society, rehabilitation, vocational training, and assistance in work settings are essential. Counselors who work in community settings for psychiatric rehabilitation need additional training to meet the myriad needs of people with severe psychiatric disabilities.

Abuse.   Unfortunately, individuals with disabilities are victimized at a higher rate than that of the general population. Women with disabilities, regardless of age, race, or class, are assaulted, raped, and abused at a rate 2 times greater than women without a disability, and the risk of being physically or sexually assaulted for adults with developmental disabilities is 4 to 10 times higher than it is for other adults (NVAA, 1999). Also, children with disabilities, regardless of the specific type, are approximately twice as likely to be physically or sexually abused as children without disabilities (National Clearinghouse on Child Abuse and Neglect Information, 2002). Counselors working with people with disabilities need to be alert to any signs indicating abuse and advocate for the rights of their clients.

Other issues.   Cultural values and expectations influence beliefs about disabilities. In some cultures, mistaken beliefs about causal factors can lead to greater stigmatization of people with disabilities. For example, many Latino/a families have a fatalistic view about their lives, which may make rehabilitation more difficult (W. Lee, 1999). Also, some Asian cultures attribute disability to the behavior of one's ancestors, making the disability a source of shame. Within certain Native American tribes (e.g., the Dine'h), attributional beliefs may be attached to specific disabilities, such as the belief that seizures are caused by incest between siblings (W. Lee, 1999). Culturally based beliefs and attitudes like these can complicate the counseling process and need to be addressed sensitively.

Although people with disabilities share some common concerns, specific needs and counseling goals relate directly to the nature, duration, and severity of the disability (Livneh & Wosley-George, 2001). Although it is beyond the scope of this chapter to describe specific disabling conditions and recommended interventions, readers are encouraged to consult additional sources to gain more in-depth knowledge about counseling people with particular disabilities.

SUMMARY AND CONCLUSION

In this chapter, we have examined counseling issues related to three areas of diversity: culture and ethnicity, sexual orientation, and disability. There is a wealth of material in the professional literature portraying the general concerns of each group and describing the counseling theories and techniques most appropriate for working with these populations and topics. Indeed, specialty courses and counseling concentrations that focus on one or more of these groups are offered in many graduate counselor education programs.

Although information about a special population may appear unrelated to other populations, it is not. A common theme is that counselors who work with a variety of clients must be knowledgeable about them collectively and individually in order to deal effectively with their common and unique concerns. All too often, stereotypes and prescribed roles are assigned to members of distinct ethnic and racial groups, sexual minorities, and people with disabilities. Cultural limitations restrict not only the growth of the people involved in them but also the larger society. Overcoming prejudices, fears, and anxieties and learning new skills based on accurate information and sensitivity are major challenges of counseling in a multicultural and pluralistic society.

When working with specific groups, counselors need to be aware of uniqueness and common concerns. They must also realize the limitations and appropriateness of counseling interventions they employ. Counselors must constantly ask themselves how each of their clients is similar to and different from others. What are within- and between-group universals and uniquenesses? They must concentrate on increasing their sensitivity to global issues as well as to individual concerns. When clients differ significantly from counselors, extra attention and skill must be devoted to establishing and cultivating the counseling relationship and to selecting and implementing appropriate interventions.

REFERENCES

American Counseling Association (ACA). (1995). Ethical standards of the American Counseling Association. Alexandria, VA: Author.

American Psychiatric Association. (1968). *Diagnostic and statistical manual of mental disorders* (2nd ed.). Washington, DC: Author.

American Rehabilitation Counseling Association. (2002). *Mission* and *Scope of Practice*. Retrieved December 2, 2002, from http://www.nchrtm. okstate.edu/ARCA/index.html

Arredondo, P., Toporek, R., Brown, S., Jones, J., Locke, D. C., Sanchez, J., & Stadler, H. (1996). *Operationalization of the multicultural counseling competencies.* Alexandria, VA: Association for Multicultural Counseling and Development.

Attneave, C. (1982). American Indian and Alaskan native families: Emigrants in their own homeland. In M. McGoldrick, J. Pearce, & J. Giordano (Eds.), *Ethnicity and family therapy* (pp. 55–83). New York: Guilford Press.

Axelson, J. A. (1993). *Counseling and development in a multicultural society* (2nd ed.). Pacific Grove, CA: Brooks/Cole.

Black, J., & Underwood, J. (1998). Young, female, and gay: Lesbian students and the school environment. *Professional School Counseling, 1,* 15–21.

Bringaze, T. B., & White, L. J. (2001). Living out proud: Factors contributing to healthy identity development in lesbian leaders. *Journal of Mental Health Counseling, 23,* 162–173.

Brinson, J. A. (1996). Cultural sensitivity for counselors: Our challenge for the twenty-first century. *Journal of Humanistic Education and Development, 34,* 195–206.

Carroll, L., Gilroy, P. J., & Ryan, J. (2002). Counseling transgendered, transexual, and gender-variant clients. *Journal of Counseling and Development, 80,* 131–139.

Cass, V. C. (1979). Homosexual identity formation: A theoretical model. *Journal of Homosexuality, 4,* 219–235.

Cass, V. C. (1984). Homosexual identity formation: A concept in need of definition. *Journal of Homosexuality, 10,* 105–126.

Chen-Hayes, S. F. (2000). Social justice advocacy with lesbian, bisexual, gay and transgendered persons. In J. Lewis & L. Bradley (Eds.), *Advocacy in counseling: Counselors, clients, and community* (pp. 89–98). Greensboro, NC: ERIC/CASS.

Cheung, F. K. (1991). The use of mental health services by ethnic minorities. In H. F. Myers, P. Wholford, L. P. Guzman, & R. J. Echemendia (Eds.), *Ethnic minority perspectives on clinical training and services in psychology* (pp. 23–31). Washington, DC: American Psychological Association.

Chung, R. C., & Bemak, F. (2002). The relationship of culture and empathy in cross-cultural counseling. *Journal of Counseling and Development, 80,* 154–159.

Cohen, M. N. (1998, April 17). Culture, not race, explains human diversity. *Chronicle of Higher Education,* B4–B5.

Coleman, H. L. K. (1998). General and multicultural counseling competency: Apples and oranges? *Journal of Multicultural Counseling and Development, 26,* 147–156.

Corsini, R. J., & Wedding, D. (Eds.). (2000). *Current psychotherapies* (6th ed.). Itasca, IL: F. E. Peacock.

D'Andrea, M., & Daniels, J. (2001). Facing the changing demographic structure of our society. In D. C. Locke, J. E. Myers, & E. L. Herr (Eds.), *The handbook of counseling* (pp. 529–540). Thousand Oaks, CA: Sage.

Degges-White, S., Rice, B., & Myers, J. E. (2000). Revisiting Cass's theory of sexual identity formation: A study of lesbian development. *Journal of Mental Health Counseling, 22,* 318–333.

Epp, L. R. (1998). The courage to be an existential counselor: An interview with Clemmont E. Vontress. *Journal of Mental Health Counseling, 20,* 1–12.

Foster, S. (1996). October is National Disability Employment Awareness Month. *Counseling Today, 39*(4), 18.

Fujiura, G. T. (2001). Emerging trends in disability. *Population Today, 29,* 9–10.

Garske, G. G. (1999). The challenge of rehab counselors: Working with people with psychiatric disabilities. *Journal of Rehabilitation, 65,* 21–25.

Geertz, C. (1973). *The interpretation of cultures.* New York: Basic Books.

Hayes, P. A. (1996). Addressing the complexities of culture and gender in counseling. *Journal of Counseling and Development, 74,* 332–338.

Hershenson, D. B. (1998). Systemic, ecological model for rehabilitation counseling. *Rehabilitation Counseling Bulletin, 42,* 40–50.

Ho, D. Y. F. (1995). Internalized culture, culturocentrism, and transcendence. *The Counseling Psychologist, 23,* 4–24.

Holiday, M., Leach, M. M., & Davidson, M. (1994). Multicultural counseling and intrapersonal value conflict: A case study. *Counseling and Values, 38,* 136–142.

Holmes, J. F. (1999). U.S. population, a profile of America's diversity: The view from the Census Bureau, 1998. In *The world almanac and book of facts.* Mahwah, NJ: Primedia Reference.

Horowitz, J. L., & Newcomb, M. D. (1999). Bisexuality, not homosexuality: Counseling issues and treatment approaches. *Journal of College Counseling, 2,* 148–164.

Lee, C. C. (Ed.). (1997). *Multicultural issues in counseling* (2nd ed.). Alexandria, VA: American Counseling Association.

Lee, C. C. (2001). Defining and responding to racial and ethnic diversity. In D. C. Locke, J. E. Myers, & E. L. Herr (Eds.), *The handbook of counseling* (pp. 581–588). Thousand Oaks, CA: Sage.

Lee, W. M. L. (1999). *An introduction to multicultural counseling.* Ann Arbor, MI: Taylor & Francis.

Lidderdale, M., & Whitman, J. S. (March 2000). *Counselor education on gay, lesbian, and bisexual issues.* Paper presented at the American Counseling Association Annual Conference, Washington, DC.

Livneh, H., & Evans, J. (1984). Adjusting to disability: Behavioral correlates and intervention strategies. *Personnel and Guidance Journal, 62,* 363–368.

Livneh, H., & Wosley-George, E. T. (2001). Counseling clients with disabilities. In D. Capuzzi & D. R. Gross (Eds.), *Introduction to the counseling profession* (3rd ed., pp. 435–462). Needham Heights, MA: Allyn & Bacon.

Locke, D. C. (1990). A not so provincial view of multicultural counseling. *Counselor Education and Supervision, 30,* 18–25.

Locke, D. C. (2001). ACES at its best: Celebrating the human spirit. *Counselor Education and Supervision, 40,* 242–251.

Lustig, D. C., Rosenthal, D. A., Strauser, D. R., & Haynes, K. (2000, Spring). The relationship between sense of coherence and adjustment in persons with disabilities. *Rehabilitation Counseling Bulletin, 43,* 134–141.

Martin, E. D., Jr. (1999). Foundations of rehabilitation. In G. L. Gandy, E. D. Martin, Jr., & R. E. Hardy (Eds.), *Counseling in the rehabilitation process: Community services for mental and physical disabilities* (2nd ed., pp. 5–31). Springfield, IL: Thomas.

McReynolds, C. J., & Garske, G. G. (Oct.–Dec. 1999). Psychiatric rehabilitation: A survey of rehabilitation counseling education programs. *Journal of Rehabilitation, 65,* 45–49.

Middleton, R. A., Rollins, C. W., & Harley, D. A. (1999). The historical and political context of the civil rights of persons with disabilities: A multicultural perspective for counselors. *Journal of Multicultural Counseling and Development, 27,* 105–120.

Miller, J. L., & House, R. M. (2001). Counseling gay, lesbian, and bisexual clients. In D. Capuzzi & D. R. Gross (Ed.), *Introduction to the counseling profession* (3rd ed., pp. 386–414). Needham Heights, MA: Allyn & Bacon.

Moursund, J., & Kenny, M. C. (2002). *The process of counseling and therapy* (4th ed.). Upper Saddle River, NJ: Prentice Hall.

National Clearinghouse on Child Abuse and Neglect Information (2002). In focus: The risk and prevention of maltreatment of children with disabilities. Retrieved November 26, 2002, from http://www.calib.com/nccanch/pubs/prevenres/focus.cfm

National Institute of Mental Health. (1999). Sociocultural and environmental processes. Retrieved July 1, 2002, from http://www.nimh.nih.gov/publicat/baschap7.cfm

National Organization on Disability. (2000). *Survey of the status of people with disabilities in the United States: Employment.* Washington, DC: Author.

National Victim Assistance Academy (NVAA). (1999). Victimization of individuals with disabilities. Retrieved November 11, 2002, from http://www.ojp.gov:80/ovc/assist/nvaa99/chap14.htm

Nwachuka, U., & Ivey, A. (1991). Culture-specific counseling: An alternative model. *Journal of Counseling and Development, 70,* 106–111.

Okun, B. F., Fried, J., & Okun, M. L. (1999). *Understanding diversity: A learning-as-practice primer.* Pacific Grove, CA: Brooks/Cole.

Palma, T. V., & Stanley, J. L. (2002). Effective counseling with lesbian, gay, and bisexual clients. *Journal of College Counseling, 5,* 74–89.

Parker, W. M., Archer, J., & Scott, J. (1992). *Multicultural relations on campus.* Muncie, IN: Accelerated Development.

Pedersen, P. B. (1977). The triad model of cross-cultural counselor training. *Personnel and Guidance Journal, 56,* 94–100.

Pedersen, P. B. (1978). Four dimensions of cross-cultural skill in counselor training, *56,* 480–484.

Pedersen, P. B. (1990). The constructs of complexity and balance in multicultural counseling theory and practice. *Journal of Counseling and Development, 68,* 550–554.

Pedersen, P. B. (2002). Ethics, competence, and other professional issues in culture-centered counseling. In P. B. Pedersen, J. G. Draguns, W. J. Lonner, & J. E. Trimble (Eds.), *Counseling across cultures* (5th ed., pp. 3–27). Thousand Oaks, CA: Sage.

Pinterits, E. J., & Atkinson, D. R. (1998). The diversity video forum: An adjunct to diversity sensitive training in the classroom. *Counselor Education and Supervision, 37,* 203–216.

Robinson, T. L., & Howard-Hamilton, M. (2000). *The convergence of race, ethnicity, and gender: Multiple identities in counseling.* Upper Saddle River, NJ: Merrill/Prentice Hall.

Roland, J. (1994). *Families, illness and disability.* New York: Basic Books.

Rothrock, J. A. (1999). A personal experience of acceptance and adjustment to disability. In G. L. Gandy, E. D. Martin, Jr., & R. E. Hardy (Eds.), *Counseling in the rehabilitation process: Community services for mental and physical disabilities* (2nd ed., pp. 204–217). Springfield, IL: Thomas.

Sager, J. B. (2001). Latin American lesbian, gay, and bisexual clients: Implications for counseling. *Journal of Humanistic Counseling, Education, and Development, 40,* 13–33.

Smith, E. M. J., & Vasquez, M. J. T. (1985). Introduction. *Counseling Psychologist, 13,* 531–536.

Sophie, J. (1987). Internalized homophobia and lesbian identity. *Journal of Homosexuality, 14,* 53–65.

Sue, D. W. (1981). *Counseling and the culturally different: Theory and practice.* New York: Wiley.

Sue, D. W. (1992, Winter). The challenge of multiculturalism. *American Counselor, 1,* 6–14.

Sue, D. W., Arredondo, P., & McDavis, R. J. (1992). Multicultural counseling competencies and standards: A call to the profession. *Journal of Counseling and Development, 70,* 477–486.

Sue, D. W., Ivey, A. E., & Pedersen, P. (1996). *A theory of multicultural counseling and therapy.* Pacific Grove, CA: Brooks/Cole.

Sue, D. W., & Sue, D. (1999). *Counseling the culturally different: Theory and practice* (3rd ed.). New York: Wiley.

Surgeon General. (2002). Overview of cultural diversity and mental health services. Retrieved May 30, 2002, from http://www.surgeongeneral.gov/library/mentalhealth/chapter3/sec5.html

Swartz-Kulstad, J. L., & Martin, W. E., Jr. (1999). Impact on culture and context on psychosocial adaptation: The cultural and contextual guide process. *Journal of Counseling and Development, 77,* 281–293.

Thomas, R. (2002). Supreme Court limits ADA disability definition. Retrieved November 15, 2002, from http://www.ppspublishers.com/biz/ada.htm

Tyiska, C. (1998). Working with victims with disabilities. *Office for Victims of Crime Bulletin,* Washington, DC: U.S. Department of Justice, Office for Victims of Crimes.

Turner, J., & Helms, D. (1994). *Lifespan development* (5th ed.). Chicago: Holt, Rinehart & Winston.

U.S. Census Bureau. (2000). Retrieved December 8, 2002, from http://landview.census.gov/population/www.cen2000/phc-t1.html

Vontress, C. E. (1996). A personal retrospective on cross-cultural counseling. *Journal of Multicultural Counseling and Development, 16,* 73–83.

Walsh, R. (2000). Asian psychotherapies. In R. J. Corsini & D. Wedding (Eds.), *Current psychotherapies* (6th ed., pp. 407–444). Itasca, IL: F. E. Peacock.

Weinrach, S. G., & Thomas, K. R. (1996). The counseling profession's commitment to diversity-sensitive counseling: A critical reassessment. *Journal of Counseling and Development, 73,* 472–477.

Weinrach, S. G., & Thomas, K. R. (1998). Diversity-sensitive counseling today: A postmodern clash of values. *Journal of Counseling and Development, 76,* 115–122.

Weinrach, S. G., & Thomas, K. R. (2002). A critical analysis of the Multicultural Counseling Competencies: Implications for the practice of mental health counseling. *Journal of Mental Health Counseling, 24,* 20–35.

West-Olatunji, C. A. (2001). Counseling ethnic minority clients. In D. Capuzzi & D. R. Gross (Eds.), *Introduction to the counseling profession* (3rd ed., pp. 415–434). Needham Heights, MA: Allyn & Bacon.

Winter, J. M. (February 2002). *Counseling lesbian, gay, and bisexual clients.* Paper presented at the North Carolina Counseling Association Annual Conference, Greensboro, NC.

Wrenn, C. G. (1962). The culturally encapsulated counselor. *Harvard Educational Review, 32,* 444–449.

Wright, K. C., & Martin, E. D., Jr. (1999). The rehabilitation process: A perspective for the rehabilitation counselor. In G. L. Gandy, E. D. Martin, Jr., & R. E. Hardy (Eds.), *Counseling in the rehabilitation process: Community services for mental and physical disabilities* (2nd ed., pp. 117–129). Springfield, IL: Thomas.

Yeh, C. J., & Hwang, M. Y. (2000). Interdependence in ethnic identity and self: Implications for theory and practice. *Journal of Counseling and Development, 78,* 420–429.

CHAPTER 11

Counseling Adults

My father tells me
   my mother is slowing down.
He talks deliberately and with deep feelings
   as stooped shouldered he walks to his garden
    behind the garage.
My mother informs me
   about my father's failing health.
"Not as robust as before," she explains,
   "Lower energy than in his 50s."
Her concerns arise as she kneads dough for biscuits.
Both express their fears to me
   as we view the present from the past.
In love, and with measured anxiety,
   I move with them into new patterns.

Gladding, S. T. (2003). *Family Therapy: History, Theory and Practice* (3rd ed., p. 145). Upper Saddle River, NJ: Prentice Hall.

People are defined both by their age and by the age in which they grew up. Thus, emphases and adjectives get attached to individuals and generations that may only partly be descriptive of them and may even discriminate against them. For example, Americans born between 1946 and 1964 ($n = 78$ million) are collectively known as "baby boomers," and those born between 1965 and 1976 ($n = 44$ million) are known as "baby busters," "Generation X," or "Thirteenth" generation (Dunn, 1993).

In working with adults of all ages, it is crucial that counselors keep in mind that individuals, as well as groups, change over time. What once may have been accurate in assessing a person or persons in a particular decade may lose validity over the years. Table 11–1 shows how generations in the 20th century have been characterized. It is useful in becoming more aware of people and the mindsets that have accompanied the times in which they lived. By being sensitive to both descriptors and changes, counselors can remind themselves that collectively and individually people continue to grow throughout their lives—not just in childhood and adolescence.

To examine the development of adults and their needs in a community context, a counselor should begin by conceptually examining the word *development*. *Development* is traditionally defined as any kind of systematic change that is lifelong and cumulative (Papalia, Olds, & Feldman, 2001). Individuals develop throughout their lives on a number of levels: cognitively, emotionally, and physically. When events occur and develop within an expected time dimension, such as getting a first

Table 11–1
The generational diagonal in twentieth-century America

	Inner-Driven Era 1901–24	Crisis Era 1925–42	Outer-Driven Era 1943–60	Awakening Era 1961–81	Inner-Driven Era 1982–2003
AGE 66+	PROGRESSIVE (Adaptive) sensitive	MISSIONARY (Idealist) visionary	LOST (Reactive) reclusive	G.I. (Civic) busy	SILENT (Adaptive) sensitive
AGE 44–65	MISSIONARY (Idealistic) moralistic	LOST (Reactive) pragmatic	G.I. (Civic) powerful	SILENT (Adaptive) indecisive	BOOM (Idealist) moralistic
AGE 22–43	LOST (Reactive) alienated	G.I. (Civic) heroic	SILENT (Adaptive) conformist	BOOM (Idealist) narcissistic	THIRTEENTH (Reactive) alienated
AGE 0–21	G.I. (Civic) protected	SILENT (Adaptive) suffocated	BOOM (Idealist) indulged	THIRTEENTH (Reactive) criticized	MILLENIAL (Civic) protected

Note. From William Strauss & Neil Howe. The cycle of generations. *American Demographics,* April 1991, p. 27. © American Demographics, Inc. Reprinted with permission.

job somewhere in their 20s, individuals generally have only minor transitional or adjustment problems, if at all. However, if life events are accelerated, delayed, or fail to materialize (i.e., become nonevents) the well-being of persons and those associated with them may be negatively affected (Schlossberg, Waters, & Goodman, 1996). For example, if individuals do not develop a positive self-esteem by young adulthood, they may act out in delinquent, defiant, and inappropriate ways.

Theorists and researchers such as Jean Piaget, Lawrence Kohlberg, Erik Erikson, Carole Gilligan, Nancy Schlossberg, Elinor Waters, Jane Goodman, and Jane Myers have addressed issues associated with developmental stages of life. The Association for Adult Development and Aging (AADA), a division of the American Counseling Association, particularly focuses on chronological life-span growth after adolescence. In this chapter, developmental issues surrounding adults at different ages and stages are addressed. At times, developmental issues related to adults are overlooked because it is sometimes assumed that development prior to reaching adulthood is more important. However, life is a continuously evolving experience, and it is important that the developmental needs of adults are addressed by counselors.

YOUNG AND MIDDLE ADULTHOOD

Adulthood is a somewhat nebulous term (Broderick & Blewitt, 2003). It implies that a person has reached physical, mental, social, and emotional maturity. Yet, researchers, such as Levinson, Darrow, Klein, Levinson, and McKee (1978), note that adulthood is a multidimensional stage of growth characterized by a certain unevenness and unpredictability (Neugarten, 1979). There is little uniformity to it (Hudson, 2000). Indeed, as Allport (1955) stated, human beings are "always becoming," and what may be appropriate behavior in one period of adulthood may be considered inappropriate at a later time.

In this section, two periods of adulthood are considered: *young adulthood* and *middle adulthood*. During *young adulthood* (20 to 40 years), identity and intimacy are two primary developmental issues, whereas in *midlife* (40 to 65 years), needs related to generativity become the main focus (Erikson, 1963). Although it is somewhat artificial to divide adulthood into age categories, many counseling services for adults are conducted around themes that center on issues related to particular ages and issues in life. Therefore, in this section, these two divisions of adulthood are treated separately. Wrenn (1979) advises counselors to "learn to work more effectively with adults" (p. 88). This means understanding universal life stages as well as novel transitional experiences. Overall, aging is as much a mental process of considering one's self older, as it is a biological phenomenon composed of physiological changes.

Young Adulthood

Young adults (those in their 20s and 30s) struggle with many issues. One of the most important according to Erikson (1963) is establishing intimacy with the emphasis on achieving close interpersonal relationships. Other major concerns of young adults involve independence/dependence, choosing a career, deciding about marriage or partnership, developing a healthy lifestyle, finding meaning in life, and dealing with loneliness, disappointment, and potential (Corey & Corey, 2001; Robbins & Wilner, 2001).

Early in adult life, at least in the United States, the focus is on personal promise. Young adults are expected to live up to their potential by making good decisions, working hard, adjusting, and achieving proper roles and status. It is a time of maturation and transition. If all goes well, young adults usually make a smooth transition into gainful employment and into either single or couples life. Career development (which will be dealt with in a later chapter) is also important.

The three most prevalent lifestyles of young adults are singlehood, newly married, and parents of preschool children. Most young adults enter these lifestyles sequentially; however, circumstances such as separation and divorce may modify the order.

Singlehood.   The first stage in the lives of most young adults is singlehood. It involves leaving home and initiating processes whereby one becomes independent. A major task of this period is to disconnect and reconnect with one's family on a different level while simultaneously establishing one's self as a person (Haley, 1980). This double focus is often difficult to achieve. Some young adults start the process by continuing their education, joining the armed forces, or getting their first job and moving in with other young people.

Being single requires a person to strike a balance between a number of choices, such as education, career, and/or marriage. Ambitions are continuously influenced by a desire for personal autonomy. In the past, singlehood was considered a transitional stage in life. However, "being single is now a more accepted status than it was in the past," and its popularity as a lifestyle appears to be growing (Corey & Corey, 1990, pp. 303–304). For example, in 2000 the number of single adults over the age of 18 in the United States population living alone was approximately 25 percent of the population. At the same time only 52 percent of adult Americans were married (U.S. Department of Commerce, 2001).

Therefore, singlehood is a viable alternative to marriage. Indeed, singles are usually the second happiest group (married couples being the happiest), ranking above gay/lesbian couples, unmarried couples, and others. Singlehood can be as fulfilling as marriage, depending on the needs and interests of the individual (Gullotta, Adams, & Alexander, 1998). Being single and mentally healthy requires that individuals establish social networks, find meaning in their work or avocations, and live a balanced life physically and psychologically. Singles must also develop coping strategies to avoid becoming overwhelmed by stress, loneliness, or isolation (Kleinke, 2002). Living a healthy single life requires making adjustments to cultural demands and realizing that culture is a phenomenon to which one must accommodate. A major challenge for singles is overcoming internal and external pressures to marry or form partnerships, especially if they do not wish to or are not developmentally ready.

Because of the demands and pressures of singlehood, it is a challenge for community counselors to deal with this population. Mental health services to singles must be well thought out. The freedom to choose one's actions is a major attraction and benefit to this lifestyle and one that counselors, especially those from an existential background, can utilize in working with singles.

Newly married.   The newly married lifestyle—less than 2 years of marriage—begins with courtship, where couples test their compatibility through dating. The process of dating and coupling may involve a number of partners before one becomes committed to marriage. Generally, individuals tend to be most comfortable with those at the same or similar developmental level (Gladding, 2002; Rice, 2001). That is why relationships between dissimilar people rarely last.

As a group, single women usually have better mental and physical health than their counterparts (Apter, 1985). (The reason is related to a number of variables, including that some emotionally unstable women marry, whereas emotionally unstable men most likely do not because of the rejection power of women.) However, in new marriages, the mental health of men usually improves, and for women the reverse may occur. A factor influencing the mental health of newly married women and men is whether women cater to the wishes of their husbands at the expense of meeting their own needs or whether household duties are shared.

In general, the early stages of a couple's relationship are characterized by idealization and adjustment. Both men and women initially idealize each other and relate accordingly. This idealization is likely to dissipate naturally because of adjustments that must be made. If it does not, marital dissatisfaction and discord may occur. Overall, the new couple stage of the family life cycle in young adulthood is one filled with challenge and compromise. For example, new couples must learn how to share space, meals, work, leisure, and sleep activities. They must accommodate to each other's wishes, requests, and fantasies. The process takes time, energy, and good will. Couples that are most satisfied are those whose partners believe they are receiving as much as they are giving.

It is not surprising that the new couple stage of marriage is one of the most likely times for couples to divorce, due to an inability of individuals to resolve differences or make adaptations (Quinn & Odell, 1998). On the other hand, it is a time of life when couples may experience the greatest amount of satisfaction in their marriage, especially if they negotiate satisfactory arrangements early and have children later (Glenn & McLanahan, 1982). The new couple is free to experiment with life and to engage freely in a wide variety of activities. Financial and time constraints are the two main limitations for couples during this period. Adjustment difficulties from the past or present circumstances, which are most often interpersonal, are the two primary reasons new couples seek counseling.

Parenthood with young children.   Becoming a parent marks the beginning of a third phase of young adulthood. Parenting, especially when children are under 3 years old, is a physical, psychological, and social event that alters a couple's lifestyle dramatically (Bauman, 2002). The arrival of a child can have an impact on a couple's lifestyle (e.g., place of residence), marital relationship (e.g., sexual contact), and paternal/maternal stress (e.g., new demands) (Hughes, 1999). When a newborn enters a family, the family becomes unbalanced, at least temporarily. Couples have to readjust the time they spend working outside the house, socializing with friends, and engaging in recreational activities. They also have to decide who will take responsibility for the child, when, where, and how. A rebalancing occurs in a couples' investment of time, energy, and focus (Bradt, 1988).

One of the most important tasks for young adult families is meeting the physical demands involved in having preschool children. This challenge becomes especially great when both partners are working outside the home, which is the case with a large percentage of the couples in the United States with children under the age of 6 (Bauman, 2002). In such arrangements, childcare responsibilities are more likely to be shared to some extent, but women frequently are the primary caregivers (Darling-Fisher & Tiedje, 1990). Juggling multiple roles can lead to frustration and dissatisfaction, unless necessary adjustments are made. To increase marital and family satisfaction and fulfillment, it is important for partners to develop egalitarian gender-role expectations and negotiate effective methods of role sharing (Rosenbaum & Cohen, 1999).

Strategies for Dealing With Young Adulthood

Regardless of the lifestyle chosen, many of the tasks engaged in during young adulthood, such as developing an identity and establishing intimacy, continue over the life span and influence future life outcomes. Therefore, young adults are under considerable pressure to do well. Although society will tolerate some delays in making adult commitments, young adults who do not respond appropriately in meeting the challenges of this time are discounted, disregarded, severely criticized and/or ostracized (Worth, 1983).

It is little wonder then that many young adults attempt to avoid entering this life stage by staying at home in a delayed adolescence. Others fail to take calculated or needed risks and do not progress in forming a new or expanded identity. Yet, a third group physically separates from their families of origin but simply flounders vocationally and interpersonally. A final unproductive strategy at this life stage is to short-circuit the developmental process of independence by marrying prematurely and assuming new and often overwhelming family responsibilities (Aylmer, 1988).

Prevention.   Prevention is one of the best ways to help young adults in any lifestyle. One way prevention can be implemented is through psychoeducation, where young adults are made aware of some of the normal and expected changes that may occur in their lives. For example, if young couples with preschool children expect their lives to be more hectic and less intimate, they may be prepared to deal with their circumstances and not get discouraged with or withdraw from their relationship. Forewarning young adults of the consequences of too much change can also be helpful. Consequently, young adults may realize that they cannot do everything at once and thus learn to decline as well as accept opportunities.

Another preventive strategy in working with young adults is to explore their personal, marital, and career ambitions and the changes that will have to occur in their lives to meet these goals, with a focus on growth and development. In most types of growth there is "change in the direction of greater awareness, competence, and authenticity" (Jourard & Landsman, 1980, p. 238). Within individuals, regardless of their marital status, growth can be a conscious process that involves courage, that is, the ability to take calculated risks without knowing the exact consequences (Sweeney, 1999). When planned strategies and activities are outlined and accomplished as a part of growth, young persons understand the past more thoroughly, live actively and fully in the present, and envision possibilities of the future more clearly.

A third preventive strategy is to help young adults explore patterns within their families of origins, so they can understand and avoid making past mistakes as they develop their own lifestyles. One way to do this is to draw a genogram, such as the one shown in Figure 11–1.

A genogram is a visual representation of a person's family tree depicted in geometric figures, lines, and words (Gladding, 2002; Sherman, 1993). Genograms include information about items such as a family's employment, health, and marriage, as well as about family relationships over at least three generations. Genograms help people see and understand patterns in the context of historic and contemporary events (McGoldrick, Gerson, & Shellenberger, 1999). The tangibility and nonthreatening nature of this process helps counselors and clients gather a large amount of information in a relatively brief period of time. Furthermore, genograms can increase "mutual trust and tolerance" among all involved in their construction (Sherman, 1993, p. 91).

Basically genograms allow young adults "to go 'back, back, back; and up, up, up' their family tree to look for patterns ... getting not just information but a feel for the context and milieu that existed during each person's formative years" (White, 1978, pp. 25–26). This process promotes the shift from emotional reactivity to clear cognition. Data in a genogram are scanned for (a) "repetitive patterns," such as triangles, cut-offs, and coalitions; (b) "coincidences of dates," such as the death of members or the age of symptom onset; and (c) "the impact of change and untimely life cycle transitions," such as "off-schedule" events like marriage, deaths, and the birth of children (McGoldrick et al., 1999, p. 60).

A fourth preventive strategy helpful for young adults (and older adults) is group work. Within growth and support groups, young adults can gauge their own and other's reactions to issues related to the total process of being an adult. A group setting where people talk about and identify with others in similar situations usually helps young adults connect with peers. Psychoeducational and counseling groups are primarily used in exploring issues of young adulthood and the transitions that go with them. Group counseling with adults is essentially a process of using group facilitation to help adult group members deal with transitions relevant to their life-cycle changes (Gladding, 2003).

Young adults experiencing life problems are also helped if they can be persuaded by counselors to make "a game" of them. Language games appear to be especially beneficial. Metaphorical language or concrete symbols are used in such games to enable the release of pent-up emotions; take more control of life; plan appropriate

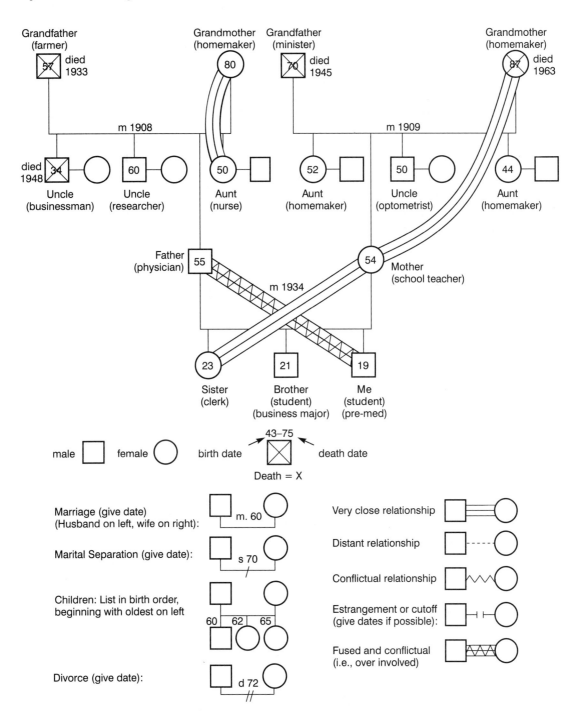

Figure 11–1
Genogram: Three generations of the Smith family (as of 1965)

strategies for addressing predictable situations; and, equally important, have fun and laugh at some less serious follies. Structured appropriately, games can help bring out the best in young adults and keep them from ruminating over situations they cannot control. Further, many games empower adults to take charge of the parts of their lives that parallel the games they have played and where they feel they can make positive contributions (Duhl, 1983).

Treatment.   As with other stages of life, young adults respond to a number of treatment modalities. Among the most prevalent are individual, group, or marriage/family counseling. Each has its place, depending on the problem or predicament. For instance, infidelity within a couple relationship might best be addressed with individual and marriage counseling, and career indecisiveness might be best addressed through an individual and a group approach.

A frequently used type of treatment for young adults is individual counseling. In one-on-one situations, young adults may evaluate their situations, put them in perspective, and also learn new skills either directly or indirectly. Sometimes individual counseling of this kind involves homework. One of the best examples of a playful counseling homework technique for young adults is a "shame attack" (Ellis & MacLaren, 1999). In shame attacks people display behaviors of which they have been fearful. Clients frequently see that the world does not collapse or fall apart if they make a mistake or do not get what they want. For example, a young adult might ask for a glass of water in a restaurant without ordering food or might intentionally fall down at a shopping mall and see what happens.

In prison populations that contain a high percentage of young adults, one successful treatment modality that is similar to but more structured than a shame attack is drama therapy (Bergman, 2000). It can be conducted on either an individual or a group level. This type of counseling has been shown to be quite effective in reducing rates of recidivism. In it, inmates play out scenes they are likely to encounter and ways they may positively react to certain situations. Although the use of drama is not effective for all young adults who are incarcerated, Ryder (1976) reported a recidivism rate of about 15 percent for inmates who participated in a drama project he conducted. Such a rate is far below the national level.

Counselors in other agencies have also found drama techniques to be quite effective. Enactment is a major dramatic tool of most marriage and family counselors. In this process, a counselor "constructs an interpersonal scenario in the session in which dysfunctional transactions among family members are played out." Within this scenario the counselor can observe "the family members' verbal and nonverbal ways of signaling to each other and monitoring the range of tolerable transactions. The therapist can then intervene in the process by increasing its intensity, prolonging the time of transaction, involving other family members, indicating alternative transactions, and introducing experimental probes. . . ." (Minuchin & Fishman, 1981, p. 79). The drama that occurs in presenting the problem and in finding successful resolutions decreases the power of symptoms and empowers the family of the young adult to be innovative and to change.

An interesting, interdisciplinary, positive-wellness model for self-selected young adults is the jogging group (Childers & Burcky, 1984). This approach is built on the premise that physical exercise is an important element that contributes to people's abilities to perform better in all areas of life (Freund & Seligman, 1982; Gerler, 1980). The jogging group combines an hour of exercise, in the form of walking, jogging, or running, with another hour of group process. The group is co-led by a counselor and a health facilitator (e.g., a physician or an exercise physiologist) and follows Lazarus's (1976, 1981) multimodal BASIC ID concept, which focuses on behavior, affect, sensation, imagery, cognition, interpersonal relationships, and drugs/biological factors. Jogging seems to hasten the group's developmental growth, and although research is lacking, the authors report that jogging groups function more like marathon groups than extended groups, because of the high energy invested in the physical exercises before the group experience.

Middle Adulthood

Middle adulthood begins somewhere between the late 30s and the early 40s and ends in the early to mid-60s (Willis & Reid, 1999). Individuals at this time realize that "life is half over and death is a reality" (Worth, 1983, p. 240). It is a time for evaluating, deciding, and making adjustments. This process is known as the *midlife transition.* It is a difficult time for many individuals as they give up the dreams of adolescence and come to terms with their own mortality (Marmor, 1982). Once they get through the thought process of having reached midlife, they typically settle down and enjoy themselves (Sheehy, 1976). However, those who do not successfully integrate the reality of this period into their lives will often try three other ways of coping:

1. Denial by escape (frantically engaging in activities)
2. Denial by overcompensation (engaging in sexual adventures)
3. Decompensation (being depressed and angry) (Marmor, 1982)

Overall, there is some physical decline in men and women during middle adulthood, including losses in hearing, sight, hormonal level, height, and attractiveness. Yet, there are some gains, too, including an improvement in crystallized intelligence (the ability to do something as a result of experience and education) and freedom from early childrearing responsibilities and/or novice job demands (Kogan & Vacha-Haase, 2002). Women as a group become more assertive and achievement oriented, and men as a group become more nurturing and emotional (Neugarten, 1968). These behavioral changes support Jung's (1971) belief that men and women achieve a more balanced personality during this time. A prime developmental task for all individuals at this stage is to enhance their expression of generativity (creativity in their lives and work for the benefit of others) and to work toward self-actualization (realistically living up to their potential). A failure to do so results in stagnation and self-absorption (Erikson, 1963; Maslow, 1968).

Predictable crises that occur in midlife include coping with aging parents, the emancipation of children, reestablishing and/or evaluating one's work career, and bereavement (Kimmel, 1976; McCullough & Rutenberg, 1988). Midlifers are often sandwiched between caring for the needs of their children and those of their parents (Chisholm, 1999). They must constantly readjust to losses and gains in a manner secondary only to the rapid changes of adolescence. "For most people the middle years are quite busy, which may explain why some arrive at the end of this period with surprise that the journey is finished so quickly" (Worth, 1983, pp. 242–243).

Prevention.   There are a wide variety of approaches for working with adults in midlife. In the area of psychoeducation, Parker (1975) reports on the use of systematic desensitization within a leadership group for the purpose of helping adult members become less anxious about public speaking. After participating in five sessions, participants noticed a decrease in anxiety about public speaking and a more relaxed attitude in their personal lives in general. Bisio and Crisan (1984) used a 1-day group workshop with adults to focus on nuclear anxiety and hidden stress in life. They emphasized principles of Victor Frankl's (1962) logotherapy and helped participants create a renewed sense of hope and purpose in life. Although members of both of these groups did not express a desire for counseling, the groups were therapeutic in addressing areas of immediate concern. By modifying the group format as needed, counselors can address a range of midlife concerns.

Another way of promoting positive mental health and fostering the prevention of disorders in midlife is through the use of the creative arts, such as music. Besides offering adults sounds to relax by, research suggests that music is an enhancer of physical endurance, especially if "movement is rhythmically coordinated with a musical stimulus" (Thaut, 1988, p. 129). Therefore, adults who are athletes or who regularly exercise can enhance their efforts by coordinating their physical movement with certain sounds. The reason for the positive effect of music is that it either distracts people's perceptions by causing them to selectively focus on pleasant stimuli or it physically inhibits negative feedback transmissions (i.e., fatigue) because of the pleasurable electrosensory reactions it generates. Regardless, music is a prime ingredient in helping midlifers maintain physical and mental health. Music also facilitates the enhancement of experiences. It promotes growth to the fullest (Maslow, 1968). Through music the rhythm of life events, and life itself, is appreciated more.

An interesting adaptation of music is the use of humorous rational songs. By employing these songs, overly serious adults are able to relax more and see their problems as more resolvable (Watzlawick, 1983). Ellis (1980) has written many humorous songs to familiar tunes. However, creative individuals can also write their own words and/or music. For example, to the tune "I've been working on the railroad," an adult once wrote the following:

> I've been working on my problems/All the live long day/I've been working on my problems/Just to pass the time away/Can't you hear the problems growing/Rise up so early in the morn/Can't you hear me as I'm shouting/"This is how I blow my horn."

Regardless of the artistic nature of songs by adults, actions that encourage playfulness can be essential in gaining perspective. Counseling prevention techniques with a playful quality are healthy and helpful for midlife individuals often squeezed between too many demands and not enough time or resources.

Treatment.   A good deal of treatment for midlife adults is conducted in groups, although individual and family work are also a part of such efforts. Groups are used frequently because of the commonality of many problems that arise in midlife and the power of groups to help individuals struggling with these common concerns.

For adults who have grown up in families where at least one parent abused alcohol, heterogeneous groups based on Yalom's (1995) therapeutic factors, especially altruism and imitative behavior, can be empowering (Corazzini, Williams, & Harris, 1987). Such groups allow adults to question and change any of the four common roles (i.e., hero, scapegoat, lost child, and mascot) that adult children of alcoholics (ACoAs) tend to play out in order to survive the instability, confusion, and fear they experienced growing up (Wegscheider, 1981). Groups of this nature also increase the support and reference network these individuals have within their lives.

Because alcoholic families tend to be rather isolated (Steinglass, 1982), this extended system of group support is invaluable for ACOAs who wish to continue their growth toward more functional behavior and to break the three rules Black (1981) identifies as universal for these individuals: (a) don't trust, (b) don't talk, and (c) don't feel. Corazzini et al. (1987) recommend that groups of this nature work best when conducted in an open format. Whitfield (1987) further notes that "many clinicians who work with ACOAs or other troubled or dysfunctional families believe that group therapy is the major choice for recovery work" (p. 142). Such work should be combined with a psychoeducational approach to the dynamics related to addiction, dysfunction, and recovery, as well as with individual and family counseling.

Groups may also be used to help grown-up abused children (Courtois & Leehan, 1982). Victims of abuse (whether physical, psychological, sexual, or neglect) have a number of common characteristics, such as low self-esteem, self-blame, unresolved anger, and an inability to trust. Groups help them share their stories and feel emotional relief. In addition, group members can help each other focus on resolving present, problematic behaviors that would be difficult to resolve individually. "The sharing and empathy derived from common experiences and reactions, as well as the analysis of the interactions between members, are of great therapeutic value" (Courtois, 1996, p. 244).

In short, groups help victims of abuse to break the cycle of isolation so common to this population and to interrelate in a healthy, dynamic way. "Many survivors come to view the group as a new family in which they are reparented as they help to reparent others" (Courtois, 1996, p. 247). Courtois and Leehan (1982) recommend that no more than six members be included in such groups in order to give everyone adequate "air time" (p. 566).

A final type of remedial service for adults in midlife that is both psychoeducational and psychotherapeutic involves career change (Zimpfer & Carr, 1989). Midlifers are pressured both from within and without to advance in their life's work. Some midlife adults, especially those at the middle management level, think the best way to advance is to change careers. Persons who usually consider such a strategy have the following personal characteristics: high achievement motivation, a steady and successful work record, high need for advancement, career challenge and individual satisfaction, a positive self-image, a high energy level, and a sense of limited chances for advancement in their present position (Campbell & Cellini, 1980). They may also face increased pressure for different behavior from their spouses (McCullough & Rutenberg, 1988). Joining a career change group or working on career change individually with a counselor may help midlife participants sort out the reasons for pursuing a new career and evaluating whether some alternative course of action may be more healthy for them. Effective career change treatment is holistic in nature and explores personal and professional aspects of individuals' lives.

LATE ADULTHOOD

Age 65 has traditionally marked the beginning of late adulthood because it is the time when people have, until recently, retired from work and collected social security or pension funds. However, old age is a concept that continues to change. According to some researchers (e.g., Neugarten, 1978), there are two major periods within this category. The first is the young–old: those between ages 55 and 75 who are still active physically, mentally, and socially, whether they are retired or not. The second period is the old–old: those individuals beyond age 75 whose physical activity is far more limited. The effects of decline with age are usually more apparent in the old–old population, though patterns of aging are clearly unique. Other developmental theorists categorize late adulthood according to functional age: the young–old elderly appear physically young for their age, and the old–old elderly appear frail and show signs of decline (Berk, 2001). Regardless of age or categorization, members of senior populations have developmental issues that collectively and individually are complex and in need of attention by community counselors and other mental health workers (Hill, Thorn, & Packard, 2000).

The need for counselors trained to work with older adults can be seen in recent and projected figures of their numbers. In 2002, persons over age 65 constituted approximately 13 percent of the U.S. population. By the year 2030, the number of people aged 65 and older will constitute about 20 percent of the U.S. population (Administration on Aging, 1998; Sandberg, 2002). The growth of older Americans and their percentage of the total population are due primarily to the maturation of the so-called baby boomers of post–World War II and improved health care.

To work with older adults, counselors and other helpers need to know several prominent theories of aging. Birren and Schaie (2002) view aging from a biological, psychological, and social perspective, recognizing that the multidimensional process of this time may be uneven. Both Erikson (1963) and Havighurst (1959) propose that aging is a natural part of development. They believe also that individuals have specific tasks to accomplish as they grow older. For example, Erikson views late adulthood (after age 65) as a time when individuals enter a stage where they either achieve integrity (i.e., an emphasis on integrating life activities and feeling worthwhile) or they become despairing. According to Havighurst (1959), older adults must learn to cope successfully with (a) the death of friends and/or spouses, (b) reduced physical vigor, (c) retirement and the reduction of income, (d) more leisure time and the making of new friends, (e) the development of new social roles, (f) dealing with grown children, and (g) changing living arrangements and/or making satisfactory living arrangements.

In general, older adults in the United States must deal with a broad range of complex issues in their transition from midlife to senior citizen status (Cox, 1985; Tinsley & Bigler, 2002). Some of the required changes associated with aging are gradual, such as the loss of physical strength. Others are abrupt, such as death. Transitions that involve a high level of stress are those connected with major loss, such as the death of a spouse, the loss of a job, or the contraction of a major illness (Sinick, 1979). In handling the death of a spouse, for instance, many older adults struggle due to the lack of a peer support group through which to voice their grief and work through emotions (Morgan, 1994). Not all transitions are traumatic, however, and some may even involve a gain for the individual, such as becoming a grandparent. Regardless, the changes that are a part of aging have the potential to spark an identity crisis within the person for better or worse. In general the developmental demands of older adults are probably second only to those of young children (Pulvino & Colangelo, 1980).

Many older adults do not successfully accomplish the necessary developmental tasks required for a smooth transition into this later stage of life. They fail to develop and maintain a stabilizing functional life perspective (Kasterbaum, 1969). In such cases, preventive and treatment strategies by counselors can be helpful and productive.

Prevention.   To effectively offer preventive services to older adults, counselors must understand their needs. Old age is a unique life stage and involves continuous growth. When older clients are treated with respect and with empathy, services are more likely to be effective.

One preventive strategy for promoting positive mental health in older adults is to combat pervasive negative attitudes and messages about aging, such as viewing old age as an undesirable time of physical, cognitive, and emotional decline (Lee, 1999). These attitudes, also called *ageism,* influence older people's attitudes about themselves, creating a predisposition toward vulnerability. Many older adults act old because their environments encourage and support such behavior. American society "equates age with obsolescence and orders its priorities accordingly" (Hansen & Prather, 1980, p. 74). Therefore, counselors must become educators and advocates for change in societal attitudes, if destructive age restrictions and stereotypes are to be overcome. "We need to develop a society that encourages people to stop acting their age and start being themselves" (Ponzo, 1978, pp. 143–144).

Counselors can also help older adults deal with specific and immediate environmental demands. Services for the elderly are most helpful if they are portable and practical (Tomine, 1986). An educational, problem-solving model is very useful to this age group. For example, Hitchcock (1984) reviewed successful programs to help the elderly obtain employment. A particularly successful program was a job club for older job seekers, where at regular meetings participants shared information about obtaining employment. Other effective prevention strategies include helping older adults find ways to reduce isolation through participating in community activities, engaging in physical exercise, being involved in church, and volunteering (Lee, 1999; Myers & Schwiebert, 1996).

A structured life review process has also proven beneficial in working with the elderly and may be a form of primary or secondary prevention (Beaver, 1991; Haight, Michel, & Hendrix, 1998). This technique helps older adults integrate the past and prepare themselves for the future. It is particularly useful in fostering a sense of ego integrity (Myers, 1989; Sweeney, 1999). The use of photographs from the past is an excellent way to help the older clients participate in the life review process. The procedure used to introduce this activity can vary depending on the work setting. For example, a counselor employed in an older adult day care center can ask members to bring in photographs of their lives. However, a counselor employed in an inpatient facility where clients do not have ready access to their personal possessions may have to be more active and find some "representative photographs." Regardless of how it is done, the idea is to accentuate the positive and help clients recall early recollections. Negative experiences can be reframed by labeling them "learning times" instead of "failures" or "defeats." Through such means, self-esteem may be built.

Playing or making music with the elderly is another preventive strategy. Its mental health benefits include the promotion of social interaction, the enhancement of self-worth, the facilitation of self-expression, and the recall of past events (Bruscia, 1987; Osborn, 1989). Sessions may be conducted formally or informally, with either individuals or small groups. In formal sessions clients usually follow a schedule and personal or interpersonal gains may become secondary to performance. In informal sessions, however, performance may become secondary to creativity and interaction. Music may also be used with the elderly to help them achieve better functioning of their movements. Rhythmic music, for example, acts as a stimulus for helping elderly patients with gait disorders improve the flow of their movement (Staum, 1983). In this process, the beat of the music serves as a cue for individuals in anticipating a desired rate of movement.

Treatment. Counseling with older adults historically has been a misunderstood and neglected area. For instance, Sadovy, Lazarus, Jarvik, and Grossberg (1996) estimated that approximately 2.7 percent of clinical services are provided to older adults, even though that group represents more than 11 percent of the population.

One reason older people do not receive more attention from counselors and other mental health specialists is due to the investment syndrome (Colangelo & Pulvino, 1980). The premise behind this syndrome is that some counselors feel their time and energy are better spent working with younger people "who may eventually contribute to society" (p. 69). Professionals who display this attitude are banking on future payoffs from the young and may have either misinformation about the elderly or an irrational fear of old age that keeps them at a psychological distance (Neugarten, 1971).

In treating older adults, it is important to recognize general concerns associated with aging as well as specific concerns germane to individual clients (Duffy, 1999). Five major problems associated with aging, most of which are treatable, include loneliness, physical illness, retirement, idleness, and bereavement (Shanks, 1982). In addition, a large number of persons over age 60 suffer some degree of depression often related to these problems (Blazer, 2002; Myers & Schwiebert, 1996). Because older people may emphasize the physical signs of depression (e.g., lack of appetite, fatigue, headaches, and breathing difficulties) rather than feelings of sadness, depression may go undetected (Myers & Schwiebert). When depression is diagnosed, cognitive–behavioral interventions have been shown to be most successful (Lee, 1999). For example, rational emotive behavior therapy can help increase rational thinking and decrease anxiety about aging (Keller, Corake, & Brooking, 1975).

Members of aging populations may suffer more incidents of psychosis as they grow older: 30 percent of the beds in psychiatric hospitals are occupied by the elderly. For older adults with Alzheimer's disease, counseling based on Rogers' theories and Carkhuff's practical application is beneficial in the early stages of the disease, whereas group counseling, based on Yalom's existential writings, may be productive in helping family members cope as the disease progresses (LaBarge, 1981).

A trend in working with the elderly is to get them physically, as well as emotionally, involved in their treatment. One way to do this is through developmental drama therapy. In this approach, the counselor works especially to help disoriented or depressed older adults connect with their past, their present, and with each other in a positive way. A group format is used to implement this process, and group members are actively engaged in a sustained manner (Johnson, 1986). The developmental and sequential nature of drama progresses from a greeting stage, to unison activities, to the expression of group themes, to personification of images, to playing, to closing rituals. In this process, older adults are encouraged to interact with their fellow group members and to recognize and own their emotions through structured exercises, such as "phoning home." In phoning home a group member calls a significant person is his or her life and either resolves difficulties of the past or expresses gratitude.

In reminiscing or in present-oriented self/social treatment groups, music may be the key to encouraging the discussion of past or present feelings and thoughts about events, such as learning, romance, loss, and family life. Typically, music is initially played that revolves around a particular theme, but only after the group as a whole has warmed up by participating in a brief sing-along of familiar songs that includes their own accompaniment of clapping and foot-tapping sounds. In a maximum participation group, members select their own music and themes. In less democratic groups, much of the selection process is made by the leaders with particular foci in mind. Songs such as Barbara Streisand's "The Way We Were" and early American ballads like "My Old Kentucky Home" are used to set a tone and a mood that encourages talk and interaction after the singing has stopped.

Some popular group therapies can be effective in the treatment of adults, ages 65 and older:

- *Reality-oriented groups* help orient confused group members to their surroundings.
- *Remotivation therapy groups* are aimed at helping older clients become more invested in both the present and the future.

- *Reminiscing groups* assist members in becoming more personally integrated through conducting life reviews.
- *Psychotherapy groups* are geared toward specific problems that often accompany aging, such as loss.
- *Member-specific groups* focus on particular transition concerns of individual members, such as hospitalization or dealing with in-laws. (Gladding, 2003)

In working with senior populations, counselors often become students of life, and older persons become their teachers (Kemp, 1984). When this type of open attitude is achieved, clients are more likely to deal with the events in their lives that are most important, and counselors are more prone to learn about a different dimension of life and be helpful in the process.

SUMMARY AND CONCLUSION

In this chapter the issues and problems of adults throughout the life span have been examined on a number of levels. Prevention and treatment of these problems have also been explored.

Specific developmental issues are associated with adulthood (ages 20 to 40) and midlife (ages 40 to 65). Each has a different focus: young adults concentrate on intimacy and becoming established in a productive lifestyle; midlifers face their own mortality, settle down, and work more toward generativity and self-actualization. Prevention activities for young adults include psychoeducation, exploration of goals, family-of-origin work, group work (such as support groups), and conceptualizing problematic situations as games or puzzles to be solved. Prevention activities for midlifers include psychoeducation, marriage and family enrichment, and use of the creative arts (especially music).

Treatment for young adults includes individual counseling situations, the use of drama, and jogging groups. Group treatment is especially effective for adults in midlife. Groups that focus on adult children of alcoholics, victims of abuse, and career change are popular.

Older adults are often misunderstood or avoided because of a lack of information or irrational fears. Yet, the elderly are an important and growing segment of the U.S. population (about 13 percent). Older adulthood can be divided into two groups: the young–old (ages 55 to 75) and the old–old (ages 75 and above). The young–old have more flexibility and are generally in better health than the old–old, but both groups need help from community counselors and others. Collectively and individually, older adults must work to achieve integrity in their lives and to deal with loss (of friends, physical strength, and/or spouse), as well as changing roles with their children and/or environments.

Preventive services for older adults can take many forms. Most important, however, is the need to treat older adults with respect and dignity. Counselors and others can advocate for the elderly by taking action to help modify the attitudes of nonsupportive people and systems that surround them. It is also beneficial to promote social interaction among older adults through activities such as music and life review groups. In treatment, cognitive theories may be helpful for some clients, and existential theories can be employed with their families. Physical involvement as well as mental involvement of older adults facilitate treatment and may be achieved in a variety of ways, including the use of developmental drama. Various forms of group work with older adults can also be effective.

Just as childhood and adolescence are marked by unique developmental challenges and opportunities, so are the various stages of adulthood. In working with adults throughout the life span, counselors and community workers often learn as much as they teach and help themselves as much as they help others.

REFERENCES

Administration on Aging. (1998). *Profile of older Americans.* Washington, DC: Author.

Allport, G. W. (1955). *Becoming: Basic considerations for a psychology of personality.* New Haven, CT: Yale University Press.

Apter, T. (1985). *Why women don't have wives.* New York: Schocken.

Aylmer, R. C. (1988). The launching of the single young adult. In B. Carter & M. McGoldrick (Eds.), *The changing family life cycle* (2nd ed., pp. 191–208). New York: Gardner.

Bauman, S. S. M. (2002). Promoting parenting and child-rearing skills. In C. L. Juntenen & D. R. Atkinson (Eds.), *Counseling across the lifespan* (pp. 227–242). Thousand Oaks, CA: Sage.

Beaver, M. L. (1991). Life review/reminiscent therapy. In P. K. H. Kim (Ed.), *Serving the elderly: Skills for practice* (pp. 67–89). New York: Aldine de Gruyter.

Bergman, J. (2000). Creating new cultures: Using drama therapy to build therapeutic communities in prisons. In P. Lewis & D. R. Johnson (Eds.), *Current approaches to drama therapy* (pp. 303–330). Springfield, IL: Thomas.

Berk, L. E. (2001). Development through the lifespan (2nd ed.). Needham Heights, MA: Allyn & Bacon.

Birren, J. E., & Schaie, K. W. (Eds.). (2002). *Handbook of the psychology of aging* (5th ed.). New York: Academic Press.

Bisio, T. A., & Crisan, P. (1984). Stress management and nuclear anxiety: A structured group experience. *Journal of Counseling and Development, 63,* 108–109.

Black, C. (1981). *It will never happen to me.* Denver: M.A.C. Printing.

Blazer, D. (2002). *Depression in late life* (3rd ed.). New York: Springer.

Bradt, J. O. (1988). Becoming parents: Families with young children. In B. Carter & M. McGoldrick (Eds.), *The changing family life cycle* (2nd ed.), (pp. 235–254). New York: Gardner.

Broderick, P. C., & Blewitt, P. (2003). *The life span: Human development for helping professionals.* Upper Saddle River, NJ: Prentice Hall.

Bruscia, K. E. (1987). *Improvisational models of music therapy.* Springfield, IL: Thomas.

Campbell, R. E., & Cellini, J. V. (1980). Adult career development. *Counseling and Human Development, 12,* 1–8.

Childers, G. H., Jr., & Burcky, W. D. (1984). The jogging group: A positive-wellness strategy. *AMHCA Journal, 6,* 118–125.

Chisholm, J. F. (1999). The sandwich generation. *Journal of Social Distress and the Homeless, 8,* 177–191.

Colangelo, N., & Pulvino, C. J. (1980). Some basic concerns in counseling the elderly. *Counseling and Values, 24,* 68–73.

Corazzini, J. G., Williams, K., & Harris, S. (1987). Group therapy for adult children of alcoholics: Case studies. *Journal for Specialists in Group Work, 12,* 156–161.

Corey, G. & Corey, M. S. (1990). *I never knew I had a choice* (4th ed.). Pacific Grove, CA: Brooks/Cole.

Corey, M. S., & Corey, G. (2001). *Groups: Process and practice* (6th ed.). Pacific Grove, CA: Brooks/Cole.

Courtois, C. A. (1996). *Healing the incest wound: Adult survivors in therapy.* New York: Norton.

Courtois, C. A., & Leehan, J. (1982). Group treatment for grown-up abused children. *Personnel and Guidance Journal, 60,* 564–566.

Cox, B. J., & Waller, L. L. (1991). *Bridging the communication gap with the elderly.* Chicago: American Hospital Association.

Cox, H. G. (1985). *Later life: The realities of aging.* Upper Saddle River, NJ: Prentice Hall.

Darling-Fisher, C. S., & Tiedje, L. B. (1990). The impact of maternal employment characteristics on fathers' participation in child care. *Family Relations, 39,* 20–26.

Duffy, M. (Ed.). (1999). *Handbook of counseling and psychotherapy with older adults.* New York: Wiley.

Duhl, B. S. (1983). *From the inside out and other metaphors.* New York: Brunner/Mazel.

Dunn, W. (1993). *The baby bust: A generation comes of age.* New York: American Demographic Books.

Ellis, A. (1980). *Rational humorous songs: A garland of rational songs.* New York: Institute of Rational Emotive Therapy.

Ellis, A., & MacLaren, C. (1999). *Rational emotive behavior therapy: A therapist's guide.* New York: Impact Publishers.

Erikson, E. H. (1963). *Childhood and Society* (2nd ed.). New York: Norton.

Frankl, V. (1962). *Man's search for meaning: An introduction to logo-therapy.* New York: Washington Square Press.

Freund, P., & Seligman, M. (1982). Group jogging and emotionally disturbed clients. *Journal for Specialists in Group Work, 7,* 194–198.

Gerler, E. R., Jr. (1980). Physical exercise and multimodal counseling groups. *Journal for Specialists in Group Work, 5,* 157–162.

Gladding, S. T. (2002). *Family therapy: History, theory, and practice* (3rd ed.). Upper Saddle River, NJ: Prentice Hall.

Gladding, S. T. (2003). *Group work: A counseling specialty* (4th ed.). Upper Saddle River, NJ: Prentice Hall.

Glenn, N., & McLanahan, S. (1982). Children and marital happiness: A further specification of the relationship. *Journal of Marriage and the Family, 43,* 63–72.

Gullotta, T., Adams, G., & Alexander, S. (1998). *Today's marriages and families: A wellness approach.* Pacific Grove, CA: Brooks/Cole.

Haight, B. K., Michel, Y., & Hendrix, K. (1998). Life review: Preventing despair in newly relocated nursing home residents: Short- and long-term effects. *International Journal of Aging and Human Development, 47,* 119–142.

Haley, J. (1980). *Leaving home: The therapy of disturbed young people.* New York: McGraw-Hill.

Hansen, J. C., & Prather, F. (1980). The impact of values and attitudes in counseling the aged. *Counseling and Values, 24,* 74–85.

Havighurst, R. J. (1959). Social and psychological needs of the aging. In L. Gorlow & W. Katkovsky (Eds.), *Reading in the psychology of adjustment* (pp. 443–447). New York: McGraw-Hill.

Hill, R. D., Thorn, B, L., & Packard, T. (2000). Counseling older adults: Theoretical and empirical issues in prevention and intervention. In S. D. Brown & R. W. Lent (Eds), *Handbook of counseling psychology* (3rd ed.), (pp. 499–531). New York: Wiley.

Hitchcock, A. A. (1984). Work, aging, and counseling. *Journal of Counseling and Development, 63,* 258–259.

Hudson, F. (2000). *The adult years: Mastering the art of self-renewal.* San Francisco: Jossey-Bass.

Hughes, F. P. (1999). *Human development across the life span* (rev. ed.). Upper Saddle River, NJ: Merrill/Prentice Hall.

Johnson, D. R. (1986). The developmental method in drama therapy: Group treatment with the elderly. *Arts in Psychotherapy, 13,* 17–33.

Jourard, S. M., & Landsman, T. (1980). *Healthy personality* (4th ed.). New York: Macmillan.

Jung, C. G. (1971). The stages of life. In J. Campbell (Ed.), *The portable Jung.* New York: Viking.

Kasterbaum, R. (1969). The foreshortened life perspective. *Geriatrics, 24,* 126–133.

Keller, J. F., Corake, J. W., & Brooking, J. Y. (1975). Effects of a program in rational thinking on anxieties in older persons. *Journal of Counseling Psychology, 22,* 54–57.

Kemp, J. T. (1984). Learning from clients: Counseling the frail and dying elderly. *Personnel and Guidance Journal, 62,* 270–272.

Kimmel, D. C. (1976). Adult development: Challenges for counseling. *Personnel and Guidance Journal, 55,* 103–105.

Kleinke, C. L. (2002). *Coping with life challenges* (2nd ed.). Prospect Height, IL: Waveland.

Kogan, L. R., & Vacha-Haase, T. (2002). Supporting adaptation to new family roles in middle age. In C. L. Juntenen & D. R. Atkinson (Eds.), *Counseling across the lifespan* (pp. 299–327). Thousand Oaks, CA: Sage.

LaBarge, E. (1981). Counseling patients with senile dementia of the Alzheimer type and their families. *Personnel and Guidance Journal, 60,* 139–142.

Lazarus, A. A. (1976). *Multimodal behavior therapy.* New York: Springer.

Lazarus, A. A. (1981). The practice of multimodal therapy. New York: McGraw-Hill.

Lee, W. M. L. (1999). *An introduction to multicultural counseling.* Ann Arbor, MI: Taylor & Francis.

Levinson, D. J., Darrow, C. N., Klein, E. B., Levinson, M. H., & McKee, B. (1978). *The seasons of a man's life.* New York: Knopf.

Marmor, J. (1982). Transition to the empty nest. In L. Allman & D. Gaffe (Eds.), *Reading in adult psychology: Contemporary perspectives.* New York: Harper & Row.

Maslow, A. H. (1968). *Toward a psychology of being* (2nd ed.). New York: Van Nostrand Reinhold.

McCullough, P. G., & Rutenberg, S. K. (1988). Launching children and moving on. In B. Carter & M. McGoldrick (Eds.), *The changing family life cycle* (2nd ed.), (pp. 285–309). New York: Gardner.

McGoldrick, M., Gerson, R., & Shellenberger, S. (1999). *Genograms: Assessment and intervention.* New York: Norton.

Minuchin, S., & Fishman, C. H. (1981). *Family therapy techniques.* Cambridge, MA: Harvard University Press.

Morgan, J. P., Jr. (1994). Bereavement in older adults. *Journal of Mental Health Counseling, 16,* 318–326.

Myers, J. E. (1989). *Infusing gerontological counseling into counselor preparation.* Alexandria, VA: ACA.

Myers, J. E., & Schwiebert, V. L. (1996). *Competencies for gerontological counseling.* Alexandria, VA: American Counseling Association.

Neugarten, B. L. (Ed.). (1968). *Middle age and aging.* Chicago: University of Chicago Press.

Neugarten, B. (1971, December). Grow old along with me! The best is yet to be. *Psychology Today,* pp. 48–56.

Neugarten, B. L. (1978). The wise of the young-old. In R. Gross, B. Gross, & S. Seidman (Eds.), *The new old: Struggling for decent aging,* pp. 47–49. New York: Doubleday.

Neugarten, B. L. (1979). Time, age and the life cycle. *American Journal of Psychiatry, 136,* 887–894.

Osborn, C. (1989). Reminiscence: When the past eases the present. *Journal of Gerontological Nursing, 15,* 6–12.

Papalia, D. E., Olds, S. W., Feldman, R. D. (2001). *Human development* (8th ed.). New York: McGraw-Hill.

Parker, C. L. (1975). A desensitization group for adult community leaders. *Personnel and Guidance Journal, 54,* 48–49.

Ponzo, Z. (1978). Age prejudice of "act your age." *Personnel and Guidance Journal, 57,* 140–144.

Pulvino, C. J., & Colangelo, N. (1980). Counseling the elderly: A developmental perspective. *Counseling and Values, 24,* 139–147.

Quinn, W. H., & Odell, M. (1998). Predictors of marital adjustment during the first two years. *Marriage and Family Review, 27,* 113–130.

Rice, F. P. (2001). *Human development: A life-span approach* (4th ed.). Upper Saddle River, NJ: Prentice Hall.

Robbins, A., & Wilner, A. (2001). *Quarterlife crisis: The unique challenges of life in your twenties.* New York: Penguin.

Rosenbaum, M., & Cohen, E. (1999). Egalitarian marriages, spousal support, resourcefulness, and psychological distress among Israeli working women. *Journal of Vocational Behavior, 54,* 102–113.

Ryder, P. (1976). Theatre as prison therapy. *Drama Review, 20,* 60–66.

Sadovy, J., Lazarus, I. W., Jarvik, L. E., & Grossber, G. T. (Eds.). (1996). *Comprehensive review of geriatric psychiatry* (2nd ed.). Washington, DC: American Psychiatric Press.

Sandberg, J. (2002). Our aging selves. *Family Therapy Magazine, 1*(6), 10–15.

Schlossberg, N. K., Waters, E. B., & Goodman, J. (1996). *Counseling adults in transition: Linking practice with theory* (2nd ed.). New York: Springer.

Shanks, J. L. (1982). Expanding treatment for the elderly: Counseling in a private medical practice. *Personnel and Guidance Journal, 61,* 553–555.

Sheehy, G. (1976). *Passages: Predictable crises of adult life.* New York: Dutton.

Sherman, R. (1993). The intimacy genogram. *The Family Journal, 1,* 91–93.

Sinick, D. (1979). Adult developmental changes and counseling challenges. In M. L. Ganikos, K. A.

Grady, & J. B. Olson (Eds.), *Counseling the aged, a training syllabus for educators* (pp. 31–44). Washington, DC: American Personnel and Guidance Association.

Staum, M. (1983). Music and rhythmic stimuli in the rehabilitation of gait disorders. *Journal of Music Therapy, 20,* 69–87.

Steinglass, P. (1982). The roles of alcohol in family systems. In J. Oxford & J. Harwin (Eds.), *Alcohol and the family* (pp. 127–150). New York: St. Martin's Press.

Sweeney, T. J. (1999). *Adlerian counseling: A practitioner's approach.* Philadelphia: Taylor & Francis.

Thaut, M. H. (1988). Rhythmic intervention techniques in music therapy with gross motor dysfunctions. *Arts in Psychotherapy, 15,* 127–137.

Tinsley, D. J., & Bigler, M. (2002). Facilitating transition in retirement. In C. L. Juntunen & D. R. Atkinson (Eds.), *Counseling across the lifespan* (pp. 375–397). Thousand Oaks, CA: Sage.

Tomine, S. (1986). Private practice in gerontological counseling. *Journal of Counseling and Development, 64,* 406–409.

Watzlawick, P. (1983). *The situation is hopeless, but not serious.* New York: Norton.

Wegscheider, S. (1981). *Another chance: Hope and health for the alcoholic family.* Palo Alto, CA: Science & Behavior Books.

White, H. (1978). Exercises in understanding your family. In *Your family is good for you.* New York: Random House.

Whitfield, C. L. (1987). *Healing the child within: Discovery and recovery for adult children of dysfunctional families.* Pompano Beach, FL: Health Communications.

Willis, S. L., & Reid, J. D. (Eds.). (1999). *Life in the middle: Psychological and social development in middle age.* San Diego, CA: Academic Press.

Worth, M. R. (1983). Adults. In J. A. Brown & R. H. Pate, Jr. (Eds.), *Being a counselor: Directions and challenges* (pp. 230–252). Pacific Grove, CA: Brooks/Cole.

Wrenn, C. G. (1979). Proposed changes in counselor attitudes: Toward your job. *School Counselor, 27,* 81–90.

Yalom, I. D. (1995). *The theory and practice of group psychotherapy* (4th ed.). New York: Basic Books.

Zimpfer, D. G., & Carr, J. J. (1989). Groups for midlife career change: A review. *Journal for Specialists in Group Work, 14,* 1–8.

CHAPTER 12

Counseling Children and Adolescents

There you sit Alice Average
   midway back in the long-windowed classroom
      in the middle of Wednesday's noontime blahs,
Adjusting yourself to the sound of a lecture
   and the cold of the blue plastic desk that supports
      you.
In a world full of light words, hard rock, Madonnas,
   long hair, high tech, confusion, and change
      dreams fade like blue jeans
And "knowing" goes beyond the books and disks
   that are packaged for time-limited consumption
      and studied until the start of summer. . . .

Gladding, S. T. (1980/1995). Thoughts on Alice Average midway through the mid-day class on Wednesday. *Humanist Educator, 18,* 203. © 1980, 1986 by ACA. Reprinted with permission. No further reproduction authorized without written permission of ACA.

Poverty, violence, illness, school difficulties, and family disruption, as well as typical transitions associated with development, are factors that influence the mental health and well-being of a growing number of children and adolescents. Whether the increased prevalence of mental health issues in this population is due to a higher level of vulnerability or to increased efforts to identify problems, currently more young people are in need of mental health services than they were in years past (Kaffenberger & Seligman, 2003). According to the Surgeon General's Report (2000), approximately 20 percent of children and adolescents are estimated to have mental disorders of some type, and 5 to 9 percent of youth have serious emotional disturbances. However, an estimated 80 percent of young people who need treatment do not receive the mental health services they need.

- Childhood is a time of transition and reorganization. It is important to assess children's mental health within the context of familial, social, and cultural expectations about age-appropriate thoughts, feelings, and behaviors.
- The range of "normal" is wide. Even so, there are children who develop mental disorders that fall out of the normal range. Approximately 20 percent of children and adolescents experience the signs and symptoms of a DSM-IV disorder during the course of a year. Only about 5 percent, however, experience "extreme functional impairment."
- Mental health problems appear in families of all social classes and of all backgrounds.
- A wide array of factors place children at risk for mental health problems, including intellectual disabilities, low birth weight, physical problems, family history of mental disorders, multigenerational poverty, and caregiver separation or abuse and neglect.
- Preventive interventions (e.g., educational programs for young children and parent education programs) help reduce the impact of risk factors and improve social and emotional development.
- Several efficacious psychosocial and pharmacological treatments exist for children's mental health problems, including ADHD, depression, and disruptive behavior disorders.
- Primary care facilities and schools are important settings in which professionals can recognize mental problems in young people. Options for referral to specialty care, however, are limited.
- For youth with "serious emotional disturbance," a systems approach in which multiple service sectors work collaboratively (i.e., systems of care) can be effective.
- Families are essential partners in the provision of mental health services to children and adolescents.
- Cultural differences can compound the general problems of access to appropriate mental health services.

Figure 12–1

Summary of the Surgeon General's Report on Children's Mental Health (2000)

Mental health problems appear in youth of all social classes and backgrounds. Some children are at greater risk than others because of a wide range of factors, including genetic vulnerability, temperament, family dysfunction, poverty, caregiver separation, and abuse (Surgeon General Report, 2000; Figure 12–1). Community counselors who work with children and adolescents need to be aware of these risk factors, as well as of the developmental factors that impact mental health. They also need to be skilled at implementing prevention and intervention strategies that target multiple levels, including the individual, the family, and the broader community.

We begin this chapter by describing developmental and bioecological influences on children's mental health. Next, we focus on the counseling process as it applies to children and adolescents. Following that, we provide an overview of some of the specific issues that affect children and adolescents living in today's society and describe treatment suggestions for working with those issues.

DEVELOPMENTAL CONSIDERATIONS

Childhood and adolescence are characterized by dramatic developmental changes physically, cognitively, socially, and emotionally. To a large degree, mental health during these years is defined by achieving expected developmental milestones, establishing secure attachments, negotiating relationships with family members and peers, and learning effective coping skills (Surgeon General Report, 2000). Community counselors who work with young people need to be guided by developmental theory as they select strategies for prevention and treatment.

Development is multidimensional and complex, and is marked by qualitative changes that occur in many different domains. A summary of developmental theories and counseling implications is presented in Table 12–1. Whereas it is not our intent to describe the full range of developmental characteristics associated with children and adolescents, in this next section, we provide an overview of some general characteristics of early childhood, middle childhood, and adolescence.

Early Childhood

Children between the ages of 2 and 6 are in the *early childhood stage,* sometimes called *the play years* (Berk, 2001). During this period, motor skills are refined, children begin to build ties with peers, and thought and language skills expand rapidly. To understand the way young children think and use language, it is helpful to refer to Jean Piaget's stage-constructed theory of cognitive development. Although current research indicates that the stages of cognitive development are not as discrete and clear-cut as Piaget hypothesized, his descriptions of cognitive development provide a relatively accurate picture of how children think and reason at different ages (Bjorklund, 2000).

Table 12–1
Developmental theories and emerging developmental trends

Developmental Theories	Founder	Key Concepts	Implications for Counseling
Cognitive theory	Piaget, Elkind	Divided cognitive development into four stages: Sensorimotor (birth to 2), Preoperational (2 to 7), Concrete operations (7 to 11), Formal operations (begins after 11).	Counselors can adjust their approach and select interventions to match the child's level of cognitive functioning. For example, counselors working with young children will want to use some form of play media.
Theory of moral development	Kohlberg, Gilligan	Kohlberg identified three levels of moral development, beginning with a punishment and obedience orientation and progressing to higher stages of moral reasoning. Gilligan posited that feminine morality emphasizes an ethic of care, focusing on interpersonal relationships.	Counselors can use their understanding of moral reasoning to help children learn self-control and to help parents with discipline issues. Girls and boys may make moral judgments in different ways.
Psychosocial development	Erikson	Identified seven psychosocial stages and their associated developmental tasks (for example, from birth to 1 year of age, the central task is trust).	Counselors can help clients obtain the coping skills necessary to master developmental tasks so they can move forward in their development.
Developmental psychopathology	Kazden, Kovacs, and others	Study of child and adolescent psychopathology in the context of maturational and developmental processes.	The theory provides a framework for understanding child psychopathology as unique from adult psychopathology, aiding in accurate assessment.
The classic theories	Freud, Adler, and Jung	The theories of personality posited by the classic theorists emphasize the role of early life experiences on child and adolescent development.	The classic theories help counselors understand the dynamics of behavior *before* selecting counseling techniques to promote change.
Attachment theory	Ainsworth, Bowlby, and others	Focuses on the relationship between the emotional bond between a parent and child and the child's psychosocial development over the life span.	An understanding of attachment relationships can provide useful insights into how to move toward optimal psychosocial development.
Emotional intelligence	Salovey and Mayer	Focus is on the role that emotions play in social and psychological functioning.	Counselors can help promote emotional intelligence through such activities as social skills training in groups.

Source: From *Introduction to Counseling: An Art and Science Perspective* (pp. 274, 279), by M. S. Nystul. Published by Allyn and Bacon, Boston, MA. Copyright © 2002 by Pearson Education. Adapted by permission of the publisher.

According to Piaget, children between 2 and 7 years of age are *preoperational,* which means they are developing the ability to represent objects and events through imitation, symbolic play, drawing, and spoken language. They are likely to be egocentric, implying that they cannot see the viewpoint of another. Preoperational children may attribute lifelike qualities to inanimate objects and have difficulty with abstract nouns and concepts, such as time and space (Vernon, 1999). For the first time, they are entering into a stage where they are able to represent and recall their feelings. As they near the end of the preoperational stage, their emotional self-regulation improves.

Erik Erikson's psychosocial theory provides another way to understand children's development. Erikson described development as a series of psychological crises that occur at various stages. The manner in which the crisis is resolved, along a continuum from positive to negative, influences healthy or maladaptive outcomes at each stage (Berk, 2001). Young children are in the process of resolving the developmental crisis of *initiative versus guilt. Initiative* refers to being enterprising, energetic, and purposeful. Children in this stage are discovering what kinds of people they are, particularly in regard to gender. Because of their increased language and motor skills, they are capable of imagining and trying out many new things. To navigate this period successfully, children need to be given a variety of opportunities to explore, experiment, and ask questions. The guidance of understanding adults can help young children develop self-confidence, self-direction, and emotional self-regulation.

Play is an extremely important activity for children in this age group. Through play, children find out about themselves and their world. Counselors who work with young children will want to use some form of play when counseling them. Play provides a way for children to express feelings, describe experiences, and disclose wishes. Although young children may not be able to articulate feelings, toys and other play media serve as the words they use to express emotions (Landreth, 1993). Materials used to facilitate play include puppets, art supplies, dolls and dollhouses, tools, and toy figures or animals.

Middle Childhood

Children between 7 and 11 years of age are in *middle childhood*. During this time period, children develop literacy skills and logical thinking. Cognitively, they are in Piaget's *concrete operational* stage, meaning that they are capable of reasoning logically about concrete, tangible information. Concrete operational children are able to mentally reverse actions, although they can only generalize from concrete experiences. They grasp logical concepts more readily than before, but they typically have difficulty reasoning about abstract ideas. Children in this stage learn best through questioning, exploring, manipulating, and doing (Flavell, 1985). As a rule, their increased reasoning skills enable them to understand the concept of intentionality and be more cooperative.

From a psychosocial perspective, children in this age group are in the process of resolving the crisis of *industry versus inferiority*. To maximize healthy development, they need opportunities to develop a sense of competence and capability. When adults provide manageable tasks, along with sufficient time and encouragement to complete the tasks, children are more likely to develop a strong sense of industry and efficacy (Thomas, 2000). Alternatively, children who do not experience feelings of competence and mastery may develop a sense of inadequacy and pessimism about their capabilities. Experiences with family, teachers, and peers all contribute to children's perceptions of efficacy and industry.

Negotiating relationships with peers is an important part of middle childhood. Acceptance in a peer group and having a "best friend" help children develop competence, self-esteem, and an understanding of others (Vernon, 1999). Some of the interpersonal skills children acquire during middle childhood include learning to get along with age mates, learning the skills of tolerance and patience, and developing positive attitudes toward social groups and institutions (Havighurst, 1972). Community counselors can help children develop their interpersonal skills by implementing preventive strategies targeted toward social skills development.

Adolescence

Adolescence is the period when young people transition from childhood to adulthood. During adolescence, youth mature physically, develop an increased understanding of roles and relationships, and acquire and refine skills needed for performing successfully as adults (Crockett & Crouter, 1995). In many modern societies, the time span associated with adolescence can last for nearly a decade (Berk, 2001). Puberty marks the beginning of adolescence, with girls typically reaching puberty earlier than boys. As adolescence ends, young people ideally have constructed an identity, attained independence, and developed more mature ways of relating to others. Although in years past, adolescence was referred to as a time of *storm and stress,* current research indicates that "although some teenagers encounter serious difficulties, emotional turbulence is not a routine feature of adolescence" (Berk, p. 351).

As young people enter adolescence, they begin to make the shift from concrete to formal operational thinking. The transition takes time and usually is not completed until at least age 15 (Schave & Schave, 1989). Adolescents moving into the *formal operational* stage are able to deal with abstractions, form hypotheses, engage in mental manipulation, and predict consequences. As formal operational skills develop, they become capable of reflective abstraction, which refers to the ability to reflect on knowledge, rearrange thoughts, and discover alternative routes to solving problems (Bjorklund, 2000). Consequently, counseling approaches that provide opportunities to generate alternative solutions are more likely to be effective with adolescents than with younger children.

A new form of egocentrism often emerges during adolescence, characterized by a belief in one's uniqueness and invulnerability (Elkind, 1984). This may be reflected in reckless behavior and grandiose ideas. Consequently, preventive strategies addressing such issues as substance abuse, teenage pregnancy, and HIV/AIDS and other sexually transmitted diseases are warranted.

Also related to a heightened sense of uniqueness is the adolescent phenomenon of feeling constantly "on stage" or playing to an imaginary audience. It is not uncommon for adolescents to feel that everyone is looking at them, leading to increased anxiety and self-consciousness. These feelings tend to peak in early adolescence and then decline as formal operational skills improve (Bjorklund, 2000).

The onset of puberty often triggers the psychosocial crisis of *identity versus role confusion* (Erikson, 1968). A key challenge during adolescence is the formation of an identity, including self-definition and a commitment to goals, values, beliefs, and life purpose (Waterman, 1985). To master this challenge, adolescents need opportunities to explore options, try on various roles and responsibilities, and speculate about possibilities. Sometimes adolescents enter a period of role confusion, characterized in part by overidentification with heroes or cliques, before they develop a true sense of individuality and recognize that they are acceptable to society (Thomas, 2000).

Spending time with peers continues to be important throughout adolescence. As they develop self-confidence and sensitivity, adolescents base their friendships on compatibility and shared experiences. Intimate friendships increase, as do dating and sexual experimentation. Counseling may involve helping these young people deal with issues of complex relationships and decision making about the future.

It is important to keep in mind that developmental generalizations may not be applicable to all ethnic or cultural groups. For example, the search for self-identity may be delayed, compounded by a search for ethnic identity, or even nonexistent among certain groups of adolescents (Herring, 1997). Also, research on Piagetian tasks suggests that some forms of logic do not emerge spontaneously according to stages but are socially generated, based on cultural experiences (Berk, 2001). Developmental theories provide useful guides for understanding children and adolescents; however, no theory provides a complete explanation of development, nor does any theory take into account all cultural perspectives. In the next section, we examine some of the biological, environmental, and sociocultural influences on child and adolescent adjustment.

BIOECOLOGICAL CONSIDERATIONS

> *The characteristics of the person at a given time in his or her life are a joint function of the characteristics of the person and of the environment over the course of that person's life up to that time.* (Bronfenbrenner, 1989, p. 190)

Bronfenbrenner's (1979, 1989, 1995) bioecological model illustrates the way development is influenced by multilayered interactions of specific characteristics of the child (e.g., genetic, biological, and psychological factors), the immediate environment (e.g., family, school, peers, neighborhood, and community), and the more global culture, or macrosystem, within which the young person lives. These systems are not static, but instead are constantly changing. To work effectively with children and adolescents, counselors need to assess individual, environmental, and cultural factors, and their interactive effects on development and adjustment. Teasing the different influences apart can be difficult, if not impossible. In this section, specific influences on young people's mental health are described. Although the various factors are presented as separate entities, it is important to keep in mind the fact that influences are reciprocal and interactive.

Psychological, Biological, and Genetic Influences

A wide array of individual characteristics, including physical appearance, personality traits, cognitive functioning, and genetic predisposition, influence the manner in which children and adolescents adjust and adapt to their environments. A key factor affecting children's development is *temperament,* which refers to specific traits with which each child is born and which influence the way the child reacts to the surrounding environment (Surgeon General Report, 2000). Defined more simply, temperament refers to a person's *emotional style* (Berk, 2001). Temperament includes traits such as attention span, goal orientation, activity level, curiosity, and emotional self-regulation. Differences in temperament are evidenced when one child is easily excitable and impulsive, another is shy and withdrawn, and a third is calm and attentive. Although there is some continuity in temperamental traits across the life span, temperament may be modified during development, particularly through interaction with family members (Thomas & Chess, 1977).

In addition to temperament, cognitive factors, including intelligence, information processing skills, and neurological conditions, influence child and adolescent adjustment and well-being. Cognitive skills can serve as protective factors, increasing children's chances for success in school and ability to solve problems effectively. In contrast, neurological deficits and lower levels of intellectual functioning increase the risk of school failure, thereby placing youth at a greater risk for delinquency (Calhoun, Glaser, & Bartolumucci, 2001). Genetic factors and biological abnormalities of the central nervous system caused by injury, exposure to toxins, infection, or poor nutrition can lead to deficits in cognitive development.

Faulty cognitive processing skills, such as attributional bias, can adversely affect an individual's reactions to people and situations. For example, juvenile offenders often attribute hostility to others in neutral situations, resulting in unwarranted acts of aggression (Calhoun et al., 2001). As another example, depressed youth often have negative attributional styles, believing that they are helpless to influence events in their lives and that they are responsible for any failures or problems that are experienced. In contrast, young people with more accurate attributional styles tend to be more adaptable and less likely to form misperceptions, leading to more effective coping and adjustment.

Just as genetic inheritance influences individual characteristics such as temperament and cognitive functioning, it also has an influence on mental health. Although the precise manner in which heredity influences mental health is not fully understood, certain mental health illnesses, including depression, anxiety, and substance abuse, appear to have a genetic component. For example, children of depressed parents are three times as likely as children of nondepressed parents to experience a depressive disorder (Surgeon General Report, 2000). It is theorized that multiple gene variants act in conjunction with environmental factors and developmental events to make a person more likely to experience mental health problems (National Institute of Mental Health [NIMH], 2000). Children and adolescents who are genetically vulnerable to specific conditions may benefit from prevention efforts targeted toward certain areas, such as increasing self-esteem or improving coping responses.

Contextual Influences

Whereas genetic inheritance and other biological factors help determine individual traits and set the stage for child development, they are not the only influences. The many contexts in which young people live and interact have powerful effects on their mental health and well-being. The family, school, and peers are examples of contextual factors that influence psychological adjustment.

Family influences.   One of the most significant influences on the development of young people is the family, where interactions typically occur on a daily basis. Within the family, unique bonds are formed that serve as models for relationships in the greater community. Family relationships are complex and influence development both directly and indirectly. A number of family-related variables have been identified as risk factors for adverse mental health, including severe parental discord, parent psychopathology, overcrowding, and economic hardship (Surgeon General Report, 2000). In contrast, healthy interactions among family members can lead to positive outcomes as well as buffer against negative influences, such as illness or poverty, over which the family has little control.

The quality of the relationship between children and their caregivers is of principal importance to well-being across the life span. Parent–child interactions have been associated with a wide range of developmental outcomes, including self-confidence, academic achievement, psychological health, and conduct. In particular, parent–child interactions that are marked by high levels of parental support and behavioral control help children develop mastery and competence (Maccoby & Martin, 1983). Supportive behaviors are those that facilitate socialization through warmth, nurturance, responsiveness, and open communication. Controlling behaviors, including rule-setting, negotiating, and consistent discipline, help establish guidance and flexibility within the power hierarchy of the family. By combining the dimensions of support and control according to high and low extremes, parenting styles can be classified into four types: authoritative, authoritarian, indulgent, and neglecting (Baumrind, 1971; Maccoby & Martin, 1983). These four parenting types are depicted in Figure 12–2.

Authoritative families are characterized by emotional support, high standards, appropriate autonomy granting, and clear communication (Darling & Steinberg, 1993). Authoritative parents monitor their children and set clear standards for conduct. Disciplinary methods are inductive rather than punitive, and parental responses are consistent. Children are listened to and participate in family decision making. Goals for children in an authoritative family include social responsibility, self-regulation, and cooperation (Baumrind, 1991).

Authoritative parenting has been linked with a wide range of positive child outcomes, including social competence, psychological well-being, fewer conduct problems, and higher scholastic performance (e.g., Baumrind, 1991; Hein & Lewko, 1994; Lamborn, Mounts, Steinberg, & Dornbusch, 1991). Systematic efforts to educate parents about effective parenting processes and authoritative parenting practices can help improve the quality of family life and parent–child relationships. A

Support

		Accepting, responsive, child centered	Rejecting, unresponsive, parent centered
Control	**Demanding, Controlling**	AUTHORITATIVE Reciprocal, high in bidirectional communication	AUTHORITARIAN Power-assertive, high in control
	Undemanding, Low in control attempts	INDULGENT Permissive, warm, noncontrolling	NEGLECTING Ignoring, indifferent, uninvolved

Figure 12–2

A two-dimensional classification of parenting patterns

Source: Adapted from E. E. Maccoby and J. A. Martin, Socialization in the Context of the Family: Parent–Child Interaction, in E. M. Hetherington (Ed.), *Handbook of Child Psychology: Vol. 4, Socialization, Personality, and Social Development* (4th ed., p. 39), New York: Wiley. Copyright 1983. This material is used by permission of John Wiley & Sons, Inc.

variety of forums can be used to implement the teaching of parenting skills, including community-based parent education programs and school-sponsored clinics for parents.

In addition to parenting styles and practices, several other family-related factors influence child adjustment. Family structure (i.e., divorced, single-parent, married), family size, socioeconomic status, the amount of time family members spend together, and issues such as neglect and abuse all impact adjustment in various ways. Community counselors who work with children and adolescents need to be aware of these influences, help families build on strengths, and target areas in which improvement is needed.

School influences.   The unique characteristics of the school context give it special prominence in child and adolescent development. Through interactions with peers, teachers, and other adults in the school, young people make judgments about themselves, their capabilities, and their goals for the future. Consequently, experiences in school play a major role in the development of individual differences in children and adolescents.

Schools in which support, trust, respect, optimism, and intentionality are demonstrated foster the development of positive student attitudes and behaviors (Purkey, 1991). In particular, supportive teachers can positively influence students' self-confidence and performance (Newsome, 1999). Also, schools that are orderly and organized, with consistent and fair enforcement of rules, are conducive to positive student behaviors, although excessive teacher control and discipline can be detrimental to adolescent adjustment and achievement (Eccles, Lord, & Midgley, 1991). Other factors that contribute to positive outcomes in youth include:

- Communication between teachers and parents
- Providing tasks that are challenging but not overwhelming
- Communicating the importance of effort in success
- Stressing individual progress and self-improvement
- Small classes that permit teachers to provide individualized support for mastery
- Cooperative learning and peer tutoring
- Accommodating individual and cultural differences in learning styles (Ames, 1992; Eccles, Wigfield, & Schiefele, 1998)

It is important for counselors to be aware of the powerful influence the school context has on young people. Community and agency counselors can work collaboratively with school counselors, teachers, and other school personnel to optimize child and adolescent development.

Peer influences.   Relationships with peers—at home, at school, and in the community—become increasingly important as children grow older. Peer interaction plays a key role in helping children learn to take different perspectives and understand other points of view. Peer acceptance, which refers to being liked by other children, shapes the views children have of themselves as well as their views of others.

Whereas some children are well liked and make friends easily, others are rejected or neglected. Unfortunately, some children are the victims of frequent verbal and/or physical attacks by other children. Such victimization leads to a variety of adjustment difficulties, including depression, loneliness, and school avoidance (Ladd, Kochendorfer, & Coleman, 1997). Counselors can intervene at various levels to assist children who are having difficulties with peers. Depending on the situation, it may be necessary to help children develop social skills or assertiveness skills. Individual and group counseling interventions can include coaching, modeling, reinforcing positive social skills, and teaching perspective taking. It also may be necessary to intervene systemically by working collaboratively with schools to develop codes against bullying and by conducting parent education groups to help ameliorate the problem.

During adolescence, young people begin spending more time with peers and less time with family members. Typically, friendships are formed with peers who have similar interests, values, and behaviors. Most often, peer group association positively influences well-being, as teenagers learn adaptive skills that benefit adjustment. In some cases, however, the peer group provides a negative context in which antisocial behaviors are the norm. For example, young people who were aggressive and rejected as children and who feel distanced from their families are likely to become involved with deviant peers and engage in antisocial behaviors (Berk, 2001). Difficult temperament, low intelligence, poor school performance, peer rejection in childhood, and being involved with antisocial peer groups are associated with juvenile delinquency, a widespread problem that affects over 2 million children and adolescents in the United States (U.S. Department of Justice, 1997). Research also has shown that substance-abusing adolescents tend to seek out substance-abusing friends, making intervention more difficult (Steinberg, Fletcher, & Darling, 1994).

Normative and nonnormative life events.   Many of the developmental challenges young people face are expected: physical changes, school transitions, emerging sexuality, changes in cognitive functioning, and changes in family and peer relationships. Developmental transitions of this nature are considered normative; that is, they are anticipated generic challenges that everyone encounters. In some contexts, developmental challenges are compounded by chronic stressors, which are enduring aspects of the environment that involve deprivation or hardship. Poverty, physical disability, and family dysfunction are examples of chronic stressors that can exert taxing demands on families.

Whereas normative life events are expected, nonnormative life events are those unexpected, acute demands that may alter the course of development, either directly or transactionally (Compas, 1987). Nonnormative life events include parental divorce, death of a family member, onset of illness or disability, and loss of a job. Catastrophic phenomena—sudden, powerful events that require major adaptive responses from the groups sharing the experience (e.g., natural disasters, accidents, and terrorism)—also are considered nonnormative events (McNamara, 2000). Nonnormative events are not necessarily negative, however. Examples of positive events include inheriting a large amount of money or being selected for a coveted position.

Normative and nonnormative events occur in multiple contexts and have a wide range of effects on the people experiencing them. Frequency, intensity, and timing of the events can affect youth's mental health, with outcomes being moderated by subjective perceptions, parental and peer support, and coping skills (Newsome & Whitlatch, in press). To understand young clients' developmental trajectories, counselors need to assess the normative and nonnormative life events they have experienced. They can help children handle negative life events by implementing stress management interventions that are tailored toward helping children use active, problem-focused coping strategies.

Cultural influences.   Another ecological factor that exerts a strong influence on the development and adjustment of young people is the broader culture in which they live. Cultural beliefs, values, and institutions compose what Bronfenbrenner (1979, 1995) referred to as the *macrosystem*. In Chapter 10, we described the multidimensional aspects of culture. On one level, children are influenced by the dominant culture of a society: its values, laws, customs, and resources. When children are members of one or more minority groups, they are impacted not only by the belief system of the dominant culture but also by the values that guide the minority cultures. The various sociocultural influences interact, and sometimes conflict, to shape the developing child's subjective worldview.

McClure and Teyber (2003) illustrate the effects cultural influences can have on the counseling process in the following examples:

> An adolescent, African American male who is "paranoid" around authority figures is often accurately discerning a persecutory or hostile environment given his life experiences. A

counselor who diagnoses him as paranoid (which frequently occurs) and focuses on helping him see "reality" (i.e., the *counselor's* subjective worldview) would quickly lose credibility. Similarly, encouraging a young adult from a traditional Asian family to emancipate and become more autonomous from her family may only engender increased distress. (pp. 7–8)

Competent counselors are aware of the array of cultural issues that influence child and adolescent development. They recognize the importance of evaluating which cultural aspects are relevant to a particular individual and plan interventions that build on cultural strengths (Liu & Clay, 2002).

Summary

In this section, we have discussed developmental considerations that need to be taken into account when counseling children and adolescents. We also have described some of the bioecological factors that influence development. With that background in mind, we next focus on ways to counsel effectively with young people.

COUNSELING CONSIDERATIONS

Working effectively with young people requires a special knowledge of child development, contextual influences, and child-related counseling procedures. Children's needs, wishes, behaviors, and ways of viewing the world differ significantly from those of adults. Indeed, interventions that are appropriate for adults may be ineffective or even detrimental when applied to children and adolescents (Sherwood-Hawes, 1993). Through all stages of the counseling process, counselors need to take into account universal developmental principles as well as the unique, subjective way in which each child views the world.

Building a Counseling Relationship

The key to any successful counseling experience is developing an effective working relationship based on mutual trust and acceptance. Ways to go about establishing such a relationship with adults are described in Chapter 5. But how are therapeutic relationships built with children? Perhaps the most important first step is being willing to enter completely into the child's world, with no preconceptions, expectations, or agenda. All judgment needs to be suspended so that the counselor can remain open to what the child is sharing, either verbally or nonverbally. As the therapeutic relationship is being established, listening and observational skills are more important than questioning skills (Erdman & Lampe, 1996). By listening carefully to what young clients have to say, giving them undivided attention, and responding sensitively to feelings, reactions, and cultural cues, counselors can create bridges of trust and understanding.

Establishing rapport.   To build relationships successfully, counselors need to tailor their responses and interactions to fit the specific needs of each child, taking into account developmental experiences, sociocultural background, and reasons for referral (McClure & Teyber, 2003). With these considerations in mind, the counselor can select from a variety of approaches to help establish rapport. When working with young children who have difficulty verbalizing, play and art media can be especially effective. With older children, games like Jenga or "in-house" basketball can provide a nonthreatening introduction to the counseling process. I (DN) like to use a dry erase white board and markers with children, inviting them to draw pictures or symbols that illustrate things they would like me to know about them. As a variation, I ask young clients to create an *About Me* collage by decoratively writing their names in the center of a piece of poster board. Then I invite them to draw or select magazine pictures that describe different aspects of themselves, including strengths, interests, relationships, or other characteristics they want to reveal at that point. Their choices serve as a springboard for further discussion and provide a lens for glimpsing their subjective worlds.

One of the factors that makes building a relationship with children different from building a relationship with adults is that children often do not understand what counseling is. They may be confused about the nature and process of counseling, fearful of being in an unknown situation, and/or resistant to talking about issues with a stranger. Typically, children are brought to counseling by parents or by other significant adults in their lives, and it is these adults, not the children, who want change to occur. This is particularly true when children or adolescents are referred because of behavioral patterns that bother adults (Sommers-Flanagan & Sommers-Flanagan, 1997). The counselor's task is to find ways to involve the child in the counseling process, first by clarifying the counseling role.

Clarifying the counseling role.   During the initial session, counselors need to find ways to explain to the child what counseling is all about. Any delay in getting to the reason for counseling can cause undue anxiety for children (Muro & Kottman, 1995). After introducing myself, I (DN) try to find out why children think they are meeting with me. Although some children have had past experiences in counseling, many have not. Some of the responses children have given me include, "My mom said you are a doctor, but I'm not sick," "It's because I get mad too much," and the most frequent answer, "I don't know!" A short explanation of the counseling role can help establish structure, set expectations, and initiate the development of a collaborative therapeutic relationship. A counselor might say something like, "My job is to help children with lots of different things. Sometimes people have uncomfortable feelings they want to talk about. Other people might want help figuring out a problem. I wonder what I might be able to help you with?"

Many times, parents or caregivers are included in the initial sessions with children. When this is the case, it is helpful to clarify the counseling role with everyone involved. It is especially important to dissipate any misconceptions about the purpose of counseling, such as beliefs that counseling will "fix" the child. It also is wise to let parents know that things may get worse before they get better. Depending on the child's age, it may be helpful to meet with everyone together at the outset and then meet separately with the child and the caregiver.

Explaining confidentiality.   Issues related to confidentiality can create challenging legal and ethical dilemmas for counselors who work with minors (Lawrence & Robinson Kurpius, 2000). As discussed in Chapter 3, the assurance of confidentiality is fundamental to the counseling process. Counselors have a responsibility to protect information received through confidential counseling relationships with all clients, including children. However, this responsibility often conflicts with legal rights of parents or guardians, which include the right to determine the need for counseling, the right to access pertinent information about their children's treatment, and the right to control the release of information that results from counseling (Glosoff, 2001). It is important to clarify with parents and their children the conditions and limits of confidentiality before counseling begins. Ethical and legal guidelines related to confidentiality and other topics pertinent to counseling with minors are presented in Figure 12–3.

Box 12–1
Suggestions for Counselors Working With Minors

- Practice within the limits of your abilities, based on education, training, and supervised practice.
- Be thoroughly familiar with state statutes regarding privilege, informed consent, and child abuse reporting.
- Clarify policies regarding confidentiality with the child and the parents before beginning counseling. Ask everyone to sign a written statement of these policies.
- If you work with a minor without the parent's informed consent, ask the minor to provide informed assent in writing. Be aware of potential legal risks.
- Keep accurate and objective records of all counseling sessions, decisions, and interactions.
- Maintain adequate professional liability coverage.
- When in doubt, confer with other professionals and have legal assistance available.

—Lawrence and Robinson Kurpius, 2000

In many cases, it is in the child's best interest to involve the parents in the counseling process. Taylor and Adelman (2001) maintain that keeping information from parents can impede the counselor's efforts to help the child. They recommend orienting the parents to the counseling process, educating them about confidentiality with minors, and letting them know that any vital information that affects their child's well-being will be shared. By orienting parents in this way, they are more likely to support the process and respect their child's right to privacy (Welfel, 2002).

The way a counselor approaches the issue of confidentiality with children depends on their age. Young children typically do not have an understanding of confidentiality or the need for it (Remley & Herlihy, 2001). It is important to explain the

Professional Competence: The American Counseling Association (1995) *Code of Ethics* mandates that counselors practice only within their bounds of competence, based on education, training, supervised practice, and appropriate experience (ACA, 1995, C.2.a). Knowledge and skills needed to work effectively with minor clients differ from those needed to work with adult clients. Counselors who work with children need to be trained in child development and child counseling theory, as well as have an understanding of child psychopathology.

Informed Consent: Informed consent is "the formal permission given by a client that signals the beginning of the legal contractual agreement that allows treatment to be initiated" (Lawrence & Robinson Kurpius, 2000, p. 133). Legally, minor clients cannot enter into contracts. The ACA Code (1995) states that when minors or other individuals cannot give voluntary, informed consent, parents or guardians should be included in the counseling process (B.3). Ideally, if clients are minors, counselors should obtain signed informed *consent* from the parent(s) and *assent* from the minor client (Glosoff, 2001).

There are some instances in which minor clients can enter into treatment without parental consent, although the exceptions differ from state to state, depending on legal statutes. Typical exceptions include:

- Mature or emancipated minors: A mature minor is usually over the age of 16 (in some states, 14) and is capable of understanding the nature and consequences of agreeing to a proposed treatment. An emancipated minor is a child under the age of 18 who lives separately from parents or guardians and manages his or her own financial affairs (American Bar Association, 1980).
- In some states, parental informed consent may not be required when the minor is in treatment for drugs or narcotics, for sexually transmitted diseases, for pregnancy and birth control counseling, or when waiting for parental consent would endanger the minor client's life or health.

Confidentiality: Counselors have the *ethical* obligation to protect minor clients' privacy. However, parents and guardians have the *legal* right to determine the need for treatment and the right to access pertinent information about their child's treatment. At times, ethical dilemmas arise trying to balance legal requirements and ethical responsibilities. Because state laws differ, counselors need to be familiar with the legal requirements of the state in which they practice. Counselors can motivate minor clients to disclose on their own when such disclosures would be beneficial and can involve the parents in creating mutually agreed on guidelines for disclosure (Lawrence & Robinson Kurpius, 2000).

Counselors need to discuss confidentiality and its limits with the parents and the child before counseling begins. Minor clients need to know that if they make a threat to hurt themselves or others, the counselor will be required to breach confidentiality. In some instances, duty to warn also applies to threats to destroy property (e.g., *Peck v. Counseling Service of Addison County,* 1985).

Figure 12–3
Legal and ethical issues related to counseling minors
From Glosoff, 2001; Lawrence and Robinson Kurpius, 2000; and Remley and Herlihy, 2001.

> **Reporting Abuse**:   All states have statutes requiring counselors and other profes-
> sionals to report suspected child abuse and neglect (Kemp, 1998). Counselors are
> advised to become familiar with the wording of the statute for their particular state.
> In general, statutes require counselors to report if they have reason to believe that
> (a) a child is currently being abused or neglected, or (b) the child has been abused
> or neglected in the past. Requirements for reporting past abuse differ when the
> child is no longer in danger. Reporters are protected from liability as long as reports
> are made in good faith. When making the decision to report, it may be helpful to
> consult with professional colleagues or to gain legal advice. As with other counsel-
> ing decisions, it is important to document the report and the reasons for making it.

Figure 12–3   *continued*

concept in words the child can understand. Therefore, the counselor might say,
"Most of the things you and I talk about in here are between you and me, unless you
tell me that you are planning to hurt yourself or someone else. If you tell me something that I think your mom (dad, other caregiver) needs to know, you and I will talk·
about it first" (Newsome & Gladding, 2003, p. 216).

Adolescents often have a heightened concern about privacy and confidentiality
in the counseling relationship. Sommers-Flanagan and Sommers-Flanagan (1997)
emphasize the importance of making sure that teenagers understand the counselor's explanation about how privacy will be maintained. It may be helpful to present confidentiality information in a modified or even humorous manner, as in the
following illustration:

> So if you're planning on doing something dangerous or destructive, such as dissecting
> your science teacher, it's likely that we'll need to have a meeting with your parents or
> school officials to talk that over, and it's the law that I would need to warn your science
> teacher. But day to day stuff that you're trying to sort out, stuff that's bugging you—even
> if it's stuff about your parents or teachers or whoever—we can keep that private. (p. 40)

It is not unusual for community counselors to encounter dilemmas related to
the requirements of confidentiality and the counselor's responsibilities to parents or
other caregivers. By keeping the lines of communication open and taking responsibility for knowing state and federal law, it may be possible to circumvent potential
problems before they arise (Freeman, 2000).

Assessment and Evaluation

Assessment is an integral part of the counseling process. As described in Chapter 6,
assessment is an ongoing process in which counselors gather information about
clients from several different sources and then use that information to make decisions about treatment planning. Assessment also provides a way to evaluate counseling progress and outcomes. Assessment methods, which can be formal or informal,
help counselors understand children's current problems or concerns within the context of their unique developmental histories.

Interviews.   Initial assessment typically begins with an intake that involves the child and the child's parents or guardians. The amount of time spent with everyone together versus time spent with each individual depends on the age of the child, the nature of the problem, the family dynamics, and agency policy. During the intake session, the types of rapport-building activities described earlier can be used to gather important information about the child. In many agencies, intake forms are available for use with children and families.

Early and ongoing assessment is necessary for accurate case conceptualization and effective intervention planning. Orton (1997) suggests conducting a complete developmental assessment that provides counselors with the following information:

- **The Specific Concerns That Brought the Child to Counseling**. The manifestation, intensity, frequency, and duration of the concerns should be explored. In what settings or around which individuals are the concerns evidenced? Expression, manifestation, and course of a disorder in children may be quite different from adults (Surgeon General Report, 2000). Certain behaviors may be normal at one age but represent a problem at another age (e.g., temper tantrums exhibited by a 3-year-old child versus tantrums exhibited by a 6-year-old child). Assessment, diagnosis, and treatment planning need to occur within the context of the child's overall development (Orton, 1997).

- **Physical, Cognitive, Emotional, and Social Development**. Evaluating each of these areas of development is essential to conducting a thorough assessment. Counselors will want to obtain information about the child's medical history, perinatal history, motor development, cognitive functioning, and ability to express and regulate emotions. They also will want to gather information about socioeconomic and sociocultural factors that have affected development. To facilitate information gathering, counselors can ask parents or guardians to complete an information form, which includes questions about the child's physical, cognitive, emotional, and social development, prior to or immediately following the initial counseling session (Orton, 1997). The counselor can use the form to guide exploration of any areas that may be contributing to the problem.

- **Relationships Between the Child and His or Her Parents, Siblings, and Peers**. Understanding the nature and quality of relationships the child has with family members and peers is a key component of child assessment. Topics to be addressed include the child's living arrangements, home responsibilities, parental methods of discipline, the child's response to discipline, and typical family activities (Orton, 1997). Interview questions or qualitative assessment methods such as the genogram or the Kinetic Family Drawing can provide rich information about relationships, as can ongoing observation of interactions as the counselor works with the child and the family.

- **The Child's School Experiences, Including Academics, Attendance, and Attitude**. Academic and social successes or failures play an important part in children's overall development. Children who experience repeated failures often have poor self-esteem and may engage in disruptive behaviors as a way of compensating (Orton, 1997). Also, school failure may signify a learning disorder that typically requires formal testing for diagnosis. Because of the pervasive effect school has on children's lives, it is advisable to ask parents to sign a consent form for release of information so that the school can be contacted early in the counseling process.

- **The Child's Strengths, Talents, and Support System.** Implementing a strengths-based approach to assessment can help take the focus off the problem so that it is possible to begin moving toward solutions. Creative activities, checklists, and various qualitative assessment methods provide useful tools for evaluating strengths and supports. After learning about children's special skills and interests, counselors can incorporate them into treatment planning. For example, if a child enjoys art, the counselor can select expressive art interventions to facilitate the change process.

Informal and formal assessment.   Informal assessment includes direct observation and qualitative assessment methods. As discussed in Chapter 6, qualitative assessment emphasizes holistic procedures that typically are not standardized and do not produce quantitative raw scores (Goldman, 1990). A variety of qualitative assessment methods can be used with children and adolescents, including informal checklists, unfinished sentences, decision-making dilemmas, writing activities, games, expressive arts, storytelling, role-play activities, and play therapy strategies (Vernon, 1993, 1999). Informal assessment procedures of this nature can reveal patterns of thoughts and behaviors relevant to concerns and issues. Such methods are especially helpful with young children, who may not know exactly what is bothering them or lack the words to express their concerns verbally (Orton, 1997).

Formal assessment instruments that have been standardized and have sound psychometric properties provide a way for counselors to gain a somewhat more objective view of children's behaviors or attributes than do informal methods of assessment (Orton, 1997). Whereas some instruments are designed to assess specific disorders (e.g., the *Children's Depression Inventory,* Kovacs, 1992), others assess a full range of behavioral and emotional symptoms and disorders (e.g., the *Achenbach Child Behavior Checklist* and *Teacher Report Form,* Achenbach, 1991). A number of questionnaires, scales, and checklists designed to assess attributes, behaviors, interests, and emotional states of children and adolescents have been published in recent years. To learn about different options, counselors can refer to resources such as the *Mental Measurements Yearbook,* published by the Buros Institute, which provides descriptions and reviews of a wide range of published instruments. Carefully selected formal assessment tools can supplement and enhance the information counselors gather through less formal methods of assessment.

By appraising counseling needs through interviews, informal assessment, and formal assessment, the counselor gains a better understanding of the child's development and concerns. This understanding can then be used to set goals, design and implement interventions, and evaluate the counseling process (Orton, 1997; Whiston, 2000). As with adults, the information gained through assessment sometimes leads to a diagnosis, using an established diagnostic classification system, such as the *Diagnostic and Statistical Manual of Mental Disorders* (*DSM-IV-TR,* American Psychiatric Association [APA], 2000) (see Chapter 6). However, the criteria for diagnosing many mental disorders in children are derived from adult criteria, and less research has been conducted on children to verify their validity (Surgeon General

Report, 2000). Consequently, diagnosing childhood mental disorders is a challenging task and requires training and supervision.

Designing and Implementing a Treatment Plan

Several factors affect treatment planning for child and adolescent clients. The age and characteristics of the child; the nature of the presenting issue; and the counselor's theoretical approach, past training, and current skills all influence the selection of interventions. Competent counselors take each of these factors into consideration. If they realize that the presenting issue is out of their bounds of competence, they take steps to match the child with a counselor who is prepared to work with the issue.

Intentionality and flexibility.   Counselors who work with children and adolescents need to be intentional and flexible as they conceptualize cases and design interventions (Newsome & Gladding, 2003). Being intentional refers to taking steps to set counseling goals collaboratively with the child and, in many cases, the child's parents or caregivers. Being flexible refers to the counselor's ability to adapt strategies to meet the specific needs of the child in his or her context. No single counseling approach is best for all children or all problems. Counselors who are familiar with a wide array of interventions and child-based counseling strategies can personalize the treatment plan so that the possibility of a positive outcome is enhanced.

One way counselors can intentionally plan interventions is by asking specific questions related to the following areas (Vernon, 1993):

a. *Vision.* What could be different? How could things be better? What would be ideal?
b. *Goal Setting.* What is going well? What needs to be worked on?
c. *Analysis.* What is enabling or interfering with achieving these goals? What is getting in the way of solving the problem?
d. *Objective.* What specifically does the child want to change?
e. *Exploration of Interventions.* What has already been tried, and how did it work? Who else will be involved in the counseling process? What types of activities does the child respond to best? What has research shown to be the most effective interventions for this type of concern?

Selecting interventions.   Using information gathered through assessment and goal setting, counselors can begin making decisions about which intervention to implement. No one theoretical approach to counseling children and adolescents has been found to be generally more effective than another (Bergin, 1999; Sexton, Whiston, Bleuer, & Walz, 1997). Instead, a systematic, eclectic approach enables counselors to work constructively with the many different needs and concerns that bring young people to counseling.

Although outcome-based research has been conducted less with children than with adults, a body of information is beginning to accumulate matching efficacious interventions with specific concerns and needs. Consequently, counselors will want to be familiar with current research on efficacious treatment when selecting interventions. For example, an empirically supported approach to providing treatment for children with attention-deficit/hyperactivity disorder (ADHD) is a multimodal, multisystemic approach that involves parent training, counseling, and school interventions (Edwards, 2002). For adolescents with conduct disorder, a promising treatment is multisystemic therapy (MST), an intensive home- and family-focused treatment (Surgeon General Report, 2000). MST integrates empirically based treatment approaches such as cognitive skills training into an ecological framework that addresses the family, peer, school, and community context (Schoenwald, Brown, & Henggeler, 2000). Other examples of efficacious treatments include play or art therapy for sexually abused children and cognitive–behavioral approaches for children who are depressed or anxious. It is the counselor's responsibility to keep up with current research so as to provide the best possible care for their young clients.

Creative Interventions

Using expressive arts with children and families.   Counseling young people effectively often requires a departure from traditional talk therapy. In many cases, an integrative approach that uses a variety of techniques, including art, music, clay, puppetry, storytelling, drama, bibliotherapy, sand play, and other forms of directive and nondirective play therapy can guide the counseling process and promote healing and growth. Counselors who work with children are encouraged to refer to the many excellent resources that are available so as to enhance their expertise in using play and expressive arts in counseling.

Box 12–2

Expressive arts have been a part of my counseling since I began working as a counselor. I have worked with different ages and in different settings, and I have found that expressive arts easily transfer everywhere. My clients quickly come to understand that I may ask them to draw, paint, string beads, tell stories, act things out, or play, in addition to traditional talking. I may initially encounter surprise, disbelief, reluctance, or fear, but I have yet to be turned down.

What I have found by using creative arts is that my clients relax, have a sense of playfulness, and open up more quickly. I have used creative arts to draw out depressed clients who are locked up in their despair; gain trust with a mistrustful child; help a family learn to positively interact with one another; give an adolescent a chance to express herself in new ways; calm an anxious parent; and join a group together. The possibilities are only as limited as my mind. When I encounter my own limitations, I ask my clients for options. They often come up with the most creative ideas.

There are also personal advantages for me in using expressive arts as a counselor. I find my sessions to be exciting and packed with energy. I look forward to helping people find new ways to express themselves. As a counselor, I feel it is important to be myself. Being creative is a natural part of who I am. Using expressive arts in counseling is a perfect match for me.

—Elizabeth Vaughan, M.A.Ed., LPC, Community Counselor

CONCERNS AFFECTING CHILDREN AND ADOLESCENTS

Community counselors who work with children and adolescents are likely to see a wide range of presenting problems, including mood disorders, anxiety disorders, attention-deficit/hyperactivity disorder (ADHD), aggressive or antisocial behaviors, learning disorders, and eating disorders. They also are likely to work with young people coping with family disruption, abuse, violence, unemployment, and grief. In this section, we provide an overview of three disorders that may be experienced by young people: depression, eating disorders, and ADHD. We also describe three common concerns associated with childhood and adolescence: parental divorce, death of a loved one, and child maltreatment. Other childhood disorders and concerns are listed in Appendix B. To work effectively with the many issues that affect children and adolescents, counselors need to consult resources that deal specifically with children's mental health issues and participate in additional educational experiences, training, and supervision.

Depression[1]

Depression is a mood disorder that can affect thoughts, feelings, behaviors, and overall health (National Institute of Mental Health, 2002). It can impact relationships, academic performance, sleeping, appetite, self-esteem, and thought processes. The onset of major depressive disorders typically is between the ages of 13 and 19, with depression being one of the most common psychological problems of adolescence (Birmaher, Ryan, & Williamson, 1996). Unless treated, early onset of depression can predict more severe and negative symptoms later in life. Untreated mood disorders also increase the risk of suicide, particularly during the adolescent years (Surgeon General Report, 2000).

Manifestation of depression.   Levels of depression in young people can vary, ranging from depressed mood, which is not a clinical disorder, to more severe diagnosable mood disorders. Approximately one third of adolescents experience depressed mood for short or extended periods of time. Depressed mood is characterized by negative emotions, which may include sadness, anxiety, guilt, disgust, anger, and fear (Petersen, Compas, & Brooks-Gunn, 1992).

For depression to be considered a clinical disorder, a collection of symptoms must be evidenced that meet specific diagnostic criteria according to standardized classification systems, such as the DSM-IV-TR, (APA, 2000). Diagnosis is based on the intensity and duration of a set of symptoms serious enough to interfere with one's level of functioning. Examples of depressive disorders include major depressive disorder, dysthymic disorder, adjustment disorder with depressed mood, bipolar disorder, cyclothymic disorder, and mood disorder due to medical condition or substance

---

[1]Portions of this section were taken from the chapter, *Helping Students With Depression,* written by Debbie Newsome, which is in the book, *Handbook of Professional School Counseling,* edited by B. T. Erford (in press). Adapted with permission of ERIC/CASS.

abuse. In this section, the focus is on symptoms and interventions associated with major depression, dysthymia, and adjustment disorder with depressed mood.

Identifying depression in young people may be challenging because the symptoms are often masked. Although the key defining features of major depressive disorder are the same for youth as for adults, it may be difficult for them to identify or describe their feelings (NIMH, 2000). Instead, depressed children and adolescents may appear irritable, act out, or withdraw from family and friends. They also may display more anxiety symptoms and somatic complaints. A list of common signs and symptoms of depression in young people is presented in Figure 12–4.

Some two thirds of children and adolescents with clinical depression also have another clinical disorder (Surgeon General Report, 2000). The most commonly associated disorders include anxiety disorders, disruptive disorders, eating disorders, substance abuse, and personality disorders. When a young person has more than one disorder, depression is more likely to begin after the onset of the other disorder, with the exception of substance abuse. Counselors will want to be alert to the possibility of dual or multiple diagnoses and be prepared to plan interventions accordingly.

Etiology and risk factors.   Several factors are associated with the etiology of depression, including biological, cognitive, and environmental variables. Biological

Figure 12–4
*Signs and symptoms of depression
in children and adolescents*
From NIMH, 2000; and Rice and
Leffert, 1997

- Feeling sad, empty, or hopeless
- Increased emotional sensitivity
- Lack of interest or ability to engage in pleasurable activities
- Decreased energy level
- Physical complaints (headaches, stomachaches, tiredness)
- Frequent absences from school (or poor performance)
- Outbursts (shouting, complaining, crying)
- Being bored
- Substance abuse
- Fear of death
- Suicide ideation
- Sleep/appetite disturbances
- Reduced ability to think clearly and make decisions
- Increased irritability, anger, or restlessness
- Failure to make expected weight gains
- Reckless behavior
- Difficulty with relationships

explanations focus on the role of genetics and biochemical factors associated with depression. Genetics appear to make individuals more vulnerable to depression and other disorders, with children of depressed parents being three times more likely than other children to experience at least one major depressive episode (Garber & Robinson, 1997). Also, biochemical factors involving the neurotransmission of certain brain chemicals, including serotonin and norepinephrine, have been linked with depression. In some cases, antidepressant medications are prescribed to help with neurotransmission difficulties and bring about relief from depressive symptoms. The class of medications known as selective serotonin reuptake inhibitors (SSRIs) may be recommended when a young person suffers with a type of depression that does not respond well to counseling interventions alone (McWhirter & Burrow, 2001).

Cognitive models of depression (e.g., Beck, 1976) demonstrate the link between an individual's thoughts and his or her emotions and behaviors. According to cognitive theory, people's interpretations of events, rather than the events themselves, trigger emotional upsets and mood disturbances. These interpretations affect the way a person views self, the world, and the future. Depressed children tend to foster inaccurate and negative perceptions, which may be characterized by negative attributional styles or cognitive distortions (Asarnow, Jaycox, & Tompson, 2001; Kendall, 2000). Counselors can help depressed children learn to correct faulty perceptions and process information more accurately.

Other explanations of depression emphasize the role played by stressful life events. Youth who experience numerous stressors may be more likely to experience depression than those who do not. Stressors can be categorized as normative life events (expected changes, such as school entry and puberty), nonnormative events (divorce, abuse, moving away), and daily hassles (conflict with friends, excessive schoolwork). Exposure to stress triggers several physical, emotional, and cognitive changes in the body, and long-term exposure can lead to physical and psychosocial difficulties, including depression (Sharrer & Ryan-Wenger, 2002). The manner in which stress is experienced varies greatly from child to child. Preventive strategies, such as teaching constructive coping skills, can help children manage stress more effectively.

Other risk factors.   A number of other factors have been linked with depression, including family conflict, the emotional unavailability of parents, poor peer relationships, being considered "different," loss of a loved one, breakup of a relationship, chronic illness, and abuse (NIMH, 2000; Rice & Leffert, 1997). A thorough developmental assessment can alert counselors to the presence of conditions that might make children more vulnerable to depression and thus can inform treatment planning.

Treatment strategies.   Counselors who work with depressed young people typically involve both the individual and the family (McWhirter & Burrow, 2001). In some settings, counselors conduct group interventions, which can be especially effective with older children and adolescents.

Research has demonstrated the efficacy of certain approaches, especially cognitive–behavioral therapy, in alleviating depressive symptoms in young people (NIMH, 2000; Reinecke, Ryan, & DuBois, 1998). The goal of CBT is to help clients develop cognitive structures that will positively influence their future experiences (Kendall, 2000). The cognitive component of CBT helps individuals identify and change negative, pessimistic thinking, biases, and attributions. Examples of cognitive based strategies include:

1. Recognizing the connections among thoughts, feelings, and behaviors
2. Monitoring negative automatic thoughts
3. Examining evidence that refutes distorted automatic cognitions
4. Substituting more realistic interpretations for distorted cognitions
5. Regulating emotions and controlling impulses (McWhirter & Burrow, 2001, pp. 201–202)

When young people are depressed, they often withdraw from activities and interactions with others. Withdrawing from peers and family members and avoiding activities that formerly were pleasurable can exacerbate feelings of depression and loneliness. Behavioral strategies, which are a key part of the CBT model, can include helping children identify pleasurable activities and then make commitments to participate in those activities between sessions (Stark & Kendall, 1996). Other behavioral strategies include relaxation training, social skills training, and behavioral rehearsal (McWhirter & Burrow, 2001).

A cognitively based approach may be less effective with younger children because higher order thinking skills may not have developed yet (McWhirter & Burrow, 2001). When working with young children, counselors can use play therapy, games, and expressive arts to help them learn to identify feelings and cope more effectively with negative emotions. Behavioral strategies developed in conjunction with parents can help ensure that children remain engaged in pleasurable activities and find healthy ways to regulate negative emotions.

Another individual counseling approach that is used to treat depression in young people is interpersonal psychotherapy for adolescents (IPT-A). IPT-A is a brief, time-limited treatment that was originally developed for adults and then modified to meet the specific developmental and interpersonal needs of depressed adolescents (Mufson, Moreau, Weissman, & Klerman, 1993). Depression is viewed as a conflict taking place in the context of interpersonal relationships (Mufson & Fairbanks, 1996). Two primary goals of IPT are to reduce depressive symptoms and improve disturbed relationships that may contribute to depression. In treatment, five potential areas of concern are addressed: grief, interpersonal role disputes, role transitions, deficits in interpersonal skills, and single-parent families.

Research on the efficacy of IPT-A, while still in its beginning stages, has been promising (Mellin & Beamish, 2002). Although additional research is needed to establish its efficacy, IPT-A is an approach that has demonstrated encouraging results; consequently, counselors who work with adolescents may want to pursue training in that area.

Family interventions.   Concurrent family consultation or family counseling is nearly always indicated when working with depressed children and adolescents (McWhirter & Burrow, 2001). Frequently, counselors need to consult with parents to educate them about depression and help them learn ways to encourage their child's use of new skills (Stark, Sander, Yoncy, Bronik, & Hoke, 2000). At times, family counseling is required to make systemic changes that are contributing to the child's depression. Significant goals may include developing communication skills, enhancing family interactions, and sharing information about specific issues.

Child and adolescent depression is a serious but treatable condition that has received considerable attention during the past 3 decades. Early identification and treatment of depression can help alleviate symptoms and put young people on a healthy developmental trajectory. Through individual, group, and family counseling, community counselors can help depressed youth address dysfunctional cognitive processes, learn strategies for dealing with interpersonal concerns, and develop skills for coping with stress and negative emotions.

Eating Disorders

Eating disorders often appear for the first time in pre- or early adolescence or during the transition to young adulthood. Eating disorders involve serious disturbances in eating behaviors (e.g., unhealthy reduction of body weight or severe overeating) as well as feelings of distress or excessive concern about body shape or weight (NIMH, 2001). A struggle with unmet needs appears to be at the core of destructive eating behaviors (McClure & Teyber, 2003). Girls and young women tend to exhibit eating problems at a much higher frequency than do boys or young men, although the prevalence rate in males has increased in recent years (Kalodner & Van Lone, 2001). Also, although eating disorders have been more frequently associated with young, affluent, white females, it appears that disorders exist among various ethnic and cultural minority groups (Kalodner & Van Lone). Counselors need to be aware of early warning signs in all populations so that preventive interventions can be implemented when necessary.

Types of eating disorders.   The two main types of eating disorders are anorexia nervosa and bulimia nervosa. Anorexia typically arises during the transition to adolescence, whereas bulimia is more likely to develop during the transition to young adulthood (Attie & Brooks-Gunn, 1995). A third category, eating disorders not otherwise specified, includes people with eating problems that do not fit the criteria for the other two diagnoses. Eating problems that fall into this third category are much more prevalent than are anorexia and bulimia.

Individuals with anorexia nervosa weigh less than 85 percent of what is considered normal for their age and height (APA, 2000). They have a resistance to maintaining minimally normal weight, an intense fear of gaining weight or becoming fat, and a distorted view of their own bodies and weight. Youth with anorexia often stop (or fail to start) menstruating. Unusual eating habits develop, such as avoiding food, picking out only a few foods and eating them in small quantities, or weighing food servings. Whereas some young people with anorexia severely restrict eating, others engage in compulsive exercise or purge by means of vomiting or use of laxatives. Youth with anorexia tend to deny that they have a problem, making treatment difficult.

Bulimia nervosa is characterized by recurrent episodes of binge eating, typically twice a week or more, followed by attempts at compensating by purging or exercising (APA, 2000). Binge eating is defined by excessive, rapid overeating, often to the point of becoming uncomfortably full. An episode of binge eating is usually accompanied by a sense of lack of control, as well as by feelings of disgust, depression, or guilt (Kalodner & Van Lone, 2001). Subsequently, the individual engages in activities to compensate for overeating: vomiting or laxative use for the purging type of bulimia and excessive exercise or fasting for the nonpurging type. Youth with bulimia do not meet the severe underweight criterion associated with anorexia; indeed, they may appear to be within the normal weight range for their age and height. However, they are dissatisfied with their bodies and desire to lose weight or fear gaining weight.

Youth with eating disorders tend to be high achievers and sensitive to rejection. Often, other psychological issues are concurrent with the eating problems, including depression, anxiety disorders, personality disorders, and substance abuse (McClure & Teyber, 2003). To make sure that these issues are addressed in treatment, clinicians need to conduct a thorough developmental assessment.

A number of physical complications are associated with eating disorders. In anorexia, the physical problems are related to malnutrition and starvation. Common physical symptoms include fatigue, cold intolerance, and abdominal pain. In more severe cases, major organ systems in the body are affected. The mortality rate associated with anorexia is 10 percent: higher than almost any other psychiatric problem (APA, 2000). In bulimia, the medical complications are due to vomiting or the use of laxatives or diuretics and can include dental problems, esophageal inflammation, and metabolic imbalances.

Etiology and risk factors.   An interplay of biological, psychological, and sociocultural factors are thought to contribute to the development of disordered eating. As stated earlier, anorexia often arises during the transition to adolescence, when young people are undergoing intense physical and psychological changes. During this time, the chief developmental task is identity formation—a task that can be perceived as extremely challenging. Peer pressure, puberty, self-esteem issues, and societal messages that glorify thinness may all coalesce to trigger problematic eating patterns in young people. Some of the factors that appear to be linked to eating disorders include:

- The continuing media promotion of thinness as healthy and a sign of success
- Perfectionism
- Highly competitive environments that stress body thinness and high performance
- Experiences of loss in personal relationships (e.g., family breakups or death)
- A low sense of self-esteem
- Heightened concern for appearance and body shape during adjustment to the changes associated with puberty (Manley, Rickson, & Standeven, 2000, p. 228)

As stated earlier, eating disorders often reflect struggles with unmet needs, including the need to be loved, cared for, and respected. Eating problems may stem from an individual's desire to be perfect, compliant, or highly regarded. Regulating food intake may represent a way to exert control and meet those needs. People with eating disorders often have difficulty acknowledging and expressing feelings, and in some cases, disordered eating becomes a means of coping with feelings that are painful (McClure & Teyber, 2003).

Family theorists describe eating disorders as symptoms of family dysfunction (e.g., Minuchin, Rosman, & Baker, 1978; Schwartz, Barrett, & Saba, 1984). Family characteristics associated with anorexia in young people include enmeshment, overprotectiveness, and rigidity. Boundaries are not well established, and the child may feel unable to individuate. Such families also do not tolerate conflict or disagreement well and may avoid topics that are controversial. Consequently, family therapy is the preferred treatment for adolescents who live at home (Kalodner & Von Lone, 2001).

Treatment strategies.   When eating disorders are treated early, positive outcomes are more likely (NIMH, 2001). A comprehensive treatment plan is required that involves medical care and monitoring, counseling, nutritional consultation, and, at times, medication management. In some cases, when body weight is dangerously low, hospitalization is required. Treatment involves a team process, with the counselor working closely with the young person's physician and nutritionist. Counseling can take place individually, with families, in groups, or in some combination of the three methods.

To treat anorexia, the National Institute of Mental Health (2001) recommends three phases:

1. Restoring weight lost to dieting and purging
2. Treating psychological disturbances, including body image distortion, self-esteem issues, and interpersonal conflicts
3. Achieving long-term remission and rehabilitation, or full recovery. This includes promoting healthy eating attitudes, behaviors, and activity levels (Goldner & Birmingham, 1994).

Families are often included in the counseling process. Often, family members are distressed about the issue of low weight and food refusal. The responsibility to gain weight needs to be put on the individual with anorexia. To help, family members can be encouraged to allow the young person to eat foods that he or she selects (Kalodner & Van Lone, 2001).

For bulimia, the primary treatment goal is to reduce or eliminate binge eating and purging behaviors (NIMH, 2001). Nutritional rehabilitation and psychosocial intervention can be used to help the young person develop healthier patterns of thinking, feeling, and behaving. The counselor works collaboratively with the client to:

1. Establish a pattern of regular, nonbinge meals
2. Improve attitudes related to the eating disorder
3. Encourage healthy but not excessive exercise
4. Alleviate co-occurring conditions such as mood or anxiety disorders

Cognitive–behavioral approaches, interpersonal psychotherapy, and group counseling that uses a cognitive–behavioral approach can be used effectively to help young people with bulimia. At times, medications such as the selective serotonin reuptake inhibitors (SSRIs) have been helpful, particularly when anxiety or depression are involved (NIMH, 2001).

Young clients with eating disorders usually enter treatment reluctantly, denying the extent of their problems and reluctant to give up their primary method of coping. The counseling process can be challenging, as the counselor helps the young person accept the reality of the problem, feel accepted, and develop new, more flexible ways of coping with feelings and relating to others. Counselors who work with young people with eating disorders need to participate in training and supervision to ensure that they are providing the most efficacious treatment.

Attention-Deficit/Hyperactivity Disorder

Attention-deficit/hyperactivity disorder (ADHD), the most common neurologically based disorder of childhood, can influence children's emotional, behavioral, and social adjustment. Between 40 and 50 percent of referrals to child health care professionals are due to suspected ADHD (Barkley, 1998; Cantwell, 1996), making it essential for community counselors to be aware of diagnostic criteria and treatment procedures. ADHD typically first appears in early childhood, with children exhibiting symptoms of inattention, impulsivity, and hyperactivity (APA, 2000). An estimated 3 to 7 percent of school-age children have the disorder, with boys diagnosed more frequently than girls. (Ratios vary from $2:1$ to $9:1$, depending on the subtype.) Fifty to 80 percent of children with ADHD will continue to have symptoms of the disorder through adolescence, and many will carry the symptoms into adulthood (Barkley, 1996).

The *Diagnostic and Statistical Manual of Mental Disorders* has changed its description and definition of ADHD over the years, thereby creating some confusion about the name and nature of the disorder (McClure & Teyber, 2003). Initially referred to in the DSM-II as *hyperkinetic reaction of childhood,* the name was changed to *attention deficit disorder* (ADD) in the DSM-III and then to ADHD in the DSM-III-R, with undifferentiated ADD listed as a separate category. In the current DSM, the disorder is generally classified as *attention-deficit/hyperactivity disorder* (ADHD) with three subtypes: predominantly inattentive, predominantly hyperactive–impulsive, or a combination of both symptoms (APA, 2000).

The two symptom clusters used to diagnose ADHD are the *inattention cluster* and the *hyperactivity–impulsivity cluster* (Figure 12–5). A child must exhibit at least six of the nine behaviors in the cluster to be considered significantly inattentive or hyperactive (APA, 2000; Brown, 2000). Children with the combined subtype of ADHD, which is the most common presentation, exhibit six or more symptoms in both categories. For all subtypes, symptoms must be evidenced for at least 6 months in two or more settings, with some of the symptoms present before the age of 7 years (APA, 2000).

Children with ADHD are thought to have an underdeveloped inhibition of behavior, thus making it a disorder of impulse control (Barkley, 1997). They typically have difficulty staying on task for more than a few minutes, are disorganized, and

Inattentive Type

Six (or more) of the following symptoms of **inattention** have persisted for at least 6 months to a degree that is maladaptive and inconsistent with developmental level:

a) often fails to give close attention to details or makes careless mistakes in schoolwork, work, or other activities
b) often has difficulty sustaining attention in tasks or play activities
c) often does not seem to listen when spoken to directly
d) often does not follow through on instructions and fails to finish schoolwork, chores, or duties in the workplace (not due to oppositional behavior or failure to understand instructions)
e) often has difficulty organizing tasks and activities
f) often avoids, dislikes, or is reluctant to engage in tasks that require sustained mental effort (such as schoolwork or homework)
g) often loses things necessary for tasks or activities (e.g., toys, school assignments, pencils, books, or tools)
h) is often easily distracted by extraneous stimuli
i) is often forgetful in daily activities

Hyperactive-impulsive type

Six (or more) of the following symptoms of **hyperactivity-impulsivity** have persisted for at least 6 months to a degree that is maladaptive and inconsistent with developmental level:

Hyperactivity

a) often fidgets with hands or feet or squirms in seat
b) often leaves seat in classroom or in other situations in which remaining seated is expected
c) often runs about or climbs excessively in situations in which it is inappropriate (in adolescents or adults, may be limited to subjective feelings of restlessness)
d) often has difficulty playing or engaging in leisure activities quietly
e) is often "on the go" or often acts as if "driven by a motor"
f) often talks excessively

Impulsivity

a) often blurts out answers before questions have been completed
b) often has difficulty awaiting turn
c) often interrupts or intrudes on others (e.g., butts into conversations or games)

Figure 12–5
Two symptom clusters for attention-deficit/hyperactivity disorder
Source: From *Diagnostic and Statistical Manual of Mental Disorders* (4th ed., text rev., p. 92). Copyright 2000 American Psychiatric Association. Reprinted with permission.

often ignore social rules. Children who have the inattentive type have difficulty focusing (e.g., listening, following directions) and sustaining attention (staying on task, completing assignments). They frequently lose things and are forgetful. Children who have the hyperactive–impulsive type may act as though they are "always on the go." They have difficulty sitting still and taking turns. Their social skills tend to be impaired, as evidenced by excessive talking, interrupting, and blurting out answers in class (McClure & Teyber, 2003).

ADHD can create numerous difficulties for children, their families, and their teachers. Due to impaired social skills and lack of behavioral control, children with ADHD may experience peer rejection, academic difficulties, and negative family interactions. Coexisting conditions associated with ADHD include oppositional-defiant disorder, conduct disorder, anxiety or depressive symptoms, substance abuse, and learning disabilities (Brown, 2000). Careful assessment is needed to ensure that counselors "look beyond the hallmark symptoms of the disorder and consider interventions that address comorbid problems as well" (Nigg & Rappley, 2001, pp. 183–184).

Etiology and risk factors.   Despite years of research, there is still no conclusive proof of what causes ADHD (McClure & Teyber, 2003). Some of the causal factors attributed to the development of ADHD include neurological factors, hereditary, pre- and postnatal factors, and toxic influences (Brown, 2000). In particular, physical differences in brain structure and brain chemistry appear to play roles in the myriad symptoms associated with ADHD (Lyoo et al., 1996). Family factors also have been attributed to the development of ADHD; however, stressful home life does not cause ADHD. Instead, the disruptions brought about in the family as a result of the expression of ADHD symptoms can cause family stress and disorganization, which can then exacerbate the preexisting symptoms.

Treatment strategies.   A multimodal, multicomponent approach to treatment is recommended for children with ADHD (e.g., Brown, 2000; Edwards, 2002; Nigg & Rappley, 2001). Prior to treatment, a comprehensive assessment is conducted that includes a developmental history, interviews with the child and significant adults, child observation, and a medical examination by the child's physician. Typically, behavior rating scales such as the Conners' Rating Scales (Conners, 1997) or the Behavior Assessment System for Children (BASC; Reynolds & Kamphaus, 1992) are used with parents and teachers to supplement information gathered during clinical interviews. If the assessment indicates that the child has ADHD, multimodal interventions that address the child, the family, and the environment are suggested. To develop a comprehensive treatment program, the following areas should be considered:

• Behavioral interventions in the family that include parent and child education about ADHD, parent training for behavior management, and ancillary family counseling when necessary are essential to treatment (Nigg & Rappley, 2001). Helping families develop predictable daily routines, organized households, and firm but affectionate discipline can improve family functioning. Barkley (1997) has developed a comprehensive training program for parents that can be especially helpful.

- Individual and group counseling can provide a setting in which children feel understood and where issues of self-esteem and social relationships can be addressed. Although research on individual and group counseling indicates that typical counseling approaches and play therapy have not successfully remediated the core deficits of ADHD (DuPaul & Stoner, 1994), certain approaches used in conjunction with other interventions may prove helpful. Examples include *cognitive–behavioral self-regulation approaches* to help children control their behavior and *social-skills training* to help children learn to take turns, follow rules, and develop hobbies or sports activities (McClure & Teyber, 2003).

- Medication can be particularly effective in addressing the core symptoms of ADHD, although it is a controversial intervention for some educational and mental health professionals (Edwards, 2002). Medication often results in increased attentiveness and decreased impulsivity (Brown, 2000). Stimulant medications, such as methylphenidate (Ritalin), dextroamphetamine (Dexedrine), and pemoline (Cylert), are usually the first medication choices for ADHD. When children do not respond to stimulant medication, other medications such as tricyclic antidepressants, selective serotonin reuptake inhibitors, and clonidine (a hypertensive) are sometimes considered. Not all children with ADHD need medication, and the decision to use it depends on several factors. Counselors need to be up to date on the latest medication, their uses, and potential side effects as they work with the child, the family, and the prescribing physician.

- School interventions are often instigated by community counselors as they work with teachers and school counselors to coordinate the child's treatment plan (Edwards, 2002). Counselors can consult with teachers about behavior management and academic interventions. Pfiffner and Barkley (1998) have suggested a number of classroom interventions that can help children with ADHD experience school success.

- Intensive summer camp programs may benefit children with ADHD (Edwards, 2002). Such programs include sports-skill training, behavior management interventions, and opportunities for positive peer interactions.

As with any disorder, training is needed for counselors to work effectively with children that have ADHD and with their families. Counselor expertise needs to be considered as decisions are made regarding treatment. With training, community counselors can coordinate multimodal, multicomponent treatment approaches that include parent management training, counseling, school interventions, and medication.

Specific Issues of Concern

Young people in today's society are faced with a myriad of issues that can affect development and adjustment. Child abuse, drug and alcohol abuse, changing family situations, life-threatening illnesses, and the death of loved ones are just some of the many concerns that may affect children and precipitate a need for counseling. Community counselors need to be familiar with these issues, their effects on children, and potential interventions.

Children of divorce.   Postdivorce family relationships are among the most common issues seen by counselors who work with young people (McClure & Teyber, 2003). Nearly half of all first marriages end in divorce, affecting over 1 million children (Thompson & Rudolph, 2000). Research indicates that children of divorce are often confronted with a wide range of adjustment challenges. Many studies document negative consequences for children whose parents divorce, particularly in regard to psychological adjustment, academic achievement, and behavior problems (e.g., Amato, 1993; Hetherington, 1993; Zill, Morrison, & Coiro, 1993). However, there is a marked variability in children's responses to divorce, with some children adjusting well and even showing improved behavior after the breakup (Amato, 1993).

Some of the factors that influence young people's responses to divorce include their developmental level at the time of the separation, social support systems, individual resilience and coping styles, the level of parental conflict prior to and during the divorce, parenting quality after the divorce, and the degree of economic hardship experienced. There also may be gender differences in responses, with some studies indicating that boys appear to experience greater adjustment difficulties (e.g., Morrison & Cherlin, 1995; Wallerstein & Blakeslee, 1989).

Although responses vary, the initial experience of family disruption is painful for most children. Their responses to the pain tend to differ based on their developmental level. Preschoolers may feel frightened and insecure, experience nightmares, and regress to more infantile behaviors. Children between the ages of 6 and 8 may experience pervasive sadness, view the divorce as their fault, feel rejected, fear abandonment, and hold unrealistic hopes for reconciliation. Older children are more likely to feel anger and anxiety, develop psychosomatic symptoms, blame one parent or the other, and engage in troublesome behavior. Responses vary even more in adolescents than in younger children. Some adolescents feel betrayed, disengage from the family, and become depressed. Others show a positive developmental spurt and demonstrate maturity, compassion, and helpfulness toward their parents and younger siblings (McClure & Teyber, 2003).

It is important for counselors and parents to remember that adjusting to divorce takes time and requires continued efforts of patience and reassurance. During the adjustment period, children may benefit from individual or group counseling. Counselors can help children with the adjustment process by giving them opportunities to express their feelings and concerns. They also can assist children as they work through the following psychological tasks:

* Acknowledging the reality of the marital breakup
* Disengaging from parental conflict and distress and resuming typical activities
* Resolving the loss of what used to be
* Resolving anger and self-blame
* Accepting the permanence of the divorce
* Achieving realistic hope regarding the relationship. (Thompson & Rudolph, 2000; Wallerstein & Blakeslee, 1989)

Counselors may also work with the parents of children involved in divorce. Parent support groups and counselor–parent consultation can help parents cope more effectively with the changes brought about by the divorce. Counselors can encourage parents to:

- Talk with children about the divorce in a way that is developmentally appropriate, making sure that they do not consider the divorce their fault
- Plan for ways to make the child's life as stable and consistent as possible
- Arrange for regular visits from the absent parent
- Talk with children about the future. Involve them in the planning, without overwhelming them
- Avoid asking children to take on responsibilities beyond their capabilities. (Thompson & Rudolph, 2000)

Grief and loss.   At one time or another, all children are affected by death, either of a pet, a grandparent, a parent or sibling, or a friend. Accepting the reality of death as part of life is a developmental task that often needs to be facilitated in counseling.

Children may experience a range of physical and emotional responses to grief experiences. Some of the physical reactions to loss include headaches, chest pains, or stomachaches. They may experience a distortion in time or find it difficult to start new projects or begin new relationships. Some children regress to an earlier period in development, in which they felt safer. Emotional responses may vary widely, ranging from feelings of anger or guilt to those of sadness, fear, or denial of pain.

As with divorce, several factors influence children's responses to death, including their developmental level, support systems, and the manner in which the adults in their lives deal with grieving. The grief process is unique for each individual, and it is important not to assume that children in the same age group will respond in the same manner. Counselors can let children take the lead in sharing their grief experiences by requesting, "Help me find ways to help you tell me about what you feel." One of the most beneficial things a counselor can do is listen carefully to the child, trusting the child's wisdom and giving him or her unhurried time to express thoughts, feelings, and concerns.

In addition to listening carefully, the following counseling strategies can help children dealing with loss through death:

- Allow children to express their grief, talk freely, and ask questions. Play therapy, creative expression, puppetry, bibliotherapy, imagery, and letter writing are just a few of the methods that facilitate children's expression of death.
- Help the child commemorate the loss and say good-bye, perhaps through compiling a scrapbook of their loved one or memorializing the loss in some significant way.
- Work collaboratively with parents to help the child learn more about the process of death and dying. Child-appropriate books about death, which are available in most libraries, can help answer questions, stimulate conversation, and provide new understanding (Redcay, 2001).

- Help families work to reduce stress in the child's life by maintaining structure and being aware of the possibility of regression. Family counseling may be needed.
- Be aware of triggers of grief, including birthdays, holidays, and the anniversary of the death.
- Help children give themselves permission to go on with life without feeling guilty (Costa & Holliday, 1994; Thompson & Rudolph, 2000).

Child maltreatment.   Child maltreatment is a complex problem that affects large numbers of children each year (Miller-Perrin, 2001). Approximately 879,000 cases of substantiated maltreatment were documented in the year 2000, with reports of abuse to Child Protective Services agencies numbering 3 million (National Clearinghouse on Child and Neglect, 2002). Maltreatment categories and associated statistics include neglect (63 percent), physical abuse (19 percent), sexual abuse (10 percent), and psychological maltreatment (8 percent). Descriptions of each category are presented in Figure 12–6.

Every state has laws requiring professionals who work with children to report suspected child abuse or neglect to local child protective services (see Figure 12–3). Also, each state and most counties have social services agencies that provide protective services to children. Counselors who work with children need to be aware of the agencies in their region to contact in cases of suspected abuse.

Victims of child maltreatment differ in regard to their preabuse histories, the nature of the abuse experiences, family and system responses to the abuse, available social supports, and individual coping resources (Miller-Perrin, 2001). They also differ in regard to the types of symptoms displayed, with some children displaying many symptoms and others displaying few or none. Consequently, there is no single treatment approach that is appropriate or effective for all clients. Depending on the individual client's presentation, clinicians should consider treatment approaches that include the following (Miller-Perrin):

- *Managing Negative Thoughts and Feelings Associated With the Maltreatment, Including Guilt, Anxiety, Shame, Fear, and Stigmatization.* Counseling should give children opportunities to diffuse negative feelings by confronting the abuse experience within the safety of the therapeutic relationship. Older children and adolescents may be able to talk about their experience. For younger children, reenacting the experience through play or art may be helpful.
- *Providing Clarification of Cognitions and Beliefs That Might Lead to Negative Attributions.* Confronting issues of secrecy and stigmatization are important. Cognitive–behavioral approaches that help children restructure their beliefs about themselves (e.g., being "different," being at fault) can be effective. Group counseling may facilitate cognitive restructuring.
- *Reducing Problem Behavior.* Behavioral problems such as impulsivity, aggression, and sexualized behavior often need to be addressed in counseling. Parent training typically accompanies the counseling process.

Child Neglect	Physical Abuse
• Deliberate failure by a caretaker to provide a child with shelter, food, clothing, education, supervision, medical care, and other basic necessities. • Represents an ongoing pattern of inadequate care. • Physical signs and symptoms: poor hygiene, poor weight gain, inadequate medical care, dressing inadequately for weather, chronically late or absent from school, constant complaints of hunger, severe developmental lags. • Affective-behavioral signs and symptoms: low self-esteem, aggression, anger, frustration, conduct problems.	• Any act which results in a non-accidental physical injury. Such acts include punching, beating, kicking, burning, cutting, twisting limbs, or otherwise harming a child. • Often represents unreasonable and unjustified punishment to a child from a caregiver. • Physical signs and symptoms: bruises, burns, and fractures. • Affective-behavioral signs and symptoms: aggression, hopelessness, depression, low self-esteem, defiance, running away, property offenses, delinquency, substance abuse.
Sexual Abuse	Psychological Maltreatment
• Any act of a person that forces, coerces, or threatens a child to have any form of sexual contact or engage in any type of sexual activity. • Includes both touching and non-touching offenses (e.g., indecent exposure). • Physical signs and symptoms: genital bleeding, odors, eating or sleep disturbances, somatic complaints, enuresis or encopresis. • Affective-behavioral signs and symptoms: anxiety, nightmares, guilt, anger/hostility, depression, low self-esteem, sexualized behavior, aggression, regression, hyperactivity, self-injurious behavior, delinquency, running away, substance abuse.	• A pattern of behavior that can seriously interfere with a child's positive emotional development. • Acts that communicate to a child that he or she is worthless, unloved, or unwanted. • Includes emotionally neglectful behaviors and emotionally abusive behaviors. • Affective-behavioral signs and symptoms: self-abusive behavior, aggression, anxiety, shame, guilt, anger/hostility, pessimism, dependency • Social deficits: insecure attachments, poor social adjustment

Figure 12–6
Definitions, signs, and symptoms of child maltreatment
From American Humane Association, 1996; and Miller-Perrin, 2001.

• *Empowering the Child Survivor.* Prevention training that includes self-protection skills is often necessary. Self-protection skills include teaching children to identify potential abuse situations, providing them with protective responses, and encouraging them to disclose any abuse experiences.

- *Enhancing Developmental Skills.* Children may have deficits in problem-solving skills and social skills. Depending on the age of the child when the abuse occurred, there also may be developmental lags in regard to psychosocial development (e.g., learning to trust). Individual and group counseling can facilitate growth in these areas.

- *Improving Parenting Skills.* In many cases of child maltreatment, parent-focused interventions are warranted. Such interventions include educating parents about developmental processes to correct misperceptions and unrealistic expectations, teaching parents about appropriate disciplinary techniques, and teaching anger management and stress reduction skills.

Due to the complex nature of child maltreatment, counselors should consider accessing community resources and services to help families manage difficult situations more effectively. Examples of such services include substance abuse treatment, money management training, crisis hotlines, respite care services, preschool services, and parent education classes.

Other issues.   Divorce, grief, and abuse are just a few of the many issues with which children and adolescents may struggle. Other issues include living in alcoholic families, being homeless, living with chronic or terminal illness, managing teenage pregnancy, dealing with bullying or violence, and engaging in delinquent activities. Although it would be beyond the scope of this chapter to cover all of the concerns faced by young people, counselors who work with this population are encouraged to develop the expertise needed to meet the needs of their clients in the most effective way possible.

Box 12–3

My first counseling job was as a drug prevention and intervention counselor in a small, rural school district in North Carolina. My individual involvement with a client named "Carl" (not his real name) began soon after he started high school. He was flunking his classes, defying his parents, and usually finding better things to do with his day than attend school . . . such as getting stoned or drunk. What set Carl apart from the other "users" I worked with was his intelligence and his wit. His test scores were off the charts, and his humor was sharp, sarcastic, and biting (just like mine!). After a drug offense at school, Carl became involved in a group of mine and became an individual client as well. For whatever reason, Carl formed a real attachment to me during this time. He would hang out in my office before school, seek me out at lunch, and give me "high fives" in the hallway between classes. He was never a great group member, usually choosing to sabotage a serious discussion with a well-placed but inappropriate joke. I found that my best individual sessions with Carl were not ones where we talked about his using, or getting in trouble, or even what things were like at home. The best sessions were when he read me a poem he'd written over the weekend entitled, "What It's REALLY Like To Be Me"; or when we talked about his favorite rock group; or his "secret" dreams for what he would do with his life after high school (he thought he'd make a good lawyer or maybe a stand-up comedian); or the 10 reasons he felt his friends were such losers (his words, not mine). I tried

(continued)

different "traditional" counseling interventions with him, but he would usually tell me to "stop trying to fix him," and we'd go back to just shooting the breeze.

By the end of his freshman year, Carl's grades started going up. He started going to school more, and I heard less and less about drug offenses. He was more likely to be seen hanging around the basketball court than spending time on the skipping trail. At the end of the year, which was also my last year in this particular job, Carl came by to shoot the breeze for a while. We talked about his summer plans (he was going to be a camp counselor) and how he was going to "survive" a summer at home with his parents. "So where does hanging out with your friends and getting high fit into this summer?" I asked. Carl just shrugged, and said that probably wasn't going to be a big priority. "I think I have better things to do," he said. As he got up to leave, we shook hands. "Thanks," he said, and left.

As with most counseling outcomes, I never know what to attribute change to; or if I even had a hand in it at all. With Carl, I certainly felt my curricula and interventions were not terribly effective. I did, however, feel that I showed Carl respect. I showed him that I valued his sense of humor, and that I recognized his possibilities. I didn't lecture, I didn't judge, and I didn't tell him "NOT" to do anything. He came to that on his own. I learned from Carl that counseling is less about "doing," and more about "being." Thanks, Carl.

—Kelly Coker, Ph.D., LPC, Counselor Educator

SUMMARY AND CONCLUSION

Working with children and adolescents provides unique and exciting challenges for community counselors. Clinicians who work with this population need to have a comprehensive understanding of the developmental issues that influence young people's well-being. They also need to be aware of the various contextual influences on development, including the family, school, peers, life events, and culture.

Counselors use their knowledge of development and bioecological influences to frame the manner in which they counsel children and adolescents. When counseling young people, special attention needs to be given to building a therapeutic relationship, assessing and evaluating, and selecting and implementing developmentally appropriate interventions. For many children, the use of expressive arts or play in counseling can be especially effective.

Young people in today's society are confronted with a wide array of issues, ranging from diagnosable mental health disorders to specific concerns related to life events. Some of the disorders discussed in this chapter included depression, eating disorders, and ADHD. Other concerns that may precipitate the need for counseling include parental divorce, death of a loved one, and child maltreatment. These are just a few of the multiple concerns that may bring young people to counseling. We encourage counselors who plan to work with children and adolescents to participate in ongoing training, education, and supervision so that they are equipped to provide effective prevention and intervention services for this population.

REFERENCES

Achenbach, T. M. (1991). *Manual for the Child Behavior Checklist/4–18 and 1991 profile*. Burlington: University of Vermont, Department of Psychiatry.

Amato, P. R. (1993). Children's adjustment to divorce: Theories, hypotheses, and empirical support. *Journal of Marriage and the Family, 55*, 23–38.

American Bar Association. (1980). *Standards relating to the rights of minors*. Cambridge, MA: Ballinger.

American Counseling Association. (1995). *Ethical standards of the American Counseling Association*. Alexandria, VA: Author.

American Humane Association: Children's Division. (1996). *Fact sheets*. Englewood, CO: Author.

American Psychiatric Association. (2000). *Diagnostic and statistical manual of mental disorders* (4th ed., text rev.). Washington, DC: Author.

Ames, C. (1992). Classrooms: Goals, structures, and student motivation. *Journal of Educational Psychology, 84*, 261–271.

Asarnow, J. R., Jaycox, L. H., & Tompson, M. C. (2001). Depression in youth: Psychosocial interventions. *Journal of Clinical Child Psychology, 30*, 33–45.

Attie, I., & Brooks-Gunn, J. (1995). The development of eating regulation across the life span. In D. Cicchetti & D. J. Cohen (Eds.), *Developmental Psychopathology, Vol. 2: Risk, disorder, & adaptation* (pp. 332–368). New York: Wiley.

Barkley, R. A. (1996). Attention deficit hyperactivity disorder. In E. J. Mash & R. A. Barkley (Eds.), *Child psychopathology* (pp. 63–112). New York: Guilford Press.

Barkley, R. A. (1997). Behavioral inhibition, sustained attention, and executive functions: Constructing a unifying theory of ADHD. *Psychological Bulletin, 121*, 65–94.

Barkley, R. A. (1998). *Attention deficit hyperactivity disorder: A handbook for diagnosis and treatment*. New York: Guilford Press.

Baumrind, D. (1971). Current patterns of parental authority. *Developmental Psychology Monographs, 4*, 1–103.

Baumrind, D. (1991). The influence of parenting style on adolescent competence and substance use. *Journal of Early Adolescence, 11*, 56–95.

Beck, A. T. (1976). *Cognitive therapy and the emotional disorders*. New York: International Universities.

Bergin, J. J. (1999). Small-group counseling. In A. Vernon (Ed.), Counseling children and adolescents (pp. 299–332). Denver, CO: Love.

Berk, L. E. (2001). *Development through the lifespan* (2nd ed.). Needham Heights, MA: Allyn & Bacon.

Birmaher, B., Ryan, N. D., & Williamson, D. E. (1996). Depression in children and adolescents: Clinical features and pathogenesis. In K. Shulman, M. Tohen, & S. P. Kutcher (Eds.), *Mood disorders across the life span* (pp. 51–82). New York: Wiley.

Bjorklund, D. F. (2000). *Children's thinking: Developmental function and individual differences* (3rd ed.). Belmont, CA: Wadsworth.

Bronfenbrenner, U. (1979). *The ecology of human development*. Cambridge, MA: Harvard University Press.

Bronfenbrenner, U. (1989). Ecological systems theory. In R. Vasta (Ed.), *Six theories of child development: Revised formulations and current issues* (pp. 187–249). London: Jessica Kingsley.

Bronfenbrenner, U. (1995). The bioecological model from a life course perspective: Reflections of a participant observer. In P. Moen, G. H. Elder, & K. Luscher (Eds.), *Examining lives in context: Perspectives on the ecology of human development* (pp. 599–647). Washington, DC: American Psychological Association.

Brown, M. B. (2000). Diagnosis and treatment of children and adolescents with attention-deficit hyperactivity disorder. *Journal of Counseling and Development, 78*, 195–203.

Calhoun, G. B., Glaser, B. A., & Bartolomucci, C. L. (2001). The juvenile counseling and assessment model and program: A conceptualization and intervention for juvenile delinquency. *Journal of Counseling and Development, 79*, 131–141.

Cantwell, P. D. (1996). Attention Deficit Disorder: A review of the past 10 years. *Journal of the American Academy of Child and Adolescent Psychiatry, 35*, 978–987.

Compas, B. E. (1987). Stress and life events during childhood and adolescence. *Clinical Psychology Review, 7*, 275–302.

Conners, C. K. (1997). *Conners Rating Scales–Revised*. Toronto: Multi-Health Systems.

Costa, L., & Holliday, D. (1994). Helping children cope with the death of a parent. *Elementary School Guidance and Counseling, 28*, 206–213.

Crockett, L. J., & Crouter, A. C. (1995). Pathways through adolescence: An overview. In L. J. Crockett & A. C. Crouter (Eds.), *Pathways through adolescence* (pp. 1–12). Mahway, NJ: Lawrence Erlbaum.

Darling, N., & Steinberg, L. (1993). Parenting style as context: An integrative model. *Psychological Bulletin, 188,* 487–496.

DuPaul, G. J., & Stoner, G. (1994). *ADHD in schools.* New York: Guilford Press.

Eccles, J. S., Lord, S., & Midgley, C. (1991). What are we doing to early adolescents? The impact of educational contexts on early adolescents. *American Journal of Education, 44,* 521–542.

Eccles, J. S., Wigfield, A., & Schiefele, U. (1998). Motivation to succeed. In N. Eisenberg (Ed.), *Handbook of child psychology: Vol. 3. Social, emotional, and personality development* (5th ed., pp. 1017–1095). New York: Wiley.

Edwards, J. H. (2002). Evidence-based treatment for child ADHD: "Real-world" practice implications. *Journal of Mental Health Counseling, 24,* 126–139.

Elkind, D. (1984). All grown up and no place to go: Teenagers in crisis. Reading, MA: Addison-Wesley.

Erdman, P., & Lampe, R. (1996). Adapting basic skills to counsel children. *Journal of Counseling and Development, 74,* 374–377.

Erikson, E. H. (1968). *Identity: Youth and crisis.* New York: Norton.

Flavell, J. H. (1985). *Cognitive development* (2nd ed.). Upper Saddle River, NJ: Prentice Hall.

Freeman, S. J. (2000). *Ethics: An introduction to philosophy and practice.* Belmont, CA: Wadsworth.

Garber, J., & Robinson, N. S. (1997). Cognitive vulnerability in children at risk for depression. *Cognition and Emotion, 11,* 619–635.

Glosoff, H. L. (2001, November). Ethical practice in a complex era: Clients' rights, counselors' responsibilities. Workshop presentation at Wake Forest University, Winston-Salem, NC.

Goldman, L. (1990). Qualitative assessment. *The Counseling Psychologist, 18,* 205–213.

Goldner, E. M., & Birmingham, C. L. (1994). Anorexia nervosa: Methods of treatment. In L. Alexander-Mott & D. B. Lumsden (Eds.), *Understanding eating disorders* (pp. 135–157). Washington, DC: Taylor & Francis.

Havighurst, R. J. (1972). *Developmental tasks and education* (3rd ed.). New York: David McKay.

Hein, C., & Lewko, J. H. (1994). Gender differences in factors related to parenting style: A study of high performing science students. *Journal of Adolescent Research, 9,* 262–281.

Herring, R. D. (1997). *Multicultural counseling in schools.* Alexandria, VA: American Counseling Association.

Hetherington, E. M. (1993). An overview of the Virginia longitudinal study of divorce and remarriage with a focus on early adolescence. *Journal of Family Psychology, 7,* 39–56.

Kaffenberger, C. J., & Seligman, L. (2003). Helping students with mental and emotional disorders. In B. T. Erford (Ed.), *Transforming the school counseling profession* (pp. 249–284). Upper Saddle River, NJ: Prentice Hall.

Kalodner, C. R., & Van Lone, J. S. (2001). Eating disorders: Guidelines for assessment, treatment, and referral. In E. R. Welfel & R. E. Ingersoll (Eds.), *The mental health desk reference: A sourcebook for counselors and therapists* (pp. 119–128). New York: Wiley.

Kemp, A. (1998). *Abuse in the family: An introduction.* Pacific Grove, CA: Brooks/Cole.

Kendall, P. C. (2000). Guiding theory for therapy with children and adolescents. In P. C. Kendall (Ed.), *Child and adolescent therapy: Cognitive-behavioral procedures* (2nd ed., pp. 3–27). New York: Guilford Press.

Kovacs, M. (1992). *Children's Depression Inventory.* North Tonawanda, NY: Multi-Health Systems.

Ladd, G. W., Kochenderfer, B. J., & Coleman, C. C. (1997). Classroom peer acceptance, friendship, and victimization: Distinct relational systems that contribute uniquely to children's school adjustment? *Child Development, 68,* 1181–1197.

Lamborn, S. D., Mounts, N. S., Steinberg, L., & Dornbusch, S. M. (1991). Patterns of competence and adjustment among adolescents from authoritative, authoritarian, indulgent, and neglectful families. *Child Development, 62,* 1049–1065.

Landreth, G. (1993). Child-centered play therapy. *Elementary School Guidance and Counseling, 28,* 17–29.

Lawrence, G., & Robinson Kurpius, S. E. (2000). Legal and ethical issues involved when counseling minors in nonschool settings. *Journal of Counseling and Development, 78,* 130–136.

Liu, W. M., & Clay, D. L. (2002). Multicultural counseling competencies: Guidelines for working with children and adolescents. *Journal of Mental Health Counseling, 24,* 177–187.

Lyoo, K., Noam, G. G., Lee, C. K., Lee, H. K., Kennedy, B. P., & Renshaw, P. F. (1996). The corpus callosum and lateral ventricles in children with attention-deficit hyperactivity disorder: A brain magnetic resonance imaging study. *Biological Psychiatry, 40,* 1060–1063.

Maccoby, E. E., & Martin, J. A. (1983). Socialization in the context of the family: Parent–child interaction. In R. H. Mussen (Series Ed.) & E. M. Hetherington (Vol. Ed.), *Handbook of child psychology: Vol. 4. Socialization, personality, and social development* (pp. 1–101). New York: Wiley.

Manley, R. S., Rickson, H., & Standeven, B. (2000). Children and adolescents with eating disorders: Strategies for teachers and school counselors. *Intervention in School and Clinic, 35,* 228–231.

McClure, F. H., & Teyber, E. (2003). *Casebook in child and adolescent treatment: Cultural and familial contexts.* Pacific Grove, CA: Brooks/Cole.

McNamara, S. (2000). *Stress in young people: What's new and what can we do?* New York: Continuum.

McWhirter, B. T., & Burrow, J. J. (2001). Assessment and treatment recommendations for children and adolescents with depression. In E. R. Welfel & R. E. Ingersoll (Eds.), *The mental health desk reference* (pp. 199–205). New York: Wiley.

Mellin, E. A., & Beamish, P. M. (2002). Interpersonal theory and adolescents with depression: Clinical update. *Journal of Mental Health Counseling, 24,* 110–125.

Miller-Perrin, C. L. (2001). Child maltreatment: Treatment of child and adolescent victims. In E. R. Welfel & R. E. Ingersoll (Eds.), *The mental health desk reference* (pp. 169–177). New York: Wiley.

Minuchin, S., Rosman, B., & Baker, L. (1978). *Psychosomatic families: Anorexia in context.* Cambridge, MA: Harvard University Press.

Morrison, D. R., & Cherlin, A. J. (1995). The divorce process and young children's well-being: A prospective analysis. *Journal of Marriage and the Family, 57,* 800–812.

Mufson, L., & Fairbanks, J. (1996). Interpersonal psychotherapy for depressed adolescents: A one-year naturalistic follow-up study. *Journal of the American Academy of Child and Adolescent Psychiatry, 35,* 1145–1155.

Mufson, L., Moreau, D., Weissman, M. M., & Klerman, G. L. (1993). *Interpersonal psychotherapy for depressed adolescents.* New York: Guilford.

Muro, J. J., & Kottman, T. (1995). *Guidance and counseling in the elementary and middle schools.* Madison, WI: Brown & Benchmark.

National Clearinghouse on Child Abuse and Neglect Information. (2002). National Child Abuse and Neglect Data System (NCANDS) summary of key findings from calendar year 2000. Retrieved on November 26, 2002, from http:///www.calib.com/nccanch/pubs/factsheets/canstats.cfm

National Institute of Mental Health. (2000). Depression in children and adolescents: A fact sheet for physicians. Retrieved May 28, 2002, from http://www.nimh.nih.gov/publicat/depchildresfact.cfm

National Institute of Mental Health. (2001). Eating disorders: Facts about eating disorders and the search for solutions. Retrieved December 1, 2002, from http://www.nimh.nih.gov/publicat/eatingdisorder.cfm

National Institute of Mental Health. (2002). Let's talk about depression. Retrieved May 28, 2002, from http://www.nimh.nih.gov/publicat/letstalk.cfm

Newsome, D. W. (1999). *Parental and school influences on adolescent academic achievement.* Unpublished doctoral dissertation, University of North Carolina, Greensboro.

Newsome, D. W. (in press). Helping students with depression. In B. T. Erford (Ed.), *Handbook of Professional School Counseling.* Greensboro, NC: ERIC/CASS.

Newsome, D. W., & Gladding, S. T. (2003). Counseling individuals and groups in school. In B. T. Erford (Ed.), *Transforming the school counseling profession* (pp. 209–230). Upper Saddle River, NJ: Prentice Hall.

Newsome, D. W., & Whitlatch, N. H. (in press). Helping students manage stress. In B. T. Erford (Ed.), *Handbook of Professional School Counseling.* Greensboro, NC: ERIC/CASS.

Nigg, J. T., & Rappley, M. D. (2001). Interventions for attention-deficit/hyperactivity disorder. In E. R. Welfel & R. E. Ingersoll (Eds.), *The mental health desk reference* (pp. 183–190). New York: Wiley.

Nystul, M. S. (1999). *Introduction to counseling: An art and science perspective.* Needham Heights, MA: Allyn & Bacon.

Orton, G. L. (1997). *Strategies for counseling with children and their parents.* Pacific Grove, CA: Brooks/Cole.

Peck v. Counseling Service of Addison County, 499 A.2d (Vt. 1985).

Petersen, A. C., Compas, B. E., & Brooks-Gunn, J. (1992). Depression in adolescence: Current knowledge, research directions, and implications for programs and policy. New York: Carnegie Corporation (ERIC Document Reproduction Service No. ED358384).

Pfiffner, L. J., & Barkley, R. A. (1998). Treatment of ADHD in school settings. In R. A. Barkley (Ed.), *Attention deficit hyperactivity disorder: A handbook for diagnosis and treatment* (pp. 458–490). New York: Guilford Press.

Purkey, W. W. (1991). *What is invitational education and how does it work?* Paper presented at the Annual California State Conference on Self-Esteem, Santa Clara, CA. (ERIC Document Reproduction Service No. ED 334 488).

Redcay, S. (2001). Helping children deal with loss. *The Counseling Corner from the American Counseling Association.* Retrieved July 24, 2002, from http://www.counseling.org/site/PageServer?pagename=publications_ccorner_corner801

Reinecke, M. A., Ryan, N. E., & DuBois, D. L. (1998). Cognitive–behavioral therapy of depression and depressive symptoms during adolescence: A review and meta-analysis. *Journal of the American Academy of Child and Adolescent Psychiatry, 37,* 26–34.

Remley, T. P., Jr., & Herlihy, B. (2001). *Ethical, legal, and professional issues in counseling.* Upper Saddle River, NJ: Prentice Hall.

Reynolds, C. R., & Kamphaus, R. W. (1992). *Behavior Assessment System for Children.* Circle Pines, MN: American Guidance Services.

Rice, K. G., & Leffert, N. (1997). Depression in adolescence: Implications for school counselors. *Canadian Journal of Counselling, 31,* 18–34.

Schave, D., & Schave, B. F. (1989). *Early adolescence and the search for self: A developmental perspective.* New York: Praeger.

Schoenwald, S., Brown, T., & Henggeler, S. (2000). Inside multisystemic therapy: Therapist, supervisory, and program practices. *Journal of Emotional and Behavioral Disorders, 8,* 113–128.

Schwartz, R. C., Barrett, M. J., & Saba, G. (1984). Family therapy for bulimia. In D. M. Garner & P. E. Garfinkel (Eds.), *Handbook of psychotherapy for anorexia nervosa and bulimia* (pp. 280–307). New York: Guilford Press.

Sexton, T. L., Whiston, S. C., Bleuer, J. C., & Walz, G. R. (1997). *Integrating outcome research into counseling practice and training.* Alexandria, VA: American Counseling Association.

Sharrer, V. W., & Ryan-Wenger, N. A. (2002). School-age children's self-reported stress symptoms. *Pediatric Nursing, 28,* 21–27.

Sherwood-Hawes, A. (1993). Individual counseling: Process. In A. Vernon (Ed.), *Counseling children and adolescents* (pp. 19–50). Denver, CO: Love.

Sommers-Flanagan, J., & Sommers-Flanagan, R. (1997). *Tough kids, cool counseling.* Alexandria, VA: American Counseling Association.

Stark, K. D., & Kendall, P. C. (1996). *Treating depressed children: Therapist manual for ACTION.* Ardmore, PA: Workbook Publishing.

Stark, D. D., Sander, J. B., Yoncy, M. G., Bronik, M. D., & Hoke, J. A. (2000). Treatment of depression in childhood and adolescence: Cognitive–behavioral procedures for the individual and family. In P. C. Kendall (Ed.), *Child and adolescent therapy: Cognitive–behavioral procedures* (2nd ed., pp. 173–234). New York: Guilford Press.

Steinberg, L., Fletcher, A., & Darling, N. (1994). Parental monitoring and peer influences on adolescent substance use. *Pediatrics, 93,* 1060–1064.

Surgeon General Report. (2000). Children and mental health. Retrieved February 28, 2002, from http://www.surgeongeneral.gov/library/mentalhealth/chapter3/sect.html

Taylor, L., & Adelman, H. (2001). Enlisting appropriate parental cooperation and involvement in children's mental health treatment. In E. R. Welfel & R. E. Ingersoll (Eds.), *The mental health desk reference: A sourcebook for counselors and therapists* (pp. 219–224). New York: Wiley.

Thomas, R. M. (2000). *Comparing theories of child development* (5th ed.). Belmont, CA: Wadsworth.

Thomas, R. M., & Chess, S. (1977). *Temperament and development.* New York: Brunner/Mazel.

Thompson, C. L., & Rudolph, L. B. (2000). *Counseling children* (5th ed.). Belmont, CA: Wadsworth.

U. S. Department of Justice: Office of Juvenile Justice and Delinquency Prevention. (1997). *Juvenile offenders and victims: 1997 update of violence.* Washington, DC: U.S. Government Printing Office.

Vernon, A. (1993). *Developmental assessment and intervention with children and adolescents.* Alexandria, VA: American Counseling Association.

Vernon, A. (1999). Counseling children and adolescents: Developmental considerations. In A. Vernon (Ed.), *Counseling children and adolescents* (2nd ed., pp. 1–29). Denver, CO: Love.

Wallerstein, J. S., & Blakeslee, S. (1989). *Second chances.* New York: Ticknor & Fields.

Waterman, A. S. (1985). Identity in the context of adolescent psychology. In A. S. Waterman (Ed.), *Identity in adolescence: Processes and contents* (pp. 5–24). San Francisco: Jossey-Bass.

Welfel, E. R. (2002). *Ethics in counseling and psychotherapy: Standards, research, and emerging issues* (2nd ed.). Pacific Grove, CA: Brooks/Cole.

Whiston, S. C. (2000). *Principles and applications of assessment in counseling.* Belmont, CA: Wadsworth.

Zill, N., Morrison, D., & Coiro, M. (1993). Long-term effects of parental divorce on parent-child relationships, adjustment, and achievement in young adulthood. *Journal of Family Psychology, 7,* 1–13.

PART IV

Community Counseling Practice: Settings and Services

CHAPTER 13

Community Mental Health Centers, Medical Settings, and Specialized Agencies

As our sessions go on you speak of your scars
and show me the places where you have been burned.
Sadly, I hear your fiery stories
reliving with you, through your memories and words,
all of the tension-filled blows and events
that have beaten and shaped your life.
"I wish I were molten steel," you say,
"And you were a blacksmith's hammer.
Maybe then, on time's anvil, we could structure together
a whole new person, with soft smooth sounds,
inner strength and glowing warmth."

Gladding, S. T. (1977). Scars. *Personnel and Guidance Journal, 56,* 246. © 1977 by ACA.
Reprinted with permission. No further reproduction authorized without written permission of
ACA.

During the past 3 decades, community counselors' opportunities for employment have increased significantly. Prior to the passage of the Community Mental Health Act of 1963 (Title II, Public Law 88-164), counselors worked primarily in educational settings. With the passage of the Community Mental Health Act, funding was provided for the nationwide establishment of community mental health centers, thereby opening the door for large numbers of counselors to work in agency settings. Today, community counselors are employed in many different community sites, including government-funded agencies, hospitals, rehabilitation agencies, family service agencies, shelters for victims of domestic violence, and probation settings, to name just a few. Within these settings, counselors provide a wide range of direct and indirect services to people of all ages who struggle with problems ranging from developmental transitions to serious mental disorders.

In this chapter, we describe some of the publicly and privately funded, typically not-for-profit settings in which community counselors might be employed: community mental health centers, health care facilities, child and family agencies, and other not-for-profit agencies. Other community settings, including career counseling centers, employment assistance programs, and private practices, are discussed in Chapter 14.

COMMUNITY MENTAL HEALTH CENTERS

Prior to 1963, people with mental illness were primarily hospitalized in state institutions. Unsafe and inhumane conditions in many of these institutions precipitated a reform movement that led to the enactment of the Community Mental Health Centers Act (CMHC Act) of 1963, resulting in the deinstitutionalization of people with chronic and severe mental illness. The CMHC Act provided federally matched funds for the state construction of community mental health centers in *catchment* areas—geographic areas of 75,000 to 200,000 people (MacCluskie & Ingersoll, 2001). These community-based agencies were expected to provide a comprehensive continuum of care to all Americans in need of mental health services. Five core elements of service were identified: outpatient, inpatient, consultation and education, partial hospitalization, and emergency/crisis intervention. In addition to providing a comprehensive system of care, community agencies were expected to engage in outreach to the community and form linkages with other service providers. A primary purpose of community mental health centers was to serve as many clients as possible in the least restrictive setting (MacCluskie & Ingersoll).

In subsequent years, funding of community mental health centers (CMHCs) shifted from federal monies to primarily state and local funding. By 1981, with the passage of the Omnibus Budget Reconciliation Act, federal funding of mental health services was allocated through block grants "to be used by states as they saw fit" (MacCluskie & Ingersoll, 2001, p. 230). Block grants were grouped into nine areas of preventive health, with one of the largest being the alcohol, drug abuse, and mental health block grant (ADAMHA). Currently, although states still bear the primary funding burden for mental health services, federal government funds help finance mental health care through Medicaid, Medicare, and federally funded special programs for adults with serious mental illness and children with serious emotional disability (Surgeon General Report, 2000).

Although community mental health centers were designed to provide a broad range of community care, community members often need more support than the CMHCs can provide, resulting in many people not receiving treatment and increased rates of homelessness and rehospitalization. The Surgeon General Report on Mental Health (2000) states that approximately one in five Americans experiences a mental disorder and 15 percent of the adult population uses mental health services in any given year. Providing adequate support to all people in need of mental health assistance continues to be a challenge for community mental health centers (Viger, 2001). Many CMHCs currently are in a state of organizational transition, as attempts are made to manage human and financial resources as efficiently as possible.

Services of Community Mental Health Centers

CMHCs provide a comprehensive system of care designed in partnership with the community, service providers, and payers. The following principles guide community mental health practices:

1. Services should be accessible and culturally sensitive to those who seek treatment.
2. Services should be accountable to the entire community, including the at-risk and underserved.
3. Services should be comprehensive, flexible, and coordinated.
4. Continuity of care should be assured.
5. Treatment providers should utilize a multidisciplinary team approach to care (Administration on Aging [AOA], 2001).

Multidisciplinary teams that provide services typically include psychiatrists, psychologists, counselors, social workers, psychiatric nurses, and paraprofessionals. The following areas of service are frequently offered at CMHCs:

• **Outpatient Counseling Services**. The goal of outpatient services is to help clients improve personal and social functioning through the use of individual, group, and/or family counseling, and possibly medication management. Most often, social workers, counselors, and psychologists provide these services, which address both acute and chronic mental health needs.

• **Day Programs**. Day programs provide intensive treatment to clients who do not need 24-hour care but have significant impairment due to psychiatric, emotional, behavioral, and/or addictive disorders. These programs provide a combination of individual and group therapy, psychoeducation, recreational therapy, life-skills training, vocational rehabilitation, medication management, and other activities designed to help participants acquire skills needed for adjustment to everyday-life tasks and roles (Hershenson, Power, & Waldo, 1996; Viger, 2001). In many CMHCs, day programs include two types of service: *partial hospitalization programs* (PHPs) and *intensive outpatient programs* (IOPs). PHPs provide brief, intensive structured treatment for individuals who can maintain some degree of independence, whereas IOPs usually serve more stable individuals who still need structured treatment programs but on a more flexible basis.

- **Emergency Services/Crisis Intervention.** These services provide for the delivery of center- and community-based crisis intervention in psychiatric emergencies. Services are available on a 24-hour basis through telephone crisis lines, walk-in treatment, or agencies specifically designated to provide emergency care (AOA, 2001).

- **Substance Abuse Services.** Substance abuse services address the recovery of individuals who are controlled by addiction, dependence, or the abuse of substances. Addictive substances can include alcohol, prescription medication, or illegal drugs. Because recovery is an ongoing process, treatment may include outpatient services, residential care, inpatient treatment, emergency care, and the coordination of community drug abuse resources. In addition, counseling and educational programs for family members are usually available to help the family understand and cope with the effects of a substance abuse environment (CenterPoint Human Services, 2002).

- **Case Management and Outreach.** Case management links clients to essential services and supports in the community. Essential services include securing financial benefits, health care, and psychiatric treatment. Goals of case management include preventing hospitalization, improving quality of life and levels of functioning, and empowering clients to maximize their independence (MacCluskie & Ingersoll, 2001). Outreach involves engaging people in need of services who are unable or unwilling to seek services on their own (Viger, 2001).

- **Education and Consultation.** These services include support for family members of clients who are mentally ill, community-wide education programs on the nature of mental health, preventive programs that teach participants about skills such as stress management, and informational programs describing ways to link with various community resources (Lewis, Lewis, Daniels, & D'Andrea, 2003). Education and consultation play key roles in primary and secondary prevention, which are geared toward promoting and maintaining mental health.

- **Residential Programs.** Residential programs include transitional facilities where individuals recently discharged from hospitals learn to function in the community, youth homes for troubled or delinquent adolescents, and other residential homes that vary in the degree to which clients are supervised. Residential supervision can range from 24-hour staffed supervision to independent living options that allow participants to receive care based on their level of functioning. In some cases, intensive outpatient programs for substance abuse and other disorders provide a temporary residential option for clients during the course of treatment.

- **Inpatient Services.** Most community mental health centers are affiliated with either community or state hospitals that provide intensive, inpatient mental health services to stabilize symptoms of acute mental illness and prepare clients to return to community-based care. During the past 3 decades, the number of state psychiatric institutions providing inpatient services has shrunk dramatically, resulting in the discharge of many individuals who are severely mentally ill from hospitals into nursing homes or board-and-care homes that are inadequately prepared to provide necessary services (Duffy & Wong, 2000).

Table 13–1

Direct and indirect community and client services in community mental health agencies

	Community Services	**Client Services**
Direct	Educational programs on the nature of mental health Preventive education programs that teach about mental health and life skills	Counseling and crisis intervention services Outreach programs for persons dealing with life transitions and other high-risk situations
Indirect	Helping the local community organize to work for positive environmental change Taking action on policies affecting community mental health	Advocacy for groups such as people who have experienced chronic mental health problems Consultation within clients' helping networks Promoting self-help programs Linkage with other helping systems in the community

Source: From *Community Counseling: Empowerment Strategies for a Diverse Society* (3rd ed.), by J. A. Lewis, M. D. Lewis, J. A. Daniels, and M. J. D'Andrea, 2003, Pacific Grove, CA: Brooks/Cole. Adapted with permission of Wadsworth, a division of Thomson Learning: www.thomsonrights.com. Fax 800 730-2215.

Counselors in community mental health settings provide services that focus on prevention and promotion of mental health as well as on treatment of mental disorders and dysfunctions. Lewis et al. (2003, p. 259) categorized the services provided by counselors working in community mental health agencies as direct and indirect, and targeted toward clients or to the community at large. Examples of services that might be provided by community counselors are illustrated in Table 13–1.

Necessary Skills

To provide direct and indirect services effectively, counselors who work in community mental health centers must have basic counseling skills as well as specialty skills related to particular populations and problems. They need to be skilled in assessment and diagnosis, which includes having a comprehensive knowledge of the DSM-IV-TR (American Psychiatric Association [APA], 2000) and its classifications. They also need to be familiar with medications and their common side effects used to treat mood, anxiety, substance abuse, and psychotic disorders. Other essential skills include being able to plan, implement, and evaluate prevention programs designed for individuals, groups, and the community at large. Community mental health centers treat a diverse set of clients, many of whom come from lower socioeconomic backgrounds and present with a broad spectrum of issues. Consequently, multicultural awareness, knowledge, and skills are essential.

In most CMHCs, mental health workers are expected to meet the organization's productivity expectations, which vary from agency to agency (MacCluskie & Ingersoll, 2001). *Productivity* refers to the number of "billable hours" a clinician

The greatest challenge of working in a community mental health center (CMHC) is to effectively meet administrative (agency) and clinical (consumer) needs without burning out over time. All settings have paperwork and difficult clients, yet a CMHC, as a public agency, is subject to a high volume of documentation requirements and high volume of clients. There is also the burden of meeting productivity expectations (quotas) each month. This is not an easy task when 50 percent of new clients no-show for first appointments. The challenge is to work with as many clients as you can, as skillfully as you can, and not get behind in paperwork, productivity, or passion.

Many days the benefits of working in a CMHC setting outweigh the struggles. These include the ease of consulting with, and referring clients to, colleagues under the same roof; stable work hours; and no personal responsibility for emergency crisis coverage. Additionally, the pay is good, the organization values high practice standards, and clients do improve. A CMHC is a great place to grow professionally and make a difference in the lives of those who seek therapy.

—Ellen Nicola, Ph.D.
Senior Psychologist/Team Leader
CenterPoint Human Services

Figure 13–1
Urban community mental health: Adult outpatient services

generates. Many agencies have a specified number of client hours that must be averaged over a period of time and often affect salary and promotion. Being able to meet productivity expectations, complete paperwork requirements, provide crisis intervention when needed, and attend staff meetings and supervision can prove to be challenging, making it all the more necessary for counselors to practice self-care to maintain wellness and avoid burn out (Figure 13–1).

Professional Affiliation and Certification

Counselors who work in mental health settings may choose to affiliate with the American Mental Health Counselors Association (AMHCA), a division of the American Counseling Association (ACA). Members of AMHCA have been active in supporting federal and state legislation that recognizes mental health counselors as core practitioners, or reimbursable providers of services. They also have helped define the areas in which mental health counselors work and establish guidelines for involvement in those areas. AMHCA has initiated several different task forces that focus on prevention and treatment in relation to specific populations and concerns. Such concentrations are important because they enable counselors who work in mental health settings to obtain in-depth knowledge and skills in particular areas. The organization also publishes a quarterly periodical, the *Journal of Mental Health Counseling,* which provides readers with up-to-date information on prevention, treatment, and emerging issues in the mental health field.

AMHCA was instrumental in establishing the certified clinical mental health counseling credential (CCMHC), a specialty credential within the field of professional counseling. Professional counselors who have become Nationally Certified Counselors (NCCs) and have met the requirements stipulated by the Academy of Clinical Mental Health Counselors (ACMHC) are eligible for the CCMHC title. Requirements include a 60-semester-hours master's degree (or the equivalent in coursework) from a regionally accredited institution, 2 years of post-master's clinical practice that involves 3,000 hours of direct client contact in a supervised clinical setting, submission of a taped and critiqued recording of a clinical counseling session, and an examination for certification as a clinical counselor (Clawson & Rhodes, 1999). For counselors who work in mental health settings, as well as in many other community settings, becoming a certified clinical mental health counselor may enhance employability and professional credibility.

HOSPITALS AND HEALTH CARE SETTINGS

Many community counselors work in hospitals and other health care facilities, which are essential components of community health care systems (Browers, 2001). Medical facilities may be public or private and may operate for profit or not for profit. Most hospitals offer behavioral health care or psychiatric services to assist people struggling with mental health issues, and many provide preventive and maintenance programs for patients with cardiac disease, diabetes, stroke, or other illnesses (Browers). Hospitals and other health care settings also provide counseling through programs such as cancer patient support, rehabilitation services, AIDS clinics, and hospice. When people receiving treatment in medical settings are referred to, the term *patients* is used more frequently than is the term *clients,* a term which may be uncomfortable for counselors initially but which can facilitate communication with other helping professionals (Barker, 2001). It is important to many behavioral health care systems to show their commitment to quality standards by seeking accreditation from organizations such as the Joint Commission on Accreditation of Healthcare Organizations (JCAHO) or the Commission on Accreditation of Rehabilitation Facilities (CARF).

Inpatient Medical Settings

Inpatient services are designed to treat patients with mental health disorders such as major depression, bipolar disorder, schizophrenia, substance abuse, and dementia. Inpatient services provide crisis stabilization, evaluation, and intensive monitoring based on medical assessment conducted by a multidisciplinary team. Team members include psychiatrists, psychiatric nurses, social workers, counselors, occupational therapists, and other health professionals. Usually within 24 hours of admission, patients are given a complete medical, nursing, and psychosocial assessment. Each team member participates in the assessment process, and team members work together to formulate a diagnosis and treatment plan.

The patient's treatment plan is developed collaboratively by team members and, whenever possible, by the patient and the patient's family members (Barker, 2001).

The treatment plan, which is reviewed periodically by team members, includes a description of patient problems and assets, goals and objectives, target dates, interventions and outcomes, and discharge information. Interventions may include medication; individual, group, and/or family counseling; psychoeducation; recreation therapy; and support groups. To provide a continuum of care, after patients have been stabilized in an inpatient setting, they may be discharged and then moved to another level of treatment, such as the ones described in the next section.

Other Behavioral Health/Psychiatric Services

Many hospitals offer a broad spectrum of treatment options, including some of the same services described in the previous section on community mental health centers. Partial hospital programs (PHPs) and intensive outpatient programs (IOPs) provide services to patients who continue to need intensive treatment but do not need 24-hour supervised care. An additional service, the 23-hour observation bed, is an option for intensive monitoring and evaluation without formal admission into the inpatient unit and associated expensive inpatient costs. Residential treatment programs provide supervised housing and treatment for specific problems, particularly for substance abuse. Outpatient clinics or services provide individual, group, and/or family counseling, based on the patient's need. Examples of outpatient, partial hospitalization, and residential treatment services that may be found in hospitals include:

- Marital and family therapy clinics, providing services to families and couples
- Memory disorders clinics, which assist in the evaluation of individuals with declines in memory, concentration, and thinking, followed by appropriate referral
- Sleep centers, which evaluate sleep disorders and recommend treatment
- Substance abuse intensive outpatient programs, which help patients recovering from chemical dependency. Services may include detoxification, medication management, dual diagnosis treatment, 12-step orientation, family education, and relapse prevention
- Child and adolescent outpatient services, which use multimodal approaches to treat the needs of youth and their families
- Child and adolescent partial hospitalization services, which help reduce psychological symptoms and improve the psychosocial functioning of troubled youth
- Residential treatment for sexually aggressive children and adolescents, where treatment focuses on relapse prevention in a safe, structured, supportive environment
- Sexual abuse clinics, which provide evaluation and treatment for children who may have been abused sexually, prevention services for preschool youth, and education to the community
- Older adult substance abuse programs, which facilitate recovery from chemical dependency as well as counseling focused on life transitions, grief and loss, and leisure and recreation (Wake Forest University Baptist Medical Center, 2002)

Whereas the services provided through hospitals' psychiatric and behavioral care programs are geared toward helping people with chronic or acute mental health disorders, other services offered in hospital and health care facilities are geared toward patients and family members dealing with physical illnesses. An example of this type of service is cancer patient support, which is described next.

Cancer Patient Support Services

Box 13–1

Receiving a diagnosis of cancer is a little like being pushed out of a helicopter into a jungle war without any training, any familiarity with the terrain, or any sense of how to survive.

—(Lerner, 1994, p. 28)

Box 13–2

The ultimate goal of successful treatment for cancer is not just survival but a quality of survival, which is the ability to transcend the trauma of being diagnosed and treated for cancer, to create a lifestyle that is compatible with having a chronic illness, and to renew the process of achieving life goals.

—(Henderson, 1997, p. 188)

Statistics indicate that men have a one in two risk and women a one in three risk of developing cancer during the course of a lifetime, with three out of four families in the United States being affected by some form of cancer (American Cancer Society, 2002). When cancer is diagnosed, feelings of fear, anxiety, and confusion often emerge, placing the patient and frequently the entire family in a state of crisis (Johnson, 1997). In many medical settings, oncology clinics provide counseling and other forms of psychosocial support to help families through the diagnosis, treatment, and posttreatment process. Examples of the services provided by cancer-patient-support programs include:

- New patient orientation services that provide information about the oncology center, treatment procedures, and support services
- Individual counseling to help the patient cope with the cancer diagnosis, treatment ramifications, and related life issues
- Family counseling that focuses on helping family members learn ways to help the patient and themselves as they cope with new stresses on the family system
- Support and educational groups for caregivers, cancer patients, and cancer survivors. For example, a *Coping with Breast Cancer* group can help group members with lifestyle adjustments specific to breast cancer
- Appearance consultation to assist patients receiving chemotherapy who may need help with various appearance-related issues, including the provision of wigs, turbans, and hats
- Resource rooms that provide information for patients and family members on all aspects of cancer care, including diagnosis, treatment, and coping strategies. Resources may include books, brochures, videotapes, and computer access to Internet information

Many cancer-patient-support programs use mental health professionals and volunteers as service providers. When interviewed about her role as associate director of a cancer patient support program, a professional counselor who works primarily with inpatient leukemia patients stressed the importance of just being there to listen—to let people tell their stories. She explained, "You just see them visibly relax. Telling their stories gives them a sense of control: It is something that they need to do time and time again." She went on to say, "Even though many people in today's society are cancer survivors, there is still a feeling in the general public that a diagnosis of cancer is a death sentence. A lot of what I do is to normalize what they are experiencing" (DeChatelet, personal communication, July 15, 2001).

Counselors who work with cancer patients and their families need to be aware that the impact cancer has on the family system varies, depending on the nature of the cancer diagnosis, the phase of the clinical course of the cancer, and the developmental stage of the family (Veach & Nicholas, 1998). With this understanding, counselors can facilitate healthy adjustment to cancer more effectively. Counselors also need to have worked through their own issues related to cancer, illness, and loss so that they are capable of helping others facing difficult circumstances.

Other Hospital-Based Counseling Services

Other counseling services offered in hospital settings include pastoral counseling, caregiver support programs, rehabilitation facilities, and employee assistance programs, which are discussed in the next chapter. In addition, community counselors work in a variety of public and private not-for-profit agencies or clinics that have a medical connection, including AIDS clinics, retirement or nursing homes, hospice programs, and substance abuse agencies. A brief overview of programs offering hospice care and substance abuse treatment is provided next.

Hospice and Palliative Care

Box 13–3

The great events of life, as we observe them, are still clearly recognizable as journeys. . . Out of centuries of experience has come the repeated observation that death appears to be a process rather than an event, a form of passage for human life.

—*Sandol Stoddard* (The Hospice Movement: A Better Way of Caring for the Dying, 1992)

Although hospice and palliative care programs function outside of hospitals, they are connected with the medical world and hence are included in this section. Hospice and palliative care programs assist individuals and their families as they cope with grief, loss, and change. *Hospice care* specifically refers to the care needed by an individual during the last months or weeks of his or her life. *Palliative care* includes hospice care and refers to a compassionate, comprehensive, team approach to care that focuses on quality of life for anyone coping with a serious illness, including the patient and the family members (Hospice and Palliative Care Center, 2002). Hospice and palliative care centers provide help to families dealing with many different diseases, including Alzheimer's, arterial lateral sclerosis (ALS), cancer, chronic lung disease, AIDS, pediatric conditions, and congestive heart failure. Hospice team members traditionally include nurses, physicians, social workers, counselors, clergy, art and music therapists, physical and occupational therapists, nutritionists, pharmacists, and trained volunteers (Stoddard, 1992).

An important role of hospice and palliative care centers is to provide bereavement support services, including counseling, to individuals and families who are facing or have faced the death of a loved one. The types of bereavement support services offered through the centers vary, depending on the resources available at the particular site. Support can include home visits, grief workshops, support groups, individual counseling, telephone calls, and the provision of brochures and other materials that describe how individuals deal with the sorrow and uncertainty surrounding death (Foliart, Clausen, & Siljestrom, 2001) (Figure 13–2). Hospice services also include partnerships with other community organizations to help families engage in advanced planning about end-of-life care issues.

Unhelpful Comments	Helpful Comments
I know exactly how you're feeling.	I am sorry that you are going through this painful process.
I can imagine how you are feeling.	It must be hard to accept that this has happened.
I understand how you are feeling.	It's okay to grieve and be really angry with God and anyone else.
You should be over it by now. It's time you moved on.	Grieving takes time. Don't feel pushed to hurry through it.
You had so many years together. You are so lucky.	I did not know _____; will you tell me about him? What was your relationship like?
You're young; you'll meet someone else.	What is the scariest part about facing the future alone without _____?
At least her suffering is over. She is in a better place now.	You will never forget ____, will you?
He lived a really long and full life.	It's not easy for you, is it? What part of your relationship will you miss the most?
How old was he?	He meant a lot to you.

Figure 13–2
Unhelpful and helpful comments in speaking with the bereaved
Source: From *Heavenly hurts: Surviving AIDS-related deaths and losses,* by S. Klein, 1998, New York: Baywood Publishing Company. Adapted with permission.

An excellent example of a specialized bereavement program is the Carousel Center, which is part of the Hospice and Palliative Care Center in Winston-Salem, North Carolina. The Carousel Family Center offers programs specifically designed to meet the needs of individuals and families experiencing a life-limiting illness, an anticipated death, or a death-related loss. Established in 1990, the Carousel Center provides ongoing grief and bereavement counseling to children and their families, specialized children's programs, art therapy, support groups, and a summer weekend camp for children and adults in the community who are grieving the loss of a loved one. Other services include community educational presentations and a bereavement library with books, videos, tapes, and other resources on grief and loss. All services are provided at no charge. The staff at the Carousel Center includes an art therapist, certified grief therapists, a clinical psychologist, and professional counselors. Susanna Lund, a licensed professional counselor and registered art therapist for the Carousel Center, describes her work with grieving children in this way:

> Children go through a grieving process just like adults, but often are not sure how to verbally connect the emotional dots. Expression through art gives them another way to express and understand their feelings. Art is recognized as being less threatening than words, therefore providing a safe outlet for expression of feelings. Art can allow for the cathartic expression of emotions of grief, allowing the healing process to begin. (Art from the Heart, 2002, p. 1)

Counselors working in hospice programs need to be skilled in grief and bereavement counseling, knowledgeable about death education, aware of their own feelings and beliefs about death, and capable of maintaining personal and professional boundaries. Issues related to countertransference, dealing with loss of a client, and fostering overdependence can be especially difficult to manage. Counselors working in hospice programs can navigate boundary issues more effectively by asking themselves the following questions (Hampton, 2002):

- Have I experienced less patience and increased irritability?
- Am I giving out any telephone number other than my work number?
- Is the family becoming overly dependent on me? (or vice versa)
- Do I feel like no one can support the family like I can?

By maintaining healthy boundaries, working as part of a team, and engaging in consultation or supervision when needed, community counselors can play vital roles in meeting the needs of hospice patients and their families.

Substance Abuse Treatment Programs

Substance-related disorders represent the most commonly occurring mental health problem in the United States (Pidcock & Polansky, 2001). It is estimated that approximately 30 percent of the population will experience some type of substance use disorder (SUD) at some point in life (Evans, 1998). An estimated one in ten adults has significant problems related to the use of alcohol, with rates being higher among certain ethnic groups (Miller & Brown, 1997). Other substances that frequently are abused include marijuana, cocaine, heroin, and a wide range of prescription drugs. Problems related to substance use transcend gender, ethnicity, socioeconomic levels, geography, and almost all other domains (Stevens-Smith & Smith, 1998). Unfortunately, many people with substance use problems are in denial and their conditions often go undiagnosed and untreated.

When people with substance use disorders do present for treatment, either voluntarily or involuntarily, they typically are diagnosed with either a *substance abuse* or a *substance dependency* disorder. *Substance abuse* is characterized by continued use of a substance in the presence of significant adverse consequences. An individual who exhibits one or more of the following symptoms within a 12-month period is considered to have a substance abuse problem:

- Substance use is responsible for failure to fulfill major role obligations at work, school, or home.
- Recurrent substance use occurs in situations in which it is physically hazardous.
- Legal problems related to substance use recur.
- Continued substance use occurs despite the difficulties it is causing in significant relationships (APA, 2000).

Substance dependence refers to the repeated, nonmedical use of a substance that harms the user or precipitates behavior in the user that harms others and is characterized by physical or psychological dependence. Dependence is diagnosed when three or more of the following symptoms are evidenced:

- Tolerance (increased amounts of the substance are needed to experience the desired effect).
- Withdrawal (when withdrawal symptoms occur or when individuals continue to use the substance to avoid withdrawal symptoms).
- The substance is taken in larger amounts or over a longer period of time than was intended.
- There is a persistent desire to cut down or control substance use.
- A lot of time is spent trying to acquire the substance.
- Important work, social, or leisure activities are given up or reduced because of the substance use.
- Substance use continues despite knowledge of recurrent physical or psychological consequences (APA, 2000).

Frequently, individuals with substance-related disorders have co-occurring mental health issues, including mood disorders, anxiety, personality disorders, sleep disorders, posttraumatic stress disorder, psychotic disorders, and other psychological disorders. The coexistence of substance abuse and mental disorders is referred to as *dual diagnosis,* a condition that can be particularly intractable to treatment. Clients with a dual diagnosis are at greater risk for relapse, and those who do relapse are more likely to develop depression (Pidcock & Polansky, 2001). Another condition that makes the already complex issue of substance use disorders more difficult to assess, diagnose, and treat is *polysubstance abuse,* which refers to the abuse of two or more substances simultaneously.

People with a substance dependency are considered to have an *addiction*. Addiction is a complex, progressive behavior pattern with biological, psychological, sociological, and behavioral components (Scott, 2000). It has been defined as "a persistent and intense involvement with and stress upon a single behavior pattern, with a minimization or even exclusion of other behaviors, both personal and interpersonal" (L'Abate, 1992, p. 2). Addictive disorders, which can include gambling, workaholism, sexual addictions, and Internet addictions, continue to be major problems in the United States (L'Abate, Farrar, & Serritella, 1992). Counselors may work in sites that specialize in treating any of these addictions. In this section, however, the focus is on the treatment of addictions to or abuse of chemical substances, including alcohol, illegal drugs, and prescription drugs.

Treatment for individuals who abuse substances primarily occurs in two general settings: substance abuse treatment facilities and community mental health centers (Von Steen, Vacc, & Strickland, 2002). Some facilities provide public or private not-for-profit services, whereas others provide for-profit services. Professionals and paraprofessionals, including rehabilitation counselors and other professional counselors, often are employed in substance abuse treatment centers. Many centers provide education, prevention, and consultation services about substance use as well as about treatment and rehabilitation services for substance abuse.

Whereas it is important for all community counselors to have some training in addictions and substance abuse, counselors who work in substance abuse treatment facilities need specialized training and certification (e.g., Certified Clinical Addiction Specialist, Certified Substance Abuse Counselor, and Certified Substance Abuse Prevention Consultant). The number of academic programs that educate counselors with an emphasis on substance abuse is growing (Hollis, 2000), and since 1994, the National Board of Certified Counselors (NBCC) has provided a certification process for becoming a certified master addictions counselor (MAC). Counselors who work in the substance abuse field need to participate in ongoing education and training to be able to work effectively with diverse clients presenting with complex issues (Thombs & Osborn, 2001).

The dominant model for treating chemical dependence is the Minnesota Model of Chemical Dependency Treatment (Benshoff & Janikowski, 2000). The model is based on the disease concept of dependency, which asserts that chemical addiction is a treatable disease with specific origins, symptoms, progression, and outcomes. The multidisciplinary model ascertains that recovery is only possible through abstinence accompanied by major emotional and spiritual changes, a belief that has been disputed by some professionals but serves as the underpinning for most treatment programs. In addition to advocating abstinence, the model places a strong emphasis on life change utilizing 12-step programs (e.g., Alcoholics Anonymous [AA] and Narcotics Anonymous [NA]); provides a combination of didactic, educational, and psychotherapeutic interventions; and values personal confrontation. Initially designed for the treatment of alcoholism, the model is now used to treat all forms of dependency. It is characterized by a continuum of care that includes detoxification, inpatient and outpatient services, and aftercare services (Benshoff & Janikowsi, 2000).

• *Detoxification* is the first phase of dependency treatment. Three forms include *medical detoxification* (when withdrawal can be life-threatening, thus requiring the help of medical professionals), *social detoxification* (when withdrawal symptoms are less severe, enabling detoxification to occur in a residential, nonmedical setting), and *self-detoxification* (unmanaged, unsupervised detoxification that often is unsuccessful). Detoxification serves as a gateway to treatment, with formal detoxification typically lasting from 3 to 5 days.

• *Residential treatment* can occur in medical or nonmedical residential facilities, halfway houses, and therapeutic communities. The most widely recognized residential settings utilize the Minnesota Model, or 28-day programs, such as the Betty Ford Center and Hazelden. Other settings, which are less costly, are referred to as freestanding programs. They offer residential care in a community-based setting with lower levels of direct medical monitoring. During the course of treatment, abstinence is required and group therapy and psychoeducation are emphasized, although some programs also provide individual counseling. Residential programs focus on the attainment of short-term goals in treatment and the development of longer term goals for posttreatment. In these confrontational but supportive environments, clients have an opportunity to live and act productively in a drug-free manner.

• *Outpatient treatment* is designed to follow more intensive inpatient or residential treatment as part of the continuum of care plan. In the past, outpatient treatment for substance abuse was either unlimited or had very liberal limits, allowing clients to continue in treatment for an indefinite period of time. However, insurance companies and funding agencies now impose stricter limits on the number of outpatient visits covered per year or per policy. An additional problem associated with outpatient treatment, particularly if it is not preceded by more intensive forms of treatment, is a high rate of missed appointments and relapse because the individual has not been removed from the pressures of the drinking or drug-using environment in which he or she lives. To address this problem, many sites offer intensive outpatient programs (IOPs), which may provide temporary housing for people in treatment. IOPs are the predominant level of care for clients in treatment for chemical dependency and consist of 3 to 5 days or evenings per week, ranging from 3 to 10 weeks of care. Counseling and psychoeducation in IOPs tend to be group focused, intensive, and multidimensional, in accordance with the Minnesota Model. Family members often are encouraged to participate, and clients are asked to attend AA or NA meetings during and after treatment.

• *Aftercare.* When a client successfully completes a chemical dependency treatment program, he or she is not *cured;* instead, recovery has just begun and is considered to be a lifelong process. According to Prochaska, DiClemente, and Norcross's (1992) *transtheoretical model of change* (described in Chapter 5), clients who successfully complete treatment are in the *maintenance stage,* in which there is still much work to accomplish. During the first few months of maintenance, clients are especially vulnerable to relapse. Continued vigilance and support are needed to help clients maintain their new lifestyle. Many treatment programs offer aftercare support groups that meet on a weekly basis. To help with recovery and to prevent relapse, 95 percent of inpatient addiction treatment programs in the United States incorporate AA and NA into plans for treatment and follow-up care (Bristow-Braitman, 1995). These peer support groups provide guidance, support, sustenance, and solace to individuals seeking help with substance-related disorders (Benshoff, 1996). Typically, AA, NA, and other support groups, which are adjunctive to a comprehensive continuum of care, have at their foundation the 12 Steps, which are listed in Figure 13–3. The 12 Steps utilize important counseling concepts, including *problem recognition* (Step 1), *hope* (Step 2), *help seeking* (Steps 3, 5, and 7), *insight development* (Steps 4, 6, and 10), *restitution* (Steps 8 and 9), and *adoption of new consciousness and forms of behavior* (Step 12) (Benshoff & Janikowski, 2000).

Working with clients who have substance-related disorders can be challenging for many reasons. *Denial,* which involves minimizing the effects of substance abuse on oneself or others, is a common defense mechanism and can sabotage successful treatment. Related to denial is the client's degree of motivation, or readiness for change. When clients are court-ordered to receive treatment for substance use, they

---

1. We admitted that we were powerless over alcohol—that our lives had become unmanageable.
2. Came to believe that a Power greater than ourselves could restore us to sanity.
3. Made a decision to turn our will and our lives over to God *as we understood Him.*
4. Made a searching and fearless moral inventory of ourselves.
5. Admitted to God, to ourselves and to another human being the exact nature of our wrongs.
6. Were entirely ready to have God remove all these defects of character.
7. Humbly asked Him to remove our shortcomings.
8. Made a list of all persons we had harmed and became willing to make amends to all of them.
9. Made direct amends to such people wherever possible, except when to do so would injure them or others.
10. Continued to take personal inventory, and when we were wrong promptly admitted it.
11. Sought through prayer and meditation to improve our conscious contact with God *as we understood Him,* praying only for the knowledge of His will and the power to carry that out.
12. Having had a spiritual awakening as a result of these steps, we tried to carry this message to alcoholics and to practice these principles in all our affairs. (Alcoholics Anonymous, 2001, pp. 2–3)

Figure 13–3
The 12 Steps of Alcoholics Anonymous

may not be at a point where they are willing to acknowledge that they have a problem or consider changing their behaviors. According to Prochaska et al. (1992), such individuals are in the *precontemplation stage* of change. Counselors working with clients in this stage are advised to use strategies such as motivational interviewing to help clients become more aware of their emotional response to the negative consequences associated with their substance use habits (Prochaska & Norcross, 1999). Various forms of client resistance, unhealthy family dynamics, negative environmental influences, and stressful living conditions are other factors that can make working with this population problematic. Counselors who work with substance-abusing clients will want to seek ongoing consultation and supervision so that they can provide optimal services to their clients and avoid burnout.

Box 13–4
Chemical dependency treatment center

The challenges of work in chemical dependency counseling are often mixed with the rewards. What may be frustrating suddenly leads to a breakthrough insight. Never boring, chemical dependency counseling often presents the counselor with many opportunities. Relapses are prevalent and knowing some clients lose their life while relapsing is perhaps one of the hardest aspects of chemical dependency work. Skillful preparation, teamwork, and helpful supervision are invaluable as the nature of addiction challenges the counseling relationship.

The benefits of chemical dependency counseling include being a part of a person's discovery of sobriety. Recovery from chemical dependency is often a difficult struggle, and as a counselor in that process, it is both an honor and a daunting responsibility to provide our best work. Helping people learn how to live life on life's terms, take responsibility for their own recovery, and make amends to loved ones equally scarred by addiction are just the beginning. Other benefits involve leading group processes where clients share and thereby lessen pain, conducting family counseling that leads to a better understanding of enabling behaviors, and facilitating sessions with clients who had been obsessively ruled by chemicals as they sense their new freedom to live clean and sober. Just being a part of the many miracles of those whose lives change as they discover, sometimes for the first time, the joy of being alive makes chemical dependency counseling a rewarding occupation.

—Laura Veach, Ph.D., LPC, NCC
Certified Clinical Addiction Specialist, Certified Clinical Supervisor
Assistant Professor, Department of Counseling, Wake Forest University

OTHER SPECIALIZED NOT-FOR-PROFIT SETTINGS

Whereas centralized community mental health centers and medical facilities provide a wide array of treatment options, other agencies intentionally provide a more narrow range of specialized services. *Specialized agencies* usually focus on a specific problem (e.g., domestic violence, substance abuse) or a specific group (e.g., older adults, children, at-risk youth; Lewis et al., 2003). Examples of specialized services include support for Alzheimer's patients and their caregivers, AIDS care centers, child abuse prevention services, drop-in crisis counseling centers, child and family services, and services for at-risk youth, to name just a few. A review of community resources in a midsized southeastern city revealed over 200 not-for-profit agencies, of which over 60 provided counseling-related services (First Line, 2001). In this section, attention is given to agencies that provide services to families, with a focus on issues of domestic violence and abuse.

Child and Family Service Agencies

Many communities have not-for-profit agencies that specialize in treating the needs of children, couples, and families. Funding sources for child and family service agencies vary, with many of the private agencies getting support from the United Way, religiously affiliated organizations, charities, private endowments, or grants (Browers, 2001). Community counselors with a background in family counseling may find excellent opportunities in agencies that specialize in child and family services. Depending on the agency, family services may include combinations of any of the following services:

- Child and family assessment
- Individual counseling
- Couples counseling
- Family counseling
- Parent education
- Pregnancy testing and support/education services
- Shelters for women and children who are victims of domestic violence or sexual assault
- Victim assistance counseling
- Counseling and support groups for abusers
- Counseling and support groups for adult survivors of sexual abuse or incest
- Supervised, structured visitation for parents who are not allowed to be alone with their children
- Family preservation programs
- Counseling and support for abusive or potentially abusive families
- Community education programs to help prevent abuse and neglect

Counselors who work in child and family settings need to have a comprehensive understanding of systems-based counseling. Systems-based counseling, as described in Chapter 9, embraces a circular causality approach and assumes that interactions within families are dynamic rather than static or linear. For counseling to be effective, both the family system and the larger systems within which the family is embedded need to be taken into account. Popular family counseling approaches include structural, strategic, experiential, solution focused, and narrative.

Domestic violence.   Domestic violence—also referred to as intimate partner violence, abuse, and battering—is a pervasive problem that affects approximately 2 million women in the United States annually, although estimates range from 1 million to 4 million cases of serious assault by an intimate partner (American Psychological Association, 1996; James & Gilliland, 2001). Eighty-five percent or more of the victims are women (U.S. Department of Justice, 2000; Walker, 2000), so although there are instances of women abusing men, the reverse phenomenon is more common. Also of concern are violent relationships among gays, lesbians, and bisexuals; abusive treatment of elders or children; and the witnessing of violence by children.

Victims of violence are at increased risk for mental health problems as well as for physical injury and death (Surgeon General Report, 2000). Anxiety, posttraumatic stress disorder (PTSD), depression, suicide, eating disorders, and substance abuse are among the many mental health issues associated with being abused. Children who witness abuse are at a greater risk for short- or long-term emotional disturbances, including nightmares, PTSD, depression, learning difficulties, and aggressive behavior.

Due to the prevalence and severity of domestic violence, many family service agencies include services designed to prevent domestic violence from occurring or recurring and to protect victims of domestic violence. To accomplish these goals, comprehensive family service agency programs may provide anger management programs, counseling groups for abusers (also called batterers), support groups for people who have been abused, and protective shelters for women and children.

What is abuse?   According to the National Council Against Domestic Violence (NCADV, 2002), *abuse* is a pattern of behavior used to establish power and control over another person through the use of fear and intimidation. Abuse occurs when one person believes that he or she is entitled to control another person. Three major categories of abuse are:

   a. *Physical Abuse,* which can range from bruising to murder. Many times, physical abuse begins with trivial injuries that then escalate over time
   b. *Sexual Abuse,* which refers to any forced sexual activity
   c. *Psychological Abuse,* which includes constant verbal abuse, harassment, extreme possessiveness, deprivation of resources, isolation, and the destruction of physical property

A number of social, psychological, and cultural theories have been posited to explain battering and abuse. Among the more prominent among those theories are attachment theory, feminist theory, social learning theory, and systems theory (James & Gilliland, 2001). Counselors providing domestic violence services will want to be familiar with theoretical frameworks about causes of battering so that they can work more effectively with perpetrators and victims.

Who are batterers?   Domestic violence cuts across socioeconomic, geographic, cultural, and religious barriers. Several psychological and behavioral characteristics are associated with batterers, although no single typology characterizes all people who abuse. Men who abuse women may exhibit some of the following characteristics, attitudes, and behaviors:

- *Objectify women.* Women are not respected but instead are viewed as property.
- *Exhibit low self-esteem.* Batterers often feel inadequate or powerless.
- *Blame their behavior on external causes.* They may blame their behaviors on a "bad day," alcohol, or drugs.
- *Deny the severity of the problem and its effects on their families.*
- *Be characterized as jealous, possessive, demanding, and aggressive.*
- *Abuse alcohol or other drugs.*
- *Were abused as children or saw their mothers abused.*
- *Have strong, traditional, patriarchal beliefs.*
- *Tend to overreact; have a short fuse.*
- *Be likely to use force or violence to solve problems.*
- *Cycle from being hostile, aggressive, and cruel to being charming, manipulative, and seductive, depending on the situation.*
- *Have unrealistic expectations of marriage, their spouses, and relationships in general* (James & Gilliland, 2001; NCADV, 2002).

Why do women stay?   Reasons to remain in or terminate a relationship are seldom simple. In cases of domestic violence, reasons typically are quite complex. Often, the act of leaving is dangerous, as many batterers will attempt to retaliate (Walker, 2000). It has been noted that most women leave an abusive relationship an average of three to six times, with varying degrees of permanency (James & Gilliland, 2001). Some of the reasons a woman might choose to stay in an abusive relationship include:

- She would suffer shame, embarrassment, and humiliation if her secret were revealed.
- She fears repercussion from her partner.
- Financial circumstances make leaving difficult.
- Early role models of an abusive parent may have warped her view of the nature of relationships.
- She may not have access to safety or support.
- She may hold strong beliefs against separation or divorce.
- She may believe that her partner will reform.
- She may focus on the good times rather than the battering (James & Gilliland, 2001; NCADV, 2002).

What services are available?   During the last 25 years, as consciousness about domestic violence has been raised, programs have been established that target both the victim and the abuser. Crisis lines, shelters, and support groups are

- Knowledge about the phenomenon of partner abuse (definitions, prevalence rates, types of abuse, dynamics and consequences of abuse)
- Knowledge of the explanatory theories of abuse and violence
- Knowledge of feminist-informed and culturally sensitive theories and practices pertaining to partner abuse
- Effective assessment protocols for partner abuse
- Knowledge of the experiences, needs, and risks faced by battered individuals (including symptoms of PTSD)
- Key principles and practices for individual treatment
- Services and resources available for victims and abusers

Figure 13–4
Knowledge and skills needed to work with victims of domestic violence
From Haddock, 2002.

common forms of assistance for victims. Counselors who work with domestic violence issues need to be well trained in crisis intervention as well as in other forms of intervention appropriate for victims of violence. Examples of knowledge and skills that should be acquired by counselors who work with this population are listed in Figure 13–4. Ensuring the victim's safety is of primary concern, regardless of the setting. Counselors also often serve as victim advocates by providing assistance with legal, economic, housing, and parenting issues (NCADV, 2002). To advocate effectively, counselors need to understand the legal system and have a strong networking alliance so that help can be obtained quickly (James & Gilliland, 2001).

Many communities have created programs to treat people who have abused their partners, recognizing that treatment is necessary for change to occur. Although not all counselors who work in family services will choose to work with victimizers, it is important to be aware of the types of services available to domestic abusers. Most batterers, especially those who are adjudicated, do not enter treatment willingly and often exhibit denial, minimization, justification, or projection of blame (James & Gilliland, 2001). The prevalent mode of treatment for batterers is court-ordered group counseling, which provides opportunities for social learning, anger management, confrontation, and support. Groups typically are designed to help abusers learn to accept responsibility for their behavior, recognize the spectrum of abuse, resolve conflict without violence or abuse, and address personal concerns (James & Gilliland, 2001; Golden & Frank, 1994). A professional counselor who began working with batterers during a community counseling internship describes his experiences in Figure 13–5.

Child abuse services.   In Chapter 12, we describe some of the issues related to child abuse and neglect. In many communities, specialized agencies focus on

"They" were not the people I expected to meet. I expected "them" to be the stereo-type—uncaring, manipulative, harsh, and antisocial. I took the assignment because I needed the hours. I was already working with sexually and physically abused boys. I told myself I would only do the groups for a short time, just until the end of my internship. My first group was almost 7 years ago and I am still with the program.

Some male batterers personify the stereotype—a noxious soup of bullying, selfishness, narcissism, and sociopathology. They always try to tell me what they think I want to hear. They always think they can hide their true selves. They can't see themselves accurately, and they assume that I am similarly impaired. Their problems are always caused by others and the deck is always stacked against them.

The majority of male batterers I encounter, however, value family, love their partners, and acknowledge that some of their behaviors are inappropriate. Many of these men enter the group believing that control will prevent abandonment, and the opposite is true. Many batterers enter the group believing that "taking care of her" is respectful and appropriate, and the opposite is true. Intimate relationships pro-duce a frustrating paradox for most of these men. The harder they try, the more conflict, frustration, and failure they experience.

The purpose of the program is to produce a safer world for women and chil-dren. The goal is to educate and change beliefs. The process is one of engage-ment, confrontation, and encouragement. Success is measured with attendance, homework returned, and in-session behavior. Throughout the process, I always hope for healing and changes of heart.

—*Robin Daniel, Ph.D., LPC, NCC*

Figure 13–5
Group counseling with male batterers

the prevention and treatment of child abuse. These agencies provide support ser-vices for abusive or potentially abusive families, parent training programs, and community education programs regarding the recognition of abuse and neglect (Figure 13–6). Lewis et al.'s (2003) community counseling model, which was described earlier, provides a helpful framework for conceptualizing the types of services that might be offered at a child abuse prevention and treatment agency (see Table 13–2).

Home-based services.   Home-based services provide intensive interventions within the homes of children and youth with emotional disturbances. In most cases, home-based services are provided through the child welfare, juvenile justice, or community mental health systems (Surgeon General Report, 2000). Three major goals of home-based services are to (a) prevent out-of-home placements; (b) connect youth and their families with community resources, thereby creating an outside support

Working with victims is an ultimate challenge, considering that their need for therapy is always the result of their exposure to some trauma. Some of the challenges to be dealt with in therapy are lack of trust, low self-esteem and the absence of autonomy, fear of reprisal from the person or persons responsible for the trauma, and the possible absence of a viable and healthy support system. An additional hidden challenge is the possibility that, in an effort to survive, the victims may have acquired some of the characteristics of the person or persons responsible for the trauma; i.e., they may be cunning, manipulative, and coercive. The challenge then is for the therapist to recognize these behaviors in the clients, help the clients to recognize these behaviors in themselves and acknowledge the source of the behaviors, and help the client adapt more appropriate coping skills.

The rewards of working with this population are many, including seeing the victims learn to trust; witnessing their elevated self-esteem and evidence, though small at times, of their movement toward self-nurturing; and observing the growth of courage to assign responsibility for their trauma to its rightful owner. The ultimate reward is when they no longer see themselves as victims but as survivors.

—Dorothy Walton Walker, M.S., LPC, NCC
Director, StaSafe (Systemic Treatment after Sexual Abuse for Families) Exchange/SCAN

Figure 13–6
Counseling with victims of sexual abuse

Table 13–2
Direct and indirect community and client services in a child abuse prevention and treatment agency

	Community Services	**Client Services**
Direct	Community education programs regarding the recognition of abuse and neglect. Parent training classes offered to the community-at-large.	Individual and family counseling for children and parents. Assessment of and treatment for sexual offenders.
Indirect	Sponsoring community awareness events to make families aware of abuse and neglect issues. Working with local and state legislators to advance children's rights.	Sponsoring parent support groups that focus on effective parenting skills. Working with DSS to provide supervision and structured intervention for visits between children and parents who are not allowed to be alone with their children.

Source: From *Community Counseling: Empowerment Strategies for a Diverse Society* (3rd ed.), by J. A. Lewis, M. D. Lewis, J. A. Daniels, and M. J. D'Andrea, 2003, Pacific Grove, CA: Brooks/Cole. Adapted with permission of Wadsworth, a division of Thomson Learning: www.thomsonrights.com. Fax 800 730-2215.

system; and (c) strengthen the family's coping skills and capacity after crisis treatment is completed (Stroul, 1988). Services provided through these programs include evaluation, assessment, counseling, skills training, and coordination of services.

Two primary types of home-based services are family preservation programs and multisystemic therapy programs (MST) (Surgeon General Report, 2000). Family preservation programs provide family-based services designed to keep dysfunctional families together. For example, the Surgeon General Mental Health Report (2000) describes the Homebuilders Program in Tacoma, WA, and family reunification programs in both Washington State and Utah. The success of these programs was attributed to:

- Delivering services in a home and community setting
- Viewing family members as colleagues in defining a service plan
- Making back-up services available 24 hours a day
- Building life skills based on individual needs of family members
- Offering marital and family interventions
- Efficiently coordinating community services
- Assisting with basic needs, such as clothing, food, and housing

MST (Henggeler, Schoenwald, Borduin, Rowland, & Cunningham, 1998) are intensive, short-term, home- and family-focused treatment services for youth with behavioral and emotional disturbances. MST is based on Bronfenbrenner's (1979, 1995) bioecological theory, which was described in Chapters 2 and 12. Originally implemented with juvenile delinquents, MST intervenes directly in the young person's family, school, neighborhood, and peer group by identifying factors that contribute to the problem behaviors (Surgeon General Report, 2000). Major goals of MST are to (a) empower caregivers with the skills needed to address the difficulties that accompany parenting youth with behavior problems and (b) empower youth to cope more effectively with family, peer, school, and neighborhood difficulties. By working intensively with the young person, the family, and the larger community, skills are developed across all groups that lead to improved behaviors and mental health. The efficacy of MST has been attributed to the fact that it is clearly specified, based on solid empirical research, and uses quality assurance mechanisms to ensure that treatment protocol is followed (Schoenwald, Brown, & Henggeler, 2000).

Other not-for-profit services.   Opportunities for community-based counselors exist in numerous settings, depending on the counselor's training, skills, interests, and professional certification. In addition to the sites already mentioned, opportunities for employment include wellness centers, for-profit agencies, private practice, prisons, and alternative healing centers. Some of those settings and related services are discussed in Chapter 14. We conclude this section with narratives from counselors working in two diverse settings: an ecumenical, not-for-profit, counseling center; and a state prison. Both counselors describe some of the challenges and rewards that are inherent in their work.

Box 13–5
Directing and counseling in a private, not-for-profit community center

Trinity Center, Inc., is a small, ecumenical community counseling center that operates on a budget of approximately $360,000 annually. Trinity Center is staffed by 2 full-time administrative and support staff, two employees who are part-time clinicians/part-time administration, 13 part-time contract clinicians, 1 part-time (4 hours per week) medical director, and a 16-member Board of Directors. One of the rewards of directing the Trinity Center is working alongside talented, committed professionals who bring creativity and energy into the work they do with their clients, each other's lives, and the life of the Center. An ongoing challenge is continually adapting to changes that come from professionals' evolving interests and the profession's evolving standards of acceptable practice. It is a challenge to hold both of these goals in the balance—sacrificing neither procedural predictability and accountability nor professional creativity and growth.

Another challenge is maintaining financial stability as we combine the model of a standard private practice (clients able to pay the full fee for services either through insurance or self-pay) with that of a not-for-profit agency (serve all appropriate clients, regardless of ability to pay, soliciting missing revenue from donors and foundations). The richness inherent in the variety of client issues and the reward of bringing professional expertise and talent to the community continue to make this the model of choice for those of us involved at Trinity Center. For almost 20 years, we have shared the financial challenges as well as the professional enrichment—learning and adapting as we have grown.

—Ann Dixon Coppage, M.A. Ed., LPC

Box 13–6
Group counseling in a prison setting

There are some barriers to providing an effective group experience to inmates in a prison setting. For instance, a disadvantage is the limited amount of privacy, with closed-circuit television and windowed doors. Institutional furniture in a room with tables and no carpeting ordinarily are not conducive to physical comfort and emotional closeness. Materials used in the group must be approved in advance and examined by prison guards. Out-of-group contact also can be a problem, even in a very large institution.

Some counselors might be reluctant to hold groups in this milieu due to concerns for personal safety. Though unfounded, these fears may be difficult to overcome until trust has been established. Also, there is ambivalence in society as to whether an inmate, who is in prison for punishment, is entitled to grief groups.

The advantages, however, greatly outweigh the disadvantages. The prison chaplains publicize the group, interview prospective members, and collect evaluations after the group ends. A mixture of self-referrals and men encouraged by the psychologist or social worker brings a variety of experiences and awareness to the group. Many of the participants have experience with groups and have learned to communicate directly and with great insight. They are enthusiastic about (and have time for) homework assignments, often taking great care with written activities such as letter writing and closing comments. They are open to experiential exercises, genuine with each other, and appreciative of facilitators who treat them as "real people." Our experience with these groups has been growth promoting for the facilitators as well as the participants.

—*Margaret (Peg) J. Olson, Ph.D., Counselor Educator*
—*Margaret (Peg) A. McEwen, MSN, Family Nurse Practitioner*

SUMMARY AND CONCLUSION

In this chapter, we have described a variety of community settings in which counselors may be employed. Some of the venues, such as community mental health centers and hospitals, provide many different treatment options to diverse clientele who present with a spectrum of issues. Other settings, including family service agencies, hospice programs, and substance abuse agencies, allow counselors to focus on a specific population or mental health issue. Services in CMHCs, hospitals, clinics, and agencies can include inpatient treatment and day programs, residential treatment, outpatient services, home visits, prevention efforts, and multisystemic interventions.

Regardless of the setting in which they practice, community counselors will want to engage in ongoing training and supervision to update knowledge, skills, and professional certifications. The counseling profession and community health services continue to evolve, both as a result of changes in the profession itself and as a consequence of government and public policy. It is incumbent upon counseling professionals to be cognizant of those changes, remaining open to new approaches, interventions, and service options.

REFERENCES

Administration on Aging. (2001). Community mental health services. Retrieved December 28, 2002, from http://www.aoa.dhhs.gov/mh/report2001/chapter2.html

Alcoholics Anonymous World Services, Inc. (2001). *AA fact sheet*. Grand Central Station, NY: Author.

American Cancer Society. (2002). Statistics for 2002. Retrieved December 30, 2002, from http://www.cancer.org/

American Psychiatric Association. (2000). *Diagnostic and statistical manual of mental disorders* (4th ed., text rev.).

American Psychological Association (1990). Violence and the family: Report of the American Psychological Association Presidential Task Force on Violence and the Family, 10.

Art from the Heart. (2002, Fall/Winter). *The Circular* (Hospice and Palliative Care Center), *1,* 7.

Barker, S. B. (2001). Counseling in medical settings. In D. C. Locke, J. E. Myers, & E. L. Herr (Eds.), *The handbook of counseling* (pp. 373–390). Thousand Oaks, CA: Sage.

Benshoff, J. J. (1996). Peer self-help groups. In W. Crimando & T. F. Riggar (Eds.), *Utilizing community resources: An overview of human services* (pp. 57–66). Delray Beach, FL: St. Lucie Press.

Benshoff, J. J., & Janikowski, T. P. (2000). *The rehabilitation model of substance abuse counseling*. Belmont, CA: Wadsworth.

Bristow-Braitman, A. (1995). Addiction recovery: 12-step programs and cognitive-behavioral psychology. *Journal of Counseling and Development, 73,* 414–418.

Bronfenbrenner, U. (1979). *The ecology of human development*. Cambridge, MA: Harvard University Press.

Bronfenbrenner, U. (1995). The bioecological model from a life course perspective: Reflections of a participant observer. In P. Moen, G. H. Elder, & K. Luscher (Eds.), *Examining lives in context: Perspectives on the ecology of human development* (pp. 599–647). Washington, DC: American Psychological Association.

Browers, R. T. (2001). Counseling in mental health and private practice settings. In D. Capuzzi & D. R. Gross (Eds.), *Introduction to the counseling profession* (3rd ed., pp. 316–338). Needham Heights, MA: Allyn & Bacon.

CenterPoint Human Services. (2002). Substance abuse services. Retrieved December 28, 2002, from http://www.cphs.org/sa.htm

Clawson, T. W., & Rhodes, K. K. (1999). Certified clinical mental health counselors: History, development, and future. In J. S. Hinkle (Ed.), *Promoting optimum mental health through counseling: An overview* (pp. 25–30). Greensboro, NC: CAPS Publications.

Duffy, K. G., & Wong, F. Y. (2000). *Community psychology* (2nd ed.). Needham Heights, MA: Allyn & Bacon.

Evans, W. N. (1998). Assessment and diagnosis of the substance use disorders (SUDS). *Journal of Counseling and Development, 76,* 325–333.

First Line. (2001). *Directory of community resources*. United Way of Forsyth County, NC.

Foliart, D. E., Clausen, M., & Siljestrom, C. (2001). Bereavement practices among California hospices: Results of a statewide survey. *Death Studies, 25,* 461–467.

Golden, G. K., & Frank, P. B. (1994). When 50-50 isn't fair: The case against couple counseling in domestic abuse. *Social Work, 39,* 636–637.

Haddock, S. A. (2002). Training family therapists to assess for and intervene in partner abuse: A curriculum for graduate courses, professional workshops, and self-study. *Journal of Marital and Family Therapy, 28,* 193–202.

Hampton, D. (2002). *Grief counseling: It's all about loss*. Unpublished manuscript.

Henderson, P. A. (1997). Psychosocial adjustment of adult cancer survivors: Their needs and counselor interventions. *Journal of Counseling and Development, 75,* 188–194.

Henggeler, S. W., Schoenwald, S. K., Borduin, C. M., Rowland, M. D., & Cunningham, P. B. (1998). *Multisystemic treatment of antisocial behavior in children and adolescents*. New York: Guilford Press.

Hershenson, D. B., Power, P. W., & Waldo, M. (1996). *Community counseling: Contemporary theory and practice*. Needham Heights, MA: Allyn & Bacon.

Hollis, J. W. (2000). *Counselor preparation, 1999–2001* (10th ed.). Philadelphia: Taylor & Francis.

Hospice and Palliative Care Center. (2002). *Programs and services at a glance* [Brochure]. Winston-Salem, NC: Author.

James, R. K., & Gilliland, B. E. (2001). *Crisis intervention strategies* (4th ed., pp. 282–383). Belmont, CA: Wadsworth.

Johnson, L. S. (1997). Developmental strategies for counseling the child whose parent or sibling has cancer. *Journal of Counseling and Development, 75,* 417–427.

L'Abate, L. (1992). Introduction. In L. L'Abate, G. E. Farrar, & D. A. Serritella (Eds.), *Handbook of differential treatments for addiction* (pp. 1–4). Boston: Allyn & Bacon.

L'Abate, L., Farrar, G. E., & Serritella, D. A. (Eds.). (1992). *Handbook of differential treatments for addiction*. Boston: Allyn & Bacon.

Lerner, M. (1994). Training for cancer: An interview with Michael Lerner. *The Journal of Mind-Body Health, 10,* 27–37.

Lewis, J. A., Lewis, M. D., Daniels, J. A., & D'Andrea, M. J. (2003). *Community counseling: Empowerment strategies for a diverse society* (3rd ed.). Pacific Grove, CA: Brooks/Cole.

MacCluskie, K. C., & Ingersoll, R. E. (2001). *Becoming a 21st century agency counselor*. Belmont, CA: Wadsworth.

Miller, W. R., & Brown, S. A. (1997). Why psychologists should treat alcohol and drug problems. *American Psychologist, 52,* 1269–1279.

National Coalition Against Domestic Violence. (2002). National Coalition Against Domestic Violence Web site. Retrieved December 30, 2002, from http://www.ncadv.org/

Pidcock, B. W., & Polansky, J. (2001). Clinical practice issues in assessing for adult substance use disorders. In E. R. Welfel & R. E. Ingersoll (Eds.), *The mental health desk reference: A sourcebook for counselors and therapists* (pp. 128–135). New York: Wiley.

Prochaska, J. O., DiClemente, C. C., & Norcross, J. C. (1992). In search of how people change: Applications to addictive behaviors. *American Psychologist, 47,* 1102–1114.

Prochaska, J. O., & Norcross, J. C. (1999). *Systems of psychotherapy: A transtheoretical analysis.* Pacific Grove, CA: Brooks/Cole.

Schoenwald, S. K., Brown, T. L., & Henggeler, S. W. (2000). Inside multisystemic therapy: Therapist, supervisory, and program practices. *Journal of Emotional and Behavioral Disorders, 8,* 113–127.

Scott, C. G. (2000). Ethical issues in addiction counseling. *Rehabilitation Counseling Bulletin, 43,* 209–214.

Stevens-Smith, P., & Smith, R. L. (1998). *Substance abuse counseling: Theory and practice.* Upper Saddle River, NJ: Merrill/Prentice Hall.

Stoddard, S. (1992). *The hospice movement: A better way of caring for the dying* (rev. ed.). New York: Random House.

Stroul, B. A. (1988). *Series on community-based services for children and adolescents who are severely emotionally disturbed, Vol. I: Home-based services.* Washington, DC: CASSP Technical Assistance Center, Georgetown University Child Development Center.

Surgeon General Report. (2000). Mental health: A report of the Surgeon General. Retrieved December 1, 2002, from http://www.surgeongeneral.gov/Library/MentalHealth

Thombs, D. L., & Osborn, C. J. (2001). A cluster analysis study of clinical orientations among chemical dependency counselors. *Journal of Counseling and Development, 79,* 450–458.

U.S. Department of Justice. (2000). Domestic violence. Retrieved May 16, 2001, from http://www.usdoj.gov/domesticviolence.htm.

Veach, T. A., & Nicholas, D. R. (1998). Understanding families of adults with cancer: Combining the clinical course of cancer and stages of family development. *Journal of Counseling and Development, 76,* 144–156.

Viger, J. (2001). Community mental health centers. Retrieved December 28, 2002, from http://www.echoman.com/knowledgesource/Community_Mental_Health_Centers.htm

Von Steen, P. G., Vacc, N. A., & Strickland, I. M. (2002). The treatment of substance-abusing clients in multiservice mental health agencies: A practice analysis. *Journal of Addictions and Offender Counseling, 22,* 61–71.

Wake Forest University Baptist Medical Center. (2002). Patient care/department of psychiatry and behavioral medicine. Retrieved December 28, 2002, from http://www.wfubmc.edu/psychiatry

Walker, L. E. (2000). Battered woman syndrome (2nd ed.). New York: Springer.

CHAPTER 14

Counseling in Other Community Settings

Far in the back of his mind he harbors thoughts
*   like small boats in a quiet cove*
*   ready to set sail at a moment's notice.*
I, seated on his starboard side,
*   listen for the winds of change*
*   ready to lift anchor with him*
*   and explore the choppy waves of life ahead.*
Counseling requires a special patience
*   best known to seamen and navigators—*
*   courses are only charted for times*
*   when the tide is high and the breezes steady.*

From "Harbor Thoughts," by S. T. Gladding, 1985, *Journal of Humanistic Education and Development, 23,* p. 68. © 1985 by ACA. Reprinted with permission. No further reproduction authorized without written permission of the American Counseling Association.

This chapter examines three counseling specialties that appeal to many community counselors—career counseling, employee assistance program (EAP) counseling, and private practice. The activities of counselors who engage in these specialties are conducted in a variety of settings ranging from those that are primarily educational to those that are affiliated with business or government agencies.

Career counselors assist clients in determining what occupations they are best suited for and help them prepare for finding employment. EAP counselors work with companies and institutions on either in an in-house or on a referral basis to offer counseling, referral, or prevention-based initiatives to workers in employment settings. Finally, private practitioners are counselors who work independently or in a group with other clinicians. They are both counseling and business minded. Many such counselors are generalists; however, some private practitioners specialize in helping people with specific disorders or concerns, including grief, depression, anxiety, eating disorders, and family transitions, to name just a few.

Thus, community counselors who choose any of the specialties and settings just described have universal and unique foci. On a universal level, they engage in activities that overlap one another, such as administering and interpreting assessment instruments or finding helpful resources within their respective communities. On a unique level, their work environments and orientation to client needs impact how they interact and where they choose to focus their attention.

CAREER COUNSELING

Choosing a career is more than simply deciding what one will do to earn a living. Occupations influence a person's whole way of life, including physical, mental, and emotional health. Work roles and other life roles are often interconnected (Imbimbo, 1994). Thus, income, stress, social identity, meaning, education, clothes, hobbies, interests, friends, lifestyle, place of residence, and even personality characteristics are linked to one's work life (Herr & Cramer, 1996). In some cases, work groups serve as cultures in which social needs are met and values developed (Tart, 1986). The nature and purpose of a person's work are related to his or her sense of identity, well-being, and life satisfaction (Burlew, 1992). Qualitative research indicates that individuals who appear most happy in their work are committed to following their interests; exhibit a breadth of personal competencies and strengths; and function in work environments that are characterized by freedom, challenge, meaning, and a positive social atmosphere (Henderson, 2000).

Yet, despite evidence highlighting the importance of work, many individuals do not systematically explore and choose their careers. In surveys commissioned by the National Career Development Association (NCDA) and the National Occupational Information Coordinating Committee (NOICC), it was found that approximately 40 percent of adults selected their careers by conscious planning and nearly 70 percent of adults would investigate job options more thoroughly if they were starting the process over again (cited in Brown, 2003). Therefore, it is important that individuals obtain career information early and enter the job market with knowledge and flexibility in regard to their plans.

Box 14–1

"It is so important to plan your career and not drift wherever the wind blows," says Friedberg, who is a New York-based career coach with the Five O'Clock Club, a national career counseling organization, and has a private practice in the city. "You must do some careful long-term strategic assessment, think about what you might need at each stage of your life, commit to a plan, and accept the fact that there will be some trade-off along the way. Too often, people try to fit themselves into a job and end up patterning their lives after it. What they should do instead is find a job that fits them and fits into their lives."

—(cited in Hayes, 2001)

A variety of factors, some unique and others common, influence the process of career development. For instance, personality styles, developmental stages, values, skills, and cultural factors all impact career development and career choice (Drummond & Ryan, 1995). Serendipity and happenstance (Guindon & Hanna, 2002; Miller, 1983), family background (Helwig & Myrin, 1997), gender (Hotchkiss & Borow, 1996), giftedness (Rysiew, Shore, & Leeb, 1999), and age (Canaff, 1997) may also affect the selection of a career. Other influential factors include local and global economic conditions, trends in the workplace, and the accessibility of career information (Borgen, 1997; Brown, 2003).

The National Career Development Association (NCDA; formerly the National Vocational Guidance Association [NVGA]) and the National Employment Counselors Association (NECA) are the two divisions within the American Counseling Association (ACA) primarily devoted to career development and career counseling. The NCDA, the oldest division within the ACA, traces its roots back to 1913 (NCDA, 2001). The association is made up of professionals in business and industry, rehabilitation agencies, government, private practice, and educational settings. Its mission is to promote the career development of all people across the life span by providing services to the public and to professionals involved in career development (NCDA, 2001). NECA, which also is comprised of a diverse membership, was founded to offer professional leadership to people who counsel in employment services or career development settings and to people employed in related areas of counselor education, research, administration, or supervision (NECA, 2003). Until 1966, NECA was an interest group of NCDA (Meyer, Helwig, Gjernes, & Chickering, 1985). Both divisions publish quarterly journals: the *Career Development Quarterly* (formerly the *Vocational Guidance Quarterly*) and the *Journal of Employment Counseling,* respectively.

Another group that promotes career development is the National Occupational Information Coordinating Committee (NOICC). NOICC is not a professional counseling organization; instead, it is a federal interagency organization that works with the Department of Defense, the Department of Labor, and the Department of Education to promote excellence in the way occupational information is compiled and delivered (Brown, 2003). A State Occupational Information Coordinating Committee (SOICC) exists in each state and works in conjunction with NOICC to accomplish overarching national goals.

Career Counseling and Related Terminology

Career counseling is a hybrid discipline, often misunderstood and not always fully appreciated by many professionals or the public. Changes that have taken place in society and the world-of-work have resulted in changes in the practice and definition of career counseling. Several current definitions of career counseling are worth examining. The NCDA (1997) defines *career counseling* as "the process of assisting individuals in the development of a life-career with focus on the definition of the worker role and how that role interacts with other roles" (p. 1). Niles and Harris-Bowlsbey (2002) describe career counseling as a formal relationship in which a counselor helps a client or group of clients find ways to cope more effectively with career concerns, including making a career choice, handling career transitions, and managing job-related stress. Career counseling can also be viewed as "a series of general and specific interventions throughout the life span" dealing with issues pertaining to self-understanding, work selection and satisfaction, work site behavior, and life style issues (e.g., balancing work, family, and leisure) (Engels, Minor, Sampson, & Splete, 1995, p. 134).

Each of the above definitions illustrates the broad scope of career counseling—a complex process that is both a counseling specialty and a core element of general counseling practice. By necessity, career counselors in the 21st century possess a wide range of competencies that encompass general counseling skills as well as skills, knowledge and awareness specific to the career domain (Niles & Harris-Bowlsbey, 2002).

Throughout its history, career development and career counseling have been known by several different names, including *vocational guidance, occupational counseling,* and *vocational counseling.* Differences in terminology reflect changes in viewpoints about the meaning of work and its significance in our society. To understand the process of career counseling as it is conceptualized in the 21st century, it is first important to clarify terms associated with *career* and *career counseling.*

Three terms associated with the term *career* are *job, occupation,* and *vocation.* A *job* is merely an activity undertaken for economic returns (Fox, 1994), whereas an *occupation* may be defined as a group of similar jobs found in different industries or organizations (Herr & Cramer, 1996). The term *vocation,* which is sometimes used synonymously with *occupation,* implies a psychological commitment or calling to a particular field. Each of these terms is somewhat limited in scope. In contrast, the term *career* is broader, more modern, and more inclusive than other terminology and is discussed next.

Career development specialists have defined *career* in a number of ways. According to Sears (1982), a career is the totality of work one does in a lifetime. It is a lifelong process that encompasses psychological, sociological, educational, economic, physical, and chance factors. Brown (2003) adds to Sears's definition by emphasizing the importance of cultural factors to the career development process. Super's (1976) classic definition of *career* incorporates many of these same factors. Super defined *career* as:

> . . . the course of events that constitutes a life; the sequence of occupations and other life roles which combine to express one's commitment to work in his or her total pattern of self-development; the series of remunerated and nonremunerated positions occupied by a person from adolescence through retirement, of which occupation is only one. A career

includes work-related roles such as those of student, employee, and pensioner together with complementary avocational, familial, and civic roles. Careers exist only as people pursue them; they are person-centered. (p. 4)

Although not disagreeing with Super, McDaniels (1984) broadens the definition to emphasize the importance of leisure as a life role. He contends that leisure will occupy an increasingly important role in the lives of all individuals in the future. According to McDaniels, the integration and interaction of work and leisure in a person's career over the life span are fundamental and can be expressed in the formula "Career equals Work plus Leisure" ($C = W + L$). Similarly, Liptak (2001) emphasizes the interaction between work and leisure activities, maintaining that effective career counseling involves helping clients fuse work and leisure experiences in order to gain greater life satisfaction.

Four additional terms related to the process of career counseling include *career education, career information, career intervention,* and *career coaching.* To help build a foundation for what follows, we define each term briefly here, and then provide elaboration in subsequent sections of the chapter:

- *Career Education:* a systematic attempt to influence the career development of students and adults through various educational strategies, including providing occupational information, infusing career-related concepts into the academic curriculum, and offering career planning courses (Brown, 2003).
- *Career Information:* information about the labor market, including job trends, industries, and comprehensive information systems. In the 21st century, a primary source of career information is the Internet (Brown, 2003).
- *Career Intervention:* a deliberate act designed to empower people to cope effectively with career development tasks (Spokane, 1991). Career interventions include individual and group career counseling, career development programs, computer information delivery systems, and career education (Niles & Harris-Bowlsbey, 2002).
- *Career Coaching:* a term used in business and industry that refers to managers' efforts to facilitate the career development of employees (Brown, 2003).

Just as it is important for community counselors to be familiar with current terminology related to career development and career counseling, it also is essential for them to be informed about the different theories of career development that guide career counseling practice. Although it would be beyond the scope and purpose of this text to elaborate on each of the theories that has contributed to our knowledge about career development, in the next section, we summarize the central concepts of four theories that have influenced past and current research and practice.

Career Development Theories

Career development theories try to explain why individuals choose careers. They also deal with the career adjustments people make over time, because people living in the 21st century are likely to change jobs several times over their life span. Modern theories, which are broad and comprehensive in regard to individual and occupational development, began appearing in the literature in the 1950s (Gysbers,

Heppner, & Johnston, 2003). The theories of Donald Super and John Holland are perhaps the most utilized and/or recognized theories of career development (Weinrach, 1996), although a number of other career theories have been generated and some are currently evolving (Zunker, 2002). The theories described here (i.e., trait-and-factor, developmental, learning, and social–cognitive) and the counseling procedures that go with them are among the most prominent.

Trait-and-factor theory.   The origin of trait-and-factor theory can be traced back to Frank Parsons. The theory stresses that the traits of clients should first be assessed and then systematically matched with factors inherent in various occupations. Its most widespread influence occurred during the Great Depression when E. G. Williamson (1939) championed its use. Trait-and-factor theory fell out of favor during the 1950s and 1960s but has resurfaced in a more modern form, which is best characterized as "structural" and is reflected in the work of researchers such as John Holland (1997). The trait-and-factor approach has always stressed the uniqueness of persons. Original advocates of the theory assumed that a person's abilities and traits could be measured objectively and quantified. Personal motivation was considered relatively stable. Thus, satisfaction in a particular occupation depended on a proper fit between one's abilities and the job requirements.

In its modern form, trait-and-factor theory stresses the interpersonal nature of careers and associated lifestyles as well as the performance requirements of a work position. Holland (1997) identifies six categories in which personality types and job environments can be classified: realistic, investigative, artistic, social, enterprising, and conventional (RIASEC) (see Figure 14–1). According to prestige

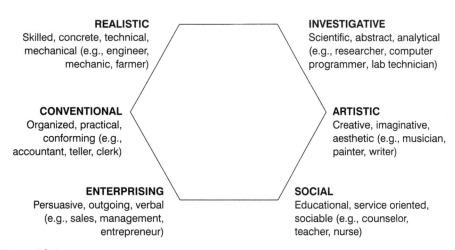

Figure 14–1

Holland's six categories of personality and occupation

levels, investigative (I) occupations rank highest, followed by enterprising (E), artistic (A), and social (S) occupations, which have roughly the same level of prestige. The lowest levels of prestige are realistic (R) and conventional (C) occupations (Gottfredson, 1981).

Personal satisfaction in a work setting depends on a number of factors, but among the most important is the degree of congruence between personality type, work environment, and social class (Gade, Fuqua, & Hurlburt, 1988; Holland & Gottfredson, 1976; Savickas, 1989). Also as a general rule, with notable exceptions, "women value language-related tasks more, and men value mathematics-related tasks more" (Trusty, Robinson, Plata, & Ng, 2000, p. 470). Some nonpsychological factors, such as economic or cultural influences, account for why many professional and nonprofessional workers accept and keep their jobs (Brown & Brooks, 1991; Salomone & Sheehan, 1985).

Nevertheless, as Holland emphasizes, it is vital for persons to have adequate knowledge of themselves and of working environments in order to make informed career decisions. According to Holland, a three-letter code represents a client's overall personality, which can be matched with a type of work environment. Three-letter codes tend to remain relatively stable over the life span beginning as early as high school (Miller, 2002). For example, a profile of **SAE** would suggest that a person is most similar to a social type, then to an artistic type, and finally to an enterprising type. However, it is the interaction of letter codes that influences the makeup of the person and his or her fit in an occupational environment. Miller (1998) suggests that instead of using the three highest scores on Holland's hexagon for such a purpose that the top two, middle two, and lowest two scores be paired and presented to give the client a more complete picture of his or her personality profile and similarity to others in a given career. When only the first three letters are examined, Donald Super's profile would be S/I/R, whereas John Holland's profile would be A/E/IRS (representing a tie for the third letter in the code). However, when Miller's criterion is followed, Super's profile is represented as SI/RA/EC, with Holland's profile being AE/IR/SC (Weinrach, 1996).

Developmental theories. Two of the most widely known developmental theories are those associated with Donald Super and Eli Ginzberg. Both theories focus on personal growth and development. The original developmental theory proposed by Ginzberg and his associates has had great influence and has been revised to reflect a more comprehensive life span approach (Ginzberg, 1972). But Super's theory is examined in detail here because it has been researched and implemented more extensively.

Compared to other approaches, developmental theories are generally more inclusive, more concerned with longitudinal expression of career behavior, and more inclined to highlight the importance of self-concept. Super's life-span, life-space approach (1957, 1980, 1990) posits that career development is the lifelong process of implementing a self-concept. People's views of themselves are reflected in what they do. Super suggests that vocational development unfolds in five stages, each of which contains a developmental task to be completed (see Table 14–1). The first stage is *growth* (from birth to age 14). During this stage, with its substages of fantasy (ages 4–10), interest (ages 11–12), and capacity (ages 13–14), children form a mental picture of themselves in relation to others. During the process of growth, children become oriented to the world of work.

The second stage, *exploration* (ages 15–24), has three substages: tentative (ages 15–17), transition (ages 18–21), and trial (ages 22–24). The major tasks of this stage include a general exploration of the world of work and the specification of a career preference.

The third stage is known as *establishment* (ages 25–44). Its two substages, trial (ages 25–30) and advancement (ages 31–44), constitute the major task of becoming established in a preferred and appropriate field of work. Once established, persons can concentrate on advancement until they reach the top of the professions, tire of their job, or are forced to change jobs.

The fourth stage, *maintenance* (ages 45–64), has the major task of preserving what one has already achieved. The final stage, *disengagement* (formerly called *decline;* age 65 to death), is a time for detaching from work and aligning with other sources of life satisfaction. Tasks associated with this stage include deceleration, retirement planning, and retirement living (Niles & Harris-Bowlsbey, 2002).

Super (1990) also suggested that a small (mini) cycle takes place when people transition from one stage to the next or each time they are destabilized by downsizing, illness or injury, or other socioeconomic or personal events. Consequently, "adults may recycle through various career development stages and tasks, depending on their situations in life" (Niles & Harris-Bowlsbey, p. 33). For example, if a 40-year-old man loses the job he has had with a particular company for the past 20 years, he is likely to re-enter the *exploration* stage, as he re-examines options and opportunities.

Whereas Super's concept of *life span* is characterized by five stages and recycling, the concept of *life space* refers to the combination of life roles in which people participate (Super, 1980). These roles include those of son or daughter, student, leisurite, citizen, worker, spouse (or partner), homemaker, parent, and pensioner. People participate in various roles in specific arenas, such as the home, the school, the workplace, and the community. The degree of salience people attach to different roles, the amount of time allotted to each, and the extent to which life-roles overlap and/or interact all influence life satisfaction. When life seems out of balance or stressful, it may be due to attempts at balancing multiple roles in a manner that is not satisfying.

The major contributions of developmental career counseling are its emphases on the importance of the life span in career decision making and on career decisions that are influenced by other processes and events in a person's life. This "life pattern paradigm for career counseling encourages counselors to consider a client's aptitudes and interests in a matrix of life experiences, not just in comparison to some normative group" (Savickas, 1989, p. 127).

Table 14–1
Super's stages

Growth	Exploration	Establishment	Maintenance	Disengagement
Birth	**14 years**	**24 years**	**44 years**	**64 years**
Self-concept develops through identification with key figures in family and school; needs and fantasy are dominant early in this stage; interest and capacity become more important with increasing social participation and reality testing; learn behaviors associated with self-help, social interaction, self-direction, industrialness, goal setting, persistence.	Self-examination, role try-outs and occupational exploration take place in school, leisure activities, and part-time work.	Having found an appropriate field, an effort is made to establish a permanent place in it. Thereafter changes which occur are changes of position, job, or employer, not of occupation.	Having made a place in the world of work, the concern is how to hold on to it. Little new ground is broken, continuation of established pattern. Concerned about maintaining present status while being forced by competition from younger workers in the advancement stage.	As physical and mental powers decline, work activity changes and in due course ceases. New roles must be developed: first, selective participant and then observer. Individual must find other sources of satisfaction to replace those lost through retirement.
Substages	**Substages**	**Substages**		**Substages**
Fantasy (4–10) Needs are dominant; role playing in fantasy is important.	*Tentative* (15–17) Needs, interests, capacities, values and opportunities are all considered; tentative choices are made and tried out in fantasy, discussion, courses, work, etc. Possible appropriate fields and levels of work are identified.	*Trial-Commitment and Stabilization* (25–30) Setting down. Securing a permanent place in the chosen occupation. May prove unsatisfactory resulting in one or two changes before the life work is found or before it becomes clear that the life work will be a succession of unrelated jobs.		*Deceleration* (65–70) The pace of work slackens, duties are shifted, or the nature of work is changed to suit declining capacities. Many find part-time jobs to replace their full-time occupations.
Interest (11–12) Likes are the major determinant of aspirations and activities.		*Advancement* (31–44) Effort is put forth to stabilize, to make a secure place in the world of work. For most persons these are the creative years. Seniority is acquired; clientele are developed; superior performance is demonstrated; qualifications are improved.		*Retirement* (71 on) Variation on complete cessation of work or shift to part-time, volunteer, or leisure activities.
Capacity (13–14) Abilities are given more weight and job requirements (including training) are considered.				

Tasks

Developing a picture of the kind of person one is.

Developing an orientation to the world of work and an understanding of the meaning of work.

Task—Crystallizing a Vocational Preference

Transition (18–21) Reality considerations are given more weight as the person enters the labor market or professional training and attempts to implement a self-concept. Generalized choice is converted to specific choice.

Task—Specifying a Vocational Preference

Trial–Little Commitment (22–24) A seemingly appropriate occupation having been found, a first job is located and is tried out as a potential life work. Commitment is still provisional, and if the job is not appropriate, the person may reinstitute the process of crystallizing, specifying, and implementing a preference. Implementing a vocational preference. Developing a realistic self-concept. Learning more about more opportunities.

Tasks

Finding opportunity to do desired work.
Learning to relate to others.
Consolidation and advancement.
Making occupational position secure.
Settling down in a permanent position.

Tasks

Accepting one's limitations.
Identifying new problems to work on.
Developing new skills.
Focusing on essential activities.
Preservation of achieved status and gains.

Tasks

Developing nonoccupational roles.
Finding a good retirement spot.
Doing things one has always wanted to do.
Reducing working hours.

Source: From *Career Guidance and Counseling Through the Life Span: Systematic Approaches* (5th ed.) by Edwin L. Herr and Stanley H. Cramer. Published by Allyn and Bacon, Boston, MA. Copyright © 1997 by Pearson Education. Reprinted by permission of the publisher.

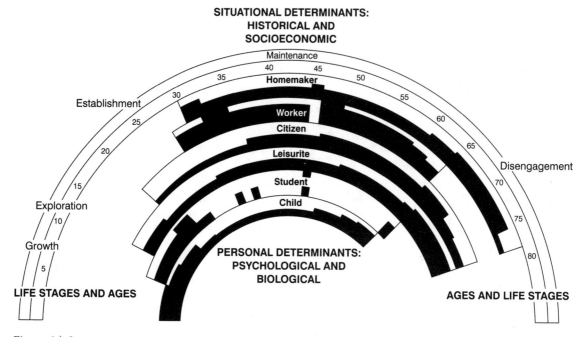

Figure 14–2
Super's rainbow theory: Six life roles in schematic life space
Source: From "Career and Life Development," by D. F. Super, 1990, *Career Choice and Development: Applying Contemporary Theories to Practice* (2nd ed.) San Francisco: Josey-Bass. © 1990 by Donald Super. Used with permission of Jossey-Bass.

The developmental approach can be conceptualized as career-pattern counsel-ing (Super, 1954). Although this method has been criticized for its historical and descriptive emphases, these features, along with the conceptual depth of the theory, have also been considered strengths (Herr, 1997). Overall, developmental career counseling is strong and continues to grow beyond the comprehensive *rainbow theory* that Super conceptualized toward the end of his life (Super, 1990; Super, Thompson, & Lindeman, 1988) (see Figure 14–2).

Learning theory of career counseling.   A third influential career development the-ory was originally proposed by John Krumboltz in 1979, at which time it was called the *social learning theory* of career decision making and was based on Bandura's (1977, 1986) social cognitive theory. In recent years, Krumboltz and his colleagues have developed the theory further to include specific applications of social learning theory to the practice of career counseling. The expanded theory is called the *learning theory of career counseling* (LTCC).

According to LTCC (Mitchell & Krumboltz, 1996), four factors influence a person's career decision making: genetic endowment (innate traits and abilities), environmental conditions and events (which may be planned or unplanned), learning experiences (instrumental and associative learning), and task-approach skills (work habits, expectations of performance, cognitive processes, and emotional response patterns). As a result of the interaction of these four factors, people form beliefs about their own abilities (self-observation generalizations) and beliefs about the world (worldview generalizations). These generalizations affect actions and decisions relevant to the career-planning process.

The goal of career counseling from an LTCC perspective is to help clients develop skills, interests, beliefs, values, work habits, and personal qualities that will enable them to have satisfying lives within a dynamic work environment (Swanson & Fouad, 1999). Often, career counselors serve as coaches or mentors as they help clients develop new beliefs, attitudes, and skills. Interventions may be developmental and preventive (e.g., career education, job clubs) or targeted and remedial (directed toward cognitions and behaviors).

Recently, Mitchell, Levin, and Krumboltz (1999) have amended the learning theory of career counseling to include the construct of *planned happenstance*. The term, which at first glance appears oxymoronic, refers to the "creating and transforming of unplanned events into opportunities for learning" (Mitchell et al., 1999, p. 117). Career counselors can help clients develop attitudes that enable them to recognize, create, and use events that happen by chance as career opportunities. Moreover, counselors can help their clients learn to be comfortable with ambiguity and indecision, thereby making it possible for them to capitalize on unforeseen future events.

Social cognitive career theory.   An emerging theory of career development that has been the subject of much current research is social cognitive career theory (SCCT). Proposed by Lent, Brown, and Hackett (1994), SCCT provides a framework for explaining career development that focuses on the "(a) formation and elaboration of career-relevant interests, (b) the selection of academic and career choice options, and (c) performance and persistence in educational and occupational pursuits" (Lent et al., 1994, p. 79). Like Krumboltz's LTCC theory, SCCT derived from Bandura's (1977, 1986) social cognitive theory. As with LTCC, a primary assumption of SCCT is that a complex array of factors, including culture, gender, genetic endowment, and health, affect people's beliefs, interests, and subsequent career decision-making behaviors. However, Lent et al. emphasize two additional constructs—self-efficacy beliefs and outcome expectations—in a manner that differs from Krumboltz's approach.

Self-efficacy refers to an individual's beliefs about his or her ability to successfully perform a particular task (Bandura, 1977, 1986). Outcome expectations are the consequences a person expects to occur following a particular course of action (Bandura, 1986). According to SCCT, self-efficacy beliefs and outcome expectations influence the development of career-related interests. These interests, in turn, influence the development of career-related aspirations and goals (Lent et al., 1994).

Two other key constructs believed to influence career interests and goals are people's perceptions of barriers and their perceptions of supports (Lent, Brown, & Hackett, 2000). To illustrate, even if a person possesses high levels of self-efficacy, high expectations, and interests that match a particular career, that person may avoid pursuing the career if barriers toward that pursuit appear insurmountable. In contrast, an individual's perception of certain supports (e.g., family, community) may enhance the likelihood that he or she will embark on a particular career path.

SCCT has particular relevance for addressing the unique factors that shape the career development of women, ethnic minorities, gay and lesbian individuals, and others who are members of cultural minorities (McWhirter & Flojo, 2001). Career counselors who follow an SCCT approach acknowledge the influence of contextual factors on cognitions, interests, and goals. Counselors working from this perspective may implement interventions that help clients:

- Identify options that may have been foreclosed due to unrealistic or faulty self-efficacy beliefs or outcome expectations.
- Identify perceived barriers that may have led clients to eliminate career possibilities prematurely and then examine how realistic those perceptions of barriers are.
- Modify and counteract faulty beliefs and expectations as well as faulty occupational information (Swanson & Fouad, 1999).

Theories of career development serve as road maps to help counselors understand their clients' career-related beliefs, behaviors, and aspirations (Krumboltz, 1994). Theoretical approaches help career counselors make sense of the information clients bring them about work-related issues (Swanson & Fouad, 1999). Many career counselors adopt a holistic approach to career counseling that integrates key constructs from various theories that have particular relevance for particular clients dealing with particular issues. A strong understanding of career development theories and their applications guides counselors as they become skilled in implementing effective career interventions.

Career Counseling Process and Skills

As mentioned previously, career counseling is a complex process that has evolved throughout the years. Niles and Harris-Bowlsbey (2002) highlight a number of factors that have contributed to rapid change in the world-of-work and the delivery of career counseling services, including:

- An interdependent global economy
- Continued advancement in technology, especially Internet services
- An increasingly diverse workforce
- Higher levels of unemployment
- Corporate downsizing
- An increased number of dual-career families and number of people working from locations away from the workplace.

Box 14–2
Career coaching by telephone

As a part of the relocation package offered to employees of our client companies, my job was to contact the "trailing" spouse and offer assistance in his or her own career move. The service was available without charge to the spouse and could include any or all of the following: the *Myers-Briggs Type Indicator* (MBTI) and *Strong Interest Inventory* (SII) administration and interpretation, rèsumè critiques, practice interviews, job search strategies and contact information for potential employers. All of the services were provided over the telephone—in the vast majority of cases, I never met the client in person.

That was the primary challenge—establishing rapport with the client via the telephone. Also, because some clients were only available at night or on weekends, it was hard to separate working hours and personal time.

The benefits included the ability to work from home and in one's casual clothes or even pajamas. The company that employed me provided great support in the form of test administration and research about targeted industries. There were personal rewards as well. Often the spouse was surprised and pleased to find out there was someone interested in his or her own employment challenges and personal reaction to the upcoming move.

—Pamela Karr, M.A.Ed., NCC, LPC

To meet the needs of clients seeking help with career-related issues, career counselors need to be skilled in several areas. According to Brown (2003), some of the more important skills career counselors need to develop include the following:

*   Understanding the career development process across the life span
*   Knowing how to locate and access career information and evaluate its usefulness
*   Understanding how to integrate career assessment into career counseling
*   Understanding trends that will shape the workplace over the next decade
*   Understanding the processes by which people locate and secure jobs using Internet sources
*   Being able to implement culturally sensitive career counseling skills.

The NCDA has developed and revised a set of career counseling competency statements designed to guide the practice of professional career counselor. The competency statements, which can be accessed at www.ncda.org/pdf/counselingcompetencies.pdf, focus on a broad range of general counseling and specific career-related skills. In this section, we highlight three essential skill areas: conducting career-related assessment, providing career information, and counseling diverse clientele.

Career assessment.   It is not uncommon for clients to enter career counseling with the misconception that the counselor will give them tests that will magically reveal the perfect career match. Perhaps this misconception stems from the early days of trait-and-factor theory, when Frank Parson's model of career counseling predominated. The Parsonian model encouraged career counselors "to objectify interests, values, and abilities through the use of standardized assessment to guide people in identifying where they fit within the occupational structure" (Niles & Harris-Bowlsbey, p. 10). In today's society, the complex process of career counseling goes well beyond the "test and tell" method, and counselors recognize the limitations associated with standardized testing. Therefore, it is important for career counselors to clarify their role from the outset, so that the client understands the purposes and limits of career counseling and assessment.

Although career assessment does not act as a crystal ball, it does serve a key role in career counseling. As stated in Chapter 6, assessment is an ongoing activity that takes place throughout the entire counseling process, from referral to follow-up (Hohenshil, 1996). Formal and informal methods of assessment help counselors gather information to determine the nature of clients' issues, the prevalence of their problems, and their strengths and skills, (Whiston, 2000). Similarly, career-related assessment may be formal or informal, is used to gather client information, and helps evaluate individual strengths and areas of concern. Spokane (1991) suggested that "the purposes of career assessment are to unearth congruent career possibilities, to assess conflicts and problems, to motivate constructive behavior, to acquire a cognitive structure for evaluating career alternatives, to clarify expectations and plan interventions, and to establish range of abilities" (cited in Whiston, 2000, p. 190).

Conceptually, it is helpful to divide career assessment into two major categories: assessment of individual differences and assessment of the career choice process (see Betz, 1992 and Whiston, 2000). Assessment of individual differences is conducted to increase client self-awareness in multiple areas, including interests, values, needs, personality attributes, and skills and abilities. In contrast, assessing the career choice process involves measuring where clients are in the decision-making process. Assessment in this area may include measuring degree of career maturity or level of decidedness (Whiston). A plethora of career assessment instruments have been published during the past several decades, some of which have stronger psychometric properties than others. Publications such as *A Counselor's Guide to Career Assessments* (4th ed.) can be especially helpful in describing characteristics of various instruments, including purpose, reading level, validity, reliability, and cultural fairness (Niles & Harris-Bowlsbey, 2002).

Computer-assisted assessment in career counseling is likely to become even more prevalent during the 21st century. Career assessment can be conducted online, or instruments can be purchased for computerized administration and interpretation. When computers are used in career assessment, scoring errors are avoided and results are obtained quickly, thus saving time for professionals and eliminating the wait period for clients. However, several concerns have been raised in regard to computer-assisted assessment. Whiston (2000) summarizes some of those concerns by stating:

> With the ease of computer-generated reports, clinicians may be lulled into a false sense of security and use the computer-generated results without becoming educated about the instrument. Instruments used in counseling are validated for specific purposes; therefore, a counselor cannot in isolation use a general computer-generated report. The American Counseling Association's *Code of Ethics and Standards of Practice* (ACA, 1995) clearly states that clinicians must be trained in the construct and the specific instrument prior to using a computer-generated report. . . . Simply using a computer-generated report

without knowledge of the instrument's strengths and limitations is negligent and unprofessional. Computer-generated reports are designed to supplement or complement the clinician's interpretation of the results, not replace them. (pp. 353–354)

Qualitative methods of assessment, which encourage active client participation, are especially applicable to career counseling. Qualitative approaches can be used alone or in conjunction with quantitative instruments (McWhirter & Flojo, 2001). Through qualitative assessment procedures, clients have opportunities to tell their stories and explore the meaning they take from those stories (McMahon, Patton, & Watson, 2003). There are several examples of qualitative assessment processes, including card sorts, lifelines, and career genograms. The career genogram is similar to the family genogram described in Chapters 9 and 11 in that it creates a graphic representation of a client's family spanning three generations. It "is particularly useful because it provides a direct and relevant framework for use with clients to shed light on many topics, including their worldviews, possible environmental barriers, personal-work-family role conflicts, racial identity status and issues, and levels of acculturation" (Gysbers, Heppner, & Johnston, 2003, p. 202). The career genogram provides a venue through which the client can describe family relationships and prevailing attitudes about the various occupations that have been charted.

Qualitative and quantitative forms of career assessment can help clients clarify values, interests, skills, and personality traits that affect career development and choice. In summarizing important points related to the use of assessment in career counseling, Niles and Harris-Bowlsbey (2002) remind us that:

- The results of assessment tools are only one piece of data that the client and counselor use to consider career options. They should be interpreted in conjunction with other data, including the client's self-knowledge, past experiences, and knowledge about world of work.
- Using assessment to identify new concepts of self, areas of potential growth, and possibilities for exploration is preferable to using assessment for making predictions.
- It is best to work collaboratively with the client in making decisions about whether to engage in assessment, in determining what procedures to use, and in interpreting results.

Career information and planning.   Career information refers to the many types of resources available in print and electronic form that can be used to help clients make informed career choices (Niles & Harris-Bowlsbey, 2002). The NCDA has developed a comprehensive set of guidelines describing counselors' responsibilities in regard to selecting high-quality information resources of all types. These guidelines can be accessed through the NCDA Web site (www.NCDA.org) under the section titled *NCDA Policy Statements.*

In the past, *The Dictionary of Occupational Titles* (DOT), published by the U.S. Department of Labor, was considered the definitive source of occupational information. In 1994, the U.S. Department of Labor began the process of developing a new occupational classification scheme to replace the DOT. The new system, called the *Occupational Information Network* (O*NET), replaced the DOT in

2001. O*NET is a computer-based career information system that provides the "most up-to-date source of [occupational] information available today" (Brown, 2003, p. 16). It can be accessed at the following Web site: http://www.doleta.gov/programs/onet. The Department of Labor now places all its major publications, such as the *Occupational Outlook Handbook,* online, and it maintains a group of four Web sites that comprise *America's Career Kit* (i.e., *America's Learning Exchange, America's Job Bank, America's Talent Bank,* and *CareerInfoNet*).

Although many people in the Information Age have ready access to computers and the Internet, technology is not the only source of career information. Many print resources that provide valuable career information are available through libraries, bookstores, and educational sites. Some self-help books, such as Bolles's (2002) *What Color Is Your Parachute?*, outline practical steps most individuals, from late adolescence on, can follow to define personal values and successfully complete career-seeking tasks, such as writing a rèsumè. These books also provide a wealth of information on how to locate positions of specific interest.

In addition to selecting high quality career-related resource materials, career counselors also are responsible for making the resources known to clients in as user-friendly a manner as possible. Moreover, they are responsible for helping clients process the information that has been gathered (Niles & Harris-Bowlsbey, 2002). When career information is not processed accurately or adequately, clients may have difficulty making career decisions effectively. It also is important for counselors to discuss the nature of the career decision process with their clients, reminding them that career decidedness develops over time and the decision-making process is complex, not simple (Krieshok, 1998). Knowledge of career information and of the processes associated with it does not guarantee self-exploration in career development, but good career decisions cannot be made without these data. A lack of sufficient or up-to-date information is one reason that individuals fail to make career decisions or make unwise choices.

A number of *computer-assisted career guidance systems* (CACGS) offer career information and help individuals sort through their values and interests or just find job information. One of the beauties of computer-based career planning systems is their accessibility: they are available in many settings and to diverse clientele across cultures and the life span (Harris-Bowlsbey, 1992; Sampson & Bloom, 2001). Two of the better known CACGS include SIGI-Plus (*System of Interactive Guidance and Information,* with "Plus" indicating a refinement of the system) and DISCOVER, which has been adapted for varying age levels. Ways of enhancing computer-assisted career guidance systems are constantly being implemented. No matter how sophisticated the programs are, however, it is wise to have trained career counselors available to assist people who may make use of this technology but still have questions about its applicability to their lives (Walker-Staggs, 2000).

Skilled career counselors know how to access, evaluate, and utilize various types of printed and electronic career-related resources. Knowledge alone, however, is not sufficient. Effective career counselors also are able to work collaboratively with the client so that the information retrieved can be translated into something that is meaningful and useful.

Career counseling with diverse populations.   Community counselors who conduct career counseling are likely to work with a wide variety of individuals in diverse settings. They may work at job placement services, rehabilitation facilities, employment offices, businesses and industries, or in private practice (Brown, 2003). Typically, career counselors in community settings work with adults, rather than children, while counselors in educational settings focus on career development interventions and activities for young people. In this section, we direct attention to the unique career counseling needs of specific groups of adult clients: women, ethnic minorities, and gay/lesbian/bisexual individuals.

Career counseling with women and ethnic minorities.   "Many of the assumptions inherent in traditional theories of career development fall short in their application to women and ethnic minorities" (Luzzo & McWhirter, 2001, p. 61). Women and ethnic minorities have historically received less adequate career counseling than have European American males, and they have faced more barriers in pursuit of their careers (Brown, 2002). The reason has often involved stereotypical beliefs and practices connected with these two groups (Herr & Niles, 2002). For example, society has generally assumed that women will have discontinuous career patterns to accommodate their families' needs. Likewise, ethnic minorities have often been viewed as interested in only a limited number of occupations. The growing social activism among women and ethnic minority groups, combined with a growing body of research, are helping to challenge constraining negative forces and create models of career counseling for these populations (Peterson & Gonzalez, 2000).

Women.   Gender-based career patterns for women have changed for several reasons. For one thing, "children are being exposed to greater and more varied career choices. Additionally, women have moved into careers previously reserved for men, thereby creating a broader range in the role models they provide girls" (Bobo, Hildreth, & Durodoye, 1998, pp. 40–41).

Since 1970, there has been a dramatic rise in research on and interest in the career development of women (Luzzo & McWhirter, 2001; Scott & Hatalla, 1990; Walsh & Osipow, 1994). This trend parallels the increase in women's participation in the civilian work force, from roughly 20 percent in 1900 to 50 percent in the 1970s to approximately 75 percent at present.

> Research on women's career development has identified both internal and external barriers associated with women's career development, documenting that the process of career decision making and maintaining a career are more complex and restricted for women than for men (Sullivan & Mahalik, 2000, p. 54).

Unfortunately, most theories of career development, with the exception of SCCT, cannot be appropriately applied to women because they were formulated for men or are incomplete (Cook, 1993; Cook, Heppner, & O'Brien, 2002; Jackson & Scharman, 2002). Therefore, in working with women, counselors need to realize they are often entering new territory and must watch out for and resist *occupational sex-role stereotyping,* even at the elementary school level (McMahon

& Patton, 1997). Common stereotypes include viewing women primarily as mothers (nurturing), children (dependent), iron maidens (hard driving), and sex objects (Gysbers et al., 2003), or mistakenly assuming that as a group, females prefer social, artistic, and conventional occupations (as opposed to realistic, investigative, and enterprising occupations); (Tomlinson & Evans-Hughes, 1991). In addition, there is the *"glass ceiling" phenomenon* in which women are seen as able to rise only so far in a corporation because they are not viewed as being able to perform top-level executive duties. When these myths are accepted, girls and women are not challenged to explore their abilities and possibilities, and as a result, some women fail to develop their abilities or gifts to the fullest. Consequently, they never work; develop a low or moderate commitment to work; or focus on "safe," traditional, female-dominated occupations such as teaching, clerical work, nursing, or social services (Betz & Fitzgerald, 1987; Brown, 2002; Walsh & Osipow, 1994).

Other barriers outside of these myths must also be considered, too, in career counseling for women. For instance, a company culture may revolve around the expectation of working far more hours than what may be described in a job, in attending certain events, or being "one of the guys." Thus, women must overcome these realities, as well as the myths that surround them, in order to achieve career goals (Luzzo & McWhirter, 2001). Counselors may advise them that they may more readily find a job that is not in a female-dominated occupational field by socially contacting men rather than women (Mencken & Winfield, 2000). However, overcoming barriers and misperceptions and finding balance are essential parts of the counseling process.

To understand how women may combine a career and a family, Jackson and Scharman (2002) studied a national sample of "26 women identified as having creatively constructed their careers to maximize time with their families" (p. 181). Eight different themes emerged as to how these women managed to construct family-friendly careers. Their strategies ranged from "peaceful trade-offs" to "partner career flexibility." However, "each participant found satisfying solutions to combining career and family that did not require an either/or choice" (p. 184). Overall, these women demonstrated remarkable self-efficacy (i.e., confidence in themselves to cope with or manage complex or difficult situations). This ability is becoming an increasingly important factor in the career development of women. Career self-efficacy is something that can be increased through working with women in groups to address factors that compose it such as performance accomplishments, vicarious experiences, emotional arousal, and verbal persuasion (Sullivan & Mahalik, 2000).

Another helpful career counseling strategy in working with women, especially if they are depressed and indecisive about a career, is to offer "*career plus life counseling,* meaning that in counseling they [the women] focus on personal and relationship issues in addition to explicit career issues" (Lucas, Skokowski, & Ancis, 2000, p. 325). An ecological perspective, where career counselors work with women on career development issues in the context and complexity of the environment in which they live, is increasingly gaining recognition as a way of helping women become more empowered and shape their futures (Cook et al., 2002).

Cultural minorities.   Cultural minorities are so diverse that it is impossible to focus on all the factors that career counselors must deal with in working with them individually or collectively. Many cultural minorities have difficulty obtaining meaningful employment because of employers' discrimination practices, lack of marketable skills, and limited access to informal networks that lead to good jobs (Leong, 1995). In addition, the interest patterns of cultural minorities (as a group) have tended not to fall within Holland's (1997) hexagonal RIASEC ordering in the same way European Americans have, thus presenting challenges for many career counselors in regard to helping them (Osipow & Fitzgerald, 1996). Whereas about 27 percent of adults in the United States express a need for assistance in finding information about work, the rate is much higher among specific minority populations: African Americans (44 percent), Asian/Pacific Islanders (36 percent), and Hispanics/Latinos (35 percent); (NCDA, 1990).

Counselors must remember that cultural minorities have special needs in regard to establishing themselves in careers. Thus, counselors must be sensitive to such issues and at the same time help individuals overcome artificial and real barriers that prohibit them from maximizing their potential. For instance, some African American young people who have lived in poverty all their lives are characterized as vocationally handicapped because "they have few positive work-related experiences, limited educational opportunities, and frequently lack positive work role models" (Dunn & Veltman, 1989, pp. 156–157). Structured programs for these individuals use positive role models and experiences to affirm cultural or ethnic heritage and abilities, thus working to address and overcome traditional restrictions (Drummond & Ryan, 1995; Locke & Faubert, 1993). In the process, counselors help these youth, as they do others, to distinguish between barriers over which they have control and responsibility for transcending and those that they may not have the capacity to overcome (Albert & Luzzo, 1999).

Career awareness programs for Chinese American and Korean American parents have also proven beneficial (Evanoski & Tse, 1989). In these Asian cultures, parents traditionally make career decisions for their children, regardless of the children's interests. By staging neighborhood workshops to introduce parents to American career opportunities, a greater variety of choices is opened to all concerned. The success of such workshops is due to bilingual role models and career information materials written in the participants' language.

Career counseling with gays/lesbians/bisexuals.   Special diverse groups not often considered in career counseling are gays, lesbians, and bisexuals. These individuals face unique concerns as well as many that are common to other groups. Of special concern to many gays, lesbians, and bisexuals is whether to be overt or covert in disclosing their sexual orientation at the workplace (Chojnacki & Gelberg, 1994). Persons with minority sexual orientations may face personal and professional developmental concerns, including discrimination, if they openly acknowledge their beliefs and practices.

Although traditional career-counseling methods are usually appropriate with individuals of all sexual orientations, special attention should be given to helping gays, lesbians, and bisexuals assess the fit between their lifestyle preferences and specific work environments. Sexual orientation cannot be ignored as an important variable in career counseling if the process is to be constructive (Croteau & Thiel, 1993).

In working with members of this population, career counselors must assess both their own attitudes and those of the surrounding community toward gays, lesbians, and bisexuals. In such an assessment, they must gauge personal, professional, and environmental bias toward people who are not heterosexual. In addition, they need to use nonbiased language and become familiar with support networks that are within their communities for members of these groups. Furthermore, they need to become informed about overt and covert discrimination in the workplace, such as blackmail, ostracism, harassment, exclusion, and termination. The *"lavender ceiling"* also needs to be discussed with gays, lesbians, and bisexuals. This barrier to advancement in a career is the equivalent to the "glass ceiling" for women, where a career plateaus early due to discrete prejudice by upper management against the person because of beliefs about them related to their sexual orientation (Friskopp & Silverstein, 1995; Zunker, 2002).

Summary

Career counseling in the 21st century is a complex process that combines general counseling skills with specific, career-related skills. Many changes in society and in the workplace have impacted the delivery of career counseling services, making it essential for career counselors to affiliate with professional organizations such as the NCDA or NCEA to stay abreast of current developments and emerging trends in the field. Effective career counselors have a strong understanding of career development theories and career assessment and intervention skills. They know how to access career information resources and are accomplished at counseling from a multicultural perspective.

Before concluding this section on career counseling, we want to add a note about the importance of integrating career counseling with personal counseling—a topic that has been the focus of much research and dialog during the past decade (For example, Imimbo, 1994; Krumboltz, 1993; Manuele-Adkins, 1992). Although distinctions are sometimes drawn between career counseling and personal counseling, the two processes are not dichotomous but instead are intricately related. Often, a client will present with a career-related issued that is rooted in personal problems (For example, anger management problems leading to job loss). Or the reverse can occur, where stress brought on by a toxic work environment results in decreased coping skills that negatively affect family interactions. Competent career counselors are able to work holistically with clients, helping them deal effectively with personal issues and career-related issues that arise during the counseling process (Liptak, 2001).

EMPLOYEE ASSISTANCE PROGRAMS

After the bombing of the Alfred P. Murrah Federal Building in Oklahoma City on April 19, 1995, the Kerr-McGee Corporation, an energy company whose headquarters is only two blocks from the attack, "spent many hours and tens of thousands of dollars offering counseling and other services to help employees cope" (Hightower, 1995, p. A22). Kerr-McGee contracted with an external company, Crisis Management International of Atlanta, to bring 18 counselors on site to work with its employees. In addition, it set up a command center, held group and individual counseling sessions, and established a phone tree to update information to its workers. Problems that employees had in the wake of the bombing included grief, anger, depression, fatigue, nightmares, survivor guilt, and trouble eating and concentrating.

Although the actions of Kerr-McGee may seem unusual or dramatic, they are not. Since the 1940s, but especially accelerating in the 1970s, business, industry, government, educational, and private/public institutions in the United States have exhibited a strong interest in the overall health of employees (Herlihy, 2000). In many cases, they have made mental health and other health services offered to employees a part of their fringe benefits package (Del Campo, Del Campo, & Gorman, 2002).

The reasons for this interest are both humanistic and financial in nature. Through documented studies, employers have found that workers who are healthier and less stressed are better performers and subject to less absenteeism and accidents. They have further discovered that between 10 percent and 18 percent of workers normally experience some mental or emotional problems that detrimentally influence their on-the-job behavior (Masi, 1984). Thus, counseling, health, and referral programs, commonly referred to as Employee Assistance Programs (EAPs), have been set up by a variety of companies to help employees in addressing personal problems, such as alcoholism, drug abuse, family adjustments, divorce, financial pressures, retirement planning and adjustment, and distress resulting from exposure to traumas and crises ranging from violence to departmental reorganization and change (Cooper, Dewe, & O'Driscoll, 2003; Hoffman, 2000; Plaggemars, 2000).

Employee assistance counselors operate on either an in-house or referral basis. As a general rule, large companies and institutions offer EAP services on their premises (i.e., in-house), whereas smaller operations will usually rely on EAP counselors who serve a number of companies and institutions (i.e., outsource); (Sciegaj, et al., 2001). Virtually all of the Fortune 500 companies in the United States have an EAP program, with most EAP programs offering *fourth-party payments* (from companies themselves) to counselors.

Becoming an EAP Counselor

There are approximately 15,000 employee assistance programs (EAPs) in the United States and the number continues to rise. In a national survey of EAP programs, over 60 percent of the externally administered programs reported hiring counseling graduates with master's and doctoral degrees (Hosie & Spruill, 1990). This percentage was topped only slightly by EAP programs hiring master's-level social workers. From these statistics, it is evident that the need exists for counselors to provide preventive and remedial services to employees and to train supervisors to recognize troubled workers and refer them for help. Counselors can also actively contribute to the conceptual development of EAP prevention and intervention programs. Being a community resource for referrals from EAPs is yet a third venue through which counselors interact with EAP programs. "Clearly, counselors have the potential to play an important role in the EAP arena" (Gerstein & Bayer, 1988, p. 296).

To enter the employee mental health care field, particularly EAPs, counselors have to utilize their basic counseling skills while learning new ways of professionally relating to people in business.

> Many EAP organizations expect counselors to have knowledge of business and organizational practices and solid competencies in consultation, program management and evaluation, and marketing. Expertise in dealing with alcohol-related problems is also commonly expected of counselors working in all types of EAPs. (Hosie, West, & Mackey, 1993, p. 359)

Indeed, many EAP programs were primarily established to deal with troubled employees, especially workers dealing with difficulties that were alcohol-related (Van Den Bergh, 2000). Many programs still focus on preventing alcohol problems associated with the work environment. Their initiatives include finding ways to reduce stress, decrease alienation, and lessen pressure from subcultures that promote the consumption of alcohol or illicit drugs (Cook & Schlenger, 2002; Roman & Blum, 2002).

Work as an EAP Counselor

Employee assistance counselors recognize that there are multiple ways of bringing about change in employees and institutions. One way is for EAP counselors to take a preventive approach and collaborate with others in their organization. The focus of such an effort is to have the workplace culture reflect the company's mission so there is congruence between what employees expect from their work and what they find (Kennedy, 2001). If this type of harmony is reached, workers are more likely than not to be pleased with their work environment.

A second approach is to work with employees directly. In this type of arrangement, EAP counselors attempt to move employees beyond their present range of behavior and help them find new solutions through developing relationships with them. Specific ways in which employees are served are dependent on the counselors' skills, employees' needs, and institutional resources (Sandhu, 2002). One general way for EAP counselors to be effective is to set up programs that deal with a variety of subjects in which employees have an interest; for example, retirement planning. EAP counselors can conduct such seminars themselves or they may invite outside experts to make presentations at convenient times. In either case, arrangements for follow-up should be a part of the plan, because one-shot efforts at helping may not be entirely satisfactory.

In addition, EAP counselors typically offer short term counseling services to employees who may be experiencing difficulties. These services are usually time limited (e.g., 3–6 sessions). As experts in community resources, EAP counselors may also make referrals to mental health professionals or outside agencies that can offer employees more extensive services than can be provided through the EAP program.

Box 14–3

Rewards and challenges of EAP counseling

Employee Assistance Programs (EAPs) are work-based programs that address the personal problems of employees and their members in order to improve the productivity of the workforce. The EAPs grew out of the Occupational Alcohol Programs of individual companies in the 1940s. They originally addressed alcohol issues but broadened in scope in the 1970s to include other drug issues, psychiatric issues, and a range of personal problems that do not conform to a DSM-IV diagnosis. Today, most EAP work is done by an agency that provides the service to contracted companies.

Working as an EAP counselor is something I find rewarding for several reasons, including:

1. EAP counseling is short-term. A key emphasis in EAP work is on conducting a comprehensive assessment to determine the client's needs and the appropriateness of EAP counseling. I generally conduct three to six sessions, using brief counseling interventions, many of which are solution-focused. When short-term counseling is not appropriate, I am responsible for referring the client to other services.
2. Efforts are made to impact the employer, not just the employee. EAP counselors design and implement various training programs and workshops, which can include Stress Management, Substance Abuse, and Sexual Harassment, just to name a few. We also consult with managers, supervisors, and human resource professionals about issues that influence work performance. These consultations may be about individual employees or about the impact of policies, procedures, or external events on the workplace.
3. EAP counseling is free to employees and their family members. As an EAP counselor, you do not get direct payment from the client. Instead, you generally contract with the client's employer to provide counseling services. This means that issues related to a client's ability to pay do not interfere with the counseling relationship or process.

As with any career, this one also comes with challenges. The biggest challenges for EAP counselors are protecting confidentiality and setting appropriate boundaries. This is due largely to the fact that EAP counselors work with more than one set of clients. For example, I may be working with a client in my office, but I also have an obligation to the company for whom that client works. This means that I must be very aware of confidentiality issues and articulate those issues to clients and the company. At times, the need to maintain confidentiality may mean losing a contract with a particular company.

Boundary and competency issues can occur when the EAP counselor is expected to take on ever-expanding roles that may go well beyond his or her level of expertise. The counselor must be aware of personal and professional limits when making promises about providing services. Sometimes, it is necessary to direct the client or

continued

the company to other resources. This can be difficult, given the pressure that some companies may place on having certain services performed by the EAP. It is important, however, to maintain integrity of self, integrity of the program, and integrity in the relationships that one has with various clients and customers. Ultimately, this will determine the counselor's long-term success in the EAP field.

—Jay Hale, LPC, CEAP

Balance and Wellness: Current Emphases of EAP Programs

As noted, graduates in counseling continue to find increased opportunities for employment in EAP settings. Among the present emphases in EAP settings are programs that focus on prevention, especially the balance between work and family life and wellness.

Achieving a good balance between one's work and family life is not always easy. The reasons are many, including increased responsibilities at work and/or home, self-imposed demands for perfection in either or both areas, family and friend support, and lack of adequate time for self or others. To prevent the transmission of work and family problems from entering into the other domain, EAP counselors can initiate comprehensive work/life balance programs. These initiatives can include a focus on employees' strengths that is personalized, the establishment of a cultural climate that is supportive and understanding of employee needs, and a solution-focused, empowerment-oriented approach to working with employees who have diverse needs (Herlihy, 2000; Hobson, Delunas, & Kesic, 2001; Kennedy, 2001; Van Der Berg, 2000).

Positive wellness approaches (i.e., health-related activities that are both preventive and remedial and have a therapeutic value to those individuals who practice them consistently) represent another current emphasis in EAP programs. Wellness approaches include such activities as eating natural foods, taking vitamins, going to health spas, meditating, and participating in regular exercise (O'Donnell, 1988). "For the person to be a whole, healthy, functioning organism, one must evaluate the physical, psychological, intellectual, social, emotional, and environmental processes" (Carlson & Ardell, 1988, p. 383). Signs of the holistic movement toward health and well-being in the workplace are apparent everywhere and are spilling over in their impact on Americans of all ages. Therefore, EAP counselors today concentrate on wellness as well as on treatment services (Bennett & Lehman, 2003).

Research validates the need for this movement and in some ways leads it. In an extensive review of the literature on the effectiveness of physical fitness on measures of personality, Doan and Scherman (1987) found strong support for the belief that regular exercise can have a beneficial effect on people's physical and psychological health. Their review supports counselors who prescribe health habits to accompany regular counseling practices. Other strategies for working from a wellness perspective include having EAP counselors (a) emphasize positive, life-enhancing activities; (b) alter traditional screening to include more emphasis on overall health; (c) conduct more research; and (d) highlight the physical feature dimension as one aspect of what Lazarus (1989) calls "multimodal therapy" (i.e., BASIC ID: behavior, affect, sensation, imagery, cognition, interpersonal relationships, and drugs/biology).

PRIVATE PRACTICE COUNSELING

Private practice counselors have a less formalized history than either career or EAP counselors. The involvement of mental health practitioners in private practice pre-dates the existence of licensed professional counselors (LPCs) (Ginter, 2001). Currently, however, most counselors involved in private practice are licensed professional counselors LPCs, licensed mental health counselors (LMHCs), or licensed clinical professional counselors (LCPCs).

Community counselors in private practice work for themselves in an individual or group practice unaffiliated with an agency. Many private practitioners specialize in distinct areas of treatment, such as helping clients with depression, anxiety, or grief issues. Others take a more generalist approach that may involve working with children, adolescents, or adults and working with them "in the context of individual, couple, family, or group counseling" (Ginter, 2001, p. 356).

In decades past—before insurance, third-party payments, and managed care—the professional lives of private practitioners were less complex than they are today. Clinicians were reimbursed on a fee-for-service basis, comparable to the way in which physicians were reimbursed. They operated a counseling business and did so for the freedom and opportunity it afforded them. That arrangement changed dramatically in the 1980s as managed care began to replace fee-for-service arrangements.

Despite changes in the ways clinicians are now reimbursed for service, private practice is still popular. When many students first enroll in a counseling program, they aspire to set up a private practice. Indeed, doctoral graduates of counseling programs indicate that private practice is their preferred venue of service delivery (Zimpfer, 1996; Zimpfer & DeTrude, 1990). Often counselors conceptualize that a private practice setting will give them more control over their lives and be more rewarding financially. Indeed, a private-practice can be a wonderful experience. However, it usually takes a great deal of work to begin such a practice unless a professional buys into or is invited into an already established practice.

Difficulties Setting Up a Private Practice

To be successful as a private practitioner, a counselor needs a number of abilities beyond clinical expertise. Some of the most salient of those abilities include the following:

* Being able to balance business skills with counseling skills or able to find a competent business manager.
* Being able to build support networks in the community (Such networks are less necessary in agencies, where one is often surrounded by colleagues who can supply needed information on treatment plans or give referrals to appropriate specialists.)
* Being able to overcome or avoid the use of restrictive covenants or noncompetitive agreements that some agencies put in their contracts with counselors. Such

contracts prohibit counselors from setting up a private practice within a certain geographic area or within a certain time period after leaving the agency (Wyatt, Daniels, & White, 2000).

- Being willing to invest time and hard work in "pull marketing" relationships [that is, in making oneself attractive by offering services to specialized groups and meeting regularly with other community professionals to increase referral possibilities (Crodzki, 2002)].
- Being willing to donate services and participate in endeavors for the public good in order to build up a reputation and a practice, for as Allen Ivey remarked: "There is just a very small window for private practitioners to make big money" (Littrell, 2001, p. 117).

Advantages in Establishing a Private Practice

There are opportunities for counselors to enter private practice and succeed. Indeed, mental health agency administrators view "private practitioners . . . as the greatest competitors for insured clients" (Wyatt, et al., 2000, p. 19). Among the advantages private practitioners have are the following:

- A growing dissatisfaction among consumers with mental health managed care. In such an environment, consumers are most likely to begin paying directly for services when they can afford it and not go through a managed care arrangement. Such an arrangement may benefit counselors in private practice and portions of the public.
- A chance for counselors in private practice to become known in their communities as professionals who provide quality service and thus to gain excellent reputations.
- An opportunity for counselors to set up their office hours for times that are most convenient for them.
- A chance for counselors to become specialists in treatment, especially if they live in large urban areas where there are abundant numbers of clients with specific problems.

Overall, while private practice has some drawbacks, it will continue to be a setting in which community counselors elect to work.

SUMMARY AND CONCLUSION

This chapter has covered information on various aspects of career counseling, EAP program counseling, and private practice. Influential theories of career counseling— trait-and-factor, developmental, learning, and social-cognitive—were reviewed. Specific skills associated with career counseling were described, with a focus on conducting career assessment, providing career information, and working with diverse groups of clients. Among the many functions that career counselors perform are:

- Administering and interpreting tests and inventories
- Conducting personal counseling sessions

- Developing individualized career plans
- Helping clients integrate vocational and avocational life roles
- Facilitating decision-making skills
- Providing support for persons experiencing job stress, job loss, or career transitions

Employee assistance program counselor services sometimes overlap those of career counselors. However, these professionals have a multitude of counseling responsibilities outside of career services in working with employees of companies either at the employee's business setting or at a convenient location. Employees may self-refer or be referred to counselors in these programs through their supervisors. To function well as EAP counselors, clinicians need to be proactive and knowledgeable regarding the institutions with which they work. Moreover, they must have a comprehensive understanding of community resources in addition to knowing how to handle a wide variety of problems or concerns.

The final group discussed in this chapter, private practitioners, share common interests with career counselors and EAP counselors in that they may deal with vocational and general counseling concerns. Many counselors in private practice choose to align themselves with one or more specialty areas. However, private practitioners are unique in that they must be strong business managers as well as skilled counselors. Practitioners who are energetic, disciplined, and able to balance the demands of running a business with the demands of counseling are likely to find private practice a fulfilling venue in which to work.

REFERENCES

Albert, K. A., & Luzzo, D. A. (1999). The role of perceived barriers in career development: A social cognitive perspective. *Journal of Counseling and Development, 77,* 431–436.

American Counseling Association. (1995). *Ethical standards of the American Counseling Association.* Alexandria, VA: Author.

Bandura, A. (1977). Self-efficacy: Toward a unifying theory of behavioral change. *Psychological Review, 84,* 191–215.

Bandura, A. (1986). *Social foundations of thought and action.* Upper Saddle River, NJ: Prentice Hall.

Bennett, J. B., & Lehman, W. E.-K. (Eds.). (2003). *Preventing workplace substance abuse: Beyond drug testing to wellness.* Washington, DC: American Psychological Association.

Betz, N. E. (1992). Career assessment: A review of critical issues. In S. D. Brown & R. W. Lent (Eds.), *Handbook of counseling psychology* (2nd ed., pp. 453–484). New York: Wiley.

Betz, N., & Fitzgerald, L. (1987). *The career psychology of women.* New York: Academic Press.

Bobo, M., Hildreth, B. L., & Durodoye, B. (1998). Changing patterns in career choices among African American, Hispanic, and Anglo children. *Professional School Counseling, 1*(4), 37–42.

Bolles, R. N. (2002). *What color is your parachute?* (32nd ed). Berkeley, CA: Ten Speed Press.

Borgen, W. A. (1997). People caught in changing career opportunities: A counseling perspective. *Journal of Employment Counseling, 34,* 133–143.

Brown, D. (2002). The role of work and cultural values in occupational choice, satisfaction, and success: A theoretical statement. *Journal of Counseling and Development, 80,* 48–56.

Brown, D. (2003). *Career information, career counseling, and career development* (8th ed.). Boston: Allyn & Bacon.

Brown, D., & Brooks, L. (1991). *Career counseling techniques.* Boston: Allyn & Bacon.

Burlew, L. (1992, Winter). My job, my mind. *American Counselor, 1,* 24–27.

Canaff, A. L. (1997). Later life career planning: A new challenge for career counselors. *Journal of Employment Counseling, 34,* 85–93.

Carlson, J., & Ardell, D. B. (1988). Physical fitness as a pathway to wellness and effective counseling. In R. Hayes & R. Aubrey (Eds.), *New directions for counseling and human development* (pp. 383–396). Denver: Love.

Chojnacki, J. T., & Gelberg, S. (1994). Toward a conceptualization of career counseling with gay/lesbian/bisexual persons. *Journal of Career Development, 21,* 3–9.

Cook, E. P. (1993). The gender context of life: Implications for women's and men's career-life plans. *Career Development Quarterly, 41,* 227–237.

Cook, E. P., Heppner, M. J., & O'Brien, K. M. (2002). Career development of women of color and White women: Assumptions, conceptualization, and interventions from an ecological perspective. *Career Development Quarterly, 50,* 291–305.

Cook, R., & Schlenger, W. (2002). Prevention of substance abuse in the workplace: Review of research on the delivery of services. *Journal of Primary Prevention, 23,* 115–142.

Cooper, G. L., Dewe, P., & O'Driscoll, M. (2003). Employee assistance programs. In J. C. Quick & L. E. Tetrick (Eds.), *Handbook of occupational health psychology* (pp. 289–304). Washington, DC: American Psychological Association.

Croteau, J. M., & Thiel, M. J. (1993). Integrating sexual orientation in career counseling: Acting to end a form of the personal-career dichotomy. *Career Development Quarterly, 42,* 174–179.

Crodzki, L. (2002, May/June). Practice strategies. *Family Therapy Magazine, 1,* 43–44.

Del Campo, R. L., Del Campo, D. S., & Gorman, D. (2002). Employee assistance: Some background and employment opportunities. *Annals of the American Psychotherapy Association, 5,* 15–17.

Doan, R. E., & Scherman, A. (1987). The therapeutic effect of physical fitness on measures of personality: A literature review. *Journal of Counseling and Development, 66,* 28–36.

Drummond, R. J., & Ryan, C. W. (1995). *Career counseling: A development approach.* Upper Saddle River, NJ: Merrill/Prentice Hall.

Dunn, C. W., & Veltman, G. C. (1989). Addressing the restrictive career maturity patterns of minority youth: A program evaluation. *Journal of Multicultural Counseling and Development, 17,* 156–164.

Engels, D. W., Minor, C. W., Sampson, J. P., Jr., & Splete, H. H. (1995). Career counseling specialty: History, development, and prospect. *Journal of Counseling and Development, 74,* 134–138.

Evanoski, P. O., & Tse, F. W. (1989). Career awareness programs for Chinese and Korean American parents. *Journal of Counseling and Development, 67,* 472–474.

Fox, M. (1994). *The reinvention of work: A new vision of livelihood for our time.* San Francisco: Harper.

Friskopp, A., & Silverstein, S. (1995). *Straight jobs gay lives.* New York: Scribner's.

Gade, E., Fuqua, D., & Hurlburt, G. (1988). The relationship of Holland's personality types to educational satisfaction with a Native-American high school population. *Journal of Counseling Psychology, 35,* 183–186.

Gerstein, L. H., & Bayer, G. A. (1988). Employee assistance programs: A systemic investigation of their use. *Journal of Counseling and Development, 66,* 294–297.

Ginter, E. J. (2001). Private practice: The professional counselor. In D. C. Locke, J. E. Myers, & E. L. Herr (Eds.), *The handbook of counseling* (pp. 355–372). Thousand Oaks, CA: Sage.

Ginzberg, E. (1972). Toward a theory of occupational choice: A restatement. *Vocational Guidance Quarterly, 20,* 169–176.

Gottfredson, L. S. (1981). Circumscription and compromise: A developmental theory of occupational aspirations. *Journal of Counseling Psychology, 28,* 545–579.

Guindon, M. H., & Hanna, F. J. (2002). Coincidence, happenstance, serendipity, fate, or the hand of God: Case studies in synchronicity. *Career Development Quarterly, 50,* 195–208.

Gysbers, N. C., Heppner, J. A., & Johnston, J. A. (2003). *Career counseling: Process, issues, & techniques* (2nd ed.). Boston: Allyn & Bacon.

Harris-Bowlsbey, J. (1992, December). Building blocks of computer-based career planning systems. *CAPS Digest,* EDO-CG-92-7.

Harris-Bowlsbey, J., & Niles, S. G. (2002). *Career development interventions in the 21st century.* Upper Saddle River, NJ: Prentice Hall.

Hayes, C. (2001). Choosing the right path. *Black Enterprise, 31,* 108–112.

Helwig, A. A., & Myrin, M. D. (1997). Ten-year stability of Holland codes within one family. *Career Development Quarterly, 46,* 62–71.

Henderson, S. J. (2000). "Follow your bliss": A process for career happiness. *Journal of Counseling and Development, 78,* 305–315.

Herlihy, P. A. (2000). Employee assistance and work/family programs: Friends or foes? *Employee Assistance Quarterly, 16,* 33–52.

Herr, E. L. (1997). Super's life-span, life-space and its outlook for refinement. *Career Development Quarterly, 45,* 238–246.

Herr, E. L., & Cramer, S. H. (1996). *Career guidance and counseling through the lifespan* (5th ed.). New York: Harper Collins.

Herr, E. L., & Niles, S. G. (2002). Multicultural career guidance in the schools. In P. Pedersen & J. C. Carey (Eds.), *Multicultural counseling in schools.* Boston: Allyn & Bacon.

Hightower, S. (1995, May 7). Helping cope: Counselors brought to Oklahoma City company. *Winston-Salem Journal,* A22, A24.

Hobson, C. J., Delunas, L., & Kesic, D. (2001). Compelling evidence of the need for corporate work/life balance initiatives: Results from a national survey of stressful life-events. *Journal of Employment Counseling, 38,* 38–44.

Hoffman, C. (2000). Dependent care in the 21st century: Broadening the definition for employee assistance practice. *Employee Assistance Quarterly, 16,* 15–32.

Hohenshil, T. H. (1996). Role of assessment and diagnosis in counseling. *Journal of Counseling and Development, 75,* 64–67.

Holland, J. L. (1997). *Making vocational choices: A theory of vocational preferences and work environments* (3rd ed.). Odessa, FL: Psychological Assessment Resources.

Holland, J. L., & Gottfredson, G. D. (1976). Using a typology of persons and environments to explain careers: Some extensions and clarifications. *Counseling Psychologist, 6,* 20–29.

Hosie, T., & Spruill, D. (1990, November). *Counselor employment and roles in three major types of EAP organizations.* Paper presented at the Southern Association for Counselor Education and Supervision Convention, Norfolk, VA.

Hosie, T. W., West, J. D., & Mackey, J. A. (1993). Employment and roles of counselors in employee assistance programs. *Journal of Counseling and Development, 71,* 355–359.

Hotchkiss, L., & Borow, H. (1996). Sociological perspective on work and career development. In D. Brown, L. Brooks, & Associates (Eds.), *Career choice and development* (3rd ed.). San Francisco: Jossey-Bass.

Imbimbo, P. V. (1994). Integrating personal and career counseling: A challenge for counselors. *Journal of Employment Counseling, 31,* 50–59.

Jackson, A. P., & Scharman, J. S. (2002). Constructing family-friendly careers: Mothers' experiences. *Journal of Counseling and Development, 80,* 180–187.

Kennedy, S. (2001). Organizational change affects work stress and work-family balance. *Australian and New Zealand Journal of Family Therapy, 22,* 105–106.

Krieshok, T. S. (1998). An anti-introspectivist view of career decision making. *Career Development Quarterly, 46,* 210–229.

Krumboltz, J. D. (1979). *Social learning and career decision making.* New York: Carroll.

Krumboltz, J. D. (1993). Integrating career and personal counseling. *Career Development Quarterly, 42,* 143–148.

Krumboltz, J. D. (1994). Integrating career and personal counseling. *Career Development Quarterly, 42,* 143–148.

Lazarus, A. A. (1989). Multimodal therapy. In R. J. Corsini & D. Wedding (Eds.), *Current psychotherapies* (4th ed., pp. 503–544). Itasca, IL: F. E. Peacock.

Lent, R. W., Brown, S. D., & Hackett, G. (1994). Toward a unifying social cognitive theory of career and academic interest, choice, and performance. *Journal of Vocational Behavior, 45,* 79–122.

Lent, R. W., Brown, S. D., & Hackett, G. (2000). Contextual supports and barriers to career choice: A social cognitive analysis. *Journal of Counseling Psychology, 47,* 36–49.

Leong, F. T. L. (Ed.). (1995). *Career development and vocational behavior of racial and ethnic minorities.* Hillsdale, NJ: Erlbaum.

Liptak, J. J. (2001). *Treatment planning in career counseling.* Pacific Grove, CA: Brooks/Cole.

Littrell, J. M. (2001). Allen E. Ivey: Transforming counseling theory and practice. *Journal of Counseling and Development, 79,* 105–118.

Locke, D. C., & Faubert, M. (1993). Getting on the right track: A program for African American high school students. *School Counselor, 41,* 129–133.

Lucas, M. S., Skokowski, C. T., & Ancis, J. R. (2000). Contextual themes in career decision making of female clients who indicate depression. *Journal of Counseling and Development, 78,* 316–325.

Luzzo, D. A., & McWhirter, E. H. (2001). Sex and ethnic differences in the perception of educational and career-related barriers and levels of coping efficacy. *Journal of Counseling and Development, 79,* 61–67.

Manuele-Adkins, C. (1992). Career counseling is personal counseling. *Career Development Quarterly, 40,* 313–323.

Masi, D. (1984). *Developing employee assistance programs.* New York: American Management Association.

McDaniels, C. (1984). The work/leisure connection. *Vocational Guidance Quarterly, 33,* 35–44.

McMahon, M., Patton, W., & Watson, M. (2003). Developing qualitative career assessment processes. *Career Development Quarterly, 51,* 194–202.

McWhirter, E. H., & Flojo, J. R. (2001). Career counseling: Counseling for life. In D. Capuzzi and D. R. Gross (Eds.), *Introduction to the counseling profession* (3rd ed., pp. 188–207). Needham Heights, MA: Allyn and Bacon.

Mencken, F. C., & Winfield, I. (2000). Job search and sex segregation: Does sex of social contact matter? *Sex Roles, 42,* 847–865.

Meyer, D., Helwig, A., Gjernes, O., & Chickering, J. (1985). The National Employment Counselors Association. *Journal of Counseling and Development, 63,* 440–443.

Miller, M. J. (1983). The role of happenstance in career choice. *Vocational Guidance Quarterly, 32,* 16–20.

Miller, M. J. (1998). Broadening the use of Holland's hexagon with specific implications for career counselors. *Journal of Employment Counseling, 35,* 2–6.

Miller, M. J. (2002). Longitudinal examination of a three-letter Holland code. *Journal of Employment Counseling 39,* 43–48.

Mitchell, L. K., & Krumboltz, J. D. (1996). Krumboltz's learning theory of career choice and counseling. In D. Brown, L. Brooks, & Associates (Eds.), *Career choice and development* (3rd ed., pp. 233–280). San Francisco: Jossey-Bass.

Mitchell, K. E., Levin, A. S., & Krumboltz, J. D. (1999). Planned happenstance: Constructing unexpected career opportunities. *Journal of Counseling and Development, 77,* 115–124.

National Career Development Association (NCDA). (1990). *National survey of working America, 1990: Selected findings.* Alexandria, VA: Author.

National Career Development Association (NCDA). (1997). *Career counseling competencies.* Columbus, OH: Author.

National Career Development Association (NCDA). (2001). *Mission statement, history, and purpose.* Retrieved May 23, 2003, from http://www.ncda.org/about/mission.html

National Employment Counseling Association (NECA). (2003). *National Employment Counseling Association.* Retrieved May 27, 2003, from http://geocities.com/employmentcounseling/neca.html

National Occupational Information Coordinating Committee (NOICC). (1994). *Program guide: Planning to meet career development needs in school-to-work transition programs.* Washington, DC: U.S. Government Printing Office.

Niles, S. G., & Harris-Bowlsbey, J. H. (2002). *Career development interventions in the 21st century.* Upper Saddle River, NJ: Merrill/Prentice Hall.

O'Donnell, J. M. (1988). The holistic health movement: Implications for counseling theory and practice. In R. Hayes & R. Aubrey (Eds.), *New directions for counseling and human development* (pp. 365–382). Denver: Love.

Osipow, S. H., & Fitzgerald, L. F. (1996). *Theories of career development* (4th ed.). Boston: Allyn & Bacon.

Peterson, N., & Gonzalez, R. C. (Eds.). (2000). *Career counseling models for diverse populations.* Pacific Grove, CA: Brooks/Cole.

Plaggemars, D. (2000). EAPs and critical incident stress debriefing: A look ahead. *Employee Assistance Quarterly, 16,* 77–95.

Roman, P. M., & Blum, T. C. (2002). The workplace and alcohol problem prevention. *Alcohol Research and Health, 26,* 49–57.

Rysiew, K. J., Shore, B. M., & Leeb, R. T. (1999). Multipotentiality, giftedness, and career choice: A review. *Journal of Counseling and Development, 77,* 423–430.

Salomone, P. R., & Sheehan, M. C. (1985). Vocational stability and congruence: An examination of Holland's proposition. *Vocational Guidance Quarterly, 34,* 91–98.

Sampson, J. P., Jr., & Bloom, J. W. (2001). The potential for success and failure of computer applications in counseling and guidance. In D. C. Locke, J. E. Myers, & E. L. Herr (Eds.), *The handbook of counseling* (pp. 613–627). Thousand Oaks, CA: Sage.

Sandhu, D. S. (Ed.). (2002). *Counseling employees: A multifaceted approach.* Alexandria, VA: American Counseling Association.

Savickas, M. L. (1989). Annual review: Practice and research in career counseling and development, 1988. *Career Development Quarterly, 38,* 100–134.

Sciegaj, M., Garnick, D. W., Horgan, C. M., Merrick, E. L., Goldin, D., Urato, M., Hodgkin, D. (2001). Employee assistance programs among Fortune 500 firms. *Employee Assistance Quarterly, 16,* 25–35.

Scott, J., & Hatalla, G. (1990). The influence of chance and contingency factors on career patterns of college-educated women. *Career Development Quarterly, 39,* 18–30.

Sears, S. (1982). A definition of career guidance terms: A National Vocational Guidance Association perspective. *Vocational Guidance Quarterly, 31,* 137–143.

Spokane, A. R. (1991). *Career intervention.* Upper Saddle River, NJ: Prentice Hall.

Sullivan, K. R., & Mahalik, J. R. (2000). Increasing career self-efficacy for women: Evaluating a group intervention. *Journal of Counseling and Development, 78,* 54–62.

Super, D. E. (1954). Career patterns as a basis for vocational counseling. *Journal of Counseling Psychology, 1,* 12–19.

Super, D. E. (1957). *The psychology of careers.* New York: Harper.

Super, D. E. (1976). *Career education and the meaning of work* [Monograph]. Washington, DC: Office of Career Education, U.S. Office of Education.

Super, D. E. (1980). A life-span, life space approach to career development. *Journal of Vocational Behavior, 16,* 282–298.

Super, D. E. (1990). A life-span, life-space approach to career development. In D. Brown, L. Brooks, and Associates (Eds.), *Career choice and development: Applying contemporary theories to practice* (2nd ed., pp. 197–261). San Francisco: Jossey-Bass.

Super, D. E., Thompson, A. S., & Lindeman, R. H. (1988). *Adult career concerns inventory.* Palo Alto, CA: Consulting Psychologists Press.

Swanson, J. L., & Fouad, N. A. (1999). *Career theory and practice: Learning through case studies.* Thousand Oaks, CA: Sage.

Tart, C. T. (1986). *Waking up: Overcoming the obstacles to human potential.* Boston: New Science Library.

Tomlinson, S. M., & Evans-Hughes, G. (1991). Gender, ethnicity, and college students' responses to the Strong-Campbell Interest Inventory. *Journal of Counseling and Development, 70,* 151–155.

Trusty, J., Robinson, C. R., Plata, M., & Ng, K.-M. (2000). Effects of gender, socioeconomics status, and early academic performance on postsecondary educational choice. *Journal of Counseling and Development, 78,* 463–472.

Van Den Bergh, N. (2000). Where have we been? . . . Where are we going? Employee assistance practice in the 21st century. *Employee Assistance Quarterly, 16,* 1–13.

Walker-Staggs, J. (2000). Discover. In N. Peterson & R. C. Gonzalez (Eds.), *Career counseling models for diverse populations.* (pp. 112–120). Pacific Grove, CA: Brooks/Cole.

Walsh, W. B., & Osipow, S. H. (1994). *Career counseling for women.* Hillsdale, NJ: Erlbaum.

Weinrach, S. G. (1996). The psychological and vocational interest patterns of Donald Super and John Holland. *Journal of Counseling and Development, 75,* 5–16.

Whiston, S. C. (2000). *Principles and applications of assessment in counseling.* Belmont, CA: Wadsworth.

Williamson, E. G. (1939). *How to counsel students.* New York: McGraw-Hill.

Wyatt, T., Daniels, M. H., & White, L. J. (2000). Noncompetition agreements and the counseling profession: An unrecognized reality for private practitioners. *Journal of Counseling and Development, 78,* 14–20.

Zimpfer, D. (1996). Five-year follow-up of doctoral graduates in counseling. *Counselor Education and Supervision, 35,* 218–229.

Zimpfer, D., & DeTrude, J. (1990). Follow-up of doctoral graduates in counseling. *Journal of Counseling and Development, 69,* 51–56.

Zunker, V. G. (2002). *Career counseling* (6th ed.). Pacific Grove, CA: Brooks/Cole.

Maintaining Effectiveness as a Counselor: Managing Stress and Avoiding Burnout

Exhausted, Tanya climbed into her car and began the long drive home. Her day had been filled with back-to-back clients and staff meetings. One of her clients was suicidal and had to be involuntarily hospitalized. Another client lost his temper during the session, demanding to know why insurance wouldn't pay for continued counseling, which, according to him, "wasn't really helping, anyway." During the staff meeting, the agency director admonished clinicians to do a better job of meeting productivity quotas. "How can I possibly see more clients?" Tanya thought. "I haven't even finished writing today's case notes." As a single mother, finding the time to catch up tonight wasn't going to be easy. After all, Nicholas and Anthony deserved at least some of her attention, and Anthony would probably need help with that English assignment. Maybe they'd just eat out again this evening—or order pizza. Just thinking about trying to cook and clean up made Tanya feel even wearier. As she braked suddenly to avoid hitting the car that stopped unexpectedly in front of her, Tanya felt like crying. She wondered what had happened to her energy, her concentration, her enthusiasm, and the passion she used to have for counseling.

Community counseling provides challenges and opportunities that can be rewarding and life-enhancing. However, working therapeutically with clients day after day can also be emotionally draining and stressful. How do community counselors effectively balance the taxing demands of the profession with personal needs and responsibilities? As we near the end of this text, we address ways counselors can successfully manage stress, avoid burnout, and maximize life satisfaction personally and professionally.

STRESS AND BURNOUT IN COUNSELING

A growing body of evidence suggests that human service workers, including community counselors, experience high levels of stress in the workplace (e.g., Edwards,

Burnard, Coyle, Fothergill, & Hannigan, 2000; Kottler & Schofield, 2001; MacCluskie & Ingersoll, 2001). In addition to the "typical" stressors associated with everyday living, clinicians encounter challenges unique to mental health professionals. A full day of counseling clients can stretch one's emotional and mental resources, particularly when clients are dealing with traumatic problems such as assault, disease, and abuse (MacCluskie & Ingersoll, 2001). Other stressors that often are present in community counseling environments include long work hours, low pay, organizational demands, paperwork deadlines, and hassles related to insurance reimbursement. When professional demands are coupled with personal pressures, finding ways to cope effectively can be especially challenging.

Stress is experienced when a substantial imbalance exists between real or perceived environmental demands and an individual's response capabilities (Baird, 2002; Lazarus & Folkman, 1984). When stress is not dealt with effectively and the imbalance is not corrected, counselors may experience *burnout*. James and Gilliland (2001) described *burnout* as "a state of physical, mental, and emotional exhaustion caused by long-term involvement in emotionally demanding situations" (p. 611). It is the single-most common personal consequence of working as a counselor (Kottler, 1993). People experiencing burnout are emotionally or physically drained to the point that they cannot perform functions meaningfully. Symptoms of excessive stress and burnout can be manifested in several areas, including the following (James & Gilliland, 2001; Kottler & Schofield, 2001):

- *Cognitive Functioning.* Individuals may experience confusion, memory problems, organizational difficulties, irrational thinking, negativity, rigidity, disillusionment, and decreased creativity.
- *Emotional Functioning.* Common emotional expressions associated with burnout include irritability, sadness, anxiety, numbness, apathy, and a sense of being "out of control" or "not oneself."
- *Behavioral Functioning.* People may withdraw from colleagues, friends, and activities; be critical or detached; and engage in inappropriate risk taking. Struggles with interpersonal relationships may be evidenced, and productivity may decrease.
- *Physical Functioning.* A host of physical problems are associated with burnout, including headaches, sleep problems, nervousness, addictions, fatigue, chest or back pains, loss of appetite, and lowered resistance to illness.

Kottler and Schofield (2001) categorized sources of counselor stress and burnout into four primary areas: the work environment, specific events, client-induced stress, and self-induced stress. Stressors associated with the work environment include excessive paperwork, demanding time pressures, inflexible rules and regulations, unsupportive colleagues, and incompetent supervisors. Event-related stressors tend to stem from individuals' personal lives and may include developmental transitions (e.g., getting married, having children, entering midlife), health-related issues, and financial concerns. In contrast, client-induced stressors include difficult or resistant clients, clients experiencing trauma or crisis, and clients who terminate prematurely. Finally, examples of self-induced stressors include perfectionism, unrealistic expectations, an unhealthy lifestyle, exhaustion, and fear of failure on the part of the clinician. Kottler and Schofield remind us that all counselors will experience stress of some type. The question is not whether stress will be experienced, but instead, how will counselors choose to cope with it.

MANAGING STRESS AND AVOIDING BURNOUT

Counselors are in the business of helping clients improve their quality of life. However, to be effective helpers, it is essential for counselors to find ways to take care of themselves (Baird, 2002). Just as prevention in counseling is preferable to remediation, a proactive approach to managing stress and avoiding burnout can help counselors balance professional and personal challenges more effectively. In this section, we address four areas in which community counselors can take steps to achieve that balance: establishing limits, modeling self-care, cultivating self-awareness, and maintaining a sense of humor.

Establishing limits.   Some of the very characteristics that inspire people to become counselors—wanting to help others, idealism, and high motivation—can lead them to taking on more responsibilities than can be managed realistically or effectively. In addition to serving the needs of clients, counselors often work extra hours, engage in volunteer activities, and make themselves accessible to clients and others long after the "normal" workday is finished. Swenson (1998) labels the tendency to take on too much and continually push personal limits as *overload syndrome*. Many of us are not very adept at knowing where our limits are, and consequently, it is easy to overextend them. However, living in a state of constant overload, with no margins or buffers to protect our time and energy, can lead to exhaustion and stagnation. Setting limits at work and elsewhere is essential to healthy, effective living. The following suggestions, made by various authors (e.g., Baird, 2002; MacCluskie & Ingersoll, 2001; Swenson, 1998) can help community counselors establish and maintain limits in their personal and professional lives.

• **Use appropriate assertiveness by saying no** (MacCluskie & Ingersoll, 2001). Many people set unrealistic expectations for themselves, believing that they can accomplish more in a 24-hour period than is feasible. Other people accept additional responsibilities because they fear the repercussions of declining them. Setting necessary limits involves prioritizing what is important, recognizing that we have more control over our schedules than we realize, and learning how to say no, even to good things, to avoid overcommitment.

• **Consider doing less, not more** (Swenson, 1998). It is easy to saturate our schedules, leaving little room for empty space or margins. Overly packed schedules provide the fuel for stress responses. Counselors can intentionally create margins in their schedules by (a) ending sessions on time; (b) building in breaks during the day for note writing, physical activity, and rejuvenation; and (c) periodically pruning, or cutting out, activities that are unnecessary or unrewarding.

- **Create boundaries around the private spaces of life** (Swenson, 1998). Often, the boundary between work and home becomes blurred or even nonexistent, making burnout more likely. Belson (1992) facetiously advises counselors who want to "achieve" burnout to:

  a. Work long hours, especially weekends and evenings, telling yourself that this doesn't interfere with family relationships.
  b. Think about your most difficult cases, even when you are not at work.
  c. Worry continually about what you are not doing that you should be doing.

In contrast, counselors who maintain healthy boundaries recognize that it is desirable to establish and defend perimeters around their homes, communities, and leisure activities. Protecting boundaries provides ways to nurture relationships with family members and friends, which are essential to healthy living.

Modeling self-care.   In addition to setting limits, counselors can model physical, mental, emotional, and spiritual self-care. The counselor who pursues a wellness-oriented lifestyle is in a better position to provide services to clients and help them engage in their own self-care plans (MacCluskie & Ingersoll, 2001).

- **Physical Self-Care.** Often, counselors place their own physical self-care on the back burner as they attempt to meet the multiple demands of clients and organizations. However, the cost of physical neglect can be high, resulting in outcomes such as illness, hypertension, bodily aches and pains, fatigue, and other forms of physical or mental malaise. Engaging in physical self-care is essential to one's personal health and effectiveness as a counselor.

Sleep, nutrition, and exercise are three areas that need ongoing attention to maintain optimal health. Many of us consistently chip away at the hours needed for rest in order to "catch up." We consistently allow insufficient time for sleep, relying on alarm clocks to wake us. Ongoing sleep deprivation can lead to poor concentration, disorganization, and exhaustion. Prioritizing the need for sleep and guarding that time are essential to stress management. Similarly, carving out time to exercise regularly and eat nutritiously yields physical, emotional, and cognitive benefits. The sedentary nature of counseling combined with busy schedules that may not include formal lunch breaks increase the need for ongoing physical exercise and attention to nutrition. Counselors also will want to monitor physical tension associated with stress and find healthy ways to alleviate tension through such activities as controlled breathing, relaxation exercises, and yoga.

- **Cognitive Self-Care.** The beliefs counselors hold about themselves, their clients, and the counseling process may promote health and well-being or create stress. Evaluating and modifying irrational stress-inducing cognitions promote positive mental health (Baird, 2002). Several authors have identified faulty beliefs that may negatively impact counselor effectiveness (e.g., Baird, 2002; Freemont & Anderson, 1986; James & Gilliland, 2001; Kottler & Schofield, 2001). Examples of irrational beliefs associated with stress and burnout include:

  - My job is my life; what I do is who I am.
  - I must be totally competent and knowledgeable.

- I must help everyone all of the time.
- I must be a model of mental health.
- I need to be available at all times.
- No one can do the job like I can.
- I am responsible for client change.
- I should not be anxious or uncertain.
- Any negative feedback indicates that there is something wrong with me.
- The client is in counseling to change or get better. (Although this some-times is the case, it is not necessarily so.)
- The client should appreciate the counselor's efforts.
- The client should be different from what he or she is.

Taking the time to evaluate one's beliefs about self, the counseling process, and clients is the first step toward enhancing cognitive functioning. Counselors may want to work with a supervisor or colleague as they strive to identify and modify faulty beliefs and expectations.

- **Emotional and Spiritual Self-Care.** Some of the qualities that help make counselors effective—being empathic, sensitive, humane, people-oriented, and highly committed—also can lead to difficulties and stress. For example, empathic, sensitive counselors may also be anxious, obsessive, overly conscientious, overly enthusiastic, and susceptible to identifying too closely with clients (James & Gilliland, 2001). Counselors who work with traumatized clients may be vulnerable to experiencing vicarious traumatization, also called *compassion fatigue.* Consequently, it is crucial for counselors to monitor their emotional reactions on an ongoing basis. Baird (2002) suggests engaging in "cleansing rituals" after demanding sessions. These rituals may include stretching, walking, splashing water on one's face, or deep breathing exercises. Moreover, counselors can symbolize leaving clients at work by placing client files in the file cabinet, closing the door to the office, and literally and figuratively leaving them there.

Seeking support from friends, family members, and colleagues is a key element of emotional self-care. Taking time to nurture personal relationships with loved ones provides an important source of support. However, one of the difficulties related to counseling is the need to keep client's stories confidential, which means that much of what goes on during the day cannot be shared with those closest to us. Conse-quently, having a professional colleague or supervisor with whom one can discuss difficult or unsettling cases can be an invaluable resource. Another source of sup-port, especially when counselors are dealing with difficult personal issues, comes through personal counseling or therapy. Ironically, many counselors are reluctant or unwilling to seek help for themselves, even though they recommend it for others (Kottler & Schofield, 2001).

In addition to emotional self-care, spiritual nurturing can help counselors man-age stress more effectively. Myers and Williard (2003) define *spirituality* as "the capacity and tendency present in all human beings to find and construct meaning about life and existence and to move toward personal growth, responsibility, and relationship with others" (p. 149). Spirituality is the central component of the Wheel of Wellness model (Myers, Sweeney, & Witmer, 2000), which is presented in Chapters

4 and 7. Although religion is a form of spirituality, the construct of spirituality encompasses more than religion or religious practices (Myers et al., 2000; Myers & Williard, 2003). Finding ways to nurture and enhance one's spiritual development—whether through prayer, meditation, worship, or some other practice—can promote personal growth and facilitate optimal functioning.

Cultivating self-awareness.   One of the key characteristics of effective counselors is self-awareness. Counselors who are self-aware have an in-depth knowledge of their attitudes, values, and feelings, as well as the ability to recognize ways situations and events affect them. Self-awareness enables counselors to identify early symptoms of stress and overload and then select coping responses more effectively. Kottler and Schofield (2001) suggest that counselors use the following questions to guide reflection and increase self-awareness:

- What haunts you the most and continues to plague you during vulnerable moments?
- In what ways are you less than fully functioning in your personal and professional life?
- What are some aspects of your lifestyle that are unhealthy?
- What are your most difficult, conflicted, and dysfunctional relationships?
- How does all of this impact your work with clients? (p. 429).

Counselors can increase personal self-awareness by creating *reflective structures,* which allow time and space for self-examination (Boyatzis, McKee, & Goleman, 2002). Reflective structures provide time away from work and responsibilities for the purpose of being alone with one's thoughts. Reflection involves a conscious, disciplined effort at self-examination. It provides an opportunity to contemplate past experiences, current relationships, and future hopes. Through reflection, counselors may encounter themselves and their deepest feelings in ways that are surprising, unexpected, and perhaps a little frightening. Such encounters put counselors in a better position to take stock and move in directions that are personally and professionally enhancing.

Maintaining a sense of humor.   The physiological benefits of humor were extolled in Norman Cousins' (1979) *Anatomy of an Illness.* Having a sense of humor—being able to laugh at oneself and one's situations—can be a primary source of energy for rejuvenation. As Oscar Wilde once stated, "Life is too important to be taken seriously." Or, to paraphrase the title and content of a book by Paul Watzlawick (1983), humor allows one to know that many human problems are "hopeless but not serious" or "serious but not hopeless" and, therefore, solvable.

Humor has the remarkable ability to promote insight, generate creativity, and defuse tense situations (Gladding, 1995). It can help regulate anxiety, relieve boredom, dispel fear, boost performance, and build group cohesion (Weaver & Wilson, 1997). Laughter can stimulate the immune system and help reduce stress (Goldin & Bordan, 1999). Being able to laugh at oneself and one's mistakes can help put things in perspective and create pathways for healing.

In the following narrative, Gladding shares an example of how humor sometimes arises unexpectedly in counseling situations.

Box 1

I learned about the value of humor in counseling during my first years of work as a counselor. I had completed intake information on a man and asked him what he would like to work on in the session. He looked at me a bit negatively and simply stated: "I am not talking until you get rid of the rabbits in this room."

We were in a rural area, so I surveyed our surroundings. Not seeing any rabbits, I asked where they were. He pointed to an imaginary hare (that I assumed was wild), and I went over, grabbed it by its invisible ears, then opened the door, and threw it outside. As I went to sit down, he pointed to a second imaginary furry creature, so I proceeded to do the same thing. Again, as I went back to my chair, he pointed to a third unseeable furry critter with long ears and a cotton tail (so he said). As I approached this third imaginary hare and started to grab it by its airy ears and toss it out with a flare, I suddenly stopped and thought: "Who really needs help here?" I laughed to myself and proceeded to get my client the help he needed.

From that experience, I began to develop better confrontation skills. I probably would have eventually learned these necessary helping techniques in counseling, but the bizarre nature of my client's experience accelerated the process and gave me a laugh at myself in the process. Levity can sometimes be enlightening, and there often is a humorous side to even the most serious of situations.

Counseling is serious business. However, it also provides multiple opportunities for joy, enthusiasm, and continued mastery of personal and professional skills. As you develop that mastery, it is helpful to keep in mind the words of Robert Brown, a leader in the counseling profession who died of cancer several years ago:

> What do I have to say to counselors in the field who are trying to find their way, to create meaning in their lives? Don't take yourself seriously, but take yourself measurably. Don't take yourself in a manner that is cavalier, but take yourself in a manner that has sincerity and thoughtfulness about it. (Kottler & Brown, 2000, p. 383)

As we conclude this text, we encourage you to engage in lifelong learning, ask questions, take risks, and build professional relationships. We also encourage you to find ways to balance your professional and personal endeavors, manage stress effectively, grow in self-awareness, learn from your mistakes, and remember to laugh. In so doing, may the contributions you give to the community not only enrich the clients you serve but also rejuvenate and enhance your experiences, personally and professionally, in multiple ways.

REFERENCES

Baird, B. N. (2002). *The internship, practicum, and field placement handbook: A guide for the helping professions* (3rd ed.). Upper Saddle River, NJ: Prentice Hall.

Belson, R. (1992, September/October). Ten tried-and-true methods to achieve therapist burnout. *Family Therapy Networker, 22.*

Boyatzis, R., McKee, A., & Goleman, D. (2002). Reawakening your passion for work. *Harvard Business Review, 80,* 86–93.

Cousins, N. (1979). *Anatomy of an illness.* New York: Norton.

Edwards, D., Burnard, P., Coyle, D., Fothergill, A., & Hannigan, B. (2000). Stress and burnout in community mental health nursing: A review of the literature. *Journal of Psychiatric and Mental Health Nursing, 7,* 7–14.

Freemont, S., & Anderson, W. (1986). What client behaviors make counselors angry? An exploratory study. *Journal of Counseling and Development, 65,* 67–70.

Gladding, S. T. (1995). Humor in counseling: Using a natural resource. *Journal of Humanistic Education and Development, 34,* 3–12.

Goldin, E., & Bordan, T. (1999). The use of humor in counseling: The laughing cure. *Journal of Counseling and Development, 77,* 405–410.

James, R. K., & Gilliland, B. E. (2001). *Crisis intervention strategies* (4th ed.). Pacific Grove, CA: Brooks/Cole.

Kottler, J. A. (1993). On being a therapist. San Francisco: Jossey-Bass.

Kottler, J. A., & Brown, R. W. (2000). *Introduction to therapeutic counseling: Voices from the field* (4th ed.). Belmont, CA: Wadsworth.

Kottler, J. A., & Schofield, M. (2001). When therapists face stress and crisis: Self-initiated coping strategies. In E. R. Welfel & R. Elliott Ingersoll (Eds.), *The mental health desk reference* (pp. 426–431). New York: Wiley.

Lazarus, R. S., & Folkman, S. (1984). *Stress, appraisal and coping.* New York: Springer.

MacCluskie, K. C., & Ingersoll, R. E. (2001). *Becoming a 21st century agency counselor: Personal and professional explorations.* Belmont, CA: Wadsworth.

Myers, J. E., Sweeney, T. J., Witmer, J. M. (2000). The Wheel of Wellness counseling for wellness: A holistic model for treatment planning. *Journal of Counseling and Development, 78,* 251–266.

Myers, J. E., & Williard, K. (2003). Integrating spirituality into counselor preparation: A developmental, wellness approach. *Counseling and Values, 47,* 142–155.

Swenson, R. A. (1998). *The overload syndrome: Learning to live within your limits.* Colorado Springs, CO: NavPress.

Watzlawick, P. (1983). *The situation is hopeless but not serious.* New York: Norton.

Weaver, S. T., & Wilson, C. N. (1997). Addiction counselors can benefit from appropriate humor in the work setting. *Journal of Employment Counseling, 34,* 108–114.

APPENDIX A

DSM-IV-TR Classification

NOS = Not Otherwise Specified.

An *x* appearing in a diagnostic code indicates that a specific code number is required.

An ellipsis (. . .) is used in the names of certain disorders to indicate that the name of a specific mental disorder or general medical condition should be inserted when recording the name (e.g., 293.0 Delirium Due to Hypothyroidism).

Numbers in parentheses are page numbers.

If criteria are currently met, one of the following severity specifiers may be noted after the diagnosis:

Mild

Moderate

Severe

If criteria are no longer met, one of the following specifiers may be noted:

In Partial Remission

In Full Remission

Prior History

Source: *Diagnostic and Statistical Manual of Mental Disorders* (4th ed., text rev.). Copyright 2000 American Psychiatric Association, 1994. Reprinted with permission.

Disorders Usually First Diagnosed in Infancy, Childhood, or Adolescence (39)

MENTAL RETARDATION (41)

Note: These are coded on Axis II.

317	Mild Mental Retardation (43)
318.0	Moderate Mental Retardation (43)
318.1	Severe Mental Retardation (43)
318.2	Profound Mental Retardation (44)
319	Mental Retardation, Severity Unspecified (44)

LEARNING DISORDERS (49)

315.00	Reading Disorder (51)
315.1	Mathematics Disorder (53)
315.2	Disorder of Written Expression (54)
315.9	Learning Disorder NOS (56)

MOTOR SKILLS DISORDER (56)

315.4	Developmental Coordination Disorder (56)

COMMUNICATION DISORDERS (58)

315.31   Expressive Language Disorder (58)

315.32   Mixed Receptive-Expressive Language Disorder (62)

315.39   Phonological Disorder (65)

307.0   Stuttering (67)

307.9   Communication Disorder NOS (69)

PERVASIVE DEVELOPMENTAL DISORDERS (69)

299.00   Autistic Disorder (70)

299.80   Rett's Disorder (76)

299.10   Childhood Disintegrative Disorder (77)

299.80   Asperger's Disorder (80)

299.80   Pervasive Developmental Disorder NOS (84)

ATTENTION-DEFICIT AND DISRUPTIVE BEHAVIOR DISORDERS (85)

314.xx   Attention-Deficit/Hyperactivity Disorder (85)
   .01   Combined Type
   .00   Predominantly Inattentive Type
   .01   Predominantly Hyperactive-Impulsive Type

314.9   Attention-Deficit/Hyperactivity Disorder NOS (93)

312.xx   Conduct Disorder (93)
   .81   Childhood-Onset Type
   .82   Adolescent-Onset Type
   .89   Unspecified Onset

313.81   Oppositional Defiant Disorder (100)

312.9   Disruptive Behavior Disorder NOS (103)

FEEDING AND EATING DISORDERS OF INFANCY OR EARLY CHILDHOOD (103)

307.52   Pica (103)

307.53   Rumination Disorder (105)

307.59   Feeding Disorder of Infancy or Early Childhood (107)

TIC DISORDERS (108)

307.23   Tourette's Disorder (111)

307.22   Chronic Motor or Vocal Tic Disorder (114)

307.21   Transient Tic Disorder (115)
         Specify if: Single Episode/Recurrent

307.20   Tic Disorder NOS (116)

ELIMINATION DISORDERS (116)

———.—   Encopresis (116)
787.6   With Constipation and Overflow Incontinence
307.7   Without Constipation and Overflow Incontinence

307.6   Enuresis (Not Due to a General Medical Condition) (118)
         Specify type: Nocturnal Only/Diurnal Only/ Nocturnal and Diurnal

OTHER DISORDERS OF INFANCY, CHILDHOOD, OR ADOLESCENCE (121)

309.21   Separation Anxiety Disorder (121)
         Specify if: Early Onset

313.23   Selective Mutism (125)

313.89   Reactive Attachment Disorder of Infancy or Early Childhood (127)
         Specify type: Inhibited Type/Disinhibited Type

307.3   Stereotypic Movement Disorder (131)
         Specify if: With Self-Injurious Behavior

313.9   Disorder of Infancy, Childhood, or Adolescence NOS (134)

Delirium, Dementia, and Amnestic and Other Cognitive Disorders (135)

DELIRIUM (136)

293.0   Delirium Due to . . . *[Indicate the General Medical Condition]* (141)

———.—   Substance Intoxication Delirium *(refer to Substance-Related Disorders for substance-specific codes)* (143)

——·— Substance Withdrawal Delirium *(refer to Substance-Related Disorders for substance-specific codes)* (143)

——·— Delirium Due to Multiple Etiologies *(code each of the specific etiologies)* (146)

——·— Delirium NOS (147)

DEMENTIA (147)

294.xx* Dementia of the Alzheimer's Type, With Early Onset *(also code 331.0 Alzheimer's disease on Axis III)* (154)
  .10   Without Behavioral Disturbance
  .11   With Behavioral Disturbance

294.xx* Dementia of the Alzheimer's Type, With Late Onset *(also code 331.0 Alzheimer's disease on Axis III)* (154)
  .10   Without Behavioral Disturbance
  .11   With Behavioral Disturbance

290.xx Vascular Dementia (158)
  .40   Uncomplicated
  .41   With Delirium
  .42   With Delusions
  .43   With Depressed Mood
      Specify if: With Behavioral Disturbance

Code presence or absence of a behavioral disturbance in the fifth digit for Dementia Due to a General Medical Condition:

      0 = Without Behavioral Disturbance

      1 = With Behavioral Disturbance

294.1x* Dementia Due to HIV Disease *(also code 042 HIV on Axis III)* (163)

294.1x* Dementia Due to Head Trauma *(also code 854.00 head injury on Axis III)* (164)

294.1x* Dementia Due to Parkinson's Disease *(also code 332.0 Parkinson's disease on Axis III)* (164)

294.1x* Dementia Due to Huntington's Disease *(also code 333.4 Huntington's disease on Axis III)* (165)

294.1x* Dementia Due to Pick's Disease *(also code 331.1 Pick's disease on Axis III)* (165)

294.1x* Dementia Due to Creutzfeldt-Jakob Disease *(also code 046.1 Creutzfeldt-Jakob disease on Axis III)* (166)

*ICD-9-CM code valid after October 1, 2000.

294.1x* Dementia Due to . . . *[Indicate the General Medical Condition not listed above] (also code the general medical condition on Axis III)* (167)

——·— Substance-Induced Persisting Dementia *(refer to Substance-Related Disorders for substance-specific codes)* (168)

——·— Dementia Due to Multiple Etiologies *(code each of the specific etiologies)* (170)

294.8 Dementia NOS (171)

AMNESTIC DISORDERS (172)

294.0 Amnestic Disorder Due to . . . *[Indicate the General Medical Condition]* (175)
      Specify if: Transient/Chronic

——·— Substance-Induced Persisting Amnestic Disorder *(refer to Substance-Related Disorders for substance-specific codes)* (177)

294.8 Amnestic Disorder NOS (179)

OTHER COGNITIVE DISORDERS (179)

294.9 Cognitive Disorder NOS (179)

Mental Disorders Due to a General Medical Condition Not Elsewhere Classified (181)

293.89 Catatonic Disorder Due to . . . *[Indicate the General Medical Condition]* (185)

310.1 Personality Change Due to . . . *[Indicate the General Medical Condition]* (187)
      Specify type: Labile Type/Disinhibited Type/Aggressive Type/Apathetic Type/Paranoid Type/Other Type/Combined Type/Unspecified Type

293.9 Mental Disorder NOS Due to . . . *[Indicate the General Medical Condition]* (190)

Substance-Related Disorders (191)

The following specifiers apply to Substance Dependence as noted:

  [a]With Physiological Dependence/Without Physiological Dependence

  [b]Early Full Remission/Early Partial Remission/ Sustained Full Remission/Sustained Partial Remission

^cIn a Controlled Environment
^dOn Agonist Therapy

The following specifiers apply to Substance-Induced Disorders as noted:

^IWith Onset During Intoxication/^WWith Onset During Withdrawal

ALCOHOL-RELATED DISORDERS (212)

Alcohol Use Disorders (213)

303.90   Alcohol Dependence^{a,b,c} (213)

305.00   Alcohol Abuse (214)

Alcohol-Induced Disorders (214)

303.00   Alcohol Intoxication (214)

291.81   Alcohol Withdrawal (215)
Specify if: With Perceptual Disturbances

291.0   Alcohol Intoxication Delirium (143)

291.0   Alcohol Withdrawal Delirium (143)

291.2   Alcohol-Induced Persisting Dementia (168)

291.1   Alcohol-Induced Persisting Amnestic Disorder (177)

291.x   Alcohol-Induced Psychotic Disorder (338)
.5   With Delusions^{I,W}
.3   With Hallucinations^{I,W}

291.89   Alcohol-Induced Mood Disorder^{I,W} (405)

291.89   Alcohol-Induced Anxiety Disorder^{I,W} (479)

291.89   Alcohol-Induced Sexual Dysfunction^I (562)

291.89   Alcohol-Induced Sleep Disorder^{I,W} (655)

291.9   Alcohol-Related Disorder NOS (223)

AMPHETAMINE-(OR AMPHETAMINE-LIKE) RELATED DISORDERS (223)

Amphetamine Use Disorders (224)

304.40   Amphetamine Dependence^{a,b,c} (224)

305.70   Amphetamine Abuse (225)

Amphetamine-Induced Disorders (226)

292.89   Amphetamine Intoxication (226)
Specify if: With Perceptual Disturbances

292.0   Amphetamine Withdrawal (227)

292.81   Amphetamine Intoxication Delirium (143)

292.xx   Amphetamine-Induced Psychotic Disorder (338)
.11   With Delusions^I
.12   With Hallucinations^I

292.84   Amphetamine-Induced Mood Disorder^{I,W} (405)

292.89   Amphetamine-Induced Anxiety Disorder^I (479)

292.89   Amphetamine-Induced Sexual Dysfunction^I (562)

292.89   Amphetamine-Induced Sleep Disorder^{I,W} (655)

292.9   Amphetamine-Related Disorder NOS (231)

CAFFEINE-RELATED DISORDERS (231)

Caffeine-Induced Disorders (232)

305.90   Caffeine Intoxication (232)

292.89   Caffeine-Induced Anxiety Disorder^I (479)

292.89   Caffeine-Induced Sleep Disorder^I (655)

292.9   Caffeine-Related Disorder NOS (234)

CANNABIS-RELATED DISORDERS (234)

Cannabis Use Disorders (236)

304.30   Cannabis Dependence^{a,b,c} (236)

305.20   Cannabis Abuse (236)

Cannabis-Induced Disorders (237)

292.89   Cannabis Intoxication (237)
Specify if: With Perceptual Disturbances

292.81   Cannabis Intoxication Delirium (143)

292.xx   Cannabis-Induced Psychotic Disorder (338)
.11   With Delusions^I
.12   With Hallucinations^I

292.89   Cannabis-Induced Anxiety Disorder^I (479)

292.9   Cannabis-Related Disorder NOS (241)

COCAINE-RELATED DISORDERS (241)

Cocaine Use Disorders (242)

304.20   Cocaine Dependence^{a,b,c} (242)

305.60   Cocaine Abuse (243)

Cocaine-Induced Disorders (244)

292.89   Cocaine Intoxication (244)
         Specify if: With Perceptual Disturbances

292.0   Cocaine Withdrawal (245)

292.81   Cocaine Intoxication Delirium (143)

292.xx   Cocaine-Induced Psychotic Disorder (338)
   .11   With Delusions[I]
   .12   With Hallucinations[I]

292.84   Cocaine-Induced Mood Disorder[I,W] (405)

292.89   Cocaine-Induced Anxiety Disorder[I,W] (479)

292.89   Cocaine-Induced Sexual Dysfunction[I] (562)

292.89   Cocaine-Induced Sleep Disorder[I,W] (655)

292.9   Cocaine-Related Disorder NOS (250)

HALLUCINOGEN-RELATED DISORDERS (250)

Hallucinogen Use Disorders (251)

304.50   Hallucinogen Dependence[b,c] (251)

305.30   Hallucinogen Abuse (252)

Hallucinogen-Induced Disorders (252)

292.89   Hallucinogen Intoxication (252)

292.89   Hallucinogen Persisting Perception Disorder (Flashbacks) (253)

292.81   Hallucinogen Intoxication Delirium (143)

292.xx   Hallucinogen-Induced Psychotic Disorder (338)
   .11   With Delusions[I]
   .12   With Hallucinations[I]

292.84   Hallucinogen-Induced Mood Disorder[I] (405)

292.89   Hallucinogen-Induced Anxiety Disorder[I] (479)

292.9   Hallucinogen-Related Disorder NOS (256)

INHALANT-RELATED DISORDERS (257)

Inhalant Use Disorders (258)

304.60   Inhalant Dependence[b,c] (258)

305.90   Inhalant Abuse (259)

Inhalant-Induced Disorders (259)

292.89   Inhalant Intoxication (259)

292.81   Inhalant Intoxication Delirium (143)

292.82   Inhalant-Induced Persisting Dementia (168)

292.xx   Inhalant-Induced Psychotic Disorder (338)
   .11   With Delusions[I]
   .12   With Hallucinations[I]

292.84   Inhalant-Induced Mood Disorder[I] (405)

292.89   Inhalant-Induced Anxiety Disorder[I] (479)

292.9   Inhalant-Related Disorder NOS (263)

NICOTINE-RELATED DISORDERS (264)

Nicotine Use Disorder (264)

305.1   Nicotine Dependence[a,b] (264)

Nicotine-Induced Disorder (265)

292.0   Nicotine Withdrawal (265)

292.9   Nicotine-Related Disorder NOS (269)

OPIOID-RELATED DISORDERS (269)

Opioid Use Disorders (270)

304.00   Opioid Dependence[a,b,c,d] (270)

305.50   Opioid Abuse (271)

Opioid-Induced Disorders (271)

292.89   Opioid Intoxication (271)
         Specify if: With Perceptual Disturbances

292.0   Opioid Withdrawal (272)

292.81   Opioid Intoxication Delirium (143)

292.xx   Opioid-Induced Psychotic Disorder (338)
   .11   With Delusions[I]
   .12   With Hallucinations[I]

292.84   Opioid-Induced Mood Disorder[I] (405)

292.89   Opioid-Induced Sexual Dysfunction[I] (562)

292.89   Opioid-Induced Sleep Disorder[I,W] (655)

292.9   Opioid-Related Disorder NOS (277)

PHENCYCLIDINE-(OR PHENCYCLIDINE-LIKE) RELATED DISORDERS (278)

Phencyclidine Use Disorders (279)

304.60   Phencyclidine Dependence[b,c] (279)

305.90   Phencyclidine Abuse (279)

Phencyclidine-Induced Disorders (280)

292.89   Phencyclidine Intoxication (280)
Specify if: With Perceptual Disturbances

292.81   Phencyclidine Intoxication Delirium (143)

292.xx   Phencyclidine-Induced Psychotic Disorder (338)
  .11   With Delusions[I]
  .12   With Hallucinations[I]

292.84   Phencyclidine-Induced Mood Disorder[I] (405)

292.89   Phencyclidine-Induced Anxiety Disorder[I] (479)

292.9   Phencyclidine-Related Disorder NOS (283)

SEDATIVE-, HYPNOTIC-, OR ANXIOLYTIC-RELATED DISORDERS (284)

Sedative, Hypnotic, or Anxiolytic Use Disorders (285)

304.10   Sedative, Hypnotic, or Anxiolytic Dependence[a,b,c] (285)

305.40   Sedative, Hypnotic, or Anxiolytic Abuse (286)

Sedative-, Hypnotic-, or Anxiolytic-Induced Disorders (286)

292.89   Sedative, Hypnotic, or Anxiolytic Intoxication (286)

292.0   Sedative, Hypnotic, or Anxiolytic Withdrawal (287)
Specify if: With Perceptual Disturbances

292.81   Sedative, Hypnotic, or Anxiolytic Intoxication Delirium (143)

292.81   Sedative, Hypnotic, or Anxiolytic Withdrawal Delirium (143)

292.82   Sedative-, Hypnotic-, or Anxiolytic-Induced Persisting Dementia (168)

292.83   Sedative-, Hypnotic-, or Anxiolytic-Induced Persisting Amnestic Disorder (177)

292.xx   Sedative-, Hypnotic-, or Anxiolytic-Induced Psychotic Disorder (338)
  .11   With Delusions[I,W]
  .12   With Hallucinations[I,W]

292.84   Sedative-, Hypnotic-, or Anxiolytic-Induced Mood Disorder[I,W] (405)

292.89   Sedative-, Hypnotic-, or Anxiolytic-Induced Anxiety Disorder[W] (479)

292.89   Sedative-, Hypnotic-, or Anxiolytic-Induced Sexual Dysfunction[I] (562)

292.89   Sedative-, Hypnotic-, or Anxiolytic-Induced Sleep Disorder[I,W] (655)

292.9   Sedative-, Hypnotic-, or Anxiolytic-Related Disorder NOS (293)

POLYSUBSTANCE-RELATED DISORDER (293)

304.80   Polysubstance Dependence[a,b,c,d] (293)

OTHER (OR UNKNOWN) SUBSTANCE-RELATED DISORDERS (294)

Other (or Unknown) Substance Use Disorders (295)

304.90   Other (or Unknown) Substance Dependence[a,b,c,d] (192)

305.90   Other (or Unknown) Substance Abuse (198)

Other (or Unknown) Substance-Induced Disorders (295)

292.89   Other (or Unknown) Substance Intoxication (199)
Specify if: With Perceptual Disturbances

292.0   Other (or Unknown) Substance Withdrawal (201)
Specify if: With Perceptual Disturbances

292.81   Other (or Unknown) Substance-Induced Delirium (143)

292.82   Other (or Unknown) Substance-Induced Persisting Dementia (168)

292.83   Other (or Unknown) Substance-Induced Persisting Amnestic Disorder (177)

292.xx   Other (or Unknown) Substance-Induced
         Psychotic Disorder (338)
  .11   With Delusions[I,W]
  .12   With Hallucinations[I,W]

292.84   Other (or Unknown) Substance-Induced
         Mood Disorder[I,W] (405)

292.89   Other (or Unknown) Substance-Induced
         Anxiety Disorder[I,W] (479)

292.89   Other (or Unknown) Substance-Induced
         Sexual Dysfunction[I] (562)

292.89   Other (or Unknown) Substance-Induced
         Sleep Disorder[I,W] (655)

292.9   Other (or Unknown) Substance-Related
         Disorder NOS (295)

Schizophrenia and Other Psychotic Disorders (297)

295.xx   Schizophrenia (274)

         *The following Classification of Longitudi-
         nal Course applies to all subtypes of Schizo-
         phrenia:*

         Episodic With Interepisode Residual Symp-
         toms (*specify if:* With Prominent Negative
         Symptoms)/Episodic With No Interepisode
         Residual Symptoms
         Continuous (*specify if:* With Prominent Neg-
         ative Symptoms)
         Single Episode In Partial Remission (*specify
         if:* With Prominent Negative Symptoms)/
         Single Episode in Full Remission
         Other or Unspecified Pattern

  .30   Paranoid Type (313)
  .10   Disorganized Type (314)
  .20   Catatonic Type (315)
  .90   Undifferentiated Type (316)
  .60   Residual Type (316)

295.40   Schizophreniform Disorder (317)
         Specify if: Without Good Prognostic Features/
         With Good Prognostic Features

295.70   Schizoaffective Disorder (319)
         Specify type: Bipolar Type/Depressive Type

297.1   Delusional Disorder (323)
         Specify type: Erotomanic Type/Grandiose
         Type/Jealous Type/Persecutory Type/Somatic
         Type/Mixed Type/Unspecified Type

298.8   Brief Psychotic Disorder (329)
         Specify if: With Marked Stressor(s)/Without
         Marked Stressor(s)/With Postpartum Onset

297.3   Shared Psychotic Disorder (332)

293.xx   Psychotic Disorder Due to ... *[Indicate the
         General Medical Condition]* (334)
  .81   With Delusions
  .82   With Hallucinations

———.—   Substance-Induced Psychotic Disorder
         *(refer to Substance-Related Disorders for
         substance-specific codes)* (338)
         Specify if: With Onset During Intoxication/
         With Onset During Withdrawal

298.9   Psychotic Disorder NOS (343)

Mood Disorders (345)

*Code current state of Major Depressive Disorder or
Bipolar I Disorder in fifth digit:*

         1 = Mild
         2 = Moderate
         3 = Severe Without Psychotic Features
         4 = Severe With Psychotic Features
              Specify: Mood-Congruent Psychotic Features/
              Mood-Incongruent Psychotic Features
         5 = In Partial Remission
         6 = In Full Remission
         0 = Unspecified

*The following specifiers apply (for current or
most recent episode) to Mood Disorders as noted:*

[a]Severity/Psychotic/Remission Specifiers/[b]Chronic/
[c]With Catatonic Features/[d]With Melancholic Features/
[e]With Atypical Features/[f]With Postpartum Onset

*The following specifiers apply to Mood Disorders
as noted:*

[g]With or Without Full Interepisode Recovery/
[h]With Seasonal Pattern/[i]With Rapid Cycling

DEPRESSIVE DISORDERS (369)

296.xx   Major Depressive Disorder (369)
  .2x   Single Episode[a,b,c,d,e,f]
  .3x   Recurrent[a,b,c,d,e,f,g,h]

300.4   Dysthymic Disorder (376)
         Specify if: Early Onset/Late Onset
         Specify: With Atypical Features

311   Depressive Disorder NOS (381)

BIPOLAR DISORDERS (382)

296.xx Bipolar I Disorder (382)
.0x Single Manic Episode[a,c,f]
Specify if: Mixed
.40 Most Recent Episode Hypomanic[g,h,i]
.4x Most Recent Episode Manic[a,c,f,g,h,i]
.6x Most Recent Episode Mixed[a,c,f,g,h,i]
.5x Most Recent Episode Depressed[a,b,c,d,e,f,g,h,i]
.7 Most Recent Episode Unspecified[g,h,i]

296.89 Bipolar II Disorder[a,b,c,d,e,f,g,h,i] (392)
Specify (current or most recent episode):
Hypomanic/Depressed

301.13 Cyclothymic Disorder (398)

296.80 Bipolar Disorder NOS (400)

293.83 Mood Disorder Due to . . . *[Indicate the General Medical Condition]* (401)
Specify type: With Depressive Features/With Major Depressive-Like Episode/With Manic Features/With Mixed Features

——.—— Substance-Induced Mood Disorder *(refer to Substance-Related Disorders for substance-specific codes)* (405)
Specify type: With Depressive Features/With Manic Features/With Mixed Features
Specify if: With Onset During Intoxication/With Onset During Withdrawal

296.90 Mood Disorder NOS (410)

Anxiety Disorders (429)

300.01 Panic Disorder Without Agoraphobia (433)

300.21 Panic Disorder With Agoraphobia (433)

300.22 Agoraphobia Without History of Panic Disorder (441)

300.29 Specific Phobia (443)
Specify type: Animal Type/Natural Environment Type/Blood-Injection-Injury Type/Situational Type/Other Type

300.23 Social Phobia (450)
Specify if: Generalized

300.3 Obsessive-Compulsive Disorder (456)
Specify if: With Poor Insight

309.81 Posttraumatic Stress Disorder (463)
Specify if: Acute/Chronic
Specify if: With Delayed Onset

308.3 Acute Stress Disorder (469)

300.02 Generalized Anxiety Disorder (472)

293.84 Anxiety Disorder Due to . . . *[Indicate the General Medical Condition]* (476)
Specify if: With Generalized Anxiety/With Panic Attacks/With Obsessive-Compulsive Symptoms

——.—— Substance-Induced Anxiety Disorder *(refer to Substance-Related Disorders for substance-specific codes)* (479)
Specify if: With Generalized Anxiety/With Panic Attacks/With Obsessive-Compulsive Symptoms/With Phobic Symptoms
Specify if: With Onset During Intoxication/With Onset During Withdrawal

300.0 Anxiety Disorder NOS (484)

Somatoform Disorders (485)

300.81 Somatization Disorder (486)

300.82 Undifferentiated Somatoform Disorder (490)

300.11 Conversion Disorder (492)
Specify type: With Motor Symptom or Deficit/With Sensory Symptom or Deficit/With Seizures or Convulsions/With Mixed Presentation

307.xx Pain Disorder (498)
.80 Associated With Psychological Factors
.89 Associated With Both Psychological Factors and a General Medical Condition
Specify if: Acute/Chronic

300.7 Hypochondriasis (504)
Specify if: With Poor Insight

300.7 Body Dysmorphic Disorder (507)

300.82 Somatoform Disorder NOS (511)

Factitious Disorders (513)

300.xx Factitious Disorder (513)
.16 With Predominantly Psychological Signs and Symptoms
.19 With Predominantly Physical Signs and Symptoms
.19 With Combined Psychological and Physical Signs and Symptoms

300.19 Factitious Disorder NOS (517)

Dissociative Disorders (519)

300.12   Dissociative Amnesia (520)

300.13   Dissociative Fugue (523)

300.14   Dissociative Identity Disorder (526)

300.6   Depersonalization Disorder (530)

300.15   Dissociative Disorder NOS (532)

Sexual and Gender Identity Disorders (535)

SEXUAL DYSFUNCTIONS (535)

The following specifiers apply to all primary Sexual Dysfunctions:

Lifelong Type/Acquired Type

Generalized Type/Situational Type

Due to Psychological Factors/Due to Combined Factors

Sexual Desire Disorder (539)

302.71   Hypoactive Sexual Desire Disorder (539)

302.79   Sexual Aversion Disorder (541)

Sexual Arousal Disorders (543)

302.72   Female Sexual Arousal Disorder (543)

302.72   Male Erectile Disorder (545)

Orgasmic Disorders (547)

302.73   Female Orgasmic Disorder (547)

302.74   Male Orgasmic Disorder (550)

302.75   Premature Ejaculation (552)

Sexual Pain Disorders (554)

302.76   Dyspareunia (Not Due to a General Medical Condition) (554)

306.51   Vaginismus (Not Due to a General Medical Condition) (556)

Sexual Dysfunction Due to a General Medical Condition (558)

625.8   Female Hypoactive Sexual Desire Disorder Due to . . . *[Indicate the General Medical Condition]* (558)

608.89   Male Hypoactive Sexual Desire Disorder Due to . . . *[Indicate the General Medical Condition]* (558)

607.84   Male Erectile Disorder Due to . . . *[Indicate the General Medical Condition]* (558)

625.0   Female Dyspareunia Due to . . . *[Indicate the General Medical Condition]* (558)

608.89   Male Dyspareunia Due to . . . *[Indicate the General Medical Condition]* (558)

625.8   Other Female Sexual Dysfunction Due to . . . *[Indicate the General Medical Condition]* (558)

608.89   Other Male Sexual Dysfunction Due to . . . *[Indicate the General Medical Condition]* (558)

———   Substance-Induced Sexual Dysfunction *(refer to Substance-Related Disorders for substance-specific codes)* (562)
Specify if: With Impaired Desire/With Impaired Arousal/With Impaired Orgasm/With Sexual Pain
Specify if: With Onset During Intoxication

302.70   Sexual Dysfunction NOS (565)

PARAPHILIAS (566)

302.4   Exhibitionism (569)

302.81   Fetishism (569)

302.89   Frotteurism (570)

302.2   Pedophilia (571)
Specify if: Sexually Attracted to Males/Sexually Attracted to Females/Sexually Attracted to Both
Specify if: Limited to Incest
Specify type: Exclusive Type/Nonexclusive Type

302.83   Sexual Masochism (572)

302.84   Sexual Sadism (573)

302.3   Transvestic Fetishism (574)
         Specify if: With Gender Dysphoria

302.82   Voyeurism (575)

302.9   Paraphilia NOS (576)

GENDER IDENTITY DISORDERS (576)

302.xx   Gender Identity Disorder (576)
  .6   in Children
  .85   in Adolescents or Adults
         Specify if: Sexually Attracted to Males/
         Sexually Attracted to Females/Sexually
         Attracted to Both/Sexually Attracted to
         Neither

302.6   Gender Identity Disorder NOS (582)

302.9   Sexual Disorder NOS (582)

Eating Disorders (583)

307.1   Anorexia Nervosa (583)
         Specify type: Restricting Type; Binge-Eating/
         Purging Type

307.51   Bulimia Nervosa (589)
         Specify type: Purging Type/Nonpurging Type

307.50   Eating Disorder NOS (594)

Sleep Disorders (597)

PRIMARY SLEEP DISORDERS (598)

Dyssomnias (598)

307.42   Primary Insomnia (599)

307.44   Primary Hypersomnia (604)
         Specify if: Recurrent

347   Narcolepsy (609)

780.59   Breathing-Related Sleep Disorder (615)

307.45   Circadian Rhythm Sleep Disorder (622)
         Specify type: Delayed Sleep Phase Type/
         Jet Lag Type/Shift Work Type/Unspecified
         Type

307.47   Dyssomnia NOS (629)

Parasomnias (630)

307.47   Nightmare Disorder (631)

307.46   Sleep Terror Disorder (634)

307.46   Sleepwalking Disorder (639)

307.47   Parasomnia NOS (644)

SLEEP DISORDERS RELATED TO ANOTHER MENTAL DISORDER (645)

307.42   Insomnia Related to . . . *[Indicate the Axis I or Axis II Disorder]* (645)

307.44   Hypersomnia Related to . . . *[Indicate the Axis I or Axis II Disorder]* (645)

OTHER SLEEP DISORDERS (651)

780.xx   Sleep Disorder Due to . . . *[Indicate the General Medical Condition]* (651)
  .52   Insomnia Type
  .54   Hypersomnia Type
  .59   Parasomnia Type
  .59   Mixed Type

——.——   Substance-Induced Sleep Disorder *(refer to Substance-Related Disorders for substance-specific codes)* (655)
         Specify type: Insomnia Type/Hypersomnia Type/Parasomnia Type/Mixed Type
         Specify if: With Onset During Intoxication/
         With Onset During Withdrawal

Impulse-Control Disorders Not Elsewhere Classified (663)

312.34   Intermittent Explosive Disorder (663)

312.32   Kleptomania (667)

312.33   Pyromania (669)

312.31   Pathological Gambling (671)

312.39   Trichotillomania (674)

312.30   Impulse-Control Disorder NOS (677)

Adjustment Disorders (679)

309.xx   Adjustment Disorder (679)
.0   With Depressed Mood
.24   With Anxiety
.28   With Mixed Anxiety and Depressed Mood
.3   With Disturbance of Conduct
.4   With Mixed Disturbance of Emotions and Conduct
.9   Unspecified
           Specify if: Acute/Chronic

Personality Disorders (685)

Note: These are coded on Axis II.

301.0   Paranoid Personality Disorder (690)

301.20   Schizoid Personality Disorder (694)

301.22   Schizotypal Personality Disorder (697)

301.7   Antisocial Personality Disorder (701)

301.83   Borderline Personality Disorder (706)

301.50   Histrionic Personality Disorder (711)

301.81   Narcissistic Personality Disorder (714)

301.82   Avoidant Personality Disorder (718)

301.6   Dependent Personality Disorder (721)

301.4   Obsessive-Compulsive Personality Disorder (725)

301.9   Personality Disorder NOS (729)

Other Conditions That May be a Focus of Clinical Attention (731)

PSYCHOLOGICAL FACTORS AFFECTING MEDICAL CONDITION (731)

316   *. . . [Specified Psychological Factor] Affecting . . . [Indicate the General Medical Condition]* (731) *Choose name based on nature of factors:*

          Mental Disorder Affecting Medical Condition

          Psychological Symptoms Affecting Medical Condition

          Personality Traits or Coping Style Affecting Medical Condition

Maladaptive Health Behaviors Affecting Medical Condition

Stress-Related Physiological Response Affecting Medical Condition

Other or Unspecified Psychological Factors Affecting Medical Condition

MEDICATION-INDUCED MOVEMENT DISORDERS (734)

332.1   Neuroleptic-Induced Parkinsonism (735)

333.92   Neuroleptic Malignant Syndrome (735)

333.7   Neuroleptic-Induced Acute Dystonia (735)

333.99   Neuroleptic-Induced Acute Akathisia (735)

333.82   Neuroleptic-Induced Tardive Dyskinesia (736)

333.1   Medication-Induced Postural Tremor (736)

333.90   Medication-Induced Movement Disorder NOS (736)

OTHER MEDICATION-INDUCED DISORDER (736)

995.2   Adverse Effects of Medication NOS (736)

RELATIONAL PROBLEMS (736)

V61.9   Relational Problem Related to a Mental Disorder or General Medical Condition (737)

V61.20   Parent-Child Relational Problem (737)

V61.10   Partner Relational Problem (737)

V61.8   Sibling Relational Problem (737)

V62.81   Relational Problem NOS (737)

PROBLEMS RELATED TO ABUSE OR NEGLECT (738)

V61.21   Physical Abuse of Child (738) *(code 995.54 if focus of attention is on victim)*

V61.21   Sexual Abuse of Child (738) *(code 995.53 if focus of attention is on victim)*

V61.21   Neglect of Child (738) *(code 995.52 if focus of attention is on victim)*

———   Physical Abuse of Adult (738)

V61.12   (if by partner)

V62.83 (if by person other than partner) *(code 995.81 if focus of attention is on victim)*

———.— Sexual Abuse of Adult (738)

V61.12 (if by partner)

V62.83 (if by person other than partner) *(code 995.83 if focus of attention is on victim)*

ADDITIONAL CONDITIONS THAT MAY BE A FOCUS OF CLINICAL ATTENTION (739)

V15.81 Noncompliance With Treatment (739)

V65.2   Malingering (739)

V71.01 Adult Antisocial Behavior (740)

V71.02 Child or Adolescent Antisocial Behavior (740)

V62.89 Borderline Intellectual Functioning (740)

Note: This is coded on Axis II.

780.9   Age-Related Cognitive Decline (740)

V62.82 Bereavement (740)

V62.3   Academic Problem (741)

V62.2   Occupational Problem (741)

313.82 Identity Problem (741)

V62.89 Religious or Spiritual Problem (741)

V62.4   Acculturation Problem (741)

V62.89 Phase of Life Problem (742)

Additional Codes (743)

300.9   Unspecified Mental Disorder (nonpsychotic) (743)

V71.09 No Diagnosis or Condition on Axis I (743)

799.9   Diagnosis or Condition Deferred on Axis I (743)

V71.09 No Diagnosis on Axis II (743)

799.9   Diagnosis Deferred on Axis II (743)

Multiaxial System

Axis I   Clinical Disorders Other Conditions That May Be a Focus of Clinical Attention

Axis II Personality Disorders Mental Retardation

Axis III General Medical Conditions

Axis IV Psychosocial and Environmental Problems

Axis V   Global Assessment of Functioning

DSM-IV-TR Classification of Disorders and Conditions That Affect Children and Adolescents

DISORDERS USUALLY FIRST DIAGNOSED IN INFANCY, CHILDHOOD, OR ADOLESCENCE

Mental Retardation (Axis II)

317	Mild Mental Retardation (50–59 to 69–70 IQ)
318.0	Moderate Mental Retardation (35–40 to 50–55 IQ)
318.1	Severe Mental Retardation (20–25 to 35–40 IQ)
318.2	Profound Mental Retardation (below 20–25 IQ)
319	Mental Retardation, Severity Unspecified

Learning Disorders

315.00	Reading Disorder
315.1	Mathematics Disorder
315.2	Disorder of Written Expression
315.9	Learning Disorder NOS

Motor Skills Disorders

315.4	Developmental Coordination Disorder

Communication Disorders

315.31	Expressive Language Disorder
315.31	Mixed Receptive/Expressive Language Disorder
315.39	Phonological Disorder
307.0	Stuttering
307.9	Communication Disorder NOS

Pervasive Developmental Disorders

299.00	Autistic Disorder
299.80	Rett's Disorder
299.10	Childhood Disintegrative Disorder
299.80	Asperger's Disorder
299.80	Pervasive Developmental Disorder

Attention-Deficit and Disruptive Behavior Disorders

314.xx	Attention-Deficit/Hyperactivity Disorder
.01	Combined Type
.00	Predominantly Inattentive Type
.01	Predominantly Hyperactive-Impulsive Type
314.9	Attention-Deficit/Hyperactivity Disorder NOS
312.xx	Conduct Disorder
.81	Childhood-Onset Type
.82	Adolescent-Onset Type
.89	Unspecified Onset

313.81   Oppositional Defiant Disorder

312.9   Disruptive Behavior Disorder NOS

Feeding and Eating Disorders of Infancy or Early Childhood

307.52   Pica

307.53   Rumination Disorder

307.59   Feeding Disorder of Infancy or Early Childhood

Tic Disorders

307.23   Tourette's Disorder

307.22   Chronic Motor or Vocal Tic Disorder

307.21   Transient Tic Disorder

307.20   Tic Disorder NOS

Elimination Disorders

787.6   Encopresis With Constipation and Overflow Incontinence

307.7   Encopresis Without Constipation and Overflow Incontinence

307.6   Enuresis (Not Due to a General Medical Condition)

Other Disorders of Infancy, Childhood, or Adolescence

309.21   Separation Anxiety Disorder

313.23   Selective Mutism

313.89   Reactive Attachment Disorder of Infancy or Early Childhood

307.3   Stereotypic Movement Disorder

313.9   Disorder of Infancy, Childhood, or Adolescence NOS

OTHER CONDITIONS THAT MAY BE EVIDENCED IN CHILDHOOD AND ADOLESCENCE

Relational Problems

V61.20   Parent–Child Relational Problem

V61.8   Sibling Relational Problem

V62.81   Relational Problem NOS

Child or Adolescent Antisocial Behavior

V71.02   (The antisocial behavior is not due to conduct disorder or another mental disorder. Examples include isolated antisocial acts of children or adolescents.)

Borderline Intellectual Functioning

V62.89   (Coded on Axis II. 71 to 84 IQ)

Bereavement

V62.82   Reaction to the Death of a Loved One

Academic Problem

V62.3   Focus of attention is an academic problem that is not due to a mental disorder, or if due to a mental disorder, is sufficiently severe to warrant independent attention.

Abuse or Neglect

995.54   Physical abuse of a child, with focus on the victim

995.53   Sexual abuse of a child, with focus on the victim

995.52   Neglect of a child, with focus on the victim

Substance-Related Disorders

Mood Disorders

For example, major depressive disorder, dysthymic disorder, bipolar disorder, cyclothymic disorder, substance-induced mood disorder, and mood disorder NOS. Irritability rather than depressed mood may characterize children and adolescents who are depressed.

Anxiety Disorders

For example, panic disorder, specific phobias, social phobia, obsessive compulsive disorder, posttraumatic stress disorder, acute stress disorder, generalized anxiety disorder

Somatoform Disorders

Dissociative Disorders

Eating Disorders

Anorexia nervosa, bulimia nervosa, eating disorder NOS

Sleep Disorders

Impulse Control Disorders (not classified elsewhere)

Pyromania, trichotillomania, kleptomania

Adjustment Disorders

The development of emotional or behavioral symptoms in response to an identifiable stressor occurring within 3 months of the onset of the stressor. The nature of the stressor can be listed on Axis IV.

Personality Disorders (Axis II)

Personality disorders typically first appear during adolescence or earlier, but the diagnosis is not made until adulthood.

Schizophrenia and Related Disorders

Schizophrenia is usually manifested in adolescence or early adulthood.

APPENDIX C

Ethical Standards of the American Counseling Association

The American Counseling Association is an educational, scientific and professional organization whose members are dedicated to the enhancement of human development throughout the life span. Association members recognize diversity in our society and embrace a cross-cultural approach in support of the worth, dignity, potential, and uniqueness of each individual.

The specification of a code of ethics enables the Association to clarify to current and future members, and to those served by members, the nature of the ethical responsibilities held in common by its members. As the code of ethics of the Association, this document establishes principles that define the ethical behavior of Association members. All members of the American Counseling Association are required to adhere to the *Code of Ethics* and the *Standards of Practice*. The Code of Ethics will serve as the basis for processing ethical complaints initiated against members of the Association.

CODE OF ETHICS

Section A: The Counseling Relationship

A.1. *Client Welfare*

a. *Primary Responsibility.* The primary responsibility of counselors is to respect the dignity and to promote the welfare of clients.

b. *Positive Growth and Development.* Counselors encourage client growth and development in ways which foster the clients' interest and welfare; counselors avoid fostering dependent counseling relationships.

c. *Counseling Plans.* Counselors and their clients work jointly in devising integrated, individual counseling plans that offer reasonable promise of success and are consistent with abilities and circumstances of clients. Counselors and clients regularly review counseling plans to ensure their continued viability and effectiveness, respecting clients' freedom of choice. (See A.3.b.)

d. *Family Involvement.* Counselors recognize that families are usually important in clients' lives and strive to enlist family understanding and involvement as a positive resource, when appropriate.

e. *Career and Employment Needs.* Counselors work with their clients in considering employment in jobs and circumstances that are consistent with the clients' overall abilities, vocational limitations, physical restrictions, general temperament, interest and aptitude patterns, social skills, education, general qualifications, and other relevant characteristics and needs. Counselors neither place nor participate in placing clients in positions that will result in damaging the interest and welfare of clients, employers, or the public.

A.2. Respecting Diversity

a. *Nondiscrimination.* Counselors do not condone or engage in discrimination based on age, color, culture, disability, ethnic group, gender, race, religion, sexual orientation, marital status, or socioeconomic status. (See C.5.a., C.5.b., and D.1.i.)

b. *Respecting Differences.* Counselors will actively attempt to understand the diverse cultural backgrounds of the clients with whom they work. This includes, but is not limited to, learning how the counselor's own cultural/ethnic/racial identity impacts her/his values and beliefs about the counseling process. (See E.8. and F.2.i.)

A.3. Client Rights

a. *Disclosure to Clients.* When counseling is initiated, and throughout the counseling process as necessary, counselors inform clients of the purposes, goals, techniques, procedures, limitations, potential risks and benefits of services to be performed and other pertinent information. Counselors take steps to ensure that clients understand the implications of diagnosis, the intended use of tests and reports, fees, and billing arrangements. Clients have the right to expect confidentiality and to be provided with an explanation of its limitations, including supervision and/or treatment team professionals; to obtain clear information about their case records; to participate in the ongoing counseling plans; and to refuse any recommended services and be advised of the consequences of such refusal. (See E.5.a. and G.2.)

b. *Freedom of Choice.* Counselors offer clients the freedom to choose whether to enter into a counseling relationship and to determine which professional(s) will provide counseling. Restrictions that limit choices of clients are fully explained. (See A.1.c.).

c. *Inability to Give Consent.* When counseling minors or persons unable to give voluntary informed consent, counselors act in these clients' best interests. (See B.3.)

A.4. Clients Served by Others

If a client is receiving services from another mental health professional, counselors, with client consent, inform the professional persons already involved and develop clear agreements in order to avoid confusion and conflict for the client. (See C.6.c.)

A.5. Personal Needs and Values

a. *Personal Needs.* In the counseling relationship, counselors are aware of the intimacy and responsibilities inherent in the counseling relationship, maintain respect for clients, and avoid actions that seek to meet their personal needs at the expense of clients.

b. *Personal Values.* Counselors are aware of their own values, attitudes, beliefs, and behaviors and how these apply in a diverse society, and avoid imposing their values on clients. (See C.5.a.)

A.6. Dual Relationships

a. *Avoid When Possible.* Counselors are aware of their influential positions with respect to clients, and they avoid exploiting the trust and dependency of clients. Counselors make every effort to avoid dual relationships with clients that could impair professional judgment or increase the risk of harm to clients. (Examples of such relationships include, but are not limited to, familial, social, financial, business, or close personal relationships with clients.) When a dual relationship cannot be avoided, counselors take appropriate professional precautions such as informed consent, consultation, supervision, and documentation to ensure that judgment is not impaired and no exploitation occurs. (See F.1.b.)

b. *Superior/Subordinate Relationships.* Counselors do not accept as clients superiors or subordinates with whom they have administrative, supervisory, or evaluative relationships.

A.7. Sexual Intimacies With Clients

a. *Current Clients.* Counselors do not have any type of sexual intimacies with clients and do not counsel persons with whom they have had a sexual relationship.
b. *Former Clients.* Counselors do not engage in sexual intimacies with former clients within a minimum of two years after terminating the counseling relationship. Counselors who engage in such relationship after two years following termination have the responsibility to thoroughly exam and document that such relations did not have an exploitative nature, based on factors such as duration of counseling, amount of time since counseling, termination circumstances, client's personal history and mental status, adverse impact on the client, and actions by the counselor suggesting a plan to initiate a sexual relationship with the client after termination.

A.8. Multiple Clients

When counselors agree to provide counseling services to two or more persons who have a relationship (such as husband and wife, or parents and children), counselors clarify at the outset which person or persons are clients and the nature of the relationships they will have with each involved person. If it becomes apparent that counselors may be called upon to perform potential conflicting roles, they clarify, adjust, or withdraw from roles appropriately. (See B.2. and B.4.d.)

A.9. Group Work

a. *Screening.* Counselors screen prospective group counseling/therapy participants. To the extent possible, counselors select members whose needs and goals are compatible with goals of the group, who will not impede the group process, and whose well-being will not be jeopardized by the group experience.
b. *Protecting Clients.* In a group setting, counselors take reasonable precautions to protect clients from physical or psychological trauma.

A.10. Fees and Bartering (See D.3.a. and D.3.b.)

a. *Advance Understanding.* Counselors clearly explain to clients, prior to entering the counseling

relationship, all financial arrangements related to professional services including the use of collection agencies or legal measures for nonpayment. (A.11.c.).
b. *Establishing Fees.* In establishing fees for professional counseling services, counselors consider the financial status of clients and locality. In the event that the established fee structure is inappropriate for a client, assistance is provided in attempting to find comparable services of acceptable cost. (See A.10.d., D.3.a., and D.3.b.)
c. *Bartering Discouraged.* Counselors ordinarily refrain from accepting goods or services from clients in return for counseling services because such arrangements create inherent potential for conflicts, exploitation, and distortion of the professional relationship. Counselors may participate in bartering only if the relationship is not exploitive, if the client requests it, if a clear written contract is established, and if such arrangements are an accepted practice among professionals in the community. (See A.6.a.)
d. *Pro Bono Service.* Counselors contribute to society by devoting a portion of their professional activity to services for which there is little or no financial return (pro bono).

A.11. Termination and Referral

a. *Abandonment Prohibited.* Counselors do not abandon or neglect clients in counseling. Counselors assist in making appropriate arrangements for the continuation of treatment, when necessary, during interruptions such as vacations, and following termination.
b. *Inability to Assist Clients.* If counselors determine an inability to be of professional assistance to clients, they avoid entering or immediately terminate a counseling relationship. Counselors are knowledgeable about referral resources and suggest appropriate alternatives. If clients decline the suggested referral, counselors should discontinue the relationship.
c. *Appropriate Termination.* Counselors terminate a counseling relationship, securing client agreement when possible, when it is reasonably clear that the client is no longer benefiting, when services are no longer required, when counseling no longer serves the client's needs or interests, when clients do not pay fees charged, or when

agency or institution limits do not allow provision of further counseling services. (See A.10.b. and C.2.g.)

A.12. Computer Technology

a. *Use of Computers.* When computer applications are used in counseling services, counselors ensure that: (1) the client is intellectually, emotionally, and physically capable of using the computer application; (2) the computer application is appropriate for the needs of the client; (3) the client understands the purpose and operation of the computer applications; and (4) a follow-up of client use of a computer application is provided to correct possible misconceptions, discover inappropriate use, and assess subsequent needs.

b. *Explanation of Limitations.* Counselors ensure that clients are provided information as a part of the counseling relationship that adequately explains the limitations of computer technology.

c. *Access to Computer Applications.* Counselors provide for equal access to computer applications in counseling services. (See A.2.a.)

Section B: Confidentiality

B.1. Right to Privacy

a. *Respect for Privacy.* Counselors respect their clients' right to privacy and avoid illegal and unwarranted disclosures of confidential information. (See A.3.a. and B.6.a.)

b. *Client Waiver.* The right to privacy may be waived by the client or their legally recognized representative.

c. *Exceptions.* The general requirement that counselors keep information confidential does not apply when disclosure is required to prevent clear and imminent danger to the client or others or when legal requirements demand that confidential information be revealed. Counselors consult with other professionals when in doubt as to the validity of an exception.

d. *Contagious, Fatal Diseases.* A counselor who receives information confirming that a client has a disease commonly known to be both communicable and fatal is justified in disclosing information to an identifiable third party, who by his or her relationship with the client is at a high risk of contracting the disease. Prior to making a disclosure

the counselor should ascertain that the client has not already informed the third party about his or her disease and that the client is not intending to inform the third party in the immediate future. (See B.1.c. and B.1.f.)

e. *Court Ordered Disclosure.* When court ordered to release confidential information without a client's permission, counselors request to the court that the disclosure not be required due to potential harm to the client or counseling relationship. (See B.1.c.)

f. *Minimal Disclosure.* When circumstances require the disclosure of confidential information, only essential information is revealed. To the extent possible, clients are informed before confidential information is disclosed.

g. *Explanation of Limitations.* When counseling is initiated and throughout the counseling process as necessary, counselors inform clients of the limitations of confidentiality and identify foreseeable situations in which confidentiality must be breached. (See G.2.a.)

h. *Subordinates.* Counselors make every effort to ensure that privacy and confidentiality of clients are maintained by subordinates including employees, supervisees, clerical assistants, and volunteers. (See B.1.a.)

i. *Treatment Teams.* If client treatment will involve a continued review by a treatment team, the client will be informed of the team's existence and composition.

B.2. Groups and Families

a. *Group Work.* In group work, counselors clearly define confidentiality and the parameters for the specific group being entered, explain its importance, and discuss the difficulties related to confidentiality involved in group work. The fact that confidentiality cannot be guaranteed is clearly communicated to group members.

b. *Family Counseling.* In family counseling, information about one family member cannot be disclosed to another member without permission. Counselors protect the privacy rights of each family member. (See A.8., B.3., and B.4.d.)

B.3. Minor or Incompetent Clients

When counseling clients who are minors or individuals who are unable to give voluntary, informed consent, parents or guardians may be included in the counseling process as appropriate. Counselors act in the best interests of clients and take measures to safeguard confidentiality. (See A.3.c.)

B.4. Records

a. *Requirement of Records.* Counselors maintain records necessary for rendering professional services to their clients and as required by laws, regulations, or agency or institution procedures.

b. *Confidentiality of Records.* Counselors are responsible for securing the safety and confidentiality of any counseling records they create, maintain, transfer, or destroy whether the records are written, taped, computerized, or stored in any other medium. (See B.1.a.)

c. *Permission To Record or Observe.* Counselors obtain permission from clients prior to electronically recording or observing sessions. (See A.3.a.)

d. *Client Access.* Counselors recognize that counseling records are kept for the benefit of clients and therefore provide access to records and copies of records when requested by competent clients unless the records contain information that may be misleading and detrimental to the client. In situations involving multiple clients, access to records is limited to those parts of records that do not include confidential information related to another client. (See A.8., B.1.a., and B.2.b.)

e. *Disclosure or Transfer.* Counselors obtain written permission from clients to disclose or transfer records to legitimate third parties unless exceptions to confidentiality exist as listed in section B.1. Steps are taken to ensure that receivers of counseling records are sensitive to their confidential nature.

B.5. Research and Training

a. *Data Disguise Required.* Use of data derived from counseling relationships for purposes of training, research, or publication is confined to content that is disguised to ensure the anonymity of the individuals involved. (See B.1.g. and G.3.d.)

b. *Agreement for Identification.* Identification of a client in a presentation or publication is permissible only when the client has reviewed the material and has agreed to its presentation or publication. (See G.3.d.)

B.6. Consultation

a. *Respect for Privacy.* Information obtained in a consulting relationship is discussed for professional purposes only with persons clearly concerned with the case. Written and oral reports present data germane to the purposes of the consultation, and every effort is made to protect client identity and avoid undue invasion of privacy.

b. *Cooperating Agencies.* Before sharing information, counselors make efforts to ensure that there are defined policies in other agencies serving the counselor's clients that effectively protect the confidentiality of information.

Section C: Professional Responsibility

C.1. Standards Knowledge

Counselors have a responsibility to read, understand, and follow the *Code of Ethics* and the *Standards of Practice*.

C.2. Professional Competence

a. *Boundaries of Competence.* Counselors practice only within the boundaries of their competence, based on their education, training, supervised experience, state and national professional credentials, and appropriate professional experience. Counselors will demonstrate a commitment to gain knowledge, personal awareness, sensitivity, and skills pertinent to working with a diverse client population.

b. *New Specialty Areas of Practice.* Counselors practice in specialty areas new to them only after appropriate education, training, and supervised experience. While developing skills in new specialty areas, counselors take steps to ensure the competence of their work and to protect others from possible harm.

c. *Qualified for Employment.* Counselors accept employment only for positions for which they are qualified by education, training, supervised experience, state and national professional credentials, and appropriate professional experience. Counselors hire for professional counseling positions only individuals who are qualified and competent.

d. *Monitor Effectiveness.* Counselors continually monitor their effectiveness as professionals and take steps to improve when necessary. Counselors in private practice take reasonable steps to seek out peer supervision to evaluate their efficacy as counselors.

e. *Ethical Issues Consultation.* Counselors take reasonable steps to consult with other counselors or related professionals when they have questions regarding their ethical obligations or professional practice (See H.1.).

f. *Continuing Education.* Counselors recognize the need for continuing education to maintain a reasonable level of awareness of current scientific and professional information in their fields of activity. They take steps to maintain competence in the skills they use, are open to new procedures, and keep current with the diverse and/or special populations with whom they work.

g. *Impairment.* Counselors refrain from offering or accepting professional services when their physical, mental or emotional problems are likely to lead to harm to a client or others. They are alert to the signs of impairment, seek assistance for problems, and, if necessary, limit, suspend, or terminate their professional responsibilities. (See A.11.c.)

C.3. Advertising and Soliciting Clients

a. *Accurate Advertising.* There are no restrictions on advertising by counselors except those that can be specifically justified to protect the public from deceptive practices. Counselors advertise or represent their services to the public by identifying their credentials in an accurate manner that is not false, misleading, deceptive, or fraudulent. Counselors may only advertise the highest degree earned which is in counseling or a closely related field from a college or university that was accredited when the degree was awarded by one of the regional accrediting bodies recognized by the Council on Post-secondary Accreditation.

b. *Testimonials.* Counselors who use testimonials do not solicit them from clients or other persons who, because of their particular circumstances, may be vulnerable to undue influence.

c. *Statements by Others.* Counselors make reasonable efforts to ensure that statements made by others about them or the profession of counseling are accurate.

d. *Recruiting Through Employment.* Counselors do not use their places of employment or institutional affiliation to recruit or gain clients, supervisees, or consultees for their private practices. (See C.5.e.)

e. *Products and Training Advertisements.* Counselors who develop products related to their profession or conduct workshops or training events ensure that the advertisements concerning these products or events are accurate and disclose adequate information for consumers to make informed choices.

f. *Promoting to Those Served.* Counselors do not use counseling, teaching, training, or supervisory relationships to promote their products or training events in a manner that is deceptive or would exert undue influence on individuals who may be vulnerable. Counselors may adopt textbooks they have authored for instruction purposes.

g. *Professional Association Involvement.* Counselors actively participate in local, state, and national associations that foster the development and improvement of counseling.

C.4. Credentials

a. *Credentials Claimed.* Counselors claim or imply only professional credentials possessed and are responsible for correcting any known misrepresentations of their credentials by others. Professional credentials include graduate degrees in counseling or closely related mental health fields, accreditation of graduate programs, national voluntary certifications, government-issued certifications or licenses, ACA professional membership, or any other credential that might indicate to the public specialized knowledge or expertise in counseling.

b. *ACA Professional Membership.* ACA professional members may announce to the public their membership status. Regular members may not announce their ACA membership in a manner that might imply they are credentialed counselors.

c. *Credential Guidelines.* Counselors follow the guidelines for use of credentials that have been established by the entities that issue the credentials.

d. *Misrepresentation of Credentials.* Counselors do not attribute more to their credentials than the credentials represent, and do not imply that other counselors are not qualified because they do not possess certain credentials.

e. *Doctoral Degrees from Other Fields.* Counselors who hold a master's degree in counseling or a closely related mental health field, but hold a doctoral degree from other than counseling or a closely related field do not use the title, "Dr." in their practices and do not announce to the public in relation to their practice or status as a counselor that they hold a doctorate.

C.5. *Public Responsibility*

a. *Nondiscrimination.* Counselors do not discriminate against clients, students, or supervisees in a manner that has a negative impact based on their age, color, culture, disability, ethnic group, gender, race, religion, sexual orientation, or socioeconomic status, or for any other reason. (See A.2.a.)

b. *Sexual Harassment.* Counselors do not engage in sexual harassment. Sexual harassment is defined as sexual solicitation, physical advances, or verbal or nonverbal conduct that is sexual in nature, that occurs in connection with professional activities or roles, and that either (1) is unwelcome, is offensive, or creates a hostile workplace environment, and counselors know or are told this; or (2) is sufficiently severe or intense to be harassing to a reasonable person in the context. Sexual harassment can consist of a single intense or severe act or multiple persistent or pervasive acts.

c. *Reports to Third Parties.* Counselors are accurate, honest, and unbiased in reporting their professional activities and judgments to appropriate third parties including courts, health insurance companies, those who are the recipients of evaluation reports, and others. (See B.1.g.)

d. *Media Presentations.* When counselors provide advice or comment by means of public lectures, demonstrations, radio or television programs, prerecorded tapes, printed articles, mailed material, or other media, they take reasonable precautions to ensure that (1) the statements are based on appropriate professional counseling literature and practice; (2) the statements are otherwise consistent with the *Code of Ethics* and the *Standards of Practice*; and (3) the recipients of the information are not encouraged to infer that a professional counseling relationship has been established. (See C.6.b.)

e. *Unjustified Gains.* Counselors do not use their professional positions to seek or receive unjustified personal gains, sexual favors, unfair advantage, or unearned goods or services. (See C.3.d.)

C.6. *Responsibility to Other Professionals*

a. *Different Approaches.* Counselors are respectful of approaches to professional counseling that differ from their own. Counselors know and take into account the traditions and practices of other professional groups with which they work.

b. *Personal Public Statements.* When making personal statements in a public context, counselors clarify that they are speaking from their personal perspectives and that they are not speaking on behalf of all counselors or the profession. (See C.5.d.)

c. *Clients Served by Others.* When counselors learn that their clients are in a professional relationship with another mental health professional, they request release from clients to inform the other professionals and strive to establish positive and collaborative professional relationships. (See A.4.)

Section D: Relationships With Other Professionals

D.1. *Relationships With Employers and Employees*

a. *Role Definition.* Counselors define and describe for their employers and employees the parameters and levels of their professional roles.

b. *Agreements.* Counselors establish working agreements with supervisors, colleagues, and subordinates regarding counseling or clinical relationships, confidentiality, adherence to professional standards, distinction between public and private material, maintenance and dissemination of recorded information, workload, and accountability. Working agreements in each instance are specified and made known to those concerned.

c. *Negative Conditions.* Counselors alert their employers to conditions that may be potentially disruptive or damaging to the counselor's professional responsibilities or that may limit their effectiveness.

d. *Evaluation.* Counselors submit regularly to professional review and evaluation by their supervisor or the appropriate representative of the employer.

e. *In-Service.* Counselors are responsible for in-service development of self and staff.

f. *Goals.* Counselors inform their staff of goals and programs.

g. *Practices.* Counselors provide personnel and agency practices that respect and enhance the rights and welfare of each employee and recipient of agency services. Counselors strive to maintain the highest levels of professional services.

h. *Personnel Selection and Assignment.* Counselors select competent staff and assign responsibilities compatible with their skills and experiences.

i. *Discrimination.* Counselors, as either employers or employees, do not engage in or condone practices that are inhumane, illegal, or unjustifiable (such as considerations based on age, color, culture, disability, ethnic group, gender, race, religion, sexual orientation, or socioeconomic status) in hiring, promotion, or training. (See A.2.a. and C.5.b.)

j. *Professional Conduct.* Counselors have a responsibility both to clients and to the agency or institution within which services are performed to maintain high standards of professional conduct.

k. *Exploitive Relationships.* Counselors do not engage in exploitive relationships with individuals over whom they have supervisory, evaluative, or instructional control or authority.

l. *Employer Policies.* The acceptance of employment in an agency or institution implies that counselors are in agreement with its general policies and principles. Counselors strive to reach agreement with employers as to acceptable standards of conduct that allow for changes in institutional policy conducive to the growth and development of clients.

D.2. Consultation (See B.6.)

a. *Consultation as an Option.* Counselors may choose to consult with any other professionally competent persons about their clients. In choosing consultants, counselors avoid placing the consultant in a conflict of interest situation that would preclude the consultant, being a proper party to the counselor's efforts to help the client. Should counselors be engaged in a work setting that compromises this consultation standard, they consult with other professionals whenever possible to consider justifiable alternatives.

b. *Consultant Competency.* Counselors are reasonably certain that they have or the organization represented has the necessary competencies and resources for giving the kind of consulting services needed and that appropriate referral resources are available.

c. *Understanding with Clients.* When providing consultation, counselors attempt to develop with their clients a clear understanding of problem definition, goals for change, and predicted consequences of interventions selected.

d. *Consultant Goals.* The consulting relationship is one in which client adaptability and growth toward self-direction are consistently encouraged and cultivated. (See A.1.b.)

D.3. Fees for Referral

a. *Accepting Fees From Agency Clients.* Counselors refuse a private fee or other remuneration for rendering services to persons who are entitled to such services through the counselor's employing agency or institution. The policies of a particular agency may make explicit provisions for agency clients to receive counseling services from members of its staff in private practice. In such instances, the clients must be informed of other options open to them should they seek private counseling services. (See A.10.a., A.11.b., and C.3.d.)

b. *Referral Fees.* Counselors do not accept a referral fee from other professionals.

D.4. Subcontractor Arrangements

When counselors work as subcontractors for counseling services for a third party, they have a duty to inform clients of the limitations of confidentiality that the organization may place on counselors in providing counseling services to clients. The limits of such confidentiality ordinarily are discussed as part of the intake session. (See B.1.e. and B.1.f.)

Section E: Evaluation, Assessment, and Interpretation

E.1. General

a. *Appraisal Techniques.* The primary purpose of educational and psychological assessment is to provide measures that are objective and interpretable in either comparative or absolute terms.

Counselors recognize the need to interpret the statements in this section as applying to the whole range of appraisal techniques, including test and nontest data.

b. *Client Welfare.* Counselors promote the welfare and best interests of the client in the development, publication, and utilization of educational and psychological assessment techniques. They do not misuse assessment results and interpretations and take reasonable steps to prevent others from misusing the information these techniques provide. They respect the client's right to know the results, the interpretations made, and the bases for their conclusions and recommendations.

E.2. Competence to Use and Interpret Tests

a. *Limits of Competence.* Counselors recognize the limits of their competence and perform only those testing and assessment services for which they have been trained. They are familiar with reliability, validity, related standardization, error of measurement, and proper application of any technique utilized. Counselors using computer-based test interpretations are trained in the construct being measured and the specific instrument being used prior to using this type of computer application. Counselors take reasonable measures to ensure the proper use of psychological assessment techniques by persons under their supervision.

b. *Appropriate Use.* Counselors are responsible for the appropriate application, scoring, interpretation, and use of assessment instruments, whether they score and interpret such tests themselves or use computerized or other services.

c. *Decisions Based on Results.* Counselors responsible for decisions involving individuals or policies that are based on assessment results have a thorough understanding of educational and psychological measurement, including validation criteria, test research, and guidelines for test development and use.

d. *Accurate Information.* Counselors provide accurate information and avoid false claims or misconceptions when making statements about assessment instruments or techniques. Special efforts are made to avoid unwarranted connotations of such terms as IQ and grade-equivalent scores. (See C.5.c.)

E.3. Informed Consent

a. *Explanation to Clients.* Prior to assessment, counselors explain the nature and purposes of assessment and the specific use of results in language the client (or other legally authorized person on behalf of the client) can understand, unless an explicit exception to this right has been agreed upon in advance. Regardless of whether scoring and interpretation are completed by counselors, by assistants, or by computer or other outside services, counselors take reasonable steps to ensure that appropriate explanations are given to the client.

b. *Recipients of Results.* The examinee's welfare, explicit understanding, and prior agreement determine the recipients of test results. Counselors include accurate and appropriate interpretations with any release of individual or group test results. (See B.1.a. and C.5.c.)

E.4. Release of Information to Competent Professionals

a. *Misuse of Results.* Counselors do not misuse assessment results, including test results, and interpretations, and take reasonable steps to prevent the misuse of such by others. (See C.5.c.)

b. *Release of Raw Data.* Counselors ordinarily release data (e.g., protocols, counseling or interview notes, or questionnaires) in which the client is identified only with the consent of the client or the client's legal representative. Such data are usually released only to persons recognized by counselors as competent to interpret the data. (See B.1.a.)

E.5. Proper Diagnosis of Mental Disorders

a. *Proper Diagnosis.* Counselors take special care to provide proper diagnosis of mental disorders. Assessment techniques (including personal interview) used to determine client care (e.g., locus of treatment, type of treatment, or recommended follow-up) are carefully selected and appropriately used. (See A.3.a. and C.5.c.)

b. *Cultural Sensitivity.* Counselors recognize that culture affects the manner in which clients' problems are defined. Clients' socioeconomic and cultural experience is considered when diagnosing mental disorders.

E.6. Test Selection

a. *Appropriateness of Instruments.* Counselors carefully consider the validity, reliability, psychometric limitations, and appropriateness of instruments when selecting tests for use in a given situation or with a particular client.

b. *Culturally Diverse Populations.* Counselors are cautious when selecting tests for culturally diverse populations to avoid inappropriateness of testing that may be outside of socialized behavioral or cognitive patterns.

E.7. Conditions of Test Administration

a. *Administration Conditions.* Counselors administer tests under the same conditions that were established in their standardization. When tests are not administered under standard conditions or when unusual behavior or irregularities occur during the testing session, those conditions are noted in interpretation and the results may be designated as invalid or of questionable validity.

b. *Computer Administration.* Counselors are responsible for ensuring that administration programs function properly to provide clients with accurate results when a computer or other electronic methods are used for test administration (See A.12.b.)

c. *Unsupervised Test Taking.* Counselors do not permit unsupervised or inadequately supervised use of tests or assessments unless the tests or assessments are designed, intended, and validated for self-administration and/or scoring.

d. *Disclosure of Favorable Conditions.* Prior to test administration, conditions that produce most favorable test results are made known to the examinee.

E.8. Diversity in Testing

Counselors are cautious in using assessment techniques, making evaluations, and interpreting the performance of populations not represented in the norm group on which an instrument was standardized. They recognize the effects of age, color, culture, disability, ethnic group, gender, race, religion, sexual orientation, and socioeconomic status on test administration and interpretation and place test results in proper perspective with other relevant factors. (See A.2.a.)

E.9. Test and Scoring Interpretation

a. *Reporting Reservations.* In reporting assessment results, counselors indicate any reservations that exist regarding validity or reliability because of the circumstances of the assessment or the inappropriateness of the norms for the person tested.

b. *Research Instruments.* Counselors exercise caution when interpreting the results of research instruments possessing insufficient technical data to support respondent results. The specific purposes for the use of such instruments are stated explicitly to the examinee.

c. *Testing Services.* Counselors who provide test scoring and test interpretation services to support the assessment process confirm the validity of such interpretations. They accurately describe the purpose, norms, validity, reliability, and applications of the procedures and any special qualifications applicable to their use. The public offering of an automated test interpretations service is considered a professional-to-professional consultation. The formal responsibility of the consultant is to the consultee, but the ultimate and overriding responsibility is to the client.

E.10. Test Security

Counselors maintain the integrity and security of tests and other assessment techniques consistent with legal and contractual obligations. Counselors do not appropriate, reproduce, or modify published tests or parts thereof without acknowledgment and permission from the publisher.

E.11. Obsolete Tests and Outdated Test Results

Counselors do not use data or test results that are obsolete or outdated for the current purpose. Counselors make every effort to prevent the misuse of obsolete measures and test data by others.

E.12. Test Construction

Counselors use established scientific procedures, relevant standards, and current professional knowledge for test design in the development, publication, and utilization of educational and psychological assessment techniques.

Section F: Teaching, Training, and Supervision

F.1. Counselor Educators and Trainers

a. *Educators as Teachers and Practitioners.* Counselors who are responsible for developing, implementing, and supervising educational programs are skilled as teachers and practitioners. They are knowledgeable regarding the ethical, legal, and regulatory aspects of the profession, are skilled in applying that knowledge, and make students and supervisees aware of their responsibilities. Counselors conduct counselor education and training programs in an ethical manner and serve as role models for professional behavior. Counselor educators should make an effort to infuse material related to human diversity into all courses and/or workshops that are designed to promote the development of professional counselors.

b. *Relationship Boundaries with Students and Supervisees.* Counselors clearly define and maintain ethical, professional, and social relationship boundaries with their students and supervisees. They are aware of the differential in power that exists and the student's or supervisee's possible incomprehension of that power differential. Counselors explain to students and supervisees the potential for the relationship to become exploitive.

c. *Sexual Relationships.* Counselors do not engage in sexual relationships with students or supervisees and do not subject them to sexual harassment. (See A.6. and C.5.b.)

d. *Contributions to Research.* Counselors give credit to students or supervisees for their contributions to research and scholarly projects. Credit is given through coauthorship, acknowledgment, footnote statement, or other appropriate means, in accordance with such contributions.(See G.4.b. and G.4.c.)

e. *Close Relatives.* Counselors do not accept close relatives as students or supervisees.

f. *Supervision Preparation.* Counselors who offer clinical supervision services are adequately prepared in supervision methods and techniques. Counselors who are doctoral students serving as practicum or internship supervisors to master's level students are adequately prepared and supervised by the training program.

g. *Responsibility for Services to Clients.* Counselors who supervise the counseling services of others take reasonable measures to ensure that counseling services provided to clients are professional.

h. *Endorsement.* Counselors do not endorse students or supervisees for certification, licensure, employment, or completion of an academic or training program if they believe students or supervisees are not qualified for the endorsement. Counselors take reasonable steps to assist students or supervisees who are not qualified for endorsement to become qualified.

F.2. Counselor Education and Training Programs

a. *Orientation.* Prior to admission, counselors orient prospective students to the counselor education or training program's expectations, including but not limited to the following: (1) the type and level of skill acquisition required for successful completion of the training; (2) subject matter to be covered; (3) basis for evaluation; (4) training components that encourage self-growth or self-disclosure as part of the training process; (5) the type of supervision settings and requirements of the sites for required clinical field experiences; (6) student and supervisee evaluation and dismissal policies and procedures; and (7) up-to-date employment prospects for graduates.

b. *Integration of Study and Practice.* Counselors establish counselor education and training programs that integrate academic study and supervised practice.

c. *Evaluation.* Counselors clearly state to students and supervisees, in advance of training, the levels of competency expected, appraisal methods, and timing of evaluations for both didactic and experiential components. Counselors provide students and supervisees with periodic performance appraisal and evaluation feedback throughout the training program.

d. *Teaching Ethics.* Counselors make students and supervisees aware of the ethical responsibilities and standards of the profession and the students' and supervisees' ethical responsibilities to the profession. (See C.1. and F.3.e.)

e. *Peer Relationships.* When students or supervisees are assigned to lead counseling groups or provide clinical supervision for their peers, counselors take steps to ensure that students and supervisees placed in these roles do not have personal or adverse relationships with peers and that they understand they have the same ethical obligations as counselor educators, trainers, and supervisors. Counselors make every effort to ensure that the rights of peers are not compromised when students or supervisees are assigned to lead counseling groups or provide clinical supervision.

f. *Varied Theoretical Positions.* Counselors present varied theoretical positions so that students and supervisees may make comparisons and have opportunities to develop their own positions. Counselors provide information concerning the scientific bases of professional practice. (See C.6.a.)

g. *Field Placements.* Counselors develop clear policies within their training program regarding field placement and other clinical experiences. Counselors provide clearly stated roles and responsibilities for the student or supervisee, the site supervisor, and the program supervisor. They confirm that site supervisors are qualified to provide supervision and are informed of their professional and ethical responsibilities in this role.

h. *Dual Relationships as Supervisors.* Counselors avoid dual relationships such as performing the role of site supervisor and training program supervisor in the student's or supervisee's training program. Counselors do not accept any form of professional services, fees, commissions, reimbursement, or remuneration from a site for student or supervisee placement.

i. *Diversity in Programs.* Counselors are responsive to their institution's and program's recruitment and retention needs for training program administrators, faculty, and students with diverse backgrounds and special needs. (See A.2.a.)

F.3. *Students and Supervisees*

a. *Limitations.* Counselors, through on-going evaluation and appraisal, are aware of the academic and personal limitations of students and supervisees that might impede performance. Counselors assist students and supervisees in securing remedial assistance when needed, and dismiss from the training program supervisees who are unable to provide competent service due to academic or personal limitations. Counselors seek professional consultation and document their decision to dismiss or refer students or supervisees for assistance. Counselors assure that students and supervisees have recourse to address decisions made to require them to seek assistance or to dismiss them.

b. *Self-Growth Experiences.* Counselors use professional judgment when designing training experiences conducted by the counselors themselves that require student and supervisee self-growth or self-disclosure. Safeguards are provided so that students and supervisees are aware of the ramifications their self-disclosure may have upon counselors whose primary role as teacher, trainer, or supervisor requires acting upon ethical obligations to the profession. Evaluative components of experiential training experiences explicitly delineate predetermined academic standards that are separate and not dependent upon the student's level of self-disclosure. (See A.6.)

c. *Counseling for Students and Supervisees.* If students or supervisees request counseling, supervisors or counselor educators provide them with acceptable referrals. Supervisors or counselor educators do not serve as counselor to students or supervisees over whom they hold administrative, teaching, or evaluative roles unless this is a brief role associated with a training experience. (See A.6.b.)

d. *Clients of Students and Supervisees.* Counselors make every effort to ensure that the clients at field placements are aware of the services rendered and the qualifications of the students and supervisees rendering those services. Clients receive professional disclosure information and are informed of the limits of confidentiality. Client permission is obtained in order for the students and supervisees to use any information concerning the counseling relationship in the training process. (See B.1.e.)

e. *Standards for Students and Supervisees.* Students and supervisees preparing to become counselors adhere to the *Code of Ethics* and the *Standards of Practice.* Students and supervisees have the same obligations to clients as those required of counselors. (See H.1.)

Section G: Research and Publication

G.1. Research Responsibilities

a. *Use of Human Subjects.* Counselors plan, design, conduct, and report research in a manner consistent with pertinent ethical principles, federal and state laws, host institutional regulations, and scientific standards governing research with human subjects. Counselors design and conduct research that reflects cultural sensitivity appropriateness.

b. *Deviation From Standard Practices.* Counselors seek consultation and observe stringent safeguards to protect the rights of research participants when a research problem suggests a deviation from standard acceptable practices. (See B.6.)

c. *Precautions To Avoid Injury.* Counselors who conduct research with human subjects are responsible for the subjects' welfare throughout the experiment and take reasonable precautions to avoid causing injurious psychological, physical, or social effects to their subjects.

d. *Principal Researcher Responsibility.* The ultimate responsibility for ethical research practice lies with the principal researcher. All others involved in the research activities share ethical obligations and full responsibility for their own actions.

e. *Minimal Interference.* Counselors take reasonable precautions to avoid causing disruptions in subjects' lives due to participation in research.

f. *Diversity.* Counselors are sensitive to diversity and research issues with special populations. They seek consultation when appropriate. (See A.2.a. and B.6.)

G.2. Informed Consent

a. *Topics Disclosed.* In obtaining informed consent for research, counselors use language that is understandable to research participants and that: (1) accurately explains the purpose and procedures to be followed; (2) identifies any procedures that are experimental or relatively untried; (3) describes the attendant discomforts and risks; (4) describes the benefits or changes in individuals or organizations that might be reasonably expected; (5) discloses appropriate alternative procedures that would be advantageous for subjects; (6) offers to answer any inquiries concerning the procedures; (7) describes any limitations on confidentiality; and (8) instructs that subjects are free to withdraw their consent and to discontinue participation in the project at any time. (See B.1.f.)

b. *Deception.* Counselors do not conduct research involving deception unless alternative procedures are not feasible and the prospective value of the research justifies the deception. When the methodological requirements of a study necessitate concealment or deception, the investigator is required to explain clearly the reasons for this action as soon as possible.

c. *Voluntary Participation.* Participation in research is typically voluntary and without any penalty for refusal to participate. Involuntary participation is appropriate only when it can be demonstrated that participation will have no harmful effects on subjects and is essential to the investigation.

d. *Confidentiality of Information.* Information obtained about research participants during the course of an investigation is confidential. When the possibility exists that others may obtain access to such information, ethical research practice requires that the possibility, together with the plans for protecting confidentiality, be explained to participants as a part of the procedure for obtaining informed consent. (See B.1.e.)

e. *Persons Incapable of Giving Informed Consent.* When a person is incapable of giving informed consent, counselors provide an appropriate explanation, obtain agreement for participation and obtain appropriate consent from a legally authorized person.

f. *Commitments to Participants.* Counselors take reasonable measures to honor all commitments to research participants.

g. *Explanations After Data Collection.* After data are collected, counselors provide participants with full clarification of the nature of the study to remove any misconceptions. Where scientific or human values justify delaying or withholding information, counselors take reasonable measures to avoid causing harm.

h. *Agreements to Cooperate.* Counselors who agree to cooperate with another individual in research or publication incur an obligation to cooperate as promised in terms of punctuality of performance and with regard to the completeness and accuracy of the information required.

i. *Informed Consent for Sponsors.* In the pursuit of research, counselors give sponsors, institutions, and publication channels the same respect and opportunity for giving informed consent that they accord to individual research participants. Counselors are aware of their obligation to future research workers and ensure that host institutions are given feedback information and proper acknowledgment.

G.3. Reporting Results

a. *Information Affecting Outcome.* When reporting research results, counselors explicitly mention all variables and conditions known to the investigator that may have affected the outcome of a study or the interpretation of data.

b. *Accurate Results.* Counselors plan, conduct, and report research accurately and in a manner that minimizes the possibility that results will be misleading. They provide thorough discussions of the limitations of their data and alternative hypotheses. Counselors do not engage in fraudulent research, distort data, misrepresent data, or deliberately bias their results.

c. *Obligation to Report Unfavorable Results.* Counselors communicate to other counselors the results of any research judged to be of professional value. Results that reflect unfavorably on institutions, programs, services, prevailing opinions, or vested interests are not withheld.

d. *Identity of Subjects.* Counselors who supply data, aid in the research of another person, report research results, or make original data available take due care to disguise the identity of respective subjects in the absence of specific authorization from the subjects to do otherwise. (See B.1.g. and B.5.a.)

e. *Replication Studies.* Counselors are obligated to make available sufficient original research data to qualified professionals who may wish to replicate the study.

G.4. Publication

a. *Recognition of Others.* When conducting and reporting research, counselors are familiar with and give recognition to previous work on the topic, observe copyright laws, and give full credit to those to whom credit is due. (See F.1.d. and G.4.c.)

b. *Contributors.* Counselors give credit through joint authorship, acknowledgment, footnote statements, or other appropriate means to those who have contributed significantly to research or concept development in accordance with such contributions. The principal contributor is listed first and minor technical or professional contributions are acknowledged in notes or introductory statements.

c. *Student Research.* For an article that is substantially based on a student's dissertation or thesis, the student is listed as the principal author. (See F.1.d. and G.4.a.)

d. *Duplicate Submission.* Counselors submit manuscripts for consideration to only one journal at a time. Manuscripts that are published in whole or in substantial part in another journal or published work are not submitted for publication without acknowledgment and permission from the previous publication.

e. *Professional Review.* Counselors who review material submitted for publication, research, or other scholarly purposes respect the confidentiality and proprietary rights of those who submitted it.

Section H: Resolving Ethical Issues

H.1. Knowledge of Standards

Counselors are familiar with the *Code of Ethics* and the *Standards of Practice* and other applicable ethics codes from other professional organizations of which they are member, or from certification and licensure bodies. Lack of knowledge or misunderstanding of an ethical responsibility is not a defense against a charge of unethical conduct. (See F.3.e.)

H.2. Suspected Violations

a. *Ethical Behavior Expected.* Counselors expect professional associates to adhere to Code of Ethics. When counselors possess reasonable cause that raises doubts as to whether a counselor is acting in an ethical manner, they take appropriate action. (See H.2.d. and H.2.e.)

b. *Consultation.* When uncertain as to whether a particular situation or course of action may be in violation of Code of Ethics, counselors consult with other counselors who are knowledgeable about ethics, with colleagues, or with appropriate authorities.

c. *Organization Conflicts.* If the demands of an organization with which counselors are affiliated pose a conflict with Code of Ethics, counselors specify the nature of such conflicts and express to their supervisors or other responsible officials their commitment to Code of Ethics. When possible, counselors work toward change within the organization to allow full adherence to Code of Ethics.

d. *Informal Resolution.* When counselors have reasonable cause to believe that another counselor is violating an ethical standard, they attempt to first resolve the issue informally with the other counselor if feasible, providing that such action does not violate confidentiality rights that may be involved.

e. *Reporting Suspected Violations.* When an informal resolution is not appropriate or feasible, counselors, upon reasonable cause, take action such as reporting the suspected ethical violation to state or national ethics committees, unless this action conflicts with confidentiality rights that cannot be resolved.

f. *Unwarranted Complaints.* Counselors do not initiate, participate in, or encourage the filing of ethics complaints that are unwarranted or intend to harm a counselor rather than to protect clients or the public.

H.3. *Cooperation With Ethics Committees*

Counselors assist in the process of enforcing Code of Ethics. Counselors cooperate with investigations, proceedings, and requirements of the ACA Ethics Committee or ethics committees of other duly constituted associations or boards having jurisdiction over those charged with a violation. Counselors are familiar with the ACA Policies and Procedures and use it as a reference in assisting the enforcement of the Code of Ethics.

STANDARDS OF PRACTICE

All members of the American Counseling Association (ACA) are required to adhere to the *Standards of Practice* and the *Code of Ethics*. The *Standards of Practice* represent minimal behavioral statements of the *Code of Ethics*. Members should refer to the applicable section of the Code of Ethics for further interpretation and amplification of the applicable Standard of Practice (SP).

Section A: The Counseling Relationship

SP-1: Nondiscrimination. Counselors respect diversity and must not discriminate against clients because of age, color, culture, disability, ethnic group, gender, race, religion, sexual orientation, marital status, or socioeconomic status. (See A.2.a.)

SP-2: Disclosure to Clients. Counselors must adequately inform clients, preferably in writing, regarding the counseling process and counseling relationship at or before the time it begins and throughout the relationship. (See A.3.a.)

SP-3: Dual Relationships. Counselors must make every effort to avoid dual relationships with clients that could impair their professional judgment or increase the risk of harm to clients. When a dual relationship cannot be avoided, counselors must take appropriate steps to ensure that judgment is not impaired and that no exploitation occurs. (See A.6.a. and A.6.b.)

SP-4: Sexual Intimacies With Clients. Counselors must not engage in any type of sexual intimacies with current clients and must not engage in sexual intimacies with former clients within a minimum of 2 years after terminating the counseling relationship. Counselors who engage in such relationship after two years following termination have the responsibility to thoroughly exam and document that such relations did not have an exploitative nature.

SP-5: Protecting Clients during Group Work. Counselors must take steps to protect clients from physical or psychological trauma resulting from interactions during group work. (See A.9.b.)

SP-6: Advance Understanding of Fees. Counselors must explain to clients, prior to their entering the counseling relationship, financial arrangements related to professional services. (See A.10.a.–d.) and A.11.c.)

SP-7: Termination. Counselors must assist in making appropriate arrangements for the continuation of treatment of clients, when necessary, following termination of counseling relationships. (See A.11.a.)

SP-8: Inability to Assist Clients. Counselors must avoid entering or immediately terminate a counseling relationship if it is determined that they are unable to be of professional assistance to a client. The counselor may assist in making an appropriate referral for the client. (See A.11.b.)

Section B: Confidentiality

SP-9: Confidentiality Requirement. Counselors must keep information related to counseling services confidential unless disclosure is in the best interest of clients, is required for the welfare of others, or is required by law. When disclosure is required, only information that is essential is revealed and the client is informed of such disclosure. (See B.1.a.–f.)

SP-10: Confidentiality Requirements for Subordinates. Counselors must take measures to ensure that privacy and confidentiality of clients are maintained by subordinates. (See B.1.h.)

SP-11: Confidentiality in Group Work. Counselors must clearly communicate to group members that confidentiality cannot be guaranteed in group work. (See B.2.a.)

SP-12: Confidentiality in Family Counseling. Counselors must not disclose information about one family member in counseling to another family member without prior consent. (See B.2.b.)

SP-13: Confidentiality of Records. Counselors must maintain appropriate confidentiality in creating, storing, accessing, transferring, and disposing of counseling records. (See B.4.b.)

SP-14: Permission to Record or Observe. Counselors must obtain prior consent from clients in order to electronically record or observe sessions. (See B.4.c.)

SP-15: Disclosure or Transfer of Records. Counselors must obtain client consent to disclose or transfer records to third parties, unless exceptions listed in SP-9 exist. (See B.4.e.)

SP-16: Data Disguise Required. Counselors must disguise the identity of the client when using data for training, research, or publication. (See B.5.a.)

Section C: Professional Responsibility

SP-17: Boundaries of Competence. Counselors must practice only within the boundaries of their competence. (See C.2.a.)

SP-18: Continuing Education. Counselors must engage in continuing education to maintain their professional competence. (See C.2.f.)

SP-19: Impairment of Professionals. Counselors must refrain from offering professional services when their personal problems or conflicts may cause harm to a client or others. (See C.2.g.)

SP-20: Accurate Advertising. Counselors must accurately represent their credentials and services when advertising. (See C.3.a.)

SP-21: Recruiting Through Employment. Counselors must not use their place of employment or institutional affiliation to recruit clients for their private practices. (See C.3.d.)

SP-22: Credentials Claimed. Counselors must claim or imply only professional credentials possessed and must correct any known misrepresentations of their credentials by others. (See C.4.a.)

SP-23: Sexual Harassment. Counselors must not engage in sexual harassment. (See C.5.b.)

SP-24: Unjustified Gains. Counselors must not use their professional positions to seek or receive unjustified personal gains, sexual favors, unfair advantage, or unearned goods or services. (See C.5.e.)

SP-25: Clients Served by Others. With the consent of the client, counselors must inform other mental health professionals serving the same client that a counseling relationship between the counselor and client exists. (See C.6.c.)

SP-26: Negative Employment Conditions. Counselors must alert their employers to institutional policy or conditions that may be potentially disruptive or damaging to the counselor's professional responsibilities, or that may limit their effectiveness or deny clients' rights. (See D.1.c.)

SP-27: Personnel Selection and Assignment. Counselors must select competent staff and must assign responsibilities compatible with staff skills and experiences. (See D.1.h.)

SP-28: Exploitive Relationships with Subordinates. Counselors must not engage in exploitive relationships with individuals over whom they have supervisory, evaluative, or instructional control or authority. (See D.1.k.)

Section D: Relationship With Other Professionals

SP-29: Accepting Fees From Agency Clients. Counselors must not accept fees or other remuneration for consultation with persons entitled to such services through the counselor's employing agency or institution. (See D.3.a.)

SP-30: Referral Fees. Counselors must not accept referral fees. (See D.3.b.)

Section E: Evaluation, Assessment, and Interpretation

SP-31: Limits of Competence. Counselors must perform only testing and assessment services for which they are competent. Counselors must not allow the use of psychological assessment techniques by unqualified persons under their supervision. (See E.2.a.)

SP-32: Appropriate Use of Assessment Instruments. Counselors must use assessment instruments in the manner for which they were intended. (See E.2.b.)

SP-33: Assessment Explanations to Clients. Counselors must provide explanations to clients prior to assessment about the nature and purposes of assessment and the specific uses of results. (See E.3.a.)

SP-34: Recipients of Test Results. Counselors must ensure that accurate and appropriate interpretations accompany any release of testing and assessment information. (See E.3.b.)

SP-35: Obsolete Tests and Outdated Test Results. Counselors must not base their assessment or intervention decisions or recommendations on data or test results that are obsolete or outdated for the current purpose. (See E.11.)

Section F: Teaching, Training, and Supervision

SP-36: Sexual Relationships With Students or Supervisees. Counselors must not engage in sexual relationships with their students and supervisees. (See F.1.c.)

SP-37: Credit for Contributions to Research. Counselors must give credit to students or supervisees for their contributions to research and scholarly projects. (See F.1.d.)

SP-38: Supervision Preparation. Counselors who offer clinical supervision services must be trained and prepared in supervision methods and techniques. (See F.1.f.)

SP-39: Evaluation Information. Counselors must clearly state to students and supervisees in advance of training, the levels of competency expected, appraisal methods, and timing of evaluations. Counselors must provide students and supervisees with periodic performance appraisal and evaluation feedback throughout the training program. (See F.2.c.)

SP-40: Peer Relationships in Training. Counselors must make every effort to ensure that the rights of peers are not violated when students and supervisees are assigned to lead counseling groups or provide clinical supervision. (See F.2.e.)

SP-41: Limitations of Students and Supervisees. Counselors must assist students and supervisees in securing remedial assistance, when needed, and must dismiss from the training program students and supervisees who are unable to provide competent service due to academic or personal limitations. (See F.3.a.)

SP-42: Self-Growth Experiences. Counselors who conduct experiences for students or supervisees that include self-growth or self disclosure must inform participants of counselors' ethical obligations to the profession and must not grade participants based on their nonacademic performance. (See F.3.b.)

SP-43: Standards for Students and Supervisees. Students and supervisees preparing to become counselors must adhere to the *Code of Ethics* and the *Standards of Practice* of counselors. (See F.3.e.)

Section G: Research and Publication

SP-44: Precautions to Avoid Injury in Research. Counselors must avoid causing physical, social, or psychological harm or injury to subjects in research. (See G.1.c.)

SP-45: Confidentiality of Research Information. Counselors must keep confidential information obtained about research participants. (See G.2.d.)

SP-46: Information Affecting Research Outcome. Counselors must report all variables and conditions known to the investigator that may have affected research data or outcomes. (See G.3.a.)

SP-47: Accurate Research Results. Counselors must not distort or misrepresent research data, nor fabricate or intentionally bias research results. (See G.3.b.)

SP-48: Publication Contributors. Counselors must give appropriate credit to those who have contributed to research. (See G.4.a. and G.4.b.)

Section H: Resolving Ethical Issues

SP-49: Ethical Behavior Expected. Counselors must take appropriate action when they possess reasonable cause that raises doubts as to whether counselors or other mental health professionals are acting in an ethical manner. (See H.2.a.)

SP-50: Unwarranted Complaints. Counselors must not initiate, participate in, or encourage the filing of ethics complaints that are unwarranted or intended to harm a mental health professional rather than to protect clients or the public. (See H.2.f.)

SP-51: Cooperation with Ethics Committees. Counselors must cooperate with investigations, proceedings, and requirements of the ACA Ethics Committee or ethics committees of other duly constituted associations or boards having jurisdiction over those charged with a violation. (See H.3.)

REFERENCES

The following documents are available to counselors as resources to guide them in their practices. These resources are not a part of the *Code of Ethics* and the *Standards of Practice*.

American Association for Counseling and Development/Association for Measurement and Evaluation in Counseling and Development. (1989). *The responsibilities of users of standardized tests (revised)*. Washington, DC: Author.

American Counseling Association. (1988) *American Counseling Association ethical Standards*. Alexandria, VA: Author.

American Psychological Association. (1985). *Standards for educational and psychological testing (revised)*. Washington, DC: Author.

American Rehabilitation Counseling Association, Commission on Rehabilitation Counselor Certification, and National Rehabilitation Counseling Association. (1987). *Code of professional ethics for rehabilitation counselors.* Alexandria, VA: Author.

American School Counselor Association. (1992). *Ethical standards for school counselors.* Alexandria, VA: Author.

Joint Committee on Testing Practices. (1988). *Code of fair testing practices in education.* Washington, DC: Author.

National Board for Certified Counselors. (1989). *National Board for Certified Counselors code of ethics.* Alexandria, VA: Author.

Prediger, D.J. (Ed.). (1993, March). *Multicultural assessment standards.* Alexandria, VA: Association for Assessment in Counseling.

Name Index

Subject Index